12·27·79

This book boldly interprets colonial life and
the origins of the American Revolution.
Through a century-long history of three
seaport towns, Boston, New York, and
Philadelphia, Gary B. Nash discovers subtle
changes in social and political awareness and
relates them ultimately to revolution.

Comparing America's three largest cities in
the first half of the eighteenth century, Nash
demonstrates how the origins of the
American Revolution were deeply rooted
and shows why Boston became the first
center of insurrectionary ferment. He
describes the coming of the Revolution as
partly that of popular collective action and
partly that of challenging the gentry's claim
to rule by custom, law, and divine will. With
poverty on the rise and their share of
colonial wealth and bounty decreasing,
ordinary people forced their way into
politics through street demonstrations, mass
meetings, and intimidation of their enemies.
Their reordering of political power, running
oppositely from the redistribution of
economic power, required a new
consciousness to challenge the model of

social relations inherited from the past and defended by higher classes. Deeply affected by economic dislocations at the end of the Seven Years War, urban dwellers struggled against each other rather than working harmoniously for the mutual good. By the 1760s the internal struggles in the port towns had become intertwined with the contest with Britain.

Nash's study, based on wide research, including many previously unexploited sources, clearly and vigorously written, is a major work of reevaluation, changing the contours of colonial and revolutionary history. It takes its place among the most important books in American studies.

THE
URBAN CRUCIBLE

Social Change,
Political Consciousness,
and the Origins of
the American Revolution

Gary B. Nash

Harvard University Press
Cambridge, Massachusetts
and London, England
1979

Library of Congress Cataloging in Publication Data

Nash, Gary B
    The urban crucible.

    Includes bibliographical references and index.
        1.   United States—Politics and government—Colonial
period, ca. 1600-1775.   2.   United States—Social conditions—To 1865.   3.   United States—Economic conditions
—To 1865.   4.   United States—History—Revolution, 1775-
1783—Causes.   I.   Title.
E188.N38   309.1'73 '02   79-12894
ISBN 0-674-93056-8

To the memory
of my parents

Preface

ALTHOUGH eighteenth-century America was predominantly a rural, agricultural society, its seaboard commercial cities were the cutting edge of economic, social, and political change. Almost all the alterations that are associated with the advent of capitalist society happened first in the cities and radiated outward to the smaller towns, villages, and farms of the hinterland. In America, it was in the colonial cities that the transition first occurred from a barter to a commercial economy; where a competitive social order replaced an ascriptive one; where a hierarchical and deferential polity yielded to participatory and contentious civic life; where factory production began to replace small-scale artisanal production; where the first steps were taken to organize work by clock time rather than by sidereal cycles. The cities predicted the future, even though under one in twenty colonists lived in them in 1700 or 1775 and even though they were but overgrown villages compared to the great urban centers of Europe, the Middle East, and China.

Considering the importance of the cities as dynamic loci of change, it is surprising that historians have studied them so little. Even the fascination with urban history in the last few decades has done little to remedy this. We have at our disposal a shelfful of books on the early American inland villages, whose households numbered only in the hundreds, but have comparatively little to inform us about the colonial urban centers. Nothing written in the last generation, in fact, has gone much beyond Carl Bridenbaugh's *Cities in the Wilderness: Urban Life in America, 1625-1742* (1938) and *Cities in Revolt: Urban Life in America, 1743-1776* (1955). These were pioneering works, but while richly textured and elegantly written, they are descriptive rather than analytic, they deal primarily with institutional history, and they are based primarily on town records, newspapers, and personal accounts.

This book proceeds from a different conception of how urban societies changed in the eighteenth century and is based largely on different sources. It stems from my interest in the social morphology of America's colonial cities and how it was that urban people, at a certain point in the preindustrial era, upset the equilibrium of an older system of social relations and turned the seaport towns into crucibles of revolutionary agitation. More particularly, I have tried to discover how people worked, lived, and perceived the changes going on about them, how class relationships shifted, and how political consciousness grew, especially among the laboring classes.

What has led early American historians to avoid questions about class formation and the development of lower-class political consciousness is not only an aversion to Marxist conceptualizations of history but also the persistent myth that class relations did not matter in early America because there were no classes. Land, it is widely held, was abundant and wages were high because labor was always in great demand. Therefore, opportunity was widespread and material well-being attainable by nearly everybody. If being at the bottom or in the middle was only a way station on a heavily traveled road to the top, then the composition of the various ranks and orders must have been constantly shifting and class consciousness could be only an evanescent and unimportant phenomenon. Thus, our understanding of the social history of the colonial cities has been mired in the general idea that progress was almost automatic in the commercial centers of a thriving New World society.

Only recently has the notion of extraordinary elasticity within classes and mobility between them begun to yield to a more complex analysis of how demographic trends, economic development, the spread of a market economy, and a series of costly wars produced a social, political, and ideological transformation. Historians have begun to create a far more intricate picture of social change by studying the extent of vertical and horizontal mobility, the degree of stratification, the accumulation and distribution of wealth, the social origins of the elite, the changing nature of economic and political power, and the shaping of class, ethnic, and religious consciousness. Historians are also coming to understand the need to retreat from discussing how *the* community was affected and to consider instead how different groups within the community were affected. Armies were supplied by some urban dwellers and manned by others, and those who gained or lost were not randomly selected. Price inflation and monetary devaluation caused problems for the whole society but the burdens were not distributed evenly. A sharp rise in overseas demand for American grain might increase the profits of inland farmers and seaboard merchants but could undercut the household budget of urban laborers and artisans.

Much of this book is about those who occupied the lower levels of urban society, the people who frequently suffered the unequal effects of eighteenth-century change. This is no mere quest for aesthetic balance or for simple justice in recreating the past. Examination of the circumstances of life for the great mass of common people in every period and place and inquiry into their ways of thinking and acting are essential if we are ever to test and correct the hallowed generalizations made from the study of the select few upon which our understanding of history is primarily based. What is more, I proceed from the conviction that the success of any society is best measured not by examining the attainments and accumulations of those at the top but by assaying the quality of life for those at the bottom. If this be thought the maxim of a utopian socialist, it was also the notion of an eighteenth-century English aristocrat whose writings circulated in Boston. "Every Nation," wrote Sir Richard Cox, "has the Reputation of being rich or poor from the Condition of the lowest Class of its Inhabitants."*

In examining the lives of the lower classes in the eighteenth-century American cities I have repeatedly encountered evidence of social situations for which there is no accounting in the standard scholarship. Boston, I have found, was not only the commercial and intellectual center of New England Puritanism, as we have been taught, but also, by the 1740s, the New England center of mass indebtedness, widowhood, and poverty. By the end of the Seven Years War in 1763 poverty on a scale that urban leaders found appalling had also appeared in New York and Philadelphia. The narrowing of opportunities and the rise of poverty are two of the subthemes of this book. This is not to deny that compared with most places from which the colonists came—at least those who were white and free—the material circumstances of life were far more favorable than they had previously known. Comparisons between life in the colonial cities and life in Europe, however, like comparisons today between the plight of the urban poor in Chicago and Calcutta, miss the mark. An indebted shoemaker in Boston in 1760 took little satisfaction that for many of those who worked with hammer and awl life was worse and the future even bleaker in Dublin or London. People's sense of deprivation is not assuaged by referring them to distant places or ancient times. Like those above them, they measure the quality of their lives within their own locales and make comparisons primarily with the world of their parents.

To study those who resided at the bottom of the seaport societies it is also necessary to study those in the middle and at the top. Whether it is the reaction of the poor to the new formulae for dealing with urban poverty or the role of the crowd in the Stamp Act demonstrations of 1765, nothing is explicable without understanding the ideology and conduct of

---

*A Letter from Sir Richard Cox, Bart. To Thomas Prior, Esq.; Shewing from Experience a sure Method to establish the Linnen-Manufacture (Boston, 1750), p. 10.

men at the higher levels. It was, after all, with those who possessed economic, political, and social power that the lower orders ultimately had to
resolve matters. All urban people were linked together in a social network where power was unevenly distributed, and one part of this social
organism cannot be understood in isolation from the others. Above all,
this book is about the relationships among urban people who occupied
different rungs of the social ladder.

The concept of class is central to this book. Therefore, it is important
to specify that the term has a different meaning for the preindustrial period than for a later epoch. I employ it as both a heuristic and a historical
category. It is a term which enables us to perceive that urban people
gradually came to think of themselves as belonging to economic groups
that did not share common goals, began to behave in class-specific ways
in response to events that impinged upon their well-being, and manifested ideological points of view and cultural characteristics peculiar to
their rank. This is not to say that all carpenters or all shopkeepers occupied the same position along the spectrum of wealth or that all ship
captains or all caulkers thought alike or that merchants and shoemakers
consistently opposed each other because they occupied different social
strata. Nor can class be determined simply by notations on a tax assessor's list or by occupations given in inventories of estate. Moreover, evidence is abundant that vertical consciousness was always present in a
society where movement up and down the social ladder never stopped
and where the natural tendency of economic networks was to create a
common interest among, for example, the merchant, shipbuilder, and
mariner.

Thus, we must recognize the problems in employing the concept of
class in eighteenth-century society, for the historical stage of a mature
class formation had not yet been reached. To ignore class relations, however, is a greater problem. The movement between ranks and the vertical
linkages that were a part of a system of economic clientage did not fore-
close the possibility that horizontal bonds would grow in strength. People who had always thought of themselves as belonging to the lower,
middling, or upper ranks, but saw no reason that this implied social conflict, would gradually associate these rough identifiers of social standing
with antagonistic interests and make them the basis for political contention. One of the main tasks of this book is to show that many urban
Americans, living amidst historical forces that were transforming the
social landscape, came to perceive antagonistic divisions based on economic and social position; that they began to struggle around these conflicting interests; and that through these struggles they developed a consciousness of class. This is quite different, as E. P. Thompson points out,
than arguing "that classes exist, independent of historical relationship

and struggle, and that they struggle *because* they exist, rather than coming into existence out of that struggle."*

Hence, I am concerned with the evolving relations among different groups of urban people who were subject to historically rooted changes that may have been as perplexingly intricate to them as they have been to historians since. It is not my argument that by the end of the colonial period class formation and class consciousness were fully developed, but only that we can gain greater insight into the urban social process between 1690 and 1776 and can understand more fully the origins and meaning of the American Revolution if we analyze the changing relations among people of different ranks and examine the emergence of new modes of thought based on horizontal rather than vertical divisions in society. The shift in social alignments would continue after the Revolution, not moving with telic force toward some rendezvous with destiny in the industrial period but shaped by historical forces that were largely unpredictable in 1776.

This book is also comparative in its approach. Examining concurrently the process of change in Boston, New York, and Philadelphia has enabled me to comprehend how particular factors intertwined in each city to hasten or retard the formation of class consciousness and to give a particular texture to social discourse and political behavior. I have chosen these three cities not only because they were the largest northern maritime centers, as well as the seats of provincial government, but also because their populations differed significantly in racial and ethnic origins, in religious composition, and in the legacies of their founding generations. It should be apparent in what follows that class consciousness developed according to no even-paced or linear formula. It emerged and receded depending upon conditions, leadership at both the top and bottom, cultural traditions, and other factors. The comparative approach has also convinced me that the Marxist maxim that the mode of production dictates the nature of class relations has only limited analytic potential for explaining changes during some historical eras. It is not different modes of production that account for the striking differences among the three port towns in the historical development of class consciousness but the different experiences of people who lived within three urban societies that shared a common mode of production. Thus, it is necessary to go beyond determining objective class structures and objective productive relations to examining "the specific activities of men [and women] in real social and economic relationships, containing fundamental contradictions and variations and therefore always in a state of dynamic pro-

*"Eighteenth-Century English Society: Class Struggle Without Class?" *Social History*, 3 (1978), 149.

cess."* Bostonians, New Yorkers, and Philadelphians experienced their situations differently between 1690 and 1776 because discrete factors impinged upon them, ranging from their proximity to Anglo-French theaters of war to the development of their hinterlands to their cultural heritage.

In inquiring into the history of the common people of the northern port towns I have adopted the term "laboring classes." I do so in order to take account of the fact that before the American Revolution—in fact, for more than half a century after the Revolution—there was no industrial working *class* composed of a mass of wage laborers who toiled in factories where a capitalist class wholly owned and controlled the productive machinery. My concern is with broad groupings of people who worked with their hands but were differentiated by skills and status. Thus, the laboring *classes* included slaves, whose bondage was perpetual, indentured servants, whose unfree status was temporary, and free persons, whose independence could be altered only in unusual circumstances. The laboring ranks also ascended from apprentice to journeyman to master craftsman. Likewise, there were gradations among ill-paid merchant seamen, laborers, and porters at the bottom; struggling shoemakers, tailors, coopers, and weavers who were a step higher; more prosperous cabinetmakers, silversmiths, instrumentmakers, and housewrights; and entrepreneurial bakers, distillers, ropewalk operators, and tallow chandlers. There was, in short, no unified laboring class at any point in the period under study. That does not mean that class formation and the shaping of class consciousness was not happening in the era culminating with the American Revolution.

Despite the importance attached to economic and social change, this book argues that ideology in many instances was far more than a reflection of economic interests and acted as a motive force among urban people of all ranks. But it needs to be emphasized at the outset that ideology is not the exclusive possession of educated individuals and established groups. Nor do I believe that those at the top established an ideology that was then obligingly adopted by those below them. Slaves, indentured servants, the laboring poor, women, and the illiterate also had an ideology, although many of these people did not express ideas systematically in forms that are easily recoverable by historians two hundred years later. What I mean by ideology is awareness of the surrounding world, penetration of it through thought, and reasoned reactions to the forces impinging upon one's life. People living in communities as small as the prerevolutionary port towns, linked together as they were by church, tavern, workplace, and family, exchanged views, compared insights, and through the face-to-face nature of their associations, arrived at certain

*Raymond Williams, "Base and Superstructure in Marxist Cultural Theory," *New Left Review*, no. 82 (1973), 5-6.

common understandings of their social situations. The world for them may have always been half-seen and imperfectly comprehended, but, as is universally true, they acted upon reality as they understood it, whether they were university trained and rich or could barely keep their shop books by crooked hand in a rented room.

It is not possible to fathom the subterranean social changes that transformed the urban centers of colonial America or to peer into the minds of the mass of urban dwellers who have been obscured from historical sight by consulting only the sources that are most accessible to the historian—newspapers, municipal records, business accounts, diaries and correspondence, and published sermons, political tracts, and legislative proceedings. As vital as these sources are, they are insufficient to the task, for they most often came from the hands of upper-class merchants, lawyers, clergymen, and politicians, who, though they tell us much, do not tell all. These sources are particularly silent on the lives of those in the lower reaches of the urban hierarchy and they are only occasionally helpful in revealing the subsurface social processes at work. This is not surprising, for on the one hand the gentry was not interested in illuminating the lives of laboring-class city dwellers and on the other hand they were often unaware of, mystified by, or eager to obscure the changing social, economic, and political relationships in their cities. Buried in less familiar documents, virtually all of them unpublished and many of them fragmentary and difficult to use, are glimpses of the lives of ordinary people. The story of how life was lived and conditions changed in the colonial cities can be discerned, not with mathematical precision or perfect clarity but in general form, from tax lists, poor relief records, wills, inventories of estate, deed books, mortgages, court documents, and portledge bills and wage records. This book draws extensively upon such sources as well as upon more traditional forms of evidence. It also infers lower-class thought from lower-class action, which is justifiable when the action is adequately recorded and is repetitive.

I regret that I have not been able to deal more extensively with the history of urban women. As in the case of studying the lower classes, the problem of source materials is very great but not insuperable. Rather than plead the difficulties of research, I must affirm that after fourteen years of ferreting out and pondering the meaning of more sources than I had reason to believe existed, it seems better to leave this task to others. It should be obvious, however, that our understanding of the American cities before the Revolution must remain imperfect until questions relating to women's work, marriage patterns, roles in churches and social institutions, and behind the scenes involvement in politics are answered.

WHILE ABSORBING myself in this book, I have accumulated many intellectual debts which I happily acknowledge. The encouragement Alfred F. Young has given and the conceptual rigor he has imparted in our correspondence and conversations have been invaluable. This book, which he read and criticized in draft form, would not be the same without his generous assistance and good-humored goading. Joyce Oldham Appleby and John Murrin also read nearly every word I have written and through their deft criticisms helped me sharpen the internal logic and rescued me from a variety of errors. Richard S. Dunn, Aida D. Donald, and James A. Henretta offered valuable suggestions on the manuscript, and particular portions of it were improved through criticism tendered by Catherine Menand and Cynthia Shelton. I am also grateful to Lawrence Stone, who some years ago disabused me of the notion that this book might logically end in 1765. My debt also extends to a number of people, some anonymous, whose criticism of earlier articles and conference papers or whose own work, intersecting with my own, forced me to rethink my ideas or return to the archives for further digging. I doubt that the best scholarship is collaborative in a formal sense, but I am certain that this book owes much to the supportive criticism of a great many members of the profession, many of whom are of a different mind in interpreting the colonial past. I hereby extend my thanks as well to the graduate students at the University of California, Los Angeles, who, over the last fourteen years, have listened to my ideas, responded to them reflectively, and obliged me to discard, modify, or recast formulations which I tested on them. Elizabeth Suttell at Harvard University Press applied her considerable talents to preparing the work for publication; the final product is much the better for her attention.

Financial aid from a number of institutions enabled me to visit archives in the cities I have studied, while living on the other side of the continent, and gave me time for writing. I hereby thank the Guggenheim Memorial Foundation, the American Council of Learned Societies, the American Philosophical Society, and the Research Committee of the Academic Senate at the University of California, Los Angeles, for fellowship and research funds. Grants from the latter committee also allowed me to employ the following graduate research assistants, whose contribution went far beyond the gathering and processing of data: Peter Ball, Theresa Corbett, Jeanette Gadt, Ruth Kennedy, Laura Margolin, Andrew Morse, Joseph O'Reilly, Sharon V. Salinger, Ronald Schultz, John W. Shaffer, Cynthia Shelton, Billy G. Smith, and Margaret Strobel. Sally McMahon of Brandeis University was also of great assistance in conducting research for me in Boston, and I wish to thank Noel Diaz for the preparation of the line drawings in the appendix.

Research for this book has also been vastly facilitated by the courtesy and cooperative spirit of many archivists and librarians. Generosity was extended in Boston at the Massachusetts Archives, Massachusetts Historical Society, Boston Athenaeum, New England Historic Genealogical Society, Boston Public Library, Suffolk County Courthouse, and Baker

Library of the Harvard Business School; in New York at the New-York
Historical Society, New York Public Library, Museum of the City of
New York, and Municipal Archives and Record Center; in Philadelphia
at the Historical Society of Pennsylvania, Library Company of Phila-
delphia, City Archives, American Philosophical Society, Presbyterian
Historical Society, Friends Record Center, Pennsylvania Genealogical
Society, Carpenter's Hall, Office of the Register of Wills, Philadelphia
Historical Commission, and Philadelphia Contributionship for Insuring
Houses; in Harrisburg at the Pennsylvania Archives and the Pennsylvania Historical and Museum Commission; and in Washington, D.C., at
the Library of Congress. The University Research Library at the University of California, Los Angeles, provided a superb home base for my
studies.

G.B.N.
Pacific Palisades, California
March 1979

Contents

ILLUSTRATIONS

TABLES

FIGURES

PART ONE

GROWTH AND WAR
1690-1740

*'Tis the Lord, who has Taken away from you, what He
has Given to others.*

    Cotton Mather, *Some Seasonable Advise unto the Poor*
(Boston, 1712)

*Idleness is the Dead Sea, that swallows all Virtues
Be active in Business, that Temptation may miss her Aim
The Bird that sits, is easily shot.*

    B. Franklin, *Poor Richard Improved*
(Philadelphia, 1756)

1

The Web of Seaport Life

WATER DOMINATED the life of America's northern seaport towns in the seventeenth century, dictating their physical arrangement, providing them with their links to the outer world, yielding up much of their sustenance, and subtly affecting the relationships among the different groups who made up these budding commercial capitals. Boston was almost entirely surrounded by water. Built on a tadpole-shaped peninsula that jutted into island-dotted Massachusetts Bay, the town was connected to the mainland only by the mile-long causeway called the Neck. New York was literally an island, set in perhaps the finest natural harbor on the continent and separated from its hinterland by the East and Hudson rivers. At a time when steel bridge construction was still more than a century away, it was accessible only by ferry, barge, or small wind-propelled craft. Philadelphia was almost one hundred miles from the sea, but it was planted on a broad strip of land between the Schuylkill and Delaware rivers—the latter providing its access to the ocean.

The colonial seaports existed primarily as crossroads of maritime transport and commercial interchange. European cities had often grown up as centers of civil and ecclesiastical administration and by the early nineteenth century they would expand greatly as centers of industrial production. But Boston, New York, and Philadelphia served primarily as points of entry for immigrating Europeans and Africans and as commercial marts serving hinterland populations. The ocean was the highway connecting the Old World and the New and the seaport towns were the vital link between the two. They gathered in the timber, fish, and agricultural produce that came from the rural settlers who made up the vast majority of the colonial population, sending it off to West Indian and European markets and distributing finished European goods throughout the regions they served.[1]

At the end of the seventeenth century the seaport towns were really only overgrown villages. Boston was the largest. Growing slowly for six decades after the Great Migration of English Puritans began in 1630, it reached a population of about 6,000 by 1690. New York, founded five years before Boston by the Dutch West India Company and known as New Amsterdam until conquered by the English in 1664, increased only to 3,500 by 1674 and to about 4,500 by 1690. Philadelphia, not planted until 1681, when William Penn received an immense grant from Charles II and promoted a movement of English and Irish Quakers across the Atlantic, was still in its infancy at the turn of the century, counting only about 2,200 inhabitants.[2] None of the American port towns could compare with even the secondary commercial centers of western Europe such as Lyon, which had reached 45,000 in the 1530s, or Norwich, which had grown to 19,000 by the 1570s. Nor could they claim equal status with the cities of the Spanish and Portuguese colonies to the south, where Bahia, Cartagena, Potosi, and Mexico City, built on the ruins of ancient Indian urban centers, numbered 50,000 or more by the end of the seventeenth century.[3]

The insignificant size of these seaports in British North America did not indicate English backwardness or a preference for the pastoral, agricultural life. The port towns were small because they served regional populations that themselves were still very limited. The population of Massachusetts had not yet reached 50,000 in 1690, so it is not surprising that Boston counted only 6,000 souls. Similarly, New York and Philadelphia served agricultural populations that had grown to no more than 14,000 and 12,000 respectively.[4]

The reduced scale of life in these late seventeenth-century ports made face-to-face relationships important. Craftsmen did not produce for anonymous customers or distant markets but labored almost entirely at turning out "bespoke goods"—articles made to order for individual customers. Nor would anybody long be a stranger in a town whose boundaries could be traversed on foot in a brisk thirty-minute walk. Bostonians did not spread out across their peninsula but crowded together between Beacon Hill, Copp's Hill, and Fort Hill along the southeastern shore that faced the harbor. New Yorkers did not range across the island of Manhattan but squeezed together at its southern tip, in the area known today as Wall Street. Philadelphia, where as late as 1750 the skyline was unbroken by a single building of more than three stories, covered a tract of about 1,200 acres. But its inhabitants chose their building sites along a one-mile stretch of Delaware River frontage, penetrating inland from the river no more than three blocks in the first quarter-century of settlement. Proximity to the harbor and wharves was on everyone's mind.[5] A by-product of this mode of settlement, in what urban historians call "walking cities," was a mixing of classes, occupations, religious beliefs, and ethnic backgrounds in the early years. So personal were the relationships in towns of this kind that even by the middle of the eighteenth century, one prominent Philadelphian could remark that in his city of about 13,000 he "knew every person white & black, men, women & children by name."[6]

Face-to-face relationships also reflected societies that were strongly familial in organization and still reliant upon oral discourse rather than the written or printed word for communications. Seventeenth-century American families were generally nuclear in structure, with each conjugal family unit living in a separate household headed by a father or his widowed wife. Indentured servants, slaves, and apprentices, as well as children, were integral parts of this family network, all living in close quarters where they worked, ate, and learned together, subject to the authority of the patriarchal father-employer.[7] Learning—whether religious, vocational, or concerned with the socialization of the young—was conducted typically through intimate human interchange, the mark of all oral societies preceding the modern era.[8]

If the individual family, closely knit by affective bonds and parental authority, was the characteristic social unit, no less familial in form was the wider network that bound together individual households. Whether in the church, where individual families melded into a congregation that stood united in pursuit of a common goal, or in the organization of poor relief, where the community at large acknowledged care of the poor as a common responsibility, the kinship orientation was pervasive. The family, according to the Puritan leaders of Boston, was a "little commonwealth."[9] The town, a collection of families, was a larger commonwealth, recognizing the common good as the highest goal. And all the towns in the Bay colony made up the Commonwealth of Massachusetts. The corporate whole, not the individual, was the basic conceptual unit.

In probing the social dynamics of the early towns it is essential to recognize that these were preindustrial societies in which tradition held sway. Little about the late seventeenth-century towns would be recognizable to the twentieth-century urbanite. Cows were commonly tethered behind the crudely built wooden houses, for milk was a commodity that most householders could not afford to purchase. Hogs roamed the streets because, as scavengers of refuse, they were the chief sanitary engineers in an age when most household wastes were emptied into ditches running down the middle of the streets. Indian shell beads, called wampum, were still in use as a medium of exchange in New York at the end of the seventeenth century, and paper money was as yet unknown except in Boston where it made its first appearance in 1690. There were no newspapers printed in the colonies before 1704, when the *Boston News-Letter* was first published. Philadelphians would wait until 1719 to see a newspaper in their city and New Yorkers until 1725. Lawyers, another fixture of the modern city, were everywhere regarded with suspicion, and the few who practiced in the late seventeenth century were largely untrained, unorganized, and little respected. "There was not such a parcel of wild knaves and Jacobites as those that practised the law in the province of New York," wrote Governor Bellomont in 1699, "not one of them a barrister, one was a dancing master, another a glover, a third . . . condemned to be hanged in Scotland for blasphemy and burning the bible."[10]

We must consider the values that lay behind human behavior in the context of these premodern aspects of urban life. Superstition and belief in the supernatural were widespread, for though urban dwellers might be more worldly than their country cousins, they were still bound within an inherited mental framework that had been formed by the precariousness of life and the incomprehensibility of nature. The seaport towns were not traumatized in 1690 by the witchcraft hysteria that shook Salem, Boston's neighbor, but most town dwellers believed that witches were truly abroad in Salem. Witches were as real as the devil, and witchcraft was a crime "as definite and tangible as is treason today."[11] As late as 1727 an earthquake that shook most of New England was interpreted by the lettered and unlettered alike as evidence of God's displeasure with his people in this corner of the earth. In both Massachusetts and New York census takers met broad resistance because of the widespread belief that violation of the biblical injunction against enumerating the people would bring famine or plague—a conviction that was vastly strengthened in New York City when the census of 1703 was closely followed by a smallpox epidemic that carried away almost 10 percent of the population.[12]

Another part of the value system was the prevailing orientation toward the proper arrangement and functioning of society. How should people in different social layers interact with each other? How should wealth and power be distributed? How much opportunity for advancement did ordinary town dwellers expect? What were the responsibilities of the rich for the poor and the poor to the wealthy? Was there a unitary body of thought on such questions, subscribed to by the affluent and indigent, by merchant, artisan, and common laborer alike? Implicit in all these questions is the assumption that the history of the seaport towns cannot fully be understood without fixing our attention upon the evolution of urban class structures. We need a social anatomy of these urban places, a comprehension of their component parts and the social relationships among them. In seeking this, it is well to be mindful of the advice of the English historian E. P. Thompson that "class" is a fluid not a static phenomenon, "a social and cultural formation, arising from processes which can only be studied as they work themselves out over a considerable historical period." "Class eventuates," writes Thompson, "as men and women *live* their productive relations, and as they *experience* their determinate situations, within 'the *ensemble* of the social relations,' with their inherited culture and expectations, and as they handle these experiences in cultural ways."[13]

Virtually everyone of wealth or position in the port towns adhered to the axiom that rank and status must be carefully preserved and social roles clearly differentiated if society was to retain its equilibrium. This was a cast of thought inherited from the Old World, although some colonizers recognized that a new environment might call for alterations. Social stability was uppermost in the minds of most of these leaders and they believed that nothing counted for more in its achievement than a careful demarcation of status and privilege. John Winthrop, the leader of the Puritan occupation of Massachusetts Bay, echoed ancient thinking that social unity and political stability were the products of a hierarchical social system that preserved distances between occupational groups and limited movement between them. "In all times," he wrote, "some must be rich, some poore, some highe and eminent in power and dignitie; others meane and in subjeccion."[14] Winthrop's conception of the carefully layered society where mobility was limited was perpetuated in Boston by a long line of Puritan clergymen who exhorted their auditors in this vein for many decades to come. There was every reason for officialdom and the mercantile elite of the port towns eagerly to echo such thoughts, for they justified the position of those at the top and encouraged those at the bottom to believe that their lowly positions were divinely willed. Hence, John Saffin, a Boston merchant, wrote in 1700 that God "hath Ordained different degrees and orders of men, some to be High and Honourable, some to be Low and Despicable, some to be Monarchs, Kings, Princes and Governours, Masters and Commanders, others to be subjects, and to be commanded." If it were otherwise, Saffin concluded, "there would be a meer parity among men."[15] Where parity crept in, anarchy was not far behind.

In New York and Philadelphia it was much the same. The religious impulse that reverberated so powerfully in Boston was more subdued in the Manhattan port, the least utopian of the northern capitals, but it was widely believed by those at the apex of the social pyramid that all men, by God's design, were created unequal. In Pennsylvania, also, the "holy experiment" was thought by its founder to depend for success on orderly patterns of taking up land, economic regulation, and firm lines of authority. Equalitarianism within the Society of Friends has been much remembered by historians, but it was confined to a belief in the equal worth of each individual in the sight of God and the capacity of each person to find God within himself or herself apart from scriptural revelation or external authority. Quakers were not levelers, even though they opposed social deference when it fed arrogance and abuse of power by those who held it. Their quarrel was not with the need for a structured society but with its social conventions. "We design to level nothing but Sin," wrote an early English Quaker, and his sentiment was repeated by one of the Society's principal theoreticians, who wrote that "I would not have any

judge, that . . . we intend to destroy the *mutual* Relation, that is betwixt
Prince and *People, Master* and *Servants, Parents* and *Children;* . . . Our
Principle in these things hath no such tendency, and . . . these Natural
Relations are rather better established, than any ways hurt by it."[16]

This perpetuation of social hierarchy can be seen in many of the conventions of urban life at the end of the seventeenth century. Puritans did
not file into church on Sunday morning and occupy the pews in random
fashion. Each was assigned a seat according to his or her rank in the community. "Dooming the seats" was the responsibility of a church committee that used every available yardstick of social status—age, parentage,
social position, service to the community, and wealth—in drawing up a
seating plan for the congregation. In New York, whipping, the most
common punishment meted out by the courts for minor offenses, was not
permitted for men of rank, though the stripping away of the right to use
"Mister" before one's name, or "Gentleman" after it, may have been
more painful than the lash. In their dress, speech, manners, and even the
food on their tables, urban dwellers proclaimed their place in the social
order.

While this replication of traditional European social attitudes regarding the structuring of society was widespread, and even regarded by
many as God-ordained, it was not universally accepted; nor was it unaffected by the environment of the New World. Those already in positions
of authority or possessed of economic advantage were the principal proponents of a paternalistic system that steadfastly advocated social gradations and subordination, for they, after all, were the chief beneficiaries of
such an arrangement. Those below them in the social order were often
less eager merely to recreate the past in the new land. As early as 1651 in
Massachusetts the magistrates of the General Court expressed their "utter
detestation and dislike that men and women of meane Condition should
take upon themselves the garb of Gentlemen by wearing gold or silver,
lace or buttons, or points at their knees or to walk in bootes or women of
the same rancke to weare silke or tiffany horlles or scarfes, which though
allowable to persons of greater estates, or more liberal education, yet we
cannot but judge it intollerable in persons of like condition."[17] Here was a
signal that many early Bostonians not only were able to improve their
condition but also intended to use their newfound prosperity to enhance
their wardrobes, thereby upgrading their class identification, of which
clothes were a primary badge. Such upward striving might have been expected, for the immigrants who settled the early towns were generally recruited from the middling ranks of English society and had been drawn to
the western edge of the Atlantic because they were motivated, among
other things, by a desire to better themselves economically. The impressive quantity of late seventeenth-century jeremiads concerning the need
for order and discipline in Massachusetts is one more indication that

many colonists, especially those not at the top of the social pyramid, found the old hierarchical code out of place and out of time.

To what extent hierarchical thinking pervaded the upper ranks of seaport society and to what degree it was resisted from below cannot be measured quantitatively. It is safe to say, however, that although almost every urban dweller knew instinctively his or her relation to those below and above, there was much crossing of lines between social layers and, even by the 1690s, a long history of undeferential behavior among plebeian sorts. We employ the term deference to describe the unquestioning acceptance of the superior wisdom of an elite by the broad mass of people.[18] It is easy, however, to overstate the operation of a well-oiled set of relationships between superiors and inferiors, and the unresentful acceptance of them as natural. Many urban people deferred because their economic security was bound up with a landlord, employer, or creditor. This was economic clientage and it doubtlessly produced social deference. But the obliging comment and passive demeanor of a journeyman carpenter or merchant seaman could melt away in moments of passion or collective action and often did not extend at all to other powerful figures whose control was less direct. Many vertical links bound urban society together and inhibited the formation of solidarities that were horizontal in nature. But these interrank bonds forged by vertical loyalties and obligations were by no means all-encompassing or unchanging. Time and circumstances altered social consciousness, wore away at deferential behavior, and gave rise to feelings of solidarity that were based on occupation, economic position, and class standing.

Closely tied to attitudes about the structural arrangement of society was the urban dweller's sense of whether his or her community functioned equitably. The important gap to measure is the one between aspiration and achievement. We must tread carefully in approaching this question, for twentieth-century concepts of mobility and contemporary expectations of success will help us little in studying preindustrial people.[19] The rise from rags to riches cannot be taken as a universal expectation.

In the late seventeenth century the limits of possibility had not yet been raised very high in the minds of most urban dwellers. Few Scots-Irish or German immigrants in Philadelphia, Dutch residents of New York, or English inhabitants of Boston dreamed of becoming wealthy merchants or country gentlemen. Nor did they regard themselves as "blocked" if they, or even their sons, could not make it to the top. They were coming from a society where intergenerational movement was almost imperceptible, where sons unquestioningly followed their father's trades, where the Protestant work ethic did not beat resoundingly in every breast, and where security from want, rather than the acquisition of riches, was the primary goal. It was modest opportunity (access to sufficient capital, land, and labor to produce material well-being) rather than rapid mobility (social ascendancy at the expense of others) that was most important in their calculations of whether equity prevailed in their society.

Much of the urban laboring man's sense of what was possible was shaped by the distinctly premodern nature of economic life in the port towns. Routinized, repetitive labor and the standardized work day, regulated by the clock, were unknown in this preindustrial era. Even the Protestant work ethic could not change irregular work patterns, for they were dictated by weather, hours of daylight, and the erratic delivery of raw materials. When the cost of fuel for artificial light was greater than the extra income that could be derived from laboring before or after sunlight hours, who would not shorten his day during winter? Similarly, when winter descended, business often ground to a halt. Even in the southernmost of the northern ports, ice frequently blocked maritime traffic. In the winter of 1728-1729, 36 ships lay frozen at dockside in Philadelphia; several decades later a visitor counted 117 ships icebound in the Delaware. This meant slack time for mariners and dockworkers, just as laborers engaged in well digging, road building, and cellar excavating for house construction were idled by frozen ground. The hurricane season in the West Indies forced another slowdown because few shipowners were willing to place their ships and cargoes before the killer winds that prevailed in the Caribbean from August to October.[20] If prolonged rain delayed the slaughter of cows in the country or made impassable the rutted roads into the city, then the tanner laid his tools aside and for lack of his deliveries the cordwainer was also idle. The hatter was dependent upon the supply of beaver skins, which could stop abruptly if disease struck an Indian tribe or war disrupted the fur trade. Weather, disease, and equinoxial cycles all contributed to the fitful pace of urban labor—and therefore to the difficulties of producing a steady income. Food and housing cost money every day of the year, but in calculating his income the urban dweller had to count on many "broken days," slack spells, and dull seasons.[21]

While resettlement in America could not change the discontinuous work patterns of preindustrial European life, shifting to the other side of the ocean did bring an adjustment in thinking about what was achievable. In Europe "the frontier zone between possibility and impossibility barely moved in any significant way, from the fifteenth to the eighteenth century."[22] But it moved in America. Hector St. John Crèvecoeur, a literary Frenchman who took up the life of a country gentleman in New York late in the colonial period, wrote memorably about this. "An European, when he first arrives," he reflected, "seems limited in his intentions, as well as his views; but he very suddenly alters his scale . . . He no sooner breathes our air than he forms schemes, and embarks in designs he never would have thought of in his own country."[23] Crèvecoeur romantized

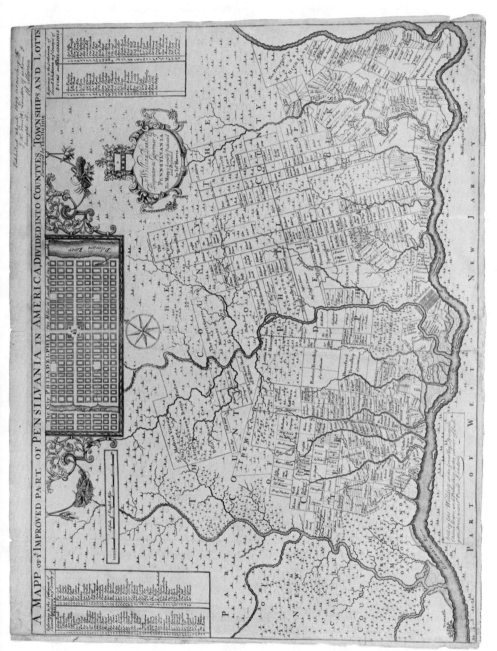

1. Map of Pennsylvania ca. 1687 by Thomas Holme

the matter somewhat, but many other observers also noted these rising expectations in North America—a psychological transformation fraught with implications for notions about the structuring of society. Land-hungry Europeans, turned loose on the western shore of the Atlantic, found river valleys spread before them beyond their wildest dreams. Their aspirations and their behavior consequently changed, and not always for the better in the view of their leaders. Roger Williams deplored the "depraved appetite after the great vanities, dreams and shadows of this vanishing life, great portions of land, land in this wilderness, as if men were in as great necessity and danger for want of great portions of land, as poor, hungry, thirsty seamen have, after a sick and stormy, a long and starving passage."[24] If this was true in New England, where religion acted as a brake on ambition more than in any other colony, what must it have been elsewhere? Williams saw the hunger for more and more land, symbolizing the raising of expectations, as "one of the gods of New England," and one "which the living and most high Eternal will destroy and famish."[25] Deplore it though he might, most would not listen, either in New England or elsewhere.

In the seaport towns it was somewhat different. Open stretches of land meant nothing to the artisan or shopkeeper, but the availability of work, the relationship of wages to prices, and the price of a lot and house meant much. In all of these matters the seaport dwellers could anticipate more favorable conditions than prevailed in the homelands that they or their parents had left. Unemployment was virtually unknown in the late seventeenth century, labor commanded a better price relative to the cost of household necessities, and urban land was purchased reasonably.[26] Upper-class urban dwellers often complained of the high cost of labor, but none suggested, as did Henry Addison, that faithful reflector of early eighteenth-century manners in England, that wages for the laboring class be lowered to the subsistence level and the poor "be supported but never relieved."[27] Labor was in shorter supply than in Europe and therefore commanded greater respect. This goes far toward explaining why one of the English holidays that did not persist in the American port towns was "St. Monday," the English laboring class's way of creating a long weekend. If more work meant only lower daily wages, as was often the case in England, then shortening the work week made perfect sense. But in the port towns "St. Monday" fell victim to the belief that opportunities were greater and that men, by the steady application of their skills, could raise themselves above the ruck.[28]

This did not mean that artisans and laborers worked feverishly to ascend the ladder of success. Craftsmen who commanded 5 shillings a day and laborers who garnered 3 knew that weather, sickness, and the inconstancy of supplies made it impossible to work more than 250 days a year, which would bring an income of about £35 to £60. Even if the margin between subsistence and saving was better than in Europe, it was still so narrow that years of hard work and frugal living usually preceded the purchase of even a small house. Hence, laboring people were far from the day when the failure to acquire property or to accumulate a minor fortune produced guilt or aroused their anger against those above them. Most artisans did not wish to become merchants or professionals. Their desire was not to reach the top but to get off the bottom. Family and community still counted more than the acquisition of wealth, and their modest ambitions were fully sanctioned by the Protestant belief that every man's calling, however menial, was equally worthy in the sight of God. Yet they expected a "decent competency," as it was called, and did not anticipate the grinding poverty of the laboring poor everywhere in Europe.

FROM ATTITUDES and aspirations we must turn to the actual structure of the late seventeenth-century port towns and reach some understanding of how they differed from the European commercial centers that the urban colonizers had left behind.

At the bottom of the social hierarchy were black slaves. The common view that slavery in colonial America was overwhelmingly a southern plantation phenomenon must be modified, for slavery took root early in the northern port towns and persisted there throughout the colonial period. By 1690, in fact, slaves represented as large a proportion of the northern urban populations as they did in tobacco-growing Maryland and Virginia. Boston was only eight years old, a town with fewer than 1,500 inhabitants, when it began its connection with the "peculiar institution." Victorious in a war of extermination against the Pequot Indians, Massachusetts shipped several hundred captive Pequot women and children to the West Indies, where they were exchanged for African slaves. A few years later, in 1645, the brother-in-law of John Winthrop counseled war against another Indian tribe, the Narragansetts, and argued "if upon a Just warre the Lord should deliver them [the Narragansetts] into our hands, wee might easily have men, women, and children enough to exchange for Moores, which wilbe more gaynefull pilladge for us than wee conceive, for I doe not see how wee can thrive untill wee gett into a stock of slaves sufficient to doe all our buisines, . . . [for] I suppose you know verie well how wee shall mainteyne 20 Moores cheaper than one Englishe servant."[29]

It was the calculation of relative labor costs that thereafter kept a small but steady flow of slaves coming into Boston. The number might have been greater if they had been more available, but Boston was at a considerable disadvantage, situated as it was at a greater distance from the source of slave labor than the West Indian or Chesapeake colonies. Even so, slaves made up about 3 to 4 percent of the population in 1690 and about one out of every nine families owned at least one slave.[30] Most of them were held by well-to-do merchants and officials of the community, who employed them as house servants, or by the best-established artisans, who taught them their skills and turned them into mastmakers, bakers, blacksmiths, seamen, shipwrights, and the like.

While the roots of slavery slowly penetrated the soil of Boston, they sank faster and deeper into that of New York. Boston's initiation to black slavery had been indirect, coming as a result of the enslavement of Indians; New York's introduction stemmed directly from the extensive early Dutch participation in the international slave trade to West Africa. Dutch New Netherland traded extensively with Dutch Curaçao, a sugar island off the coast of South America that produced a steady stream of "unworkable" slaves who were consequently transported for nonplantation labor to the mainland colony. In the last five years before the English takeover of New Netherland, more than 400 slaves entered its capital city. The English, in capturing New Amsterdam in 1664, were seizing a city whose population was 20 percent black, about four times the incidence of blacks in Virginia and Maryland at this time.[31] The English imported fewer Africans than the Dutch but they made no attempt to phase out slave labor. By 1698, when the first English census was conducted in the city, Negroes represented more than 14 percent of the population. Even more indicative of the extent to which the master-slave relationship was incorporated into the social structure was the number of slaveholding families in the society. In 1698, almost 35 percent of the heads of household owned slaves and five years later the percentage had increased to 41.[32]

It is not easy to evaluate the impact of this extensive involvement with chattel slavery upon the life of the society, but John Woolman's assessment of the connection between slavery and white personality development, made years later, deserves careful consideration. Slaveholding, wrote the northern Quaker reformer, even by the kindliest of masters, did "deprave the mind in like manner and with as great certainty as prevailing cold congeals water." The absolute authority exercised by the master over his slave established "ideas of things and modes of conduct" that inexorably affected the attitudes of children, neighbors, and friends.[33] Slavery, in short, was far more than a labor system. Beyond that, it was part of an evolving system of racial attitudes and child-rearing practices, and, ultimately, a manner of approaching human labor as something to be imported and exported, bought, bartered, and sold.[34]

In Philadelphia slavery also found its place from the beginning, although most historical accounts leave the impression that the institution was incidental to the city's development. The spirit of Quaker abolitionism was still half a century away when the earliest settlers gladly received a shipload of African slaves, who arrived only three years after the Delaware River capital had been established. Quaker settlers, engaged in the difficult work of clearing trees and brush and erecting crude houses, eagerly exhausted most of the specie brought from England to purchase the Africans. Extant inventories of estate indicate that about one of every fifteen families owned slaves in the last decade of the seventeenth century —a rate understandably below that of New York and Boston since Philadelphia was in its infancy and had not yet generated sufficient capital for the importation of large numbers of involuntary servants.[35]

Above slaves in the urban social structure were indentured servants. Trading four to seven years of their labor for passage across the Atlantic and sold at dockside to the highest bidder, they were circumscribed so thoroughly by the law that most rights regarded as basic to the English heritage were held in abeyance until their terms of service were up. They formed an important part of the labor force in New York and Philadelphia but not in Boston. Urban indentured servitude was never so debilitating and exploitative as in the early Chesapeake tobacco colonies, where most servants did not survive to breathe the air of freedom they sought and only a few of those who completed their indentures matched legal freedom with freedom from want.[36] Yet it is evident from the considerable number of suicides and the great number of runaways that the life of the servant-immigrant, who was typically between thirteen and twenty years old, was frequently miserable and often unbearable.

This was probably less true in the early years of urban settlement because many of the servants were actually nephews, nieces, cousins, and children of friends of emigrating Englishmen, who paid their passage in return for their labor once in America.[37] When John Bezar, a maltster from Wiltshire, England arrived in Pennsylvania in December 1681, for example, he brought along Joseph Cloud, the son of a friend, William Cloud, as an indentured servant. Of a sample of 788 settlers who arrived in Philadelphia between 1682 and 1687, 34 percent of all persons and 49 percent of the adult males were indentured; but a great many of these servants were related by kinship, religious ties, or prior association in small communities of England.[38] These associative ties meant life under servitude, at least for the first generation, was laborious but relatively humane and the prospect for advancement after the term of indenture was bright. It would not always be so.

Above slaves and indentured servants—bound laborers who occupied a kind of subbasement of society from which ascent into the main house was difficult or impossible—stood apprentices and hired servants. Apprentices were servants too, but they differed from indentured servants in serving in the locale where they were born, usually in a family known to their parents, and contracting out to another familial setting by consent of their parents or guardians. They were rarely bought and sold, as were indentured servants. Especially in Boston the apprentice system bolstered familial forms by training up the young in the families of friends and acquaintances who were usually coreligionists. In all the port towns the principal purpose of apprenticing was the same as it had been for generations in England—to educate the youth in the "arts and mysteries" of the various crafts, thus providing an adequate pool of skilled labor.[39]

Free unskilled laborers occupied the next rank of society. In the preindustrial era they performed the essential raw labor associated with construction and shipping. Along the waterfront, they loaded and unloaded the ships and manned the vessels that provided the lifelines between the seaports of North America and the world beyond. Each of the northern port towns, even in the early stages of development, had hundreds of such laborers. They are perhaps the most elusive social group in early American history because they moved from port to port with far greater frequency than other urban dwellers, shifted occupations, died young, and, as the poorest members of the free white community, least often left behind traces of their lives on the tax lists or in land and probate records. Grouped with them in social status were common laborers who stayed on land. In the port towns, where house, wharf, road, and bridge construction was a major enterprise throughout the colonial years, they were the diggers of basement and wells, the pavers of streets, the cutters and haulers of wood, and the carters of everything that needed moving. It is difficult to assess how large a proportion of the working force they represented, but of the 304 estates inventoried in Boston between 1685 and 1699, they constitute nearly one-fifth of the decedents.[40] Together with apprentices, indentured servants, and slaves, these free laborers probably constituted as much as half the labor force at the end of the seventeenth century.

Artisans—known also as "tradesmen," "mechanics," "artificers," and "leather apron men"—filled the wide social space between laborers and an upper-class elite. This is a group so large and diverse that historians have never quite been able to agree on how to define it in occupational or class terms. Most of them were self-employed, proudly so, and they included everyone from silversmiths and hatters to shoemakers, tailors, and mast and sailmakers. Within most of the occupational subdivisions a wide range of wealth and status existed. In part this reflected the age-old hierarchy within each craft, composed of apprentices, journeymen, and master craftsmen.[41] At each step along the way the economic security and material rewards could normally be expected to rise, so that the range of wealth that can be observed in the tax lists for carpenters in Boston or clockmakers in New York reflects to some degree the age of the particular artisan and the acquisition of skills associated with his work. Age was by no means the only or even the most important factor, however. Stephen Coleman, a Philadelphia glover, died in 1699 with an estate valued at £580, including two houses, while John Simons, also a glover of about the same age, died in the same year with an estate of only £51. In 1691 Thomas Smith, a Boston carpenter, left possessions worth £839, including four indentured servants and a house valued at £312. Seven years later, Richard Crisp, another carpenter, had personal possessions valued at only £72 and no real estate to leave his heirs.[42] Craft skill, business acumen, health, luck, and choice of marriage partner were all parts of the formula by which some prospered and others did not.

The opportunities of the late seventeenth-century urban artisan varied considerably within crafts but no more so than variations between occupational groups. A hierarchy of trades existed in all of the towns—after the Revolution this was sometimes symbolized by the marching order of the various crafts at public celebrations—and to some degree the success of individual mechanics can be predicted by the trade they followed. Everyone knew that artisans working with precious metals got ahead faster than those who worked at the cobbler's bench and that house carpenters were far more likely to become property owners than tailors and stocking weavers.[43] Nonetheless, young men chose their careers far more with reference to that of their fathers—or their uncles, older brothers, or cousins—than to a rational calculation of future material rewards. Nathaniel Adams, a Boston blockmaker since the 1650s, died in the town in 1690 but passed his skills along to his son Joseph, also a blockmaker. Joseph's son John continued the family tradition as did his son Nathaniel, who was supplying ships with maritime pulleys on the eve of the American Revolution. Along the Philadelphia waterfront the name Penrose meant shipbuilding, for four generations of the family had plied the shipwright's craft before the Revolution. Such intergenerational artisan continuity was one more proof that urban dwellers who worked with their hands retained part of the traditional mentality which held that a decent subsistence or a slow inching forward was more the norm than the rapid aggrandizement of wealth.[44]

Standing at the top of the urban pyramid were two groups, one distinguished by its high social status and the other by its wealth. The first of these was composed of the professionals—government officials, doctors, clergymen, schoolteachers, and, eventually, lawyers. Often they were rewarded more by the community's respect than by material benefits. Boston, for example, paid its public school teachers only about £25 sterling per year in the 1690s and forty years later New York had only £30 sterling to spare for a teacher's wages.[45] The congregation of Old South Church allowed its pastors, Benjamin Colman and Thomas Prince, only £73 sterling annually in 1725. Professional men sometimes did better but mostly when they drew upon social prestige to arrange a propitious marriage.[46] But nobody denied that these educated men performed vital functions in the community, and the fact that their wealth rarely approximated their prestige serves as a reminder that parallel hierarchies of wealth, power, and prestige existed and did not precisely overlap.

Held in lower regard but dominating economic life were the seaport merchants, and, to a lesser degree, the shopkeepers, who often aspired to merchant status. These were the urban dwellers who controlled the life-lines between the seaports and the hinterland and between the ports and the outside world. Without these importers and exporters, wholesalers and retailers, builders of ships, wharves, and warehouses there could have been no commercial centers. It should come as no surprise that those who controlled mercantile endeavors quickly gained a disproportionate share of economic leverage in the urban centers of colonial life, not only in dominating the flow of marketable goods but also in their control of shipbuilding, credit facilities, and urban real estate. Political power to match their economic influence was established early in all the northern ports; how this power was used would become one of the most enduring issues of the eighteenth century.[47]

The differing opportunities and abilities of men to manipulate their economic environment and to operate within the urban occupational hierarchy were eventually inscribed on the tax lists of the community, which measured each person's wealth alongside that of his or her neighbors, and in inventories of estate, which set a value on each item of a decedent's personal estate, from the clothes in the wardrobe to the tools in the shop to the implements in the kitchen and furniture in the bedroom. Tax records must be used with caution because what was taxed in one city was not necessarily taxed in another, because some adult males were not included in the tax rolls, and because the lists were based on a regressive tax system that grossly underestimated the wealth of some, particularly those at the top of the social pyramid. Inventories of estate also have shortcomings because they were made or survive for less than 50 percent of the deceased heads of household in Boston, for a still smaller proportion of Philadelphians, and for only a statistically irrelevant number of New Yorkers. Also, it is widely suspected by historians that the estates of the wealthier members of society were inventoried more frequently than those of their poorer neighbors.

In spite of these difficulties, tax lists and inventories are a generally reliable index to wealth distribution in the seaport towns and if the distortions inherent in them remained constant, they can be used to measure long-term secular change.[48] We gain confidence in the picture that these data present because of the general congruence between wealth profiles revealed by the tax lists on the one hand and the inventories of estate on the other.

One of the most obvious conclusions to be drawn from these data is that the division of wealth in the three cities, despite marked differences in their age, religious, and ethnic composition, differed only slightly at the end of the seventeenth century. Boston in 1687 and New York in 1695 were more than half a century old and had reached populations of nearly 6,000 and 4,700 respectively. Philadelphia had existed for only a decade and contained about 2,100 inhabitants. But wealth within the three communities was similarly distributed. In each of the towns the bottom 30 percent of wealthholders had only a slight hold on the community's resources, possessing about 3 percent of the total assets. On the tax lists, these were the men at the beginning of their careers, who had accumulated only meager taxable assets, and the older members of the town, such as seamen and laborers, whose wages were never sufficient to permit more than the necessities of life. In the inventories, these bottom layers of society included all persons, regardless of age or occupation, who at death possessed personal wealth from £2 to £70 sterling in Boston and £5 to £79 in Philadelphia.[49] Some of them truly lived in penury, such as Boston mariners Robert Oliver and Henry Johnson, who died in the 1690s with the clothes on their backs, a sea chest, a Bible, and a few nautical instruments.[50] But most maintained a rudimentary existence, renting a small, sparsely furnished house, and owning the tools of their trade and a few household possessions. About one in twenty had scraped together enough money to purchase real estate, usually a small lot with a rude wooden structure on it. Counted among them were a large number of merchant seamen and laborers, but there were also many widows and a scattering of carpenters, cordwainers, coopers, tailors, and joiners, as well as an occasional shopkeeper or merchant whose luck or business acumen had failed him.

The second tier of society, made up of the fourth, fifth, and sixth least wealthy deciles, contained a broad spectrum of artisans, smaller numbers of mariners who had prospered modestly, merchant-shopkeepers who had not, and the inevitable widows. At death this middle range of persons left behind personal possessions worth between £72 and £206 sterling in Boston (£87 to £292 including real property) and £79 and £246 in Philadelphia. This meant that they commanded 11 percent of Boston's collective inventoried wealth and 16.5 percent of Philadelphia's. In the Puritan capital about half of them owned real estate, usually a small lot and house valued at not more than £150. Caleb Rawlings of Boston, a house carpenter who died in 1693, stood near the median of this group and we can tell something about the conditions of life in this middling range of seaport dwellers from his inventory.[51] Rawlings owned a house and lot worth £117 sterling, which he left to his wife. The house was plainly furnished with three bedsteads, tables, chairs, and chests, but the family had done well enough to acquire pewter and brassware worth about £5, a looking glass, and a few rugs for the floor. His musket, bandeliers, and sword indicate that he may have been a militia officer, and the two spinning wheels tell us that his wife and daughters probably contributed significantly to the family economy.

Within the upper-middle tier of urban society stood the prospering merchants and shopkeepers, a sprinkling of master craftsmen, and the widows of men who had left their wives securely situated at death. In Boston almost three-quarters of these persons passed on to their heirs substantial amounts of real estate, including wharves, shops, and warehouses, as well as land and houses. The range of their wealth tells us that they lived comfortably. In Philadelphia their estates, exclusive of real property, ranged from £252 to £625; in Boston from £207 to £711.[52] Men who had achieved material success of this kind had mahogany furniture in the parlor instead of oak, slept in canopied beds with fine linen, ate from silver rather than wood or pewter, and owned imported clocks, books, and other accoutrements of the moderately affluent life. Whereas only 4.4 percent of Boston's deceased in the bottom 60 percent of society in this period owned slaves, 20 percent of those in the 61-90 percentile did. In all of the port towns this group claimed hold of about 40 percent of the collective assets in their communities.

The top 10 percent of the wealthholders, who can loosely be designated as the economic elite, were almost all officeholders, merchants, and others closely associated with mercantile pursuits or the widows of such men. Among the thirty Boston decedents between 1685 and 1699 who occupied this uppermost rank, for example, there were nineteen merchants, four sea captains, who also usually acted as importers on their own, two officeholders (including Governor William Phips), a distiller, house carpenter, brazier, butcher, miller, and minister. All but five of these men owned real estate, and most could boast of property worth £500 sterling or more.[53] Eight owned slaves and their personal wealth was valued at between £728 and £2,634. Counting real estate they had accumulated between £1,155 and £3,417 of property during their lifetimes. Their Philadelphia counterparts were also mostly men involved in commerce. If their personal estates were somewhat less than in Boston, varying between £666 and £1,978 sterling, this can be explained by the shorter time they had to accumulate worldly goods, since most of them had died within a decade of leaving England to establish a new life in the Delaware River Valley. In both towns, and also in New York, about 40 percent of the total taxable assets or inventoried wealth fell under the control of this wealthiest tenth—about the same percentage possessed by the next richest three-tenths of society.

We need not be surprised that the top tenth of society controlled 40 percent of the community's wealth and the bottom half possessed only about 10 percent. So it had been throughout history, especially in urban centers, where the division of material goods and property was almost always less even than in the countryside. It is likely, in fact, that the wealth of European towns in this period was maldistributed to a far greater degree. So long as the unequal division of wealth had proceeded only this far, it was of far less concern than the actual conditions of life and how they compared to what the previous generation had known. Laboring people had never controlled more than a tiny fraction of the community's total wealth and did not imagine that social relationships were deranged because assets were disproportionately concentrated at the top of society. What mattered to them was that in some places in the world the laboring poor lived in abject misery while in others they knew a spare but decent existence.

In the American port towns of the 1690s life at the bottom compared favorably with conditions in any of the English, Irish, and Scottish towns from which urban dwellers or their parents had come. Mariners, laborers, and many of those at the lower levels of the artisanry labored long hours under unpleasant and often unhealthy conditions; and at the end of their lives they had little to show for their efforts by modern standards. But they did not starve or go unclothed and unhoused. They were far better off than their counterparts in the late seventeenth-century English towns, where unemployment and acute poverty were major problems and political economists were busily planning workhouses to sponge up the jobless poor and set them to hard labor that would relieve taxpayers of supporting them through the poor rates. The incidence of poverty, in fact, was extremely low and was confined for the most part to the widowed, disabled, and orphaned, who were decently cared for. Thoroughly Elizabethan in their attitudes to the poor, townspeople regarded the small number of indigents as wards of the community, whose members should collectively assume responsibility for those in distress. Little stigma was attached to being poor, for it was generally due to circumstances beyond the individual's control.[54] If Widow Chambers in Boston was old, infirm, and without children to care for her, the selectmen saw to it that wood was delivered to her door during the winter months. In New York in 1683 legislation was passed directing local officials to "make provision for the maintenance and support of their poor." In Philadelphia the law until 1700 required the justices of the peace to see to the needs of the indigent. Within a social system fundamentally based on family and kinship, remedies for dealing with the community's unfortunates were familial in form. Most often, persons in need remained in their homes or in the homes of others and were given "out-relief" there— clothes, firewood, bread, and often small weekly cash payments. In all of the port towns poverty was not regarded as a social defect and a sense of social responsibility pervaded poor relief measures.[55]

In none of the towns did poor relief burden the taxpayers. On average, less than £100 per year was spent by Boston on poor relief in the 1690s and in Philadelphia the figure was probably less than half of that.[56] In 1688 only £20 was required for the care of the needy in New York.[57] Only twice in the late seventeenth century did widespread deprivation appear in the seaports and in both cases it was the ravages of war, not the internal functioning of the economy, that was responsible. The first crisis came when Indian tribes in Massachusetts devastated dozens of inland communities in 1676, sending refugees streaming into Boston in search of safety and aid. Bostonians, however, did not graciously apply the rule of corporate responsibility to the larger community of Massachusetts Bay. In a foreshadowing of later events, Boston's leaders tried to convince the General Court to allow the eviction of these "strangers"—those who had neither been born nor established residence in the town. It was thus revealed that the other side of caring for one's own poor was hardhearted exclusion and punishment of those judged to be vagabonds, idlers, or the itinerant poor. But the crisis soon passed and Boston returned to the traditional system of caring for its small number of resident indigents. When war broke out with France in 1689, the town received a second taste of distress. By excluding refugees from border towns along the Canadian frontier or by "warning them out," a legal procedure that permitted them to take up residence but disqualified them from public relief, the town again acted to hold down taxes. But Boston found that it now had a resident poverty problem of unprecedented proportions. The disastrous Canadian expedition of 1690, designed to level Quebec, left in its wake the widows and children of scores of Boston seamen and foot soldiers, volunteers who had lost their lives in an abortive offensive against French Catholic power in North America. Bostonians alone among the late seventeenth-century urban dwellers knew at first hand the debilitating effects of war, but even in the New England capital there was still no reason to believe that poverty would become a permanent urban problem or to view the poor as anything but unfortunates whose condition was to be pitied and communally relieved since it was no fault of their own.

If life at the bottom of northern seaport society put laboring people ahead of their European relatives, life at the top left the colonial economic elite far behind. Just as a subbasement for slaves and indentured servants had been added, the colonial structure lacked a tower full of glittering diamonds and gold. Even the richest merchants of Boston, New York, and Philadelphia cut a poor figure compared to the overseas traders of Bristol, Hull, Cork, Dublin, and Edinburgh. The point is important because the gap between rich and poor was one of those measures by which ordinary town dwellers and even upper-class leaders judged equity and virtue in their society. Nobody, at least at this time, questioned the right of the rich to their worldly goods. But too much wealth was suspect, especially in Boston and Philadelphia, where the Puritan notion that making money was legitimate only when profits were put to public uses and the Quaker emphasis on "plain living" subtly curbed the aggrandizement of large fortunes.[58] Religious restraints on the aggressive accumulation of riches were strengthened by a pervasive secular feeling that transplanted Europeans were building a better kind of society in the New World, one where neither jewel-bedecked lords nor impoverished vassals would be known. There was no inconsistency between adherence to social hierarchy and disdain for too great a gap between rich and poor. Hierarchy was best preserved from challenges, in fact, when the social spectrum did not include degrading indigency at the lower end and sumptuous wealth at the upper.

The opportunities for amassing great wealth were, in fact, few in the late seventeenth-century port towns, so the fortunes of even the handful of affluent merchants and landowners were hardly a match for the wealth of a prospering London entrepreneur. Even the wealthiest men were primarily rich on paper, since their main assets were large tracts of land outside the towns, which would await a later generation to find buyers. Even urban real estate, which was appreciating in value, would not deliver rewards until the succeeding generation, when it doubled and redoubled. The inventories make clear how truncated was the pyramid of wealth. Only 3 of the 304 decedents in Boston between 1685 and 1699 left personal estates worth more than £2,000 sterling and only 1 of 84 did so in Philadelphia. Even including real estate, only 7 Bostonians left more than £2,000 and the estate of the wealthiest totaled only £3,417.[59] There were many merchants in Boston in the last decade of the century who were well on their way to accumulating more than this, but the risks of trade, the absence of a highly productive hinterland that could produce large marketable surpluses, and the generally low level of credit available to seaport entrepreneurs severely limited the opportunities for the aggrandizement of profits of a magnitude possible in European commercial capitals. Fish and lumber were the two products around which Boston shipping revolved, and shipbuilding was Boston's chief industry; but none of these activities yet had the potential to generate great wealth.[60]

Still, a small number of Bostonians accumulated minor fortunes, more often in land speculation than in trade or shipbuilding, and some had begun to convert their success into a Restoration lifestyle that shocked the town's moral guardians. Samuel Shrimpton, for example, inherited a sizeable estate from his father, an immigrant brazier who had invested in Boston real estate, and the son consolidated the family fortune by investing in the fish and logwood trade and by speculating in real estate. Shrimpton owned one of Boston's few coaches in the 1690s, and he scandalized Puritans with his sinful extravagances and public displays. Samuel Sewall, a devout merchant of modest estate, described one drunken coach ride made by Shrimpton and his friends from Roxbury to Boston where "they stop and drink Healths, curse, swear, talk profanely and baudily to the great disturbance of the Town and grief of good people. Such high-handed wickedness has hardly been heard of before in Boston."[61] Other prospering merchants, such as Andrew Belcher, arrived at balls in carriages attended by liveried slave footmen. And merchants were beginning to build Boston's first three-story brick houses in the North End.[62] But for all these pale imitations of European aristocratic life, this was still an elite very much in the formative stage.

In New York and Philadelphia the budding mercantile luminaries were less distant from the laboring sector of society than in Boston. New York's merchants gleaned their profits off a far less developed hinterland than in New England and they were caught in the late seventeenth century in a transition period, where mercantile activities were shifting from connections with Amsterdam and the Dutch empire to London, the West Indies, and other parts of the English-controlled colonial world. The merchant elite in New York in 1695 was an ethnically tripartite community with about forty-six Dutch, thirty-four English, and eighteen French traders.[63] Challenging the pre-eminent position that had been held by Dutch merchants such as Rip Van Dam, Abraham DePeyster, and Jacobus Van Cortlandt were English and French newcomers such as Richard Willett, William Merritt, Stephen DeLancey, and Gabriel Minvielle. Inventories of New Yorkers who died in this period are rare, so it is difficult to ascertain the size of mercantile fortunes; but, as in Boston, they cannot have been very great to judge by the tax lists, where the wealthiest man in 1695 was assessed for an estate of £2,610 and only six taxpayers had estates in excess of £500.[64]

In Philadelphia, sufficient time had not elapsed by the end of the century to allow for the crystallization of an elite; of the eighty-four inventoried estates before the turn of the century, only one exceeded £2,000 sterling, and in 1693 only two men paid taxes on estates larger than £1,000. This telescoped social structure was accentuated by the Quakers' emphasis on simplicity and avoidance of ostentation. Though its social structure was moving toward greater elaboration and though its wealth was divided in a manner similar to Boston's, Philadelphia in its early years disguised the gap between top and bottom as in no other town.[65] Still young and fluid, Philadelphia welcomed all comers and bid them do their best.

All three port towns by the end of the seventeenth century had evolved into bustling entrepôts through which the lifeblood of their colonies flowed. As everywhere, the benefits of a commercial way of life were shared unequally among their members. But by European standards, which, after all, provided the American urban dwellers with their frame of reference, the relationships among the constituent parts of society functioned in a generally equitable fashion. Lower-class artisans and laborers might regard upper-class leaders as too inflexibly committed to the concept of an ordered and immobile society; and upper-class merchants and professionals might see dangerous leveling tendencies in lower-class pretensions to a more genteel manner of living. But most people took satisfaction in the fact that William Phips, a sheep farmer and ship's carpenter from Maine, could rise to the governorship of Massachusetts in 1692 and that Griffith Jones, a glover from County Surrey in England, could become mayor of Philadelphia in 1704.[66] If the expectations of not every inhabitant of the port towns were fully met, there was at least a general sense that life was fulfilling in the northern English colonies and that the future was bright.

2

The Urban Polity

"WERE IT NOT for Government, the World would soon run into all manner of disorders and confusions," wrote a Puritan clergyman early in the eighteenth century. "Mens Lives and Estates and Liberties would soon be prey to the Covetous and the Cruel" and every man would be "as a wolf" to others.[1] Few persons, Puritan or otherwise, would have disagreed at this time, for the concept that government existed to protect life, liberty, and property was well established in every part of the English-speaking world.

Exactly how government achieved these ends was not so clear. Social harmony, for example, was repeatedly held up as a goal of such importance that every citizen should sacrifice individual desires in order to attain it. The members of the community should be "knitt together in this worke as one man," said John Winthrop, and his words rang as true in 1700 as they had a half-century before. Equally uncontroversial was the notion that behind all good government stood good law, for the lines between acceptable behavior and unsanctioned acts had to be precisely drawn so that offenders could be quickly apprehended and punished.[2] A third widely acknowledged tenet of government was that political authority existed not only to keep order and promote harmony but also to protect members of the community in the free exercise of their just rights —rights that had been defined over the centuries of English life and had become embodied in the common law carried to the New World. In theory, all of these precepts of government found general acceptance among the urban societies of the 1690s, just as they did within rural communities.

Between theory and practice in political life, however, lay difficult terrain. The social harmony so widely desired was rarely achieved by Englishmen either at home or overseas. Agreement was rare concerning exactly what constituted "good law." How far individual rights extended was a never-ending subject of debate. And events and circumstances had a way of driving men and women outside the boundaries of normally acceptable behavior and into kinds of political activity whose legitimacy was the subject of wide disagreement. Especially thorny was the question of how far protest against established authority could go and what forms it might take. Consensus was easy enough to reach on the illegal nature of a whole catalogue of antisocial acts, including theft, assault, murder, rape, arson, bribery, extortion, and perjury. But what were the limits of the ruler's power? When was his encroachment on the people's rightful liberties serious enough to warrant his exclusion from office? Who was to determine this and how was an unjust ruler to be ousted? What kinds of dissent should be allowed?

Such questions were especially pertinent in the colonial seaports, where provincial government in the northern colonies was centered. Legislative assemblies convened in Boston, New York, and Philadelphia; the will of the mother country was promulgated in them; and royal officials charged with its implementation resided there. The people of the maritime centers were closest to mercantilist regulations initiated in London and most affected by the policies of the home government. Among the 200,000 colonists in English North America in 1690, they were the most attuned to the wider world of politics created by the Anglo-American connection.

Political life also operated more vibrantly in the towns than in the country because the urban communities required a greater degree of government, given their size and commercial character. Larger, more diverse populations meant more officials, more ordinances, greater social and economic controls. In Chesapeake tobacco counties, widely dispersed plantations operated semiautonomously. County government played a role in building and maintaining bridges and roads and in operating the system of civil and criminal law. But nowhere near the volume of governmental activity was required as in the northern seaport towns, where population density and a more complex structure of economic relationships made local authority more visible and drew members of the community into a much more politicized world.

There is one other reason for attaching to the seaport towns an importance far beyond their share of the population, which in the northern colonies never reached even 10 percent. Social structure and economic conditions changed more rapidly in the commercial centers of northern colonial life than in the smaller towns and rural hinterland, and thus political life, which necessarily responded to these alterations, can be observed here in its most dynamic form. Many of the changes that would transform the political system as a whole appeared first in the maritime centers of prerevolutionary life. By the same token, the gap between political theory and political practice is best disclosed in the northern seaports, for it was here that rapidly changing economic and social conditions engendered new kinds of political behavior, demanded new political institutions, and led to the articulation of new political ideas.

Before we can understand these changes, we must comprehend the political world that urban dwellers inhabited at the end of the seventeenth century. It is difficult to speak of a dominant political ideology in the seaport towns, for English political theory, from which American thought was derived, was itself in the process of change, moving from medieval modes of thought in which the God-given authority of the monarch was unquestioned to adherence to a "civic humanism" in which stability was achieved by balancing the interests of monarchy, aristocracy, and democracy. The Revolution of 1688 strengthened the commitment to a carefully balanced system in which the interests of the one, the few, and the many—represented by the king, Lords, and Commons— were poised in dynamic equilibrium.[3] The governments of most of the colonies were so modeled. Equipoise would be achieved, it was hoped, by distributing power among governor, council, and assembly. The governor was appointed by the king and acted as his agent overseas; the council was appointed by the governor and sat as a pale equivalent of the House of Lords; and the assembly was elected by the freeholders, who regarded it as a replica of the House of Commons. Most inhabitants of the seaports, though not all, would probably have agreed with a Bostonian of the next generation who wrote that "the concurrence of these three forms of government seems to be the highest perfection that human civil government can attain to in times of peace . . . ; if it did not sound too profane by making too free with the mystical expressions of our religion, I should call it *a trinity in unity*."[4]

The freeholders of Boston, New York, and Philadelphia experienced this "republican" form of English government in slightly different forms. The governors of Massachusetts and New York were royally appointed in accordance with the Massachusetts Charter of 1691 and the establishment of New York as a royal colony in 1685. Pennsylvania's governor was appointed by William Penn, who had received a vast proprietary grant from Charles II in 1681. More important to seaport dwellers were differences in the manner of constituting the council and assembly, the lawmaking bodies in each colony. In Massachusetts the councilors were selected annually by the elected assembly, voting with the councilors of the previous year, the selection being subject to the veto of the governor. In New York and Pennsylvania, councilors were selected by the governor. A popular element was thus present in the election of the Massachusetts council that was absent in the other colonies.

The election of an assembly was widely regarded as the most important element of the legislative power of the people. In Boston and Philadelphia elections for the assembly were held annually, thus establishing the tradition that the electorate's interests and opinions should be determined at frequent intervals. In New York, however, assembly elections were held only when the governor pleased, although eventually a law requiring elections at least every seventh year was passed. Equally important was determining who could vote for representatives to the provincial legislatures. Since the fifteenth century in the English world civil participation had been defined by property ownership. Those who did not have real property capable of producing an annual income of 40 shillings, in addition to satisfying fundamental requirements related to age, sex, and sometimes religion, were not deemed part of the political community. This principle of enfranchisement contained two important assumptions. First, the poor and propertyless were excluded from politics because they lacked the "stake" in society that supposedly transformed unpredictable, anarchically inclined creatures into sober, responsible voters. Secondly, landed wealth was favored over liquid wealth, such as bonds, bills, book credit, mortgages, and stock in trade. This amounted to an antiurban bias, for in dynamic, commercial maritime towns liquid capital was unusually important if not dominant.

In Massachusetts, the definition of political competence underwent many changes before 1690. Given the incomplete state of the records, historians have not yet settled the question of how widespread the franchise was at various points in the seventeenth century.[5] Certainly by 1690 it was not as open as in 1655, when "Scotch servants, Irish, negers and persons under one and twenty years" were voting according to a committee of the General Court.[6] The Charter of 1691 abolished the old church membership requirement and extended the vote to holders of real property worth 40 shillings per year in rent or those who held property of any kind worth £40 sterling. If several recent scholars have correctly figured the value of property assessed on the Boston tax list of 1687, then at least 70 percent of the free adult males in the town were eligible to vote.[7] The very low number of voters turning out at this time—before 1698 apparently no more than 200 participated, or about one-sixth of the total adult white males—calls these calculations into question; but even so the franchise was undoubtedly broad by English standards and probably included a majority of the adult males.[8]

In New York, the basic suffrage requirement was also a £40 freehold, and as in Boston it seems to have embraced a majority (though not a precisely determinable proportion) of the free male members of the community. Voting statistics are scarce for this period, but we know that in 1699, 632 voters went to the polls in a population that included only 800 male taxpayers. Allowing for some absenteeism, this number of voters strongly suggests that the £40 property requirement was generally ignored or that almost everyone owned property worth £40 in New York, which is highly unlikely in view of what is known about the structure of wealth in the other seaport towns in this period.[9]

Pennsylvania also had a liberal franchise. Anyone who owned 100 acres of land, which could be purchased from Penn for £2 in the early 1680s, or who paid scot and lot, a householder's municipal tax, was eligible to vote. This undoubtedly enfranchised a large majority of the free, adult males. In 1696, when the Quaker-dominated assembly was concerned about the heavy influx of non-Quakers in Philadelphia, the franchise was redefined to exclude anyone without a £50 estate free of debts, a restriction that narrowed the suffrage but still permitted a majority of free males to participate in the electoral process.[10]

The privilege of voting for the provincial assembly was a treasured right of the urban electorate at the end of the century. The assemblies passed laws regulating the economic life of the cities, levied property taxes and duties on imported goods, and concerned themselves with many other matters of importance to the seaports. But of equal, if not greater, importance to the urban dwellers were their municipal governments. It was here, where tax assessors, tax collectors, overseers of the poor, selectmen, sheriffs, and constables operated, that people placed their primary emotional commitment. The vision of the larger community was still circumscribed, communications with other areas were poor, and the vital concerns of daily life were carried on for the most part in a local setting.

In some towns, notably Boston, the economic qualifications for voting in local elections differed from those in provincial elections.[11] More important, the range of elected urban officials and the dynamics of the municipal political systems varied markedly in the three seaports. Boston was unique because her political life revolved around the town meeting, in operation by 1634 in crude form and highly prized by most inhabitants at the end of the century as the keystone of their political system.[12] The town meeting annually elected six selectmen, who acted throughout the ensuing year as a municipal governing board. The meeting also selected assessors, constables, overseers of the poor, surveyors of the hemp, informers about deer, purchasers of grain, haywards, sheepreeves, hogreeves, town criers, measurers of salt, scavengers, viewers of shingles, sealers of leather, fence viewers, firewards, cullers of staves, and auditors, who carried the authority of the town to every inhabitant. Complaints about officials could rarely congeal into bitter enmity, for virtually every holder of even the smallest office within the town was subject to the scrutiny of a broadly composed electorate that met each March to make new appointments. A recent historian of the city calculates that of about 1,000 adult males in 1683, 101 were elected to serve the town in some capacity. Many of these did not themselves have sufficient property to vote. With one-tenth of the adult males holding office every year, nobody could gain a reputation for sobriety and industry without quickly finding himself elected to some municipal post.[13]

This widely participatory system of local government did not mean that Boston's politics were democratic in the modern sense. In fact, hierarchy characterized town affairs. The most important offices—representative, selectman, clerk, treasurer, and town meeting moderator—were regularly filled from a small pool of acknowledged leaders to whom the lesser people ordinarily deferred. A second level of offices, including the sheriff, overseers of the poor, and tax assessors, was almost always occupied by men of high social standing and economic position. Left to ordinary town dwellers were the supervisory and regulatory minor offices, which were more burdensome than honorific. This fact comes through clearly in the repeated instances of artisans and shopkeepers who preferred to pay a fine rather than serve in positions that took substantial time (and therefore income) from their trades. Nonetheless, substantial numbers of Boston's inhabitants regularly became public servants involved in making decisions and discharging responsibilities. In this they were unique among residents of the northern provincial capitals.[14]

Boston was also unique because only there were open debate permitted and decisions made by majority vote in town meetings on a wide range of issues. Moreover, the deliberations of the meeting, as distinguished from the vote, were open to all inhabitants, whether propertied or propertyless, free or bound, male or female. Bostonians gathered every March to elect a battery of town officeholders and then reconvened in May to settle town affairs. After 1715, any item brought to the meeting's attention in a petition signed by any ten inhabitants was placed on the agenda.[15] Collectively the town decided whether "to prevent playing football in the streets," whether Susanna Striker should have £10 for a kidney stone operation for her son, how much the schoolteachers should be paid, and other such matters large and small.[16] Hostility to concentrated political power would come naturally to Bostonians, who were bred in an environment where local affairs were managed in this way.

New York and Philadelphia had far less participatory town governments. The first elections for aldermen and assistants of the newly chartered municipal corporation and for constables were held in New York in 1686. The governor, with the approval of the council, appointed all other offices, including the mayor, recorder, town clerk, sheriff, tax assessors and collectors, and clerk of the market.[17] In Philadelphia, where at first the suffrage was the broadest of any of the seaport towns, the structure of municipal government was the most conservative. Under a city charter granted in 1691, sheriffs, commissioners, tax assessors, and coroners were elected annually, but the municipal corporation, the chief agency of city government, was a self-perpetuating body of aldermen and councilmen who were initially appointed by William Penn with tenure for life and who thereafter selected their own successors. This kind of city government, largely immune from public opinion, was patterned after the closed corporations in England, which exercised extensive powers, including almost exclusive jurisdiction in civil and criminal courts and the right to pass municipal laws, erect public buildings, and appoint municipal officers. Penn succumbed to the influence of a small clique of merchants in Philadelphia who had been urging him since 1684 to incorporate the town along these lines. He may also have been moved to concentrate the city's political power by the rampant factionalism and antiproprietary sentiment that embroiled his colony in internecine battling.[18]

The towns were commercial centers whose inhabitants were legatees of a traditional organization of economic life, so they willingly hedged themselves in with restrictions. Unrestrained competition, with each artisan or merchant playing for advantage to the limit of his ability, was an alien notion. It was thought of as a prescription for chaos and corruption rather than for material blessings and harmonious social relations. Commercial transactions were more than mere exchanges of goods or money; they composed "part of a network of human intercourse that held society together."[19] Traditional ties of social responsibility between master and servant, parent and child, buyer and seller, and, ultimately, the people and their government could be maintained only when economic life was pervaded by a sense of what was equitable, not simply what was profitable.

Consistent with this corporate thought, Philadelphia and New York operated carefully regulated public markets where foodstuffs and many nonperishable items were sold by schedule several times a week. "Among the corporation-owned stalls," writes one historian of Philadelphia, "strolled corporation officials employing corporation standards of weights and measures to gauge the produce sold by corporation-licensed butchers and corporation-admitted freemen. Elsewhere in the marketplace were cereals, hides, and cordwood which had travelled by corporation-owned ferry to corporation docks and had there passed the scrutiny of corporation viewers and corders, only to be carried away by corporation-appointed porters working at rates fixed by the corporation."[20]

Boston was an exception to this corporate control of public marketing, but even there economic life was managed according to the traditional ethic in many other ways. The selectmen strictly regulated the price at which bakers could sell a loaf of bread, fixing the price according to the price of flour. Tanners could not place hides on the market that did not measure up to standards set by law. Mariners received wages in accordance with schedules set by the General Court. Town officials carefully regulated weights and measures. But unlike New York and Philadelphia, Boston did not restrict vocational opportunity by limiting the number of men who could enter specific trades, and in general allowed for a freer movement of labor and goods.[21]

The structure of town government and the size of the electorate cannot alone describe the political world of the seaport towns. Also of great importance were the values and social customs that informed political discourse and legitimized political decisions. The social credo, it may be argued, ultimately counted for more than the size of the electorate or the range of decisions determinable at the polls. A broad electorate in a society where the upper class wields cultural hegemony and exercises paternalistic social control over an economically dependent laboring class is hardly a democratic electorate. Nor can we usefully employ the word "democracy" to describe a system that "demanded that every man actively and repeatedly consent to his own inequality, that by covenant and ballot he confirm his adherence to the Lord's unitary truth and the small group of laymen and clergy who were its executors."[22] The cultural context of politics, the cognitive structures of the people, must be understood in order to probe the dynamics of political life. It must also be kept in mind that as the seaports grew and conditions altered, the cultural context—the conception of what was proper and equitable—also changed. Although everyone was part of the same social web, at least ideally, it would become less and less true that all town dwellers subscribed to the same social and political ideology. This is why we must carefully differentiate between the dominant, literate, upper-class ethos, preached from the pulpits and readily recaptured in the printed sermons and political tracts of the day, and a subordinate laboring-class ethos, largely untraceable in literary sources because its subscribers' culture was aural rather than literary and its spokesmen had no access to the press. This alternative outlook is disclosed primarily in the behavior of the lower-class urban populace.

In the late seventeenth century, social and political ideas, like political theory, were in a state of flux. In fact we can hardly speak of a single ideology, subscribed to universally by town dwellers. But certain assumptions had wide currency: that those of substantial wealth and high social status were best qualified to hold positions of power; that the people en masse, however lowly in education, occupation, or material achievement, were entitled in special circumstances to make judgments regarding the actions of those entrusted with power and to act accordingly; that those who held civil power ought to promote no special interests but be zealous for the commonweal; and that partisan politics, where "factions" and "parties" competed for power, were to be avoided as a plague. Each of these precepts, which were part of a collective consciousness rather than a written doctrine, bears examination.

Everywhere in the late seventeenth-century English-speaking world it was normally assumed that those at the top of the pyramid of wealth and status were best equipped and most entitled to high political offices. Even William Penn, known as something of a social radical, wrote in 1681, as he was designing a Frame of Government for Pennsylvania, that the elective upper house should be made up of the "most eminent for vertue Wisdom and Substance."[23] It was understood that even the lower house would seat only men of considerable estate, demonstrably successful in their private affairs, and therefore deserving of public office. Philadelphia Quakers had no more difficulty than other Englishmen in reconciling spiritual equalitarianism with a traditional view of the natural layering of social classes. Early elections in Pennsylvania confirmed the notion that the men who represented Philadelphia in the assembly would be drawn from the uppermost stratum of society. Among the men elected to serve in the legislature from 1682 to 1700, a high proportion were merchants; collectively they were the men who held a preponderant share of power in the economic affairs of the burgeoning city. Some of them had come from modest backgrounds, but if they were not yet wealthy, they were the men who were accumulating estates in the budding Quaker capital and represented the best facsimile of eminence obtainable at that time. Beneath them in the elective officeholding hierarchy were sheriffs, tax assessors, and coroners. These positions usually went to men at the next level of society—shopkeepers and master artisans whose success had gained them the respect of the voters.

Boston was no different. Although town dwellers in the Puritan commonwealth insisted on electing a wide range of municipal officers, everyone "simply assumed that any man elected to high office would have to be rich to discharge his duties effectively."[24] Only at the end of the seventeenth century can we detect some tendency among the voters to challenge the assumption that the dignity of those who ruled would be diminished and the stability of the political system undermined by the election of plebeian types to major offices. Boston's selectmen occupied less elevated positions than councilors and representatives to the General Court, but they too were drawn consistently from the town's upper rank. No perfect correlation existed between wealth, status, and officeholding either in Boston or Philadelphia but a general congruency is indisputable.[25]

New York stood somewhat aside from the other towns because ethnic tension between English and Dutch partially undermined the traditional values that prescribed consonance between officeholding and socioeconomic status. Amidst a political atmosphere inflamed by ethnic factionalism, New Yorkers much more frequently elected artisans, tavernkeepers, and ship captains to the aldermanic board than was the case in Boston or Philadelphia. This was especially true in 1689, when Jacob Leisler, a minor merchant deeply alienated from the English elite, seized power, and in the heated municipal elections from 1699 to 1702, when the Leislerians, mostly Dutch, ran against anti-Leislerians, mostly English. Foreshadowing things to come, both sides made extensive popular appeals in elections that brought out an unusual number of voters. It was the need for mobilizing broad electoral support that induced the leaders of both factions to nominate more than the usual number of men from the artisan class. In Boston and Philadelphia municipal politics were only rarely contested in this period and slates of candidates were never offered to the voters. Ethnic-based, issue-oriented politics in New York cracked the traditional order in which the principal places of power were reserved for those on the top rungs of the economic ladder. Whereas in Boston virtually every selectman during the period from 1687 to 1707 was drawn from the merchant and professional community, in New York merchants and professionals occupied only 65 percent of the aldermanic seats and 47 percent of the assistants' places, while artisans, sea captains, and tavernkeepers held 35 and 53 percent of these positions respectively.[26]

Political deference, like economic clientage, involved the dependency of lesser people upon the greater. Possessing superior education and more leisure time, the few were elected or appointed to leadership roles. But the commonality retained the right to judge the actions of the elite and to enforce the social norms and obligations that were understood to exist in every community. Beyond this, when their leaders misused their power, defying common notions of what was fair and proper, the people often felt justified in badgering their betters, protesting openly, or even assuming control in order to rectify the situation. At these moments it became apparent how quickly the deferential mass could transform itself into a self-activating, purposeful crowd.[27] The political elite typically deplored such assumptions of power, decrying the street politics of the "unthinking multitude" and "the rabble." But men who worked along the wharves and in artisans' shops were not deterred by these characterizations. When leaders, elected or appointed, breached the basic rules of equity in social or economic relations, they responded in calculated and coordinated ways. 2073184

What gave special power to the townspeople who assembled for the purposes of redressing a widely felt grievance was the fragility—nearly the complete absence—of any effective agency of control. Municipal police forces were not formed in American cities until the early nineteenth century and they had no comparable equivalent in the colonial period.[28] In theory the militia was available to quell public disturbances, but urban crowds aroused by specific grievances almost always drew upon the same people who were the rank and file of the militia. Nor could those in authority count on the sheriff, constables, or the night watch for much help, for they were too few in number, usually no more than a dozen, and could rarely insulate civil leaders from organized pressure. As late as 1757 the *New-York Gazette* described the night watch as a "Parcell of idle, drinking, vigilant Snorers, who never quelled any nocturnal Tumult in their Lives."[29] The potential for political action *outside* the confines of electoral politics was never greater in the history of urban America. Most European seaports were familiar with extralegal mob activity, and their American counterparts proved to be no exceptions.

Included in virtually every urban street disturbance were hundreds of those who were not entitled to participate in organized politics—women, indentured servants, slaves, apprentices, sailors, the propertyless, and even children. Once in motion, the seaport crowd provided nearly every urban dweller a chance to influence the course of events by bringing pressure to bear on the constituted authorities. Crowd actions were frequent enough and effective enough that they achieved a kind of legitimacy of their own. The urban crowd was the watchdog of politics, always ready to chastise or drive from office those who violated the collective sense of propriety or equity.[30] Never wholly legitimized, roundly hated by the upper class, organized and led in mysterious ways that sprang from collective outrage, the seaport crowd served as an effective counterbalance in a political system where men who had secured positions of influence and trust because of their high economic and social position were far from incapable of abusing their power.

Another axiom of conventional political wisdom in the late seventeenth century was that factional or party politics were to be abhorred. Political writers of the time believed that factions and parties pursued special interests rather than the interests of the whole community. Thomas Hooker, an early Boston leader, had put it cogently in the 1630s: "For if each man may do what is good in his owne eyes, proceed according to his own pleasure, so that none may crosse him or controll him by any power; there must of necessity follow the distraction and desolation of the whole, when each man hath liberty to follow his owne imagination and humerous devices and seek his particular, but oppose one another, and all prejudice the publicke good."[31] His advice echoed down the decades and even at the close of the colonial era a great majority of political authors labeled factions and parties as dangerous and evil, the telltale symptom of a diseased body politic. Parties existed where private ambition and avariciousness replaced love of the community, service to the corporate whole, and sacrifice for the commonweal.[32]

The necessity of choosing magistrates and other officeholders who were distinguished by education, wealth, and social position was subtly tied to the inherent conflict between private interest and public good. Only those who had attained material security, asserted political writers, could keep their eyes fixed on the public good, for they alone were free of the painful necessity of scratching for their bread. The artisan or laborer could never think clearly about the good of the whole community because he was too immersed in daily toil, his views restricted by the narrowness of his circumstances and the incessant struggle for survival.

In a second way, according to the promulgators of political theory, the public interest could only be served by the eminent. In every human breast "passion" and "reason" competed for ascendancy. Passion was the unloosing of base, avaricious, worldly impulses; reason was the victory of clear thought and conscience over these brutish, barely suppressible tendencies. In every community, be it a small farming settlement or a thriving seaport, those with education and piety had conquered passion and cultivated reason. If they had not done so completely, they had accomplished this to a greater degree than the middling or lowly of their communities would ever find possible. It was not by accident that the term "the unthinking multitude" was invoked so often by those at the top of colonial society, for it placed the disqualifying badge on those beneath them and perpetuated the notion that only they were capable of legislating with the public good in mind and comporting themselves in a disinterested way.

Thus, several strands intertwined to weave the fabric of urban politics in the late seventeenth century. Generally nonrestrictive suffrage requirements allowed wide participation in provincial politics, although in the conduct of town affairs the seaports varied considerably. The limited geographical areas and small populations of Boston, New York, and Philadelphia permitted intimate contact between the rulers and the ruled. The structure of town governments, particularly in Boston, insured that matters of concern were quickly known and often acted upon by the commonality. Even in Philadelphia, where officers of municipal government were not popularly elected, the fluidity of early immigrant society meant that officeholders were men of modest wealth and only faint aristocratic pretensions. Annual assembly elections kept those with legislative authority responsive to the collective interests of the citizens. This was not democracy to be sure, for all of these facets of urban politics were contained within a framework of social deference, which insured that those of inferior rank would normally bow to their superiors, accepting the legitimacy of a structured society, even regarding it as God-ordained. But it was a system in which the contractual relationship between rulers and ruled could be breached if the rulers acted irresponsibly. At these times, which occurred far more often than is generally believed, deference quickly crumbled under the pressure of an aroused populace. How all of these elements combined depended upon time, place, and circumstances and is best understood by delving into the story of each of the seaports at particular moments in the late seventeenth century when political crisis enveloped the community.

POLITICAL TURMOIL broke out in Boston in the spring of 1689. Three years before, the English government had launched a bold administrative experiment to unify the northern colonies under a political authority more responsive to London. This was thought to be particularly necessary in the case of New England, where for two generations an autonomous spirit had reigned, not the least effect of which was widespread evasion of English commercial regulations. The instrument of English determination to rationalize and discipline her growing empire was Sir Edmund Andros, who arrived in Boston in December 1686. Escorted by a company of English grenadiers, Andros assumed the governor generalship of the Dominion of New England, the name invented for the gathering together of political authority for Massachusetts, Connecticut, Plymouth, Rhode Island, New York, New Jersey, and part of Maine.[33]

Andros was a strict and determined crown administrator with a military background that had taught him how to bring the recalcitrant to book. Bostonians soon hated him heartily. He imposed taxes without the consent of the people, who had no opportunity even to debate such issues since Andros abolished the General Court and lodged all civil power in the hands of appointed officials. Boston's cherished town meeting was muzzled by an order that it meet no more than once a year for the purpose of electing town officers. Congregationalist Puritans in Boston were also appalled at the establishment in their midst of the Church of England, against which their forefathers had rebelled. Their rage was further heightened by Andros's land policy, which required quitrents on new grants of land and called into question all old land titles. Only by petitioning the Dominion government for a new patent to their land and paying the fees specified by the governor could New Englanders be assured of valid title to their property. Employing the methods of the army officer, not the diplomat, Andros tried to impose discipline and a proper sense of mercantilist subordination on a people who for many years had blandly ignored English regulations.[34]

When news reached Boston in April 1689 that William of Orange had landed in England to end the hated Catholic regime of James II, Bostonians lost no time in overthrowing their tyrant in residence. To the beat of drums, the inhabitants streamed into the streets, formed units with the militia, and surrounded the Town House, the center of government. A committee of safety, composed mostly of merchants and ministers, assumed control and quickly seized and imprisoned Andros. No blood was shed, for the governor general was aware that his tiny garrison could not hope to overpower the town; he therefore offered no resistance. Within hours, the Bostonians had set up provisional authorities, arrested most of Andros's supporters, and issued a declaration justifying their seizure of power. On the next day Andros surrendered the fort in Boston harbor where most of his troops were garrisoned.[35]

How had the highest authority in the land been so quickly overturned? Edward Randolph, royal customs collector and crown investigator, believed that "a violent & bloudy zeal" had been "stir'd up in the Rabble, acted & managed by the preachers."[36] We must allow, however, for the

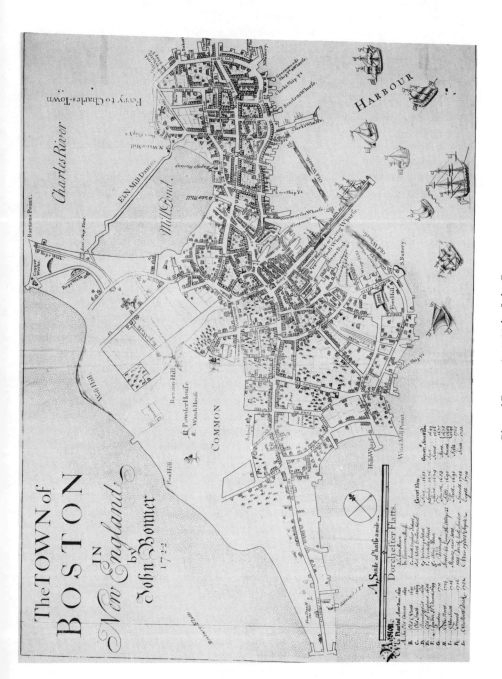

2. *Plan of Boston in 1722 by John Bonner.*

fact that the imperious Randolph regarded everyone beneath the upper class as "the rabble." Historians have agreed that preachers, along with merchants and former magistrates, led the rebellion, but they have also noted that city folk of all classes, about a thousand strong, united to overthrow the governor. They were animated by what Cotton Mather, Boston's eminent divine, hyperbolically called the "most Unanimous Resolution perhaps that was ever known to have Inspir'd any People."[37] In doing so the city people were reflecting a colony-wide animus against Andros. They were also trying to preserve their power against the threats of a thoroughly aroused countryside, which was ready to unseat Andros if the city people would not. Despite this city-country tension, New England's Glorious Revolution would be recorded in the memories of the people as the thrusting out of a tyrant who used his authority unlawfully, ignored local traditions, and trampled on the customary rights of the people. Overthrow of constituted authority was a treasonable act. But when those vested with authority perpetrated what one Bostonian called "a Treasonable Invasion of the Rights which the whole English Nation lays claim unto," then all good Englishmen, whether in London, Boston, or anywhere else, must rise in defense of these privileges.[38] Tyranny in Boston had been stopped because the mass of people had collectively taken the law into their own hands. They had done so, it is important to remember, under the leadership of the town's foremost men, who never lost control of the situation.

Self-congratulation and community consensus after the overthrow of Andros did not last long. Among the elite, the rebellion itself was more generally approved than the implication of the mass rising against oppressive authority. Though the tyrant was gone, the question of the proper relationship between rulers and ruled remained.[39] Many Bostonians from the upper class who had detested Andros and participated in his overthrow had no wish to alter the traditional axiom of politics granting those in positions of authority free rein in the formulation of public policy. Of another view were townsmen, many drawn from lower in the social structure, who now desired greater participation in public affairs. Many who had not enjoyed freemanship under the Old Charter of 1629, including non-church members of all ranks, had been in the crowd surrounding the Town House in April 1689, and they subsequently showed an unwillingness to withdraw quietly from the political arena. To the Puritan elite such perversity was alarming.

As the interim government sought to establish its authority, while awaiting instruction from England on how the post-Andros government should be constituted, these former outsiders pressed for a new role. They petitioned for a change in the colony's suffrage law that would allow the vote to qualified property owners who were not church members. The council of state acceded, granting the franchise to most pro-

perty owners. Less peaceful demands followed in July 1689 when the interim government allowed Joseph Dudley, one of Andros's chief officers,
to return home on bail from the Boston jail. Dudley was hated in Boston
for the excessive fees and fines he had imposed as chief justice under Andros, and he was particularly remembered for the words he had uttered
in 1687 when convicting John Wise, a minister from Ipswich who had
protested Andros's imposition of a tax without legislative approval:
"You must not think the laws of England follow us to the ends of Earth,"
Dudley exhorted, "you have no more priviledges left you, than not to be
sold for Slaves."[40] To allow this henchman of Andros's autocratic reign
to go free was more than Boston's populace could abide. A crowd appeared in the streets, composed of "women boyes and negros," according
to one unsympathetic observer, broke all the windows in Dudley's
house, and demanded his reincarceration.[41] Several magistrates reported
that "the tumult in the town is so great and sudden that no reason will be
heard or regarded."[42] Bowing to public pressure, the president of the interim government, who was Dudley's brother-in-law, convinced him
that he must return to jail, lest the crowd take further action. There is not
sufficient evidence to determine the social composition of the July mob.
But it takes a miscalculation of the responses of those accustomed to exercising authority to believe that the governing council would have
yielded to a street gang composed only of "women boyes and negros."
An aroused populace, more broadly based it seems clear, had abandoned
their deferential stance and taken matters into their own hands, increasing the pressure on the provisional magistrates "to justify their policies
before the people."[43]

Such a mobilization of political energy created a deep split in Boston's
ranks. Andros had proved to nearly everyone's satisfaction that the common good could be undermined by despotism. Now some town dwellers
grew convinced that the common good was also threatened by the "giddy
and enraged mob" made up of ordinary people who were no longer content merely to vote for their rulers or instruct them annually at the town
meeting but wanted to intrude themselves into day-by-day political affairs as well. "As soon as the hurry of revolution was over," wrote the
author of *Reflections upon the Affairs of New England* in 1691, the people installed in civil authority "the men that had thrown themselves at the
head of the action." But when these men did not "in all things run with
the *mad headstrong multitude* they began to be kicked at and when they
endeavored a regulation of affaires that the law might have its course it
was accounted intolerable."[44] "Anarchy" was the word chosen by Samuel Willard, minister at Boston's Third Church, to tar the popular spirit
he saw unloosed in Boston in the aftermath of Andros's ouster.[45]

It was this feeling of political importance, and the dawning notion that
the public good was better served if the common people exercised a

watchdog role rather than electing eminent men to positions of power and trusting them to exercise it for the commonweal, that marked a turning point in politics. Only a few years before, in 1676, the Harvard-trained clergyman William Hubbard had published in Boston a sermon that opined "that the greatest part of mankind are but as tools and Instruments for others to work by, rather than any proper Agents to effect any thing of themselves."[46] But by the 1690s Boston contained many people who no longer regarded themselves as mere tools in the hands of others, passive implements from whom only obedience and submission was due. The mass of people were probably never so inert as Hubbard suggested; but after 1689 their political consciousness began to grow. There were those in New England who believed that the overthrow of Andros had uncovered a "levelling, independent, democratical principle and spirit, with a tang of fifth-monarchy." It was said that some deluded New Englanders now wished to form "an Oliverian republic."[47]

Phrases of this kind bear close examination, for they were loaded with enormous emotional freight. "A tang of fifth-monarchy" and reinstituting "an Oliverian republic" called to mind the entire bloody English civil war of the previous generation, the rise to power of the radical dictator Oliver Cromwell, and the emergence of millenarianists, radical utopians, and social reformers in the 1650s and 1660s. These were events within the living memory of many Bostonians and well known, through story and book, to the younger generation. The mid-seventeenth century, in fact, had witnessed in England, "the greatest upheaval that has yet occurred" in that country.[48] At the center of the turmoil were the efforts of common people, enlisting in popular movements such as the Ranters, Levellers, Muggletonians, Quakers, Diggers, and Fifth Monarchists, "to impose their own solutions to the problems of their time, in opposition to the wishes of their betters who had called them into political action."[49] Whereas the gentry revolted against an absolutist king, arbitrary taxes, prerogative courts, and feudal tenures, the radical sects warred for a far-reaching democratization of political and legal instutitions, establishment of communal property, disestablishment of the church, and leveling of class distinctions and wealth. The Fifth Monarchy Men, who believed that the Lord Jesus would return to earth to help usher in the new era, were primarily composed of the urban lower classes and were often prepared to resort to violence to attain their goals. Twice, in 1657 and 1661, they had organized armed uprisings. They were pathetically unsuccessful and were driven underground, but like other lower-class groups that rose violently in quest of radical reform, they sent shock waves through the propertied, politically dominant upper class.[50]

Boston in 1690 was not London or Bristol in 1660, of course. But there was enough of a parallel to give credence to the fears expressed by the Boston elite about the "tang of fifth-monarchy." In both cases, the gentry had been outraged by the authoritarian, arbitrary actions of the king or his vice regent in a remote corner of the empire. In both cases monarchy or its agency had been overthrown after the gentry had called into action those beneath them in a concerted, cross-class effort to rid the body politic of the cancer of despotism. In both cases, the lower orders were not content to resume their quiescent political role but irreverently made new demands for a more basic political and economic reconstruction. The difference between Boston in 1690 and England during the Civil War was that in England lower-class reformist zeal had blossomed into a revolution within a revolution, as the call went forth, accompanied by violent uprisings, for fundamental change; whereas in Boston, the lesser people were far more moderate in their proposals and far less violent.

Almost nothing in the actions of the Boston commonality suggests that they wished to level distinctions among the inhabitants or to do away with a system of private property in favor of return to a primitive communitarianism. But enough of the spirit of Fifth Monarchy had crossed the Atlantic, albeit in watered-down form, to frighten many in the upper echelon.[51] In recoiling at the power of the common people, whose aid they had solicited in the overthrow of Andros, the gentry revealed its understanding that the rules of the political game might change if the diffusion of power that had always been permitted in the town meeting was allowed to proceed along other channels. They were witnessing an assault on the older emphasis on the primacy of social hierarchy and civil order by notions about the primacy of popular rights. The belief that those at the top of society were the true guardians of the public interest, the only truly disinterested members of the community, was in contention with the opposite belief that it was those of modest means but common sense who could best be trusted with power.

By the end of the century one prominent Bostonian whose hands had never been roughened by artisanal labor was accused of attempting "to prove that all men have equal right to Liberty, and all outward comforts of this life."[52] Samuel Sewall, Boston's famous diary-keeping merchant, had been attacking slavery when he penned a statement regarding liberty and equality. But his antagonist, John Saffin, like many upper-class Bostonians, had become prickly on these topics in the aftermath of the mini-revolution of 1689. Much had changed in Boston since 1630, but Saffin's retort to Sewall flowed from his pen as if the ghost of John Winthrop were hovering over his shoulder: "God . . . hath ordained different degrees and orders of men, some to be High and Honourable, some to be Low and Despicable, some to be Monarchs Kings, Princes and Governours, Masters and Commanders, others to be subjects and to be commanded; servants of sundry sorts and degrees, bound to obey; yea, some born to be slaves, and so to remain during their lives, as hath been proved. Otherwise there would be a meer parity among men."[53]

Saffin's vision of a society where social position was assigned on the basis of inherited status was already incongruent with the social reality of a town that included a good many important men who had risen from the bottom and a good many others who, through no fault of their own, had been reduced to poverty or had never been able to climb out of it.[54] His comment was mostly a worrisome lament against the rumblings that had been heard in Boston after 1689—rumblings that had neither taken organizational form nor emerged as a clear-cut ideology but nonetheless bespoke feelings of disdain for the gentry, a predilection for egalitarianism, perhaps even the faint echo of millenarianism.

In New York, where the hard-bitten military careerist Francis Nicholson had been deputized as Andros's lieutenant governor under the Dominion of New England, word of the Boston uprising arrived on April 26, 1689. Nicholson had inflicted few of the odious new policies upon New Yorkers that Andros had applied in Boston, mostly because it was unnecessary to do so. New Yorkers had no representative assembly to suspend, no town meeting to restrict, and had dutifully paid small quitrents on their land for years. Though he alienated some in the town by bestowing political favors on a circle of powerful Dutch and English merchants gathered around him, Nicholson was not looked upon by New Yorkers as a despot or an abrogator of ancient liberties. He was, however, regarded by some as a crypto-Catholic. This made him deeply suspect in the eyes of those who applauded Boston's revolt as part and parcel of the move on both sides of the Atlantic to drive out James II and all the other "bloody Devotees of Rome," as the Boston Declaration of Grievances against Andros declared.[55]

New Yorkers did not really overthrow Nicholson's government. It simply melted away. One flash point occurred when the governor resisted the attempt of a local militia lieutenant to station a sentry inside Fort James at the lower end of Manhattan, which was occupied by a small band of English soldiers. But when the local militia, led by Captain Jacob Leisler, a petty merchant of German origin, appeared to take over the fort on May 31, 1689, while awaiting instructions from the newly crowned monarchs in England, Nicholson offered only token resistance. Within two weeks he had quietly sailed for England. Leisler became the head of an interim government, ruling with an elected committee of safety for thirteen months until a governor appointed by the new king arrived in the colony.[56]

New York seethed with tension during this interregnum, but, unlike in Boston, it was internal conflict that caused the problem. Factional infighting was so intense that when Governor Henry Sloughter arrived in 1691 and was resisted by the Leisler party, the anti-Leislerians put Leisler and seven compatriots on trial for treason. Joseph Dudley, the target of the crowd's wrath in Boston four years before, presided over a less than impartial court, which found Leisler and his chief adjutant, Jacob Milbourne, guilty of treason. They were summarily hanged and decapitated. This did nothing to reduce the enmity coursing through the town, for the Leislerians believed that their leaders did not forfeit their lives for treason but were judicially murdered for the crime of challenging the rule of an entrenched oligarchy.[57]

The differences between the ousting of constituted authority in New York and Boston are striking. In Boston a united populace had risen against a man seen as an invader of the people's rights but one who upheld the rule of a distant authority rather than an oppressive local economic elite. In New York one part of a divided population rose to seize authority from a caretaker governor who had never reduced or struck down long-enjoyed privileges but who stood at the center of a group of local, arrogant, mercantile grandees. In both cases the takeover of power was followed by fission within the community. Whereas in Boston the division was caused by an upwelling of political activity among those who had played very little role in political affairs until then, the split in New York represented the widening of a break that predated the Glorious Revolution and was ethnic as well as economic in nature. Neither Dutch nor English New Yorkers had much of a tradition of participatory politics to draw upon, for the town's charter, allowing the election of a common council, had not been granted until 1686 and a representative assembly had existed in the colony only from 1683 to 1685, when it was abolished. But ethnic tension interlaced with class antagonism had permeated the town since the English takeover of New Amsterdam in 1664.

Rather than overthrowing constituted authority, Leisler stepped into a local power vacuum created by the Protestant revolt against James II in England. His enemies depicted him as a treasonous rebel, illegally overthrowing the legitimate government in New York. But the real conflict in the town was internecine and occurred after Leisler had established an interim government. Much of this strife had its origins in the smoldering resentment felt by Dutch inhabitants toward the English of the town. Many of the Dutch merchants had adjusted to the English government after the conquest of Dutch New Amsterdam in 1664, for business was business whether conducted under Dutch or English rule. Conversely, many incoming Englishmen, accompanied by not nearly enough English women to go around, married into Dutch families and joined the Dutch church. But beneath the upper echelon, where ethnic accommodation was facilitated by economic success, incidents of Anglo-Dutch hostility were legion. The feeling grew steadily in the 1670s and 1680s among ordinary Dutch families that they were being crowded out of an economic system which they had built.[58]

When turmoil came in 1689 the Dutch and English segments of the

population did not neatly divide into Leislerian and anti-Leislerian factions. A number of wealthy Dutch merchants who had made their peace
with the English, including Jacob DeKay, Brandt Schuyler, Frederick
Philipse, and Stephanus Van Cortlandt, opposed the renegade leader. A
few Englishmen, such as Samuel Edsell and Thomas Williams, joined
him. But leadership of the two sides split along ethnic lines to a considerable degree and among the rank and file the ethnic alignment was even
more striking. It was indicative that in a town where the Dutch composed 60 percent of the population, Leisler was tried and found guilty by
an all-English jury in the spring of 1691.[59]

Leisler's brief government radicalized New York's political life. It
created a precedent for popular politics and nurtured egalitarian resentment of parvenu merchants among laboring people. Leisler was not himself interested in traditional English liberties, as they were cherished in
Boston, and he was no political ideologue intent on transforming society
along equalitarian lines. He established virtually no contact and received
little support from the communities on Long Island where migrating New
Englanders had established town meetings and agitated for a representative assembly in previous years. When he reluctantly revived the elective
assembly, mainly because he desperately needed revenue which he dared
not raise by executive order, he was so angered by the legislators' attempts to discuss English liberties that he prorogued the first session and
rejected a measure which the second session enacted to obtain such
rights.[60] His motivation, instead, was primarily economic and religious.
A fervid, orthodox Calvinist who saw a Popish plotter lurking in every
corner, he had detested Thomas Dongan, the former Catholic governor
sent by England's closet Catholic king to New York in 1683. He frequently denounced his opponents as "Popish Doggs & Divells," vividly
reflecting the fear of Catholicism that resonated deeply in New York's
Dutch population.[61] In trying to legitimize the assumption of power it
was, of course, judicious for the Leislerians to argue that they had
cleansed the colony of Jacobitism, just as the faithful Protestants of England had driven out the tainted James II. But Leisler and his followers
lived in real fear of Popish subversion and were in deadly earnest when
they described Governor Nicholson as a "pretended protestant" who
"countenanced the Popish party" and appointed Catholics to high
places.[62]

Interwoven with Leislerian anti-Popery was a hostility toward New
York's elite that rose so suddenly after Nicholson's departure and spread
so rapidly that even Leisler was at times powerless to contain it. Soon
after their assumption of power, the Leislerians freed imprisoned debtors
in New York. Shortly thereafter, they called for the election of justices of
the peace and militia officers, who previously had been appointed.[63]
These were steps of great significance in a colony where authoritarian

and oligarchical rule had prevailed for several generations. In another move, the Leislerians tried to reshape municipal government so as to extend the role of ordinary people. The second request of Leisler's deputy, sent to England less than three months after the assumption of power to gain recognition for the interim government, was that the crown grant New York a city charter "in the like manner and with same or more priviledges as the city of Boston, being that the contents of that Charter, doth best agree with the humour and nature of those inhabitants."[64] Although the Leislerians may not have been closely acquainted with the exact workings of Boston's town government, they were clearly asking for a more participatory system with a town meeting and elective officials.

In one other respect Leisler's government in New York varied radically from past practice. It not only drew wide support from the laboring people of the town but artisans and persons of humble background were given positions of power in the new government. Joost Stoll, a dram seller, was chosen to represent the Leislerian cause in London in 1689. Henry Cuyler, a baker and tailor, was a prominent cohort of Leisler. Johannes Johnson, a carpenter, was appointed sheriff. Leisler's marshal, who could be seen marching at the head of a file of supporters when arrests of wealthy merchant opponents were made, was William Churcher, formerly a bricklayer. Jacob Milbourne, Leisler's son-in-law and chief lieutenant, had begun his career in America as an indentured servant and was the brother of William Milbourne, a radical Fifth Monarchy man in England.[65] Six of the ten members of the aldermanic board chosen in the year of Leisler's takeover were drawn from outside the merchant elite; they included a baker, innkeeper, limner, bricklayer, carpenter, and mariner.[66] It was moving testimony to Leisler's popularity among the "leather aprons" that his wealthy opponents, after sentencing him to death, could find no carpenter in the town who would furnish a ladder to use at the scaffold. Some further appreciation of the class orientation of the Leislerian struggle can be gained by the fact that no sooner were Leisler's merchant antagonists reinstalled in power in 1691 than they attempted to lower artisans' wages by law and to make the requirements for freemanship more restrictive. These were obvious acts of retaliation against the part of the population that had identified most strongly with Leisler.[67]

At times the laboring people forged ahead of their supposed leaders, belying the charge of Leisler's adversaries that the movement's success lay in his ability to delude and manipulate the "poore ignorant innocent and senseless people."[68] Leisler's initial accession to power is in part attributable to the fact that the militia captains of several regiments in the town were browbeaten by their men to join Leisler in the early days of the takeover. By late in the summer of 1689, Leislerian mobs began attacking the property of some of New York's wealthiest merchants. Although the plundering probably never reached the proportions claimed by the anti-Leislerians, the assault on the property of the rich was widespread. One of the town's principal merchants claimed that the mobs "take peoples goods out of their houses and if hindered by Justices of the peace, they come with great numbers and fetch it out of the Justices house by forse."[69] In this expropriation of property, without parallel in Boston's overthrow of Andros, "their Captains can no more Rule them," it was claimed.[70]

Attacks on the property of the rich, whether English or Dutch, are important indications of the class feeling that mixed strongly with ethnic hostility in New York. Nothing is more noticeable in the charges of the anti-Leislerians than their horror that the movement had raised up what they variously described as the "rabble," the "ignorant Mobile," the "tumultuous multitude," the "most abject Comon people," and the "drunken crue." Lower-class New Yorkers of "mean birth and sordid Educacon & desperate fortunes," according to the Anglo-Dutch elite, were perfect clay in the hands of a usurper such as Leisler, for they were too witless to understand his evil designs and the ruin he would ultimately bring upon them.[71] Claims would be made later that "almost every man of Sense, Reputation, or Estate" was against Leisler.[72] Historians who have examined the social backgrounds of the two groups have shown that there was far from a perfect correlation between class and political allegiance during the rebellion.[73] But it is equally important to note that the anti-Leislerians correctly understood how widely their enemies had appealed to the working poor, who were disproportionately Dutch in the town. In stigmatizing the revolt Leisler's enemies were at pains to show that it was people of lowly condition, in no way entitled to rebel against civil authority by themselves, who had snatched control of the government.

This conviction was summed up in the label of "Masaniello," applied to Leisler by Robert Livingston, Nicholas Bayard, and Chidley Brooke, three of the province's wealthiest and most powerful men.[74] Known in England and America, Masaniello was the peasant fishseller who in 1647 had mobilized the masses in Naples against a hated food tax that struck at the poor. For a brief period Masaniello had controlled the city, while his followers emptied the jails, attacked the rich, executed hundreds of public enemies who ground the faces of the poor, and, for a brief moment, stood the political order on its head. Masaniello became a folk hero, the courageous leader of the oppressed, an Italian Robin Hood springing from nowhere to right the wrongs of an unjust society. His ghost had surfaced in America during Bacon's Rebellion in Virginia, which the royal governor characterized as "in every respect like to that of Masaniello Except their Leader." Thirteen years later, John Coode, a small planter who led the Maryland revolt of 1689, which was also directed against Papist influence and oligarchical oppression, was proud to call himself Masaniello, indicating that among the common people the name had retained its magic.[75]

Leisler's rebellion, unlike Masaniello's, had led to little bloodshed and no executions, but in other respects it was indeed Masaniellian. It was a measure of the fear and hatred of Leisler among wealthy New Yorkers that after he surrendered the government to Colonel Henry Sloughter, the newly appointed royal governor who arrived in March 1691, Leisler was tried for treason in New York rather than being sent to England. As the best legal historians of this period of New York's history have said, Leisler "was eventually sentenced under circumstances which no amount of explanation has justified."[76] The Masaniello of New York would later be canonized by the laboring people of the town, who had been amply instructed on how far the elite was prepared to go to insure its dominance.

PHILADELPHIA staged no miniature Glorious Revolution because there was no local autocrat, appointed from afar, to oust. But all was not tranquil at the heart of William Penn's "holy experiment." Tension had been mounting, in fact, since the first settlers arrived in 1681. It was fed by the normal confusion attending migration to a new land, the lack of specie to facilitate trade, disagreements over the proper form of government, friction between council and assembly, striving for choice land and political preferment, and the departure of the charismatic Penn from the colony in 1684. A remonstrance delivered to Penn as he made final arrangements for leaving his colony dramatized the mounting disaffection. Signed by several dozen Philadelphians, the document charged the proprietor with favoritism and opportunism in his land policy and raised special objections to the distribution of town lots in Philadelphia.[77] The issues were never satisfactorily resolved and Penn spent long days after he returned to London reading reports from his proprietary officials regarding the truculent behavior of his colonists. In fact, between 1684 and 1689 Penn faced the growth of a strong antiproprietary movement centered in Philadelphia that strove to limit severely his political power in the colony and to evade the quitrents that he collected on all property.[78]

Disillusioned with the ordinary colonists, Penn tried to cultivate the support of a local elite. When this failed he unwisely appointed a Puritan disciplinarian, Captain John Blackwell of Boston, as deputy governor of the colony. It was a monumental blunder and Penn paid dearly for it. Puritans were cordially hated by the Quakers, especially in the New World where Friends were beaten, mutilated, and hanged in Boston only a few decades before. Although he had years of administrative and military experience, Blackwell was no match for the Philadelphia pacifists. Within eighteen months he resigned his commission, thoroughly shaken and convinced that the mosquitoes in Philadelphia were worse than armed men, though not nearly so nettlesome as the "men without Armes," who had found endless ways to obstruct his administration of government.[79]

Stymied in his efforts to bring orderly government to Pennsylvania or to implement proprietary land and revenue policies, Penn returned the reins of government to a circle of Quaker leaders in 1692. Many of them had been among the antiproprietary faction that had developed after Penn's departure, but at a distance of three thousand miles his alternatives were limited. Invested with power, this group, composed primarily of the wealthiest Quaker merchants, removed all officeholders who had supported Governor Blackwell and began to administer government with a highhandedness that rankled elements of the lower and middle classes. When the new government proposed a general tax on real and personal property in 1692, alienated groups in the city had an issue for expressing their discontent. The tax was very light, yet it was loudly protested. The source of dissatisfaction was not the tax itself but its intended use—a salary for the deputy governor Thomas Lloyd, a financially embarrassed Quaker merchant who stood at the center of Penn's new proprietary circle. Freemen of the Quaker capital petitioned the assembly to defeat the tax bill and the signatures reveal that the opposition to the Quaker merchant elite was composed of the town's lesser merchants, shopkeepers, and master artisans, as well as a number of non-Quakers, including Anglicans, Germans, and Swedes.[80]

Against this backdrop of civil controversy a religious schism split the Quaker community in Philadelphia wide open in 1692. Known as the Keithian controversy, it took its name from George Keith, an itinerant Quaker preacher who had emigrated from Scotland to East New Jersey in 1685. A deeply introspective, moody individual, Keith accepted an appointment as tutor of the newly established Quaker school in Philadelphia in 1689. Not long thereafter, disturbed by what he perceived as the failing commitment of Quakers to the founding principles of the Society of Friends, he began a crusade to institute more discipline and structure in church affairs. By Keith's reckoning, ordinary, untutored Quaker folk, cast into a disintegrative New World setting, would be able to preserve their faith only with a set of strict tenets to guide them and sterner tests of religious convincement to weed out superficial adherents from true believers.[81]

Keith was soon confronting most of Philadelphia's "Public Friends," the lay leaders of the Society of Friends. They hewed to a simpler faith, believing in a less structured organization of the church and the ability of each Quaker to draw upon the "inner light" in every person to fashion a godly life. They utterly rejected Keith's reform demands as "downright Popery," a phrase heavy with inference in view of contemporary fears in England of Catholic plots. Soon the controversy over Quaker doc-trine turned into an issue of where authority resided within the Society of Friends, for Keith was accusing some of the Public Friends of heretical views and demanding that they be disciplined. When he lost these bat-tles, amidst an outpouring of un-Quakerly pamphlets and broadsides, Keith and his followers established a separate meeting and in 1693 even staged a physical confrontation at the main Philadelphia meetinghouse. On a Saturday night, cloaked by darkness, Keith's partisans worked feverishly to erect a gallery from which their leader might exhort the worshippers the next morning. Keith's opponents controlled the per-manent gallery at the opposite end of the room and denied him entrance to it. The next day, as Quakers filed into the meeting, they found them-selves caught in the crossfire of two groups of impassioned Friends. Ac-cusations and counteraccusations filled the air as each side struggled to be heard. Axes appeared from nowhere and each group sought to destroy the other's gallery. Posts, railings, stairs, seats—all went down before the angry blows of the two opposed camps.[82]

The Keithian controversy was deeply rooted in issues of religious doc-trine and church organization. Yet it was more than this. The hundreds of Philadelphians who followed Keith were drawn to the passionate Scotsman not only for ideological reasons but also because political and economic tensions in Philadelphia were interwoven with disputes about Quaker belief and organization. The conjunction of religious and civil conflict was noted by one of Penn's supporters, who wrote in 1692 that "Alls a fire spiritual and temporal."[83]

An analysis of the social composition of the Keithian and Lloydian camps shows the close connection between secular and religious conflict. Among the several hundred Quakers who publicly avowed their opposi-tion to Keith, not one was known as a political opponent of Thomas Lloyd, who led the anti-Keithians. Conversely, within the network of Governor Lloyd's officeholders, the denunciation of Keith was almost unanimous. In the council, all nine Quakers opposed Keith and so did the entire membership of the Provincial Court. On the Philadelphia court only one of eight Quakers supported Keith and he was an avowed politi-cal opponent of Lloyd. Similarly, the most prominent Keithians were those men who led the political opposition against Lloyd but had lost their voice in public affairs because of their support for Penn or his dep-uty Blackwell. Keith also found considerable support among the shop-keepers and master artisans of the town and it is not accidental that these men had consistently petitioned against the Lloydian-sponsored tax of 1692. Of 87 known Keithians in Philadelphia, 71 had opposed the tax, whereas among 204 Quakers who had signed public condemnations of Keith's doctrines, only 12 joined the tax protest. Keith's strong appeal to the artisan class can also be measured. Of 78 known Quaker artisans in the city, 15 (19 percent) signified their rejection of Keith, 44 (56 percent) backed Keith, and 29 (25 percent) took no position so far as can be determined.[84]

Thus, Keithianism took on a far broader meaning for elements of Philadelphia society than Keith had initially intended in his movement to reform the Society of Friends. A stratum of lesser merchants, shopkeepers, and artisans found that Keith's program provided a means of challenging those who held high positions, who were resented for their political domination and overbearing behavior. The texture of the debates, the scurrilous language used by Quakers against each other, and the abstruseness of some of the theological issues at stake all suggest that participation in the movement was not only religiously inspired but emblematic of widely felt political and economic grievances.

The inner history of the Keithian controversy reveals a number of tendencies that were woven into the fabric of urban politics. When they went to the polls each year Philadelphians elected men who had ascended to the top of society, as measured by occupation, wealth, and reputation. At the same time they did not hesitate to oppose these figures or even William Penn, who was known and respected far beyond the boundaries of his colony. Men of middling and even lower status affixed their names to petitions, joined public demonstrations, indulged in inflammatory and hyperbolic rhetoric, refused to pay quitrents and taxes, and kept invoking the communal interest, as they saw it, in order to oppose those they viewed as authoritarian or inequitable. While they may have denied the legitimacy of factions, they readily indulged in factional politics, though carefully designating the other side as the violators of the public good.

What occurred in the early years of Philadelphia's history was to some extent related to the unleashing of energy and ambition that accompanied the exodus from England of persecuted Quakers. "More and not less [liberty]," Penn would later reflect, "seems the Reasons . . . to Plant this Wilderness." Or, he would write, "are wee come 3000 miles into a Desart of orig[inal] wild people as well as wild Beasts . . . to have only the same priviledges wee had at home?"[85] Penn's words tap the sense of anticipation felt in Philadelphia from the outset. People whose religion and humble positions in English society had made lofty aspirations unthinkable acquired almost overnight in the New World an englarged sense of self-importance and what was attainable. Agencies of authority were also less organized than at home and to a considerable degree were the instruments of the people they were supposed to direct.

In early Philadelphia, special factors relating to Quakerism may also have contributed to the tendency to balk at constituted authority. In the exercise of their beliefs in England, Friends continually defied established authority. Puritans had also rejected conventional authority and existing norms, but the Quakers far outdid them. The Friends were not unrestrained individualists; there was much in their code of values that stressed self-control and a commitment to community. But the Quaker personality had two sides, one which emphasized control, hierarchy, and community and another that celebrated freedom, individualism, and nonconformity. In Philadelphia, the centrifugal tendencies seem to have overpowered the centripetal ones, even though Quakers now had control of their own government. Penn despaired that his followers, set down on the banks of the Delaware, should be so "governmentish," so "brutish," so ready to indulge in "scurvy quarrels that break out to the disgrace of the Province." Before the first decade was over, Penn would have read so many reports from Philadelphia about "the surging waves of pestiferous apostates and runagadoes" and the seemingly unstoppable flood of litigious behavior that he would conclude that there was "nothing but good said of the place and little thats good said of the people."[86]

Religious values in Philadelphia, though of fundamental importance in the first few decades, never stifled the quest for economic and political advantage in an environment that was fluid and abundant enough to raise the level of aspiration of a large part of the community. Quakers in England, persecuted and limited in what they could achieve, looked inward. In Pennsylvania, where they controlled the government and were in the process of discovering what the limits of ambition were, they looked outward. They were not unique in this, however, as events in New York and Boston during this period show.

3

The Seaport Economies
in an Era of War

THE HALF-CENTURY between 1690 and 1740 marked the emergence of the small American seaport towns into commercial centers that rivaled such British provincial ports as Hull, Bristol, and Glasgow. Boston and New York reached about 17,000 and 9,500 inhabitants respectively, and Philadelphia more than quadrupled in size to about 9,000 during this period.[1] Boston's substantial lead, however, was deceptive, for it had reached the limits of its colonial growth by the late 1730s, while the population curve of New York and Philadelphia would continue upward through the second and third quarters of the century, leaving Boston on the eve of the American Revolution as the third largest city in British North America. The reasons for this are of more than passing interest, for the demographic history of the three port towns was closely tied to their changing economic and social conditions.

To a considerable extent the growth of the cities and the expansion of their economies during this period was dictated by the development of the hinterlands to which they were commercially linked. Boston, for example, reached out to serve the scores of towns, many of them founded in this era, that made up New England. Grain, cattle, and lumber were sent to Boston from the inland Massachusetts towns, none of which was more than thirty miles from tidewater. Boston marketed in the West Indies, Spain, and England the cod that the Massachusetts fishing fleet, sailing out of Ipswich, Marblehead, Newbury, and other fishing villages, caught in Newfoundland waters. The lumber of New Hampshire that provided the English navy with masts, yards, and planks was carried eastward across the Atlantic in Boston ships. These vessels returned to Boston with the finished goods of Scotland, Ireland, and Holland as well as England; Boston merchants then distributed them throughout New England.[2] Regional expansion caused growth at the metropolitan center. So while New England's population tripled between 1690 and 1740, from about 50,000 to 150,000, Boston's climbed correspondingly from 6,000 to nearly 17,000. Inward and outward bound shipping also grew rapidly as the level of imports and exports kept pace with rising regional population.[3]

The same relationship between seaboard commercial center and commodity-producing hinterland obtained for the ports of New York and Philadelphia. Inland New York and Pennsylvania were the great receiving areas for the waves of German and Scots-Irish immigrants sweeping in after Queen Anne's War. The province of New York increased nearly fivefold between 1690 and 1740, while Pennsylvania's population swelled more than sevenfold.[4] This alone guaranteed that the two mid-Atlantic ports would rapidly close the gap on their northern competitor. It is also important to note that by early in the eighteenth century the fertile interiors of New York and Pennsylvania had begun to establish a competitive advantage over New England with its marginal soil. This meant that their primary ports, rather than Boston, would come to dominate the West Indian and southern European foodstuffs trade and thereby earn larger balances to pay for a higher volume of imported goods than New Englanders could afford.

A simple model of urban growth tied to regional expansion and productivity can yield only an incomplete understanding of how the three seaports were evolving and why they differed so strikingly in their internal development. To comprehend why economic and social conditions in Boston, New York, and Philadelphia followed divergent paths we must also consider the impact of war on the commercial centers of colonial life. Almost continuously for a quarter-century after 1689 the colonies were involved in military conflict originating in Europe. Wars alternately stimulated and depressed trade. They also opened up new forms of entrepreneurial activity such as smuggling, piracy, and military contracting, provided the basis for new urban fortunes as well as new urban misery, altered the social structure, and exposed the towns to the vagaries of the market economy to a degree previously unknown.

International war came to America in 1689. But it did not have the same impact in each of the three regions served by the seaport towns. Boston, far more than any other colonial seaport, was involved in King William's War (1689-1697) and Queen Anne's War (1702-1713)—the two worldwide conflicts that launched the contest between Britain and France for control of North America. Shipping and shipbuilding were mainstays of its economy and both were affected by wartime conditions. Boston had more than a dozen shipyards by the turn of the century and from 1697 to 1714 they turned out an average of 1,568 tons of shipping per year.[5] War made the shipyards hum, as orders from England rolled in and the loss of local vessels to the enemy required replacement. In the peacetime years from 1697 to 1702 Boston's shipwrights constructed an average of fifteen vessels totaling 1,024 tons per year. During Queen

Anne's War the volume of construction nearly doubled.[6] After the Peace of Utrecht in 1713 this war-stimulated demand for Boston ships dropped, idling many artisans employed in the shipyards.[7]

War stimulated shipbuilding in Boston and thus contributed to the economic welfare of the entire community, but war also altered the pattern of shipowning. In a time of great risk on the high seas only those financially cushioned to withstand short-term losses could continue investing their capital. At the outbreak of King William's War 203 Bostonians owned at least a fractional share in a vessel. Most of the owners were merchants, shopkeepers, and ship captains, but also included were a handful of upwardly mobile artisans.[8] In 1698 "small" investors, those who purchased fractional shares in no more than three ships, held about 70 percent of all investments. But in the period of war that followed, their investments fell to 52 percent of the total. The five leading investors in 1698 controlled 12 percent of investments and the same top fraction of all investors increased their command of Boston shipping to 24 percent during the subsequent war years.[9] The largest vessels were held by fewer and fewer people, and the wealthiest shipowners, those who invested in ten or more vessels, obtained control of the colony's shipping. War vastly increased the risks of overseas trade and those who could not sustain the loss of one, two, or even more ships to enemy marauders on the high seas were driven from the field. Wealthier Bostonians, who could weather such losses, became a small investor community that played for high stakes. Not all of them won, of course, but those who did laid the foundations for a number of Boston mercantile fortunes of the eighteenth century.

The experiences of two Boston merchant-investors, one who won and one who lost, tell the story of how the wheels of fortune turned during an era of armed conflict. Andrew Belcher, born in 1648 to a respectable but undistinguished Cambridge family, got his start as a country peddler. The great Indian War in New England from 1675 to 1677, which had devastating effects on the region's economy, left thousands in great distress. For Belcher it was the chance of a lifetime, for he obtained provisioning contracts for the provincial militia.

Pooling his profits with a small inheritance from his wife, Belcher purchased a ship and took it to sea as both shipmaster and trader. At the advent of King William's War in 1689, Belcher was already a considerable shipowner in Boston. Through the connections he carefully cultivated with Governor Joseph Dudley, he obtained lucrative provisioning contracts for the English navy, which had made Boston its chief supply base in North America. By 1698 he had at least partial ownership of twenty-three vessels and was the second largest shipowner in the town. The Indian War of 1675 had pried open the door of opportunity; King William's War held it ajar; Queen Anne's War brought opportunities beyond all expectations for combining patriotism with profits. Belcher became one of the main royal provisioners for that part of the British fleet operating in American waters. More than £57,000 sterling was spent in Boston between 1711 and 1713 alone for supplying warships and outfitting expeditions against French Canada. As one of the favored recipients of the fruits of war, Belcher became a local titan, riding through Boston's streets in London-built coaches, erecting a fine mansion on State Street, purchasing Negro slaves to symbolize his ascent to the pinnacle of urban society. During the sixteen years after 1697, he invested in 137 ships totaling over 3,000 tons and owned 22 of them outright.[10]

That war could impoverish rich men as well as make poor men rich was amply illustrated by the career of the only man in Boston who could challenge Andrew Belcher as a shipping magnate in this period. Samuel Lillie, like Belcher, could claim no pedigree, for he was born in Boston in 1663 to a cooper, who had recently immigrated from England. Lillie may have gotten his start through an opportune marriage to Mehitable Frary, the sister of Andrew Belcher's second wife. Although his early career is obscure, the shipping register makes clear that by 1697 he was a flourishing merchant.

By that year he was the largest shipowner in Massachusetts and therefore in the American colonies. He owned more than twice as much tonnage as Belcher and continued to invest heavily during Queen Anne's War. At age forty Lillie "was easily the biggest shipowner in the western hemisphere; he probably would have ranked high on any list of European shipping magnates as well."[11] But that year marked disaster for Samuel Lillie. Many knew that his credit was overextended and when he was pressed for payment by several Boston merchants and taken to court, his empire collapsed. He made desperate attempts to plug the dike through partial payments and promises but his creditors gave no quarter. They demanded the liquidation of his fleet, and then, still insisting on payment, watched him flee to England under threat of imprisonment for debt. Twenty-two years later he returned to Boston, a broken man who had lived out most of his years in straitened circumstances.[12]

While war made some men impressively rich, broke the backs of others, and drove from the field a host of would-be merchant entrepreneurs who had to scale down their aspirations and return to shopkeeping and retail trading, it had far more deranging effects on those at the bottom of urban life. Wartime shipbuilding booms kept shipwrights, mastmakers, caulkers, ropewalk workers, blacksmiths, and others associated with ship construction fully employed; provisioning contracts for the royal navy aided bakers, distillers, and chandlers; and so long as trade was uninterrupted Boston's large population of merchant seamen, who may have numbered about 800 during this period, found berths aplenty.[13]

Beneath the established artisanry, however, resided another group of men—indentured servants, apprentices, recently arrived immigrants, migrants from hinterland towns, unskilled laborers, and younger artisans not yet established on their own. It was from these ranks of the least securely situated Bostonians that troops were recruited or pressed involuntarily into service for the assaults on the bastions of French Canadian strength. Once in military service, they died in proportions that seem staggering today. They cannot have enlisted because they regarded the pay as handsome, for the eight to ten shillings per week paid in Queen Anne's War was below the prevailing wage for common laborers.[14] Fervent antipopery, dreams of glory, and, most of all, hopes for plunder from the commercial centers of French Canada probably attracted most of them. Having little purchase on the paths that led upward, they grasped at straws or, frequently, were involuntarily pressed into service when quotas could not be met by volunteers.[15] A hefty percentage of those who sailed in the naval expeditions against Port Royal, on the fogbound west coast of Nova Scotia, or who marched overland to attack Montreal and Quebec, never lived even to collect their meager wages. None found the advertised booty, which turned out to be only a sugar plum dangled by the recruiters.

No accurate statistics are available on the number of Bostonians who died in the two wars between 1689 and 1713. It is likely, however, that one-fifth or more of the able-bodied males of Massachusetts participated in the campaigns and of these about one-quarter never lived to tell the terrors of New England's first major experience with international warfare. Within Massachusetts recruitment was particularly heavy in the coastal ports. In May 1690 an expedition of 736 men captured Port Royal, the principal town in sparsely populated Nova Scotia, with only slight casualties.[16] But the far more ambitious attack on Quebec four months later involved a flotilla of thirty-two ships and more than 2,000 men.[17] Unlike Port Royal, which fell without resistance, Quebec stood its ground against the New Englanders and the expedition limped home ravaged by smallpox and beset by the loss of three ships at sea. Jeremiah Dummer, a contemporary with wide experience in the war, later wrote that the 1690 expeditions had cost a thousand lives, mostly from camp fevers, famine, and disaster at sea.[18] Further losses were suffered in attacks made from 1692 to 1696 against French forts and Indian villages along the eastern frontier, which was becoming a kind of open vein from which the colony bled continuously. At war's end in 1697 Massachusetts was left, according to one official, "quite exhausted and ready to sinke under the Calamitys and fatigue of a tedious consuming War."[19] More than a decade later a knowledgeable Bostonian recalled that the war had cost the province an "abundance of young *chosen Men*" and left Massachusetts so burdened with debt that it "did not recover itself for many Years after."[20]

At the beginning of Queen Anne's War, much of the romance of bearding the French lion in his den was wearing thin. Governor Dudley tried hard to recruit volunteers for a British expedition against the French in the West Indies in 1702, but it was with great difficulty that he finally mustered two companies. When they were wiped out by disease, it became still clearer that the ghastly conditions prevailing on the ships and the prevalence of malignant fevers in military encampments made volunteering for garrison duty and seaborne assaults a way of signing one's own death warrant.[21] Nonetheless, Massachusetts had 1,100 in service in August 1703 and sent 550 men on a fruitless foray into Nova Scotia in 1704, when the government claimed that 1,900 men, every tenth adult male, was under arms.[22] Three years later, about 1,000 soldiers and 300 sailors, many of them pressed into service, embarked for two attacks on Port Royal. They ended in disorganization, mutiny, and craven retreat, which so enraged Bostonians that the returning troops were showered with the contents of chamber pots, as housewives called out from second-story windows: "Is your piss-pot charged, neighbour? So-ho, souse the cowards."[23]

Massachusetts mustered 1,000 men in 1709 for another Port Royal expedition, which never sailed because the expected English supporting task force failed to arrive. In the following year a combined British-New England expedition did capture the Nova Scotian port and in 1711 Massachusetts put about 2,000 men into service in the most ambitious military exploit yet conceived—an Anglo-American assault on Quebec by land and sea.[24] Admiral Sir Hovenden Walker was in charge of the expedition, which included sixty ships and about 6,000 British soldiers. When he asked Massachusetts authorities for additional seamen to replenish his disease-ridden ranks, they pointed out that the colony had already contributed one-fifth of its able-bodied men to frontier duty or the invasionary forces and could do no more.[25] Instead of dealing a knockout punch to the French, the expedition turned into a fiasco. Ships ran aground in the St. Lawrence River, heavy casualties were sustained, and the task force never reached its objective.

The emergence of a serious poverty problem in Boston by the closing years of Queen Anne's War was clearly related to this series of calamitous campaigns, which not only claimed the lives of many single men of the laboring classes but also left many war widows and their children without means of support. At the end of King William's War Cotton Mather complained that "our beggars do shamefully grow upon us," and by the end of the next war he was keeping track of eighty impoverished persons in his own church. Some of them were probably victims of a fire in 1711 but many others were widows of men whose lives were snuffed out in the monumentally mismanaged attacks on Canada. In 1712 Mather wrote that "the distressed Families of the Poor to which I dispense, or procure needful Relief, are now so many, and of such daily Occurrence, that it is needless for me here to mention them."[26]

While war stimulated employment among artisans who could avoid military service, it also affected them adversely in two ways. First, even in a day of primitive weaponry and miserable pay, military campaigns required substantial expenditures that could be met only by increasing taxes. For the expedition against Canada in 1690-1691, which cost £50,000, the legislative levied a tax twenty times the usual rate. When the campaign failed, Bostonians had only enormous tax bills on their hands and no victory over the French Catholics to compensate. The expedition's leaders hoped to seize enough enemy treasure to pay for the costs of the war, but "failure, debts, unpaid soldiers, and threats of mutiny at Boston were the actual results."[27] Among taxpayers, those of the middle and lower levels of society were probably most affected, for the method of taxation was highly regressive and struck with particular force at those with the smallest estates.

The campaigns against Canada from 1707 to 1711 also required extraordinary expenditures. Governor Dudley estimated the war costs at £30,000 per year and put a price tag of £50,000 on the 1711 expedition.[28] Bostonians in the 1690s had ordinarily paid less than £1,000 local currency in town taxes, but by 1707 they were dipping into their pockets for about £1,500 annually. From 1712 to 1714, when the town was obliged to build new fortifications to counter the threat of French attacks, local taxes exceeded £4,000 per year. Provincial taxes rose even faster. Boston's share of the province's tax burden had only occasionally exceeded £2,000 before 1704, but in the next decade it topped £4,000 in almost every year.[29] These figures are somewhat deceptive because Massachusetts currency began depreciating in 1705 and the town's population was growing steadily. For comparative purposes local currency must be converted into pounds sterling, which had a steady purchasing power in this period, and the town's total tax burden must be calculated on a per capita basis. Even with these adjustments the average householder faced taxes that showed a real increase of 42 percent between the end of the seventeenth century and the height of Queen Anne's War. For Boston artisans, who commanded wages of about 5 shillings per day and, because of the seasonality of work, could rarely earn more than £40 sterling per year, these war-related tax increases represented a significant reduction in expendable income.

Bostonians do not seem to have complained about the additional tax burden, for most of them cordially hated the French Catholic enemy and fervently hoped that the expeditions would drive the French from the continent. But by 1708 a customs officer in Boston was contending that "the warr hath extreamly impoverished them, so that the trade is now one third of what it was." Four years later the governor lamented that his people were "much impoverished and enfeebled by the heavy and almost insupportable charge of a long calamitous war which has chiefly lyen upon this Province."[30] Weighted down by war taxes, Bostonians had less to spend on imported goods. The subsequent drop in trade meant dead time between voyages and unemployment for the town's seafaring men at times when naval expeditions against the French were not underway.

The war economy of the two decades bracketing the turn of the century affected Bostonians of the laboring class in a second way. The heavy demands which war placed upon the provincial treasury could be met only by issuing paper money because taxes sufficient to subsidize military operations could never be extracted from property owners' pockets all at once. Thus, in the face of unpaid, mutinying troops in 1690, the legislature issued paper money for the first time in Massachusetts history. It was the initial experiment in deficit financing in the American colonies. In 1690-1691, £40,000 of paper bills were emitted and a decade later Governor Dudley found it impossible to undertake the war against the French without obtaining further issues of script. Between 1702 and 1710 Massachusetts printed £85,000 in paper bills, most of it to finance Queen Anne's War. With the launching of the mammoth Canadian expedition in 1711, the military appropriations spiraled higher, forcing the assembly to authorize another £317,000 in paper money over the next five years.[31]

Most economic thinkers of the day, at a time when monetary theory was in its infancy, believed that the bills of credit would retain their value so long as they were accompanied by tax legislation insuring that levies on property would be used to retire the paper currency within reasonable time limits. This meant that taxes could be paid in paper money, which would then be destroyed, or in specie or commodities, which would be exchanged for bills still in the hands of private citizens. So long as the amount of paper money in circulation was not excessive and was adequately backed by anticipated tax revenues, bills of credit would command respect. And respect was what maintained the value of paper money, for if public confidence in its worth was shaken, it would depreciate rapidly.[32]

Faced with military expenditures far beyond any they had previously known, the Massachusetts legislature gradually began to extend the time for redeeming the yearly issues of paper money. Their only alternative was a series of crushing taxes, and the experience of 1690, when such a tax had been passed but proved impossible to collect, suggested that this was folly.[33] Choosing the lesser evil, the government extended the retirement date of new issues of paper money to one year in the early years of Queen Anne's War; strung out the redemption to eighteen months in

1704; and granted a life of two or three years to the issues of 1707-1708. As more and more paper money was placed in circulation and taxes rose, legislators mortgaged income from property taxes farther into the future until by 1710 newly issued bills were scheduled for redemption by taxes levied six years hence.[34] It was a way of spreading out the costs of war over a number of years. But, unexpectedly, Massachusetts currency began to lose its value in 1705, the beginning of a depreciatory trend that was to last for two generations. This depreciation is most easily charted by the price of silver, a standard unit of measurement, in Massachusetts paper currency. Stable at 6 shillings 8 pence per ounce from 1685 to 1704, it rose slowly to 8 shillings by 1706, climbed to 9 shillings by 1714, and reached 13 shillings in 1721.[35]

To some degree the decline in sterling value of Massachusetts money represented faltering public acceptance of the bills of credit. Too much paper money, secured by taxes slated too far in the future, caused the gap to widen between the market value of the bills and their official value. But that was not the sole factor in currency depreciation. The rise in the price of silver occurred mainly after 1711, when the amount of paper money in circulation relative to the province's population changed only fractionally. Placing additional pressure on the value of local currency was the difficulty that Massachusetts's merchants had in balancing trade. Lacking a rich hinterland, the colony's residents were always scrambling for means of paying for products imported from England. Unable to make sufficient returns to England, especially in 1711 when the province imposed an embargo on its own shipping in order to assemble a fleet for the expedition against Nova Scotia, merchants bid higher and higher in Massachusetts paper money for sterling bills of exchange.[36] Massachusetts money had itself entered the competitive marketplace and fared poorly in the decade following the Peace of Utrecht in 1714.

The other side of currency depreciation, as modern readers are aware, was price inflation. In 1714, when the decline in value of Massachusetts money had only begun, Paul Dudley, the conservative son of the governor and no friend of the laboring classes, complained of the "excessive price of everything among us (and even the very necessaries of life.)" A bushel of wheat had risen to 8½ shillings, Dudley lamented, an increase of 60 percent since the early years of the century.[37] Such increases were caused in part by the heavy demand for provisions for the royal navy and the colonial military expeditions, but they were also the result of currency depreciation. Such advances in the cost of household commodities spelled misfortune for the average family unless wages rose equivalently.[38] Price-wage ratios remain an unexplored field in American colonial history, but the main authority on Massachusetts currency during this period states unequivocally that "wages did not rise proportionately with [the price of] silver."[39] Opinion at the time confirms this. "I will ask the Poor labourer, that works for *Five Shillings per* day," wrote a critic of the colony's fiscal policy in 1721, "Whether he lives better now than when he received *Four Shillings* a day in good Silver Money." Four shillings in "good silver money" would have purchased almost one bushel of wheat in the first years of Queen Anne's War.[40] By the end of the war 5 shillings in Massachusetts currency would buy about six-tenths of a bushel. Though wages had risen by one-quarter, prices had gone up even more, reducing the purchasing power of the ordinary artisan or laborer.[41]

The differential effects of increased taxes and decreased purchasing power on Boston's residents can probably never be measured with statistical precision. But it is generally conceded by economists today that in an inflationary period those at the lower levels of society are most adversely affected because it is they who spend the largest proportion of their income on the "necessities of life" and taxes. Confirmation of this can be gleaned from the inventories of estate of those who died during this era.

As a group, Bostonians among the lowest 30 percent of decedents in the first fifteen years of the eighteenth century died with much smaller estates than did their counterparts in the last fifteen years of the seventeenth century. In the earlier period personal wealth at death ranged between £2 and £70 sterling, or, with real property added, from £2 to £86. But those whose lives were completed during the era of Queen Anne's War left behind only £1 to £33 personal wealth and £1 to £55 total wealth. Other laboring-class Bostonians, who died in the decade after 1715 but whose ability to accumulate wealth was affected during this era, left between £1 and £23 personal wealth and £1 and £33 total wealth. Moving up the ladder of inventoried decedents, the same trend can be observed, with estates at death shrinking in the first quarter of the eighteenth century as measured against the wealth left by Bostonians dying in the closing fifteen years of the previous century. But the greatest proportionate decreases occurred at the bottom of the social scale, among mariners, laborers, and lesser paid artisans such as tailors, coopers, and cordwainers. Only among the top 5 percent of society, where some merchants had turned war to their advantage, did Bostonians die with larger estates than had been accumulated at a comparable level in the late seventeenth century.[42]

One of the corollaries of decreasing material wealth was decreased property ownership and the consolidation of urban real estate holdings in the hands of a rentier class. A decrease of nearly 25 percent in the rate of real property ownership occurred in Boston between 1685 and 1725 and by the end of the first quarter of the eighteenth century at least the bottom four-tenths of society did not hold property.[43]

By looking at two kinds of Bostonians who figured importantly at the bottom of Boston's social structure—mariners and widows—it is possible to glimpse some other effects of the war years.[44] Merchant seamen were by far the largest occupational group represented in the bottom 30 percent of the seaport's inventoried decedents. One of New England's most astute early historians wrote nearly a century ago that "If we could look into the living of these hardy mariners in their dingy cabins, it would be history indeed."[45] The seaports were by definition maritime centers, with merchant seamen composing at least one-tenth and often one-quarter of the adult male population. To ignore this group of struggling, disease-prone, ill-paid laboring men is to dismiss from consideration those without whose lives the wheels of maritime commerce could not have turned.[46]

Wages for mariners were notoriously low. In 1694 Massachusetts set them by law at £1.3 per month local currency for mariners in "government service," which meant those serving in the expeditions against the French. Receiving only half pay when in port, these men could probably expect an annual income no greater than £10 sterling per year. In 1713-1714 ordinary seamen on private vessels received about £2.5 per month Massachusetts money, which, when adjusted for currency depreciation, would have brought in about £12 to £14 sterling per year.[47] With wages at this level it is not surprising that the inventories of men such as Samuel Pell, Daniel Blin, and Nathaniel Fox included only the clothes on their back, a sea chest, and occasionally a set of knee buckles or an extra pair of shoes.[48]

Some mariners were able to do better. Those who survived the high mortality rates that prevailed on the ships could work their way slowly up the ladder, from ordinary seaman to second mate, and then to first mate and captain. Wages rose accordingly, although by unwritten rule captains were paid not more than twice as much as ordinary seamen. But this edge, when combined with a fortuitous marriage that brought a bit of investment capital, enabled some captains and occasionally mates to purchase partial shares in a voyage and thus lift themselves above the ruck of mere subsistence. The inventories of estate generally list the occupation of all men who went to sea as "mariner" so it is difficult to sort out those who died as ordinary seamen, mates, and ship masters. But the inventories show that about one in five (roughly the ratio of captains to crew members) left more than £400 at death, until 1716-1725 when the percentage dropped sharply. Another one-quarter to one-third left between £101 and £400. In the wake of Queen Anne's War, however, almost two-thirds of Boston's mariners died with estates worth £100 sterling or less and not even one of every five managed to leave over £200 in possessions at the end of a seafaring life.[49]

The second most numerous group among the bottom 30 percent was widows. Many of them were undoubtedly war widows and their numbers, as a proportion of all decedents at the bottom of Boston society, increased as the eighteenth century wore on. They were 14.3 percent from 1685 to 1699, 15.2 percent in the next fifteen years, and 16.0 percent from 1716 to 1725. Cotton Mather reckoned in 1718 that one-fifth of the communicants in his church were widows.[50] In the future, widowhood would create one of Boston's gravest social problems. By the end of Queen Anne's War, the rate of widowhood in the town, the product of a generation of war, was already extraordinarily high, with scores of lower-class women depending upon public and private charity.[51]

Unlike the frontier towns of Massachusetts that were sometimes ravaged by direct attack during the Anglo-French wars between 1689 and 1713, Boston did not witness war itself. But war profoundly affected the town—snuffing out the lives of hundreds who participated in a generation of fighting in Canada, Nova Scotia, and along the eastern frontier; driving up taxes to levels that were particularly onerous to the lower and middle classes; requiring the issue of huge amounts of paper money that through depreciation ate into the real wages of laboring people and others on fixed salaries; and leaving in its wake a new class of dependent poor. For some merchants and for many master artisans the wars generated substantial profits. But Boston as a whole could only view the era of war as a disaster, producing, as its pamphleteers cried out, "The Present Melancholy Circumstances" and "The Distressed State of the Town of Boston."[52]

NEW YORK'S FORTUNES were also intimately connected with war for the first two decades of the eighteenth century but in ways that differed strikingly from Boston. The Hudson River entrepôt never grew to more than two-thirds of Boston's size in this period and the volume of shipping usually measured from one-third to half of that registered in the Massachusetts port.[53] Nonetheless, shipping was the mainstay of New York's economy, and though it was often disrupted during Queen Anne's War, the overall volume of trade increased substantially.[54] But far more important in tracing the effects of war in New York is the fact that the Manhattan seaport, like the province it served, was never drawn into the actual fighting. New York raised money for the defense of its northern frontier, but the amount appropriated was less than one-eighth of that expended in Massachusetts. Consequently, paper money issues in New York were far smaller—about one-tenth as much as in the Bay colony—and the inflationary trend that had begun to erode the purchasing power of laboring-class Bostonians was largely avoided.[55] Moreover, New York contributed only token numbers of men for the expeditions against French Canada, in spite of the shrill calls for intercolonial cooperation emanating from officials in London and northern colonial governors.[56] New Yorkers even refused to attack the French across their own frontier, partly because the Hudson River town of Albany had established a profitable illegal trade with the French in Montreal and also because in 1701 the powerful and strategically located Iroquois tribes had adopted a policy of neutrality in the growing Anglo-French rivalry. Overland attack without Indian assistance was regarded in New York as unthinkable, and if the main effect of a New York attack on Canada was the interruption of the pipeline of profits, then trading with the enemy was clearly preferable to fighting him.[57] Simply by not participating in the futile attempts to drive the French from Canada, New Yorkers avoided most of the problems that struck Bostonians so severely from 1689 to 1720.

Although New York sat out the expeditionary phases of King William's and Queen Anne's wars, the town was still considerably affected. Like most wars of the eighteenth century, these conflicts were fought as much at sea as on land. In King William's War, New York benefited as one of the main suppliers of foodstuffs for the British fleet operating in the Caribbean and gained additionally from the opening of a foodstuffs trade with the Spanish colonies in the West Indies. The town's fleet almost quadrupled, growing from about 35 vessels just before the outbreak of war in 1689 to 124 ships in 1700.[58] Nor did French seapower bother New York shipping very much. In Queen Anne's War it was different. Spain outlawed the American foodstuffs trade with her Caribbean possessions, depriving New York of one of her best markets, and the French navy wrecked havoc on the town's merchant fleet. By 1704 the French had plucked off nearly thirty New York vessels, representing almost 25 percent of the fleet that had existed four years before. By 1706 the value of exports to London had dropped to one-sixth the level in 1700 and imports to two-fifths. The specie drain—the result of trade imbalance—became so serious that in 1709 its exportation was prohibited.[59] Trade with the West Indies improved after the English fleet bested the French in the Caribbean in 1706, but the war-buffeted economy recovered only slowly until the mounting of the 1711 Canadian expedition. With New York sharing the role of provisioner with Boston, an infusion of English money began to pull the seaport's economy out of the doldrums.[60]

Piracy also figured prominently in the effect of the wars on New York's economy. For years pirates had lain in wait along the main arteries of Spanish trade, intercepting the treasure ships that carried gold and silver from Peru and Mexico to Europe or from Spain to the Orient. But pirate silver and gold was only as good as what it could buy in ports where the sea bandits were welcome. Without a home port where booty could be exchanged for provisions and durable goods, gold and silver was so much ballast.[61] Before 1690, many pirates operating in the Caribbean had used Boston as their "home" port. In the sack of Vera Cruz in 1683, for example, sea marauders made off with 960,000 pieces of eight, much of which soon dropped into the tills of Boston's merchants and shopkeep-

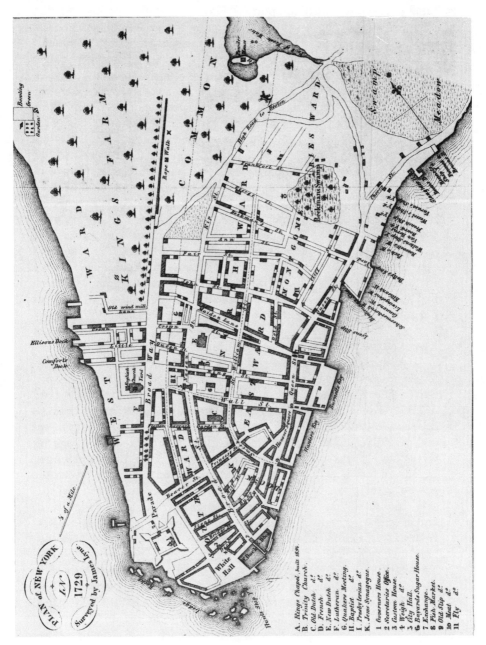

3. *Plan of New York in 1729 by James Lyne.*

ers.[62] But after 1690 the center of piratical activity shifted to the Red Sea and Indian Ocean, and New York, sending out encouraging signals, became the favorite American port.

Piracy was wholly illegal and condemned by every European government. English governors in the American colonies were strictly enjoined to offer no succor to pirates and to pack off to England any they caught so that they might be tried for treason. But from the colonial viewpoint pirates served a crucial economic function. To a considerable extent the northern colonies could relieve their severe specie shortages by blinking at English law and seizing opportunity when it presented itself. Each time a pirate ship sailed into a colonial seaport, tavernkeepers supplied liquid refreshment, ship carpenters refitted their vessels, shopkeepers sold fine goods, provisioners provisioned, and merchants and government officials gave covert support from the top. One contemporary Bostonian argued that the material impulse was so great in all the colonies that they vied with each other for smugglers and pirates who would bring more trade and hard coin. With such "confusion and anarchy" governors and legislators were "hardly safe in their Persons or Estates, if by a due and vigorous execution of the Law against Pyrats or illegal Traders, they should incense the People against them."[63] Governor William Markham in Philadelphia was so little offended by pirates that he married his daughter to one of the most notorious of the day, Captain John Avery, who was known to all seafaring men and even celebrated as the hero of Daniel Defoe's King of Pirates, published in London in 1720.[64]

Governor Benjamin Fletcher of New York stands as the shining example of how subversion of the law could be used to fatten one's own purse while aiding the local economy. Sent to New York in the aftermath of Leisler's Rebellion, Fletcher did not simply look the other way but addressed pirates directly, offering them commissions to sail as privateers and promising immunity from prosecution. He received handsome rewards for his hospitality, as did two members of his council, William Nicolls and Nicholas Bayard, who acted as intermediaries between the governor and pirate captains. One student of this form of entrepreneurship has written that "Great estates had been made by selling wine, rum, and ammunition to the pirates" and that the profit margin "seemed incredible."[65] Many of New York's mercantile fortunes took a sharp upward turn during the 1690s as a result of complicity with the pirates. Nicholas Bayard, Frederick Philipse, Stephen DeLancey, Gabrielle Minvielle, William Nicolls, William "Tangier" Smith, and Thomas and Richand Willett were only some of the town's leading merchants who engaged in this early American version of white-collar crime.

It is difficult to estimate how deeply the benefits of trading with the pirates ran in New York's social structure. Certainly, the marauders enjoyed fairly broad support, for they brought into the seaport vast amounts of badly needed specie, estimated as high as £100,000 annually.[66] Piratical profits, however, may have fallen mostly into the hands of a chosen few. Fletcher's council, composed of the largest merchants of the Anglo-Dutch elite, was squarely behind the governor on the pirate issue. When the pirate ship *Jacob* arrived in 1698, for example, the council recommended that the governor permit the men ashore because the colony was "exhausted in men as well as money" and therefore "nothing could be worse than to drive these men to others parts."[67] But others, frozen out of the lucrative business because of the bitter Leislerian conflict, reacted differently. Fletcher was replaced in 1698 by Richard Coote, Earl of Bellomont, and when the new governor announced a crackdown on pirates he found plenty of support among the Leislerians, many of whom came forward to implicate those in the anti-Leislerian party who had abetted the pirates. Hard money was something that all New Yorkers needed, but the vigorous Leislerian support of Bellomont's campaign against the oceanic freebooters suggests strongly that the rewards of the piratical connection were by no means uniformly distributed.[68] Because they were not equal beneficiaries, the Leislerians opposed smuggling and piracy, "the beloved twins" of the seaport's Anglo-Dutch mercantile elite.[69]

The risks of wartime shipping and the benefits of smuggling and piracy seem to have consolidated economic power in the hands of a small class of wealthy merchants. No ship register exists for the town, as for Boston, but this trend can be partially seen in the custom house records for 1701 and 1702. They portray a seaport in which a large part of the shipping was controlled by about two dozen men. New York in 1703 had about 110 merchants, including some shipmasters and retailers who ventured capital in trade on occasion and styled themselves merchants. Of these, nineteen traders accounted for 57 percent of all the imports in 1701 and 1702 and the top two dozen controlled two-thirds of the city's inbound trade.[70] The risks of war, the use of larger vessels, and the increasing complexity of New York's trade, which by now was reaching out to Africa, Portugal, and South America as well as to the less distant West Indian and mainland North American ports, consolidated the power held by a handful of men within the mercantile community.

Among these fast-rising merchant princes, none was more successful or indicative of the character of late seventeenth-century mercantile life than Frederick Philipse. Born in Holland, Philipse had come to North America in the 1650s as the carpenter of Peter Stuyvesant, governor of the Dutch West India Company's tiny colony of New Netherland. Philipse was known than as Vredryck Flypsen and it was not until the English takeover of New Netherland in 1664 that he signified his cooperative posture toward the new authorities by Anglicizing his name. He had no intention of risking an already sizeable estate, acquired in the previous years by some minor trading ventures to Virginia and, more important, through marriage in 1662 to Margaret Hardenbroeck de Vries, the wealthy widow of Pieter de Vries, who had left her a handsome fortune in New York real estate and ships. Philipse had parlayed his newfound wealth into one of the Manhattan seaport's greatest estates by the time of Leisler's Rebellion.[71] Some of this fortune came from his position as New York's largest importer of African slaves. By the 1690s Philipse calculated that he could make several thousand pounds profit on a single voyage to Mozambique and Madagascar, where slaves that fetched £30 on the New York market could be obtained for 30 shillings and where rum that cost 2 shillings a gallon in New York could be sold to pirates for 50 to 60 shillings per gallon.[72]

In the early 1690s, when Governor Fletcher openly welcomed pirates in New York, Philipse was a member of his council and a willing mediator between the marauders and the royal governor. Fletcher's replacement by Bellomont, who was determined to crack down on the buccaneers, required Philipse to alter his mercantile activities slightly. Trading with pirates in New York now became impossible. But great profits could still be reaped by combining the Madagascar slave trade with the supplying of pirates outside New York. The English East India Company had a monopoly on all trade eastward of the Cape of Good Hope, but as long as Philipse's ships touched at the island of Saint Helena, off the coast of East Africa, to obtain clearance from the Company, they were entirely legal.[73] Extraordinary returns could be harvested from provisioning the Red Sea and Indian Ocean pirates from New York and then loading up with Madagascar slaves for the return voyage. Philipse had made 9,514 pieces of eight, or about £2,000 sterling, on a previous voyage of this kind, bearing out Governor Bellomont's assertion that supplying pirates could be even more profitable than turning pirate oneself.[74]

In 1698, however, Parliament passed the East India Act, which imposed tight restrictions on trade east of the Cape of Good Hope, and thus virtually sealed off Philipse's formula for amassing wealth. Unwilling to forego the fabulous profits he had been accruing, he attempted to smuggle a cargo from the Indian Ocean. He was caught red-handed but his loss was only forfeiture of the smuggled goods to the crown. This could hardly wreck the fortunes of a merchant of his means; in fact, the larger loss through his exposure as an illegal trader in 1698 was to his pride, for he was removed from the governor's council as a result of the violation.[75] When he died four years later, he left to his only son one of the great American estates of the early eighteenth century, including more than 90,000 acres of land in the Hudson River Valley, several hundred tenant farmers and slaves, a small fleet of ships, and a fortune in New York City real estate.[76] In Boston Andrew Belcher had risen to wealth through war contracting; in New York Frederick Philipse had used the slave trade, the piratical connection, and the ability to straddle the line between legal and illegal economic activity to open the gates of wealth. For both in this early period of capitalism, an eye for the main chance, as well as a generous portion of unscrupulousness, had proved the keys to success.

To some extent the wartime redistribution of power in New York that was personified in the career of the Philipse family can be seen in the tax lists that have survived for this period. In 1695 the wealthiest 10 percent of the taxpayers owned 45 percent of the seaport's taxable assets, while the bottom half could claim only about 10 percent of the total wealth. By 1703 this concentration of wealth had become slightly more pronounced.[77] Even these measurements underestimate the growing disparity between the top and bottom of society. In the aftermath of Leisler's Rebellion, when the insurgents had been driven from office and the government was placed firmly in the hands of Governor Fletcher and the Anglo-Dutch mercantile elite, the assessors began to undervalue greatly the estates of the wealthy. In 1676, just two years before Governor Edmund Andros had described "substantial" citizens as those with estates worth £500 to £1,000, forty-six persons had been assessed in this wealth range. But in 1695, by which time the leading merchants had amassed far greater wealth than this, the assessors rated only two men for more than £1,000 and four others between £500 and £1,000. By employing the reverse of the modern-day graduated income tax, the assessors placed the heaviest proportionate tax burden on the lower and middle classes and the lightest proportionate burden on those at the top. For example, Robert Skelton, a tailor, was taxed for wealth assessed at £20 in 1699; when he died in 1703 his estate actually totaled £336. Merchant Isaac Rodriques Marques, who was rated at £110 on the same tax list, died shortly thereafter with an estate totaling about £3,400. The tailor paid tax on 6 percent of his actual wealth; the merchant on 3 percent of his. The tax lists at the end of the century, moreover, show how little of the community's wealth now remained in the hands of the lesser artisans and laborers. In both 1695 and 1703 the bottom 30 percent of the taxable population held less than 5 percent of the wealth.[78]

The two wars bracketing the turn of the century had differential effects on New York society, benefiting large merchants more than small and bringing intermittent economic stagnation and uncertainty to parts of the community. New York contributed far fewer men proportionate to its population than did the Bay colony capital to the war effort; price inflation and rising taxes were generally not a part of the New York experience; and the postwar economic recovery was faster than in Boston.[79] Extant pauper lists for New York make the contrast with Boston clear. The first surviving list, from January 1700, names only thirty-five persons receiving aid. Almost all of them were orphaned, crippled, or aged. Another census of the poor, taken near the end of Queen Anne's War in

1713, lists only sixteen persons, including two children, one soldier's wife, and only two adult males. Throughout that year only twenty persons were aided by the churchwardens, who directed the care of the needy, and in 1714 their charges numbered twenty-eight. Expenditures for the relief of the impoverished, while rising from £219 in 1698 to £454 in 1714, were still lower on a per capita basis than in Boston, where about £500 had been spent in 1700 and about £1,000 by 1713.[80] Much of the 62 percent increase in per capita expenditures on the poor between 1698 and 1714 was necessitated by the yellow fever epidemic of 1702, which swept away about 10 percent of New York's population and probably hit the laboring classes with unusual severity. A household census taken just after the epidemic shows that 130 households, or 17.5 percent of all families in the town were headed by females.[81] This substantial widowing of New York obliged the assembly to double the poor rate.[82] But impoverishment did not spread very extensively, for while smallpox was a deadly killer, its victims were not so concentrated in the lower ranks as were the several hundred Bostonians who had succumbed in army encampments and on naval vessels during the years of miscalculated adventuring against French Canada.

OF ALL THE northern seaports, Philadelphia was least affected by the turn-of-the-century wars. The Quaker-controlled government argued shrewdly that the immature state of the colony, the pacifist beliefs of most of its inhabitants, and its greater distance from the northern zone of Anglo-French rivalry made Pennsylvania's participation unfeasible. So Philadelphians contributed virtually nothing by way of manpower to the war efforts and were obliged to tax themselves only lightly in order to provide token amounts of support for what were supposed to be intercolonial campaigns. Philadelphians, in fact, paid a small provincial tax in only nine of the twenty-five years between the beginning of King William's War and the end of Queen Anne's War, and paid no city taxes whatsoever before 1710.[83] On a per capita basis they contributed less than one-twentieth as much as Bostonians in town and provincial taxes in this era.[84] Spared military expenditures, Pennsylvania never had to print paper money; Philadelphians, therefore, knew none of the price inflation that depleted the pocketbooks of Bostonians.

The immunity of Philadelphia from the dislocating effects of the wars is evident in the poor relief and tax records that have recently been recovered for the year 1709. Only fourteen city dwellers received aid from the Overseers of the Poor in that year, three of them men and four of them widows. Total expenses for subsidizing the indigent were only £153. The tax list of 1709 also shows that only 5.2 percent of the households were headed by women, less than a third the rate in New York and Boston.[85]

While Philadelphia was spared the unsettling effects of the wars that especially affected the laboring classes, the city's trade, upon which economic conditions in general hinged, swung back and forth between bursts of activity and periods of recession. These ups and downs were dictated by control of the ocean routes between mainland North America and the West Indian islands where Philadelphia merchants marketed the grain, meat, and lumber that made up the colony's principal exports. For the first half of King William's War, French privateers played havoc with English shipping on the Spanish Main and off the coast of North America. Pennsylvania's trade slumped badly and land prices in Philadelphia spiraled downward in response. But when the French marauders were contained in the closing years of the war, Philadelphia merchants reaped handsome profits from the West Indian trade. In the brief interwar period the city remained prosperous.[86]

Similarly, in Queen Anne's War, French privateers infested the Caribbean waters in the early years of the conflict, and the Pennsylvania grain market, the underpinning of the economy, was badly shaken. By the fall of 1702, one of Philadelphia's leading merchants wrote William Penn that "Wheat, that while thou wast here [in 1701] was our best commodity, goes begging from door to door, and can scarcely find a buyer."[87] Some of Philadelphia's largest merchants suffered severe losses. Samuel Carpenter, whose mercantile success in the late seventeenth century had been unequaled, went bankrupt.[88] Conditions improved after 1706 and as the war drew to a close Philadelphians flourished. Population growth, spurred by the beginning of heavy Scots-Irish and German immigration after 1715, continued into the early 1720s. Per capita imports from England, which can be taken as a crude measurement of economic conditions, rose from £.45 annually between 1701 and 1710 to £.66 in the next decade, a 47 percent increase.[89] With shipping routes cleared of enemy ships, a new period of growth and prosperity came to Philadelphia.

James Logan, an Ulster Quaker who at age twenty-five had arrived in Pennsylvania in 1699 as William Penn's secretary, and Isaac Norris, son of a merchant in Port Royal, Jamaica, provide examples of the entrepreneurial possibilities in a port town where war contracting was wholly absent. Both Logan and Norris began to explore new mercantile connections in this era, selling grain in Lisbon, provisions in Carolina, rum in Newfoundland, and lumber in Mediterranean ports such as Leghorn, Italy. Whereas the West Indian provisioning trade and the tobacco trade with England had occupied earlier efforts almost exclusively, now Philadelphia's leading merchants expanded their commercial network. Both Logan and Norris had accumulated minor fortunes by the end of the war period, extensive enough, in fact, to begin construction of country seats outside the town. Logan's "Stenton" and Norris's "Fairhill," both built in the subdued elegance of early Georgian style, were erected in the immediate postwar period at a cost running close to £1,000 each.[90]

The Philadelphia probate records for the years before 1720 yield some interesting indications that in the Quaker capital, comparatively untouched by the two major conflicts of this era, ordinary artisans and shopkeepers did better than their counterparts in Boston. The pattern of wealth left by Bostonians and Philadelphians whose lives had ended in the last fifteen years of the seventeenth century was very similar. But those who died in the first quarter of the eighteenth century, whose careers had been affected by an era of war, left estates that differed markedly in the two seaports. Median wealth at every stratum except the top 10 percent dropped significantly in Boston, while in the Quaker capital wealth at death remained about the same in the bottom third of society and rose considerably in the top 40 percent of decedents. By the end of the first quarter of the eighteenth century, median wealth left by Bostonians at all levels of society except the upper tenth was half or less of that left by Philadelphians.[91]

This greater likelihood for Philadelphians to prosper should probably not be explained solely by Boston's greater involvement in the Anglo-French wars, for other factors, including Philadelphia's more productive hinterland and her more favorable proximity to West Indian markets, undoubtedly came into play. But the wars were a major factor, for they visited upon Boston higher rates of widowhood and poverty, heavier taxes, and price inflation that outran wage increases. Philadelphia's economy was not yet sufficiently developed to allow for the creation of fortunes to match those of men such as Andrew Belcher and Frederick Philipse. But this meant also that the distance between the humblest laborer and the most successful merchant was not so great as in Boston and that wealth in the Quaker town was much more evenly distributed than in the Puritan capital. In Boston, the top 5 percent of those who died between 1700 and 1715 possessed 40 percent of all inventoried wealth as compared with 25 percent in Philadelphia. In the following decade the richest twentieth of Boston's inventoried decedents possessed 48.5 percent of all inventoried wealth; in Philadelphia this group had only 31 percent of all assets.[92] In the Quaker town, population growth and economic development, carried out without significant involvement in war, was leading slowly toward a less even distribution of wealth. But though he watched his merchant neighbor forge ahead more rapidly than he, the average carpenter, shopkeeper, or mariner was leaving as much or slightly more in worldly goods than his counterpart of the previous decades. In Boston, population growth and economic development, accompanied by prolonged involvement in war, redistributed wealth less evenly and created conditions in which artisans, small retailers, and merchant seamen left less personal wealth than those who had stood in their places a generation before.

The probate, tax, and poor relief records cannot, of course, be relied upon to establish with mathematical precision the degree or exact timing of change. There can be little doubt, however, concerning the direction of change or the fact that the war period had transformed the character of urban life. To what extent urban artisans and others understood the scope and meaning of change is not easy to say, for they left in writing almost nothing of their thoughts. But in the political behavior of these seaport dwellers are ample clues that people of the time were not insensitive to the transformation of their world and did not passively accept new conditions.

4

The Rise of Popular Politics

EACH OF THE northern seaports had been shaken between 1689 and 1692 by a political disturbance that revealed the fragility of traditional beliefs that the well-born and wealthy should lead, the commonality should follow, and the eyes of all should be firmly fixed on the public good rather than on private interests. Each town witnessed some degree of turbulence, crossing of traditional lines of authority, renunciation of established leaders, mobilization of ordinary town dwellers, and cleaving of the political body into loose interest groups, if not parties. The cause of the political inflammation had differed from one town to another: in Boston it came from a disillusionment with royal authority; in New York from ethnic tension mixed with economic grievances; in Philadelphia from opposition to a proprietor and local rulers whose use of political power was thought to be highhanded.

In the first two decades of the eighteenth century the citizenry of the seaport towns fitfully made further inroads on the traditional mode of politics. New political tactics were devised, sporadic crowd action expanded the boundaries of political behavior, and the notion of a unitary political community in which the public interest rather than individual group interests was the common goal suffered new blows. It is not accidental that social disruption and political innovation proceeded fastest and farthest in Boston, where economic dislocation was most severe, and that it lagged far behind in Philadelphia, where economic problems were least noticeable. Of the three northern ports, New York had been the most buffeted by political storms in the 1690s because the overthrow of James II in England had brought to a head a decade of interconnected economic and ethnic grievances. In the quarter-century that followed, it was Boston, where economic and social life was disrupted by war, that was the most politically volatile port town.

During Queen Anne's War and in its aftermath, Boston weathered three controversies that reveal the changes overtaking urban society. The

first began in 1710 when Andrew Belcher, Boston's largest grain merchant, personally created a bread shortage in the town. Belcher had the
contract to supply 400 royal marines who were joining the Massachusetts
militia for another attack on Port Royal. Belcher, the grain merchant,
bought up most of the wheat supplied to Boston from the countryside,
held it while prices rose sharply under the pressure of new demands, and
sold it to Belcher, the commissary general, at a handsome profit. War
profiteering was one thing, but a shortage of bread in the town was another.

When Belcher began to export grain from Boston to other colonies, the
townspeople moved into the streets. Eight years before, at the beginning
of the war, the town meeting had specifically instructed the selectmen to
forbid the export of wheat and bread during wartime emergencies.[1]
When their pleas to the wealthy Belcher went unheeded, the people took
more direct action, exercising what one historian has called "the right to
be fed."[2] Under cover of night, a group of marauders descended on one
of Belcher's ships, about to sail from the harbor with 6,000 bushels of
grain, and sawed through the rudder. The ship lay disabled at her moorings and on the next night a crowd of about fifty Bostonians comman-
deered the vessel and tried to run it aground.[3] The selectmen, whose pleas
Belcher ignored, petitioned the General Court to stop the exportation of
grain. Apparently convinced by the direct action of the townspeople, the
legislature complied, although exempting the grain already on Belcher's
ship.[4]

Belcher had no intention of taking orders from the "mob." Though restricted from exporting more grain, he continued to buy up as much as he
could find, holding it in his warehouses while prices rose. By 1711, with
the huge Anglo-American expedition to Canada about to depart, the demand for wheat was so great that the selectmen were forced to use town
taxes to buy up any available wheat, flour, and corn and to sell it to the
laboring poor at prewar prices.[5] Two years later grain shortages in the
West Indies gave Belcher another opportunity to offend his townsmen.
Rather than sell flour to hungry Bostonians at a modest profit, he chose
to export grain to Curaçao, the Dutch island in the Caribbean. The selectmen pleaded with him to halt the shipment of grain and Cotton Mather
spoke authoritatively about God's love of the poor in order to raise gifts
of bread from his congregation.[6] But a crowd of about 200 did not wait
for God's love to descend. Provoked by Belcher's recalcitrance, they took
matters into their own hands, attacking and emptying his grain warehouses. The lieutenant governor discovered that the deference which the
clergy monotonously prescribed to the lower classes was a frail reed to
rely upon; when he tried to intervene he was promptly shot. Bostonians
of meager means proved that through concerted action the powerless
could become powerful, if only for the moment. Wealthy merchants who

would not listen to pleas from the community could be forced through collective action to subordinate profits to the public weal.[7]

We can see in the behavior of the Boston crowd in 1710 and 1713 the determined resistance of ordinary people to those with great economic leverage who used it in disregard of the traditional restraints on entrepreneurial activity. Some of Boston's merchants, anticipating a new era, were attempting to forge a fresh set of economic relationships that promised greater flexibility and higher profits. The old political economy, medieval in origins, rested on the assumption of a world made up of many semiclosed economies, each operating in a nearly self-sufficient way. Boston, according to this model, was connected to its hinterland, with each part of the system serving the other to some degree while remaining semiautonomous. Boston, though, by the early eighteenth century had become a part of a far wider commercial network that linked the town not only to England and other mainland colonies but also to Newfoundland, the West Indies, Portugal, and even Africa. Of course, not every Boston merchant was involved in this enlarged mercantile world. But some, like Andrew Belcher, were intent on expanding overseas trade and obtaining the flexibility to operate in a freer marketing climate where economic decisions were made not with reference to local and public needs but according to laws of supply and demand that operated internationally. This wider market was indifferent to individuals and local communities; the flow and price of commodities, as well as labor and land, were dictated by the invisible laws of the international marketplace. If grain fetched eight shillings a bushel in Curaçao and only five in Boston, then the merchant was entitled, according to the emerging ethic, to ship to the more distant buyer all the grain he could procure from the countryside.

Economic decisions made in consonance with this version of a freer and more international market ran squarely against the precepts of traditional economic thinking.[8] For decades, Bostonians had lived with the understanding that the government had the right—indeed, was obligated —to provide for the general welfare by licensing certain economic activities, prohibiting others, and overseeing prices, wages, quality controls, and many other aspects of daily economic life. Artisans had felt the hand of the law in this regard as recently as July 1711. When 11,000 men had to be supplied for the Canadian expedition, Governor Dudley issued a proclamation "to impress all bakers, brewers, coopers, &c. who cannot or will not supply the public in their way at the stated prices."[9] Serving corporate needs required subordination from below. But it also imposed obligations on those at the top. "Since every man occupied an appointed place or degree in the body politic," writes one student of the traditional economic ethic, "every man had a claim on that body to provide him with the means of livelihood. Transactions or contracts that militated against his right to subsistence, however arrived at, were unjust and in-valid. For most people the ultimate appeal in disputed dealings was to social, in contrast with economic duty."[10]

Of course, Andrew Belcher was not manufacturing new economic theory in 1710 or 1713 when he made decisions to fill overseas grain orders rather than serve the local market. For decades the economic sys-tem of the English-speaking world had been undergoing change, and the alterations were mostly in the direction of greater freedom for the local merchant from time-honored regulations of the corporate society but greater mercantilist regulation from England in economic matters that bound the colonies to the mother country. For decades, the new values had been intruding upon older mores. In the American colonies they probably lagged behind England. But change was in the air on both sides of the Atlantic, involving "a new social reality in which the self-seeking drive appeared more powerful than institutional restraints to mold peo-ple's actions."[11] It was not until a genuine crisis occurred that the full ex-tent of the conflict between the new entrepreneurial freedom and the older concern for the public weal became manifest. This happened almost exclusively during periods of war, for food shortages were never a problem in colonial America unless external demand grossly depleted homegrown supplies. During the later years of Queen Anne's War, just such a conflict developed between the profit-oriented desires of Boston's largest grain merchants and the needs of local consumers, who demanded to be fed at prices they could afford.

It is important to observe that Boston's common folk did not stand by impassively when the town's merchants attempted to substitute the laws of supply and demand for the older axiom that the public welfare tran-scended all private gain. Even though they had rarely known food short-ages, which occurred far less frequently in colonial America than in Europe, they were the inheritors of an older ethic that in Europe had provided some measure of security for the lower classes. Accordingly, they did not hesitate to take direct—even illegal—action to compel the engrossers, hoarders, and exporters to back down.[12] What is more, they not only halted Belcher's grain exports but also escaped punishment for taking government into their own hands. After the 1710 incident, the Boston grand jury, made up of substantial members of the community, returned a writ of ignoramus rather than indict the rioters who had at-tacked Belcher's ship. Several members of the grand jury asked to be dis-missed or were challenged by the attorney general, correctly in all proba-bility, as being in favor of the riot.[13] Even the council attempted to pass over the expropriation of Belcher's property by describing the attack as the work of "the inferior sort of people men & boys as well as strangers and others."[14] In effect, this was an acknowledgment that the ruling elite did not possess the power or the moral authority to restrain or punish the crowd leaders. The conservative elite in the town probably applauded Ebenezer Pemberton, who ranted in 1710 that it was "not God's people but the Devil's people that wanted Corn. There was Corn to be had; if they had not impoverished themselves by Rum, they might buy Corn."[15] But many Bostonians believed that Belcher's actions justified breaching the law in order to uphold a more fundamental, if unwritten, principle. It is not clear whether the looting of the houses of some wealthy Bostonians during a major fire in the following year was a populist act of retributory justice, but it set the clergy to exclaiming about the "Monstrous Wretches" and "Monsters of Wickedness" who were abroad.[16]

The second controversy that enveloped Boston in the era of Queen Anne's War concerned the reorganization of town government. At issue was the viability of the town meeting and the wisdom of electing a wide range of public officials, the hallmarks that distinguished Boston's municipal government from all others in colonial America. In 1708 a plan to dismantle the town meeting system was introduced by some of the selectmen, who argued for converting Boston into an incorporated municipal borough to be ruled, as were most English towns, by a mayor and board of aldermen who would appoint most local officials. The change was needed, argued some, because Boston's town meeting was too unwieldy and turbulent to make decisions efficiently and wisely. Greater discipline could be obtained in the discharge of duties by minor officeholders if these men were appointed by a borough government rather than elected at large.[17]

At the time this proposal was brought forward the town was already divided into two factions, one gathered around the royal governor, Joseph Dudley, still hated by many for his autocratic tendencies in the Andros government, and the other around Elisha Cooke, a doctor, lawyer, and landowner who was the leader of the "popular" faction.[18] The two groups were not split strictly along class lines, for well-to-do merchants and shopkeepers were numerous in each. But the Dudley party, led by Boston's wealthiest merchants, was strongly oriented toward the growing Anglican church, where the pews were filled with conservative men who looked toward England and the world outside Massachusetts.[19] Cooke's group included many younger and less established merchants, but made a strong appeal to the artisans of the town as well. Every spring, for thirteen years beginning in 1703, Governor Dudley stoked the fires of animosity between the two factions by vetoing Elisha Cooke's election to the council.

When the proposed reorganization of municipal government came before the Boston town meeting in 1708, it was rejected. Bostonians evidently preferred to disperse political power and to retain the highly participatory system they had long known. Six years later proposals for municipal incorporation were brought forward again, this time in the midst of a controversy concerning the issue of paper money. A group of investors closely associated with the Cooke faction, now under the leadership of Elisha Cooke, Jr., who had inherited the role of opposition leader from his father, wanted to create a private bank that would emit £300,000 in paper money. Subscribers could mortgage their property to the bank in return for private bills of credit issued in the amount of two-thirds of the value of the borrower's land. The proposers hoped to relieve the severe shortage of a circulating medium in Boston and also to return a profit to the organizers. The bank would also have given Cooke and his associates important leverage in their private economic struggles with Boston's more established merchants.[20]

In the midst of the battle over the private land bank, the plan to reorganize Boston's government came to a head. The Cooke faction, in appealing to the voters, carefully demonstrated the connection between the plan for a municipal borough and the economic divisions that were separating Boston into two communities. The equation was made clear in two pamphlets issued before the town meeting met to decide the issue. In one, *A Dialogue between a Boston Man and a Country Man*, the plan was blasted as an oligarchic plot because it would allow only men worth £1,000 to qualify as aldermen. Its authors were characterized as men with "Proud Spirits" and "Coveteous" of standing in high places. The plan itself was stigmatized as a transparently self-interested concoction of those who had no "fellow-feeling of every bodies Pocket in the whole Town" but "like to the Great Fish" wanted to be "lords over the Small."[21]

In the second pamphlet, the case was made even more explicit. Under cover of "pretended zeal to do the Town Service," the proponents of incorporation were said to be plotting to strip Bostonians of their most precious rights. Behind this move was seen a strong class animus, a dislike of ordinary people who had for so long participated in the governance of the town and who occasionally took the law into their own hands. "Then Farewell to all Town-Meetings," warned the author, "and to the Management of the Town Affairs by the Freeholders, Collectively; Rich & Poor Men then will no more be jumbled together in Town Offices, as they are in the Grave, no more Mobb Town-Meetings of Freeholders, (as some are pleased to call them)." Under the proposed reorganization of government the wealthy would rule and the humble submit. Economic consequences were predicted. "The Rich will exert that right of Dominion, which they think they have exclusive of all others . . . and then the Great Men will no more have the Dissatisfaction of seeing their Poorer Neighbours stand up for equal Privileges with them."[22] Fifty years later, another Boston oligarch, preoccupied with the erosion of traditional authority, wrote in his history of Massachusetts that when the incorporation plan was laid before the town meeting in 1714 "a demagogue called out, 'It is a whelp now, it will be a lion by and by, knock it in the head.' " As Thomas Hutchinson noted, "It was rejected by a great majority."[23]

Though successful in defeating the plan to abolish the town meeting, the Cooke faction failed to obtain approval for their private bank scheme. The private bank was vigorously opposed by the mercantile elite surrounding Governor Dudley, and the pamphlet war against Cooke and his associates was led by the governor's son, Paul Dudley, who occupied the position of attorney general.[24] At the largest town meeting in Boston's history, a majority of the voters opted for issuing bills of credit by a public bank under the management of the General Court rather than for incorporating a private bank.[25] Though it was a defeat for Cooke and his partners, it was not a victory for Dudley, for the governor's camp included a number of merchants opposed to both private and public banks because they thought all paper money "utterly bad and that the only salvation lay in returning to specie payment, let the people suffer as they might."[26] Moreover, the need for the private bank had been considerably diminished by the authorization of £50,000 in province bills of credit late in 1714.[27] The voters had chosen a public solution to the problem, voting for more paper money but keeping the management of the money supply in the hands of the court rather than a private group of investors.

For six years after the defeat of the private bank proposal of 1714 Boston politics revolved around monetary issues, the third controversy in the era of Queen Anne's War. Annual elections for selectmen and representatives to the General Court became contests between the Dudley and Cooke groups and the rift between them widened. The issue no longer centered on the advisability of a private bank, although merchant John Colman, its most strenuous advocate, continued to push his favorite plan. The more vital question was what to do when the large emissions of public bank bills, issued by the provincial government between 1714 and 1716, were retired in 1720.[28] The value of Massachusetts currency fell sharply after 1715, dropping by 44 percent in the next six years. This cast a great shadow over the soundness of paper money. At the same time the town was suffering a postwar recession, which was severe enough by 1720 for Colman to charge that the Boston of 1710, which "in the Opinion of All Strangers who came among us" was "one of the most Flourishing Towns in America," would shortly become "the most *miserable Town herein.*"[29]

Today the term "stagflation" is employed to describe the phenomenon of recession accompanied by inflation. Bostonians had no name for it and were unsure of the cure, but they could see its effects in idled ships, rising prices, and widespread distress. Historians have disagreed on what was happening to the Massachusetts economy but two tendencies are generally acknowledged.[30] First, the excess of imports over exports kept hard money flowing from Massachusetts to England in order to make up for the imbalance of trade; second, the sterling exchange rate, which measured the amount of Massachusetts currency required to purchase a pound sterling, inched upwards. The cause of local currency depreciation was probably a combination of flagging public confidence in New England bills of credit and the scrambling of merchants for ways to make returns to England, which drove up the sterling exchange rate.[31] Various writers in Boston suggested solutions to the problem, including a heavy tariff on imported goods (which was passed but disallowed in England), a voluntary boycott of English finished goods, the issuing of more paper money, and the reduction of the paper money supply. But nobody fully understood the colony's ailment or had a comprehensive program for dealing with it.

As in most recessions, those with the smallest margin of security were hit hardest. As trade declined, sailors could not find berths, shipbuilding slumped, and house construction must also have suffered, leaving many laborers and artisans without work. Price increases only compounded the difficulties of wage earners, while also striking at those on fixed incomes, such as clergymen, artisans whose wages were regulated by the town, and widows living on stipends set by probate courts. Also affected adversely were lessors tied to long-term leases, lessees whose landlords raised rents faster than their wages rose, and anyone indebted to a shopkeeper or merchant who demanded repayment in specie when it was in scarce supply.[32] Even the fiscal conservatives opposing Elisha Cooke's popular party recognized that the inflationary trend had "so raised the price of necessaries, that *Tradesmen and Labourers* can scarce subsist." With taxes rising alongside the price of wood, food, rent, and clothing, "many of your Laborious People . . . move out of your Town," wrote one pamphleteer.[33]

Law suits increased by leaps and bounds, reaching about a thousand in a single half-year term of the Suffolk County Court in 1720. "The vast Number of Law Suits," bewailed John Colman, "given out against good honest Housekeepers, who are as willing to pay their Debts as their Creditors would be, and have wherewith to Pay, but can't Raise Money, unless they will Sell their Houses at half Value . . . are Squeezed and Oppress'd, to Maintain a few Lawyers, and other Officers of the Courts, who grow Rich on the Ruins of their Neighbours, while great part of the Town can hardly get Bread to satisfie Nature."[34] Colman focused on the lawyers rather than the complainants at law, and he was arrested for libel for his trouble. It is important to note the tone of his pamphlet and the charges of inequity that pervade it. Some Bostonians, he pointed out, were profiting at the expense of others in a crisis whose origins lay in miscalculated and expensive expeditions against Canada. Colman pitched his appeal to the artisans and middling people. It was they, he claimed, who were forced to sell their household goods in order to buy food. He advocated a public works project to employ the poor, identified the rich as the principal opponents of proposals to issue more paper money (since it was they who benefited by its retirement), and, finally, in an inversion of the conventional thinking, urged that the people turn to men of lesser estates for leadership.[35]

The popular party of Elisha Cooke was nurtured amidst this economic dislocation and Bostonians were exposed for the first time to an extended published argument on an issue that concerned everyone's daily existence. In more than thirty-five pamphlets published between 1714 and 1721 the Cooke and Dudley factions traded blows.[36] To state their case the merchant-dominated "court party" relied heavily on conservative clergymen such as Cotton Mather, Edward Wigglesworth, and Thomas Paine, whose voices, it was thought, carried the greatest authority in the community. The line of argument they fashioned was not calculated to appeal to laboring people but to awe them into submission. Hard times had come to Boston, argued the church leaders, because of the extravagant habits of "the Ordinary sort" of people, who squandered their money on a "foolish fondness of Forreign Commodities & Fashions" and on excessive tippling in the taverns.[37] Laziness, sottishness, and a hunger for things above their station in life were at the heart of a decay in Boston that was economic in its manifestations but moral at root. Cotton Mather handed down some advice to the lower class: "It is to be demanded of the Poor that they do not indulge in an Affectation of making themselves in all Things appear equal with the Rich: but patiently submit unto the Differences, which the Maker of you Both, has put between you."[38] Boston's poor might well have cheered the night marauder who, shortly after this nostrum to the suffering, threw a bomb through Mather's window,[39] for they now found themselves chastised both for confusing the class order (amidst the growing stratification of Boston's society) and for bringing on economic problems that struck against them with special force while inconveniencing, it was said, the rest of the community.

We have no record of how ordinary Bostonians reacted to arguments of this kind, for they rarely left letters, diaries, or other kinds of direct evidence. But it is not hard to imagine that those without work or caught in the inflationary squeeze were not deceived by such accusations. They could take them, in fact, as additional proof that the rich and powerful, who only a few years before had attempted to dismantle the town meeting, now intended to impoverish them, as one pamphleteer had warned at the time.[40] Some pamphlet writers strongly defended the industriousness of laboring men and, as the debate grew more shrill, explicit warnings of class conflict rang out. A mean spirit was loose, charged a pamphleteer in 1720, whereby those with power studied "how to oppress, cheat, and overreach their neighbours." Gathering great estates and scattering "a few of their mites among the poor" for show, "the Rich, Great, and Potent, with rapacious violence bear down all before them, who have not wealth, or strength to encounter or avoid their fury. So the prodigious Monsters of the deep, extend their formidable jaws, (and lash the foaming brine,) while they scoop in whole shoals of the lesser people."[41] Picking up the thread, the egalitarian Congregational minister from neighboring Ipswich, John Wise, wrote that the people "are fully Resolved [when] it is in their own Power to Remove those who stand in their way, and supply themselves."[42]

The economic malaise that swept over Boston in the wake of Queen Anne's War had profoundly politicizing effects. To be sure, many people in all classes were probably genuinely confused on the fiscal issues, for nobody at this point in the eighteenth century had much experience with paper money and banks and there was no coherent economic theory to account for what was happening. On the one hand, Boston's local trade seemed to be hampered by an inadequate circulating medium; and on the other hand, the addition of more paper money seemed likely to erode the value of Massachusetts currency, thus cutting deeper into the buying power of wage earners. In this situation, where few Bostonians were immune from the monetary difficulties, neither class nor occupational lines were tightly drawn on the issue. But it was clear that some Bostonians suffered more than others, that the fiscal conservatives were the town's wealthiest merchants, and that they were closely tied to the conservative clergy who counseled the poor to rest content with their lot. Those who led the opposition to the court party of Governor Dudley and his successor, Samuel Shute, did not come from the ranks of artisans themselves and were not without their own axes to grind. But they recruited support among laboring men and confronted the elite with language that must have resonated deeply in the homes of mechanics and laborers. Some men, declared Oliver Noyes, an important member of the Cooke party, would "like a design to inslave a People and make a few Lord's and the rest Beggars."[43] Such language, and the attention paid them by popular party leaders, made ordinary townspeople feel that some of Boston's best were responsive to their needs.

Political controversy, raised to new heights, ushered in new political instruments. Among them, the emergence of the "political press" was of extraordinary importance. Printing was almost as old as the Bay colony itself but what came off the presses before 1714 was almost wholly religious. Campaign literature—direct appeals to the freemen at election time —was a rarity and polemics pitched to the public at large were uncommon. In Boston between 1690 and 1713 not more than fifteen political pieces appeared in print, fewer than one per year, and they were moderate in tone. The right of the government to censor all printed material was

still unbroken. But in the eight years from 1714 to 1721, economic dislocation brought forth a rush of pamphlets. Printed at the expense of political factions and often distributed free, they made direct appeals to the
people, both those who enjoyed the vote and others who participated in
the larger arena of street politics. To people who for generations had
thought of the printing press as an instrument for issuing sermons and
official documents, it must have indeed seemed, as one put it, that there
were "almost an infinite number of Pamphlets dispersed thro' the Country."⁴⁴

This increase in the use of the press had important implications not only
because of the quantity but also because the pamphlets were intended to
make politics everyone's concern. Distributed without reference to social
standing or economic position, the new political literature "accustomed
people of all classes, but especially of the middling and lower estates, to
the examination and discussion of controversial issues of all sorts."⁴⁵
Those whom even the most liberal politicians would not have formally
admitted to the political arena were drawn into it informally. It was not
only that the paper money argument, as Perry Miller has said, was showing "its true bent: it contained the threat of revolution," but also that this
message was carried into the consciousness of the people at large.⁴⁶ It was
testimony to the power behind the printed word that even those who
yearned for a highly restricted mode of politics were compelled to set
their views in print for all to read. For unless they did, their opponents
might sweep the field.

In the troubled years after 1714, one man in Boston was intent not only
on broadening the arena of politics but also on organizing that arena
with an efficiency and discipline that has earned him the title of creator of
"America's first urban political 'machine.' "⁴⁷ There was nothing plebeian
in the background of Elisha Cooke, Jr. Rather, his politics were "popular" because he came from a family with a strong tradition of entrepreneurship combined with a concern for the common people. Cooke's
father had dabbled in doctoring and lawyering; but he lived off money
earned in land dealings and poured most of his energy into politics. He
had been among the principals who overthrew Andros in 1689, and he
led the opposition against the conservative merchants who gathered
around the royal governors after 1698. Because he worked for lenient
bankruptcy laws which would "allow the poor people to escape the
clutches of hardhearted creditors among the merchants," he was known
as the "darling of the people."⁴⁸ The elder Cooke died in 1715 and his
son, a Harvard graduate and physician as well as a considerable landlord, took up where his father left off. Stung by the defeat of the land
bank on his first appeal to the electorate, he set about to mold a political
organization that could capture the town meeting and penetrate all aspects of town and provincial politics. Temperamentally, Cooke was well

suited to the task, for he was "genial, generous to needy people of all classes, and a drinking man without equal."[49]

Beginning in 1718, when he was elected to the General Court, Cooke undertook to mobilize broad-based support in Boston through a political club later known as the Boston Caucus. Although the precise date when the Caucus began is unknown, a convincing case has been made that it was formed under Cooke's direction about 1719. Its task was to draw up slates of candidates for selectmen and General Court elections, mobilize the voters, using the town's taverns as political nodal points, and disseminate political literature that would politicize the community.[50] To an extent the Caucus was the antithesis of the town meeting, for it operated secretively, dispensed quantities of free liquor in order to win votes, and was carefully managed by a small clique, whereas the town meeting was open, participatory, and sober. But if the Caucus involved political management and manipulation, its goals were definitely populistic. It was strongly oriented toward the artisans and shopkeepers whose members it hoped to bring into the political process as never before in Boston's history. It was managed by men who were large landlords in the South End of town and who had extensive contacts with laboring people, as well as exercising a degree of power over them. These leaders assumed that the political interests of the artisans and laborers were well served by the same measures from which they hoped to benefit—an increase in the supply of paper money, a strict hedging of the governor's patronage and prerogatives, and the promotion of public works projects such as the construction of a bridge across the Charles River and a canal across Cape Cod.[51] It was not against material gain that the popular leaders inveighed but privilege and narrowly concentrated power.

Governor Samuel Shute's supporters, who did their best to restrict Cooke's growing political power, complained bitterly of "that Incendiary" who tried "to poyson the Minds of his Countreymen, with his republican notions."[52] But "republicanism," though bitter as gall to a number of wealthy, Anglophile Boston merchants, was no more than an expression of the legislative power of the people at the provincial level and the maintenance of the town meeting system of politics at the local level. Much later, a prominent Boston Tory would claim that the Cooke machine controlled the elections by spending nearly £9,000 sterling in the 1720s, dispensed in the form of bribes and election-time liquid treats.[53] Control, no doubt, was what Cooke was after and the striking decrease in the turnover rate of Boston's representatives to the General Court, as well as the high degree of continuity among selectmen and tax assessors, in the 1720s indicate how well he succeeded.[54]

In creating a distinctly modern political organization, Cooke's accomplishment was not to expand the electorate but to organize and politicize it. The center of political gravity did not move downward, either in terms of the kinds of people who were elected to town offices and the General Court or in terms of those who went to the polls. Well-to-do Bostonians continued to fill the positions of representative and select-man, and the number of voters seems to have decreased. There are no regular voting statistics before 1717, but Samuel Sewall noted in 1703 that the 459 people who voted at the General Court election constituted a record turnout. Figures for other years between 1698 and 1717 suggest that the average number of voters was about 225, under 20 percent of the town's adult males.[55] In 1719, which may have been the year when the Caucus was formed, 454 Bostonians voted in the General Court election. But in the next decade turnouts were much smaller, averaging 244 per year. Considering the increase in Boston's population, from about 6,800 in 1700 to 11,000 in 1720, these figures indicate a substantial decline in electoral participation.[56] It is possible that the party of Cooke and his associates, strengthened by effective pamphlet writing and the creation of a disciplined organization, may have so overwhelmed their opposition that many who adhered to the conservative court faction simply stayed away from the polls. This is also suggested by the fact that in the decade after the Caucus probably began in 1719, fewer than a third of the Boston elections for representative to the General Court were contested.[57] By making his party responsive to the public will, exemplified by regulariz-ing the practice of voting comprehensive instructions to the General Court representatives at the town meeting,[58] Cooke proved that a "popu-lar" party could also be a carefully managed party, maintained in power by the annual endorsement of a small fraction of the community's adult male members.

IN NEW YORK the fires of ethnic politics were dampened for a few years after the hanging and beheading of Leisler and Milbourne in 1691. But the bitterness of the Leislerians, who were strongly Dutch and predomi-nantly artisan, was hardly assuaged. Oligarchical rule and ethnic aggres-sion had been at the heart of the disaffection of the Leislerians, and the public execution of their leaders could only increase their alienation. So in spite of the fact that New York suffered few of the economic difficul-ties that plagued Boston during the three decades after 1690, the town's politics remained unstable, factional, and highly inflamed. The trade recession, inflation, and spread of poverty that dictated the issues and set the tone of Boston politics had no real equivalent in New York. Instead, more subtle economic issues, cross-cutting ethnic hostility, shaped politi-cal life. Nonetheless, the direction in which urban politics evolved in New York paralleled that of Boston. Politics became a clash, as one of the ablest historians of this period has put it, "between two distinct groups of voters, campaigning as parties; recognizing leaders of those parties; answering to slogans and platforms; manipulating the patronage in a partisan fashion for party purposes; bearing party names; . . . and regimented for campaign purposes and responding within deliberative bodies to the demands of the party whip."[59]

The problem of the merchant elite in New York was how to hold in check an electorate that identified primarily with the Leislerians. The DeLanceys, Van Cortlandts, Schuylers, Livingstons, and Philipses were not, however, without weapons. They enjoyed the support of Governor Fletcher, who took office in 1693, and this advantage was quickly converted into the appointment of a set of sympathetic sheriffs, grand jurors, justices of the peace, militia officers, and other officers of government. Their economic power could also be converted into political advantage because those dependent upon them for jobs, such as shipwrights, coopers, retailers, and others, took considerable risks when they ignored their political "advice." Even these advantages were not always enough. That became apparent in the elaborate preparations for the 1695 assembly elections. The Leislerians had won a few assembly seats in 1692 and 1693 and carried New York City in the following year. Determined to regain control of the town's delegation to the assembly, the anti-Leislerians convinced the magistrates to grant "freedoms" to dozens of New York mariners under their control on the night before the 1695 election, thus entitling them to vote. On election day orders were sent to the captains of English ships in the harbor to send royal sailors to the polling place so that the Leislerians, who were heavily represented in the laboring class, would believe an impressment was imminent.[60] Pressure exerted from above on the most vulnerable members of the seaport community was sometimes enough to swing the balance. In this case it sufficed to send the Leislerian candidates down to defeat.

Between 1698 and 1702 political chicanery of this kind multiplied, turning the maritime center into a political jungle with the contending forces ferociously attacking each other as if to prove Hobbes right that men left to pursue their own interests would revert to a state of war. In April 1698, Richard Coote, Earl of Bellomont, arrived to replace Governor Fletcher. In English politics the Whig Coote had been a bitter opponent of the Tory Fletcher. If that was not enough to align him with the Leislerians, an added incentive had been provided by Parliament, which, under Whig control, had reversed the bills of attainder against Leisler and Milbourne.[61] Bellomont at first appointed a bipartisan council composed of deposed Leislerians and some of Fletcher's favorites. But in initiating legal action to repossess huge tracts of land which Fletcher had generously conferred upon his favorites and in cracking down on smuggling and piracy, he bitterly offended the merchant elite, including Nicholas Bayard, Stephanus Van Cortlandt, Frederick Philipse, William Nicolls, and Chidley Brooke. Within six months of his arrival Bellomont had dismissed them all from the council. Then, in an event of tremendous sym-

bolic importance, Bellomont authorized the reburial of Leisler and Milbourne in the Dutch church. The governor reported that 1,200 persons,
about one-quarter of the seaport's population, turned out in the pouring
rain for the disinterment and triumphant march from the potter's field,
where Leisler and Milbourne had been buried in ignominy, to the Dutch
church, the main ethnic symbol in the town.[62] Nothing could have signified more pointedly the vindication of the Leislerian movement or the return of his followers to political power.

For four years after Leisler and Milbourne's reburial, elections in New
York were hotly contested. In the process, new techniques of political
management were introduced and the nature of politics transformed.
Political clubs, the first to appear in any of the seaports, were formed in
order to coordinate and plan electoral strategy. Petitions were carried
about the streets by the aristocratic anti-Leislerians, who asked people of
all ranks to aid in their attempt to oust Bellomont, the highest authority
in the colony. Election pamphlets, virtually unknown in New York until
this time, were printed and handed about. Leading anti-Leislerians, who
previously would have thought it below their dignity, rode through the
town soliciting votes, and each side formed a "ticket" of four men whom
the voters were asked to elect *en bloc*.[63]

All of these steps, which sound innocuous in the context of modern
party politics, were daring innovations which defied the traditional
understanding of the proper relation between officeholders and the electorate. Political clubs and tickets were explicit admissions of factional
politics. Instead of going to the polls to select men who in their estimation would best serve the public interest because they were virtuous and
wise, the voters were urged to elect a set of men who would serve the
interests of one group within the body politic. The open solicitation of
votes, by means of signature gathering, pamphlet writing, and face-to-
face appeals, also reversed the conventional mode of politics, which held
it inappropriate and demeaning for those virtuous and eminent enough
to occupy positions of public trust to scramble for votes.[64]

It was because New York was the first seaport in which two distinct
and inveterately opposed interest groups emerged that the organization
and dynamics of politics changed there first. To a large extent it was
ethnic hostility, strongly linked with class interest, that had produced an
inflammatory political situation. With the community deeply split, the
leaders of both factions understood the importance of broadening their
political base. Formerly, in a society where the people at large acquiesced
in the rule of the upper stratum and social, economic, and political leadership was regarded as indivisible, political decisions could be made
quietly and privately. The elite would be held in check, of course, by
periodic tests of confidence administered by the propertied part of the
community. But when the upper layer of society split into competing fac-

tions, which were then obliged to recruit the support of those previously inert or outside the political process, politics became open, abusive in tone, and sometimes violent.

To engage in political mobilization, factional leaders often found they had to pursue a course which ran against the dictates of their social philosophy. They believed in maintaining rank and order in all human affairs and subscribed to the rationalist view that only the cultivation of the mind raised man above his naturally depraved state. Hence, to court the favor of "the lesser sorts" or involve them in politics seemed a reckless policy containing the seeds of anarchy. To activate the multitude was to energize precisely that part of society ruled by "passion"—the baser impulses in human nature—rather than by "reason." Nicholas Bayard and William Nicolls, two wealthy merchant leaders of the anti-Leislerian party, may have initially balked at the thought of riding about the town recruiting votes for their ticket or circulating petitions calling for Bellomont's removal, but curse as they might the circumstances that obliged them to violate ingrained social principles, their desires for election victories evidently persuaded them to do so.

The shattering of the political ethic that damned parties and factions as conspiracies and thus imposed an implicit limit on organized, coordinated oppositional politics had dramatic effects on the elections in New York between 1698 and 1701. In a burst of pre-election activity in 1698, 289 men, most of them artisans, paid the required fees and obtained freemanship so they could vote.[65] The election attracted 632 voters, which, in a community with about 800 free adult males, was so extraordinary a turnout as to suggest that many voted who did not meet the property qualifications.[66] In Boston, by contrast, where the adult male population was about 40 percent greater than in New York, the largest turnout of this period involved 459 voters. In the New York municipal elections of 1701 the march on the polls was even more spectacular. In the East, West, and South wards, which contained about half of the town's population, a total of 428 ballots were cast. Since the number of votes exceeded the number of male taxpayers on the tax list of 1699, it is not surprising that the defeated anti-Leislerian candidates screamed "foul."[67] That the normal conventions of politics had been abandoned became clear in the investigation of the election that followed. Specially appointed boards found that women, indentured servants, transients, minors, and the propertyless had illegally taken part in the election.[68]

The revival of Leislerian popular politics reached its peak in 1702 when an attempt was made to avenge the executions of 1691. The archenemy of the Leislerians was Nicholas Bayard, who had played a leading role in the judicial murder of Leisler and Milbourne and had continued to direct the anti-Leislerian opposition during Bellomont's governorship.[69] Learning that Edward Hyde, Lord Cornbury, had been named as Bellomont's successor, Bayard gathered signatures for a congratulatory message. He also circulated two petitions to the king and House of Commons which contained wide-ranging criticisms of the administration of the outgoing governor. When the Leislerians discovered that a number of soldiers had been induced to sign the petitions, they seized on this as an opportunity to charge Bayard and his henchmen with "incitement to mutiny and conspiracy against the government."[70] In the trial that followed Bayard and John Hutchins were convicted of treason and sentenced to death. Several other prominent anti-Leislerians were convicted of complicity in the "plot" against the government and banished from the colony.[71]

Although the Leislerians were doubtless eager to exact their pound of flesh from the wealthy Anglo-Dutch mercantile elite gathered around Bayard, there was a strong element of political theater in the trying and sentencing of their opponents. The trial was carefully staged as a replica of the infamous Leisler-Milbourne trial—with the sides reversed. Bayard and his supporters were indicted for treason under the same notorious treason clause in the 1691 law that had been passed by the anti-Leislerian legislature just ten days before the executions.[72] An all-Dutch jury, composed mostly of artisans, stood in judgment of Bayard, just as an all-English jury had been seated to try Leisler and Milbourne.[73] And in the end, after demonstrating dramatically that factional opposition could be defined as treasonable if one controlled the judicial process, the Leislerians were content to allow Lieutenant Governor Nanfan to reprieve their opponents and request a royal pardon in England. Through an extended and highly public trial, the Leislerians drove home the point that power, arbitrarily employed, could cut both ways. The political atmosphere in New York was sufficiently poisoned by the end of the trial that anti-Leislerians began fleeing the town, while some of their supporters showed their defiance of the Leislerian faction by cutting down the gallows under cover of night.[74]

Cornbury's arrival in New York in 1702 reversed the tables of partisan politics once more. Leislerian militia officers, justices of the peace, and councilors who had received their appointments from Bellomont were swept from office; most of the legislation passed by the Leislerian legislature was quickly reversed; and suits were brought against leaders of the Leislerian faction.[75] In new assembly elections the anti-Leislerians allowed English soldiers stationed at Fort James to vote, and, according to the Leislerians, they voted as instructed by their officers.[76] The assembly passed revenue bills favoring the largest merchants and repealed laws enacted under Bellomont to vacate the huge grants of land made under Fletcher. Thus, the politics of plunder and reprisal continued.

Ethnic and class division gradually faded during Queen Anne's War and by the time Governor Robert Hunter arrived in 1710 a measure of stability had returned to politics. During the next decade, when the temperature of factional politics was rising in Boston because of the serious economic difficulties that had emerged at the end of the war, New York's politics cooled off.[77] Historians usually explain this either in terms of the exhaustion of the contending factions, which had whipsawed each other under a succession of pro- and anti-Leislerian governors, or by pointing out the adroit conciliatory skills of Robert Hunter.[78] Both of these factors are important, but no small part of this calming of troubled waters was the general prosperity that returned to the town at the end of the war. New York was obliged to issue only small amounts of paper money beginning in 1709, and the price inflation that struck at the purchasing power of Boston's laboring class never became a problem. Moreover, trade expansion marked the postwar period, whereas the contraction of trade plagued Bostonians. No iron tie connected adverse economic conditions to inflamed politics, but if New Yorkers had found themselves dragged down by the problems that beset Bostonians—scarcity of metallic currency, inflation, and unemployment—the calming of the roiled political waters under Governor Hunter's administration would hardly have been possible.

What also inhibited the perpetuation of an artisan-oriented, widely participatory political party in New York after 1710 was the absence of a popular leader such as Elisha Cooke, Jr. In fact, it was left to the governor himself, Robert Hunter, to assume the role of political manager. Unlike the governors appointed in Massachusetts, Hunter shunned the wealthy mercantile elite of the seaport and developed instead a program that had broad appeal among the artisans and shopkeepers. Under Hunter's leadership, a series of laws were enacted that fixed the legal rate of interest, passed protective duties to encourage local industries such as linseed pressing and lampblack making, and encouraged shipbuilding. Allying himself with Lewis Morris, a large landowner in Westchester County, Hunter built a political machine responsive to the needs of the community at large.[79]

WHILE BOSTON's politics were conditioned by grave economic problems that seemed almost insoluble at the time and New York recovered from a period of immoderate factionalism, urban politics in Philadelphia between 1690 and 1720 were indelibly marked by conflicts over William Penn's proprietary control of his colony. At first glance the struggles that developed between proprietary and antiproprietary factions appear to have been purely political in nature, a struggle at the top for the fruits of office. Closer examination reveals that the distribution of political power was interwoven with access to economic opportunity. Philadelphia was spared the economic misfortunes that struck Boston, but nonetheless political life changed, both in style and organization, even if not nearly so drastically as in the other seaports.

Oppositional politics, originating in the early years of Philadelphia's history as a response to proprietary prerogatives and propelled to new heights in the early 1690s by the Keithian schism, continued in the last decade of the seventeenth century. When Benjamin Fletcher, who assumed the governorship of New York in 1693, was also given administrative command of Pennsylvania following the king's suspension of Penn's proprietary charter, the old faction led by Thomas Lloyd did everything possible to cripple his attempts to rule. Fletcher's authority lasted only until early 1695, when word arrived that Penn's charter had been restored, and for the next four years, until Penn's return in 1699, sparring took place between the proprietor's lieutenant governor and the principal Quakers gathered in the assembly.[80]

Penn remained in Philadelphia for less than two years before returning to England in 1701, never to see his colony again. Much of the time was spent in hammering out new articles of government that involved thorny questions of proprietary land policy, the basic constitution under which Pennsylvanians would live, and a charter for the city of Philadelphia. In all of these matters he found himself tilting with men of substance who wished to limit his proprietary prerogatives—the right to impose quit-rents on land, to control the judicial process through proprietary appointment power, and to intrude upon the legislative process by denying rights to the assembly that were customarily allowed in other English colonies. At the same time Penn was able to gather around him a considerable circle of merchants and landowners whose support of him guaranteed them important places in the government after the proprietor's departure. Compromise was the result of this struggle to determine the locus of power.

In the court system that was agreed upon, greater power was given to the county courts, appointed by the assembly, especially in equity cases which dealt with most economic disputes.[81] In the legislative system Penn's appointed council was stripped of much of its power and the elective assembly won many of the privileges that Penn had steadfastly denied the body for years. In land affairs, Penn retained his right to quit-rents, thus guaranteeing great wealth to his heirs, but land disputes were assigned to ordinary courts of justice rather than to Penn's appointed Board of Propriety. Finally, Penn approved a new charter for Philadelphia which increased the powers of the municipal government and tightened the qualifications for freemanship.

Penn conceded much in the realm of government, although a major part of what he consented to as he left the colony in 1701 had already been accomplished piecemeal without his approval during the years of his absence. By cultivating the support of a powerful phalanx of placeholders he hoped to preserve what was left to him in 1701. But these men already knew that they would have to vie for political supremacy with those who dominated the county courts and the legislature.[82]

The leader of the emerging antiproprietary faction was David Lloyd, a Welshman who had arrived in Philadelphia in 1687 bearing Penn's commission as attorney general. Lloyd's loyalty to his patron was short-lived, for he soon began to drift into opposition to the proprietary position. A brilliant orator, a gifted student of the law, an unequaled legislative draughtsman and parliamentarian, Lloyd became the Elisha Cooke of Philadelphia in the first quarter of the eighteenth century. Like Cooke, his brilliance was matched with pride, volatility, and ambition. In the early 1690s he had directed his talents at opposing the king's authority in Pennsylvania, but after Penn removed him from public and proprietary offices in 1699—at the crown's insistence—he lapsed into deep resentment of Penn and the proprietary interests. When his only child died at the hands of a servant girl, who locked the boy in a small closet in 1701, Lloyd sunk into despair. When he emerged from the slough of depression he strode forward into the antiproprietary struggle with a passion that preoccupied him for the next ten years—and to some degree for the rest of his life. Emotional and intense, he issued the call that government must exist not as an extension of proprietary authority but as the instrument of the people's will. This, of course, had been the axiom of those who struggled against Penn's prerogatives from the very beginning. Between 1701 and 1725 Lloyd gave a quality of leadership to the campaign to neutralize proprietary authority that had not heretofore been seen. He articulated the philosophy of popular government with a power and clarity that made the idea resonate with new force in Philadelphia.[83]

Pitted against Lloyd was the young Ulsterman James Logan, whom Penn had brought with him as a personal secretary when he returned to his colony in 1699. Eighteen years Lloyd's junior, Logan was as controlled as Lloyd was volatile and as imperious as Lloyd was gregarious. Like Lloyd, he was brilliant.[84] Understanding this, Penn conferred upon him the offices of provincial secretary, clerk of the council, receiver general, commissioner of propriety, and proprietary secretary. It added up to a concentration of political and administrative power that contradicted the Whig philosophy of government to which Penn, the political theoretician, could never have subscribed but which Penn, the beleaguered proprietor, readily accepted. Lloyd could match these powers, however, for by 1704 he was speaker of the assembly, justice of the Philadelphia County Court, president of the City Court, and recorder of the Corporation of Philadelphia.

Control of the city courts and the assembly provided two vital staging grounds from which to launch further attacks on the machinery of proprietary management. When the Philadelphia County Court authorized

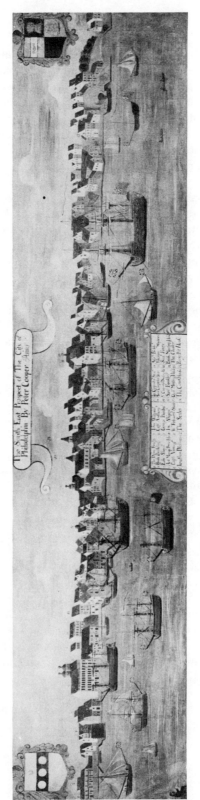

4. *Southeast Prospect of Philadelphia ca. 1720 by Peter Cooper.*

Logan's quitrent collectors to put liens on the property of tax delinquents, for example, the City Court asserted its authority in such matters and annulled the decision. Though two of Penn's appointees, the governor and the chief justice of the colony, ruled this illegal, the city government, dominated by the Lloydians, "carried it . . . by force, declaring thou [Penn] hadst given a charter, that was their expectation of it, and none whatsoever should hinder them." Logan advised Penn to "Destroy or humble" the municipal government, filled with "thy most backward friends in government."[85] But though Penn threatened to revoke the city's charter, he knew that even if such a decision could be enforced, it would only be used by Lloyd to prove the despotic tendencies of proprietary government. Controlling the assembly proved more difficult, but Lloyd's group carried every election in the decade after Penn's departure except in 1706 and 1710 and Lloyd was chosen speaker of the house in five of these years.

For eight years, from late 1701 when Penn embarked from Philadelphia, until December 1709 when James Logan took ship for England to report to Penn, Philadelphia was the center of political controversy between the proprietary and antiproprietary factions. No element of government, whether assembly, council, governor, county court, provincial court, or proprietary agency, was immune in the heated factional politics that erupted. Every component of constituted authority was challenged, deprecated, or called into question. At moments, such as in 1703 and 1708, government virtually ceased to exist as the proprietary governors gave up residence in the town, the courts lapsed for want of legislative backing, and the council was unable to act.

This decade of strife was a response to a number of factors: Penn's tangled affairs in England, the economic dislocation of the early years of Queen Anne's War, the incompetency of Penn's governors, and the personal feud between James Logan and David Lloyd. To some extent also, the factional struggles can be seen as the culminating chapter of the attempts of first-generation Quaker immigrants in Pennsylvania to assume the mantle of political responsibility. Many comments in the early eighteenth century about the endemic prickliness of Penn's colonists and their love of pitting themselves against any kind of authority, however mild its exercise of power, are reminiscent of similar descriptions in the 1680s and 1690s. Isaac Norris, one of the wealthiest merchants of Philadelphia and a staunch supporter of Penn, wrote of the "strange, unaccountable humour (almost a custom now) of straining and resenting everything, of creating monsters and then combating them."[86] Whatever the causes, they had a lasting effect on Philadelphia's political life. For in promoting the powers of the assembly and the Corporation of Philadelphia, Lloyd and his party employed strategies and rhetoric that expanded the consciousness of ordinary Philadelphians and broadened the scope of their power.

Part of this political education of the lower and middle classes came from the tendency of Lloyd and Logan to paint pictures, in their charges and countercharges, of polar opposites of government. Locked as they were in a struggle for power, it was almost a foregone conclusion that they would caricature each other's views and thus create a Manichean climate of thought. Logan, said Lloyd, took his rules of government from "Machiavel and those high flown statesmen" and his "inclination to a despotic power" led straight to the oppression of the people, the denial of their rights, and, ultimately, to the elimination of all their means of redress.[87] Lloyd, countered Logan, meant to scrap the balance of government that was the foundation of English liberty and stability and intended to throw Pennsylvania into the kind of chaos that had enveloped England during the Civil War.[88] In reality, Logan was no advocate of despotism and Lloyd no adherent of democracy. A conventional Whig, Logan believed in the mixing of popular and aristocratic elements in government, but as Penn's chief supporter and officeholder he was obliged to maximize the power of proprietary agencies and minimize the strength of the assembly. By the same token, Lloyd, who in less vexed times would acknowledge the wisdom of a government made up of counterbalancing powers, struggled to enlarge the powers of the assembly which he controlled, while attacking the agencies of government dominated by his opponents. In the heat of political battle, the two leaders spoke as if their political ideologies were worlds apart.[89]

The interminable battle of words, the endless process of assertion and counterassertion, the taking of extreme positions for the purposes of bargaining, led both antagonists farther afield than they initially wished to go. Logan grew increasingly distrustful of the people and by 1704 was declaring that the Quakers were "unfit for Government by themselves, and not much better with others."[90] He would grow even more pessimistic as the battle wore on. Lloyd too developed myopia, convincing himself that Logan and Penn intended the destruction of representative government in Pennsylvania. For those in Philadelphia who listened to the two leaders, it must have seemed that there was no middle ground, as one city dweller wrote, "between arbitrary power and licentious popularity."[91]

What was ultimately important to the political life of Philadelphia was that Lloyd's struggle against proprietary authority led to a major shift in political power. Although the fiery Welshman may not have been the "tribune of the people" that some have called him, he did much to undermine deferential attitudes toward established authority and to expand the politically relevant part of the community. It is almost impossible to say whether Lloyd tried to shift the center of political gravity downward because he was ideologically committed to a more participatory form of government or because his ends required this and could be served in no other way. In the end, no incompatibility between goals and means existed, for in learning to politicize the politically acquiescent in the service of what he regarded as "republican" and antioligarchical modes of governance, Lloyd developed a confidence in the ability of the common people to think rationally and act responsibly that his opponents would never concede. Lloyd quickly saw that the old politics denied him the constituency he needed to wage war against proprietary privilege. George Keith had faced the same problem a decade before and his answer had been to activate a part of the community that in deferential societies was rarely heard from. Lloyd followed Keith's example and then moved beyond him. He pitched his appeal in Philadelphia to those who worked with their hands and was especially successful in garnering the support of the common people who had joined Keith in significant numbers in the early 1690s.[92]

The popular party introduced various techniques that helped to cultivate the support of the laboring classes. An election law passed in 1700 had already initiated the publicizing of writs of election by requiring the sheriff to read the call to the polls in "the capital town" and to post it on the doors of every county courthouse, church, and meetinghouse in the province. In 1704 the Lloydian assembly authorized for the first time the publication of a part of the assembly's proceedings. Two years later printed copies of the minutes of legislative proceedings and the votes of the assembly were ordered sent to the coffeehouse in Philadelphia where the legislators often met and to "other Counties" for public display. This practice, which in 1711 would be extended to publishing the "Resolves, Orders, and Reports" of the assembly twice a week at the public expense, was an important step in the development of the idea that the freeholders were entitled to more than an annual opportunity to re-elect or remove from office their representatives. They were to be regularly informed of what took place in the legislative chamber so that their opinions could be immediately brought to bear upon those in whom political power had been invested.[93]

In 1706 the Lloydian assembly passed an election law that further developed the notion that society was divided into interest groups and that members of the electorate must decide wherein their interest lay. The law provided for the practice of presenting slates of candidates, who presumably held a unified view on certain issues of concern to the people. Slates of candidates meant tickets, which could be distributed before the election and brought by the people to the polls for deposit in the ballot box.[94] This "discovery of the electorate" was accompanied and facilitated by new methods of political organization that went hand in hand with the "Rattle of Rights and Privileges," as Logan disdainfully termed Lloydian politics.⁹⁵ In Logan's judgment, the new methods were important in mobilizing the support of lesser men within the body politic against merchants and large landowners. "We will never obtain a good election," he wrote in 1709, "until the recent voting law be replaced."⁹⁶ By the next year the use of the ticket was fully legitimized and Isaac Norris, an emerging leader of the conservative proprietary group, was complaining that the voter had "eight men crammed down his throat at once."⁹⁷

In expanding the politically relevant sector of society and introducing organizational strategies that encouraged the commonality to think in terms of interest groups, Lloyd had launched a kind of politics in Philadelphia which Penn and the original promoters of the colony had never anticipated. The proprietor had envisioned an annual gathering of the colony's most substantial men, known for their accomplishments in the secular world and honored for their public-mindedness. They would deliberate annually for a few days, much in the manner of the Quaker meeting, and pass such laws as were required for the common interest. Now government seemed to consist of long verbal battles between the assembly and the governor, extended legislative sessions that sometimes ran to seventy or eighty days a year, published remonstrances and accusatory letters to Penn, invective and recrimination, and long harangues on the rights of the people. For ten years, Lloyd cried out against proprietary prerogatives and upper-class privilege. The result was a chronic feeling of resentment against authority of any kind. "There is a general infatuation . . . got among us," wrote Logan, "as if we were all in a ferment and whatever was impure among the whole people rose in its filth to the top." Letter after letter reached Penn regarding Lloyd's success in stirring up the people, of a populace "drunk with wide notions of privileges."⁹⁸

Although political contention in Philadelphia became heated in the first decade of the eighteenth century, it never reached the boiling point as in Boston and New York. No angry crowds in the Quaker city moved into the streets to enforce what was equitable as opposed to what was legal; the art of pamphleteering never reached the heights it had in Boston; rampant factionalism did not turn into political violence and political violence into judicial murder as in New York; and at no time did artisans assume places of power in municipal government as in that town. But Lloyd's campaign against James Logan and the proprietary system nearly ended the possibility that in Philadelphia the generality would defer out of an inbred sense of the "natural degrees among men" to the uppermost members of society. As in Boston, that did not mean that the electorate installed artisans or men of humble standing in high offices. The representatives whom Philadelphians elected in 1709, a year when Lloydians prevailed at the ballot box, were all ranked in the top fifth of the tax list for that year and most of them were small merchants or retailers. But they were men who spoke the language of the lesser sorts, listened to their pleas, and responded.

For more than a decade after 1710 a calm descended over Philadelphia politics that paralleled the situation in New York but contrasted strikingly with that of Boston. This is not surprising in view of the fact that Philadelphia, like New York, emerged from a decade-long slump in trade at the end of Queen Anne's War and entered a period of general prosperity. As in New York, the value of annual imports from England doubled in the second decade of the eighteenth century. Shipbuilding flourished and the town enjoyed full employment. Popular politics under these conditions withered and the select group that Lloyd had been able to castigate as abrogators of the people's liberties and potential despots gained favor with the electorate. So great was their success that the Lloydians were almost always outnumbered in the assembly between 1710 and 1720 and the speakership of that body fell to a proprietary stalwart in all but one year.[99] The exhaustion of the politics of discontent cannot be wholly explained by the return of economic prosperity to Philadelphia, but the marked contrast between the Quaker city and Boston, where the deepening of economic woes was accompanied by the rise to power of Elisha Cooke and the creation of the Boston Caucus, makes clear the importance of economic distress to the perpetuation of popular politics. In both Philadelphia and New York, political activism within the lower ranks of society vanished after 1710 in an era of economic prosperity; in Boston, the thermometer rose to new heights as the town wrestled with economic problems.

By 1720 the political influence of the wealthiest Philadelphia merchants was stronger than ever it had been in the first four decades of the town's existence. Identical men, frequently linked by ties of blood, marriage, business, and religion, controlled the council and assembly, dominated the Corporation of Philadelphia, sat on the Philadelphia County and City courts, and handed down decisions from the provincial appellate court and Court of Chancery.[100] This new degree of political control did not mean that the groups which Lloyd had so effectively mobilized earlier fell into a permanent political sleep or that factions forming around interest groups had been eliminated from urban politics. The political calm, in fact, was soon to be shattered.

5

The Urban Economies
in an Era of Peace

FOR MOST OF the period from 1720 to 1740 peace reigned in the maritime centers. Only at the end of these years did the outbreak of war between England and Spain reintroduce the seaport dwellers to military conflict and disrupted international trade. But for all the perils of wartime, peace brought no guarantee of prosperity and stability. In Boston problems created by war did not disappear merely because European diplomats had signed articles of conciliation. All of the towns, in fact, learned that the vicissitudes of the peacetime international marketplace could disrupt the economy as much as did international war.

Other factors, largely unaffected by peace and war, were also at work in reshaping the contours of urban society in the second quarter of the eighteenth century. Population was one of these. Each seaport town grew more rapidly than it had between 1700 and 1720 and New York and Philadelphia demonstrated a special vigor, narrowing the gap between themselves and Boston. By 1740 New York and Philadelphia had grown to more than 9,000 and Boston to nearly 17,000.[1] Boston expanded while experiencing chronic economic difficulties; New York prospered, then stagnated and recovered; and Philadelphia burgeoned during an era of economic prosperity interrupted by one brief but wrenching period of economic recession.

Another factor in the changing faces of the towns was the composition of the urban labor force and here again the three ports differed. Boston retained the most ethnically homogeneous labor force, composed mainly of free, native-born persons, supplemented by a modest number of slaves. New York and Philadelphia, meanwhile, actively recruited immigrant slave and indentured labor. In considering this period it is best for analytical purposes to take the three seaports together in order to examine some aspects of the emerging social and economic order before turning to the economic history of each city.

Two forces that affected population growth in the maritime towns were immigration and epidemic disease. Following Queen Anne's War the largest surge of overseas migrants since the Restoration poured into the port towns. Unlike those of the post-1660 influx, these eighteenth-century immigrants were not English but German, Scots, and Scots-Irish. The first of the Palatinate Germans came to New York in 1710, and though most of them were peasant farmers, a few remained in the city, as did some of the others who followed. But the main German immigration after 1715 came through Philadelphia, the portal to the rich Pennsylvania hinterland.[2] Many of these sojourners stayed in the Quaker city, especially those who came with artisan skills from Rhineland towns. After 1720 names such as Klampffer, Brunholz, Sproegel, and Kieffer became common in Philadelphia records. James Logan marveled at this German "invasion" of Pennsylvania in the 1720s and predicted that the exodus across the Atlantic would match the Saxon inundation of Britain in the fifth century.[3] Driven from their homeland by economic misery and fear of conscription, they significantly altered the composition of Philadelphia's population.

Alongside the Germans came the Scots and Scots-Irish, with the latter far more numerous. Economic stagnation drove thousands of Scots-Irish from their homeland after the close of Queen Anne's War. A few came to Boston, more to New York, but most to Philadelphia, for immigrants learned before embarking that it was in Pennsylvania that taxes were lowest, good land most readily available, and military service unheard of because of the Quaker commitment to pacifism.[4] This high rate of immigration into and through Philadelphia was an important factor in the town's rapid growth, for many of the newcomers lodged in the Quaker capital. Even more important, those who moved inland swelled the hinterland farming population. Between 1700 and 1720, when this German and Scots-Irish immigration was just beginning, the Quaker colony's population changed only slightly in relation to that of Massachusetts. But between 1720 and 1740, when ten to twenty boatloads of immigrants landed each year at Philadelphia, Pennsylvania's population increased from 34 to 57 percent of the Bay colony's.[5] Philadelphia's rapid growth was closely linked to this immigration, for the city became the administrative and marketing center for the entire Pennsylvania region. More Pennsylvania farmers meant more Philadelphia shipwrights, coopers, blacksmiths, carpenters, shopkeepers, and merchants.

Epidemic disease also affected the urban populations, particularly that of Boston. A raging epidemic of smallpox in 1721 infected almost 6,000 Bostonians and killed about 850 persons, almost one of every twelve inhabitants.[6] Hardly a house in Boston did not fly a quarantine flag at some point during the epidemic and business was virtually suspended during April and May, when it seemed that the processions to the graveyards would never cease. Altogether, more than 1,100 burials were recorded in 1721. The smallpox returned in 1730; and though partially arrested by the acceptance of inoculation, about 400 fatalities were recorded, with total burials more than 900 in that year. From 1735 to 1737 diphtheria coursed through New England, and Boston suffered along with other towns.[7] Up until about 1700 Boston, like most New England towns, had been far freer of epidemic diseases than European urban centers. But the increase in population density meant that diseases spread more rapidly, giving Boston a mortality pattern like that in English or Continental towns. With medical knowledge not yet advanced enough to control the diseases, Boston's annual death rate climbed from thirty-six per thousand inhabitants in the early eighteenth century to forty-six by the mid-1720s. By 1736 burials were exceeding births in the town, so that only a net migratory gain could prevent demographic stagnation.[8] In addition, many families were quitting the city in fear of disease. They migrated to satellite ports such as Salem, Newbury, and Marblehead, where they could take up their urban occupations, especially in shipbuilding and distilling, while putting themselves, they hoped, beyond reach of the killer diseases.

Philadelphians and New Yorkers also suffered epidemics. But because these towns were not yet as large as Boston, and perhaps because of the accidents of history, they were spared the kind of microbic disaster visited upon Boston in 1721 and 1730.[9] Philadelphia's advantage disappeared by the end of this period because the high volume of immigration sent the death rate soaring. Typhus, typhoid, and other "shipboard fevers" contracted on the transatlantic voyage were spread to the host population when infected immigrants stepped ashore. By the late 1730s Philadelphia's overall mortality rate was higher than Boston's, although an unusual number of those who died were recent immigrants.[10] There is no way of separating these deaths from those of native-born Philadelphians, but it is clear that the initial advantage in healthful conditions enjoyed in the Quaker capital had been wiped out by the 1740s.

As the seaport towns grew in the eighteenth century the composition of their labor forces slowly changed. At the heart of this alteration was an increasing reliance on unfree labor, in New York on slaves and in Philadelphia on indentured servants. Boston lagged far behind New York and Philadelphia in recruiting bound laborers, which indicated the economic difficulties overtaking the Massachusetts port. But in all the towns householders increasingly signaled their gains by acquiring human property as well as personal possessions. The individual ownership of another human became a sign of the accumulation of capital. The collective ownership of bound laborers became a sign of a seaport's expanding opportunities for the production and distribution of goods.

Indentured servitude was closely linked to immigration since very few native-born persons were either voluntarily or involuntarily bound out.

The courts sentenced a handful of criminals and debtors to servitude and more common was binding out pauper children, who could be taken from their parents and indentured for a period of years.[11] In 1735 Boston's overseers of the poor were empowered to apprentice the children of the indigent. Intended to hold down expenditures for poor relief, this pauper apprenticing program sent about twenty poor children each year into Boston homes as indentured servants. A similar law in Pennsylvania consigned about half that number per year in Philadelphia.[12] Yet the number of bound white servants in Boston remained small, for criminals, chronic debters, and children of the poor supplied an insignificant number. It was the immigration of German and Scots-Irish servants and redemptioners who provided the vast majority of bound white laborers and Boston received few of these.[13] More than 1,600 inventories of estate recorded in Boston between 1685 and 1745 show just over one family in each one hundred owning an indentured servant. Although the inventories may not have recorded all servants, there can be little doubt that the incidence of servant owning was very low.

Immigrant indentured servants were also not very common in New York because the flow of human traffic from Ulster and the German Rhineland was directed only secondarily to that port. Occasionally a ship would arrive, as did the sloop *Garrit* in 1737, with a human cargo advertised as "Men and Women Servants, Welsh, Irish, and Germans, amongst which are several sorts of Tradesmen and Husbandmen, &c."[14] But for the most part, these immigrants, who had sold themselves into servitude in return for passage across the Atlantic, came to Philadelphia.

Indentured servants became a fixture of Philadelphia's social structure in the second quarter of the century because they were in great demand and could be readily supplied. James Logan had noted as early as 1713 that most of the arriving poor Germans and Scots-Irish could not afford their passage and therefore bound themselves out to ship captains, who auctioned them off to the highest bidders when they entered the port or sold them as a lot to a merchant dealing in human merchandise.[15] By the late 1720s most Philadelphians were answering in the affirmative the query posed by Benjamin Franklin's famous artisans' Junto: "Does the Importation of [indentured] Servants increase or advance the Wealth of our Country?"[16] A few years later the volume of this traffic increased substantially. Eighteen ships carrying German immigrants arrived in 1732 and 1733, compared with the same number of ships in the previous five years. Ship arrivals from Germany declined for several years after 1733 but beginning in 1737 and continuing until 1754 they averaged eleven per year. In the summer of 1749 twenty-four ships arrived from the Rhineland, depositing some 7,000 immigrants at the Philadelphia dockside.[17] Of about 40,000 German immigrants arriving during this period probably half to two-thirds were redemptioners or indentured servants. While most of these Palatines made their way to rural areas north and west of Philadelphia, it is clear from the sharp increase of deaths listed in the annual bills of mortality for "Dutch Calvinists," "Dutch Reformed," and "Strangers," that a substantial number remained in the city.[18]

A heavy volume of Irish and Scots-Irish indentured servants also arrived, although their number is less certain. The most informed estimate puts the total Scots-Irish immigration at about 30,000 between 1730 and 1750 and the total for the first half of the century might be twice that high.[19] As in the case of the Germans, many of the Scots-Irish who arrived as servants were sold to farmers outside Philadelphia; but hundreds were purchased by Philadelphians who put them to work not only as domestic servants but also in ropewalks, shipyards, bakeries, cordwainers' shops, cooperages, and liveries.[20] A record of all immigrant indentured servants bound in Philadelphia from October 1745 through September 1746 shows that 253 of the 430 were purchased by residents of the city. The average length of service was about three and a half years, so if this was a typical year, then by the mid-1740s Philadelphia must have contained about 885 bound white laborers among its 11,000 inhabitants. Since the free male work force numbered about 2,400 and about 80 percent of some 885 servants were male, it appears that indentured servants constituted more than one-fifth of Philadelphia's total white male work force and an even larger percentage of the people who worked with their hands.[21]

Another immigrant group was equally important in altering the composition of the urban labor forces. In the era following the Peace of Utrecht sizeable numbers of slaves, most of them Africans but some of them Native Americans, were imported into all the northern port towns. In Boston, where slaves had represented only 3 to 4 percent of the population at the beginning of the century, men with capital to invest in labor began experimenting with Indian slaves captured in South Carolina. About sixty Indian slaves can be found in inventories of Bostonians who died between 1710 and 1730 but the number sold in Boston undoubtedly reached the hundreds, for only a small percentage outlived their masters and thereby found their way into the probate records. By 1715 the truculence of these Native Americans from the coastal region of South Carolina was sufficiently worrisome that Massachusetts, along with Rhode Island and Connecticut, passed laws forbidding further importations from Charleston, the center of the Indian slaving activities. The preamble of the Massachusetts law spoke of the "malicious, surly and revengeful" behavior of the southern Indians and justified the abolition of the trade not on humanitarian grounds but because of "divers conspiracies, insurrections, rapes, thefts, and other execrable crimes [which] have been lately perpetrated in this and the adjoining colonies."[22]

If Indians could rarely be compelled to work in bondage, Africans could. The supply of black labor to the American colonies increased enormously in the first half of the eighteenth century and slaves became available in every seaport town. So much attention has been paid to the rapid growth of slavery in the southern colonies during this period that we lose sight of the fact that the northern maritime centers were also busily substituting black slave labor for free white labor. Boston's slave population rose from about 300-400 in 1710 to 1,374 in 1742, a fourfold increase in a period when the white population doubled.[23] Opposition to slavery had been expressed as early as 1700 by the town meeting, a duty of £4 per slave had been passed to discourage importation as early as 1705, and white artisans had intermittently complained about the competition of black labor; but Bostonians continued to import slaves and stepped up the pace after 1720 when the supply of Africans became more plentiful.[24] African slaves became commonplace, especially in Boston's shipyards and on ships at sea. By 1742 black slaves represented at least 8.5 percent of Boston's population.[25]

Another indication of how entrenched slavery had become is revealed by the inventories of estates. Although they are skewed somewhat in favor of the wealthier members of the community, this distortion does not seem to change significantly during the eighteenth century.[26] Even allowing for some overrepresentation of the wealthier decedents, the inventories indicate that by the second quarter of the eighteenth century about one-fifth of all Boston families owned slaves.[27]

While Bostonians accumulated slaves slowly, New Yorkers scrambled headlong into the acquisition of human property. New York had always had extensive contacts with the depots of the New World slave trade, particularly Dutch Curaçao in the West Indies, and these were augmented early in the eighteenth century when merchants such as Frederick Philipse opened a direct trade with slavers in Madagascar. Importations often exceeded two hundred slaves a year after Queen Anne's War, when the heaviest two decades of slave traffic during the colonial period began.[28] Slave auctions were held at least once a week during the trading season at the Merchant's Coffee House, Proctor's Vendue House, and other locations.[29] By 1731 more than 18 percent of the town's population was composed of black slaves and by 1746 the percentage had risen to 21. Although no household censuses exist after 1703, some indication of the extent of slaveholding can be grasped by comparing the 1703 and 1746 data. In the former year, when 14.4 percent of the population was enslaved, 41 percent of New York's families held at least one person in bondage. Four decades later the percentage of blacks in the town had increased to about 21 percent, suggesting that at least half the households owned a slave in that year and that an even higher percentage of families were involved in the master-slave relationship at some point in their lives.[30]

A series of New York censuses that differentiate inhabitants by sex and

age provide the means for tracing the rise of slave labor with an exacti-
tude not possible in the other ports. In 1703 the census listed 102 adult
male slaves and 813 white males sixteen years or older. Thus about 11
percent of the male laboring force was slave. By 1723 slaves constituted
almost 22 percent of the town's adult males and by 1746 Afro-Americans
made up almost one-quarter of the working-age male population.[31] If we
exclude from the "laboring class" the 30 percent of white males who functioned as government officials, lawyers, doctors, teachers, clergymen,
shopkeepers, merchants, and others who did not work with their
hands,[32] it appears that of every one hundred persons in the laboring
ranks, fifteen were slaves in 1703 and about thirty in 1746. Most broadly
conceived, the labor force included many women, but if we add them it
does not change appreciably the ratio of black to white workers.

New York slave masters, who eagerly bought up slaves at auction,
paid a heavy price in anxiety over the propensity of their human property for bloody rebellion. In April 1712 a group of some twenty slaves
amply fulfilled these fears by setting fire to a building in the town and
then lying in wait for the white men who came to extinguish the flames.
Wielding knives, axes, and guns, they killed nine whites and injured
others before making their escape. After the rebellion had been sup-
pressed, the plot was investigated and about seventy slaves were taken
into custody. Forty-three were brought to trial and twenty-five, including several women and Indian slaves, were convicted. The terror of black
insurrection that ran like a fever through the white community was evident in the sentences imposed: thirteen slaves died on the gallows, one
was starved to death in chains, three were burned publicly at the stake,
and one was broken on the wheel. Six others committed suicide to escape
the medieval tortures the white community prepared to mete out. The
assembly quickly passed a new slave code, which strictly regulated the
slaves' freedom of movement and stripped away most of their rights.
Thereafter the lot of New York's slaves could hardly be distinguished in
law from that of slaves in the southern colonies.[33]

The torture imposed upon the black conspirators of 1712 may have
temporarily cowed New York's growing number of slaves into submissiveness. But a generation later a wave of black unrest swept the seaboard. In 1741 the fever hit New York. A rash of fires and thefts broke
out and were attributed to slaves. Before long New Yorkers were convinced that a large part of the slave population was involved in a concerted effort to take over the town and kill all of its white inhabitants.
Under threats of torture and execution, sixty-seven confessions were extracted from terrified slaves and in the conspiracy trial that followed
eighteen slaves and four whites were sentenced to be tortured and
hanged, thirteen slaves were condemned to burn to death at the stake,
and another seventy were transported to the West Indies.[34]

In spite of rebellions and periodic pleas by prominent New Yorkers that white indentured servants should be substituted for black slaves, the town's merchants persisted in the slave trade, although it slackened after 1733.[35] They could not have done so, of course, if buyers had not been available. The reasons for the reluctance of New Yorkers to shift to white bound labor have never been clear, although the tradition of slave owning in New York went back to the Dutch founding of the city and they may have calculated that the profit in owning slaves was greater than in owning servants. White artisans complained of the extensive use of slaves as skilled craftsmen, but the objectors were probably those who could not yet afford a slave themselves. In 1737 Governor George Clarke reported that "The artificers complain and with too much reason of the pernicious custom of breeding slaves to trades whereby the honest and industrious tradesmen are reduced to poverty for want of employ, and many of them forced to leave us to seek their living in other countries." But it was other artisans who trained slaves up in crafts such as cabinetmaking, silversmithing, coopering, sailmaking, and carpentry—occupations which skilled black slaves were frequently advertised as having in the newspapers.[36] The growth of slavery in New York reflected more than the emergence of a genuinely wealthy upper class, employing slaves as coachmen, house servants, and livery grooms to signify their wealth. It also created divisions between those in the artisan class who had prospered sufficiently to substitute slaves for apprentices and others who saw their own opportunities blocked by the growing black artisanry.

In Philadelphia, where white bound labor was used more extensively than in any other seaport, slavery also took deep root. Frightened by the New York slave revolt of 1712, the Pennsylvania assembly imposed a stiff import duty on slaves which subsequently slowed the traffic. By 1729 the duty had been reduced to £2 per slave, and when it lapsed altogether in 1731 many merchants eagerly entered the slaving business. Favorable market opportunities were creating a demand for labor that could not be filled through natural increase or even by the considerable influx of indentured servants. "We have negroes flocking in upon us since the duty on them is reduced to 40 s *per* head," wrote Ralph Sandiford, an early Quaker abolitionist, whose efforts to convince Quaker merchants that the slave trade was immoral had the effect of shifting the business into the hands of merchants of other religious persuasions.[37] Both the inventories of deceased Philadelphians and burial statistics indicate that by the early 1740s about 10 percent of the town's population was black.

Following a period of relatively heavy imports in the early 1730s, the traffic in slaves slackened considerably in the Quaker town. This leveling off of the slave trade at a time when Philadelphia was growing rapidly was not due to the reinstitution of high import duties or a fall in the demand for labor. Instead, it reflected the availability of German and Scots-

Irish redemptioners and indentured servants, who flooded into the town after 1732. The marked decline of black deaths in the city after 1732 suggests that Philadelphians with resources to command the labor of another person usually preferred German or Scots-Irish indentured servants to black slaves when the former were readily available, even though indentured labor was probably somewhat more expensive. This preference may have become more pronounced after Philadelphians heard of the New York slave plot of 1741 and other insurrections up and down the coast. Not so much by planning as by the vagaries of the unfree labor market, the city contained a rough balance of white and black bound laborers by the mid-1740s. The combination of some 700 male indentured servants and about 450 male slaves in a population approaching 11,000 meant that along the wharves and in the artisans' shops more than two of every five laboring roles were filled by unfree toilers.[38]

The full meaning of the increased demand for unfree labor in New York and Philadelphia and the much smaller demand in Boston can be perceived only by placing the labor problem in a wider economic context. Did a peculiar ideological animus against slavery and servitude exist in New England, retarding the growth of an unfree labor force? Undoubtedly not, for Boston, like her southern rivals, had experimented from an early date with slaves and indentured servants. In spite of occasional criticisms of slavery, which came more often from white artisans resentful of black competition than from moral objections, Bostonians continued to import African slaves in small numbers throughout this period.[39] Nor can Boston's atypicality be explained by difficulties in New England's access to the sources of bound labor, for there was no appreciable difference in the distances from European and African sources of supply to the different northern seaports.

The crucial distinction among the three towns was one of demand, which itself was closely tied to general economic conditions. As we will see, Boston was the port town where economic difficulties were becoming chronic in the second quarter of the eighteenth century, while New York and Philadelphia, though each beset by one period of depression, were comparatively favored in their economic development. Even with their considerable natural increase in population, New York and Pennsylvania could not internally fill the demand for labor in their expanding economies. So capital was mobilized for the importation of an unfree labor force to serve ambitious men of the middling and upper ranks. New England, by contrast, was already tasting the first bitter fruit of overcrowding, the result of an expanding population competing for the resources of a relatively unproductive region. Hence, less capital was available to invest in bound labor and those who could afford additional workers could hire willing hands from the steady stream of migrants flowing into Boston from outlying towns.[40] In the northern ports those who were most free of economic difficulties were the likeliest to purchase women and men who were unfree.

This emphasis on the demand for bound labor as the crucial variable in the migratory stream from Africa and Europe to the northern port towns pays little heed to the possibility that servants could have decided where they wanted to go in the colonies to serve their time. One New Englander in 1716 implied differently, writing that servants went elsewhere because "the Land" was "so generally taken up."[41] But servants invariably went where the dealers in human cargoes knew there was a ready market. The New Englander's mention of the scarcity of uncultivated land was itself an early lament concerning the relative depletion of resources in Massachusetts, which was at the heart of the ceaseless search for adequate commodity exports to balance trade with England. No doubt indentured servants were glad enough that their new homes were in the middle colonies, where opportunities for taking up land after completing their indentures were far greater than in New England. But they were not making the choices, for power in the commercial transaction that brought bound labor across the Atlantic resided in the hands of the supplier and the buyer.[42]

In some instances ideological predispositions did affect the demand for particular kinds of bound labor, although availability was always a basic factor. When slave rebellion struck or threatened, or when the proportion of blacks in the urban population grew too great for comfort, buyers of human labor found reasons to switch to indentured servants if they were available and the price differential was not too great. On several occasions Pennsylvania forced the issue by raising import duties on slaves to prohibitive levels to encourage buyers of labor to import white servants.[43] In Boston the ideological preference was reversed, for black slaves were preferred to white servants. Bostonians imported African slaves and even Yamassee Indians from South Carolina rather than admit Scots-Irish servants. According to one account, Boston's "masters will rather be burnt in their beds by them [rebellious slaves] than suffer English servants to come hither to work, obligeing all Masters of ships to carry them back again upon their owne charge."[44] Bostonians apparently wanted their bound laborers perpetually unfree so they would never have to be incorporated into the community on the same level as their masters. If this preference had persisted and Boston's economy had been as buoyant as Philadelphia's in this period, New England's commercial capital would have eventually held the largest concentration of black slaves of any of the northern port towns.

THE COURSE of economic change in the three towns which we have prefigured in the foregoing discussion of the labor force can now be examined in fuller detail. For Boston there are contradictory economic indicators for the period from 1720 to 1740. Some suggest that the town's economy was active and healthy. Population grew from about 11,000 in 1720 to almost 17,000 in 1742; the port continued to dominate shipbuilding in New England; the physical volume of imports and exports rose; the fish market prospered, especially after New England traders were admitted to the French West Indies in 1717; and the construction trades thrived. The addition of some 700 houses and the erection of several large churches and public buildings gave employment to housewrights, plasterers, painters, masons, glaziers, and laborers.[45] Yet other indicators reveal that Boston was not able to solve the difficulties which traced back to the war years and, more fundamentally, to New England's inability to produce a staple crop. Poor relief rose, as did the number of people relieved of taxes because of poverty; the levels of wealth indicated in the probate records suggest that many struggled merely to maintain what they had; property values did not rise; and per capita imports and exports dropped.[46] Boston was not in a chronic depression during all of this period and some inhabitants reaped handsome material rewards, but for those at the lower end of the economic order life remained as precarious in peace as it had been in war. Many in the middling ranks were also squeezed by economic forces beyond their control.

Boston's immediate problem—nagging, confounding, and persistently divisive—was the depreciation of the province currency, paper notes that were used as substitutes for regular money. The total face value of paper money in circulation had been about £66,000 in 1709. It rose to £217,500 in 1718 and almost £358,000 by 1726.[47] Paper money issued in Connecticut, New Hampshire, and Rhode Island also circulated freely in Boston because trade among the four New England colonies was so extensive that none could afford to refuse the other's currency. So while Massachusetts tried hard to combat currency depreciation by retiring much of its paper money after 1730, Rhode Island continued to emit huge amounts, offsetting the attempts to return to a harder monetary standard.[48] The Bay colony kept steady the amount of paper money in circulation between 1726 and 1741 and reduced the amount per capita from about £3.4 to £2.3. But neighboring colonies, as Governor Shirley wrote in the latter years, flooded Massachusetts with their paper money "to the great profit of themselves but to the greater detriment of our community."[49] Nothing seemed to stop the plunge in value of paper bills. By 1730 it took 20 shillings of Massachusetts money to purchase an ounce of silver, compared with 12 shillings 4 pence a decade before. By 1739 the price of silver had reached 28 shillings per ounce.[50]

The problem of currency depreciation, however, was itself a symptom of an even more fundamental difficulty—Boston's deteriorating position vis-à-vis rival northern seaports as the center of the coastal and West Indian carrying trade. New York and Philadelphia possessed richer hinterlands and were blessed with shorter turnaround times to the Caribbean. Hence, they undercut Boston's former pre-eminency as the chief supplier of British goods to the American colonies and the main provisioner of the sugar islands. Boston's gradual eclipse hinged, above all, on the marginal productivity of the entire New England region. One astute observer caught the dynamic relationship between commercial center and agricultural hinterland as early as 1723. "We are all husbandmen," he wrote, "yet we want bread, drink and flesh" and "are all merchants yet have no tradeing nor one staple comodity in the whole country,"[51] Though exaggerated, this lament aptly described the growing problem of agricultural underproduction caused by the thin soils of New England, which were not renewed by sufficient manuring or crop rotation. The related problem was making returns to England to pay for imports.[52] Issuing paper money was a way of maintaining a circulating medium, but in large amounts the notes amounted to a mortgage on an uncertain future. In the long run large issues of paper money compounded the problem because currency depreciation added to the economic insecurity of particular groups in the society.

The ordinary Bostonian could do little about these structural problems, which were not fully understood even by the best minds of the day. But when women took their husbands' earnings in the form of paper notes to the shops, they were quickly apprised of the latest changes in the sterling value of Massachusetts's currency. Wheat that had sold in 1704 at 4.5 shillings per bushel was 8.5 shillings in 1719, 11 shillings in 1733, and 24 shillings by 1741. Molasses that was 2 shillings per gallon in 1720 rose to 4 shillings by 1734 and 8 shillings by 1740. Butter, available at 4 pence per pound in 1712, reached 12 pence in 1727 and 20 pence in 1739. Prices for firewood, clothes, shoes, and other basic items in the household budget rose similarly.[53]

In 1728, when the sterling value of Massachusetts currency had dropped by about half from twenty years before, a series of articles regarding the high cost of living appeared in the Boston newspapers.[54] Written to inquire why "the Country labours under such pressing Difficulties," and signed "Experience Thrifty" and "Mr. Moderator," they gave a number of household budgets for average Boston families. By taking the lowest estimate of these costs, which one letter to the printer asserted could apply "only for the lower Life," the plight of the artisans, laborers, and merchant seamen can be seen. Food for a family of nine was calculated at 6 shillings 10 pence per day; even if the family size is reduced to six, which would be below the average for this period but more typical of lower-class families, food costs would have averaged 4 shillings 3 pence per day. Candles, shoes, clothing, and washing cost another 4 shillings a day. "Experience Thrifty" left it to his readers to add the cost of taxes, firewood, house rent, medicine, repair of tools, furniture, and occasional expenses "with his Barber, Hatter, Glover, Tobacconist, and others." But even eliminating small luxuries such as gloves and tobacco and assuming that he was too poor to pay taxes, the laboring-class Bostonian had to pay out another 15 shillings per week for rent and firewood. His total household budget for six would have been about £3.7 weekly in provincial currency or about £10 sterling per person annually.[55]

Unless wages rose in tandem with the escalating cost of living, laboring-class Bostonians must have suffered a decrease in real income that wiped away savings or reduced their standard of living. There is not enough data available for this period to construct a continuous wage index but neither are we faced with an evidential void. In 1725, even before the inflationary trend of prices had become very pronounced, one writer to the *New-England Courant* grieved at the "many flourishing Familys . . . [that] have been oblig'd to fall below such as they once look'd down upon with the utmostly furnish'd tables, [and] have been reduc'd to such a humble Temper, as to be glad of plain Fare and homespun Apparrel."[56] Fourteen years later William Douglass, a staunch opponent of paper money in the 1740s, listed laboring Bostonians as first among the victims of price inflation. "How much they have suffered and continue to suffer," he wrote in 1739, "is obvious."

> For Instance, a Carpenter when Silver was at 8 s. per Oz. his Wages were 5 s. a Day all Cash. The Town House A. 1712 was built at this Rate; whereas at present A. 1739 . . . Silver being 29 s. per Oz. he has only 12 s. a Day, equal to 3 s. 4 d. of former Times; and even this is further reduced, by obliging him to take one half [his pay] in Shop Goods at 25 per Cent. or more Advance above the Money Price.[57]

Douglass pressed the point home by demonstrating that artisans' daily wages in 1712 purchased fifteen pounds of butter but by 1739 would buy only seven pounds.[58]

The wage rate that Douglass cited for carpenters was not challenged in the spate of pamphlets that appeared on fiscal policy in the late 1730s and early 1740s and can therefore be accepted with some confidence as the median wage rate of artisans in the building trades. Few outdoor workers of this kind could expect full employment for the entire year, for the severity of the New England winters, slack time between jobs, and sickness made this rare. But even if carpenters, masons, plasterers, glaziers, and other building tradesmen averaged five days' work a week throughout the year, a very optimistic estimate, their weekly income of 60 shillings would have fallen short of meeting the minimum household budget for a family of six—about 73 shillings per week in 1728. By 1739, when prices had risen at least another 30 percent, the gap between their income and expenses must have been in the range of 30 shillings a week, even when they were paid in cash. For those who were obliged to take part of their pay in "shop notes"—drafts on particular shops that employers issued at rates above current prices—the cut in spending power was even more severe.[59] Douglass's claim in 1739 that "Labourers and Trades-men" had to take half their wages in shop notes cannot be confirmed for the entire laboring population, but it is clear from the strong protests of the caulkers in 1741, who announced their refusal to work any longer for shop notes and promised to spread their protest to "other Artificers and Tradesmen," that the practice was widespread. The caulkers complained bitterly that they had for "many years labored amid great inconvenience and had suffered much damage, wrong and injury, in receiving pay for their work by notes on shops for money or goods."[60]

Another group for which wage data is available is mariners. After Queen Anne's War shipmasters were paid £5 per month in local currency and ordinary seamen about £2.5 to £2.75 in Massachusetts currency. Wages did not rise until the 1740s, with ship captains receiving £6 per month through 1735 and then £8 and seamen about two-thirds of that.[61] But these increases were proportionately less than even the building tradesmen received and could in no way meet the added expenses that inflationary price increases had fastened on the laboring classes. Ordinary seamen could expect no more than ten months employment a year, given the dead time in port while vessels were waiting for new cargoes, so annual wages in this period probably did not exceed £50 per year in Massachusetts currency. Spread over twelve months, this allowed ordinary seamen about 20 shillings per week, less than a third of the household expenses for a laboring-class family of six in 1728.

Most of the pamphlet writers of the 1730s and early 1740s beamed their arguments at the middling and upper elements of society, focusing their attention on the sufferings of those with fixed incomes such as teachers, clergymen, and widows. These people were undoubtedly pinched by the adverse wage-price trends, and one of their kind may have been the wit who sent a cow draped in silks and laces meandering through the streets in 1735 to dramatize the high cost of meat.[62] But artisans, mariners, and day laborers constituted a much more numerous class that suffered far more, going cold in the winter when they could not afford wood and scrimping on their diet. Thomas Hutchinson, one of the brightest young merchants in the town, who was beginning to accumulate a fortune in the 1730s, would later write passionately of the injuries suffered by creditors, who he claimed were "defrauded" by those who paid off old debts in depreciated currency.[63] But Hutchinson was deflecting attention from the largest class of Bostonians, those with the least cushion to protect them in adverse times and those with the lowest standard of living. In his discussion of the bitter controversy over banks and paper money Hutchinson never mentioned these groups.

As the inflationary pressure worsened in Boston, bringing many arti-

5. Southeast View of Boston in 1743 by William Burgis.

sans and laborers to the brink of crisis, the elected tax collectors, who
were acutely aware of the needs of families in their wards, began remov-
ing householders from the rolls or entering them as "non-rateables"—
persons with insufficient means to pay even the smallest tax. The population of colonial Boston reached its peak in the early 1740s when nearly
17,000 persons lived in the town. But beginning about 1735, when the
number of rateable polls was 3,637, the assessors dropped poor Bostonians from the tax rolls in sizeable numbers. While the town's population
grew, the number of taxpayers declined by 665 persons between 1735 and
1741.[64] That more than one out of every six taxpayers was stripped from
the rolls was only a pragmatic acknowledgment by elected officials that
blood could not be wrung from a stone. To extract taxes from most of
these unfortunates the collectors would have had to distrain their household goods, auction them off, and add the proceeds to the public treasury. Even the most fiscally conservative Bostonians would not have advised that.

Others who were retained on the tax rolls were reckoned too poor to
contribute to the town's coffers. The selectmen's reports in 1737 and 1742
stated that there were "a great many Polls which are not Rated and are
supported by Charity."[65] Still others who were assessed had their taxes
abated when they satisfied the collectors that they were unable to pay.
By the early 1740s roughly one of every four Bostonians had fallen sufficiently near or below the subsistence level that the public officials were
obliged to absolve them of any tax obligation.

One further way of measuring the effects of the economic doldrums is
to examine the inventories of those who died in the interwar period. It is
impossible to be precise about what level of wealth entitled eighteenth-
century urban dwellers to claim middle-class or upper-class status, but as
a general guide we can adopt the standards of a New York auctioneer
who at mid-century had brought the personal possessions of so many
families under the hammer that he felt secure in labeling the "First, Middling and Lower Classes of Householders" as those with £700, £200, and
£40-20 in New York currency in moveable possessions.[66] There are large
gaps between these wealth levels but if we arbitrarily set £100 as the upper limit of the lower class and £500 as the upper limit of the middle class
and convert these values to sterling (£56 and £280), we can measure
secular change in the personal wealth that Bostonians were able to accumulate. Among a selection of tradesmen who were broadly representative of the laboring force—bricklayers, carpenters (including joiners and
housewrights), coopers, cordwainers, glovers, masons, mastmakers,
shipwrights, and tailors—about one-third of those who died in the first
half of the century were able to make their way into the middle class; but
the percentage of those who accumulated £280 or more declined from
about one in five at the end of the seventeenth century to less than one in

twenty thereafter.[67] For laboring men who struggled in a period of economic uncertainty and price inflation, the best that could be done was to pass on to one's children artisanal skills, a few possessions, and sometimes a small house.

Not all Bostonians fell upon hard times in the interwar period. The inventories show that many merchants and urban landowners prospered. Peter Faneuil, the son of a French Huguenot immigrant who had arrived in Boston in 1691 from Rochelle, France, died in 1743 with a fortune inventoried in Massachusetts currency at the impressive figure of £44,453, which converted to sterling was still £7,557. Jonathan Waldo, merchant and land speculator, died in 1731 with an estate of £9,606 sterling, including mortgages on dozens of Boston properties. Other merchants and landowners, such as William Clarke, Simon Stoddard, John Mico, James Townsend, and Elisha Cooke, Jr., died with more than £3,000 sterling in real and personal property.[68] But the broad mass of laborers, artisans, small retailers, and professionals, not these few wealthy merchants, provide the best indication of the community's economic health.

How did lower-class Bostonians cope with shrinking real wages and economic uncertainty? The answers are not readily available in the records that survive, but the classic alternatives from which laboring people in hard times have always chosen are postponement of marriage, limitation of family size, reduction in the standard of living, acceptance of public and private charity, and craft organization. All of these seemed to have happened in this period to some degree. Craft organizing took some halting steps forward when barbers and booksellers met as groups to raise prices in 1724 and caulkers refused to take shop notes in 1741.[69] But most laboring-class Bostonians, still in an early stage of developing a collective approach to economic problems, seem to have made adjustments in their private lives rather than taking the bolder and more difficult step of organizing into craft pressure groups. "Intention to marry" statements decreased proportionate to population, as many poorly circumstanced Bostonians apparently concluded that marriage was inadvisable given the unfavorable economic conditions.[70] Postponement of marriage, which was also occurring in the towns outside of Boston, meant fewer births per marriage since young men and women were starting their families at a later age. Coupled with this may have been a decision to have fewer children. The birth rate, as measured by baptisms in the town, followed a downward trend from the 1730s on.[71] Most of all, laboring Bostonians simply tightened their belts, borrowed from friends and relatives, and hoped for better days.

While Bostonians struggled with economic hardship and the deranging effects of currency depreciation, New York and Philadelphia forged ahead in the interwar period amidst general price stability. Neither colony issued paper money in amounts reaching even 2 percent of the bills issued in Massachusetts, and, discounting short-range cyclical changes, the price level for two decades following 1720 stayed nearly horizontal—even slightly below that of the early eighteenth century.[72] The tonnage of inbound and outbound ships clearing Philadelphia more than doubled during this period, imports from England nearly tripled, and shipbuilding flourished.[73] Commercial expansion also occurred in New York, with the value of English imports more than doubling for the period as a whole.[74] Given a population increase of 73 percent in the colony of New York and 177 percent in Pennsylvania, these figures cannot be taken by themselves as evidence that boom times were on hand for all inhabitants of the seaports. But the long-range level of economic activity was relatively high and the dogged problem of declining real wages that beset Boston never had to be faced.

The interwar period was not, however, one of uninterrupted prosperity in either town. Beginning in 1720 Philadelphia suffered a serious depression. It is sometimes explained as a repercussion of the South Sea Bubble but was probably more the result of a sharp drop in grain prices in a glutted West Indian market. Wheat prices fell from about 4 shillings a bushel in 1715 to 2 shillings 8 pence by 1723. This cut sharply into farmers' profits, which in turn affected urban artisans and mariners. As a contemporary commentator on the depression wrote, the farmer, merchant, and artisan were linked together in a "Chain of mutual Dependence."[75] The assembly reported work stoppages in the shipyards, the disappearance of specie with which to carry on local trade, and falling property values. "How deplorable are the Lives of the Common People," cried one pamphleteer in 1721, who called for paper money to remedy the situation.[76] In the next year, James Logan, a fervent opponent of bills of credit, moaned along with his adversaries that "the Trade of this place is exceedingly sunk." Late in the same year, the governor described a seaport in distress: "The ship Builder & Carpenter starve for want of Employment . . . the Interest on Money is high, and the usurer grinds the Face of The Poor so that Law suits multiply, our Gaols are full, and we are justly apprehensive of falling into debt."[77]

To some extent the economic recession of the early 1720s was cushioned for Philadelphia's artisans and laborers by a decrease in rents and food prices, although this was small solace to those with no employment at all. The sting of the recession was relieved by the emission of £45,000 in paper bills in 1723 and 1724, to be lent at 5 percent interest and secured by mortgages on land and houses.[78] These bills, according to the law, were "chiefly intended for the benefit of the poor, industrious sort of people," and although they could not improve the West Indian grain market, they at least kept debtors out of the clutches of the town's wealthiest merchant-moneylenders, who "exacted Bonds of every Body at 8 per Cent."[79] When grain prices began to rise in 1724 and merchants opened new markets in Spain and Portugal, trade picked up and shipbuilding revived. A second trade recession struck Philadelphia in 1728. Convinced from the experience of 1723-1724 that a moderate issue of paper money was the antidote, the assembly issued £30,000 in paper bills. Within two years the trade doldrums had blown away.[80] Paper money, issued in large amounts as a cure for fundamental economic problems in New England, had magnified the plight of Boston's wage earners. Issued in small amounts in Pennsylvania to combat trade recession, it had proved Philadelphia's salvation.

In the 1730s Philadelphia entered a period of economic prosperity that contrasted sharply with the situation in Boston and New York. The average annual output of the town's shipbuilders almost doubled from the previous decade, while population in the seaport was increasing by about 31 percent. The average annual tonnage of shipping clearing the port rose from 4,914 tons in the 1720s to 9,563 tons in the 1730s and the value of English imports almost doubled. The layover time between voyages dropped by about 15 percent.[81] Finally, a series of fine harvests, coupled with sustained overseas demand for grain, created good years for farmers.[82] All of this meant full employment for mariners, shipwrights, mastmakers, sailmakers, coopers, and other artisans who depended on maritime trade for their livelihoods. For other artisans in the city—glovers, tailors, chair- and cabinetmakers, gold- and silversmiths, tool- and instrumentmakers, and others—agricultural prosperity created increased demands for their products. Philadelphia, a Boston newspaper enviously reported in 1735, "is in so flourishing a Condition, that there is Scarce an empty House in the Place, and . . . there are now upwards of sixty Brick Buildings carrying on in the City."[83]

This favorable condition for the artisan class in Philadelphia after the depression of the 1720s is reflected in the life stories of a few of those who came to the port town in the previous decades as inconspicuous individuals and flourished during the second quarter of the eighteenth century. Such a man was Cesar Ghiselin, a French Huguenot who arrived in Philadelphia amidst a wave of Quakers in the 1680s to take up his craft of silversmithing. By 1693 Ghiselin had established himself securely enough to purchase a slave and to rank on the tax list in the top 10 percent of the town's householders. By 1709 he was assessed for an estate of £40, which placed him midway in the hierarchy of wealth. When he died in 1733 his personal estate was inventoried at £609 sterling, which put him in the richest tenth of decedents whose estates were valued between 1726 and 1735.[84]

Among the largest merchants of the city in the 1730s, many had begun as artisans. Lionel Brittain had come to Philadelphia about 1704 as a blacksmith, had advanced to shopkeeper by 1715, and was a merchant by the third decade of the century. Thomas Coates moved from brick-making to shopkeeping and then to importing and exporting. John Palmer started even more humbly, as a bricklayer, but by 1715 he was a carter and finished his career as an important merchant. John Warder was pipemaker, then hatter, then haberdasher, and finally a merchant. William Parsons arrived as a shoemaker about 1715, was one of the original members of Franklin's Junto, and by 1741 had risen to surveyor general of the province.[85]

Such was the town to which Benjamin Franklin came from Boston in 1723 as a printer's apprentice. Not all of the ebulliency in his autobiographical account of the opportunity he found in the Quaker city can be taken at face value, for the document was written more than a half-century later and was intended as a celebration of America. But there is no doubt that in the late 1720s and 1730s Philadelphia was filled with young artisans on the make, and a number of Franklin's early friends, such as his Junto compatriots Nicholas Scull, Thomas Godfrey, and William Parsons, made it to the top, though not quite so spectacularly and stylishly as Poor Richard. Franklin became the hero of the "leather apron men" in Philadelphia. They gloried in his success, which tells us something about their pride of class. But their reverence probably would have turned to envy if many of them had not been achieving material success themselves, even though not on Franklin's scale.

It is dangerous, of course, to draw conclusions about group success from examples of individual accomplishment. But an analysis of the inventories of 103 Philadelphia craftsmen who worked in the same trades as examined above for Boston points up the high rate of artisan success in Philadelphia in the first half of the century and demonstrates the differing experiences of laboring men in the two towns. In Philadelphia these artisans were far likelier to attain a level of wealth that entitled them to think of themselves as middle class. Whereas about one-third of the Boston artisans who died between 1700 and 1745 reached this level, 60 percent of those in Philadelphia did so. The chances of doing even better—of leaving personal wealth in excess of £300 sterling—were also far higher in Philadelphia than in Boston. In the Quaker seaport about one in six did so among those who died in the first half of the eighteenth century, while in Boston the rate was hardly one in twenty.[86] Translated into the kinds of personal possessions itemized in the inventories, this difference meant that the Philadelphia artisan was eating from pewter, whereas his Boston counterpart ate from wood. In Philadelphia he was more likely to have a "seven-day clock" hanging from the wall, a few pieces of mahogany furniture in the parlor, a better quality of linen on the table, and perhaps a somewhat larger house.

The second difference between artisans' opportunities in Boston and Philadelphia was that they were increasing in the Quaker capital while decreasing in the Puritan center. Of those who died in the first half of the century in Boston, the proportion leaving £60 sterling or less personal wealth grew, while the proportion of those accumulating more than £300 fell. In Philadelphia the reverse was true, with the incidence of those leaving between £60 and £300 sterling increasing from about half between 1685 and 1715 to nearly two-thirds between 1726 and 1745.[87]

These differences in material achievement are best explained by the failure of wages to keep pace with increases in the price of household consumption articles in Boston—an adverse wage-price trend that struck hard at the fortunes of laboring people. In Philadelphia, the wage-price ratio remained nearly constant in this period, so that in an era of growth it was possible for many to save and invest. A second factor that may help to account for the difference was the ability of large numbers of Philadelphia artisans to invest profitably in urban real estate at a time when their Boston counterparts, hard hit by heavy taxes and the shrinking value of wages, were more likely to be borrowing than investing capital. For those who could plough money into Philadelphia land at any time in the first half of the eighteenth century, the returns could be gratifying—probably even more so than from trade, where the profit margin in the best of times was not very large. "Every great fortune made here within these [last] 50 years," wrote one observer of the Philadelphia scene in 1768, "has been by Land."[88] Philadelphia's artisans, with a few notable exceptions, were not among the town's real estate fortune builders, but many of them were able to buy parcels of land that appreciated handsomely after 1730 as the port underwent rapid expansion.

A few examples will indicate the possibilities. In 1683 William Penn had ordered the valuable riverfront property along the west side of Front Street to be laid out in lots with 102 feet frontage and 396 feet deep. These choice lots on the Delaware River were given as bonuses to those who purchased at least 5,000 acres of Pennsylvania land, which Penn was selling at £10 sterling per 100 acres. Almost immediately the "First Purchasers" began subdividing the Delaware River "Front Lots," which contained almost an acre. By 1689 the forty-three 102-foot lots along Front Street had become seventy smaller lots. By 1703 subdivision had further increased the number of Front Street lots to 110, with some frontages reduced to 20 feet or less. The lots were split again by running 20-foot wide alleys lengthwise through the 396-foot deep properties and facing a row of narrow tenements on each side of the alley. Thus a single one-acre lot could be subdivided into twenty to thirty lots, half of them facing on the alley and half on Front and Second Streets.[89] By the mid-1680s full-sized Front Street lots were selling for as much as £300.[90] By the end of the century one-sixth of one such lot sold for £210. Fifteen years later, in 1714, Elisha Gatchell, a cordwainer, bought one-fifth of this lot—now containing about 3 percent of the original Front Lot—with a small house on it for £140. At Gatchell's death in 1756 the lot and house were disposed of at a sheriff's sale for £400. Another tenement was built on the property, which was purchased in 1760 by Joseph Graisbury, a tailor. Less than three months later Graisbury had further subdivided the 27 by 45-foot lot into four tiny parcels of 13.5 by 22.5 feet. He held the two vacant parcels and sold the others, each with a small tenement, for £250 each to Samuel Bell, a silversmith, and William Turner, a merchant. In 1763, Bell sold to Turner for £450 the tenement he had bought three years before for £250.[91]

Such examples could be multiplied by tracing the genealogies of lots all over Philadelphia. Such transactions show that although it was predominantly the merchants who could move into the urban land market on a large scale, artisans could readily gain a foothold in real estate in the 1730s, when lots were selling for as little as £20, and throughout the 1730s, when they were still available for £32-35.[92] Land at these prices was available only on the edges of the city in the 1730s, but population growth in the next decade rapidly moved the boundaries of urban development outward. It has not been possible to determine how many of Philadelphia's artisans invested in real estate during this period, but it seems clear that they were able to do so to a much greater extent than laboring men in Boston.[93] In Philadelphia, where inflation was unknown and the 1730s brought full employment, investments were possible that could further advance artisans and others in their pursuit of what, in the eighteenth century, they called "a decent competency."

The winds of economic fortune that blew so frigidly on Boston during the interwar era and so favorably on Philadelphia by the late 1720s swept New York with alternating fair and foul gusts. For a half-dozen years after the Peace of Utrecht the Manhattan residents prospered, and this was interrupted in the early 1720s only by a short trade recession which was much less severe than in neighboring Philadelphia.[94] But in 1729 New York entered a period of serious economic stagnation that lasted for eight years. By 1734 Governor William Cosby was searching for remedies that might "give life to the expiring hopes of ship carpenters and other tradesmen, recall their unwilling resolution to depart the Province, and encourage others to come into it."[95] Some of New York's problem apparently stemmed from the competition in the carrying trade to the British West Indies, where most of New York's meat, grain, and wood products were marketed. In 1715, as a spur to local shipbuilding, the assembly had passed a tonnage duty on all ships entering the harbor that had been built elsewhere. When this law lapsed in 1720, ships registered in Bermuda began to undercut New York's trade. Partly because of the loss of this business shipbuilding languished.[96] Probably more important in the shipbuilding slump, however, was the decision of New York's wealthiest merchants to abandon this enterprise as a field of investment in favor of lending their surplus capital at 8 percent interest.[97] By 1734 it was claimed that only one or two ships per year were being built in the town and unemployment was widespread among shipwrights and others associated with maritime construction. "John Scheme" wrote in the *New-York Weekly Journal* that "the Baker, the Brewer, the Smith, the Carpenter, the Ship-Wright, the Boat-Man, the Farmer, and the Shopkeeper" all had been hurt and "our industrious Poor [forced] to seek Other Habitations so that in these three Years there has been above 300 Persons who have left New-York."[98] Houses stood empty and rents fell. New York's merchant fleet, which had numbered 124 ships in 1700 and 67 in 1715, dropped to 50 vessels by 1734. The importation of slave labor declined sharply.[99]

Economic malaise lingered on for several years. In 1735 one discouraged resident who decided to try his luck in Boston reported that 150 houses stood empty, only one vessel was under construction, and many inhabitants were resettling in Pennsylvania.[100] Two years later the governor was still lamenting adverse conditions "whereby honest and Industrious Tradesmen [were] reduced to poverty for want of employ, and many of them forced to leave us to seek their Living in Other Countrys."[101] Probably the conditions were not quite so bleak as portrayed by one newspaper correspondent, who claimed that "Our shipping are sunk. And our Ship-building almost entirely lost. Our Navigation is in a Manner gone; and Foreigners are become our Carriers, who have been continually draining us of that Money, which formerly was paid to our Seamen."[102] But the town's white population actually declined after a half century of continuous growth—almost certainly the result of out-migration because of unemployment—and per capita imports for the colony between 1728 and 1736 dropped about 11 percent below the levels of the years from 1718 to 1727.[103]

Although the shipbuilding slump rippled through the urban economy of New York, it cannot by itself explain the prolonged recession. Contributing to the decline was a serious shrinkage of trade. In 1726 and 1727 an average of 213 ships with a combined tonnage of 7,953 had cleared New York harbor. Inward-bound shipping was about the same. By 1733-1735, when the colony's population was 22 percent higher, an average of 209 ships of 7,211 tons entered and 205 ships of 7,145 tons cleared.[104] It is not clear what caused this decrease in trade, but it is unlikely that it can be explained by large absolute declines in agricultural production, given the rich harvests of the 1730s in neighboring Pennsylvania. Part of the problem may have been that the superior quality of Pennsylvania's grain and meat had now robbed New York of part of her West Indian market.[105] Probably of greater importance was the lack of a sufficient circulating medium. Ignoring the example of Pennsylvania, where modest emissions of paper money had helped to cure a recession, New York issued no paper money between 1724 and 1734. Interest rates, in the face of the scarcity, climbed to 8 percent. When £12,000 in paper money was finally emitted in 1734 and £48,350 added in 1737 to repair "the Decay of Trade & other Difficulties which this Colony has the Misfortune to have Laboured Under," the end of the economic drought was in sight. The value of English imports began to rise in 1734 and showed a 56 percent gain in the next five years from the levels recorded from 1729 to 1733. By 1739, outbound shipping had increased to 10,012 tons and inward-bound shipping to 9,738.[106]

Although the eight-year depression in New York must have caused laboring men to look enviously toward Philadelphia, the plight of New Yorkers was nowhere near as serious as for the lower class in Boston. Probably a greater part of the work force had been idled in New York than in Boston for at least part of the interwar period and for these people the situation was very bad. But in New York rents and food prices declined, thus taking the bite out of underemployment and perhaps even increasing the real income of those who managed to remain fully employed.[107] The common folk of Boston, by contrast, were losers even when trade was good and their services in demand. New Yorkers had suffered in a cyclical slump endemic to market economies whereas Boston was skidding on a downward slope that stretched indeterminately toward the future.

The data available for tracing economic change differs for each of the port towns and is not always strictly comparable, so a detailed tri-city analysis is often beyond our grasp. But in the area of poor relief enough data is recoverable from the surviving records to provide clear insights into how each town concluded the interwar period and faced the war clouds that were gathering anew in 1739.

As might be expected from what has already been said, the severity of Boston's poverty problem far exceeded that of Philadelphia, with New York occupying a midway position. By 1730, the number of completely destitute Bostonians had outstripped the capacity of the almshouse built in 1685. Poverty scarred the lives of hundreds in the town. In 1737, 270 persons were not rated by the tax assessors because of their poverty "besides many Hundreds for [the] same Reason not Entered in those [tax] Books at all." Among those who were rated, £859 in tax abatements were voted, "most of it whole Rates of poor People not able to pay."[108] Boston spent £627 sterling on poor relief in that year and probably an equal amount was contributed in private charity, both by Boston's churches and charitable institutions such as the Scot's Charitable Society, the Episcopal Charitable Society, and the Charitable Irish Society.

As poor relief costs rose in the 1730s, the selectmen and overseers of the poor looked for new solutions to the accelerating rate of pauperism. Their concern was not only caring for the poor but also caring for the dwindling resources of their constituents whose taxes underwrote all public relief. Toughening up on the poor who migrated into Boston hoping for relief was one solution and toughening up on Boston's own poor was another. In 1735 the overseers obtained a new poor law which gave the selectmen the power to eject strangers without appealing first to the county court for a warrant. The law also authorized the erection of a separate workhouse on the Boston Common where the able-bodied poor would be put to work.[109] Supported by a resolution of the town meeting in that year, the overseers specifically designated the workhouse for those who were able to work but unable to find employment, in distinction to the almshouse where the aged, infirm, and disabled received care. In the workhouse the "willing poor" would support themselves by picking oakum, weaving cloth, and making shoes, thus saving the taxpayers precious shillings. The overseers raised almost £900 sterling between 1735 and 1739, when the building was completed, almost all of it through private donations. By 1741 fifty-five persons were living in the workhouse. Although their expenses exceeded the income from their labors, an inspection committee pronounced the experiment a success since the support of this many people on out-relief would have been far costlier.[110]

In spite of the new economies achieved in Boston, the costs of poor relief kept rising. The town was not above exaggerating costs in its appeals to the legislature for tax relief. Expenditures were stated in inflated Massachusetts currency: £800 in 1727, £944 in 1729, £2,069 in 1735, £3,300 in 1737, and £4,185 in 1742. What purported to be more than a fivefold increase in fifteen years was actually about a twofold increase. Converted to sterling, expenditures rose from £256 in 1727 to about £600 in 1742. If the rapid increase in the town's population is taken into consideration, then per capita expenditures rose a little less than 50 percent.[111] But these were worrisome increases, especially at a time when fewer and fewer taxpayers were shouldering a mounting tax burden. Boston's taxables had paid an average of about 1 shilling 9 pence each for support of the poor in 1727, but the costs rose to 2 shillings 2 pence by 1735 and 4 shillings 2 pence by 1742—a 138 percent increase in fifteen years.

In New York the number of residents requiring public assistance grew slowly after 1720 and so did total expenditures for the indigent. The number of persons aided and the total funds disbursed did not approach the upward trend in Boston. It is likely that many of those thrown out of work by the severe slump in shipbuilding moved on to other ports, as one writer claimed. Their decision to leave may have been prompted in part by the tightfisted policies of the town's churchwardens and vestrymen (the counterparts to overseers of the poor in the other towns), who as yet had no precedent for supporting able-bodied artisans out of work and were unwilling to levy tax increases for this purpose. Between 1720 and 1735 the churchwardens and vestrymen relieved from twenty-eight to sixty-eight persons each year. Most of these were crippled, sick, aged, deranged, or orphaned. By building an almshouse in 1736, which admitted only twelve adults and seven children in its first year, the authorities were able to reduce the cost of caring for the poor and keep annual expenditures under £400 sterling until almost mid-century.[112]

Philadelphia also had its first taste of poverty during the depression of the 1720s. Arriving just after the slump began, one German immigrant wrote that "there are people who have been living here for 40 years and have not seen a beggar in Philadelphia."[113] Four years later, in 1728, the overseers of the poor were petitioning the assembly for funds to erect an almshouse. A "great Number of Poor from foreign Parts, and the neighboring Provinces" had entered the town, they reported, and additional cries for help came from the wives and children of "insolvent Debtors." Money for a small almshouse was appropriated in 1729 but by the time it was completed in 1732 prosperity had returned.[114]

As in New York and Boston, one of the purposes of the almshouse was to reduce the cost of caring for the destitute by sheltering them under one roof rather than supporting them individually as out-pensioners. In a further effort to keep down costs in Philadelphia the residency act of 1718 was revised in 1734 by a new poor law designed to close loopholes through which vagrants entered the town and became public charges. All in all, however, the shadow of poverty fell across the lives of few. In 1739, the overseers of the poor dispensed out-relief totaling £264 sterling to thirteen men and twenty-three women. A handful of others were cared for in the small almshouse, but the institutionalized poor were only a fraction of those in Boston. Philadelphia's poor were still the disabled, aged, and abandoned, and they were still cared for within a social system that was thoroughly familial.[115] Poverty was not yet a major social problem, as it had become in Boston, and its presence was not yet seen "as symptomatic of a basic flaw in the citizen or the society, an indicator of personal or communal failing."[116] Indigency could almost always be attributed to exceptional breeches of the family structure: the aged without relatives to care for them, widows and orphaned children without roots in the city, or the mentally ill who were shunned by their kin. The remedies were likewise familial in form: an out-relief system that kept the temporarily impoverished in their homes whenever possible and a small almshouse, constructed in the style of an ordinary home and organized like a household for a handful of chronic paupers.

By 1740 it was apparent that Boston, the oldest and most ethnically homogeneous seaport in British America, was the commercial center of the least productive region on the eastern seaboard. All of the port towns were increasingly drawn into the Atlantic network of trade, where vicissitudes of the marketplace such as falling sugar prices in the West Indies or the availability of immigrant labor could affect the health of these urban centers. But overshadowing these external forces was the productivity of the region served by each of the northern entrepôts. It was here that Boston was in a uniquely disadvantageous position, for the hinterland that the town served was beset by now with a serious decline of agricultural productivity that made it virtually impossible for the Bay colony merchants to make returns to England sufficient to maintain a balance of payments. Paper money, seen by many as a remedy to the strangling effects of the specie drain, proved only a method for placing the burdens of marginal productivity predominantly on the backs of the wage-earning urban laborers and others tied to fixed incomes. Prosperity drifted southward from New England in the first third of the eighteenth century and did not return.

6

Political Unrest
in the Interwar Period

THE THIRD and fourth decades of the eighteenth century had brought far more serious economic problems to the seaports than any experienced in the past. Although they varied in duration and intensity from town to town, these difficulties threw the interests of different social and occupational groups into sharp conflict and set the stage for further mutations in the practice and ideology of politics. The politics of deference grew shakier, artisan participation increased, important campaigning innovations tied holders of political power more closely to their constituents, and the ideology of Whig republicanism, with its emphasis on the public good, yielded further ground to the outspoken defense of private interests.

In the war period from 1690 to 1714 the vicissitudes of the economy had colored and partially conditioned the pattern of politics, but only in Boston had political discourse consistently revolved around issues of trade, prices, employment, and currency. In the era of peace that followed, economic concerns moved to the front of the political stage in all the maritime centers. They were not the only problems upon which the wheel of politics turned. Much debate continued to focus on issues that historians have traditionally emphasized: the struggle for power between the appointed governors and the elected assemblies, control of the courts, and the distribution of land. While these were important issues, the controversies around which urban political innovation and radicalization occurred typically brought antagonistic economic interest groups into combat and sent them scurrying to mobilize support, enunciating a new conception of their political universe.

In Boston two issues dominated politics in the interwar years: the economic malaise, which concerned the colony as a whole, and the question of whether Boston ought to have a regulated market. The idea of a regulated market, where the retailing of farm produce would be closely supervised and controlled, was an ancient one that went to the heart of the concept of a "moral economy." At issue was whether the supply of food at reasonable prices to the urban laboring classes was so transcendently important that it should never be compromised by considerations of private profit, either by country producers or city vendors. According to traditional, paternalist thinking, the price of country produce entering the city must be strictly controlled and the conditions under which these necessities of life were retailed should be carefully regulated. Otherwise, the nefarious practices of engrossing, forestalling, and regrating—all attempts to intercept perishables en route to the urban consumer in order to create scarcities and thus drive up prices—would creep in. Equally bad, farmers and merchants alike would take advantage of natural scarcities by charging high prices. In Europe most merchants and agricultural producers had come to favor private marketing, where each country farmer was free to sell in open competition to whomever chose to purchase his goods and where each merchant was free to buy up and hold for future sale whatever he could. Traditionalists and wage earners, on the other hand, tended to oppose the new laissez-faire approach; they called for the perpetuation of regulated public markets, surveillance of urban traders, and close attention to the needs of the laboring poor.[1]

The elaborate controls over the marketing of food in European cities were breaking down in England in the eighteenth century and they never existed in colonial American towns because the scarcity of food was an occasional rather than an endemic problem. Yet some controls were placed on the retailing of the necessities of life. Boston was unique among the northern capitals for allowing the private retailing of produce by itinerant traders rather than centralizing sales in a public marketplace. Even in Boston, however, the assize for bread—where magistrates calibrated the price that could be charged according to the current price of wheat—strictly controlled the baker's margin of profit.[2] But wheat prices in the eighteenth century increasingly hinged on overseas demand for American grain, and the price to the urban consumer fluctuated considerably. Amidst rising food prices, Bostonians argued passionately about the advantages and disadvantages of a regulated public market and the debate reached a violent climax in the 1730s.

Boston had experimented with a public market in 1696. Responding to the selectmen's recommendations, the legislature ordered a public market on Tuesdays, Thursdays, and Saturdays and set rules for market hours, weights and measures, and other matters. But many provisions were exempted from the attempt to centralize retailing and the public market lasted only a few years. It had not received the blessing of the town meeting and seems to have been backed primarily by merchants who thought they could offer produce at lower prices than the roving peddlers and small retailers who hawked individual cartloads of goods in the town.[3] In 1701 the town meeting rejected a by-law proposed by the selectmen for stricter market regulations. The merchants were back in 1714, arguing again for the public market along with the end of the town meeting system of local government. Their plans were thwarted by those who argued against centralization of power and the restriction of marketing to those who could afford licenses and fees.[4] Thus, the European alignment of interests in regard to the public marketplace was reversed in Boston. It was the small retailers and ordinary consumers who preferred the system of open marketing and viewed attempts to establish a public market as part of a movement by Boston's wealthiest merchants to aggrandize power and increase profits.

The market issue smoldered for almost two decades after 1715 before coming to a head in the 1730s.[5] Both sides resorted to the press to make their case, for by now it was standard procedure to mobilize support through the printed word. The politically conservative merchants affirmed their opposition to engrossing and profiteering but called for "carefully regulated" markets. Many saw the public market as a design to benefit the few at the expense of the many. It was apparently feared that export merchants would buy up grain and other provisions, shipping them abroad as returns against imports, while laboring families were left to scramble for their food. As recently as 1729 a crowd had gathered at dockside "to hinder the merchants from sending away ye corn as they attempted," and many Bostonians saw similar merchant self-interest lurking behind the call for public markets. Also, administering public markets would add to the tax burden and increase the likelihood of price-fixing, which would hurt the ordinary consumer who was already saddled with "Necessities of Life [that] are extravagantly dear."[6]

The market issue came to a climax because in the early 1730s a group of Boston's wealthiest merchants, many of them linked by marriage and closely allied to Governor Jonathan Belcher, chose to make their move against the aging Elisha Cooke and his popular party. Prominent among them were Thomas Hutchinson, John Colman, George Craddock, and Andrew Oliver. They intended to "reform" what they saw as Boston's chaotic and turbulent town meeting method of governing, to strengthen the prerogative party of the royal governor, and to do something about the paper money situation that continued to plague all mercantile transactions. Instituting a public market was one part of this reform scheme.[7] The 1732 election for representatives to the General Court was the most hotly contested in years, with 655 voters turning out. The selectmen elections of 1732 and 1733 swept all the popular party men from office. Elisha Cooke, only a few years from the grave, had disillusioned many of his followers by accepting a judgeship to the Suffolk County Court, which appeared to have been proferred in return for his support of the £1,000 gubernatorial salary bill long resisted by the popular party.[8] Even more important, the 1732 and 1733 elections revealed that Boston's middle-class voters, weary of the gnawing, debilitating inflation, were ready to give fiscal conservatives a chance to apply their solutions to this knotty problem.[9]

One day after the selectmen elections of 1733, voters at the town meeting elected a committee of conservative merchants to draft a plan for a public market. In two months the committee was ready with a proposal for three public markets operated under the strict supervision of salaried clerks. Both sides worked hard to get out the vote, which ended in a narrow 364 to 339 victory for the promarket side. Their victory was sweetened by the election of an eleven-man implementing committee that included ten men who held appointive offices under Governor Belcher, six of them related to him by marriage and none of them previously elected to town office by their fellow Bostonians. It was a bitter defeat for old Elisha Cooke, who had held sway in town affairs for fifteen years.[10]

Cooke was a dying man, but he was not too weak for one last fight. Regathering his forces at a town meeting on June 26, 1733, which drew a record 805 voters, Cooke pushed through a motion to refuse financing for the public markets. Having previously voted for a public market, Bostonians now declined to pay the construction costs. There the issue stood until March 1734, when 916 voters turned out to elect a new market committee that included a few Cooke supporters. Nine days later the new committee submitted a revised market plan, which gained the approval of a large majority of the voters. Every day of the week was declared a market day and retailers were not restricted from selling in the streets, even though three public markets were to be erected with public funds.[11] In effect, a mandatory public market had been transformed into a voluntary public market.[12]

The voluntary public market system, amended somewhat by the justices of the peace, began operating in June 1734. Most Bostonians indicated their attitude by boycotting the facilities and buying their produce as usual from street vendors. Nearly 400 townsmen had consistently voted against regulated markets in 1733 and 1734, and it appears from the extensive boycott that of the 60 percent or so of the adult male population that was unenfranchised by now, many were also opposed. Women were the principal marketgoers in the eighteenth century and their strong opposition was probably the most important element in the market boycott.[13]

In early 1736 it was apparent that the prerogative party's fiscal reforms were not bringing wage-price relief or revitalizing the town's commerce. The selectmen, it was reported, were crying that "Our Trades-Men of all denominations . . . are under the utmost discouragements" and that "miserable Circumstances" prevailed throughout the town. At the March town meeting voters chose to eliminate salaries for market clerks, silence the market bells, and ban paper money at the markets.[14] The markets, in effect, were abolished. The final blow came a year later when amidst rising food prices, a midnight mob, their faces blackened and some dressed as clergymen, demolished the market house near the town dock and "sawed asunder" the support posts of the market house near North Church "in a great Contempt of His Majesty's Government, in violation of the wholesome Laws of this Province, & in Terror of His Majesty's good subjects."[15] Ritually mocking the conservative clergyman Benjamin Colman, who had written in favor of the markets and whose brother had been a leading member of the original market committee, Boston's ordinary people made their power felt.

Since the public markets had already been discontinued, we must ask what the nocturnal saboteurs had in mind by destroying the market houses. It is possible that talk of reviving the markets was in the air in the spring of 1737 and that the midnight strike was meant to avert any possibility of this. There is also reason to believe that the vigilante action was a way of focusing widespread economic discontent in such a way that the rich and powerful would understand that they were not immune to the wrath of the laboring poor. The previous winter had been exceptionally severe and by March 1737 it was reported that "Provisions have grown very scarce & dear, & ye poor have been generally distress'd." There was much "murmuring against the Government & the rich People among us," reported Benjamin Colman, "as if they could (By any means within their Power, besides prayer) have prevented ye Rise [in price] of Provisions."[16] The anger and determination of the rioters can be appreciated from the public statements they posted on the Town House door and spread through the streets. They had done "what we think proper," they proclaimed. "We are so resolute, that had we any Thing further to do, we would do it, [even if] you loaded your Guns with Powder and Ball; for by the God that made you, if you come to that, we will find as much Powder and Ball as you can."[17]

The antimarket stalwarts also displayed their muscle in warning against attempts to apprehend or punish them. When Lieutenant Governor Spencer Phips promised a reward for information on the crowd leaders and ordered the sheriff to investigate the incident, the elected constables refused. They probably had wind already of a letter that was posted shortly, addressed to Sheriff Edward Winslow and warning him that if the search for the culprits went forward "you will cause them to make a Bloody Ending, and so breed a Civil War . . . If you touch One you shall [touch] All . . . and we will show you a Hundred Men where you can show One; And yet we are Resolved until Death to stand by one another yet for that good Deed." In another letter, the rioters cautioned the sheriff that "Five Hundred Men in Solemn League & Covenant" were prepared to defend the market rioters. "It will be the hardest Piece of Work that ever you took in Hand," they promised, "to pretend to Commit any Man for that Night's Work, or at least keep them when Comitted."[18] Other letters written publicly to Governor Belcher, the son of the old public enemy of 1710-1713, promised a donnybrook if he called out the militia. "None of ye Rioters or Mutineers have been yet discovered," wrote the dispirited Colman several months later, "or if suspected seem to [take] regard [of] it, their favourers being so many."[19]

The controversy over public markets provides several important insights into the attitudes of many ordinary Bostonians in this period. First, there was much uncertainty concerning what effect the public market would have on food prices, an important consideration in a period when complaints about the high price of the necessities of life were widespread. With New England's food supply becoming more uncertain, the possibility of urban merchants and country producers gaining control of the price structure through centralized marketing was not comforting. Thus, the antimarket mentality demonstrated how a long period of inflation had driven a wedge between merchants and rural producers on the one hand and urban consumers on the other.

Secondly, those opposing the market were animated as much by their opposition to the proposers of the scheme as by the idea of the market itself. It was well known that the original market committee was made up of the governor's favorites—a group of aristocratic, wealthy, ambitious men who were thought to look down on the common people while enriching themselves at their expense. Governor Belcher in 1733 had called Elisha Cooke, the leader of the popular party, "the late (now abandon'd) head of the scum," and "idol of the mob."[20] Such epithets pointed up the growing class antagonism in the town, which, by itself, was reason enough for ordinary people to oppose an innovation proposed by those whose "reforms" were seen as veils for schemes that would lead to greater disparities of condition and the concentration of political power in the hands of the wealthy.

Thirdly, the market proposal went against the grain of the deep-running traditionalism of laboring-class Bostonians. It is inaccurate to portray the political transformation of these people as foreshadowing later democratic developments or as an indication of openness to change, for most of them were profoundly conservative in a cultural sense. They hewed to an older vision of society, which they believed had been more equitable and moral. They attested to a belief in an older religion with a stricter code of conduct and resisted the creeping Arminianism of the educated class, which stressed free will more than predestination. They subscribed more to an earlier breed of clergymen, who condemned as "unregenerate" anyone who "in the General *Scramble* sieze[s] as much as he can for himself, tho it should be never so much to the Damage and Ruin of other men," than to the newer sort of churchmen such as Benjamin Colman, whose congregation at Brattle Street Church was filled with modern economic men, ambitious and successful, whose religion was an ornament to rather than a foundation of their lives.[21]

This cultural traditionalism was in many instances antirational, antiscientific, ethnocentric, and moralistic; it was also strenuously egalitarian. These were the mores of ordinary laboring people that had propelled an aroused mob in 1689 to attack the new Anglican church, shouting "Papist Doggs" at the parishioners, shattering the windows, driving the minister from town, and leaving "the Dores and Walls daubed and defiled with dung and other filth in the rudest and basest manner imaginable."[22] This was the traditionalism that arrayed ordinary people against smallpox inoculation in 1721, when it was being promoted by the best scientific minds in the midst of a catastrophic epidemic but was seen by many in the lower class as a new form of meddling in divinely willed affairs.[23] This was the spirit that had led the Cooke faction in 1729 to push through a law against dueling, which evoked agonized cries from the wealthy that class lines were being obliterated and Bostonians "putt all upon a level, so that a man is lyable to common affronts to wear a sword or to be distinguished like a gentleman."[24] It was the cast of mind that animated a crowd in the same year to pour to the waterfront to stop the landing of Irish immigrants, who were suspected of carrying infectious diseases. It is also reasonable to suspect that it was such people who demolished a whorehouse "for harbouring lewd and dissolute Persons" just fifteen days before the public markets were attacked.[25]

Finally, the market controversy provides evidence that Boston's ordinary people, many of whom were not enfranchised, continued the tradition of voting with their fists. The long struggle over public markets had been carried out in a series of stormy town meetings between 1733 and 1736 and political leaders on both sides had worked hard to turn out the vote. In the 1720s no town meeting had attracted more than 332 voters. But now, the number of ballots swelled to 500, 700, and finally, in March 1734, to 916. Even this, however, was only one-quarter of the taxable polls in Boston, which strongly suggests that the town franchise was far more restricted than is customarily believed.[26] One reason why it may have been becoming narrower is that hundreds of taxpayers who had formerly been qualified to vote had been removed from the tax rolls because of poverty. Their worsening economic condition, which relieved them of taxes, simultaneously deprived them of the vote. But this did not keep them out of the streets on the night of March 24, 1737 when the public markets were attacked. Although a majority of those entitled to participate on the formal political stage favored public markets and rallied around the prerogative party in the hope of obtaining economic remedies, a minority of voters, allied with those who claimed the streets as their political arena, won the war.

Those who represented authority at its highest—the governor, his council, and the sheriff—were obliged to back down in the face of such determined resistance. Only, as it has been written in the context of eighteenth-century English society, "if there had been a unified, coherent ruling class, content to divide the spoils of power amicably among themselves, and to govern by means of their immense command over the means of life," could the public market system have been maintained.[27] Upper-class unity never existed in Boston. Elisha Cooke's faction was led by men of considerable wealth, it enjoyed the support of many lesser merchants and shopkeepers as well as a majority of the town's artisans, and it was backed by a reserve army of disenfranchised laboring Bostonians who understood that the ballot was not the only instrument of politics and not always even the most effective.

The second issue around which political controversy pivoted in the 1720s and 1730s was paper money. Bostonians in this era were no better able to cope with the problem of depreciating paper money, or even fully to understand its causes, than they had been in the years immediately following Queen Anne's War. Nor have historians satisfactorily resolved the issue of why New England currency lost its value so rapidly. Some aspects of the problem were commonly agreed upon: that Massachusetts imported from England more than she could pay for with her exports; that she thereby suffered a continuous drain of metallic currency to make up for the deficit; and that some form of substitute currency was essential unless the people wished to return to a barter economy, which, as Cotton Mather put it in 1721, was the condition of societies where "men are brutish and savage, and nothing . . . good has been cultivated."[28] This need for paper money, which was a classic problem in expanding economies connected to more developed countries, was compounded in Massachusetts by the desire to spread out the costs of a disastrous era of war over a period of years, and to borrow against what proved to be a decreasingly productive future.

Agreement ended here. Debate raged over who should issue paper money—the government of Massachusetts or private corporations of investors. Disagreement flourished over whether more or less paper money would stabilize prices. Men argued about whether the value of paper money continued its downward spiral because of loss of confidence that the bills of credit were solidly backed—the "mean opinion people have of the current money"—or because an avaricious set of merchants manipulated the money market in mysterious ways that always seemed to redound to their benefit while hurting wage earners and those on fixed incomes.[29] And they jousted over whether the government, in a time of unemployment and hardship for laboring people, should issue more bills to underwrite public works such as the building of bridges and fortifications.

Almost all of those who wrote on these subjects, in an outpouring of pamphlets and newspaper articles between 1720 and 1728, were men of the upper class—merchants, clergymen, and officials. None of them really represented the views of laboring people, although many of them referred to the ill effects of currency depreciation on that part of society. In fact, whatever their views on solving Massachusetts's most urgent economic problem, they shared a class-biased view that it was the indulgence of the common people in buying imported European goods and falling into debt that contributed to the trade imbalance, drained the colony of specie, and thus necessitated issues of paper money, which in turn led to a depreciation of the currency. Sometimes the critics pointed their fingers at the well-to-do for living beyond their means, but most often they charged that the "ordinary people" were profligately spending themselves and their province pell-mell into ruinous stagflation. Paper money, admonished one clergyman in 1726, was meant to gratify the "gay and sensual dispositions" of the people, who were "running mad" in pursuit of "gay and costly clothing from abroad" and other items such as chocolate that only produced more "sensuality, Effeminatness, Unrighteousness, and Confusions."[30]

Many historians have taken these arguments at face value, arguing that "the real villain [of currency depreciation] was [people's] appetite for English goods," which caused Massachusetts in the eighteenth century to live "beyond her means, annually importing more than she exported."[31] This is technically true, but by focusing on the consumption of imported goods historians have diverted attention from the real problem. Massachusetts people of the middle and lower classes were no more enamoured of English goods than their contemporaries in the middle and southern colonies. Indeed, New Englanders were always known for their tight-fisted, plain living, particularly in contrast with consumption-minded southerners. In part this reflected their religious temperament, which had long inculcated the virtues of frugality and inconspicuous living even as the corollary values of industriousness called forth extraordinary energy at the workbench. Even more important, they did not have as much to spend as colonists to the south, which is evident in the much lower level of imports in New England than in the middle and southern colonies. Moreover, New Englanders did not leave nearly as much property at the end of their lives as did colonists in the middle and southern settlements.[32] There is no evidence that they ate and drank up the profits of their labor while other colonists bought nonperishable goods. So we must conclude that they left less property at the end of their lives because in fact they had accumulated less. Massachusetts's misfortune was to be saddled with a heavy war debt at a time when the growing population was placing pressure on the available agricultural resources.[33] Boston's misfortune was to be the commercial center of a debt-burdened, decreasingly productive region.

It is clear in historical perspective that New York, Pennsylvania, and

the southern colonies were spared ruinous price inflation in this period
not because they eschewed chocolate, lace, and other luxuries but because they lived in more productive regions and had not been obliged to
engage in massive deficit spending in order to mount military campaigns.
The one exception was South Carolina and it is the exception that proves
the rule. Caught up in a decade of war against the Tuscaroras and Yama-
sees, the South Carolina government issued £90,000 in paper currency
by 1717, £120,000 by 1723, and £210,000 by 1736. On a per capita basis
this was more than even Massachusetts had emitted. Just as in the Puritan colony, paper money depreciated rapidly.[34]

The myopia of the pamphlet writers of the 1720s is one indication that
all ranks of society were involved in a new social system which we call
the market economy and were still grappling for an understanding of its
workings and its social effects. Periodic downturns in the Atlantic trading world or structural weaknesses in a regional economy were diag-
nosed by employing familiar concepts. The rich, deeply suspicious of the
lower orders, complained of the heedless buying sprees of the poor. It
was hardly admissible that futile expeditions against Canada, promoted
by government officials and their merchant allies, had initiated the issuing of paper money, a process that now seemed impossible to stop. It was
much easier to fasten the blame on laboring people, who had always
been suspect. On the other side, the poor complained of the greed of the
rich, ignoring New England's declining productivity.[35] Thus, each rank
attacked the other and the argument swirled around the symptom of the
disease, currency depreciation, rather than the problem itself.

The paper money problem became acute in Boston just after the market controversy simmered down. In 1730 the Board of Trade in England,
determined to stop runaway inflation in Massachusetts and Rhode Island, issued instructions to curb sharply the emission of paper money.
No more than £30,000 per year was to be issued (roughly the annual cost
of operating the government) and by 1741 all paper money was to be retired. Recognizing that such a drastic remedy for the disease might kill
the patient altogether, Governor Belcher sidestepped his instructions in
1733 and cooperated in a scheme designed by a group of Boston merchants for privately emitting £110,000 in promissory notes redeemable
over a period of ten years in silver at the fixed rate of 19 shillings per
ounce. Known as Merchants Notes, the bills relied for their integrity
upon the solvency of the merchants who signed them. Since these were
among Boston's largest traders—men such as Edward Bromfield, Edward
Hutchinson, James Bowdoin, Joshua Winslow, and Jacob Wendell—the
notes seemed likely to increase the supply of circulating money while
maintaining a sound, stable medium of exchange. Such was not the case.
Although they were accepted in trade, the Merchants Notes could not
hold back the inflationary trend and, according to Gresham's Law, did

not remain long in circulation. Bearing a promise to pay at a fixed rate in silver, they were quickly hoarded as a hedge against inflation while provincial bills continued to drop in value.[36]

By 1736 it was clear that the prerogative party fiscal reforms, represented primarily by the Merchants Notes scheme of 1733, had failed to stabilize the provincial currency. They were seen by many as one more manipulative stratagem by which the people who could least afford it were oppressed by the richest members of society. Pamphleteers again took up the cudgels, arguing about how to comply with the English demand for the end of paper money. Some simply cried out for delivery of "the poor oppressed and distressed People out of the Hands of the Rich and Mighty."[37] A spate of compromise positions were hammered out, most of them aimed at stalling on the 1741 deadline and hoping for a change of mind in England. The configurations of the argument are difficult to follow, even with several hundred years of hindsight, and to the people of Boston the interminable debate may have been taken primarily as proof that their leaders were themselves confused on how to find their way out of the paper money morass. In 1736 the town meeting took a firm stand against deflationist plans for curbing the supply of paper money, which they proclaimed jeopardized their "laws, liberties and properties."[38] While most people supported the continuation of paper money, there was as yet no consensus on how to stop its depreciation. By June 1739, when the House of Representatives invited the public to submit proposals for privately issuing paper money to replace the public bills of credit that were to be completely banned in two years, the price of silver had reached 28 shillings per ounce in local currency. Massachusetts paper money had lost about four-fifths of its face value.[39]

The controversies over public markets and fiscal management during the 1720s and 1730s pushed further the transformation of urban politics that had begun a generation before. Leaders of Elisha Cooke's popular party reiterated the argument that men of wealth were not necessarily men of wisdom or even men animated by concern for the welfare of the community. Although Cooke was one of the wealthiest men in Boston and most of his followers who were elected as representatives or selectmen were also merchants or shopkeepers, they were careful not to parade their wealth. They dispensed money liberally to the poor, and they steadfastly maintained that the people, not a privileged elite, should manage civil affairs. Not a shred of evidence exists to suggest that they wished to broaden the electoral base in a town where only a quarter of the adult males went to the polls even in the most heated elections. But they wanted to mobilize fully this part of the community and in special circumstances they countenanced street activities by those not entitled to vote.

Increasing emphasis was placed by the popular party on the use of the printing press. It became customary for pamphleteers to analyze public issues and to discredit in strong language those whose positions they opposed—a tacit admission of the legitimacy of oppositional politics. In 1721 Cooke drew up a set of instructions for Boston's representatives to the General Court and submitted them in printed form to the town meeting for approval. Every inhabitant was now apprised of what the town expected of its representatives; thus delegates were tied more closely to their constituents and could be held more strictly accountable for their performance.[40] After 1715, the legislature published its debates and votes, distributing them at the end of each session. This gave voters and nonvoters alike a chance to pass judgment on the actions of those invested with political power. Boston's newspapers increased from one to four in the 1720s and devoted plenty of space to a discussion of politics.[41] Between 1721 and 1740, in a community where the literacy rate was probably about 80 percent, Bostonians had over fifty pamphlets and dozens of newspaper articles to inform themselves on the issues and to contemplate the arbitrary power and diminishing liberties which, according to the popular party, the governor's faction had in mind. Censorship of the press by the executive was now virtually dead, which allowed the opportunity to convert subdued expository literature into fiery political tracts.[42] The party of Elisha Cooke did not really have any answers to Boston's economic problems but they could at least remind the people that not everyone was affected equally by the derangement of the currency.[43]

IT WAS NOT by coincidence that the emergence of a highly vocal form of popular politics in Boston in the 1720s found no parallel in New York, where for the most part the governorship of William Burnet from 1720 to 1727 was placid and the laboring classes were quiescent. To be sure, the old debate over distributing the tax burden, begun under Governor Robert Hunter's administration, continued. But demands for revenue during peacetime were slight and contention mainly involved the urban-based mercantile interests, who wanted the tax to fall primarily upon land, and the rural-based landowning interests, who favored commercial taxes such as import duties.[44] Assembly elections were held infrequently —only three times in the 1720s—and common council elections saw the same men returned regularly to office. Admissions to freemanship, a kind of barometer of political activity because few men bothered to apply and pay the required 9 penny fee unless there were important choices to be made at the polls, were sluggish. An average of only 35 per year applied between 1720 and 1729 as compared with 100 per year in the stormy post-Leisler era from 1695 to 1702.[45]

The assembly election of 1727 saw a flurry of activity. Both factions, one led by Lewis Morris and Cadwallader Colden and the other by Adolph Philipse, appealed to the artisans and shopkeepers of the town by promising replacement of taxes on household commodities such as rum, salt, and molasses with taxes levied against the rich.[46] But all of these political leaders were highly aristocratic men. To the extent that they worked to mobilize the electorate in 1727 it was in behalf of their private struggles to gain political ascendancy in the assembly. In good times, given a chance to earn a "decent competency," the working people of New York were content to defer to the elite, for as yet they did not feel the need—or possess a supporting ideology—for a permanent class-based political pressure group.

When William Cosby arrived in 1732 as New York's new governor, a generation of relative political calm was abruptly shattered. For the next half-dozen years the town went through a period of political infighting that in some ways harked back to the era of Jacob Leisler, but it also brought about innovations in the relationship between governors and governed that even the Leislerians had not promoted. Historians have written profusely about this period in New York politics and their efforts have been mainly directed at spelling out how political warfare reflected struggles between the executive and legislative parts of government or between family groupings.[47]

The first sparks that flew after Cosby's arrival, for example, concerned the question of whether the Dutch merchant, Rip Van Dam, who had been acting governor for the previous thirteen months, should pay half his salary to the incoming governor.[48] The fire spread when Lewis Morris, chief justice of the provincial court, ruled against Cosby after the governor brought suit to recover the money. Cosby promptly suspended Morris, setting off a new brushfire regarding the constitutional right of the governor to interfere with the courts. When the Morrisite faction decided to take their case to the people, particularly in their new paper that spoke out with unprecedented vitriol, the government indicted its printer, John Peter Zenger, for libel. Freedom of the press was at stake and a trial ensued that became world famous.

Although constitutional questions, family politics, and high principles all were important in the highly inflamed state of politics of the 1730s, two points need to be stressed. First, these battles coincided with the most serious economic depression ever known in the town; secondly, both elite-led factions, but especially the one led by Lewis Morris, James Alexander, and William Smith, set aside personal preferences for hierarchy and narrowly based politics in order to launch a program designed to attract wide popular appeal. "The techniques and ideas which gradually took shape in the course of this conflict were sufficiently precocious, sufficiently in advance of their time, that a comparable level of political development would not again be reached until the last decade of the colonial era."[49] It is also essential to keep in mind that important political innovations occurred not simply because a handful of men at the top, for the sake of gaining office, awakened a slumbering laboring-class multitude that had lain dormant for several decades. What happened in New York in the 1730s is also attributable to the work of self-activating artisans, who were suffering from the economic depression and moved determinedly on their own behalf to bring about change.

As never before in New York's history, the press became indispensable in the political warfare of the 1730s. Fewer than a half-dozen broadsides and pamphlets had been published from 1714 to 1725 and a still smaller number between 1726 and 1731; now the ink streamed forth in the production of about forty pamphlets and broadsides between 1732 and 1736. Equally important was the founding of the *New-York Weekly Journal*, a paper specifically created in November 1733 to break the monopoly on communication held by William Bradford's *New-York Gazette*. Bradford was tied to the governor's party by his job as official government printer and was "not Suffered to insert any Thing but what his Superiors approve of" in his paper.[50] The Morris party therefore hired Bradford's apprentice, young John Peter Zenger, to print a paper beamed specifically at the artisans, shopkeepers, and laborers. The *Journal* became the mouthpiece for the antigovernment faction of Morris, Alexander, and Smith, who as its principal spokesmen left little unsaid in accusing the governor and his circle of "tyrannically flouting the laws of England and New York and of setting up personal henchmen with unlawful powers to control the judicial system of New York."[51] Zenger would soon find himself indicted for seditious libel. He was rescued from an early ending to his career by a brilliant Philadelphia lawyer, Andrew Hamilton, who was brought in by the Morris faction to convince the New York jury that he was innocent of everything but trying to inform the public of attacks on their liberties. Zenger was only a pawn in the political battle that was raging. Although he was acquitted, the jury's decision did not really change the law of libel in New York. But it did establish that the "government was the servant of the people and that open criticism was one of the important ways in which magistrates could be kept responsible to them."[52]

The Morrisite party appealed to a broad electorate by doing far more than criticizing Cosby's administration. It recommended annual assembly elections as a safeguard against entrenched political power and called for voting by secret ballot. With secret balloting ordinary people would be able to vote "for the Man they Love, and not for the haughty Tyrant they fear, and consequently hate."[53] Neither of these measures was particularly radical for the time. They had long been established in Boston and Philadelphia, but they were new for New York and promised more responsive government. Further calls went out in the town for making elective the offices of mayor, recorder, and sheriff. New York City had received a new charter in 1731 which made assessors and collectors elective for the first time. Now it was urged that this democratization be taken a step further.[54] More and more was heard about the accountability of legislators to their constituents and the power that rightly resided in the people to turn out those who proved unworthy of their trust. Election to the assembly, warned one representative in 1734, was "but like a fine laced Livery coat of which the vain Lacquey may be stript at the pleasure of his proud Master [the electorate] & may be kikt out of Doors naked."[55]

Woven through the political literature of these years, and especially evident in the direct appeals for electoral support which first appeared in the 1730s, were promises to the artisans, whose security had crumbled as depression gripped the town. The Morris-Alexander-Smith party, which also had the support of such important merchants as Rip Van Dam, Gerardus Stuyvesant, and Philip Livingston, made specific economic pledges and in fact created a kind of economic platform on which to run in the assembly election of 1734.[56]

It is difficult to determine to what extent this was voluntarily offered to the artisans and laborers and to what extent it was demanded by them. But laboring men showed they were not passive in this era, so we may conclude that what they received was no more than party leaders knew they must give in return for support from below. In the heated municipal elections of 1733 and 1734 the Morrisite party made the erection of a new almshouse and poorhouse a campaign promise and worked for the emission of £12,000 in paper money, to be used primarily in the construction of fortifications in the port.[57] These attempts to stimulate employment were supplemented with private ventures. Morris persuaded his son-in-law, Captain Matthew Norris of the royal navy, to bring his ship into New York rather than Boston for repairs. It was probably not by coincidence that Norris arrived just before the September 29, 1734 municipal election and gave orders for refitting his vessel at the expense of £900.[58] Political literature, signed pseudonymously by "Timothy Wheelwright" and "John Chissel," urged artisans to "assert their rights and liberties." Wheelwright made the class appeal unmistakably plain in a public letter that distinguished between the good, honest men of the town and the dishonest, avaricious men. It was "Shuttle" the weaver, "Plane" the joiner, "Drive" the carter, "Mortar" the mason, "Tar" the mariner, "Snip" the tailor, "Smallrent" the fair landlord, "John Poor" the tenant, and more of their kind who represented the sinews of New York. Pitted against them were "Gripe" the merchant, "Squeeze" the shopkeeper, "Spintext and Quible" the lawyer.[59]

It is possible that lawyers such as Alexander and Smith, or their merchant friends such as Stuyvesant and Livingston, coined the self-deprecating occupational labels "Gripe," "Squeeze," and "Spintext" in their efforts to recruit the artisan vote; or pamphlets of this sort may have come from the hand of laboring-class leaders. In either case, the rich were publicly attacked in a time of distress and those with their backs to the wall were urged to combine against them. "Timothy Wheelwright" revived Leislerian admonitions that "A poor honest Man [is] preferable to a rich Knave," and another writer sharpened the image of classes pitted against each other by writing that "people in Exalted Stations," who looked with contempt on "those they call the Vulgar, the Mob, the herd of Mechanicks," ought to be thrown from office.[60] Governor Cosby, hearing such leveling language, was sure that New Yorkers had been infected by "the example and spirit of the Boston people," and like others of the "court" persuasion was shocked.[61] But the artisans were tired of hearing the advice of aristocrats and their allies among the clergy that in hard times the proper remedy for a bare cupboard was prayer.

Laboring-class New Yorkers did more than listen to class appeals and vote for upper-class candidates favorable to their interest. In the municipal election of 1734 they turned out in great numbers to elect men of their own kind. New York artisans had always held offices at this level more frequently than in Boston, but in the decline of political activity after 1710 the municipal corporation had come under the control of the town's merchants. In 1733, for example, of the ten councilmen who can be identified by occupation, eight were merchants, one was a lawyer, and one was a brewer. But in 1734, in a hotly contested election, the merchants on the common council were defeated en masse by a slate of anti-Cosby men that included a painter, three bakers, a bricklayer, a bolter, and a laborer. Of the seventy-five men elected to municipal offices in 1733 and 1734, twenty-eight were not even freemen.[62]

Election of this many artisans was possible only because the franchise extended far lower in the social structure than in Boston or Philadelphia. In the 1734 municipal election, 879 voters turned out; in 1735, 812 voted and it "was supposed that every voter in the city was brought out."[63] Almost as many persons were voting in New York, where white adult males numbered about 1,500, as had cast votes in the heated public market contests in Boston, where the adult white male population was at least twice as large.[64] The feverish activity and leveling spirit that marked the elections was long remembered. William Smith, New York's first historian, wrote years later that at a pre-election evening rally in 1737, money was flung "from the windows of the house to the rabble in the streets, with a tempestuous festivity and joy." The next morning, wrote Cadwallader Colden, "the sick, the lame, and the blind were all carried to vote. They were carried out of Prison and out of the poor house to vote. Such a strugle I never saw and such a hurra[h]ing that above one half of the men in town are so hoarse that they cannot speak this day. The pole lasted from half an hour after nine in the morning till past nine at night."[65]

Although the popular party proved it could dominate municipal elec-

6. *South Prospect of New York (right-hand portion)
in 1746 by William Burgis.*

tions, it could not overpower the court party of Governor Cosby because the governor refused to hold assembly elections and was able to repulse efforts of the Morrisites in London to have him removed from office. Tuberculosis, however, struck Cosby down in November 1735, and the town erupted in a storm of argument that several times reached the edge of violence. At issue was which member of the governor's council should inherit the governor's chair until a new royal appointee arrived. The issue was finally decided in 1736 in favor of one of Cosby's supporters, George Clarke, but for the next few years the demand persisted for more broadly based government and help for the laboring classes.[66]

In the 1736 municipal election it was advocated for the first time that aldermen and councilmen act according to instructions from their constituents. Some "cautious Folks" still opposed this direct expression of positions on sensitive issues, but political liberty would be raised to its proper height, the broadside writer advised, when "in matters of the highest moment they [aldermen and councilmen] may judge it prudent and safe to act by the Advice of their Constituents."[67] This notion, that "in the Multitude of Counsel there is safety," would have shocked nobody in Boston, but in New York it was a new step toward admitting explicitly that interest groups were legitimate in politics and should be admitted as such. A further move in this direction came in the next year when the assembly agreed to record divisions on specific votes, which were then promptly reported in the newspapers so that all could know how their representative stood on a particular issue.[68]

The practice of pinning politicians down on issues that affected particular interest groups rather than electing the wisest and most eminent men and then allowing their sagacity to work mysteriously for the "public good" took still another step forward in the 1739 assembly election. In political broadsides, one slate of candidates put a series of questions to themselves on the issues involved and promptly provided answers. They promised the voters not to consent to a support bill for the governor for more than one year; not to consent to the spending of any public revenue without specific legislative appropriation; to support the printing of the legislative minutes "with the Names of all the Voters to any Material Question, if demanded by any one Member . . . that we may see who have best discharged their duty"; and to push for "frequent Electing of Representatives" and elections by ballot.[69] Their position stated, they challenged their opponents to announce where they stood on the issues.

The construction of party platforms as a basis for election appeal was accompanied by other concessions to popular politics: the revival of party "tickets," not used apparently since the Leislerian era; the first public appeals for votes in the newspapers, where candidates modestly announced that "your vote and interest are desired"; and the first exercises in admitting the entire electorate to the nomination of candidates. All of these devices, so characteristic of modern political parties, were accompanied by attacks on the rich, who, it was claimed, were riding out the depression in fine fettle while artisans and laborers suffered.[70]

The corollary of attempts to place in office men responsive to the middle and lower classes was the enactment of laws for their benefit. In 1737 the first assembly to be elected in New York in a decade passed a bundle of popular laws, including ones for remodeling the militia, holding triennial elections, establishing public schools, reducing the legal interest rate, and issuing paper money. Other laws that were passed but vetoed by the governor's council provided for more careful regulation of elections, restraint of liquor sales to apprentices and servants, reduction of officials' fees, and the appointment of an assembly agent in England. Even this spate of laws, according to New York's foremost contemporary historian, was "inadequate to the elevated expectations of the multitude and short of the intentions of their leaders."[71]

The extent of the transformation of politics in New York can be appreciated not only by the tactical innovations and legislative achievements of the popular party led by Lewis Morris, James Alexander, and William Smith but also by the response of the parties of Governors Cosby and Clarke. They fumed privately and publicly about the Morrisite attempts to "inflame the Minds of the People"; to appeal to "the lowest Canaille of the People, of no Credit or Reputation, rak'd out of Bawdy-Houses and Kennels"; and to use the press to delude the "unthinking" people with seditious libel.[72] But in the end, the aristocratic courtiers of the governor concluded that they must fight fire with fire. They too resorted to the press, though they dreaded the effects and thought they ought not "be prostituted to the censure of the mob" inflamed by the written word.[73] They too mobilized voters, even to the extent of lodging about fifteen English soldiers in private houses just before the 1734 municipal election so that they could establish their "residency" and tip the balance in the South Ward.[74] And they too, while declaring their aversion to the concept of "the Absolute Power of the People," called together "a great number of the freeholders and freemen of the . . . city" in order to choose a slate of candidates for assembly elections.[75] Even the haughty Governor Cosby learned to put aside lifelong habits in 1734 when he "became more familiar with the people & invited many of low rank to dine with him such as had never pretended or expected so much respect."[76]

Amidst such politicization it is not surprising that the time would finally come when the legitimacy of factions and private interest groups would be openly stated. In an essay that frontally attacked the notion that parties and factions were cancers on the body politic and that all holders of political power should serve only one master, the indivisible "publick good," the *New-York Gazette* pronounced the inevitability of "Parties, Cabals and Intrigues" and argued that "Parties are a Check upon one another, and by keeping the Ambition of one another within Bounds, serve to maintain the public Liberty."[77] Bostonians had been exposed to a similar theory, indirectly stated by John Wise in 1721. Now New Yorkers heard it squarely asserted that private interests, separate from those of the community, were not only legitimate but might in the end be harnessed so as to produce the greatest public good.[78] Such a notion abandoned the concept of the town as an organic unit where individual needs could be harmonized and where consensus would prevail over rancorous conflicting interests.

In truth, the new theory was a belated recognition of what had long been implicitly recognized, at least by some. To New York's artisans and unskilled laborers it had been obvious at least since Leisler's time that there was no organic unity, no consensus, no determination among those in high places to work for the common good. Such beliefs, however, had no actively continuous history. They probably always lurked to some degree in the minds of a people who, while not completely Hobbesian in their views, had little reason to be exuberantly optimistic about the nature of man. They tended to recede in years of prosperity when there was work and decent wages for all. They reappeared with new vitality in the depression years of the 1730s. It was then that the Whig ideology of advancing the common good under the direction of those at the top of society was clearly seen as a mask for protecting the interests of the economically dominant. It was the function of the new interest group ideology to expose "the contradictions between the opponents' rhetoric and his real interests" and hence to mobilize others "who seeing this conflict, might also find themselves opposed to the real interests of the ruling group."[79]

Thus, political mobilization occurred in New York in the 1730s because specific grievances were widely held and not redressed by those in power. Some of the complaints were constitutional and ideological, as in Lewis Morris's removal from the supreme court and the prosecution of Zenger for libel. But among ordinary people, who were striding to the forefront of politics, the grievances more often concerned their day-to-day welfare. Upper-class lawyers and merchants could join middle-class shopkeepers and laboring-class artisans and mariners in an opposition party. Each group held its own interests, but to promote them each could pragmatically ally against a common opponent.

It is notable that in Philadelphia, where economic depression during the interwar period was of briefest duration of any of the seaport towns, a radical ideology stressing opposition to the wealthy and the necessity of common people organizing in their own behalf flowered most fully. The leader of the movement, ironically, was an ex-Jacobite Tory placeman of aristocratic background and mien. The radicalization of Philadelphia politics in the 1720s was led by the Scottish baronet Sir William Keith, who had arrived in the town as William Penn's governor in May 1717. Within a year, Penn was dead and Keith was accountable to his widow. By 1722, when the economic winds began to blow cold on Philadelphia, he was thoroughly alienated from both her and the loyal proprietary circle that James Logan led.[80]

Only a year after Logan had sung Keith's praises to Penn's widow in England, the governor joined the dissident Lloyd and several other popular spokesmen in Philadelphia. After that he threw himself into organizing the town's artisans with a fervor to match that of Elisha Cooke in Boston. It has never been clear why Governor Keith suddenly abandoned the proprietary group in his colony and joined forces with the now aging David Lloyd, the popular leader of an earlier era. Whatever Keith's personal reasons, the political change that was looming occurred amidst the economic depression gripping the town.

By mid-1721, with trade stagnating and unemployment rising, a bill for the emission of paper money was introduced in the assembly as a palliative to the recession. Dominated by conservative Philadelphia merchants, the legislature voted the bill down. The October assembly elections were "very mobbish and carried by a Levelling spirit," Logan wrote, but the conservatives still held a thin edge.[81] A year later more of them were swept from office in an atmosphere, according to the wealthy Quaker merchant Isaac Norris, where "All Encouragement hath lately been given & all ways taken to Insult Creditors and render men of ability . . . obnoxious, in mobbish discourses & wretched argument." By the end of the year Governor Keith wrote to England that "the clamor is universall for Paper Money."[82]

For the next five years, the question of how to lift Philadelphia from the economic slump was aired in broadsides and pamphlets, as well as in the streets and taverns. The debate proved impossible to contain within narrow limits. It quickly leaped from a discussion of economic remedies to the accountability of representatives to their constituents, the organization of politics, and the nature of the body politic itself. In the 1690s George Keith, a Scottish outsider, had been at the center of a religious controversy strongly conditioned by economic considerations. In the 1720s William Keith, a Scottish insider, became the center of a political controversy that sprang directly from economic grievances. In a town where not a single political tract or election appeal had been issued since 1710, at least forty-six political screeds, many of them highly inflammatory, rolled from Philadelphia's two printing presses between 1721 and 1729.

At first glance it appears that the conflict of the 1720s might easily have been avoided since the assembly elected in October 1722 passed a bill for the emission of £15,000 of paper money and Keith gladly gave his approval. The legislature authorized a second emission, of £30,000, in the following year.[83] Fiscal conservatives such as Isaac Norris groused about "this Vile paper Currency" and "our rotten paper money," believing that the bills of credit were "the contrivance & refuge of Bankrupts & designers."[84] They seemed even more concerned at the specter of a political world turned upside down—a vision promoted by no less a man than the governor. In his opening address to the assembly elected in October 1722, Keith had set aside his class upbringing and harangued the legislators: "We all know it is neither the Great, the Rich, nor the Learned, that compose the Body of the People; and that Civil Government ought carefully to protect the poor laborious and industrious Part of Mankind."[85] He returned later with a program that included legislation not only for issuing paper money but also for reducing the interest rate, curbing lawyers' fees, and restricting the imprisonment of debtors. Adding insult to injury so far as the elite was concerned, Keith expressed doubts that "the Good of the whole Community" was best served by those with the greatest wealth and education.

James Logan, never reluctant to take up the cudgels in defense of hierarchy, social order, and wealth, eagerly struck back at the man he had recommended to William Penn in 1716. Arguing in embryonic form what two centuries later would be called the "trickle down" theory of prosperity, Logan cautioned Philadelphians that their leveling tendencies were self-destructive, for rich men were essential to the prosperity of any country. Without the rich, he argued, the poor would always be poor, for it was the rich alone "who are in a condition to assist them." Philadelphia's unemployment and new-found poverty were the products, he argued, of laboring-class perversity. It was idleness and fondness for drink that made men poor and the charging of high wages that drove away employment. Those who tried "new politics" and invented "new and extraordinary Measures" such as paper money misunderstood the roots of economic distress. The rich were rich because of their "Sobriety, Industry and Frugality"; the poor were poor because of their "luxury, Idleness and Folly."[86]

Logan's analysis of Philadelphia's recession bore a striking resemblance to arguments published in Boston in the decade after Queen Anne's War, although there is no evidence that he had read the tracts of Paul Dudley, Thomas Paine, and Edward Wigglesworth. How unemployed artisans and debt-ridden retailers reacted to this formulation of the problem can best be judged by their re-election in the next few years of the paper money legislators opposed by Logan and Norris. Their spokesman, the governor, was joined by David Lloyd, who came out of political retirement to participate in a public controversy that now began to broaden. Where Keith had hinted that men of wealth were not the "honestest Part of Mankind," Lloyd flatly stated that "a mean Man, of small Interest, devoted to the faithful Discharge of his Trust and Duty to the Government" was well enough equipped for high office and vastly preferable to wealthy, self-interested men.[87] An anonymous pamphleteer began to dig deeper into the economic motives of those who opposed paper money: "the principal Reason why you are angry with Paper-money," wrote "Roger Plowman" to "Mr. Robert Rich," is "because People who are in your Debt can raise money to pay you, without sur-rendring up their Lands for one half of what they are worth." Logan had argued that without the rich, the poor would always be poor. "Roger Plowman" now reversed the proposition, suggesting that because of the rich, the poor would remain poor. "It is an old Saying with us," he wrote, "that we must never grease the fat Sow in the Arse, and starve the Pigs."[88]

Keith's campaign to shatter the notion that those who scaled the top of the economic mountain also deserved to stand astride the political apex was accompanied by an effort at political mobilization among laboring Philadelphians such as the town had never seen. By 1723 Keith had or-ganized two political clubs, the Gentleman's Club for his more substan-tial supporters, and the "Leather Apron Club" for the artisans.[89] The Pal-atine Germans who were flooding into the colony were another obvious source of support. By 1725 Keith was sponsoring bills to naturalize them almost upon arrival—a political stratagem, Logan charged, to swing the electoral tide in his direction or, as Isaac Norris put it more graphically, to create "a sinister army" or an "Army of Mirmydons."[90] To social and fiscal conservatives the world had come unhinged. A Scottish baronet was courting the people "in the most abject manner" and in response "Ye people head and foot run mad. . . All seems topside Turvy. Our publick Speeches tell ye Country & ye World that neither knowledge or Riches are advantageous in a Country. . . The Mobb is Hallood On to render obnoxious Every Man who has any proportion of those." It was now "Criminall" to "ask for money due" and "laudable. . . to be Insolent & In-sulting in refusing paymt."[91]

Critics such as Isaac Norris and James Logan, who continued to insist that mercantile opulence was indispensable to the economic health of the community and that only the "Sot, the Rambler, the Spendthrift, and Slip Season" were in economic straits, preferred to think that ordinary Philadelphians were not educated enough to understand their own interests or that of the community at large.[92] If the commonality was "in-flamed almost to madness," it was not because of legitimate economic grievances and an accurate identification of their enemies, but because the scheming "new politicians" had deluded the people and given them a false sense of their importance.[93] In a strict sense the conservatives were correct in arguing that Philadelphia's leading merchants had not caused the depression. But unemployed and debt-ridden Philadelphians were not mistaken in their understanding of who was profiting from the situation. Nor did they fail to see that those who benefitted were also those who sanctimoniously charged that the poor had dug their own hole and now could only hope that the rich would generously pull them out. Logan paid a price for this kind of arrogance, which made sense neither in terms of economic theory nor in terms of political strategy. His house was attacked by an angry mob, which tore off the window shutters, threw bricks into his bedchamber, and threatened to level one of Philadelphia's most gracious structures.[94] Logan was publicly attacked in pamphlets for his contempt of the "poorer sort" and for leading a group of Pennsylvanians who wished to recreate, it was charged, "the Old English Vassalage." Such men dominated the courts, where justice was dispensed according to a man's wealth and status, ruled the proprietary land office, where land jobbing by the officials was the rule, and opposed paper money, which offered the best way out of an economic morass that was not of the common people's making.[95]

Unlike the common people of Boston, Philadelphians had not tasted real economic affliction before and their reaction in the 1720s is therefore of considerable interest. Political contentiousness was well known in the colony, but unemployment and chronic indebtedness were unprecedented and came as a rude shock to those who imagined that the Quaker capital was the most favored commercial center of a generally favored land. Laborers, artisans, and small retailers did not as a rule expect to grow wealthy in Philadelphia, but they anticipated that their labor would earn them a life free from want. Moreover, they believed they had seen the last of an economic world where one man's gain was another man's loss. In a preindustrial society, colonizing Europeans did not by any means suppose that the boundaries of economic opportunity were infinitely expandable. But they were gradually casting off the European conception of societies containing fixed quantities of wealth that must be distributed like a pie, so that when one man's piece was cut larger, others had to satisfy themselves with narrower slices. This older conception of economic life had not receded altogether, but it was identified mostly with the European world that had been left behind. When it was re-encountered in Philadelphia after four decades of expansion and relative prosperity, the response was passionate.

In 1727 Governor Keith touched the pulse of ordinary Philadelphians in an economic parable of rich and poor that portrayed the tribulations of a "fat unwieldy" man. Finding himself in the middle of a crowd, the fat man cried out, "Lord! what a filthy Crowd is here! Pray, good People, give Way a little! Bless me! what a De[vi]l has raked this Rabble together? What a plaguey squeezing is this? Honest Friend, remove your Elbow." After a series of such exclamations, a weaver standing next to the fat man could hold his tongue no longer: "A Plague confound you for an over-grown Sloven! and who in the De[vi]l's Name, I wonder, helps to make up the Crowd half so much as your self? Don't you consider . . . that you take up more Room with that Carcass than any Five here? Is not the Place as free for us as for you? Bring your own Guts to a reasonable Compass (and be b[un]g'd) and then I'll engage we shall have Room enough for us all."[96]

Was evocative literature of this kind an upper-class instrument for mobilizing the artisanry in Philadelphia? More likely Keith was reflecting rather than anticipating the laboring-class view, for he was writing in 1727, near the end of the period of political reawakening. In any event, such political caricatures would have had little effect if they had not fallen upon ears already finely attuned to economic problems that had disrupted the everyday lives of the people. Everyone could understand, given their personal experiences during the recession, that the fat man represented wealth, that his own insatiable appetite had created lean times for many others, and that laboring people in the crowd were entitled to cast deference aside and challenge such economic gluttons.

Keith's pamphlet is also evidence that Philadelphia's artisans and laborers looked to upper-class leaders for organizational talent and literary skills. But they were not simply passive toilers who could do nothing for themselves. Two of the first craft guilds in Philadelphia—the tanners and carpenters—were established during the depression, and the timing, one suspects, was not coincidental.[97] Leadership developed within these artisan organizations and it carried over into politics.

The popular Keithian party dominated politics in Philadelphia from 1723 to 1729. It did so by perfecting organizational and electioneering tactics that were also in use in Boston and New York. The formation of party tickets through caucuses, the recruitment of immigrant German and Scots-Irish voters (the "very scum of mankind" in the view of the conservatives), direct appeals to the electorate through broadside "advice" where positions on specific issues were announced and the wealthy denounced, outdoor political rallies that welcomed voters and nonvoters alike—all were part of the new system of popular politics.[98] In 1726, when Logan's efforts to have the governor removed finally bore fruit, Keith ran for the assembly. Amidst "Mobs, Bonfires, Gunns, Huzzas" he won a resounding victory, capped by a celebration that ended with the burning of the pillory and stocks—the symbols of authority and social control. For the opening of the new legislative session, Keith, according to his enemies, organized a parade through the town, "not of ye Wise, ye Rich or the learned . . . [but] mostly made of Rabble Butchers, porters & Tagrags." Thus far had politics fallen in Philadelphia, where the ex-governor "made his Gradations Downward . . . to an Equal with Every plain Country Member," and pleased the common people by "perambulating our citty and popping into ye dramships, tiff, & alehouses where he would find a great number of modern statesmen & some patriots settling affairs, cursing some, praising others, contriving lawes & swearing they will have them enacted cum multis aegis."⁹⁹

Politics "cum multis aegis" took on a new dimension in 1728 and 1729 when economic recession again visited Philadelphia briefly and the Keithians in the assembly pushed for a new issue of paper money. Proprietary stalwarts grumbled that the "spirit raised among the people for paper money" was the work of the master manipulator Keith. But there is no reason to believe that the people themselves were not capable of perceiving that the solution of 1723 might now work just as well. Blocked by country members of the assembly, the Philadelphia Keithians organized (or tacitly approved) street gangs who intimidated hard-money legislators in the fall of 1728 and spring of 1729. The assembly buckled under, passing an act for emitting £50,000 in paper currency.¹⁰⁰ When the governor and council announced that they would support a bill for only half this amount of paper money, the word quickly spread that several hundred country people were gathering for an armed march on Philadelphia. Rural farmers would join urban laborers "to apply first to the Assembly and then Storm the Governor, but with the Council, at least some of them it was to have been the hardest." These "unthinking People," these "misled People spirited up to Mischief," according to the governor and chief proprietary officers, were ready to club their opponents into submission and there were many in Philadelphia who "would be well content to see some scores knock'd on the Head, their estates plundered and their Houses in ashes."¹⁰¹ Keith's successor, Governor Patrick Gordon, was a man with a lifetime of military experience who knew how to beat an orderly retreat. While condemning the insurrectionists and issuing a proclamation against such unlawful assemblies, he agreed to a compromise paper money bill and privately confided to his proprietary masters that "the general Disposition which appeared everywhere for the Success of the Bill . . . obliged me to give Ground rather than exasperate the People by a flat Denial."¹⁰²

As in the other port towns, the ideal of the common good could no longer be sustained in an era of such political contention. Political spokesmen on both sides continued to inveigh against politicking on behalf of private interests, insisting that the unitary public good should be the transcendent concern.¹⁰³ But this was only a ritual affirmation of older principles which many acknowledged were no longer applicable. Whatever they thought about the desirability of serving the common good, Keithian candidates were firmly pledged to follow instructions from their constituents.¹⁰⁴ One Philadelphia assemblyman, who voted contrary to instructions in 1728, was obliged to write a pamphlet explaining that, although the usual practice was for the legislators to take "their Instructions from them [the voters] how to act in the Assembly," he had not "come under such Agreement" with others on the ticket "but thought that when I was chosen, I was at Liberty to follow the Dictates of my own Conscience."[105]

By 1730, as prosperity returned to Philadelphia, artisan-oriented politics began to wane. Never in the next decade did political discourse and electoral behavior attain the boiling point reached in the 1720s. As politics in economically depressed New York heated up in the 1730s, they cooled down in prospering Philadelphia. Andrew Hamilton, who was branded in Philadelphia as one of the three main "petty Tyrants of this Province," a "Rich Miser," an "infringer of our Priviledges," the "Conivator Pedago" who worked to reduce "the Commonality to their Duty again of eating Bread by the sweat of their Brows, without taking any Notice of their belching Curses," became the hero of the popular party in New York for his defense of Zenger, who printed the attacks of the laboring classes against monied merchant oppressors.[106]

When political debate did flare up briefly in the 1730s the ideological legacy of the previous decade became apparent. Laboring men were exhorted to stand up to those who in derision called them "Leather Aprons, the Mobb, the Scum," and to guard against every encroachment on their liberties and well-being, not just on election day but every day.[107] In the clearest enunciation of the interest group conception of politics yet heard in America, the voters were instructed that "it is your Right, to ask for anything that may be for the Publick Good, or which is the same thing, your own Good." Three years later, "Z" and "Anti-Z" squared off in the *Pennsylvania Gazette* and the *American Weekly Mercury* in a debate that codified the ripening debate over society and government. Popular government, argued Z, was the best counterpoise to power-hungry, incipient despots. Moreover, voters should cast their ballots "in Favour of themselves," for in pressing their own particular interests, "which is extremely natural," they would advance "the real publick Good," which could not be trusted to those who claimed superior knowledge in society. The conservative Anti-Z castigated such a "loose Republican Scheme," advocated a balance between "devouring Prerogatives and a licentious ungovernable Freedom," and argued that people's decisions in favor of themselves were "seditious." Who had truly known oppression, he asked? Rather, under the pretension of wrongdoing by the elite, the "inferior rank" had attempted to "usurp the necessary Prerogatives of their Superiors" and developed "mistaken Notions of their own Powers." Z acknowledged the need to obey magistrates but reminded his imperious adversary that "we are all born naturally equal" and possess the right and the duty to turn out of office those magistrates who did not rule wisely and equitably.[108]

By now Philadelphia had passed from depression to prosperity. But perceptions of how the political process actually worked, as opposed to ideal conceptions of how it should work, had been fixed in people's minds. Z's arguments were part of no new political mobilization for the achievement of specific goals. They were a clarification of changes in political ideology produced by the previous era of dislocation and class antagonism and subscribed to by many in the community. When economic difficulties and political contention returned, a clearer notion of how to respond—and an ideology sustaining the response—would already be at hand. As for the elite, such as anti-Z, they had discovered the "balance theory" by now prevalent in England, which formulated a persistent tension among the one, the few, and the many and contained the many within this conceptual structure.

Thus, in all the seaport towns the economic stress and social tensions of the 1720s and 1730s subjected the conception of an indivisible public good, or commonweal, to great pressure. The pressure, in fact, proved too great for the corporate ideology of a single harmonious community to withstand. Pursuit of the common good was evermore seen as a rhetorical cloak employed by those enjoying elevated status and material wealth to hide their covert selfish interests.

Ironically, the only solution to this abuse of service to the community was to adopt the self-interested tactics of one's self-interested enemies. If there was no organic unity, then people must struggle, whatever their social position, to defend their rights and enhance their own opportunities. Competition had replaced consensus and in a competitive world people must look to their own self-preservation.

Seaport dwellers acted according to such perceptions of the world long before they dared to enunciate an ideology justifying such a mode of behavior. This was especially true in Boston, where the ancient concept of covenant made talk of pursuing self-interest especially obnoxious. In pumping for a private land bank in 1721, John Wise ventured out of the ideological cocoon of covenant long enough to suggest guardedly that men ought to work for their own interests and that out of competing self-interests the common good might be served. But Wise was a rarity among his generation; few others could speak from an understanding that the New England way of life "had subsided from the lofty vision of the founders into getting a living."[109] Most other writers continued to invoke the traditional rhetoric of covenant and commonweal, while simultaneously participating in political partisanship that belied their pronouncements.[110] Lower-class Bostonians, harking to a simpler ethic of what was just and equitable, simply took matters into their own hands when the occasion demanded it.

In New York and Philadelphia, where the secular concept of community was not so massively reinforced by the religious concept of covenant, the ideological breakthrough proved easier. In the 1720s Philadelphia's Francis Rawle, a small merchant and pamphleteering leader of the paper money movement, found it necessary to speak against self-interest as a spring of human action and to warn against the "mis-rule of a Multitude, or a Rabble, as at Naples under Massanello."[111] Within a decade, however, the debate between Z and Anti-Z demonstrated how far not only the excusing but also the celebrating of self-interested behavior had proceeded. In order to dislodge from power or stave off threats from the conservative gentry, who continued to utter phrases about the necessity of an indivisible body politic or attempted to confine the mass of people by assigning them a share of power within a "balanced" system, the popular leaders of the seaport towns had to articulate an ideology which assumed a fractured community and thus legitimized interest group politics. The militant action of those beneath them required no less.

PART TWO

CONFLICT AND REVOLUTION
1740-1776

Wise Statesmen only, know the Rule of right
For what is just, is hid from vulgar Sight;
The silent Ox, and the lowly Ass, must bear,
Such loads as Wisdom gives them to their Share;
'The base born Herd,' the Rabble of Mankind,
By Nature too for Burdens were design'd.

New-York Journal, July 19, 1770

However meanly some People may think about the Pop-
ulace or Mob of a Country, it is certain, that the power
or Strength of every FREE Country depends entirely
upon the Populace.

Boston Gazette, July 25, 1768

7

The Renewal of War
and the Decline of Boston

Between the late 1730s and the mid-1750s the seaport towns experienced the first of two eras of boom and bust that would carry them to the eve of the American Revolution. All three had reached populations of 13,000 to 16,000 by mid-century, all were closely connected to the rapid economic development of England in this era, and all were drawn into a European war that was international in scope. Even in their earliest years, the seaboard urban centers had never been independent of economic developments overseas. Now they found themselves drawn further into worldwide commercial networks and increasingly affected by international conflict. They were becoming locked into an impersonal market world, which on the one hand promised new opportunities for wealth and material comfort and on the other produced discontinuities in the demand for goods and services, periodic economic dislocation, unemployment more widespread than ever before experienced, alterations in customary patterns of work, and a redistribution of wealth.

Urban dwellers in Boston, New York, and Philadelphia struggled to comprehend the new shape of things, to fathom the advancing market economy, to make sense of the way that urban growth and economic development were altering their lives. Part of the adjustment to change was a halting acceptance of a new system of values that legitimated private profit seeking, rationalized the abandonment of economic regulation, and projected a future economic world in which men's energies, cut loose from age-old mercantilist controls instituted to promote the good of all, would produce a common good far better. This new economic thinking was corollary to the ideas about political pursuit of self-interest.

The colonial towns were reconnoitering an ideological terrain traversed by their English cousins a generation before. By the late seventeenth century, almost a hundred years before Adam Smith published *The Wealth of Nations*, political economists were writing about the emerging market economy in which individuals responded to economic opportunities as private persons and operated outside of traditional moral restraints. Large gains in agricultural productivity and huge increases in international trade gave promise of a society which had "a comfortable margin between productive capacities and survival needs" and could therefore allow people to pursue their private gain in open competition.¹ Indeed, some economic thinkers attributed England's burgeoning wealth to the fact that traditional virtues of frugality and public-spirited restraint were being replaced by aggressive individualism and self-indulgence. The new formula for national prosperity assumed that if each individual sought his or her own improvement, all these separate efforts would produce, through a mysterious process later described by Adam Smith as the "invisible hand," a natural harmony and a prosperous, free society. "Thus the unmistakable direction of English growth," writes Joyce Appleby, "involved modes of behavior and political stances diametrically opposed to the constitutional ideal of the disinterested citizen living on his own, cultivating the public weal, and committing his virtue to the maintenance of a rightly-ordered constitutional monarchy."² By unfettering human energies, more goods would be produced and channeled into new overseas markets, which would generate more profits for investment at home, which would enrich all involved in the new economic process.

In 1714 a London physician and litterateur, Bernard Mandeville, codified almost a generation of inchoate thinking in this vein in a remarkably cynical allegory entitled *The Fable of the Bees, or Private Vices, Public Benefits*. Mandeville's beehive was economic society, filled with every kind of Englishman, including "the sharpers, the parasites, the pimps, the players, the pickpockets, and all the others who fed on their industrious neighbors."³ When moralists (the Tory politicians of the early eighteenth century who were decrying corruption, luxuriousness, and the decay of public spirit) tried to reform the hive, the bees became ascetic, moral-bound, and economically backward. The hive, though pure, was poor. England, it was implied, had reached a point in history when prosperity required an abandonment of the old virtues. Self-denial, moral rectitude, and the subordination of private to public interests lay as dead weights on the economic order. For national prosperity, something different was needed: encouragement of acquisitive appetites (though not among the laboring classes), the abandonment of an overriding concern for the public good, and acceptance of the notion that "the self-seeking drive appeared more powerful than institutional efforts to mold people's actions." Mandeville was in the forefront of those who redefined the public good as national prosperity rather than the achievement of a moral community.⁴ For the bees of England, Mandeville had curt advice: "Then leave complaints: fools only strive, To make a great, an honest hive."⁵

Of course, the new economic order in England had its dark side. The transition to a free market economy left a huge number of people caught between the old and new systems. Enclosure of land increased agricultural productivity but also threw off the land thousands of rural laborers who had to take to the roads in search of work. In the towns the capacity to offer employment was never sufficient to engage the productive energies of the class of impoverished, propertyless people who seemed to grow ever larger in numbers. By the end of the seventeenth century most towns were searching for ways to employ the poor in public workhouses where their handiwork would support them and relieve the growing pressure on property owners for poor taxes. England's rising national productivity and international trade had multiplied the collective wealth of the society but ironically left in limbo hundreds of thousands of impoverished, underemployed souls.

Nowhere could this be seen more vividly than in London. The capital city that rose from the ashes of the disastrous fire of 1666 was unmistakably a flourishing place by the early eighteenth century. But it was also a city of Hogarthian misery, where by 1750 less than one-third of the babies born to laboring people survived infancy; where disease, alcoholism, and prostitution were rampant among the lower classes; where starvation was a common sight; and where the unemployed numbered in the tens of thousands.[6] Personal ambition and the acceptance of profit seeking had replaced the rule of the magistrate as the primary incentive to economic activity, and the "liberalized" economic relations that now held sway produced a material utopia for some but a living hell for many more.

In the American coastal towns, adherence to the older notions of public spiritedness and common goals lasted much longer than in England. But the seaport dwellers could not avoid being drawn into the expanding English commercial system. The development of intensive sugar agriculture based on slave labor in the West Indies provided a growing market for North American fish and agricultural products; the growth of colonial population magnified the demand for English consumer goods; and the increasing importance of the North American colonies in the British empire produced a swelling flow of English credit, English traders, and English officials who intruded more and more on local economies. By the second quarter of the eighteenth century the commercial penetration of the market was well advanced. In one way the American colonists had far less reason to resist the new economic thinking, for their environment had been abundantly blessed, giving rise to the optimistic notion that private acquisition might be pursued at nobody's expense. One man's gain need not be another man's loss. Yet the traditional communitarian thinking hung on stubbornly, for, after all, Boston and Philadelphia were the centers of two of the boldest utopian experiments in modern history.

Even if they had not fulfilled the dreams of their founders, the City on the Hill and the City of Brotherly Love were still regarded by their inhabitants as moral outposts in a corrupt world.

This view would on occasion receive a kind of negative support from occurrences in England. One such event was the South Sea Bubble of 1720. Organized by a group of shrewd financial capitalists, the South Sea Company had offered to buy up government debts of some £9 million in exchange for a monopoly of trade to the South Seas. Chartered under the Tory government in 1711, the company embarked on a series of financial manipulations that by 1720 put it at the center of the speculative mania overtaking France and England. In that year the company's directors announced audacious plans to take over the entire national debt and expand their operations to Africa. Shares in the company began to soar in price, from about £128 in January 1720 to more than £1,000 in August. England was caught up in a frenzy of speculation, with new joint-stock companies being founded every week, fortunes being made overnight by avid speculators, and the idea spreading that so long as credit was infinitely expandable, as it seemed to be, something could be made out of nothing.[7] "Credit was the new alchemy," one historian has written, and as long as public confidence remained no end was in sight.[8] Public confidence, however, lasted only until August 18, 1720. On that day, as investors frantically began to unload their South Sea Company stock amidst rumors that many of the speculative joint-stock companies were worthless, the collapse began. Fortunes had been made by some and lost by others. But for Tory critics of finance capitalism in England, and for many Americans, the bursting of the South Sea Bubble was a sober warning that the new economic spirit was a national disease instead of a formula for national prosperity. Speculating, stockjobbing, and unbridled economic ambition were revealed as forms of a public-be-damned mentality that led to chaos and corruption.

As the two conceptions of economic life contended for ascendancy in the English mind, the merchants, shopkeepers, land speculators, and some ambitious artisans of the American seaport towns hewed more and more to the new economic dictates, although they continued to mouth the old precepts of the corporate community. Speculation on the scale witnessed in Augustan England was hardly possible and there were no fantastic schemes such as the South Sea Company to allure those infected with the speculative fever. But on a smaller scale the integration of the seaport economies into a more international and more volatile network of commercial transactions had the same effect—the creation of a world in which "men's livelihoods depended on their success in selling goods, labor, and land, which, insofar as the market was concerned, were commodities and not aspects of social relations."[9] "*Let no man seek his own, but every man another's wealth,*" Cotton Mather preached in 1710. "For men to *overreach* others, because they find them *ignorant*, or screw grievously upon them, only because they are poor and low, and in great necessities; to keep up the *necessaries* of human life . . . at an immoderate price, merely because other people want them . . . *'tis an abomination!'*[10] By the 1740s and 1750s the modernized clergy of the urban centers could rarely be heard enunciating such thoughts.[11]

In the period from 1739 to 1754 war was the most powerful engine of change and when it came it affected all three seaports, whereas earlier in the century it had mainly touched only Boston. The effects of the war, however, differed from port to port, for proximity to the enemy and connections with West Indian and European markets were key variables in the experiences of the three towns. Also interacting with the economic alterations produced by war were local conditions peculiar to the regional economies served by each of the ports.

The renewal of international conflict began formally in October 1739, when England declared war on Spain. The immediate cause of hostilities was the ear of an English sea captain, Robert Jenkins, deprived of that appendage in 1731 by Spanish authorities who rightly charged that he was a smuggler trading English goods to the Spanish Main in violation of the *asiento* agreement of 1713 between the two commercial rivals.[12] Jenkins did not bother to bring his severed ear before the public until 1738, and when he did it was as a crude but effective promotional trick for whipping up war fever against Spain, who English policymakers had decided must be chastened for the decision to transfer certain commercial privileges in the Spanish colonies from England to France. The real cause of the war was not the heavy-handed search procedures that the Spanish employed in trying to stop British smugglers but the English desire to stifle the trade of its European rivals and gain commercial hegemony in the Atlantic basin. It was thus to be expected that the Anglo-Spanish War, which began in 1739, should merge five years later into a much larger war between England and France.[13]

In Boston, the advent of hostilities provided an immediate tonic to shipbuilding and shipfitting, since much of the commercial war against Spain was to be fought by privateers—ships with commissions called letters of marque and reprisal which authorized them to attack enemy shipping and bring captured vessels into port for condemnation and sale. Beginning in the summer of 1739, business boomed along the waterfront for shipwrights, gunsmiths, blacksmiths, sailmakers, mastmakers, and caulkers, as about a dozen merchant ships of 100 tons and more were refitted for naval war.[14] Boston's shipyards hummed with activity and full pay was the rule. According to one report 164 ships were on the stocks in 1741, in contrast to some 40 to 50 constructed annually in the late 1730s.[15]

Wartime privateering not only benefitted artisans associated with ship construction but held out the possibility of spectacular rewards for the most impoverished men in society as well. The letter of marque and reprisal was what transformed the pirate, who committed robbery and violence at sea, into a legal plunderer of vessels belonging to the enemy of the government which commissioned him. Any ship flying the flag of the enemy was fair game and any prize brought back to the home port was promptly sold off and the spoils divided among the privateer's owners, ship captain, and crew. Moreover, the line separating legal and illegal piracy was difficult to maintain since no government, once it had commissioned a privateer, could "prevent him from broadening out his operations into piracy, especially if a merely privateering cruise was proving unprofitable."[16] Privateering on a small scale had occurred since the seventeenth century, but it was only in 1739 that it became regarded as a major field of entrepreneurial activity in the American seaports. The war against Spain laid open the possibility that the stupendous cargoes of bullion "that regularly accumulated at American terminals, such as Porto Bello and Cartagena, awaiting shipment across the Atlantic," could enrich the inhabitants of Boston, New York, Philadelphia, and every other American port town.[17] Through the agency of the privateer, who violently expropriated private property, profits could be reaped on a scale that was unthinkable in the realm of mundane business transactions, where profits accrued slowly from the margin between the purchase and sale price of a commodity. Privateering epitomized the pursuit of private gain, for it literally impoverished some while enriching others and was allowed only because of ruptures within the international community.

The pot of gold at the end of every privateer's rainbow proved agonizingly elusive, however, for most Boston buccaneers. The mortality rate on all seagoing vessels was extraordinarily high in the eighteenth century, not so much from enemy fire as from shipboard epidemics. Hence, many would-be overnight fortune builders never saw their home port again. Even when rich prizes were captured, the dividend for the ordinary sailor was surprisingly small. In the most spectacular capture of the war, the seizure in 1746 of the 400-ton French *Soleil*, which was carrying a cargo valued at £30,000, the share of the prize for each ordinary seaman was only £78.[18] Obtaining prize money often took months or even years. Cases were frequently contested and adjudications by vice-admiralty courts were drawn-out affairs. Sailors who had little capital to live on while awaiting a court decision were often obliged to sell their claims to prize money at a discount in order to meet current expenses.[19] Finally, because most seamen received no wages on privateers, but signed on solely for "shares" in any prizes taken, many came home empty-handed after a year or more at sea.

Although they cannot be measured precisely, the rewards of privateering seem to have fallen chiefly to the mariners who resisted the main chance and contented themselves with berths aboard merchant vessels. Privateering created a temporary boom for merchant seamen because it took a hundred men or more to man a heavily armed privateer, whereas merchant ships usually sailed with crews of five to ten.[20] This enormous enlargement of demand for the services of seamen brought a rapid rise in wages. By 1745 merchants were offering more than double the prewar pay and in the next year, according to the selectmen of Boston, mariners' pay was at "an Extravagant height."[21] Less unpaid layover time in port also aided seamen. In peacetime mariners often had to wait weeks for a ship to obtain a full cargo. Now the situation was reversed; fully loaded ships waited for crews, sometimes, as one Boston merchant complained, until "their Cargo have been almost or quite Ruined."[22]

The risks and rewards of wartime entrepreneurial activity operated at a different level for members of the merchant community. For those with only small amounts of capital to invest, decent returns could be realized from small-scale war contracting. Thus, Benjamin Hallowell profited modestly when he landed a contract in 1748 to build the first frigate type man-of-war in America for the royal navy, a ship of over 400 tons carrying twenty-eight guns on her 110-foot frame.[23] Larger gains came through provisioning contracts that were usually garnered by cultivating connections with men of importance in the British military establishment. Benjamin Colman, son of merchant John Colman, and his brother-in-law, Nathaniel Sparhawk, started a Boston mercantile house in 1741 and soon had the contract for uniforms for the Massachusetts troops bound for an assault on Louisbourg as well as a contract for supplying the Anglo-American garrison after it captured the French stronghold. Colman and Sparhawk got these contracts not through competitive bidding but because Sparhawk was married to the daughter of William Pepperell, who commanded the New England forces in Canada.[24] Such favors did not guarantee financial success, for many of those who played for higher stakes overextended themselves. If they were caught short when their creditors made demands or if their ships fell prey to Spanish or French privateers, they could plummet from the heights and live out their days in bankruptcy. Such was the case with Benjamin Colman, who was in financial difficulties by the end of the war.[25]

For the shrewdest men, war offered incredible opportunities. In Boston one of the masters of the new era of economic opportunism was Thomas Hancock, upon whose war-built fortunes his less commercially astute nephew, John, would later construct a shining political career. Hancock began as a minister's son, which in the eighteenth century gave him status but not financial leverage. In the decade before the outbreak of the Anglo-Spanish War, he started shakily on a business career as a bookseller. Marriage to the daughter of a well-to-do Boston merchant provided a toehold in the larger commercial arena and perhaps enough capital to invest in shares in several vessels in the early 1730s. Small successes led to larger ones and by the end of the decade Hancock was one of the town's most successful traders. Money came in from trading voyages to Newfoundland, where rum was exchanged for whale oil and fish; from cargoes of New England wood products and food supplies sent to the West Indies, where they were exchanged for sugar; and not least of all from cargoes of tea smuggled into Boston from Dutch and French ports in the West Indies.[26] Not every year was better than the last, but by 1735 Hancock had amassed enough wealth to pay £1,000 in local currency for a large lot where he began building a house worthy of a London merchant. It was not located near the docks, where men of all classes mixed, but on a pasture on Beacon Hill above the bustle of seaport life. Local artisans erected the structure itself, but for ornamentation such as marble hearths and wallpaper decorated with tufts of wool only London imports would do.[27]

When war came, Hancock was ready to send out privateers in pursuit of rich prizes, to supply military expeditions, and to increase profits on inflated prices that usually went with wartime demand. When the first big campaign of the war took shape—a naval expedition in 1740 against Cartagena and Havana, Spanish strongholds in the Caribbean—Hancock was one of the suppliers of beef and pork. When a group of Boston merchants decided to invest in a small fleet of privateers in order to engage in private warfare for legal profit, Hancock was prominent among them. And so long as enemy privateers did not infest the northern waters, which were controlled by France rather than Spain, Hancock's usual trading voyages returned excellent profits.[28]

The entry of France into the war in 1744 made European and West Indian trade far more risky because the French filled the seas with privateers that harassed Anglo-American shipping. Patrolling the northern Atlantic waters from St. Lawrence ports, the French intercepted Boston shipping, sent the cost of imported goods soaring, and vastly increased the risk of all oceanic voyages. But for well-connected merchants such as Hancock, these importunities of war were more than offset by military contracting on a level never before known in the colonies. In the contest against the French, the British shored up their military outposts in Newfoundland and Nova Scotia and then in 1745 planned the largest assault ever attempted on the pivot of France's North American empire—the fortress of Louisbourg on Cape Breton Island, guarding the approach to the St. Lawrence River. As his biographer has said, Hancock "hungered" for the supply contracts associated with this attempt to wipe the French from the North American map and "toiled greedily to win them."[29] Getting business depended on the quality of one's connections in London with officials of the Board of Ordnance, the paymaster general, and the

Treasury. "The history of these army supplies," writes one historian, "is a sorry tale, in which spiteful rivalry and slim intrigue are blended with servility, bungling, and corrpution."[30] Bribes, hours of letter writing, and lavish entertainment of those in strategic positions to influence English officialdom were a part of the game, but it was a game in which the stakes were so exceptionally high—£200,000 sterling for the Louisbourg expedition alone—that Hancock and other Boston merchants were willing to play it as they had never played before.[31]

By the end of the war Hancock had amassed profits that probably exceeded £12,000 sterling. All of Boston witnessed what war could do, for the man who had sold books from a tiny shop on Drawbridge Street fifteen years before was now placing an order in London for a four-horse chariot with the interior lined in scarlet and the doors emblazoned with a heraldic shield. Hancock also instructed his London agent to send a London coachman, for a man of Hancock's affluence could no longer make do with a body servant recruited from the lower class of his own town. It was not coincidence that at war's end the three wealthiest men in Boston —Hancock, Charles Apthorp, and John Erving—were the town's three largest war contractors.[32]

While Thomas Hancock surveyed what war could yield from his Beacon Hill mansion, the scene in the crooked streets of the North End of Boston was not so roseate. Among roughly the bottom quarter of society, where economic dislocation and price inflation had impoverished many in the prewar years and made ascent up the economic ladder almost impossible, the war promised one main opportunity—service in the cause against Spain and France, either by shipping out on privateers or enlisting for the volunteer army. More than a thousand men were recruited in and around Boston in August 1740 for the naval expedition against Porto Bello, Panama and Cartagena, Columbia, and, according to Thomas Hancock, "had 2000 been wanted wee could have had 'em."[33] That so many men of eastern Massachusetts were available at low pay indicates how effectively war could serve as a sponge for mopping up the unemployed and underemployed. Some of the recruits were adventurous young bloods in search of glory and inspired by the thought of marching off as Christian warriors to smash the papist enemy. They also dreamed of sharing in the mountains of gold and silver that recruiting agents assured them could be plundered from the Spanish. Another 500 men were recruited for Caribbean service in 1741 and 1,000 more were added between 1742 and 1744 for campaigns against the Spanish enemy and on the northeastern frontier. An even larger number found themselves involuntarily serving the king after being caught in the impressment dragnet that the royal navy ships threw over Boston during these years. Of some 3,500 Massachusetts men recruited during the Anglo-Spanish War, it is likely that a sixth were drawn from the streets of Boston. Many of them were apprentices, servants, and underage sons, but hundreds of others were men from the laboring classes.[34]

When the Spanish War widened into a conflict with the French in 1744, a second phase of military recruitment began. Once the decision had been made to unleash a mighty expedition against the massive French fortress at Louisbourg, the "Gibraltar of the New World," the problem was to raise 3,000 volunteers as Massachusetts's quota for the combined New England forces. The pay was less than ordinary seamen received in peacetime, only 25 shillings per month and an enlistment bounty of £1. But Massachusetts filled its quota. Attempts were made to raise still another 3,500 men for an overland expedition against Quebec in 1746, but by this time most of the available manpower within the lower levels of eastern Massachusetts society had been exhausted.[35] War had temporarily solved the problem of underemployment in maritime Massachusetts but in a way that was to compound prewar difficulties.

The recruitment for the 1745 Louisbourg expedition and the fate of its participants and their families provide an important window through which to view the differential effects of war on urban society. From the very beginning there was strong opposition to the expedition because it was seen as the brainchild of the ambitious militarist governor William Shirley and was thought to be beyond the human and financial resources of Massachusetts, even if the French fortress, which had been under construction since 1720, could be overawed. When Shirley proposed his plan to the House of Representatives in January 1745, it was voted down, for most of the members were "struck with amazement at the proposal" and thought it had "no rational prospect of success." Only after considerable lobbying by Boston's merchants and by the fishermen of Marblehead, Salem, and other coastal towns, whose trade had been interrupted by French privateers, was the plan narrowly approved.[36] Primarily, they saw the expedition as an opportunity to drive the French from the lucrative cod fisheries off the Newfoundland coast, thus guaranteeing a New England monopoly in that area. "By the possession of Cape Breton," wrote one apologist for the Louisbourg campaign, "we are become, or have it in our Power to become, entire Masters of the cod-fishery, which, as Charlevoix asserts, is of more value than the Mines of Peru."[37] The hope of larger profits in the fish trade and "the pleasant prospect of large supply orders to fill" finally changed opposition to Shirley's plan into grudging approval.[38]

Recruiting 3,000 volunteers became the major problem once the decision was made. Since the colony was still ridden with debts incurred in similar expeditions a generation before, it could not support high wages for the recruits. So Shirley and his supporters launched a propaganda campaign to implant the notion that the supposedly impregnable French citadel was protected by a demoralized army eager to surrender to anyone who would deliver them from the miseries of garrison life, and, even more important, it was widely advertised that merchants, army officers, and others at Louisbourg possessed such a rich store of money and goods that every volunteer who shared in the plunder would become a wealthy man. Some of Boston's ministers lent their support to the enlistment efforts by making ringing appeals to Protestant duty and talking up the glory of defeating the anti-Christ of the north. But according to the main student of the recruitment campaign, the extant letters and journals written by the Louisbourg volunteers show "that the desire for plunder was by far the most important motivating factor as far as enlisting in the expedition was concerned."[39] Those with families were assured that if they were killed, their widows would receive four months pay. Though Louisbourg was not quite Havana or Cartagena, there would be riches aplenty for all.

By February 1745 about 3,000 Massachusetts men had been enlisted for the expedition.[40] Now it was necessary to recruit another 1,000 seamen to man the transports that would carry them to Cape Breton Island. At first, £8 per month "old tenor" (worth £1.1 sterling) was proposed, slightly under the pay offered the land troops. But the recruitment of soldiers and naval impressments had so depleted the poorest ranks of eastern Massachusetts society that, according to the chairman of the General Court's Commission of War, "we are put to it to get 'em" for double the pay.[41] Finally, the mariners were rounded up and fifty-one transports and armed sloops weighed anchor from Boston on Sunday, April 4, 1745 in the largest expeditionary force ever launched from the American colonies. George Whitefield, the fiery evangelist preacher, was at dockside to inspire the recruits with a passionate sermon. Not by coincidence, Whitefield took as his text: "As many as were distressed, as many as were discontented, as many as were in debt, came to David, and he became a captain over them."[42] Fired with patriotic zeal and antipopery, which were hallmarks of the Protestant lower classes on both sides of the Atlantic, an expeditionary force primarily composed of the most dispossessed elements in New England society sailed east under a flag emblazoned with Whitefield's motto, "Nil desperandum Christo duce." Neither the motto nor the farewell sermons, however, could conceal the fact that the grand design against Louisbourg was still strongly opposed by many in Massachusetts, had been refused aid by Pennsylvania, New Jersey, and New York, and stood primarily to profit its merchant suppliers.

All New England rejoiced in June 1745 when news arrived in Boston that the impossible had been achieved: a six-week siege of the French fortress had brought surrender by its commander. Boston's ministers saw God's guiding hand at work, maritime men smiled at the prospect that the lucrative northeastern fisheries would now be solely in American hands, and all New Englanders rejoiced that the Indians allied with the French would no longer attack the New England frontier. Once the flush of victory passed, Boston confronted the costs of war. Long before the Louisbourg expedition sailed, it was known how staggering the losses could be in protracted amphibious operations, for of the 3,600 Americans recruited for the Cartagena expedition in 1740-1741 not more than one-fifth had returned. Among the 500 Massachusetts volunteers, only about one-tenth survived yellow fever, dysentery, and outright starvation.[43]

Historians have made only tentative efforts to count up Massachusetts's losses in the campaigns of 1745-1746. William Douglass, who wrote most extensively on the war, believed that of the 3,600 army volunteers who served at Louisbourg only about 150 died in the fighting; but in the eleven months of garrison duty that followed, dysentery killed "one half of our militia . . . like rotten sheep."[44] Another Bostonian, who commanded some of the Massachusetts troops in Nova Scotia, thought that the "northern Colonies" "have lost above *seven thousand* of their most active and industrious Inhabitants" in five years of war with France. Surveying the human wreckage at the end of the war, Douglass claimed that nearly one-fifth of the province's adult males had been lost. This would have been about 8,000 men and if correct would have amounted to a social and demographic crisis.[45] Even if we cut the casualty estimate by more than half, figuring about 450 fatalities at Cartagena, 2,000 at Louisbourg, 500 in camp while awaiting the abortive attack on Quebec in 1746 and in frontier garrison duty throughout the war, and 500 at sea on privateers, merchantmen, and royal navy ships, the losses were very great, amounting to about 2 percent of the colony's population or about 8 percent of the males sixteen years and older. It seems likely that Boston, which contributed more heavily to the war in proportion to its population than inland areas, lost at least 400 men. There can be little doubt of the punishing blow which this loss of life struck at the colony's productive capacity, for such casualty rates exceed the accepted statistics for the death rate in the colonies during the American Revolution and in the Union during the Civil War.[46]

The social ravages of war can be seen indirectly in a number of surviving records. A census taken in Boston in 1742 reported some 1,200 widows, "one thousand whereof are in low circumstances."[47] If these figures are accurate, then 30 percent of Boston's adult women were widowed, many by the disastrous Cartagena expedition. The Louisbourg campaign added hundreds of new widows to the town's poor rolls.[48] Even three years after peace was declared Boston's tax assessors reported 1,153 widows in the town, "of which at least half are very poor."[49] Boston's enormous contributions to the war account in part for the drop in the number of taxable polls during this period. They fell from 3,395 in 1738 to 2,972 in 1741 to about 2,660 in 1745.[50] War had shortened the list of taxable inhabitants and lengthened the list of those requiring poor relief. Before the attack on Louisbourg, some critics predicted that if Governor Shirley's grand strategy failed, as they expected, "such a shock would be given to the province that half a century would not recover us to our present state."[51] Ironically, the expedition triumphed, but in succeeding it brought such human and financial devastation that it was lamented for years thereafter. For hundreds of Boston families the glory of bringing French Catholic power to its knees in the frozen Canadian wilderness was slight comfort, for they had to reflect upon the victory in homes that were fatherless, husbandless, and dependent upon charity for food and fuel. Even among those who returned, there was little to celebrate, for the promised plunder never materialized and Louisbourg itself, earned with the blood of several thousand New Englanders, was promptly handed back to the French at the end of the war.[52]

For a large number of Bostonians, located between the prosperous war contractors of Hancock's circle and the impoverished war widows, tl Anglo-French conflict meant full employment and steady income. But as in the wars of the previous generation, high wages were tempered by the imposition of hefty war taxes and the last reeling stages of the currency crisis. Taxable Bostonians had paid an average of about 12 shillings annually from 1730 to 1734 and about 20 shillings sterling from 1735 to 1739. Nearly three-quarters of this went for town taxes since provincial expenses in peacetime were insubstantial. From 1740 to 1744, as the costs of war sent provincial expenditures soaring, the burden per taxable averaged almost 33 shillings. In the next five years, at the height of the war economy, 50 shillings were extracted annually from the average taxpayer —a fourfold increase in fifteen years.[53] Increases of this magnitude were so onerous that the collectors had great difficulty in collecting the assessments. Tax arrearages grew and the selectmen began borrowing money from wealthy merchants to pay immediate expenses, while abating the taxes of the insolvent. War taxes, William Douglass believed, had cost Bostonians one-quarter of their estates, and the selectmen sighed that taxes were "so very Burthensome, that many, even of the Richest of the Inhabitants are groaning under the Weight of them."[54]

Coupled with taxes was the continuing depreciation of Massachusetts currency. Despite contractionary measures to reduce the amount of paper in circulation instituted under Governor Shirley's leadership in the early 1740s, the value of Massachusetts currency continued to plummet. By 1741 it took 28 shillings of Massachusetts money to purchase one ounce of silver. When the Anglo-French War began in 1744, all pretenses of limiting the supply of paper money were laid aside, for nothing less than running the printing presses could finance the war. Between June 1744 and March 1746, £346,000 in "new tenor" (or £1,384,000 old tenor) bills of credit were issued. The expedition against Quebec required still more. From mid-1746 to mid-1748 another £354,000 (£1,416,000 old tenor) was issued. Faith in the new currency was badly undermined; its value continued the downward flight until by 1749 it took 60 shillings in provincial bills to buy a single ounce of silver. The sterling value of Massachusetts currency had fallen to less than one-tenth of its face value.[55]

No respecter of the laws of equity, hyperinflation distributed its burdens unequally. Those on fixed incomes, such as clergymen, schoolteachers, and sometimes widows, were usually heavy losers because their money would buy less and less. An anonymous clergyman wailed publicly in 1747 that when his congregation had voted him £100 per year a decade before, he could buy his weekly provisions for £1.5. The same articles now, with shoes selling at 60 shillings and milk at 4 shillings a gallon, brought his shopping bill to £15. His congregation had tripled his salary but prices had gone up ninefold.[56] Wage earners also suffered, though not quite so heavily since they demanded wage increases to match rising prices. "Merchants, Tradesmen and Labourers rise in their Demands," one writer explained, "whereas Salary-men . . . lie at the Mercy of others."[57] On the other hand, anyone who ran into debt was assured that the longer he postponed payment, the more he had to gain. The repeated efforts of the legislature to pass laws allowing an adjustment of debts according to the sterling exchange rate tell much about the lobbying of creditors, who resisted the notion that they should have to accept depreciated bills in settlement of accounts.[58] We cannot analyze precisely how the price inflation of the 1740s redistributed wealth in Boston, but it is generally assumed that those whose income goes almost entirely for the necessities of life are the most likely to suffer in such a situation. Even farther up the social scale, Boston's selectmen warned, "the Middling Sort of People are daily decreasing, many of them sinking into extream Poverty."[59]

The plight of those in the lower ranks of Boston society can be partially comprehended by examining the price of bread, the most important single item in their diet. Wheat prices had remained steady at about 14 shillings per bushel in the late 1730s but began to rise sharply in April 1740, propelled upward by what the *Boston Evening Post* called the "pernicious Practice" of some merchants who bought up large amounts of grain for immediate resale abroad. By June 1741 wheat hit an all-time high of 29 shillings per bushel. Prices declined to about 21 shillings by mid-1742 and remained there for the next four years. Then a second upward surge set in, again touched off by heavy overseas demand associated with the war. By late 1747 wheat in Boston cost 40 shillings per bushel. Not until it topped 50 shillings per bushel in 1749 did the upward trend subside. Profits for grain producers and merchants rose handsomely but for Boston's laboring poor the situation was vastly different.

A penny's worth of household bread measured six ounces in 1740, four ounces in 1745, three ounces in early 1747, two ounces by November 1747, and hardly an ounce in 1749.[60]

Bostonians struggled in the closing years of the war to understand the forces that had been unloosed in their society. In pamphlets and newspaper accounts they lamented the "continual Depreciation of the Bills of Credit" that made wages "fall greatly short of their real Value" and unfairly punished creditors.[61] They looked for the culprits upon whom public censure could be heaped. But they resisted the idea, which might have sufficed as an explanation in previous generations, that they had displeased their God. Nathaniel Appleton, a Cambridge clergyman, was certain that "oppression" against the many had been perpetrated. How had it come to pass? Unlike the ministers in the aftermath of Queen Anne's War, he did not attribute it to the profligacy of ordinary people who consumed more imported luxury goods than they could afford. Perhaps it was the "Merchants and other Traders" who "ran down" the intrinsic value of the paper bills, thus causing them to decline in value. Or perhaps it was the fault of the common people who purposely went into debt, hoping to pay off their obligations at a later date in depreciated bills. Whoever was to blame, one thing was clear. The long experience with paper money and the era of war had shattered all sense of community and commonweal. "A covetous selfish Spirit" now ran through the people and "every Man looks at his own Things, and not at the Things of others." Gone was a "publick Spirit" and in its place stood a "greedy Desire of Gain."[62]

The Boston clergy, of course, had been decrying the decline of public mindedness for generations. What was new in Appleton's jeremiad was the vision of a society in which interest groups pitted against each other produced not only moral decline but economic distress. Clergymen had long warned that for lack of a "publick spirit" the people of Massachusetts would lose their souls, prosper as they might. Appleton warned not only of spiritual decay but of economic oppression as well.

The same vision of society coming unhinged in its economic relations was portrayed by secular writers in the Boston press. Writing in the *Boston Evening Post* in 1748, an anonymous author analyzed the rapid rise of food prices. He noted that prices had been driven up by the heavy demand for provisions to supply the large Anglo-American garrison at the captured Louisbourg fortress and argued that the problem was compounded because the heavy loss of life among the Massachusetts soldiers had drained off agricultural manpower and thus cut into farm production. Alongside these uncontrollable effects of war he identified two ghastly examples of economic self-interestedness that also played a role in the rising cost of food. All around Boston, he charged, men were turning from their professions to become buyers and butchers of livestock.

They understood that by intercepting Boston's supplies and holding them for a time, they could drive up prices and take over the function of the town's butchers and hucksters. A thousand men in adjacent towns were practicing this kind of forestalling in a sort of economic warfare between rural and urban society.[63] The war against the hated French had not unified Massachusetts but had set one element against another in the pursuit of private gain.

The breakdown of an interdependent economic community was equally visible in the action of merchants in other colonies. Foodstuffs exporters in New York and Philadelphia piled up profits by engaging forty or fifty ships to sail under flags of truce in an illegal trade with the French and Spanish in the West Indies.[64] Bostonians paid more for their food because of shortages which could have been alleviated by grain and livestock from the middle colonies. Instead these merchants diverted commodities to the Caribbean, primarily to feed the enemy's slave populations there. Policymakers had prohibited this trade in hopes of starving France and Spain's West Indian colonies into submission, but northern merchants, seeking profit rather than humanitarian relief of the slaves, smuggled in cargoes at great profit. "How surprizing it is that for the Sake of Private Gain, his Majesty's declared Enemies should be thus openly assisted to destroy his Subjects," cried the *Post*. Here was the ultimate betrayal of the public good by private economic interest, a betrayal reflected in the food bill of every Bostonian. War had spurred the growing tendency of the free market, with everyone from the lowliest tar aboard a privateer to the largest war contractor and merchant smuggler seeking to capitalize on the new opportunities for self-aggrandizement.[65]

In both Philadelphia and New York the Anglo-Spanish and Anglo-French Wars brought prosperity that spread downward through the urban ranks in a way that made their experience far different from Boston's. Repeating the precedent of the last generation's wars, neither colony contributed much manpower to the expeditions against the Spanish Main and French Canada and thus were spared the personal anguish and public cost of large numbers of war widows.[66] Nor did either colony make large financial contributions to these expeditions. So, while the average Bostonian watched his annual tax bill rise to £2.5, New Yorkers paid an average of £1.2 from 1745 to 1749 and Philadelphians only 4 shillings.[67] Both middle Atlantic ports were concerned only to build fortifications to guard their harbors against French marauders and these were financed by public lotteries, which obviated the need to tax heavily or issue large amounts of paper money.[68] Instead of contributing money and lives to large-scale attacks against the centers of Spanish and French power, the seaports of the middle colonies concentrated on privateering and trade.

In New York, the Spanish War also spurred the economy. Governor

Clarke may have been overly enthusiastic when he wrote late in 1741 that New York was "never in so flourishing a condition as it is now," but it was true that housebuilding had resumed, shipbuilding had revived, and trade was on the mend.[69] Ship registrations stood at 53 on the eve of the war; by 1749 they had almost tripled to 157. Imports from England, which had averaged £114,000 sterling from 1736 to 1740, rose in the next two five-year periods to £124,000 and £195,000 respectively.[70] Much of this economic revival can be attributed to New York's emergence as the premier North American port for privateering and illegal trade. More than sixty privateers were commissioned between 1743 and 1748. In August 1744 four of them returned with six prizes worth £24,000 sterling. The fever of instant wealth grew so great that shares in privateering voyages were traded in the coffee houses, in a kind of early stock market where prices rose and fell on rumors of fabulous captures of enemy ships or losses to the enemy.[71] From 1739 to 1744 the Admiralty Court in New York condemned 32 prizes sold at vendue for about £167,000 sterling. In the next four years 213 prizes, worth £450,000, were condemned and sold in the city. New York, as one historian puts it, was the "grand beneficiary" in the wartime sweepstakes.[72]

The profits of legalized piracy were handsomely supplemented by the rewards of illegal trade. A "Fair Trader" of the port complained in 1748 that hardly a week went by that illicit traders did not sail with supplies for the enemy.[73] Bribing officials and gaining the compliance of the royal governor was fundamental to engaging in illegal trade but this proved no problem throughout the war. Thus, illegal trade with the French and Spanish kept shipbuilding craftsmen, merchant seamen, ship chandlers, bolters, coopers, and others humming at their daily work. Their pockets filled with shillings, they could repair by night to the taverns to toast the defeat of the papist enemy. Men of the artisan class could not expect to reap the kinds of profits that fell to well-connected New York war contractors such as John Watts, Peter Livingston, and James Alexander, but they could take satisfaction in full employment and steady income.

When the call came from Massachusetts in 1745 for aid in raising expeditionary forces against Louisbourg, New Yorkers proved how overwhelmingly economic interest outweighed patriotism. The assembly debated Massachusetts's request for aid and listened respectfully to their governor's strenuous appeals. But in the end they refused to raise troops and appropriated only a token £3,000 for supplies. In a rage, Clinton dissolved the assembly and called new elections, but he was only able to persuade the new legislature to cough up the not very impressive sum of £5,000—less than 1.5 shillings per inhabitant. In 1746, New York was more generous. Spurred by the devastation of the frontier town of Saratoga in November 1745, the legislature committed £40,000 and raised 1,600 men for the overland Quebec expedition.[74]

New York's stinginess was wholly related to its legislators' perception of their economic welfare. A few merchants were still involved in the Albany fur trade, which funneled beaver skins trapped in Canada down the Hudson River to New York where they were shipped to London. But the value of exportable furs had dropped drastically in the 1730s and by now accounted for an insignificant part of New York's trade with England. Governor Clinton and his party noisily admonished their antiwar opponents, who they claimed were refusing to make military appropriations because they knew that if New York were drawn into the war the pipeline of profits from Montreal to New York would be smashed. The larger economic motive, however, was simply the desire to avoid heavy war taxes and concentrate on the private war at sea against French shipping.[75]

PHILADELPHIA's prosperity in the 1740s was not so closely linked to the war as was New York's. Many of the town's merchants were Quakers and their consciences did not permit them to participate in any kind of violence. So private warfare by privateers was left to those with fewer scruples. A small number of men made fabulous fortunes, such as Captain John Sibbald, whose ship brought in prizes worth £135,000 sterling.[76] But Philadelphia had many fewer privateers than New York. The town's merchants, in fact, may have lost more ships to French and Spanish privateers than they took themselves. One of the town's wealthiest merchants claimed in 1745 that "Our Vessels are Reduced to about one Third of the number we had belonging to the Port att the Beginning of the Spanish war, since when we have had lost and taken that we know of about Sixty Sail!"[77] If this estimate is accurate, then some Philadelphia merchants suffered heavy losses. But for most, the intensified demand for bread, flour, and meat in the West Indies, which drove prices to all-time highs during the war, meant exceptional profit margins. Mariners' wages also rose sharply because privateers had scoured the waterfronts clean in all the port towns.[78] Increased demand along the normal lines of commerce, bolstered by illegal trade with the French West Indies, kept the town alert to the advantages of war while politicians shielded it from the adverse effects.

The other source of Philadelphia's prosperity during the war came from the building boom associated with the continuing heavy immigration of Germans and Scots-Irish. The famine and rural dislocation in their homelands that had forced them to look westward since the early eighteenth century only intensified during this period, and privateers did little to disrupt the flow because little was to be gained by stopping ships loaded with poor indentured servants, redemptioners, and other immigrants. Thus, the Anglo-Spanish and Anglo-French wars coincided with the greatest influx of immigrants in Philadelphia's history. Many of these newcomers were from urban backgrounds and took up residence in the town. Along with natural increase, this influx swelled Philadelphia's population from about 8,000 in 1734 to almost 14,000 in 1751. In a period when Boston's population remained static and New York's was slowly recovering from the slump of the 1730s, Philadelphia's increased by fully 75 percent.[79]

The population boom in Philadelphia meant full employment for almost everyone associated with the building trades—brickmakers, carpenters, masons, bricklayers, painters, plasterers, glaziers, joiners, carters, stonecutters, and laborers. "We have a very great number of houses building," one Philadelphian reported in 1746.[80] Employment was also provided by public construction, including additions to the statehouse in the 1740s, the erection of the New Building, a huge tabernacle built for the evangelical followers of George Whitefield in 1740, the Moravian Church in 1742, and a two-story brick Market House in 1745. Even if the handsomest profits went to urban real estate investors, who erected houses to rent to arriving immigrants, Philadelphia's artisans shared in the prosperity.

The contrast between Philadelphia and Boston can be seen plainly in the tax and poor relief records of the two towns. While Boston was losing nearly a thousand taxpayers from the rolls between 1735 and 1745, Philadelphia's taxables increased from 1,420 in 1734 to about 2,075 in 1746.[81] Unlike in Boston, the tax collectors in the Quaker center reported only small numbers of people too poor to pay the minimum levy—47 in 1731, 120 in 1742, and 141 in 1753.[82] Boston's overseers of the poor had to struggle with conditions that by 1742 put 146 persons in the almshouse and workhouse and left hundreds of others on out-relief. Philadelphia, by contrast, had only a few dozen out-reliefers and perhaps thirty persons in the small almshouse during the era of war.[83]

JUST AS King George's War had affected the port towns differently, bringing full employment everywhere but distributing the social benefits far more evenly in New York and Philadelphia than in Boston, the postwar peace, which was to last for only six years after the Treaty of Aix-la-Chapelle in 1748, had widely varying ramifications. Philadelphia was afflicted by a business slump beginning late in 1749, which sent an unusual number of merchant houses reeling into bankruptcy. Then in 1753-1754 another cyclical down-turn slowed commerce in Philadelphia and hit New York even harder. The level of English goods imported by New York in 1754 was the lowest in nearly a decade. But these trade fluctuations primarily affected merchants and country farmers, for they were basically caused by falling demand in the West Indies and southern Europe for the foodstuffs that made up the bulk of the New York and Pennsylvania export trade.[84] For the laboring classes of the Middle Atlantic

port towns the level of ship and house construction was far more important to full employment. In both cities, shipbuilding flourished. Philadelphia's tonnage output in the five years between 1748 and 1752 was more
than double that of any previous five-year period and would not be exceeded until the years just preceding the Revolution, when the population was much larger.[85] No continuous data is available for New York in
this period but the number of ship registrations, which roughly reflects
shipbuilding output, rose dramatically between 1749 and 1762.[86]

House construction followed a similar trend, with both port towns
building rapidly in the interwar period to accommodate substantial population increases. The building trades in Philadelphia constructed about
eighty houses a year, as urban settlement began to spread rapidly to the
adjacent areas of Southwark and the Northern Liberties.[87] This high volume of construction brought the largest rewards to urban landowners,
who could sell lots at prices unheard of in the 1720s and 1730s, and to
those with capital to build and rent new houses. Edward Shippen, for
example, who had plunged more than £4,000 into Philadelphia real
estate during King George's War, including the purchase of an entire city
block for £2,102, sold off lots at gratifying profits in the years following
the peace treaty. Samuel Powel played the booming urban real estate
market so well that when he died at the beginning of the Seven Years
War in 1755, he left his son more than ninety houses with a rental income
of several thousand pounds per year.[88] But almost all artisans benefitted
to some degree, for when the building trades flourished, tailors, shoemakers, tanners, metalsmiths, cabinetmakers, and many others also did
a flourishing business. In Philadelphia, the opportunities for artisans are
reflected in the large number of indentured servants they purchased in
1745-1746, the frequency of artisan names recorded in the deed books of
this era, and the relatively high level of wealth left at death by Philadelphia artisans compared to their counterparts in Boston.[89]

New York and Philadelphia found peace almost as prosperous as war
because they were centers of trade for rapidly growing hinterlands, and
they grew accordingly. Boston, however, had hardly completed the victory celebrations after the fall of Louisbourg when it began to slip into a
disheartening commercial decline that compounded all its other troubles.
At the root of this decay was the loss of much of the shipbuilding and distilling business—keystones of the town's economy. Since the seventeenth
century shipbuilding in New England had been centered in Boston. From
fourteen shipyards and six ropewalks came a large proportion of the
small fishing craft that brought in the cod, the coastal vessels that traded
from Penobscot to Savannah, the sloops and schooners that sailed the
West Indian route, and the brigantines and ships that plied the transatlantic trade. About 47 percent of all vessels produced in New England
from 1706 to 1714 came from the shipyards of Boston. By the 1730s the

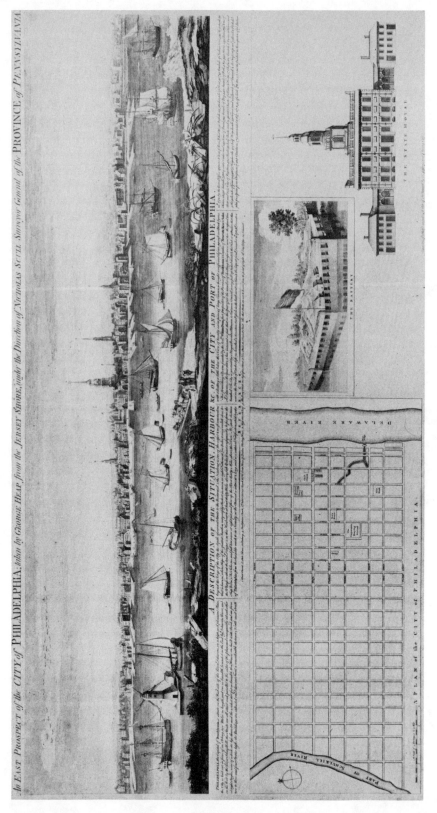

7. *East Prospect of Philadelphia in 1754 by George Heap.*

annual tonnage built often reached 6,000 tons, about four times the volume in Philadelphia, and during one twelve-month period near the end of the war, 10,140 tons slid off the ways.[90]

At the end of King George's War, however, Boston shipbuilding was struck by what one citizen called "a galloping consumption." In 1749 only fifteen ships totaling 2,450 tons were built, and three years later the selectmen were petitioning the legislature for tax relief because the pall over shipbuilding and distilling—"almost the whole Manufacture, the Town of Boston ever pretended to carry on"—was spreading.[91] To some extent the slump reflected the drying up of ship orders, which were unusually high during times of war. But more important was the fact that satellite ports in eastern Massachusetts were cutting deeply into Boston's hold on New England shipbuilding. Almost all large ships "till of Late" had been built in Boston, the selectmen reported in 1752, but now orders were going to Marblehead, Salem, and Newport, Rhode Island, where shipbuilders boasted that they could turn out vessels 20 percent cheaper than in Boston. By the mid-1750s Newport, according to the selectmen, was constructing five times as much tonnage as Boston "in proportion to the bigness of the Two Towns." By 1753 it was claimed that Boston produced only one-quarter of the region's shipping; two years later only 2,162 tons of shipping came out of Boston's yards.[92]

Compounding the loss of shipbuilding was an exodus of butchers, bakers, tanners, distillers, and glovers. The selectmen reported in 1756 that the town's thirty or forty butchers and victuallers had shrunk to "3 or 4," bakers had declined by two-thirds, the number of hides tanned had dropped from 30,000 per year at the end of the war to 6,000 "for several years past," and many of the fifty persons who had turned out 1,000 dozen pairs of gloves annually from 1746 to 1748 "are now maintained by Charity in the Alms House." Distilling and sugar baking had fallen to half the level of eight years before and coopers' work had fallen by two-thirds.[93]

Even allowing for some exaggeration on the part of elected officials seeking tax relief, we must ask why peace had wrought such economic havoc upon Boston. The selectmen themselves provided two answers and historians have added several more. First, the war left Boston with an unprecedented number of poor widows and their children. The heavy town taxes levied to support them, when combined with the onerous provincial taxes passed to pay for the Canadian expeditions, put great pressure on the middling artisans of the town. The selectmen specifically pointed to rising taxes as the reason why many were leaving Boston and argued that "unless the heavy Burthen be lightened there will be no such Town as Boston."[94] The Louisbourg expedition had been seen by many as a way of recouping their fortunes, but military success had further impoverished a large part of the town. Poverty bred poverty, for as the

number of poor who had to be maintained rose, officials were obliged
to levy heavier taxes upon those who themselves were struggling to make
ends meet. In this situation, many artisans apparently decided to try their
luck in outlying towns, where the selectmen claimed tax rates were sometimes only one-fifth as much as in Boston.

Adding to the problem caused by the high rate of poverty and the tax
burden was the tapering off of military supply contracts, which had provided gunsmiths, bakers, coopers, cordwainers, and tailors with work.
Boston's merchant seamen also found berths more difficult to come by,
for peace brought a lull in trade, a drop in wages, and an increase in dead
time between voyages. Wages for mariners, which had risen as high as 90
shillings per month in 1746, were back down to 42 shillings by 1754.
Added to all of this was high food prices, caused by a drought in 1749-
1750 so severe that Boston merchants were ordering wheat and hay from
London in a reversal of the normal flow of the grain trade.[95]

As if Boston's economic problems were not enough, a smallpox epidemic struck the town in January 1752. By March the General Court had
moved to Cambridge, in April the Suffolk County Court fled to Dor-
chester, and by May nearby towns were flooded with refugees. In the
seaport "all business is laid aside . . . , the streets desolate, many of the
shops shut up, and the people universally spend their time to attend to
the sick."[96] By the end of July, 5,566 Bostonians had contracted the
dreaded disease and 569 had succumbed to it. Some 1,850 inhabitants
fled as the death toll mounted. Those who remained paid high prices for
food and wood because country people feared to enter the town to market their goods. Many who left apparently never returned. They had had
enough of heavy taxes, sporadic employment, and disease. The loss of
many substantial taxpayers only increased the burden on the rest of the
community, leaving the selectmen to bray pathetically in 1753 that adverse conditions had "carried away from us many of Our most Industrious, frugal and provident Inhabitants, who have left us a number of
thoughtless Idle and Sottish Persons, who have very soon" become public charges.[97]

One final factor that drove shipbuilding craftsmen and mariners from
Boston to neighboring ports was the fear of impressment on British ships.
English ship captains were chronically short of crew because of the high
desertion rate that occurred whenever a ship of the royal navy cast
anchor in an American harbor. They tried to make up their losses by
raiding the streets and taverns of the port towns, not always staying
within the law that allowed impressments only with the consent of the
provincial governor and that carefully exempted provincials who were
already in service on privateers, merchant ships, or coastal vessels.[98]

Bostonians fought press gangs with a passion throughout the war years
of the 1740s. But pressing went on, and by 1745, when every mariner in

Boston was shipping out for high wages on merchant vessels and every fortune-seeking country stripling had been recruited for the Louisbourg flotilla, press gangs began scooping artisans into their nets.[99] Impressment on a ship of the royal navy was regarded as something approximating a death sentence because of the miserable conditions that prevailed, and it was this fear that drove many shipwrights and other artisans to satellite ports, according to the town meeting in 1746.[100]

This almost biblical series of misfortunes explains why the population of Boston dropped from nearly 17,000 in 1742 to less than 16,000 a decade later. In 1753 one writer bemoaned the burden of poverty and high taxes and described "The Houses of the Poor" where "Scenes of Distress do we often behold! Numbers of Wretches hungry and naked, shivering with Cold, and, perhaps, languishing with Disease."[101] Never since John Winthrop had landed in Boston in 1630 at the head of a dedicated band of Puritan immigrants had the expectations of life in America seemed so sickeningly unrealizable as in Boston in 1753. War and peace had both delivered crushing blows. By the end of the interwar period the Massachusetts seat of government had unparalleled numbers of impoverished inhabitants, the heaviest taxes in history, and little notion of how the decay of shipbuilding and other industries could be remedied.

Bostonians did not stand idly by as their waterfront community reeled under the successive shocks of war casualties, hyperinflation, fiscal retrenchment, peacetime trade recession, and epidemic disease. They struggled to understand the causes of their misery and worked to find solutions. But no Bostonian, of any political persuasion, could find a formula for economic recovery. Unable to reach the roots of the malady, they focused on the symptoms, in particular on the problem of poverty. The remedies they devised for its relief involved a transformation of thinking about indigency and its amelioration that had profound implications for the future.

Five attempts to grapple with the city's soaring poverty rate were made in the difficult years between the end of King George's War and the outbreak of the Seven Years War. One expedient was to bind out the children of the poor. Since 1704 the poor had been legally defined as persons who were not rated for town or provincial taxes. Their children could be taken from them and bound out to other families in the town in the manner of indentured servants. Taxpayers would thereby be relieved of the expense of maintaining the children of the indigent. It was thought that an added advantage of pauper apprenticing was "reintegrating the poor into society as useful working members" rather than letting them learn from their idle parents that life without work was the normal state.[102] The idea was not new to Bostonians; it had roots in the Elizabethan era, when apprenticing the children of the poor was employed as a means of holding down the costs of poor relief.

After 1735 it was the responsibility of the overseers of the poor, appointed for each of Boston's twelve wards, to take poor children from their parents and indent them to taxpayers. The practice was never extensively employed, possibly because of the resistance of poor families themselves. In the 1740s 178 Boston children were bound to other families, most of them outside the town. The number decreased slightly in the 1750s, indicating that even in worsening times the overseers were reluctant to separate parents and children, especially in families who had long lived in the community.[103]

A second expedient in the war against poverty was to "warn out" the hundreds of sick, weary, and hungry souls who tramped the roads into the town. To be warned out did not mean eviction. It was a device dating back to the general Indian War of 1675, when refugees from outlying towns had streamed into Boston. Warning out relieved the town of any obligation to support newcomers who were in need or might become so in the future. Migrants warned out of Boston could vote, hold office, and pay taxes; but they could not qualify for poor relief from the town coffers that they helped to fill.[104] From 1721 to 1742 the authorities had warned out an average of about 25 persons per year.[105] But the "Warning Out Book" that begins in 1745—a remarkable register of human misfortune during this period—lists an average of 65 persons per year from 1745 to 1752 and then much larger numbers in the years just before the outbreak of the Seven Years War—181 in 1753, 176 in 1754, and 222 in 1755.[106]

Most of these transients were part of a growing class of the "strolling poor," who had taken to the roads in search of jobs or greater opportunities. Eastern Massachusetts was becoming reminiscent of East Anglia a century and a half before, with large numbers of persons on the road in search of something better and each community warning out migrants from neighboring areas. Whereas in England it had been population growth and the consolidation of land holdings that had thrown people off the land, in Massachusetts it was the breaking up of family holdings into smaller and smaller parcels, as each generation produced more children to be provided with land. Declining crop yields, the result of over-utilizing available acreage, and the depletion of the supply of arable land set hundreds of people on the road each year, "moving very short distances from town to town and job to job."[107] Many of them decided to try their luck in New England's largest seaport, regardless of reports that must have been circulating concerning Boston's troubled economy. From 1753 to 1755 almost two-thirds of those warned out came from towns in Massachusetts, mostly within twenty miles of Boston. Another 16 percent arrived from elsewhere in New England and the remainder from more distant places such as Halifax, Philadelphia, Albany, and the West Indies.[108] By mid-century the warning out system in the various towns of eastern Massachusetts was processing people in merry-go-round fashion. Boston authorities warned out families coming southward from the Essex County towns of Salem, Marblehead, Newbury, Beverly, and Ipswich. The authorities in these towns, in turn, warned out Bostonians who were headed northward. Each town tried to spare itself the burden of the other's poor at a time when its own swollen relief rolls were driving taxes skyward.[109]

A third palliative employed by Boston's leaders was to exhort the affluent members of the community to greater and greater charitable contributions in order to alleviate the distress of the poor. Several historians have argued recently that because "poverty was regarded as an essentially public evil, remediable at public expense," the "rate of giving to charity . . . declined significantly" in eighteenth-century New England.[110] Boston's record during the interwar period does not fit this formulation. As town expenditures for poor relief rose, so did private contributions, which were centered in the churches rather than in charitable trusts or philanthropic societies. By 1752 the selectmen reported that "private Charity" equaled or surpassed public relief.[111] Although the rate of charitable bequests revealed in wills may have decreased in New England as a whole, wealthy Bostonians, who had amassed great fortunes during the war years, gave large amounts to ameliorate the condition of the town's poor. For example, Samuel Cooper, minister at Brattle Street Church, spared no pains in calling his flock to their eleemosynary duties. Cooper's parishioners controlled at least one-quarter of Boston's mercantile wealth and they rested easily under their pastor's assurances that "religion is a friend to outward Prosperity" and that "they that are poorer in worldly state should and must give way to the Rich." But Cooper also cajoled them into contributing liberally to the relief of the unfortunate.[112]

Boston's leaders tried one other expedient for ameliorating economic adversity at mid-century: they appealed repeatedly to the General Court for tax relief. Pointing out that Boston groaned under the heaviest taxes in the province because of its poverty problem, they argued that the city should pay a smaller percentage of the provincial taxes. While the number of "Rateable Inhabitants" had fallen by nearly a thousand, they pleaded, Boston laid out more in poor relief than the rest of the province combined and perhaps even more than "all the Governments of New England put together, exclusive of Boston." By the reckoning of those best acquainted with such matters, they argued in 1753, Boston's outlays were double those of any town of equal size "upon the face of the whole Earth."[113]

As loudly as the selectmen exhorted, the General Court, dominated by rural interests, mostly turned a deaf ear in the 1750s. Sympathy was hard to arouse among representatives who came from areas with much lower per capita wealth than Boston. Tax relief came in the 1760s, but in the 1750s the House of Representatives apparently thought that Boston's aggregate wealth was great enough for it to solve its own problems without turning to outlying areas, which had difficulties of their own and boasted no wealthy merchant princes who lived in urban mansions and rode in liveried carriages.[114]

In the end, none of the tactics employed by Boston's leaders was equal to the problem at hand. Despite efforts to keep migrant strangers from swelling the poor rolls and to marshal aid for those already in difficult straits, more and more Bostonians were caught in the web of poverty. So in the end, men turned from the benevolent desire to help the poor to the idea that the poor should help themselves.

The roots of such an approach to poverty are very tangled. New England Puritans, like their Elizabethan forebears, had always maintained a hearty distaste for the dependent poor, especially those who were thought to prefer public alms to hard work and self-support. Cotton Mather reflected this attitude perfectly when he wrote that "for those that Indulge themselves in *Idleness*, the Express Command of God unto us, is *That you should Let them Starve.*" As late as 1721 Mather was complaining that in the salubrious "Hive" of New England it was lamentable that there should be "any Drones."[115]

But by the 1740s it had become clear that the problem in Boston was not one of able-bodied persons who refused to work but persons for whom little work was available. On a very small scale Boston had faced this problem as early as 1656 and by 1700 the selectmen had taken a tentative step toward a practice extensively employed in England—creating work-relief programs for the poor so that they would earn their own keep in facilities provided and supervised by public authorities.[116] Many English writers at this time abandoned an earlier view that economic recessions and depressed wages were the main causes of indigency and began to blame the poor themselves for their plight. The lower class, it was said, was naturally lazy and would work only when forced to by hunger and extreme poverty. Therefore, well-intentioned lawmakers who passed relief statutes were only cultivating dependency and encouraging sloth. William Petty, one of the most respected economic writers of the late seventeenth century, even promoted a scheme for perpetually maintaining an artificial famine by storing food in government granaries. Kept at the edge of starvation, he believed, the laboring classes would develop an urge to work that was constitutionally absent in them.[117]

Out of this new climate of thought came the public workhouse movement. By 1723, when workhouses were operating in almost every sizable English town, thousands of impoverished persons were taken off out-relief and forced to move from their homes. Taken to the workhouses, they were set to spinning flax, weaving linen, and picking oakum. It was hoped that through hard labor the poor would pay for their own support and in the process gain a taste for the rewards of industry and frugality. The workhouse would benefit the middle and upper classes by reducing the poor rates; it would aid the poor by reprogramming them for a more satisfactory way of life. Some English writers also recommended transferring the management of the poor to private corporations formed by investors who might turn a profit from appropriating the labor of the poor, even as they rehabilitated them. The English workhouse became a cultural artifact of the early eighteenth century, an institution arising from a moral analysis of poverty and committed to reducing the taxpayers' load in maintaining the impoverished. John Bellers, a Quaker merchant of London, dignified these workhouses with the name "colleges of industry," and a number of other authors with whom Bostonians were familiar, including Henry Fielding, William Temple, William Petty, Charles Davenant, and Bernard Mandeville, also plumped for the new system.[118]

In 1735, with poverty spreading, Boston undertook a major experiment in working the poor. The town meeting decided to build a separate workhouse where the able-bodied poor would be segregated, relieved, and rehabilitated. Over the next few years private subscriptions were solicited, about £900 sterling in all. In 1739 the brick Workhouse on the Common opened its doors.[119] Nineteen months later an inspection committee reported that income of £360 sterling was exceeded by expenses of £466 sterling and that forty-eight adults and seven children were employed in the house, mostly picking oakum, carding, and spinning. In 1742 thirty-six persons were in the house and the number from that point on does not seem to have exceeded fifty.[120]

Obviously, the overseers were not going to cure Boston's poverty problem by institutionalizing about 5 percent of the town's distressed persons. So we must ask why so few persons were assigned to an experiment that had attracted 126 donors and gained the approval of the town meeting and provincial legislature. The answer cannot lie in the incommodiousness of the workhouse, for it was one of the largest buildings in Boston. Two stories high and 140 feet long, it was capable of holding several hundred impoverished and unemployed persons.[121] The difficulty, apparently, was that many of Boston's poor refused to be taken from their homes. In 1740 a visitor remarked that the overseers of the poor were "very tender of exposing those that have lived in a handsome manner; and therefore give them good relief in so private a manner, that it is seldom known to any of their neighbors."[122] This statement provides us with a clue to why the workhouse would not work. Many of the poor were widows with children still at their sides.[123] Many of them had lived decently, if not "handsomely," in the past. Hence, it is not difficult to understand that they would rebel at the notion of giving up their lodgings, however cramped and cold, and repairing to the workhouse, where poverty was compounded with indignity and their ties with friends, relatives, and neighborhood life would be broken.

The most unfortunate of Boston's impoverished—the aged, sick, crippled, and insane who had no families to care for them—had no choice but to go to the almshouse, as did about one hundred Bostonians each year in the 1740s. Another forty or fifty persons could be induced to go to the workhouse, especially if they did not have children or had been apprehended for prostitution or other crimes. But most of Boston's poor regarded themselves above such treatment and preferred to starve at home if the authorities cut off out-relief and ordered them to the workhouse. They refused to brook the strict regimen of the workhouse, with its rules against free coming and going and its provisions for gagging and bread and water diets for "wanton and lascivious Behaviour." Moreover, they must have found it ungenerous that the selectmen allowed them only one penny out of every shilling they earned—and that "to be disposed of by the Overseers for their greater Comfort."[124] Alarmed at the spiraling cost of relief and affronted by the challenge to order and harmony that hundreds of pauperized and idle townspeople evoked, Boston's leaders erected a substantial building that could not be filled. As in the case of the public markets, which could not be forced on the common people, the workhouse experiment failed because it underestimated the resistance of ordinary people, who had their ways of defending themselves against attempts to alter their way of life.[125]

In 1748 Boston's leaders made another attempt to deal with the widowed poor and their dependent children, whose numbers had continued to grow during King George's War. If they would not trade their mean lodgings for the workhouse, perhaps the indigent could be persuaded to go to a "manufactory" during the day, where their labor would contribute to their own support and lighten the taxpayer's burden. Thus was born the United Society for Manufactures and Importation, the first American experiment in female factory labor. Its subscribers intended to put the unemployed poor to work, halt the rise of property taxes, and make a profit off the cheap labor of poverty-stricken women and children.[126] Public authorities had been unable to make the dependent poor self-supporting; now private hands were to have a try.

The Society for Manufactures was, in reality, planning a textile factory. Its proponents, who were drawn from the ranks of Boston's most successful merchants and entrepreneurs, concluded that of the various kinds of work that might be done by women and children, spinning was the most feasible. This notion was especially attractive because Massachusetts annually imported from England cloth worth thousands of pounds. The production of cloth by the poor, it was thought, not only would end idle pauperism and reduce taxes but also would improve the province's balance of trade by cutting back on imports. It would also, the society hoped, turn a profit for its investors.

But what kind of cloth? Woolens seemed not to be the answer because, although they were widely used, sheep grazing was only marginally profitable in New England and it took considerable craft skill, beyond the capacities of a shifting, casual labor force, to produce the worsted materials favored by city people in contrast to the rough homespuns that country folk found adequate for their needs.[127] Linen was the alternative and had much to recommend it. Flax grew well in New England and linen was widely imported—to the value, according to contemporary estimates, of £20,000 to £60,000 per year. Thirty years before, a group of Scots-Irish immigrants had demonstrated the art of spinning flax in Boston and set off a mild "spinning craze." These Ulster immigrants had remained only briefly in Boston before setting out for the New Hampshire frontier, where they founded the town of Londonderry and soon proved that linen could be profitably produced.[128] More important, linen production had been promoted extensively in Ireland since the late seventeenth century and was now regarded there as the sure-fire method of curing urban poverty. Here, perhaps, was the answer to a whole bundle of problems besetting the town. As the successors to the United Society pronounced, the "palliatives" of poor relief would be replaced by "a lasting and permanent Scheme, that may be expected to reach the Root of this Malady."[129]

Despite these optimistic hopes, nothing went easily for the organizers of the manufactory. The initial call for investors in 1748 brought only thirty-six subscribers and about £200 sterling—some indication of the chariness that many felt about the prospects of success. Linen weavers and loom builders were not to be found in Boston and had to be advertised for abroad.[130] Nor were spinners available, for contrary to the conventional understanding of historians, urban women and children who could spin were the exception rather than the rule.[131] It took until December 1750 to lease a building, set up "sundry looms," and open several free spinning schools for teaching pauper children the art of the distaff and wheel.[132] By this time the United Society for Manufactures and Importation had reorganized and changed its name to the more benevolent sounding Society for Encouraging Industry and the Employment of the Poor.

To stir up enthusiasm for the opening of the manufactory, the society published an extraordinary pamphlet late in 1750. It had a cumbersome title—*A Letter from Sir Richard Cox, Bart. To Thomas Prior, Esq.; Shewing from Experience a sure Method to establish the Linnen-Manufacture, and the Beneficial Effects it will immediately produce*—but inside the covers was an exciting tale of poverty and progress. Sir Richard was none other than the grandson of the former Lord Chancellor of Ireland and his tract described a fifteen-year experiment to bring prosperity and peace to the vale of tears he found on the River Bandon, where the two tiny towns of Kinsale and Bandon-bridge lay.[133] Cox had been disheartened in 1733 to find that the natives of his inherited estate "had contracted such a Habit of Idleness" that they would not work and their children had imbibed "their pernicious Example." Naked beggars roamed the streets, people lived from hand to mouth, houses tumbled down in disrepair, and hope was nowhere to be found. Sir Richard vowed to alter the dismal situation. Hence, he embarked on an industrial experiment, turning his estates into a social laboratory and studying human motivation until he found the formula for putting everyone to work, from the oldest members of the community down to little children who had just "quit their Leading-Strings." It had taken time, but by 1749, when Sir Richard published his pamphlet in London, Kinsale and Bandon-bridge were thriving towns where prosperity and contentment had replaced poverty and despair. The key to it all was the manufacture of linen.[134]

The pamphlet, like most promotional tracts, was somewhat overblown, for the linen industry in southern Ireland, although it revived the economy for a short time, was to collapse within a generation.[135] But the promoters of the manufactory in Boston were convinced that linen production would solve Boston's problems and were doubtless glad to get such a glowing account of its success elsewhere. They had received it fortuitously from an old hometown boy, Benjamin Franklin, who had sent it to friends in Boston shortly after receiving it from a London friend.[136] It was quickly reprinted in Boston with a preface explaining that "The Circumstances of this Province, and those of Ireland, tho' not altogether similar, are in so many Respects alike." They trusted, said the society's officers, that the public would be swayed to support the manufactory, now almost ready to open.

The public that needed to be swayed, of course, was composed of the unemployed and impoverished members of the community. It is not probable that very many of them read the *Letter from Sir Richard Cox*, but it is likely that most were privately urged by the overseers of the poor and the clergy to contribute themselves to the experiment. Their response was not gratifying. A few months after the manufactory opened its doors in 1751 notices appeared in the papers describing the sermon preached at a public meeting of the society. "It is earnestly wished by all Lovers of their Country," pleaded Joseph Sewall, that the poor "would exert themselves at this Time" by working in the manufactory. "Great Numbers of Persons," if they would step forward, might now be "useful both to themselves and the publick, who have heretofore been a dead Weight upon . . . this poor Town."[137] Six months later the society reported that Bostonians were producing 5,000 yards of linen per year, two-thirds of it by women working for the society.[138] This was only about sixteen yards per work day, a not very impressive output for a town whose pauper population approached a thousand souls.

At the very time when the society was reporting limited progress in putting the indigent to work, smallpox struck so severely at the lower class that it "entirely destroyed the Linnen Manufacture."[139] Undaunted, the society redoubled its efforts when the epidemic passed. A campaign for subscriptions to erect a large new building began and some of Boston's most prestigious ministers, including Samuel Cooper at Brattle Street Church and Charles Chauncy at First Church, were enlisted in the cause. The latter argued that because of the society's praiseworthy efforts "some hundreds of Women and Children have . . . been kept at Work, whereby they have done a great deal towards supplying themselves with Bread, to the easing the Town of its Burthen in providing for the poor." Cooper, who was Boston's most accurate reflector of the growing philosophy of economic self-interest, made a naked appeal to the pocketbooks of the affluent. Nobody, he wrote, was "actuated by a kind of mad good Nature" that led him to devote himself "to the Gratification of others, without any concern or Relish for his own private Happiness." But Bostonians could indulge their natural and legitimate "self-love" while simultaneously subscribing to the new enterprise because the manufactory was designed to "advance our private interest" by lowering taxes and turning a profit while giving employment to the idle.

Ministerial urgings, however, could not unlock Boston's mercantile wealth. Some merchants may have feared that textile production would cut into trade profits, for cloth was a major import item. Others may have questioned whether the manufactory could operate at a profit, and they could point to the society's own report of March 1752 that the operation was £500 in debt.[140] Unable to attract enough private capital, the society's officers turned to government and got the response they sought. In March 1753 the town meeting voted to lend £130 sterling toward the construction of a new building and in June Boston's representatives persuaded the General Court to impose a luxury tax on coaches, chariots, and other wheeled vehicles for five years in order to raise £1,125 more.[141] Newly capitalized, the society started afresh. By fall the Linen Manufactory House on Tremont Street was ready to open.[142] To whip up enthusiasm the society staged a spinning exhibition on the Common in August. "Near 300 Spinsters, some of them 7 or 8 years old and several of them Daughters of the best Families among us," reported the *Boston Gazette*, "made a handsome Appearance on the Common." High upon a stage erected for the occasion sat a number of weavers, one at work at his loom.[143]

All of the bright hopes that the linen manufactory would rid Boston of poverty were shattered within a few years after the new facility opened its doors. Boston's leading ministers continued to promote the enterprise with annual sermons and the number of looms in operation rose from nine to twenty-one. But by 1758 operations at the manufactory were grinding to a halt. When Thomas Barnard gave the annual sermon in September 1758, he noted that economic affliction was still growing in Boston and that the thousands of men being recruited for the new war in progress would create an even greater need for putting women to work. He urged the society's members to continue their work even "tho' you should lose on the Balance," for their losses would be offset by lower poor taxes and the knowledge that they were helping to banish idleness.[144] But nobody was listening. In the next year the General Court, unable to meet the cost of the new manufactory from the luxury tax receipts, which were doggedly resisted by the wealthy, ordered the building sold at auction in order to recover the costs. But who would buy a linen factory that would not work? No bids were made and all the province could do was lease a part of its white elephant to two Boston weavers who wanted to try their own textile experiment.[145] Not until the British troops eyed it as a barracks in 1768 could anyone think of a use for the manufactory.

Why had the linen manufactory failed? Cheap labor, sufficient capital, and technology were the prime factors that led to success in Scotland and Ireland. All were available in Boston. During its existence, in fact, the society produced more than 17,000 yards of cloth.[146] Yet the enterprise failed financially because it could not produce linen as cheaply as it could be imported. In part, this may have been because, as the society claimed, the government did not provide subsidies as in Ireland. There were also problems of synchronizing labor and procuring ample supplies of flax.[147] But much of the manufactory's failure must be charged to the resistance of the supposed recipients of the society's efforts. As in the case of the workhouse, women and children showed great reluctance to toil in the manufactory. They would spin at home, working as time allowed to produce what they could within the rhythm of their daily routine and accepting small piecework wages. But removal to an institutional setting, even for daytime labor, involved a new kind of labor discipline and a separation of productive and reproductive responsibilities that challenged deeply rooted values.[148]

To understand how extensively routinized labor in the manufactory might change the work experience of laboring-class women we need to apprehend how they previously contributed to the family economy. This is extraordinarily difficult, for we are operating in a vacuum of secondary literature not only concerning the work experience of preindustrial American women in urban areas but also the day-by-day working life of the wives and daughters of artisans and laborers. We do know from studies of England and France in this period that laboring-class women typically supplemented their husbands' wages in an economy where large numbers of people regularly lacked an adequate supply of food. Domestic service and manufactory labor were the types of work most frequently performed by young, unmarried women in Europe, but married women resisted factory labor, preferring domestic manufacturing, especially spinning at home. Spreading rapidly in eighteenth-century European towns, domestic spinning helped the laboring poor to establish a viable family economy while at the same time "it allowed women to fulfill what they defined as their primary role, their family duties."[149]

We cannot transpose the European experience directly to Boston; but the wider context of the urban work experience of eighteenth-century women does provide insights into the world of Boston's women. As the wives of artisans, mariners, and laborers, they had probably always contributed to the family economy by helping in their husbands' shops, taking in washing, serving as seamstresses for middle- and upper-class families, and doing daytime domestic labor in the houses of the well-to-do. After the 1720s, when the economic security of laboring-class families was steadily undermined, supplemental income from wives and older daughters probably became even more imperative. Domestic service may have been particularly important because, unlike Philadelphia and New York, Boston lacked the substantial labor pool of female slaves and indentured servants who performed household work in those cities. New York in 1756 had 695 female slaves over sixteen years of age and 443 under that age—a total of 1,138 slave women to serve a white population of 10,768. Philadelphia in 1767 had about 600 female slaves and indentured servants for a white population of about 18,500 and families of means also had at their command a substantial pool of free, unmarried immigrant women who entered the city each year. Boston, by contrast, received only a trickle of poor Scots-Irish and German immigrants and contained only 301 black females and 16 Indian females in 1765 for a white population of 14,672.[150] Much of the demand for domestic labor, it seems, must have been filled by young, unmarried women and by the wives of lower-class men, especially if they were childless.

Older women with young children may have taken in boarders as a second major way of supplementing the family income. There is a striking difference in the number of people per house in Boston and in the other two port towns in this period, and we can infer from this either that Boston families were larger or that many householders rented rooms and furnished board to transients, unmarried mariners, and other families from the ranks of the laboring poor. In 1741 Boston had 9.53 persons per house and in 1765 9.26 persons. This contrasts sharply both with Philadelphia, where there were 6.51 inhabitants per house in 1749 and 6.26 in

1760, and with New York, where there were 6.72 persons per house in 1753.[151] All of the data available indicates that the birthrate in Boston was lower than in the other northern ports, for the mid-century wars took a fearful toll on a generation of young males, leaving a surplus population of young women whose childbearing potential was cut short by the loss of a husband or who remained single and childless altogether for lack of marriagable men. Hence, it is reasonable to conclude that the large number of persons per house in Boston, which exceeded the New York and Philadelphia averages by about 50 percent, primarily represents the taking in of single boarders and even families. For many Boston women, especially widows, this may have been the primary means of providing a family income.

Both in daytime domestic service and in maintaining boarders Boston's poor widows, who represented the major problem for the administrators of poor relief, had previously been able to combine maternal responsibilities with intermittent work, which brought a modest income but had to be supplemented with out-relief. Factory labor, however, required a workplace that was far less amenable to the discharge of women's familial responsibilities. Even when children of seven years and older were taken to the factory to assist in preparing flax for spinning, the problem of managing younger children remained. If spinning could be done in the home, it could be fit into the maternal work rhythm of the woman; in the factory it could not.

The evidence of resistance to the new work system, though fragmentary and sometimes indirect, is compelling. No records are extant that show how many spinners and weavers worked in the manufactory, but the company's accounts show that in 1757 twenty-one looms and sixty wheels were in the building. Hundreds of spinners had been trained in the previous years and twenty-one looms would have required yarn from the wheels of several hundred of them. Many, it appears, had accepted the society's suggestion that they work at home, or, to reverse the causality, had obliged the society to accept this modification of the original plan. Even so, the pre-epidemic production level, which was hardly impressive, was not being met in early 1753, and later that year it was reported that almost as many people were spinning for themselves as for the society.[152] With their initial plan falling apart, the society began offering free house rent and firewood to those who would weave linen cloth in their homes.[153] By 1760, according to the society's records, twice as much cloth had been produced over the previous nine years for "Private persons" as for the society, a sharp reversal of the situation in the opening years of the experiment. Several merchants began to purchase privately produced cloth, and apparently most of the poor preferred to work for them, as their domestic responsibilities allowed, rather than work for or in the manufactory.[154] If they had been fully supported by wages, perhaps women and children could have been induced to go to the manufactory. Since they could not live on the wages offered, about 7 shillings per week for spinners, they chose to stay at home, working at their wheels in their free time, selling their yarn to independent weavers, and counting on private and public relief to supplement their wages.[155]

The resistance of these women is all the more remarkable considering the pressure they were under from the town's leading figures, who were intent on making the manufactory succeed. This upper-class determination is most revealingly articulated in the sermons given at the annual meetings of the society by some of eastern Massachusetts's best-known clergymen. In a sermon launching the society's new subscription drive in August 1752, Chauncy took as his text the Christian Law, "Thus we commanded you, that if any would not work, neither should he eat." He decried "the Swarms of Children, of both Sexes, that are continually strolling and playing about the Streets of our Metropolis, cloathed in Rags, and brought up in Idleness and Ignorance"; he lamented the "lazy and indolent, who are both healthy and strong"; and he warned against giving money to the idle poor, because charity of this kind, far from helping, would be "a great Hurt to a Community."[156] Samuel Cooper reiterated the emerging ideology that public out-relief or private charity for widows and their children was money "worse than Lost." The only justifiable charity, he pronounced, was that which was directed toward "an Employment for honest Poverty, [that] chases away moaping Idleness, and meagre Want; and introduces chearful Industry and smiling Plenty in their Stead."[157]

Inherent in these strictures was the threat of cutting off public relief and discouraging private charity, thus forcing impoverished women to adapt themselves to factory labor or go hungry. Such finger wagging at the poor, though it may have cheered propertied Bostonians who welcomed any work program that would bring taxes down, met with considerable resistance among the lower class. Widowed women had little reason to subscribe to the notion that they were "lazy" or "idle" or lived parasitically on "promiscuously" distributed charity or that their children needed to be "trained up, not only to endure but to love a constant Employment." Such allegations must have been deeply resented by those whose misfortunes were not of their own making. The most vulnerable, to be sure, submitted to the new factory work discipline. Impecunious migrants entering Boston, such as Henry Neal, his wife, and children, were hustled off to the manufactory by the overseers of the poor and did not resist.[158] Nor, perhaps, did young lower-class women, who could find no marriage partners in a town where the sex ratio had been badly skewed by war casualties. But many poor women refused to submit to a work routine that disrupted traditional ways of life and split the dual functions of laboring-class women—work and family—into two separate spheres.

Boston's DECLINE, caused initially by deep-rooted problems of productivity and compounded in the 1740s by war, brought into sharp relief the possibilities and pitfalls created by the increasingly pervasive market economy. Nobody had foreseen the adverse social consequences of participating in the dynamic Atlantic trade world; rather, it had been assumed that interregional and international trade would provide the sinews of strength for a burgeoning population. Nor had merchants and land speculators been regarded with suspicion, for in spite of the old Puritan animus toward nonproductive labor it was widely anticipated that all urban dwellers would share in the larger rewards which vigorous commercial activity brought to the community. If mercantile wealth was produced by men who possessed the basic entrepreneurial attributes— organizational ability, perseverance, sound judgment, and the nerve to take reasoned risks—then it was expected by a broad spectrum of smaller enterprisers and independent artisans that they too would share in the largesse provided by a world cast free of the traditional limitations on individual enterprise. Entrepreneurial achievement per se in Boston was not resented but was broadly admired, as the repeated election of the town's wealthiest merchants to public offices tells us.

Yet the new system, which promised so much, had not obliterated older ways of conceiving of the community and social relationships within it. A kind of crisis of belief was produced when war dislocated the economy, brought impoverishment to many, and at the same time elevated a few to pinnacles of wealth never before seen. It was then that echoes of the traditional social system, where mutual obligations rather than the free exchange of goods and labor governed behavior, began to be heard. It is impossible to know how many wished to return to the traditional, corporate society, where immobile social ranks were as distinguishing a mark as limitations on wealth-aggrandizing individual enterprise. But particularly in the lower reaches of the laboring classes, where the contributions to the war had been heaviest and inflation pinched most severely, resistance to the new order and a longing for a passing system registered most clearly. This was primarily visible in Boston, where the market economy had distributed its rewards least evenhandedly. It showed itself in resistance to the new methods of poor relief, and, even more dramatically, in an evangelical re-evocation of the lost spirit of community and a rising chorus of voices against entrepreneurial wealth and abuse of power.

8

Religious Revival
and Politics at Mid-Century

THE DYNAMICS of politics differed substantially in the three seaport towns between the late 1730s and the early 1750s. Boston's severe wartime dislocation and postwar depression produced a tempestuous, street-filled form of politics, while New York and Philadelphia's general prosperity led to an era of stable, elite-dominated political affairs. It was not, however, all upheaval in Boston and all placidity in the other ports. In each town struggles for power within the elite as well as political activity in the plebeian ranks insured that the hurly-burly of public affairs inherited from the previous generation continued. Each of the towns, moreover, was moved by a religious revival that sent hundreds of souls "flying to Christ." It was in Boston that economic decline kept the political cauldron bubbling, while in New York and Philadelphia it simmered quietly, occasionally becoming heated, but never reaching the boiling point of the 1720s and 1730s. Likewise, it was Boston where religious revivalism was most intense and where it manifested itself most clearly as an expression of social discontent.

IN EACH of the northern towns new techniques of political organization that had been initiated in the first third of the century acquired further legitimacy. Party caucuses met to draw up slates of candidates, which at least in theory gave voters a real choice at the polls. In New York the private nomination of assembly candidates was replaced in 1739 by an outdoor rally that was staged for the purpose of nominating candidates. The affair was probably managed with care by the leaders of the Morrisite faction, but the participants at least had the sense that "great numbers constituted as good a political asset as great names."[1] Boston's popular Caucus never opened its doors to the multitude in this period, and in Philadelphia political factions waited until 1754 to follow New York's example. For about fifteen years before that time the Quaker party drew up a slate of candidates at its annual religious meeting—a tactic that one proprietary party leader bitterly attacked as "the finest Scheme that could possibly be projected for conducting political Intrigues, under the Mask of Religion."[2] But in 1754 it was the conservative proprietary party, yielding to the realities of political life, that advertised in the *Pennsylvania Gazette* for a public turnout to choose candidates for the upcoming assembly elections.[3] Ideological consistency collapsed as a Quaker writer of the popular party attacked this popularization of politics, only to be answered by a spokesman of the conservative party who defended this method of preserving the liberties of the people.[4] Seeing an opportunity for electoral success for the first time in two decades, proprietary leaders put scruples aside and resorted to tactics that heretofore had offended their most deeply held political convictions.

In another concession to popular politics candidates publicly advertised for votes, a tactic that chipped away at the deferential model of society, which had no place for a political leader who deigned to solicit votes from the commonality. At least once in the 1730s candidates in New York had requested votes in the newspapers, but it became regular practice in the assembly elections of the 1740s.[5] In Philadelphia, canvassing for votes began in 1744 in the sheriff's elections. "Tho it has not till this Time been customary, to request your Votes in Print," wrote Nicholas Scull with a tone of chagrin, "yet that Method now being introduced, I feel myself obliged in this publick Manner . . . to acquaint you that I intend to stand a Candidate, for the Sheriffs Office, and request your Votes and Interest, at the next Elections."[6] Assemblymen in Philadelphia still did not descend to advertising for votes in the newspapers but sought support through the slightly more dignified political broadside or pamphlet.

Even more significant in pushing forward the transformation of politics from a private to a public affair was the further development of the political press. By the 1740s the printed word had become an indispensable part of both campaigning for office and pressuring legislators who were considering controversial bills. In every contested election, pamphleteers industriously alerted the voters to the awful consequences of a victory by the other side. In 1754, as the Massachusetts legislature considered a liquor excise bill aimed at merchants and distillers, seventeen pamphlets appeared in the streets of Boston to rally public support against it.[7] The controversy over chartering King's College in New York in 1750-1751 kept the city's two printers busy with the publication of several dozen tracts.[8] More and more the urban newspapers, which were increasing in number in this era, were filled with polemical literature and election appeals. By 1750 the leader of New York's popular party exclaimed that the forthcoming election had "produced a violent paper war here [which had brought forth] a dozen different papers."[9] Counting newspaper articles, about forty partisan pieces in all were printed.

It is not easy to determine precisely who read or was affected by this literature. But the literacy rate was high in colonial America and especially widespread in the cities. Population density made it easy to pass broadsides and pamphlets from hand to hand or to read them aloud in the taverns. Also contributing to the wide circulation of political literature was the low cost of printing. For as little as £1 sterling an interested politician could supply every eligible voter in a seaport town with a copy of an election broadside.[10] Even lengthy pamphlets were often distributed gratis. Half of the 1,000 copies of John Smith's *Doctrine of Christianity*, a Quaker plea for noninvolvement in war, were distributed free in 1748 so "that it might have the more universal Influence over the Province." On the opposing side William Smith circulated 2,300 free copies of his *Brief History of the Rise and Progress of a Charitable Scheme for Relief and Instruction of Poor Germans*, a straightforward appeal in 1756 for the German vote.[11]

Another sign of the widespread influence of the political press is the anguished cries of political leaders about the dangerous implications of this increasingly potent weapon. Most members of the elite, whether they belonged to the popular or conservative faction, had ambivalent feelings about courting the electorate in print. A few optimists such as Benjamin Franklin and Elisha Cooke looked upon fiery pamphlets and newspaper fusillades as instruments "to prepare the Minds of the Publick."[12] But most leaders assumed that people easily succumbed to their basest instincts and that the "unthinking multitude," which was thought to include a vast majority of the population, was moved by boisterous passion rather than cool reason. Guided by these views, most of the elite considered exhortatory literature a threat to the social order. Conservative politicians frequently attacked what they called irresponsible attempts "to inflame the minds of the common people" or "to breed and nourish Discontent, and to foment Faction and Sedition."[13] Yet by the 1740s and 1750s even the most conservative leaders could not resist resorting to the press. The same men who earlier had lamented its use, such as James DeLancey of New York, eagerly employed scurrilous broadsides and pamphlets by mid-century. Their opponents, long accustomed to wielding the poisoned pen, could only shake their heads in dismay, charging that attempts were being made to propagate "Clamour & Slander" and turn the heads of "ignorant people & others who are not well acquainted with the publick affairs." That said, they took up the pen again themselves.[14] Richard Peters, a proprietary leader in Philadelphia, wrote that "I never knew any good come to the honest & right side of the Question in the Province by Publick Papers," but in a few years Peters and his colleagues, who espoused social conservatism and repeatedly warned about the anarchic and leveling designs of the Quaker politicians, raised the art of pamphleteering to new heights of sophistication.[15]

No one in Philadelphia in this era could match the imperious William Smith, an Anglican clergyman and future president of the College of Philadelphia, for statements about the necessity of the ordered, deferential society; but no one did more to make the abusive pamphlet a part of the eighteenth-century political arsenal, all the while professing that "the Appeal to the public was against my Judgment."[16]

The critics of the political press were not inventing bogeymen when they expressed fears that bombastic political literature would have a dangerous effect on ordinary people. "When all *Order* and *Government* is endeavoured to be *Trampled on*, *Reflections* are cast upon Persons of all Degrees, must not these things end in Sedition?" asked James DeLancey.[17] The answer depended upon how one defined sedition. To conservatives it was the erosion of deference, attacks on the wealthy and educated, and the intrusion into politics of laboring men. Elitists imagined that such people were manipulated by the press into an artificial anger. Cadwallader Colden of New York wrote of the "prejudices & republican notions artfully instill'd into numbers of peoples minds," as if to suggest that ideas could be implanted mechanically through pamphlets and broadsides.[18] While they may have been wrong in their conception of how laboring-class resistance was sparked, they were right about the effect of the burgeoning political press. Through the printed word untapped sources of political energy could be reached. In addition, printed political tracts sharpened the ability of ordinary people to criticize those above them in social rank and strengthened their feeling of power.[19] Thus, there was some truth in the equation made by conservatives between "scribbling" and "leveling," though the conservatives too were obliged to scribble on in pursuit of votes.

Not only a quantitative leap in the production of political literature but also an escalation of rhetoric made the press a particularly potent weapon by mid-century. As political literature proliferated, the quality of language and the modes of argumentation changed markedly, for a broader audience was being addressed. Many of the early eighteenth-century pamphlet writers, perhaps mindful of the revolutionary potential of the printed word, and beaming their arguments to the upper stratum, had couched their arguments in legalistic terms. Boston readers of the numerous pamphlets on the currency issue in the 1720s encountered nothing more virulent than charges that the opposition view was "strange and Unaccountable," "intolerable," "unreasonable and unjust," or that writers on the other side were guilty of "bold and wilful Misrepresentation." But by 1754 the antiexcise pamphleteers in Boston were painting images of the opponents as "Little pestilent Creature[s]," "dirty miscreants," and unspeakably horrible creatures ready to "cram [their] . . . merciless and insatiable Maw[s] with our very Blood, and bones, and Vitals," while making sexual advances on wives and daughters.[20] In New

York, the appearance in 1752 of the *Independent Reflector*, the first American magazine created for political exposé rather than amusement, brought vituperative politics to a new height. In the Kings College controversy the New York City Anglican clergy was bitterly vilified and granted no semblance of integrity. In phrases that made Zenger's *New-York Weekly Journal* of the 1730s seem polite by comparison, "Philo-Reflector" warned his readers of the clergymen's "ghastly juggling, their Pride, and their insatiate Lust of Power" and cautioned them to keep a weather eye out for the "Seduction of Priest-craft," the "dark and horrible Plot for usurping the sole Rule of the College," for "our intended Vassalage" and for "clerical Rubbish and Villainy."[21] Not even in Philadelphia, the pacifist center of the American colonies, could politicians avoid rhetorical violence. Factional leaders hurled insults at each other, charging opponents with "Inveterate Calumny, foul-mouthed Aspersion, shameless Falsehood, and insatiate Malice." When William Smith attacked Benjamin Franklin, the artisans' hero, his opponents wrote that "the Vomitings of this infamous Hireling . . . betoken that Redundancy of Rancour, and Rottiness of Heart which render him the most despicable of his Species."[22]

In effect, the conservatives' worst fears concerning the use of the press were confirmed, as the tactics of printed political discourse changed from attacking the legality or wisdom of the opposition's policies or pleading for the election of public-minded men to assailing the character and motives of those on the other side. The effect of the new political rhetoric was circular, as each increase in the brutality of language brought an equivalent or greater response from the opposition. Gradually the public was given reason to suspect not simply the wisdom or constitutional soundness of one side or the other, but the motives, morality, and even sanity of its leaders. The same high-placed individuals to whom the rank and file was supposed to defer were exposed as the most corrupt and loathsome members of society.

Another facet of the new politics in the 1740s and 1750s was the growing involvement of religious figures. Most urban leaders, both secular and clerical, deplored this but nonetheless caused it to happen. The clergy had never been isolated from political life in the early history of the towns, but their efforts to influence public affairs had ordinarily been conducted discreetly and privately. When clergymen published pamphlets on political subjects, they usually did so anonymously. The traditional belief that it was inappropriate for church leaders to mix religion and politics was clearly articulated in 1722 in Boston when Cotton Mather and John Wise were exposed as two of the principal controversialists in the heated currency debate. "Some of our Ecclesiasticks of late," wrote an anonymous pamphleteer, "have been guilty of too officious a meddling with State Affairs. To see a Clergy-man (Commedianlike) stand belabouring his Cushion and intermixing his Harrangue with THUNDERBOLTS, while entertaining his peaceable Congregation with things whereof he is . . . Ignorant . . . how ridiculous is the Sight and the Sound."[23]

Attacks on clerical involvement in politics continued throughout this period. In Philadelphia Quaker leaders complained that the proprietary party was promoted at election time "even from the pulpitt." But John Kinsey, the clerk of the Society of Friends Yearly Meeting, did not cavil to read a letter from Friends in London regarding the forthcoming elections "in ye Lobby of ye Assembly Room."[24] In the 1750s both factions in Philadelphia complained about attempts to make religion the servant of politics. The Quakers charged that "the utmost efforts have been used and the Pulpit and Press exercised against us," while their opponents complained that "Quaker Preachers and other Political Engines" had rolled into action in order to defeat an important bill before the assembly.[25] In spite of the lingering feeling that politics and religion should occupy separate spheres, the urban clergy became more and more politicized as contending secular leaders urged them to enter the arena of public controversy.

To some extent the line between politics and religion became blurred because some of the most burning issues of the period could not be confined to either the civil or religious sphere. In Philadelphia the issue of war and defense appropriations in 1748 brought the first full-scale exchange on a secular question between opposing denominational spokesmen. In a dozen signed pamphlets, Anglican and Presbyterian clerics took on Quaker leaders in a public dialogue on the necessity of military defense in the face of a threat of French and Spanish invasion. This battle of words thrust the clergy squarely into the political arena. The first sermon given by the fiery revivalist Gilbert Tennent on the justification for defensive war was published, he claimed, at the request of the leaders of the anti-Quaker party.[26] Before the controversy was over the political role of the Philadelphia clergy had been greatly magnified and the precedent established for their open participation in public affairs. The corollary was that denominational groups from this point on would frequently perform as political pressure groups rather than simply as religious organizations. Once that process commenced churches began to split on political questions. Only a decade after the Anglican church of Philadelphia began to involve itself in the primary political issues of the day, its leaders and laity divided irretrievably on the question of whether the vast landholdings of the proprietors of Pennsylvania ought to be subject to the same war taxes as the property of others.[27]

In New York the Kings College controversy similarly provided the occasion for the rapid obliteration of the line separating religion and politics. A group of Anglicans who were politically sympathetic to the conservative governor James DeLancey hoped to establish a college supported by public taxes. Although the Anglicans had the backing of much of the Dutch Reformed church, they ran into a hornet's nest of opposition from the Presbyterians, who intended to stop this creeping Anglicanism.

From 1753 to 1755 the issue raged and the presses poured forth vitriolic literature, much of it written by clergymen themselves. "I was not ignorant," wrote one Presbyterian, "that whole Hosts of the Cloth, . . . had a Hand in far the greatest Part of all the Lampoons and Libels, all the Malice and Calumny discharg'd at those invincable Writers" who opposed the college. The Anglicans struck back with all the power of their pens and even launched a new newspaper, the *New York Mercury*, labeled by the opposition as the "partial, party, paltry, and priestly Newspaper."[28] In the end, Kings College was finally chartered and run under Anglican direction without public support. But the side effects may have been more important than the main issue because, as with the question of war appropriations in Philadelphia, the controversy politicized the churches and politicians learned to look at religious congregations as new fields upon which to stage political battles. By mid-century church leaders were learning that they need not apologize for "preaching politics," as Jonathan Mayhew of Boston put it.[29]

Nowhere did the lines between religion, economics, and politics crumble more swiftly or completely than in the experiential and ideological upheaval connected with the Great Awakening—the firestorm of religious enthusiasm that broke over the northern colonies in the mid-1730s and continued for almost a decade. More than a religious movement, the Awakening must be seen as a profound cultural crisis involving the convergence of political, social, economic, and ideological forces that had been building for several generations. This was especially true in Boston, where social change had proceeded more swiftly and corrosively than in the other towns and where, correspondingly, the Great Awakening erupted with the greatest seismic force.

More than two centuries after the Great Awakening we still lack an adequate sociological and psychological model for interpreting this cultural earthquake.[30] Least of all do we understand the outpouring of religious energy in the urban centers of colonial life, for the wave of revivalism has been studied primarily as a rural phenomenon. Its influence, to be sure, could not be contained geographically, but it undeniably had powerful effects in the seaport towns. It was here that fiery preachers such as George Whitefield, Gilbert Tennent, and James Davenport concentrated their efforts and had their greatest success; and it was here that they published their sermons and coordinated their itineraries.

At its core the Great Awakening was "a search for new sources of

authority, new principles of action, new foundations of hope" among
people who had come to believe that "the churches as institutions no
longer met the spiritual needs of the people."[31] The Awakeners preached
that the old sources of authority were too effete to solve the problems of
the day, too encrusted with tradition, self-indulgence, hypocrisy, and
intellectualism to bring a sense of hope and faith to a generation that was
witnessing the rapid transformation of the world of their fathers. At a
time of cultural crisis, a new wellspring of authority was desperately
needed, and that source, the evangelists preached, was the individual
himself. Like the seventeenth-century Quakers who immigrated to Philadelphia, the Awakeners believed that God did not operate through an
elite corps of vice-regents composed of the learned clergy and the aristocracy. All individuals, from whatever their stations in life, could seek
and find God, barren though they might be of special learning or lofty
status. Like the Quaker "inner light," given by God to every man and
woman, the "new light" within the awakened enabled them to achieve
grace through the conversion experience.[32] From experiential religion,
which every woman, man, and child was capable of achieving, a new
sense of community could be forged, a new brotherhood of man achieved,
the city on the hill restored.

The urban appeal of the revivalists was apparent from the first American tour of the master itinerant, George Whitefield. A diminutive man
with a magnificent voice, Whitefield was the son of an English tavern-
keeper. He had worked his way through Oxford in a state of chronic
alienation from the self-indulgent, extravagant gentlemen scholars whose
class background always kept him on the defensive. Shortly after matric-
ulating at Oxford, he was converted to Methodism, which would become
the new religion of the English laboring class. From that point on Whitefield became a master of open-air preaching, as he trekked across the English countryside. He crossed the Atlantic to preach briefly in the new
colony of Georgia in 1737, returned to England in 1738, and then re-
crossed the ocean again in late 1739. Only twenty-five years old then, he
began a barnstorming trip that evoked a mass response of dimensions
never before witnessed in America.[33]

In his triumphant American tour in 1739-1740 Whitefield, as one contemporary wrote, "chiefly confined his Labours to the populous
towns."[34] His first urban appearance was in Philadelphia where he
preached a series of outdoor sermons in November 1739 to crowds of
6,000 or more. He returned to the Pennsylvania capital later that month
and again in the spring of 1740, exhorting throngs that filled the streets.[35]
Moving north, Whitefield delivered a series of outdoor sermons to sizeable gatherings in New York over a four-day period in December, although he was excluded from all municipal buildings and only the small
Wall Street Presbyterian congregation opened its doors to him.[36] But it

was in Boston, which he reached in September 1740, where Whitefield received his most spectacular reception. The town was primed to embrace him, for his sermons had been widely distributed, newspaper accounts of his tour filled the newspapers, and a dedicated group of evangelical clergymen had been actively pressing their auditors to seek the "new birth." Boston and the surrounding countryside, wrote one aged Puritan, "stand ready to receive him as an angel of God."[37]

Whitefield preached his first sermon in Boston at Benjamin Colman's fashionable Brattle Street Church. By the evangelist's estimate 4,000 persons crammed into the meetinghouse. A series of appearances followed at other Boston churches and then, on a Saturday afternoon, "about fifteen thousand flocked to hear him on Boston Common." For three weeks Whitefield barnstormed the Boston area, appearing seventeen times in Boston churches and drawing huge crowds whenever he preached outdoors. On Sunday, October 12, the South Church was so tightly packed that Whitefield had to clamber in a window in the front of the church to deliver his sermon. His farewell appearance on Boston Common drew 20,000 by the most conservative estimates and has been reckoned by a recent historian as "the largest audience seen in America before Webster's performance on Bunker Hill."[38] When he left Boston, the town was quivering with excitement about the imminent Second Coming of Christ.

Whitefield's extraordinary appeal can be partially accounted for by his genius for histrionic performances, his perfection of the art of advance publicity, and his ability to simplify theological doctrine and focus the attention of masses of people on one facet of religious life—the conversion experience. In his electrifying performances, where written sermons were cast away, where frenetic body movements and magnificent voice control replaced dry, logical, rigidly structured theological lectures, thousands experienced the desire to be "born again." But it was the message as well as the medium that explains why large portions of colonial America's urban populations flocked to see Whitefield. He frontally challenged traditional sources of authority, called upon people to become the instruments of their own salvation, and implicitly attacked the prevailing upper-class notion that the uneducated mass of people had no minds of their own.

When Whitefield began his American tour in 1739, the social dynamite buried deep in his message was not yet clearly perceived by the elite. After all, his preaching produced thousands of conversions and filled to overflowing the churches that had been languishing for more than a generation. After his 1740 visit to Boston, Thomas Prince, minister of the Old South Church, wrote that "great numbers in this town were so happily concerned about their souls, as we had never seen anything like it before, except at the time of the general earthquake [in 1727]." The people "were excited to hear ministers more than ever; so that our assemblies, both on lectures and Sabbaths, were surprizingly increased."[39] William Cooper of Brattle Street Church claimed that more parishioners came to him for spiritual guidance in one week after Whitefield's preaching than in the preceding twenty-four years. Whitefield had magnified the importance of religion in the lives of almost all Bostonians, so it is no wonder that he was welcomed as "an angel of God, or as Elias, or John the Baptist risen from the dead."[40] For civil leaders, Whitefield also appeared at first as God-sent. Religion had long been thought of by eighteenth-century leaders as the handmaiden of social control. Happily, the master evangelist was not only filling the empty pews that clergymen had brooded about, but seemed to be ushering in a new era of discipline, morality, and social harmony. Thus, he was received as royalty by figures no less important than Governor Belcher in Boston and John Penn, Pennsylvania's resident proprietor, in Philadelphia.[41]

The enthusiastic reception of Whitefield in Boston in 1740, however, did not conceal serious opposition to his preaching. Of the town's fifteen Congregational ministers, three remained cool toward his performances and three opposed him outright.[42] The town's three Anglican ministers also vocally criticized him because Whitefield, although an ordained Anglican priest, was highly critical of the church's policies and seemed to take special satisfaction in attacking the Church of England, praising Puritan religiosity, and berating the Bishop of London's policy of sending Anglican ministers to New England to proselytize in the middle of the Puritan camp.[43] But there is no gainsaying the stupendous success of his first New England tour, which triggered the greatest mass outpouring of religious feeling in the history of that religiously oriented society.

With Whitefield's departure from Boston in October 1740 and the arrival of his American field lieutenant Gilbert Tennent, whom he had instructed "to blow up the divine fire lately kindled there," enthusiasm for the Awakening diminished rapidly among the clerical and civil establishment.[44] Tennent was the son of the Scots-Irish founder of the Presbyterian "Log College" in Neshaminy, Pennsylvania, "a burly, salty, downright man" who preached, according to one contemporary, "like a Boatswain of a Ship, calling the Sailors to come to Prayers and be damned."[45] Many of Boston's Congregational ministers had been glad enough to invite Tennent to "water the seed sown by Mr. Whitefield."[46] But shortly after he arrived on December 13, 1740 it became apparent that he was a different sort of spellbinder than his English mentor. In the midst of the cruelest winter in Boston's history, townspeople stood for hours in deep snow to hear this Son of Thunder, whose highly agitated manner of preaching produced emotional writhings and faintings that had not been a part of Whitefield's performances. Worse than this, Tennent began to attack the established clergy as unregenerate and to encourage people to forsake their ministers. "The sapless Discourses of such dead Drones" were worthless, he proclaimed.[47] Worst of all, Tennent invested his exhortations with a social radicalism that was absolutely frightening to the upper orders of society. Whitefield had taken occasional cuts at aristocratic fashion and criticized the religious lassitude that came, he said, with the accumulation of material wealth. But his American successors, Tennent first among them, adapted his message to the social landscape they knew so well and infused evangelical preaching with a radical egalitarianism that left many former supporters of Whitefield grasping for their pens. Tennent confirmed all the suspicions of those who had been cool to Whitefield, and by the time the Presbyterian evangelist left Boston in March 1741 the conservative reaction against revivalism was in full swing. Tennent was called "a monster! impudent & noisy," a man whose "Beastly brayings" were having even more dangerous effects upon the humbler people of the town than had Whitefield's preaching.[48]

What had started out in Boston in 1739 as a religious revival that cut across class lines was becoming a class-specific movement. As the implicit social content of the evangelists' message became more explicit, support from the upper and middle levels of Boston society fell away. But the enthusiasm of the lower orders only grew more powerful and ecstatic. Instead of unifying Boston's economically troubled, politically divided society, as appeared possible at first, the Awakening was fragmenting it further. It was becoming clear that among the multitude the most important aspects of evangelical religion were "emotionalism, miracle, will of God, millennialism, perfectionism, evangelism, pietism," all of which smacked strongly of "antinomianism, fanaticism, radicalism, anti-institutionalism, [and] Christian liberty." On the other side stood the "old lights," the rationalists of middle- and upper-class backgrounds for whom "organic development, law and order, restraint and control" were eminently important. More and more the opponents of the Awakening began to predict "anarchy, levelling, and dissolution," if matters continued their course, "while the evangelical side argued that without drastic reformation" in society there would be "tyranny, persecution, and suppression."[49]

The growing polarization in Boston in 1741 and the increasingly class-linked sources of evangelical support became more painfully apparent in the following year, as Tennent was succeeded by the man who became the bête noire of the clerical establishment—James Davenport. Only sixteen when he was graduated from Yale College and only twenty-five when he arrived in Boston on June 27, 1742, Davenport combined impeccable credentials with a temperament reminiscent of the radical sectarians of mid-seventeenth century England.[50] His great-grandfather had been a founder of New Haven and his father was the greatly respected pastor of the Congregational Church in Stamford, Connecticut. Davenport had been infected with emotional religion while at Yale and was inspired by the news of Whitefield's first triumphant tour in America to initiate revival meetings in his own parish at Southold, Long island. In 1740 Davenport traveled to Philadelphia to meet Whitefield and Tennent, and accompanied the former on his tour from New York to Philadelphia in the fall of that year. By mid-1741 his own itinerant journeys were drawing thousands at every stop. Everywhere he went throngs turned out for street singing, all-night revival meetings, and emotional outpourings that often left dozens prostrated on the ground. Congregations split into pro- and antienthusiasts wherever he went, and by the spring of 1742 his incendiary preaching was regarded as so dangerous that he was arrested, tried, and deported from Hartford, Connecticut amidst a near riot.[51]

When Davenport reached Boston, even the most evangelical clergymen joined their conservative colleagues in denying their pulpits to the young spellbinder and in signing a declaration against his preaching there. This mattered little to Davenport, for his natural amphitheater was the street or field rather than the meetinghouse, and he could measure his strength in the large number of people who took no heed of the ministerial declaration against him. To proscribe him from the top of society was, ironically, to recommend him to the bottom, for deference was crumbling like dry leaves among "God's people," as the radical revivalists called the poor and dispossessed.

No sooner had Davenport entered the city than a noisy procession—a "Rabble of Men, Women, and Children," according to the conservative *Boston Evening Post*—followed him through the streets.[52] When he began daily appearances on Boston Common, it was clear that the clergy's fears were well founded, for Davenport proved his extraordinary ability to create religious hysteria and to provoke hatred of Boston's chief figures of authority. The people, he expostulated, should drink rat poison rather than listen to the damnifying preachments of the corrupt, "unconverted" clergy.[53] The Boston press tried hard to curb Davenport's popularity by characterizing his followers as "chiefly made up of the idle or ignorant Persons, and those of the lowest Rank." In the end it was only by indicting him before the Grand Jury "on the charge of having said that Boston's ministers were leading the people blindfold to hell" that the conservative leaders were able to get Davenport deported from town. In handing down a verdict of *non compos mentis* the Grand Jury gave the conservatives less than they wanted, but it was enough to drive the fiery Davenport from the city.[54]

On the surface Davenport's threat to Boston's leaders was directly related to his attacks against the clergy. This may have bruised egos, but it was not actually the main threat, for the city's clergymen were not losing their flocks as a result of Davenport's preaching. He was cordially hated for his "unjust and hard Speeches belch'd out against [Boston's] own proper Pastors," but Davenport was even more dangerous because he hotly indicted the rich and powerful, criticized the yawning gap between the rich and poor, and exhorted ordinary people to resist those who exploited and deceived them.[55] Only then, he cried, would the Lamb Jesus return to earth. Even before he arrived, the conservative press was ridiculing the new lights for pursuing "Porters, Cobblers, [and] Barbers"— the bottom layer of the laboring class. After his arrival, Charles Chauncy, lofty minister of the wealthy First Church and generalissimo of the anti-revivalists, expressed the near-hysterical conviction that radical revivalism was making "strong attempts to destroy all property, to make all things common, wives as well as goods."[56] Other critics raised the specter of England's Fifth Monarchy uprising during the seventeenth century civil war and noted the connection between religious enthusiasm and social leveling.[57]

Historians have rarely been willing to take Davenport seriously, agreeing with the Boston Grand Jury that he was judicially insane.[58] The twentieth-century celebration of rationality and the corollary disdain of mysticism, emotionalism, and uninhibited body movements have diverted attention from his appeal and that of other enthusiasts who provoked crying, writhing, swooning, and screaming among their auditors. The strength of feeling he inspired in Boston and his ability to evoke a joyous collective spirit among a mass of common people accounts for the alarm voiced by his critics. "Were you to see him in his most violent Agitations," wrote the *Boston Evening Post*, "you would be apt to think, that he was a Madman just broke from his Chains; But especially had you seen him returning from the Common after his first preaching, with a large Mob at his Heels, singing all the Way thro' the Streets, he with his Hands extended, his Head thrown back, and his Eyes staring up to Heaven, attended with so much Disorder, that they look'd more like a Company of *Bacchanalians* after a mad Frolick, than sober Christians who had been worshipping God."[59] Such descriptions convinced respectable Bostonians that revivalism had gotten out of hand and that social control of the lowest layers of society was now dangerously threatened. Masses of people were flocking daily to Boston Common to hear a man that the established leaders declared insane, they were deriving from him a spiritual satisfaction they had never received before, and they were forging a communal experience that was profoundly threatening to the established culture, which stressed order, discipline, and submissiveness from the laboring classes.

Boston's leaders were probably correct in charging that Davenport had "few admirers among the sober judicious Part of the Town," but it must be understood that by "sober" and "judicious" they meant the middle and upper classes. His people were those at the bottom of the urban hierarchy

—laborers, seamen, the impoverished, slaves, indentured servants, and the young—those who in the counterpart Wesleyan movement in England were called "Christ's poor."[60] Davenport's processions and ringing denunciations of the rich and powerful offered them some succour from their dismal lot and gave them a way of expressing intensely felt emotions.[61] Street processions, unconventional singing, and emotional outpourings on the common were displays of folk solidarity, of egalitarian instincts, of opposition to conventional modes of expression, and of the moral superiority of common people over the town's middle and upper classes, who had been inspired by Whitefield but could not abide the more radical preachings of Tennent and Davenport.

By 1742 Boston had become a magnet attracting a procession of itinerant gospelers and haranguers, all of them labeled social incendiaries as well as religious mystics by the established clergy. Andrew Crosswell, Samuel Buell, Eleazar Wheelock, Nathaniel Rogers, and other tramping evangelists made Boston the highlight of their pilgrimages, for no other place in New England could offer the crowds, the response of the dispossessed, or the opportunity to attack the most eminent of the colonies' entrenched clergy as could the capital of Puritanism.[62] Among the itinerants who torched Boston with the Lord's truth in the spring and summer of 1742, Andrew Crosswell was especially important. He attracted huge crowds across the river in Charlestown and triggered a fierce barrage of newspaper criticism. A friend of the dispossessed, Crosswell preached against cruel treatment of prisoners in the jails and against slavery.[63] To many "respectable" citizens it seemed as if Boston had turned into a cauldron of lower-class religious enthusiasm and social disintegration. Deference crumbled as men and women ignored their daily work, flocking to the common or to fields on the edge of town to hear the itinerant exhorters, who preached morning and evening, every day of the week.[64]

Of all the manifestations of social leveling that accompanied the Great Awakening, the one that summed up the reckless social thrust of evangelicalism in the view of conservatives was the practice of public, lay exhorting. Within the structured Protestant churches there was no room for lay persons to compete with the qualified ministry in preaching the word of God. Nor was there room for "self-initiated associations of the people meeting outside of regularly constituted religious or political meetings," for to do so was to relocate authority collectively in the mass of common people.[65] Awakeners such as Davenport not only condemned the established clergy as unconverted, but insisted that ordinary people should share their religious experiences publicly, gathering as they pleased and preaching if they felt moved to all who would listen. The danger of this new breed of self-proclaimed preachers was evident in their popularity. Though the exhorters were usually "raw and unskilful, in the word of righteousness," at least in the eyes of the trained ministry, they were highly popular "among the multitudes of people; who chose rather to *hear them*, than their old teachers."[66] Eastern Massachusetts by mid-1742 seethed with lay exhorters. "It is impossible to relate the convulsions into which the whole Country is thrown," wrote a minister in nearby Salem in 1742, "by a set of Enthusiasts that strole about harangueing the admiring Vulgar in *extempore* nonsense, nor is it confined to these only, for Men, Women, Children, Servants, & Nigros are now become (as they phrase it) Exhorters."[67]

Lay exhorting was deeply hated and feared, for it shattered the monopolistic hold of the educated clergy on religious discourse, put all people on a plane in the area of religion, gave a new importance to the oral culture of common people, whose spontaneous outpourings contrasted sharply with the literary culture of the gentry, established among them the notion that their destinies and their souls were in their own hands instead of the hands of the elite clergy, and turned the world upside down in allowing those who had traditionally been consigned to the bottom of society to assume roles customarily reserved for educated, adult men. In lay exhorting class lines were crossed and sexual and racial roles were defied. Because of such obliteration of hierarchical boundaries the concentration of power and prestige in the elite was gravely undermined. The open-field revivalism of Davenport, Crosswell, and others provided a forum where struggling and despairing Bostonians could articulate their experiences, express their discontent, and imbibe a sense of moral superiority in relation to those to whom they had traditionally been taught to defer.[68]

THE THREAT posed by Tennent, Davenport, and other radical evangelists cannot be fully appreciated without understanding the political crisis that Boston was passing through at this time. Since 1739, the burning issue had been what to do about the province's greatly inflated paper currency, which by orders from England was to be completely retired by 1741. Many believed that Massachusetts would have to defy England, for with its chronic trade imbalance the withdrawal of paper money would leave the colony without a circulating medium. In 1739 two proposals were put forward as an answer to the knotty question. One was for a Land Bank, which would issue the equivalent of £600,000 in "old tenor" bills of credit, secured by land mortgaged to the bank. Any subscriber could borrow as much as £2,000 in paper money, properly backed by land, and repay the loan in notes or enumerated commodities over twenty years at 3 percent interest. The plan circumvented the English prohibition against government-issued paper money by proposing that private citizens do it themselves. In effect, the Land Bank refurbished a proposal for privately issued bills of credit put forward more than twenty years before. Its chief organizer, in fact, was the same John Colman who had promoted a private bank along similar lines in 1714. The Land Bankers were proposing what had been suggested then—to solve Massachusetts's monetary problem by converting land, the province's most valuable resource, into a circulating medium.[69]

Rivaling the Land Bank scheme was a Silver Bank, organized by a group of wealthy Boston merchants who wanted a far less inflationary scheme, one that would increase the supply of coin, which they needed to balance accounts in London. They planned to issue the equivalent of £120,000 "old tenor" in bills of credit backed by silver and redeemable in fifteen years, much in the manner of the Merchants Notes of 1733. Around these competing plans politics reached a fever pitch in 1740 and 1741. The proponents of the Land Bank swept the May 1740 provincial elections, but both banks published their plans and began emitting bills late that summer, even though they had no legislative approval for doing so.[70] Boston's international merchants "damned the [Land] Bank as merely a more invidious form of the soft money panacea typically favored by the province's poor and unsuccessful," and publicly vowed that they would not accept the Land Bank bills.[71] Land Bank supporters attacked the Silver Bank as another scheme of the rich to throttle the poor. Governor Belcher, trying hard to implement an unpopular policy set in London, issued a proclamation banning both banks and prohibiting officers of government from accepting the bills of either. Provincial politics turned into guerrilla warfare, as the inflationist house battled the deflationist governor and council, each seeking ways of outwitting the other in a constitutional chess game that was ultimately decided in London, where Parliament in 1741 outlawed all private banks from issuing currency in Massachusetts. Boston learned this in late May, along with the news that William Shirley, a long-time resident of the town and a man known for his skills as a mediator, had become the colony's new governor.[72]

Controversy over the Land and Silver Banks divided Boston deeply. The split was neither so clear nor as morally based as William Douglass saw it at the time: the *"Idle & Extravagant* who want to borrow Money at any bad Lay" arrayed against the *"Industrious and Frugal,* our considerable foreign Traders and rich Men."[73] There were hundreds of Bostonians who were industrious and frugal but not rich merchants and hundreds more who were not extravagant but still saw their interests best represented by the Land Bankers. The Silver Bank was the handiwork of Boston's import-export merchants, who believed that the Land Bank favored debtors against creditors because paper money, backed by land, was sure to depreciate in value. According to Gresham's Law, they said, men would hoard their gold and silver, thus decreasing the availability of coin for use in international trade. The Land Bank was favored by those who did not need coin for their transactions: local traders, many shopkeepers and artisans, and probably a large majority of the working poor. It is also possible that many of the middling people probably favored the Silver Bank, for they had been badly hurt by currency depreciation and saw a restricted currency, backed by silver, as the lesser of two evils.[74]

Although the alignment of Boston's populace on the currency issue cannot be determined precisely, it is clear that enough townspeople were deeply angered by the refusal of the "Foreign Traders" to accept the Land Bank bills in late 1740 and early 1741 to support rumors flying through eastern Massachusetts about impending civil war. The governor worried at the widespread defiance of the proclamation against Land Bank bills, while reports circulated that a thousand Bostonians would join thousands of men from the countryside to force the merchants to accept Land Bank bills. Grain prices were also increasing alarmingly and wheat was in short supply, giving rise to the report that the angry mobs assembling for a march on Boston would also seize any grain they could find in merchant warehouses.[75] William Shirley, who succeeded the unpopular Belcher, defused the situation with promises of a new economic policy, but years passed before the rancor engendered by the Land Bank controversy dissipated altogether.

It is important to note that Whitefield's arrival in Boston coincided with the furor over the Land and Silver Banks. His initial sermons were preached only a few weeks after Boston's leading merchants announced that they would not accept the Land Bank bills, and his stay in Boston overlapped the public attacks on the merchants as "gripping and merciless usurers" who "heaped up vast Estates" at the expense of the common people.[76] In this atmosphere, Whitefield's ability to call the masses to worship must have been seen at first by conservatives as a positive gain, for the experience of a common religious exaltation might serve as an antidote to economic tension and incipient class conflict. The evangelist was asking all town dwellers to unite in the work of God and to redirect their energy from earthly matters to concerns of the soul.

However, the issues that affected one's ability to put food on the table and clothes on the backs of children could never be permanently subsumed in religious ecstasy. This became clear with the arrival of the itinerant evangelists who invaded Boston after Whitefield's departure. Their openhanded attacks on wealth and vested authority encouraged those who felt oppressed to challenge their enemies. Whitefield had increased the self-esteem of the lower classes by preaching that the rich were "as deeply tainted with Adam's sin as the poorest and most illiterate persons" and by arguing that heaven was populated more by the poor than the rich since "the Lord had a special preference for the poor."[77] Davenport went far beyond that, excoriating the rich and powerful and howling at his audiences to "Pull them down, turn them out, and put others in their Places."[78] Davenport preached the gospel of antiauthoritarianism and leveling, and in the context of the Land Bank controversy there could be no strict compartmentalization of religious and economic discontent. By the time he had been banished from Boston, the wealthy opponents of the Land Bank were being cursed openly in the streets as "carnal Wretches, Hypocrites, Fighters against God, Children of the Devil, cursed Pharisees." The religious flavor of such epithets, which were employed by lower-class Bostonians to indict those on one side of the currency debate, demonstrates vividly how economic exploitation and religious degeneracy were linked in the minds of many. William Douglass saw order crumbling, as the managers of the Land Bank "spirit the People to Mutiny, Sedition, and Riots."[79]

Thus, the Great Awakening in Boston represented far more than a religious earthquake. When studied carefully, its manifestations tell us a great deal about the disposition of ordinary people as they haltingly enunciated a distinctive popular ideology that challenged inherited cultural norms. Many historians have seen in the Great Awakening a ground swell of individualism, an outcry against a "static, stratified view of class structure," a kind of protodemocratic spirit that anticipated the Revolution.[80] There is some truth in this, but what we need is a more careful distinction between the new forms of protest and the protesters' goals, as well as an understanding of the meaning of the Awakening for well-situated Awakeners as distinct from the evangelized laboring poor. For almost all the awakened, but especially for those from the lower echelons, the revival years involved an expansion of political consciousness and a new feeling of self-importance, as people partook of spontaneous meetings, assumed a new power in ecclesiastical affairs, and were encouraged repeatedly from the pulpit to adopt an attitude of skepticism toward dogma and authority. The leaders of the Great Awakening were preaching a radical message: that religion was at a low ebb in America because the ministry was effete, corrupted by participation in creeping materialism, and intellectually bankrupt in their capitulation to Arminian theology, which stressed that man could gain his own salvation through "good works" rather than through God's mysterious saving grace. The revivalists urged reform and regeneration upon the established clergy, but warned the parishioners themselves not to bow passively to a corrupt religious hierarchy. Ordinary people must take matters into their own hands. The Awakeners thus encouraged doctrinal controversy and sanctified the casting out of unconverted leaders by the people. It was precisely this message that frightened so many upper-class city dwellers and led them to charge the revivalists with preaching levelism and anarchy. "It is . . . an *exceeding* difficult gloomy Time with us," wrote one disgusted antirevivalist; "Such an *enthusiastic, factious, censorious*

Spirit was never known here . . . Every *low-bred, illiterate* Person can resolve Cases of Conscience, and settle *the most* difficult Points of Divinity, *better* than the most learned Divines."[81]

Toward what ends was this new popular power to be employed? This is a thorny question, for revivalism evoked passionate religious commitment from a wide variety of people with different experiences and different needs. Many of those who joined Boston's established churches in large numbers from 1740 to 1744 probably regretted and resented the narrowing of economic opportunity. But they did not disavow the market economy that increasingly ruled their lives. Instead, they sought means for competing on more equal terms within it. The Land Bank represented a modern response to economic constriction, promising to allow those who had been squeezed hard in the competitive world to strive for gains on a more equal footing. We cannot correlate supporters of the Land Bank with the wave of converts into Boston's churches, but it seems likely that many shopkeepers, craftsmen, and others from the hard-pressed middling ranks were a part of both these movements.

Beneath these people was another group of Bostonians who experienced the Awakening differently and hoped for the advent of a much different world. These were the lowliest town-dwellers, including slaves, servants, the impoverished, and many who struggled to gain a foothold on the treacherous slopes of economic security. It was not toward democratic bourgeois revolution that these people pointed, but backwards to an earlier age when it was conceived that individuals acted not for themselves, always striving to get ahead at the expense of their neighbors, but pulled together as a community. The crowds that followed Davenport, Crosswell, and the other radical evangelists seem to have been primarily composed of these dispossessed Bostonians. Charles Chauncy, who defended the profit motive and the pursuit of self-interest and made his church a comfortable gathering place for those with established fortunes and others striving for higher places, called these people the "idle and Ignorant," "the rabble," persons of "the lowest rank." Though some of the terms were derogatory, they accurately defined the social position of those who marched through the streets behind the radical itinerants. For these people economic freedom meant little; their struggle was concerned with a more basic need simply to survive. In the Great Awakening, Gilbert Tennent's "Common People" not only liberated themselves from "the contumely of their self-appointed betters" but also "glimpsed the possibility of a people's acting to make their united will prevail as the guarantor of the common good."[82]

This antientrepreneurial tone was permeated by communalism and a concern with economic justice. That is why the humblest of the awakened harkened to the message of the most radical social critics of the revival era. Preachers such as Tennent had no way of analyzing tax lists or probate records to determine how the distribution of wealth was changing in the towns. But it was obvious that while new almshouses and workhouses were built and relief rolls were swelling, some men were erecting lavish mansions and importing coaches, chariots, and luxurious house furnishings from London. The revivalist preachers sensed the social effects of the new economic order; they were sure that a contumnacious pursuit of self-interest ate at the vitals of a community. Jonathan Mayhew, another of the Congregational ministers who spoke for the entrepreneurial fortune-builders of Boston's best-heeled churches, might declare that the "publick happiness is nothing but the happiness of a *number of individuals* united in society." But the Awakeners cringed at such an atomistic conception of society and answered back that he who was "governed by regard to his own private interest" was thereby committed to "act the part of an enemy to the public."[83] In any truly Christian society, wrote Tennent, "mutual *Love* is the *Band* and *Cement* . . . For Men, by the Neglect of its Exercise, and much more by its Contrary, will be tempted, against the *Law of Nature*, to seek a *single* and independent State, in order to secure their *Ease* and *Safety*."[84]

These two fundamentally different conceptions of society defined the responsibilities of the upper class in sharply different ways. The "old light" or rationalist clergy (and some of the "new light" ministers such as Benjamin Colman, who wished to infuse their affluent congregations with new religious energy) pragmatically countenanced the emerging capitalist ethic. The radical Awakeners, on the other hand, were thoroughly uncomfortable with the acquisitiveness of the urban elite. The motive behind such materialism, as Tennent understood it, was the desire "to be a little demigod in the World, a sort of independent Being, by having many depending on thee, courting thy Smiles, and trembling at thy frowns." Of humble stock himself, Tennent heaped scorn on "the Grandees" of America and warned that men "grow in Wickedness in Proportion to the Increase in their Wealth."[85] But fortune-building, which the new commercial ethic condoned, was even more fundamentally evil in its flaunting of the principle of human equality. It would take another generation for the notion to become general in the port towns that the rich were getting richer *because* the poor were getting poorer. But the belief that an organic connection existed between the growth of wealth and poverty was already being expressed in Boston during the Awakening. The Awakeners "stood in judgment on acquisitiveness and even strongly implied the need for redressing inequities in the division of colonial wealth. The evangelical critique of the business ethic remained at bottom a lament for society's departure from its pristine natural equality."[86]

In defining the responsibilities of the affluent for the poor the radical Awakeners and the rationalists also disagreed. The latter, speaking for securely positioned Bostonians and those who strived for positions in the competitive world, spent most of their energy counseling the poor to be content with their lot and "sought to minimize the wealthy man's obligations to his fellows."[87] In an individualistic society, and in an economic environment that hypothetically offered abundance to every diligent person, well-meaning charitable instincts might defeat the very purpose of charity by encouraging the lazy to remain idle in the expectation of public support. The Thessalonian Christians, wrote Charles Chauncy, had made this mistake. "The extraordinary Charities, common in that Day, might encourage those, who were before disposed to be idle, to neglect the Business of their proper Callings."[88] Hence, it was best to cut the laboring poor off from charity so that they would learn that starvation, not public aid, would be the fate of idlers.

The radical Awakeners and some moderates, by contrast, preached the obligations of the fortunate to the indigent. A "private niggardly spirit," wrote Jonathan Edwards, "is more suitable for wolves, and other beasts of prey, than for human beings." Edward Holyoke, president of Harvard, lashed out in 1741 at the sharp dealings of many merchants whose "Extortion, their private Cheats, and their secret Covetousness, and defrauding both GOD and the poor of their Dues" had made New England "stink in the Nostrils of the People of other Countries."[89] The Awakeners' law of charity demanded that the rich give freely of their wealth and recognized that except by the grace of God and human accident they might stand in the places of the poor themselves.

Whitefield, Tennent, Edwards, and even radicals such as Davenport and Crosswell, were not preaching class revolt. What they urged was "a thorough reconsideration of the Christian ethic as it had come to be understood in the America of the 1730s."[90] Nor were those who listened to the Awakeners inspired to foment social revolution, for in fact the seeds of overt political radicalism were still in the germinative stage. But the multitudes who harked to the revivalist message in Boston were strengthened in their conviction that it was justifiable in extraordinary circumstances to take matters into their own hands. This is why even Edwards was seen by the commercial elite and its clerical allies as "The grand leveler of Christian history," even though sedition and leveling were not what he had in mind.[91]

It was no wonder, then, that Whitefield, who had been so enthusiastically welcomed in Boston in 1740 by the clerical establishment, was bitterly disapproved of when he returned in 1744. A number of ministers in Boston and the surrounding area who had gladly opened their pulpits to him four years before now clamped shut their doors. A barrage of bitter attacks issued from the press, and the faculty of Harvard College reviled him as an "enthusiast, a censorious, uncharitable person, and a deluder of the people." Its president chastised him for his "furious zeal," which had "burnt up the vitals of religion" and brought "multitudes" into "a censorious, unpeaceable, uncharitable" frame of mind.[92] The nervous arbiters of Boston's culture might have saved their energy, for by now war with France was imminent. Lower-class religious enthusiasm would shortly be redirected to maiming the anti-Christ of the north and Whitefield would be induced to use his influence with the lower orders to spur enlistments. The "rabble," whose form of religious passion was so greatly feared from above, were now to become Christian soldiers.

THE GREAT AWAKENING in New England was not caused by economic dislocation, spreading poverty, or currency problems that affected some parts of society more than others. Its roots reached far deeper into the subsoil of Calvinist Puritan culture. But the response to the Awakening was strongly conditioned by these phenomena, just as the evangelists responded "to the emergence in colonial America of disparities of wealth, as well as ways of life, unknown to earlier, and presumably purer, generations."[93] This is made unusually clear by comparing the Awakening in Boston with religious enthusiasm in New York and Philadelphia. In neither of these towns was the Awakening experienced as strongly, as enduringly, or as messianically as in Boston. In no small part this can be explained by the relative economic prosperity that both towns had enjoyed over the past generation. There were poor and buffeted persons in both New York and Philadelphia, to be sure, but their numbers were small.[94] This is not to say that large crowds did not assemble whenever Whitefield or Tennent preached. They did and they often responded ecstatically. But the more radical exhorters, whose message contained far more social dynamite than Whitefield's, never had the impact in New York and Philadelphia that they did in Boston.

In New York, the absence of widespread economic want was joined by another factor which dampened the effects of the Awakening. The clergymen of that city were almost unanimous in their opposition to Whitefield, Tennent, and their followers, and did everything possible to close their pulpits to them and minimize their influence. Twenty years before they had invited a young emigrant evangelist from Holland, Theodorus Frelinghuysen, to preach in the town. They had not liked what they heard. Frelinghuysen's passion and conviction that only the conversion experience transformed sinners into regenerate persons attracted the young and the poor but appalled the well-to-do. Whitefield's humanitarian statements on behalf of slaves also offended many New Yorkers, for they held captive in their midst the largest urban black population in America.[95] So on his three visits to New York in 1739 and 1740 Whitefield preached in the fields to only moderate crowds and on one occasion to the small Wall Street Presbyterian congregation. Joseph

Tracy, the first thorough student of the Awakening in the nineteenth century, concluded that Whitefield "produced no very remarkable effect in New York, till his visit in 1764."[96]

The case was much the same in Philadelphia. Presbyterian revivalism had begun in the Pennsylvania hinterland even before Jonathan Edwards had ignited the flames of revival in Northampton, Massachusetts. The Presbyterian revival had much to do with questions of denominational organization and doctrinal interpretation.[97] But in Philadelphia itself the impact of the Awakening contrasts sharply with Boston. At times, as during the five-day Presbyterian Synod that convened in May 1740 to resolve a cluster of hotly disputed issues, the mass feeling of a "new birth" was spectacular. William and Gilbert Tennent, Samuel Blair, James Davenport, and John Rowland preached fourteen times during the five days, both in churches and on Society Hill, where vast interdenominational crowds assembled. When he returned in November 1740 after his extraordinary New England tour, Whitefield preached six times in the New Building, a huge tabernacle erected by his supporters, though the crowds by this time had diminished.[98] But the steam was already going out of the revivalistic wave. During 1741 and 1742, when Boston was seething with lower-class religious emotionalism, Philadelphia was sedate.[99] No street processions, midnight revels, or mass singing occurred. Nor was the Philadelphia press, in contrast to Boston's, filled with attacks on the revivalists for disrupting society, inverting the class order, and kneading the people into a state of radical insubordination.[100]

Benjamin Franklin, who was a friend of Whitefield's but felt no need to be "born again," described how the Awakening worked a kind of reverse magic in his town from what occurred in Boston. "It was wonderful to see the Change soon made in the Manners of our Inhabitants; from being thoughtless or indifferent about Religion, it seem'd as if all the World were growing Religious; so that one could not walk thro' the Town in an Evening without Hearing Psalms sung in different Families of every Street."[101] Later Franklin wrote that "The Alteration in the Face of Religion here is altogether surprizing. Never did the People show so great a Willingness to attend Sermons, nor the Preachers greater Zeal and Diligence in performing the Duties of their Function. Religion is become the Subject of most Conversations. No Books are in Request but those of Piety and Devotion; and instead of idle Songs and Ballads, the People are every where entertaining themselves with Psalms, Hymns and Spiritual Songs."[102] Though such statements also apply to Boston in 1740, religious enthusiasm in that town shortly became a divisive, socially explosive force with strong class overtones. In Franklin's Philadelphia it remained a cohesive, socially stabilizing force, as provincial leaders hoped it would. Doctrinal controversy rended the Presbyterian church, but in an atmosphere of economic prosperity the Awakening never became invested with the kind of social meaning it held for the laboring poor of Boston.[103]

JUST AS street religion took deeper root in Boston during the Great Awakening than in the other port towns, so did street politics in the aftermath of the revival. The backdrop for this was economic dislocation. Civil war had been rumored during 1741 in connection with the dismantling of the Land Bank, and in the closing years of the decade Boston went twice more to the precipice of wholesale disorder. The first crisis came in November 1747 when Charles Knowles, commodore of the royal navy in North American waters, brought his fleet to Boston for reprovisioning in preparation for cruising in the West Indies. Life in the British navy was not likely to get a sailor even to middle age, and colonial ports provided many a tar with the opportunity to begin a better life. So, as was usual wherever the royal navy went, desertions left Knowles's fleet shorthanded after a stay in port. On the evening of November 16 press gangs set out to fill the crew vacancies from Boston's waterfront populace.[104]

Knowles was almost within his rights. Ships could not sail unmanned or even seriously undermanned, and ship captains were therefore authorized to impress colonial subjects into service for the crown. But after 1696 captains had to have an order from the provincial governor to send press gangs ashore. A 1707 law, still in force according to Americans but denied by the English, also prohibited the impressment of any mariner, on ship or shore, in American waters.[105] The matter was usually academic except in time of war because only then was the British navy present in American waters. In sending his press gangs to work, Knowles, in effect, was resorting to a policy that had long been unpopular in the colonies but represented the only alternative at his disposal.

Knowles doubtless knew that his press gangs had their work cut out for them, for lower-class Bostonians had fiercely resisted pressing since 1741. In that year, when the man-of-war *Astrea*, its ranks depleted by fifty deserters, was thought to be preparing a sweep of Boston's docks, a crowd of about 300 men armed with "axes, clubs and cutlasses" surrounded the house of the commanding officer, threatened his life, and promised to destroy his landlord's house if he pressed Boston's citizens. Later that year a riotous assembly pummeled Edward Winslow, Suffolk County sheriff, and stoned Anthony Stoddard, justice of the peace, for their aid to the commander of H.M.S. *Portland*, who was pressing men to fill his depleted crew. In March 1742 Captain James Scott of the *Astrea* returned from the West Indies and seized eight men from a wood sloop and several small coasters. This infuriated even the governor and council, who demanded the release of the men, threatened to cannonade the ship when Scott refused to comply, and attempted to bring the gnarly English captain ashore for trial. Five of the men were released before

Scott sailed away to the West Indies. More violence erupted in 1745 when a crowd attacked the commander of H.M.S. *Shirley* and beat him and the Suffolk County deputy sheriff senseless in Milk Street in retaliation for pressing. Seven months later two resisting Massachusetts sailors were murdered by a press gang in a North End tavern.[106] Violence begat violence in New England's largest seaport, which the man-hungry press gangs of the royal navy seemed to have made a special target. When the judicial system failed to protect denizens of Boston's waterfront, these men moved outside the law to thwart the English body-snatchers as best they could.

All of this was a prelude to Knowles's decision in November 1747 to initiate a major press. Considering the years of bitterness surrounding the issue, he must have anticipated trouble. But he could hardly have imagined that he would touch off the most massive civil disobedience in Boston's history. Knowles's press gangs swept ashore before dawn, gathering up shipbuilders, servants, slaves, and others, while other royal mariners raided the crews of vessels at anchor in Boston harbor. By mid-morning a crowd of Bostonians was sweeping through the streets in search of British seamen. Several officers were nabbed, and when others took refuge in the governor's house a crowd surrounded the mansion and verbally abused the governor. Attempting to stop the crowd, the sheriff and his deputies were badly mauled. The militia, called to arms by the governor and instructed to "suppress the Mob by force, and if need be, to fire upon 'em with Ball," showed no intention of responding. By dusk a crowd estimated by Thomas Hutchinson at "several thousand" answered the governor's attempt to issue a proclamation for dispersing the mob by stoning the government house free of its windows. Shirley and his merchant allies did what they could to appease the assemblage, but the throng now surged toward the waterfront to burn a 20-gun vessel being built for the royal navy. They satisfied themselves with dragging what they thought was a royal barge from one of the ships in the harbor to the courtyard of the governor's house, where it was burned amidst cheers. Enraged at these actions, Commodore Knowles threatened to bombard Boston from his warships. Only determined negotiations, which after several days of tumult led to the release of the impressed Bostonians, averted a showdown.[107]

In the investigations of the impressment riot, Boston's leading citizens pretended that the "Riotous Tumultuous Assembly" was composed of "Foreign Seamen, Servants, Negroes, and other Persons of Mean and vile Condition." These, of course, were precisely the targets of any press gang. But in this case the dragnet seems to have spread much farther, even into a few middle-class Boston homes, and to have evoked a response from more than "the Rabble." The governor himself was convinced that the mob had been "secretly Countenanc'd and encourag'd by some ill minded Inhabitants and Persons of Influence in the Town," and Thomas Hutchinson wrote that while "the lower class were beyond measure enraged," the press was resented by "men of all orders." The fact that the General Court refused to condemn the riot during the two days when the crowd controlled the town is further evidence that those who were in the streets had the tacit approval of many who were not.[108] Later, after Knowles had released most of the press gang captives and the crowd had evaporated, the middle- and upper-class elements in the General Court and town meeting expressed their "Abhorence of such Illegal Criminal Proceedings" and condemned "this infamous Insult upon the King's Peace." The most thorough historians of the incident interpret this as a cover-up, an attempt to exonerate the "respectable" people by pinning the blame on those of "Mean and Vile Condition." Little, in fact, was done to indict or prosecute those who had been plainly seen leading the crowd in its assault on the Province House and the royal barge.[10]

The impressment riot, though not directly linked to the lower-class enthusiasm of the Great Awakening, extended one of the central social thrusts of evangelicalism. In defying a commodore of the royal navy and the royal governor a mass of ordinary Bostonians engaged in a supreme kind of antiauthoritarianism. Both the rich and powerful, who experienced a new taste of the people's power, and the rioters themselves, whose extralegal activity had in the end obtained the release of the impressed Bostonians without reprisals, could appreciate this. It was a limited kind of class victory, to be sure, for the rescue of the impressed townsmen had been accomplished with the tacit cooperation of men of standing. This should not obscure the fact that in acting autonomously and extralegally, the common people demonstrated a consciousness squarely in the tradition of the earlier crowd actions over grain exports and public markets. Such bold defiance of the highest authorities, moreover, accorded well with the vision that the Awakeners had called forth, of ordinary people rising against constituted authority to redress grievances perpetrated by power-hungry, morally bankrupt figures who misused their power.

Less than two weeks after peace returned to Boston's waterfront, a hard-hitting pamphlet in plain language was on the streets. Signed by "Amicus Patriae," the publication vigorously defended the "natural right" of the townspeople to band together for defense against illegal presses. But the author, well versed in Lockean principles concerning individual rights, went much farther in attacking some of the town's wealthy for defending the impressment action and the governor's condemnation of the people's spirited fight against it. "Some of Figure and Interest among us," he charged, "live at Ease upon the Produce" of the lower ranks, whose members had been coerced into service in the royal fleet. These wealthy defenders of royal impressment were "Tools to arbitrary Power, . . . Slaves to their present petty Advantages, . . . so lost to all Sense of Goodness, and so abandon'dly Vicious" that they should be "obliged to serve, as a common Seaman, for seven Years, on board the worst Ship of War, and under the worst Commander, the King has in his Service."[110]

The pamphlet was the work of a growing anti-Shirley group that was attempting to revive the populistic politics of the Elisha Cooke era. One of its leaders was Samuel Adams, Jr., whose father, one of the principal Land Bankers, had been financially ruined by its liquidation and driven from office by Governor Belcher.[111] As part of their campaign, the Adams group launched an antiadministration newspaper, the *Independent Advertiser*, which began appearing on January 4, 1748. Its pitch to the laboring classes was obvious from the first issue. "Liberty can never subsist without Equality," it pronounced, "So when Men's Riches become immeasurably or surprizingly great, a People who regard their own Security, ought to make strict Enquiry, how they came by them . . . But some will say, is it a Crime to be rich? Yes, certainly, At the Publick Expense."[112] Taken verbatim from *Cato's Letters*, the hard-hitting attacks on Walpolean government and the new capitalist economy in England by John Trenchard and Thomas Gordon, this was the most explicit formulation ever heard in Boston that the rise of a wealthy elite was causally connected with the miseries of so many in the lower and middle ranks. Several issues later, still defending the impressment uprising, the *Independent Advertiser* linked it to internal economic problems. The people were warranted in taking the law into their own hands because they had watched "Their Estates crumbling to Nothing, their Trade stagnate, and fail in every Channel, their Husbandry and Manufactures render'd for Want of Hands almost impracticable, and insupportable Weight of Taxes," meanwhile witnessing "Others thriving at their Expense, and rising to Wealth and Greatness upon their Ruin."[113] In language reminiscent of the vitriolic phrases of the radical awakeners, the *Independent Advertiser* essayists played to feelings of social inequity in Boston and explicitly made the links between increasing stratification of wealth and growing political despotism.

On the heels of the impressment riot came the dénouement of the currency question that had been in the forefront of Boston's politics for years. After taking office in August 1741 Governor Shirley had been spared by King George's War from the unpleasant duty of enforcing the parliamentary demand that Massachusetts restrict its issue of paper money and withdraw the bills of credit in circulation by the end of that year. Wars could not be fought without running the printing press, and this was the most expensive war by far in the province's history. By 1747, when England called a halt to any further attacks on Canada and ordered demobilization, almost £3 million (old tenor) of paper currency had been issued. Taxes to retire these notes had been scheduled as far ahead as 1760. Runaway depreciation was the result, with the value of the Massachusetts pound plummeting to about one-tenth of its English equivalent by 1747. But one bright star shone on the horizon. For several years it had been understood that Parliament would reimburse Massachusetts and the other New England colonies for the unprecedented war expenses by making sterling payments that could be used to retire the flood of paper money. In 1748, after elaborate audits of military expenditures, Parliament granted Massachusetts £183,649 sterling as compensation for the war effort. Silver was to be shipped to the colony and used to sink the massive issues of paper money. It was hoped that Massachusetts could reorganize its monetary system, returning to a hard money currency for the first time in more than half a century.[114]

What at first seemed a boon nearly turned into the colony's bane, for Massachusetts rocked with controversy over how to employ the sterling grant from Parliament. The question was not whether the specie should be used to accomplish monetary reform, which everyone knew was necessary to halt the sickening depreciation of provincial currency, but how the reform should be accomplished. Governor Shirley and a group of wealthy merchant supporters called for an immediate retirement of all paper bills, professing a belief that paper money was inherently evil and inevitably inflationary. Their opponents, who saw the province's imbalance of trade as the root of the long-standing problems with paper currency, called for the gradual retirement of paper money over a period of years. If paper money was abolished in one fell swoop, they argued, local trade would be disrupted, specie would flow out of Massachusetts again to pay for trade deficits, and the colony would start again down the road it had traveled for the past two generations.

The issue also involved a question of social equity. Many Bostonians believed that a drastic deflationary policy would enrich some men and impoverish others. Those with the most to gain were wealthy merchants and government officials who, in anticipation of the redemption of paper money, had been gathering in as many depreciated bills of credit as possible, hoping to exchange them at a rate that would bring fat profits. Even Christopher Kilby, one of the Massachusetts agents in London, complained that sudden redemption would greatly enrich those who were speculating in the depreciated bills and "inevitably ruin those in trade with but small or middling capital."[115] English merchants also protested "that many persons in the administration have bought up the depreciated bills and hope to receive double the sum they paid." Even Thomas Hutchinson, who drafted the immediate redemption bill and was known as the leader of the wealthy fiscal conservatives, reported in his *History of Massachusets-Bay* that the common people believed the £183,000 of silver would "fall to the share of men of wealth, and would either be exported or hoarded up, and no part of it would go to the labourer, or the lower class of people, who must take their pay in goods, or go without."[116] A *Boston Evening Post* writer, speaking as a "poor Journeyman Tradesman," drove home the point. The poor, who the wealthy merchants called "shiftless," would get none of the silver that had been sent to redeem paper money that had been earned with the blood of the lower classes on the Canadian expeditions. "It would be esteem'd an Act of most heinous Sacrilege," he wrote with passionate class feeling, "to suffer it [the silver] to be touch'd by the prophane dirty Paw of a low born Mechanic, unknowing and unworthy to know the true Use of such precious Stuff; because his views are so low, as to seek it *only* in Payment for his *Labour*, and to satisfy the pressing Necessities of Life."[117]

The conviction was widespread among ordinary Bostonians that windfall profits at the expense of the masses was what the wealthiest merchants had in mind. The town seethed with resentment against the drastic redemption bill, and the General Court thought social disorder imminent enough to rush through a "drastic law against rioting" while the paper money was redeemed in coin.[118] Hutchinson and Boston's other merchant representatives who had voted for the redemption bill were summarily voted out of office at the May 1749 elections, an indication of how far opposition to the redemption act reached into the middle class.[119] In the fall, when the British ship arrived with the silver, crowds roamed the streets, threatening Hutchinson with physical harm and convincing him that he had best retire to his summer mansion at Milton, outside the city, in order to avoid being mobbed by his townsmen.[120] Hutchinson had good reason to fear his neighbors. On the previous May Day, when his house caught fire mysteriously, a crowd had gathered in the street, cursing the colony's most avid deflationist and shouting, "Let it burn! Let it burn!" A rump town meeting in December sardonically elected Hutchinson and fifteen other wealthy merchants as tax collectors, a job that would take them out of their mansions and into the streets, where they might personally see how ordinary Bostonians were faring during hard times.[121] The Boston press spewed forth bitterness toward wealthy war profiteers, who had now found a way of turning even postwar depression to their own ends. An anonymous pamphleteer wrote that "Poverty and Discontent appear in every Face, (except the Countenances of the Rich), and dwell upon every Tongue." A few men, fed by "Lust of Power, Lust of Fame, Lust of Money," had grown rich by supplying military expeditions during the war and had now devised a monetary system guaranteed to heap their gains higher. "No Wonder such Men can build Ships, Houses, buy Farms, set up their Coaches, Chariots, live very splendidly, purchase Fame, Posts of Honour," railed the author. But such "Birds of prey . . . are Enemies to all Communities—wherever they live."[122]

These expressions of class hostility, born of economic dislocation caused by war and nurtured by the rhetoric of the antibourgeois Awakening evangelists, reflected not only an agitated state of mind but social reality in Boston as well. The war and the postwar depression had greatly intensified the problems of Boston's laboring people and hobbled the middle class while enriching the war contractors and speculators—the vanguard of the new entrepreneurial age. All Bostonians could see this. In their small city it was impossible to disguise the distress of poor women and children who were being urged to labor in the linen manufactory, or the plight of unemployed artisans and financially ruined middle-class families. Equally well, every eye could see the wartime gains of the few, perhaps most grossly registered by the return in 1749 of Edmund Quincy's privateering vessel with 161 chests bursting with 300,000 pieces of Spanish gold and silver, which were trundled under armed guard from Quincy's wharf to his house.[123]

ONE SEARCHES in vain for expressions of such antipathy for the wealthy and for evidence of street politics in either New York or Philadelphia during the 1740s. To a large extent, politics in Manhattan revolved around the figure of James DeLancey and his opposition to New York's participation in a land war against the French in Canada. DeLancey was the eldest son of Stephen DeLancey, a French Huguenot emigrant of the 1680s who built one of the city's great commercial fortunes. The son, not concerned with earning money since his inheritance was so large, pursued politics as a career. After an English education at Cambridge and the Inns of Court he was appointed chief justice of the colony in 1733, becoming a member of Governor William Cosby's inner circle. From this position he built a political power base that extended into the county courts, the governor's council, and the assembly. DeLancey faithfully served Governor Cosby and his successor George Clarke. But when George Clinton replaced Clarke on the eve of the Anglo-French War, De-Lancey began a new phase of his career. Clinton became a passionate exponent of throwing New York's resources into the war against French Canada in 1744. For DeLancey, who was tied to mercantile interests and associated with the economic recovery that New York had made since the mid-1730s, Clinton's war policy promised only heavy taxes, economic disruption, and the risk of unraveling a half-century of stable Indian relations, which might be shattered if the Iroquois were bullied into participating in a land war against Canada.[124]

Thus DeLancey the former courtier and enemy of the popular Morrisite faction of the 1730s turned into DeLancey the leader of the antiadministration party that controlled the New York assembly. When Governor Clinton decided to match DeLancey blow for blow, pamphlet for pamphlet, election appeal for election appeal, and caucus for caucus,

New York City was treated to the clearest case that had yet emerged in urban politics of a bifurcated elite, both halves of which worked to mobilize popular support. DeLancey used the *New-York Evening Post* to reach the electorate; Clinton used the *New-York Post Boy*. Political pamphlets tumbled from the presses by the dozens in the four assembly elections held between 1745 and 1752. Each side courted the middle and lower classes, accusing their opponents of representing wealth and privilege to the detriment of the common people.[125] At the same time each blasted the other for demeaning politics by hobnobbing with the poorer sort and soliciting their votes.

The Clinton party chastised the DeLanceyites in the 1748 election for campaigning like "sturdy Beggars" as they hurried around the town in old clothes soliciting votes from the lower class. At the same time they maintained that DeLancey and his merchant allies were self-indulgent rich men who had not accumulated their fortunes "by the honestest means" and cared little for "the Misfortunes of their Neighbours."[126] "True roman virtue was allmost totally extinguished," wrote Cadwallader Colden, Clinton's chief political writer, "before their great or rich men went about to court the common people for their votes." When the lower rank "take it as favour to be call'd by their names by their rich men & to be shook by the hand," they were unknowingly allowing the shackles of slavery to be slipped on their wrists and ankles, for those who "could sell their Liberty to the highest bidder" were already slaves "in their minds."[127] Clinton's party worked equally hard, seeking middle- and lower-class support in spite of private lamentations that DeLancey attempted to obtain "the applause of the Mob by their licentious harangues and by propagating the Doctrine that all authority is derived from the People."[128] Aristocrat though he was, Clinton "plunged into local politics with a fervor unmatched by any previous New York governor," all the while charging that DeLancey headed "a seditious faction composed of men of republican and levelling principles."[129]

What is remarkable about the politics of New York at mid-century is that in spite of these rousing attempts to mobilize the people, election turnouts were very low and radical street politics conspicuously absent. Applications for freemanship, one of the best indicators of artisans' attempts to control the political process, were far below the level of the depression years of the 1730s. Only 176 votes were cast in the city in the assembly election of 1745.[130] This must be explained primarily in terms of laboring men's willingness to allow the nabobs of the DeLancey party to control politics in an era when economic prosperity was widespread, a costly war had been avoided, and no specific economic grievances were present. The governor's party had to seek assembly seats primarily outside New York City, so strong was the merchant-led DeLancey party in the town.[131]

Only once in this era did laboring-class New Yorkers take to the streets. This was in 1753, when at the instigation of about fifty merchants the legislature considered a law for devaluing the English half-pence. In order to attract specie to New York the assembly had legislated an artificially high value to the coins in local currency.But feeling that they were the losers in the overvaluation of pennies, merchants decided to change the local exchange rate from 12 to 14 to the shilling. Pennies had become plentiful in the city and were commonly used in payment of artisans' wages, so in effect this amounted to a substantial decrease in wages. A riot protesting the proposed change broke out, and one newspaper proclaimed that "all Labouring Men" were hurt by the impending measure. DeLancey, whose well-oiled political machine had relied heavily in the 1740s on laboring-class support, showed his true colors by suggesting that the way to quell the riot was to shoot people down in the streets. By this time he had been appointed lieutenant governor and the Grand Jury report on the "tumultuous Assembly" assured him that the riot was the work of ignorant people, many of them not inhabitants of the city.[132] Nonetheless, the riot was a small and isolated disturbance in comparison with Boston, where the issues of economic depression, currency reform, and impressment kept the town in turmoil for most of the 1740s.

IN PHILADELPHIA, where economic conditions were the most favorable of any of the port towns in the 1740s and early 1750s, politics were generally unmarked by the violence and polarization that prevailed in Boston. Only King George's War seemed to provide a basis for challenging the dominant Quaker party in the assembly. Even war proved an ineffective basis for oppositional politics because non-Quakers had no desire to see heavy taxes imposed to fight a far-off enemy. Privateering, as in New York, was welcomed, for it cost taxpayers nothing and promised plunder to the lucky. But shipping, shipbuilding, and house construction were the sinews of the seaport's economic strength, and few within the electorate, as the proprietary party found out, could be diverted from following these pursuits.

Nonetheless, the officeholders and friends of the proprietary governor attempted to fashion a political party that would break the long domination of the Quakers in the assembly, where they refused to pass defense appropriations early in the Anglo-Spanish War and fought attempts by the governor to enlist indentured servants without adequate compensation for their masters. But the party's only issue was military preparedness, and unless the threat of the French invasion was more than theoretical, they had little hope of success at the polls.[133] The one bloc of potential voters they might exploit was the Germans, who by 1740 represented about one-third of the population. But the proprietary leaders were not working virgin territory. The Society of Friends had long before wooed the Germans to its side, promising that Quaker pacifism would keep them safe from military conscription and onerous taxes, which had plagued their existence in the home country. For the Quakers the problem in the 1740s was how to maintain influence in a society where they were fast becoming a minority. For the proprietary adherents the problem was how to develop popular sources of support in order to overcome Quaker domination of the assembly. Both parties, therefore, began thinking more systematically about the German vote. Neither the Quaker-dominated "assembly" party nor the Anglican-based proprietary party welcomed the inundation of German immigrants, for Englishmen of both groups regarded them as crude, alien, and too numerous. But neither could afford to leave the politicization of the Germans (who were more interested in farming and family than politics) to the other side.

With great misgivings the proprietary party began courting the German community in 1740. In private discourse and correspondence its leaders continued to refer to the Germans as "an uncultivated Race" of uncouth peasants, incapable, as one put it, "of using their own Judgment in matters of Government.[134] Nonetheless, they worked hard to mobilize the votes of the Germans. Although they were able to convert a few German leaders, such as the Indian agent Conrad Weiser, they never made substantial inroads on the allegiance of the Germans to the Quakers.[135] In 1740, when the proprietary party made its first concerted effort to challenge the Quaker party, the most important German printer in the colony convinced most of the Germans that "there was a [proprietary] Design to enslave them; to force their young Men to be Soldiers, make them serve as Pioneers, and go down to work upon our Fortifications.[136] The proprietary party's attempt to split the German vote failed miserably in Philadelphia County as the Germans "came down in shoals and carried all before them." But the effect on electoral participation was dramatic. Fewer than 600 persons had voted in the city and county of Philadelphia in 1739; in 1740, the year of the great German mobilization, more than 1,800 persons voted.[137] Although the proprietary party turned out far more voters than at any previous election, the Quakers countered with "about 400 Germans who hardly ever came to elections formerly."[138]

For two years after 1740, the proprietary party courted the electorate and attempted to break the Quaker stranglehold on the German vote. The dangers inherent in abandoning the gentlemanly politics which its leaders preferred became frighteningly apparent on election day in 1742 when Philadelphia was shaken by a bloody riot at the polls.[139] Rumors had been circulating that the Quaker party intended to maintain its majority in the assembly not only by garnering the German vote but also by steering unnaturalized German immigrants to the polls. Counter-rumors spread that the proprietary party would thwart this attempt by engaging a pack of toughs to frighten away these intruders. The stories proved to have substance, for when the leaders of the two political factions could not agree on procedures for supervising the election, heated words and curses were exchanged and seventy sailors suddenly appeared in the Quaker crowd assembled before the courthouse wielding clubs and shouting "down with the plain Coats & broad Brims." As the Quaker leaders retreated inside, the sailors filled the air with bricks. A counterattack was launched by Germans and younger Quakers, who momentarily forgot their pacifist principles. "Blood flew plentifully around," the proprietary secretary later reported. The Quaker assembly, after conducting investigations, concluded that the riot had been engineered by the leaders of the proprietary party. Officially this was denied but two of the proprietor's chief officials in Philadelphia admitted as much to Thomas Penn.[140]

Unlike the popular disturbances in Boston, which were set against a background of economic distress and involved large numbers of people acting out of their own consciousness, the Philadelphia election riot was a managed affair conducted by hired toughs in the employ of some of the city's most eminent men for a cause that was not their own. The riot revealed no economic dislocation in Philadelphia but rather the lengths to which a minority party would go to defeat its enemies. Chastened by the experience and discouraged at their abysmal failure to syphon off much of the artisan and German vote in Philadelphia, the proprietary inner circle ran only perfunctory campaigns for the assembly for more than a decade after 1742, never offering a full slate of candidates and only occasionally winning as much as 30 percent of the vote. For some years, a committee of the assembly wrote in 1753, the proprietary party had commanded "no formidable Share of the People's Love and Esteem" and had not bothered to contest elections.[141] Only the threat of French and Spanish privateers operating off the Delaware Capes in 1747, accompanied by the rumor of an invasion of Philadelphia, could disturb the political calm. And this issue was laid to rest by the agile footwork of Benjamin Franklin, who successfully organized a voluntary military association, while the Quaker-dominated assembly saved their principles and their constituents' pocketbooks by refusing to countenance war appropriations or the raising of a provincial militia.[142]

Franklin's extraordinary success in influencing public opinion in 1747 is worthy of notice because his campaign for a voluntary association of militiamen demonstrates how effectively the artisans and shopkeepers of Philadelphia could be recruited by someone outside the established circle of political leaders. With an attack on Philadelphia by French and Spanish privateers rumored and the Quaker assembly unwilling to take action, Franklin published *Plain Truth* in November 1747. His pitch was to the commonalty, as the title page, signed "A Tradesman," signified. They had always been the heart of civic improvements, he argued, and now must solve for themselves a problem which their leaders had cravenly evaded. Attacking the Quaker leaders for obstinacy in the face of real danger and the proprietary leaders—"those Great and rich Men, Merchants and others"—who criticized the Quakers but did nothing themselves despite their "Wealth and Influence," Franklin called upon the "middling People, the Farmers, Shopkeepers and Tradesmen" to establish their own militia on a volunteer basis.[143] Two thousand copies of *Plain Truth* were distributed free. Four days later Franklin called the tradesmen and mechanics to a meeting in a sail loft. He presented them with a printed agreement for a voluntary association of the "middling people." Persuasive man that he was, he soon had the laboring population four-square behind him. Within a few days more than 1,000 Philadelphians—about one-third of the adult white males—had signed their names to the agreement and began forming themselves into militia companies.[144]

The Associators, as they called themselves, became a symbol in Philadelphia of artisan strength and unity. Called into being by the artisan par excellence among them, acting where upper-class leaders had failed, organized into companies that elected their own officers, they never engaged the enemy but conferred upon themselves, nonetheless, an enormous collective strength. Individually, Franklin argued, the artisans and mechanics "are like separate Filaments of Flax before the Thread is form'd, without Strength because without Connection, but UNION would make us strong and even formidable." Even if they were opposed by "the *Great* . . . from some mean Views of their Own, yet, if we resolve upon it, . . . it *may* be effected."[145]

Here was an ennobling thought and one that raised the consciousness of the laboring people, though not to the degree experienced in Boston. In the Massachusetts capital the ravages of war had deeply divided the town, leading to the most explicit statements of class hostility in the history of the American port towns. Many Bostonians truly believed, in the words of one anonymous pamphleteer, "that War, is a great Calamity" that "always brings on Scarcity, Devastation and Distress of every kind," but had visited special misfortunes upon ordinary citizens because a handful of wealthy merchants had "aggrandize[d] their own Private Fortunes, in order to make the Commonality Slaves and Vassals, and themselves Lords of the Mannors."[146] In Philadelphia, where there was no war-disordered economy, the threat of privateers cannonading the town had brought a unification of laboring people and the rise of a belief that when difficult work needed to be done, it was the tradesmen and mechanics who could best do it. Boston emerged from the era of King George's War bruised and battered, its population declining, its tax base dwindling, and its streets filled with poverty and resentment against the wealthy. New York and Philadelphia emerged prosperous and expanding, unburdened by heavy taxes or severe poverty and facing the future confidently.

9

Prosperity and Poverty:
The Seven Years War and Its Aftermath

THE SEVEN YEARS WAR, known also as the French and Indian War and the Great War for the Empire, is remembered primarily as the climactic military struggle in which Anglo-American arms finally overcame the hated French and claimed Canada. No longer would the frontiers of New England and New York be exposed to French marauders; no longer would the northern fishing banks be a field of incessant Anglo-French rivalry; no longer would the powerful interior Indian tribes be able to play off one European power against another; and no longer would the trans-Allegheny west—the land reserve for the the generations to come— be poised precariously between French and English traders and settlers. England, and more immediately her American colonists, had now achived the impossible dream: control of North America from the Atlantic Ocean to the Mississippi River and from Florida to Hudson's Bay.

For the northern seaport towns, however, the Seven Years War was a far more traumatic and paradoxical event than is generally supposed. Epic victories of geopolitical significance often take on a starkly different appearance when we shift our gaze from the global to the local context. The years of bloody fighting on land and at sea lifted each of the northern commercial centers from business depression in 1750-1754, stimulated shipbuilding, meliorated underemployment in Boston, and drove up wages of artisans and mariners in New York and Philadelphia. Then, after a series of triumphant victories over the French in 1759 and 1760, all three port towns suffered a general depression of great severity. This was the war that convinced the American colonies of their growing strength and maturity, yet ironically left them weakened in manpower and debt-ridden at its end. It brought the greatest infusion of English capital in their history, yet rendered them unusually sensitive to the disadvantages of the British mercantile connection. It drove forward the commercialization of life in the port towns, yet exposed in stark detail the social costs of the transition to a capitalistic economy. The Seven Years War was Queen

Anne's War and King George's War writ large. Not only did it magnify all the difficulties that had cropped up in Boston during and after these earlier wars but it visited these problems on New York and Philadelphia as well. In the economic history of the port towns the Seven Years War marks the watershed, bringing together all the tendencies of the past seven decades and setting the maritime centers on a course from which there would be no return short of revolution.

THE SHORT peace between the Treaty of Aix-la-Chapelle and the outbreak of Anglo-French hostilities in 1748 was really only a time out from war for the purpose of regathering strength. France immediately began rebuilding its navy; the Anglo-French commission for determining the boundaries between French Canada and English New England could agree upon nothing; and American fur traders, linked to seaboard merchants, pushed deep into the Ohio Valley, establishing outposts on the Ohio River and its tributaries in a move that the French recognized as an attempt by the Anglo-Americans to win the allegiance of the trans-Allegheny Indian tribes.[1] It was obvious that the English were challenging the French where the French interest was vital, and that just behind the fur traders stood the land speculators, themselves the advance guard of a population growing by geometric proportions in the eighteenth century. "Each side now envisioned the other in the form of a scheming, implacable aggressor, determined to end the game at last by gaining all."[2] France had no intention of surrendering the continent to the English, as was apparent from the fort-building program that the French initiated almost immediately after the peace of 1748.

By 1752 armed hostility replaced diplomatic maneuvering and fort construction. The French attacked English trading posts in the Ohio Valley, won the allegiance of several Indian tribes there, and threatened to encircle the American colonists from the west. Internal division crippled colonial attempts to respond to the bold French campaign, as was dismayingly revealed at the Albany Congress of 1754. This was the first major effort of the colonies to unify for military purposes and through united action to woo the all-important Iroquois out of their long-held position of neutrality. But while representatives of the colonies labored to perfect a plan of confederation, land agents from Connecticut and Pennsylvania wallowed deep in intrigue over the purchase of Iroquois lands west of the Susquehanna River.[3] In the end, the attempt to unite the colonies fell to pieces and the Iroquois left the conference in disgust.

It was decided in the capitals of Europe, not America, to force a showdown. In London the ministry dispatched General James Braddock, a seasoned veteran, with two regiments in 1754 and instructed him to recruit two American regiments when he reached the colonies. This united force was to march against the French in the Ohio Valley, restoring to

English control areas formerly dominated by Virginia and Pennsylvania traders. The French countered with 4,000 regulars, ordered to the Canadian strongholds at Louisbourg and Quebec. The year that it took Braddock to make his way across the Atlantic and then lead his army, reinforced by American enlistees, across Virginia and into the western wilderness was the last of his life. Less than twenty miles from Fort Duquesne, Braddock's objective, the French and their Indian allies ambushed the British-Americans. The reputedly invincible army was routed by a force one-third as large. Two-thirds of the English and Americans lay killed or wounded on the field of battle. Survivors fled, leaving artillery, horses, cattle, and supplies behind.[4]

Braddock's defeat was the first of a long string of British-American disasters. For three years, until 1758, the English suffered one loss after another, in spite of putting into the field far greater numbers of men and materiel than had ever been deployed against the French in a century and a half of North American rivalry. Then the tide turned. Louisbourg, on Cape Breton Island, and Fort Frontenac, at the eastern end of Lake Ontario, fell before Anglo-American assaults. Capturing these strategic centers of French power, at opposite ends of the St. Lawrence River, proved the turning point in the war. Impressed by the English victories, the Iroquois began moving away from their neutral position. Other British victories in 1759—annus mirabilis—beginning with the seizure of Fort Niagara at the western end of Lake Ontario, continuing with the capture of the rich sugar island of Martinique, and culminating with Wolfe's dramatic victory at Quebec, all but decided the issue. With the fall of Montreal in 1760 French power was irretrievably shattered. Peace was not formally recognized until 1763, when the Treaty of Paris brought an end to almost two hundred years of French presence on the continent.[5]

Measuring the impact of the Seven Years War on the port towns is an intricate piece of calculus because Boston, New York, and Philadelphia, though all drawn into the military operations, were affected in different ways. As in earlier wars, what was good for one urban group did not always benefit another. From the onset of hostilities in 1754 one advantage became clear: British military operations in North America brought huge war contracts to all the seaports. New York was especially favored because the British strategy against French Canada, involving a two-pronged offensive through the Mohawk Valley and across Lake Champlain, made that city the logical supply base and communications center for the British army.

British troops arrived in the northern ports in numbers that by previous standards were staggering. Two thousand arrived in 1755, 11,000 in 1757, and 12,000 in 1758. A huge fleet, which in 1758 alone was manned by some 14,000 mariners, also made Boston and New York its new home ports.[6] This created a demand for food, alcohol, clothing, boots, and other supplies that made fortunes for war contractors and created employment all the way down the line. John Cruger, Peter Van Brugh Livingston, James Alexander, William Bayard, Oliver DeLancey, John Watts, and Henry White were among the New York merchants whose political connections brought them lucrative supply contracts.[7] In Boston, Andrew Oliver, Thomas Hancock, John Erving, Charles Apthorp, and others profited in a similar way. For even the smallest New England expedition, the assault on Fort Beauséjour in Nova Scotia in 1755, Hancock supplied provisions worth £20,000 sterling, and for the entire war £105,000 worth of business flowed through his firm.[8] In Philadelphia, David Franks, William Plumstead, Thomas Willing, Reese Meredith, and Robert Morris led the victualers and suppliers. A host of others benefitted on a smaller scale, such as Joseph Fox, master builder, who received an £8,000 contract for constructing British army barracks in the Northern Liberties of Philadelphia in 1758 and John Baynton, who won a £4,500 contract to construct a warship for the colony.[9] British expenditures in the northern colonies in 1760 alone were £1,344,309, and spending for the entire war likely topped £5 million. To this must be added another £1.4 million that Parliament granted in subsidies to the colonies for their war effort.[10]

Even merchants who were not major recipients of war contracts did a booming business. With military spending at an all-time high, general prosperity enveloped New York and Philadelphia, creating a strong demand for imports from England. For example, James Beekman, a rising New York merchant, imported English goods worth £1,622 on average from 1753 to 1755. But the wartime boom generated buying power so great that he imported £4,183 of goods in 1756, £10,904 in 1757, and averaged £7,219 in imports between 1756 and 1760.[11] His orders in England fell precipitously after the climactic Anglo-American victories of 1759, for when the British forces were reassigned to the Caribbean most of the war contracts left with them. What was reflected in the ledger books of Beekman generally held true for the rest of the mercantile community. Imports from England, one of the most reliable indicators of economic conditions, jumped spectacularly during the war as northern consumers purchased English commodities as never before.[12] New York and Philadelphia got most of the military spending, but all the urban centers benefitted.

While provisioning contracts made merchant princes of a few well-connected men, privateering enriched others. As in the previous war, New York stood first among the northern ports as a center for the sea marauders. The majority of merchants made more from privateering than from war contracting.[13] "War is declared in England—Universal joy among the merchants," wrote New Yorker William Smith in his diary in July 1756. "Privateering engrosses the Coffee House."[14] As soon as word of the declaration of war reached the city, men with capital bombarded Governor James DeLancey with applications for letters of marque and reprisal, the privateer's license to conduct private war at sea. Within five months, twenty-four privateers were fitted out and dispatched to stalk French shipping. By January 1757 thirty New York ships cruised the western Atlantic and ten more were emerging from the shipyards. A year later the governor described "almost a kind of madness to go privateering," a view confirmed by the fact that some 224 privateers took to sea before hostilities ceased, about three times the number as in King George's War.[15] Not every seaborne soldier of fortune returned a profit to his landborne investors, but 149 prizes were taken in the first two years of the war. One group of seven prizes brought a return of about £100,000 (local currency), and New York's marauders, in capturing 401 prizes, poured more than £2 million into the coffers of the city's investors and prize crews.[16]

Boston and Philadelphia figured much less prominently in this lucrative form of enterprise, although an occasional seadog such as John Mac-Pherson of the Quaker city snared eighteen French vessels on a single voyage in 1758. The fortune he earned gave him claim to the reputation of the greatest parvenu in Philadelphia's history. So vast was MacPherson's haul that he could afford to pour £14,000 sterling into creating Mt. Pleasant, a hundred-acre estate outside the city to which this son of a Scottish immigrant retired in Georgian splendor.[17]

By 1759 New York's privateers had plucked the seas so clean of French vessels that they spent their time chasing each other instead of the enemy.[18] The solution to diminishing profits was to divert privateers into illegal trading. Having interdicted most of the French trade to the West Indies, the American merchants now began provisioning the island-bound enemy, which was willing to pay extraordinary prices for foodstuffs rather than starve. "Some of the most prominent merchants in New York had recourse to this method of cutting their losses," and the same was true in Philadelphia and Boston.[19] Because they were armed and masked their real intent with letters of marque and reprisal, privateers who carried illegal goods could obtain lower insurance rates, thus insuring greater profits.

Such dubious patriotism by merchants who were fattening their purses on English supply contracts infuriated British military commanders. They could do little about it, however, for even if indicted the offending parties could count on acquittal by local juries. Even to inform on smugglers was hazardous, as one New Yorker found out when he attempted to publish an exposé on trade with the enemy. The city's printers turned him away, a mob "hauled him through the streets in a cart," bystanders showered him with "filth and offal," the authorities threw him in jail, and the supreme court of judicature—two of whose justices he had implicated in the smuggling racket—left him there to rot.[20] Even the British navy's attempts to stop illegal trade by intercepting American shipping as it approached French West Indian ports proved futile, for the northern merchants merely rerouted their ships to neutral Dutch entrepôts such as St. Eustatius and Curaçao. On several occasions during the war British commanders temporarily blocked trading with the enemy by declaring an embargo on all foodstuffs leaving the northern ports. But it proved impossible to seal the ports for very long, while at the same time obtaining the cooperation of the northern colonies for the land war in progress.[21]

Pennsylvania's wartime governor, William Denny, proved that even the highest appointed officials could be blinded by the vision of war profits. Rather than trading with the enemy, Denny attempted to secure his fortune by selling flags of truce, which enabled the merchant to ship goods to the enemy under the pretext that the vessel was engaged in prisoner exchange. This created a fierce demand for French prisoners, who were spread as thin as possible in order to cover the maximum number of ships carrying foodstuffs to the French West Indies. When the prisoner supply dried up, naturalized Frenchmen in the English ports hired themselves out as surrogate captives. Here was a form of entrepreneurship in which the upper-class official, the middle-class trader, and the lowly French laborer could join hands. Denny began peddling flags of truce in such numbers that they were traded speculatively on the New York market by 1759.[22] When James Hamilton relieved Denny of his governorship in Philadelphia in the following year, he found "a very great part of the principal Merchants of this City, engage in a trade with the French Islands in the West Indies."[23] Like water seeking its level, mercantile activity flowed where profits beckoned. Neither patriotism nor imperial authority proved powerful enough to stop the supply of the Caribbean enemy with whom the Anglo-American forces were engaged in the bloodiest war in the history of North America.

While merchants gathered in windfall profits from war, artisans, mariners, and laborers in New York and Philadelphia also found their earning power enhanced. The enormous demand for new ships and the refitting of merchant vessels for naval war meant full employment and sharply higher wages throughout some twenty crafts associated with ship construction. The frenzied shipyard activity enlarged the Manhattan port's fleet from 157 vessels in 1749 to 477 in 1762 and the combined tonnage from 6,406 to 19,514. This increase of 320 ships in thirteen years meant that New York artisans built more than twenty vessels annually, a hefty increase from previous years.[24] The demand for shipbuilding craftsmen drove wages up to a level not exceeded in any of the port towns before the Revolution. Merchant investors tried hard in 1758 to hold the line on wages at 8 shillings per day for ship carpenters and 4 shillings for laborers

about double the prewar rate. This was thought sufficient to lure shipyard workers "in the Country, and the neighbouring Provinces, to repair
to the City of New-York."[25] But a year later merchant John Watts was
still complaining about the shortage of shipwrights, carpenters, and
other artisans, a lament echoed in Philadelphia.[26]

For mariners too these were flush times. Dead time between voyages,
so prevalent in the trade recession of 1750-1754, was a thing of the past,
as the privateering boom put a premium on the mariner's labor and
drove wages up. As early as November 1756 one merchant was writing
about the "Scarcity of seamen as Most of them are gone privateering."
Although thousands of farm boys flocked in from the countryside to join
the fortune seekers, the demand for maritime labor intensified as the war
wore on.[27] In 1757 the sheriff of Newport, Rhode Island estimated that
10,000 men had been lured to privateering in the northern ports and the
commander in chief of the British forces believed that 3,000 operated out
of New York alone.[28] So many mariners and landsmen had been attracted to sea banditry that the huge British expeditionary fleet gathered
in New York that spring was shore-bound because of a shortage of men
to hoist the sails. Only the most massive pressing operation ever staged
in eighteenth-century America, involving about 3,000 British soldiers
who cordoned off the city in the dead of night and plucked clean "the
Taverns and other houses, where sailors usually resorted," put the ships
to sea. "All kinds of Tradesmen and Negroes" were hauled in, nearly 800
in all, according to printer Hugh Gaine, and about 400 were "retained in
the service."[29]

By 1758 privateering had syphoned off so many laboring men that
New York's merchants were obliged to offer 5 shillings per day for regular voyages, more than triple the peacetime rate, and the government
paid common sailors £5 per month—a master's pay in peacetime—for
troop transport service. In Philadelphia mariners' pay doubled between
1754 and 1760, also reaching £5 per month.[30] With such unexampled
wages available at sea, who would enlist for military service on land?
Desperately trying to attract recruits, New York's assembly kept upping
the enlistment bounty, from £1.6 in 1755 to £5 in 1756 to £10 in 1758,
and finally in 1759 to £15, the equivalent in peacetime to at least half a
year's wages for common laborers. The unscrupulous played both sides
of the street. After pocketing their enlistment money for army service,
they deserted, headed for the port towns, and signed on the privateers.[31]

New York, one might imagine, was providing the proverbial pot of
gold at the end of the rainbow for thousands of struggling members of
the lower class who had never seen such chances to propel themselves
upward in colonial society. But we must be careful to separate dreams
from reality. Reports that New York's privateers scooped up £2,000,000
in prize money make it appear that every privateersman retired in co.

fort at the end of the war, spinning out yarns in front of a crackling fire-place about exploits at sea. Lord Loudoun, the British commander in chief, seemed to believe as much, writing in 1757 that the New York privateers "have been extremely successful [and] all make Fortunes."[32] But if we do some simple arithmetic, the case appears in a different light. Taking the highest estimate of prize money accrued, about £2 million, and subtracting 10 percent for court costs and 60 percent of the remain-der that went to the owners, captain, and mates, we are left with £720,000, which was divided among the common tars.[33] Their numbers in New York have been estimated at about 15,000 to 20,000. Even if we take a lower figure of 10,000 it turns out that on average these sea adven-turers garnered only about £11 each over the course of eight years of war. One historian estimates that one of every two or three privateers-men suffered injury, imprisonment, or death, so the average reward to those who survived may have been higher.[34] But the dreams, it is clear, were mostly only that, for the main rewards went to the owner-investors, the officers, and the maritime artisans ashore, who, as a result of the rush to scoop up French riches from an English dominated sea, received un-paralleled wages while enjoying a safe billet.

Prosperity along the waterfront also meant good times for artisans in other sectors of the economy. Tailors' needles flashed as clothing con-tracts came in, cordwainers stitched to an unprecedented demand for their boots and shoes, and bakers found armies clamoring for bread. The war had hardly begun in 1755 when New York's bakers, aware that 50,000 pounds of bread was needed for the incoming British army, jacked up prices by 2 shillings a hundredweight—a hefty 14 percent in-crease. Refusing to bow to opportunism of this kind, the contracting merchant shifted his business to Philadelphia, so it was bakers in that city who ultimately profited.[35] Other artisans and shopkeepers enlarged their purses simply from the spending power of the British soldiers and sailors, whose pay was wretched individually but who collectively dropped thousands of shillings into the tills of smiling tavern-keepers, barbers, and others in the service trades. By 1757 the British had at least 25,000 army and navy personnel operating in the American theater and from 1758 to 1760 the numbers exceeded 40,000.[36] Most of them left their meager pay on American shores. Other artisans profited from the busi-ness prosperity generated out of this massive military spending machine. House construction increased in New York and boomed in Philadelphia during the war, which meant full employment and wages about 25 per-cent higher than prewar levels for housewrights, bricklayers, stone-masons, glaziers, plasterers, painters, carvers, carters, and ordinary la-borers.[37]

While New York and Philadelphia basked in wartime prosperity that reached up and down the occupational ladder from lowly laborer to princely merchant, Boston struggled through the years of conflict, attempting to regain the economic equilibrium that for so long had eluded its grasp. The immediate prewar years had been dismal ones; trade sank nearly to the level of forty years before (when the town was only two-thirds as large), housebuilding virtually ceased, and ship construction declined sharply.[38]

War provided a mild tonic, momentarily pulling the town from the depths of depression. But after the expedition against Fort Beauséjour was mounted from Boston in mid-1755, the staging grounds for military operations shifted southward. Not until 1758, when the assault on Louisbourg was launched, did New England's main seaport get much war business again. Equally dismaying, the prewar loss of shipbuilding to competing maritime centers proved impossible to reverse. Part of the problem may have been self-inflicted, for Thomas Hancock, one of the town's premier merchant investors, wrote on a number of occasions between 1747 and 1755 that he could buy a ship in London for two-thirds the cost in Boston.[39] If other merchants were following Hancock's advice to place their ship orders elsewhere, then part of the town's suffering was attributable to this decision by Boston's own mercantile leaders to succumb to the play of the free market.

By February 1756, when ship construction was booming in New York, Boston was crying to the legislature for help. Compounding the disheartening decay of shipbuilding, the output of the distilleries and sugar bakeries (also mainstays of the town's economy) dropped to less than half the 1746 level. A further blow was struck by the resumption of British impressments, which so disrupted the fishing enterprise that codfish exports fell from 39,756 barrels in 1754 to 22,113 in 1757 and four years later sagged to about 16,000 barrels.[40] With these basic industries crippled and town taxes to support the burgeoning poor weighing heavily on those who could find work, many master craftsmen from the middle ranks gave up the ghost.[41] The baking business, the selectmen reported, fell by one-third. Tanners looked for work elsewhere, for they had only about 6,000 skins per year to dress from 1754 to 1756 as compared with 30,000 per year from 1746 to 1748. Many of the town's fifty glovers, who had produced 1,000 pairs of gloves per year, were "now maintained by Charity in the Alms House." Coopers' work fell by two-thirds.[42] By 1757, according to the selectmen, the unemployed poor were only slightly worse off than a large number of Bostonians "who are . . . in such poor Circumstances that Considering how little business there is to be done in Boston they can scarcely procure from day to day daily Bread for themselves & Families."[43] In the previous war established artisans had full employment, but rampant currency depreciation tore cruelly at their pocketbooks. In this war the purchasing power of artisans' wages remained stable but work was pitiably hard to find.[44] When Thomas

Pownall, the successor to Governor Shirley, arrived in August 1757, he found not the "rich, flourishing, powerful, enterprizing" colony that had been described to him but a province "ruined and undone."[45]

There is a good deal of evidence indicating how sharply the war imperiled the economic security not only of those at the bottom of society but also of many in the middle strata, composed of master craftsmen, shopkeepers, and lesser merchants. Labor shortages in the other port towns, especially in the maritime sector, sent wage rates up sharply, but in Boston, amidst rising food prices, they remained nearly static.[46] This represented a serious decline of real income for many. Twenty-eight merchants, shopkeepers, and artisans published bankruptcy notices between November 1757 and July 1758, as the war reached its height. In 1757 the town reported that "the Poor supported either wholly or in part by the Town in the Alms-house and out of it will amount to the Number of about 1000."[47] With every seventh adult receiving poor relief, poor taxes soared, saddling middle-class Bostonians with heavier burdens. Expenditures from 1744 to 1750 had averaged £682 sterling; they climbed to £1,161 from 1751 to 1755 and to £1,362 from 1756 to 1760.[48] In a town where the number of those able to pay taxes was declining, this meant that poor rates, already by far the highest of any town in North America, more than doubled. The plight of the independent artisans and shopkeepers can be surmised from the fact that even sixteen of Boston's wealthiest merchants threatened to relocate in towns with lower tax rates if the legislature would not provide relief. With many middling taxpayers falling into arrears by 1757, the town was obliged to borrow £3,000 from the General Court to pay its schoolteachers, night watchmen, constables, and other municipal employees.[49]

With its local economy badly dislocated and with supply contracts going to New York and Philadelphia, Boston's main contribution to the war proved to be raw manpower. Thomas Hancock believed at the beginning of the war that "this Province is Spirited to Go every third man to do the work of the Lord."[50] Events proved him correct. Massachusetts men flocked to the military banners as in no other colony with the possible exception of Connecticut. In 1755, the colony raised nearly 8,000 men from a population of about 195,000. New York, with half as many people, raised only 500, and Pennsylvania, with 150,000 inhabitants, recruited fewer than that. In 1756 and 1757 respectively, about 5,000 and 7,500 Massachusetts men answered the call to arms, while New York recruits numbered 1,700 and 900 and those in Pennsylvania about the same. In 1758 and 1759, at the height of the land war, Massachusetts raised some 6,000 troops, New York about 2,500 and Pennsylvania 2,800. In the latter year, Massachusetts also claimed to have another 3,500 men engaged in frontier duty or serving as rangers, batteaux men, or military construction workers.[51] Nearly every fourth man had been recruited or pressed into wartime service and, according to Massachusetts's agent in London, during the entire course of the war "one-third part" of men able to bear arms had "become your Majesty's soldiers."[52]

It is possible to view Massachusetts's far greater contribution of manpower to military service as evidence that the flame of patriotism and antipopery burned brighter in the Bay colony than in New York or Pennsylvania. To some extent this is probably true, for geographical location, generations of frontier conflict with the French enemy, and a two-century heritage of rabid antipapist feeling made it easier for the recruiting officers to do their work in New England than farther south.[53] But there is reason to believe that economic necessity was at least as important as doing the "work of the Lord" in the minds of thousands of Massachusetts recruits, for nowhere in the northern colonies did so many men stand without opportunity and in dire need of employment. We can best understand this interplay of ideological and economic forces by looking comparatively at the alternatives available to laboring men in the three port towns.

Philadelphia's mechanics, whether they were masters, journeymen, or apprentices, found steady employment and rising wages. Those who yearned to travel faster roads to fame and fortune could take their chance at privateering, either in their own city or in nearby New York. Philadelphia's artisans would eagerly muster a thousand strong under Benjamin Franklin's leadership for militia training in 1755, but when it came time to exchange the drill grounds, where camaraderie prevailed and danger seldom lurked, for combat service in the provincial forces or the British army, they shook their heads and returned to their workbenches. The city's contribution to the biggest land war in colonial history consisted mostly of a few hundred indentured servants who ran from their masters to join the British colors and a number of recent immigrants who responded to the liberal enlistment bounties that were offered for provincial service.[54] Philadelphia's artisans may have hated the French but they evidently hated even more the prospect of long marches, wretched provisions, camp fevers, and the prospect of a French or Indian musket ball buried in their flesh.

New York's established artisans found the notion of fighting in the wilderness of Lake Ontario or Lake Champlain even less attractive. War contracts and the rapid growth of shipbuilding ensured excellent wages for almost all craftsmen, and in the heads of the unmarried, younger men danced visions of plundering richly laden French and Spanish ships. At the height of the war New York and Philadelphia contributed no more than 300 and 180 men per year respectively to the provincial troop quotas, and the muster rolls show that a large majority of them were foreign-born—about 90 percent of the New York recruits and 75 percent of the Philadelphians.[55] The muster rolls also show that most of them were recruited from the lowest ranks of the laboring class, with mariners, laborers, shoemakers, weavers, and tailors filling from two-thirds to three-quarters of the places in the files that marched off to engage the French.[56] As privateering bottomed out in 1760, mariners in New York headed for the army, lured by the £15 enlistment bounty and faced with unemployment as an alternative. So far as the established artisans of New York and Philadelphia were concerned, the bloody work of bearing arms against the French was best left to fleeing indentured servants and unskilled immigrants who had disembarked in their cities in recent years.

In Boston it was different. Shipbuilding and house construction were both in the doldrums and the handful of privateers engaged the services of only a few hundred men. Consequently, British army recruiters and provincial officers worked in fertile fields and were successful in sponging up Boston's jobless and underemployed by the hundreds. Neither the bounties nor the pay was half as good as in New York during the first four years of the war, but Boston men like cordwainer Ebenezer MacIntosh, housewright William Curtis, and laborer Obadiah Chandler flocked to the standard.[57] They hated the French enemy, of course, and Boston's authorities were eager to pump up these prejudices by welcoming back the old hero of the lower classes, George Whitefield, who preached movingly on the "imminint Gallic menace" in 1754 and was awarded an honorary degree at Harvard, where only ten years before he had been excoriated.[58] But antipopery was heightened by the fact that for many in the artisan ranks the best choice was to collect an enlistment bounty each season, which by 1759 represented half a year's wages, and hope to survive a six-month campaign in the northern wilderness. Among the Boston recruits for the Crown Point expedition in 1756, four of every five enlistees were artisans or small shopkeepers, including eighteen carpenters, fifteen tailors, twelve shoemakers, ten ropemakers, seven blacksmiths, and even a few chandlers, distillers, tobacconists, and bookkeepers. This was a striking contrast to the New York and Philadelphia regiments. Likewise, nearly 70 percent of the Boston recruits had been born in New England, as distinct from the men of the Philadelphia and New York regiments.[59] The latter two cities sent their indentured servants and immigrants off to fight; Boston sent mostly native sons from the ranks of independent craftsmen.

Driven by necessity into army service, Bostonians paid the price in greater war casualties than those suffered in the other port towns. Privateering carried many a New Yorker and Philadelphian to a watery grave, but the mortality rate at sea was not nearly so high as in the frontier campaigns at Oswego, Ticonderoga, Montreal, Quebec, and Louisbourg. How many Bostonians lost their lives through battle wounds and camp fevers has never been ascertained. But we know from the enlistment records and muster rolls that, in addition to the hundreds of men who served on transport ships or were impressed into the royal navy, hefty percentages of Boston's males of fighting age signed up or were pressed into service from 1754 onward. The Crown Point expedition in late 1755 included 137 of the city's sons, 316 more served at Lake Champlain in the 1756 campaign, and 112 were at the disastrous defeats at Fort William Henry on Lake George and at Crown Point in 1757. In the following year 517 Bostonians joined the offensive against Canada and the siege of Louisbourg, 275 served in the following year, and 514 marched against the French once more in 1760. The muster lists reveal that fully 95 percent of those who served were between the ages of seventeen and forty-three, so it appears that nearly every laboring-class Bostonian tasted military service at some point during the long war.[60] Hundreds of them never returned. Casualties were not as severe as in the previous war so far as can be ascertained from the sketchy figures available, but it is likely that about 10 percent of those who served, or at least 300 Bostonians, died at sea, on the battlefield, or in a disease-wracked garrison. Combined with the losses suffered in the war from 1739 to 1748 these casualties meant that Boston had experienced the equivalent of two twentieth-century world wars in a single generation.

The cumulative magnitude of the war losses can be indirectly measured by examining the 1764 census, taken the year after the peace treaty was signed. Among whites who were sixteen years and older, Boston counted 2,941 males and 3,612 females, whereas males under sixteen outnumbered females by 4,109 to 4,010.[61] Maritime towns always had a high mortality rate among adult males compared with inland areas because of the dangers of the sea, where perhaps a fifth of the male labor force made its living. But the deficiency of almost 700 men in a town with 2,069 families indicates how freely Boston had given its blood, only to be left by the early 1760s, as it had been at the end of the previous war, with a monumental poverty problem and no solution for putting to work the large number of husbandless women and fatherless children. Boston's 2,069 families contained more than 8,100 children in 1764 but not nearly enough breadwinners.[62] Entering the war as a maritime center in difficult straits, the Massachusetts capital suffered as did no other port town. But Boston was the only northern part not lifted from prewar business depression by the epic conflict.

Boston's wartime difficulties were capped by one final disaster, as if malevolent forces were at work to heap misfortune upon misfortune. Shortly after midnight on March 20, 1760 a fire broke out near the center of town. Boston's ten fire companies fought doggedly against flames and wind, but the blaze raged out of control. The smoke did not clear for four days. "A great part of it now lies in a ruinous heap of ashes," reported one newspaper, "and Boston now looks like a frightful skeleton."[63] Nearly 400 buildings were in ashes, property worth at least £100,000

sterling was reduced to rubble, and nearly every fifth Boston householder suffered losses, both to the fire and to looters who helped themselves to what remained. Of the 377 victims who received aid, which
poured in from churches, private individuals, provincial legislatures, and
London merchants, 58 percent were classified as poor. Among widows,
who made up almost 30 percent of the sufferers, 82 percent were poor, a
final indication of how war had left Boston a poor, widowed city in more
than one sense.[64]

IN THE AFTERMATH of the North American phase of the Seven Years War,
depression gripped all three northern seaports. In relative terms Boston
suffered the least, but that was only because it had known no wartime
prosperity. It did not plummet from the heights but merely continued on
in difficult straits. There were a few hopeful signs. For many artisans in
the building trades (more than half of whom did not own their own
houses) the devastating conflagration of March 1760 was an unexpected
blessing, for it revived the flagging construction industry.[65] Trade also
increased for several years beginning in 1762, but only to the extent that
the tonnage entering and clearing the harbor returned to the levels of the
early 1750s, which were considerably depressed from earlier years.[66]
With the end of wartime impressments the fishing industry regained
some of its former vigor.

The gains, however, must be reckoned against some severe setbacks
to the town's economy. The softest sector was the West Indian trade,
always vital to Boston's well being, particularly to the importers of
French molasses and the sugar bakers, distillers, and coopers connected
to them. Angered by colonial evasions of the Trade Acts during the war,
English bureaucrats perfected their reform plans when peace came, sending warships to patrol the northern ports, beefing up the corps of customs officials, and serving notice that they expected the Americans to
pay for the maintenance of 10,000 British soldiers who remained on the
continent after the Peace of Paris.[67] Boston merchants did their best to
buy off the customs collectors sent to enforce the old Molasses Act of
1733 and bitterly fought the writs of assistance, the general search warrants that enabled conscientious collectors to ferret out smuggling merchants with illegal molasses in their warehouses. But the pay-off system
got harder and harder to play as England toughened its resolve to enforce
the law.[68]

The new Sugar Act of 1764 lowered the duty on foreign molasses from
6 to 3 pennies per gallon, but the 3-penny duty strictly enforced was
more costly than the penny per gallon previously slipped to the corrupt
collectors as an honorarium for their poor eyesight when ships with illegal cargoes entered the harbor. Combined with the severe contraction of
British credit after 1762, the effective policing of the sugar trade con-

vulsed the West Indian part of the Boston trading community and affected all the trades associated with it. Merchants John Scollay and Joseph Scott declared bankruptcy in 1764 and in January 1765 Nathaniel Wheelwright stopped payment on debts of £70,000 sterling.[69] John Hancock called it "the most prodigious shock ever known in this part of the world." Wheelwright's collapse touched off an epidemic of bankruptcies among lesser men who could not survive without the money he owed them.[70] By summer it was reported that the number of vessels employed in the West Indian trade had dropped by 80 percent, a heavy blow to all in the maritime crafts and to merchant seamen. One merchant signaled the discouragement of his colleagues when he informed his Philadelphia correspondent that he was "heartsick" at the slumping trade and now intent upon "flying from this Dying Town" to take up life as a simple country storekeeper in Sudbury.[71]

If it was any comfort, Bostonians could look southward to the mid-Atlantic emporiums of New York and Philadelphia and see them stunned by the most serious economic derangement in their histories. The wartime boom that had provided full employment and handsome wages for most men came to a shuddering halt by the end of 1760. War contracts for uniforms, weapons, and provisions evaporated after the capture of Montreal and the subsequent shifting of military operations to the Caribbean. Moreover, the withdrawal of the British army and navy, which by now numbered 18,000 seamen and 22,000 troops in the American theater, meant that English shillings no longer clanked into the tills of tavernkeepers and shopowners. Instead, former indentured servants and British deserters, many of them broken by army service, drifted into the cities in search of employment. As the liberal inflow of specie dried up, credit began to contract and overseas trade languished. The hard money pocketed from the pay of British soldiers and sailors drained back to England. One of Philadelphia's leading dry goods merchants wrote in May 1760, as the war was winding down, that the conflict "hath occasioned such a plentiful Circulation of Cash in this & the neighboring Provinces that the demand of the Inhabitants for European goods is beyond what any Person not fully acquainted therewith can conceive."[72] But six months later Philadelphia's merchants were sending up cries of distress as the sudden slump in trade heralded the beginning of a prolonged economic depression. Merchants dunned shopkeepers for debts while desperately stalling their English creditors. As credit lines were tightened from London, everyone was caught in the contractionary cycle. "Thus the consumers break the shopkeepers," wrote John Dickinson in 1765; "they break the merchants, and the shock must be felt as far as *London*."[73]

Compounding Philadelphia's problem was the resumption of Irish and German immigration. Before the Seven Years War immigrant ships had brought thousands of newcomers to Philadelphia each year. Those who possessed urban skills often remained in the city, but most headed west to the frontier. In 1760, after a five-year hiatus, seven ships from Scotland and northern Ireland arrived with immigrants; soon the transatlantic traffic returned to prewar levels. From late 1761 through 1763 at least thirty-three ships arrived from Belfast, Londonderry, Cork, Sligo, and Ballycastle, depositing thousands of poor immigrants in a city that was attempting to cope with the postwar economic slough.[74] These Daniel O'Neals, Rachel Rhumburgs, and Patrick McGuires found high prices, few jobs, and reports of spreading conflict between frontier colonists and Native Americans in the areas of new settlement where immigrants generally headed.[75] Many European immigrants who had come to take up farming in western Pennsylvania consequently may have been forced to seek temporary work in the city at a time when the postwar recession was affecting the fortunes of even the best established families.

Philadelphia's merchants had no resources to combat such business shocks. They had overextended their credit in England in building up large inventories during the war and now, when a credit crisis led to a rush on American merchants to balance their accounts, they could only send back anguished pleas for more time. When these were answered with stony demands for payment, the most precariously situated were forced to declare bankruptcy. Daniel Clark and William Griffiths closed their doors in Philadelphia in the spring of 1761, John Reed in November, and Samuel Wallace in May 1762. Then, in the "greatest break we ever knew anything of on this side of the water," Scott and McMichael collapsed in December 1763, defaulting on debts of £40,000.[76]

Economic depression broke the backs of the frailest mercantile houses and hit small retailers harder than import merchants; but hardest hit of all were artisans and laborers. Idle ships meant unemployment for large numbers of merchant seamen and maritime artisans. Not since the 1720s had Philadelphians experienced such a slump, which battered those in the middle ranks as well as those at the bottom. Philadelphia was spared even greater economic misfortune because the level of house construction remained high.[77]

In New York the postwar down-turn also struck with a vengeance. Because New York had been the center of military provisioning, the departure of British troops magnified the boom and bust cycle there as in no other port. New York got its last contracts as the British fleet fitted out for expeditions against Martinique and Dominica in May 1761. There ended the wartime glory days for the Manhattan port.[78] "The Tipling Soldiery that use to help us out at a dead lift," signed merchant John Watts, "are gone to drink it in a warmer Region, the place of it's production."[79] Privateering and illegal trade, the other mainstays of the economy, also dried up as the British fleet in the Caribbean drove French ships from the water and the invigorated British customs service cracked

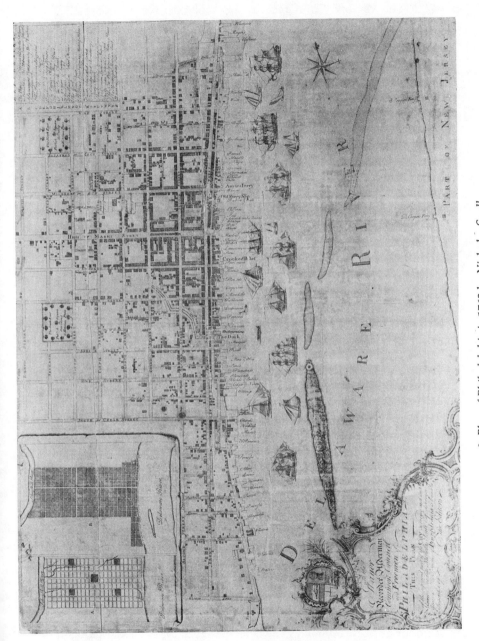

8. Plan of Philadelphia in 1762 by Nicholas Scull.

down on American smugglers. "Every thing is tumbling down," cried one of New York's leading merchants early in 1764, "even the Traders themselves."[80] The Mayor's Court records speak of this. Never before 1760 had actions for debt exceeded sixteen in any one year. By 1763 there were forty-six and three years later the number had risen to eighty.[81] "Trade in this part of the world," lamented a New Yorker in 1765, "is come to so wretched a pass that you would imagine the plague had been here, the grass growing in most trading streets; and the best traders so far from wanting the assistance of a clerk, rather want employment for themselves." Another put it bluntly: "The weak must go to the Wall. Frequent Bankruptcies and growing more frequent."[82] Building construction also bottomed out after 1763, but sustained shipbuilding mercifully kept that sector of the economy relatively immune from the depression.[83]

In all the seaport towns the greatest hardships imposed by the post-1760 slump fell upon the laboring classes, which included many established craftsmen who occupied positions on the middle rungs of the economic ladder. It was they who had the smallest savings and the thinnest margin between profit and loss. They devoted the largest proportion of their household budgets to food, rent, clothing, and fuel—expenses that could not be trimmed much when times worsened. How quickly their margin of security could be erased is evident in Philadelphia, where a leading merchant noted only a few months after the depression began that "many very poor people," unable to pay property taxes, were "disposing of their huts and lots to others more wealthy than themselves."[84] How many Philadelphians joined the ranks of the propertyless thereafter cannot be ascertained, but the rapid rise of forced sales of property beginning in 1762 and continuing for the next five years indicates that the number was substantial. Never before 1762 had foreclosures listed in the *Pennsylvania Gazette* totaled more than 50 a year, but they reached 81 in 1763, 90 in 1764, and 111 in 1765.[85]

The plight of the lower and middle classes was compounded by the rising cost of food, firewood, and taxes. Wartime demand for food to feed British forces in the North American and Caribbean theaters and the beleaguered French islands in the West Indies, as well as food shortages in the British Isles, started pushing grain and meat prices upward in 1757. The price index for Philadelphia wheat, which stood at 101 in May of that year, rose to 172 by mid-1759. Beef, pork, and bread also climbed, though less rapidly. Then, after leveling off from 1759 to 1761, prices began a precipitous ascent, driven upward by crop failures caused by extended drought. Wholesale wheat jumped from an index of 143 in May 1761 to 220 in July 1762, bread from 139 to 218. Beef and pork, which had sold for 42.5 and 60 shillings a barrel in May 1757, were marketing in Philadelphia for 62.5 and 95 shillings in July 1762.[86] Milk, customarily sold at 8 pence per gallon, rose to 12 pence. The price of nineteen "market basket" items, weighted according to the diet of the laboring classes, rose 29 percent in Philadelphia between 1755 and 1763.[87] In New York, prices followed a similar trend, bringing demands in 1763 that the common council establish "just prices" through instituting the assize. It was intolerable, cried "Plebeanus," that beef should sell at 7 or 8 pence per pound. In both New York and Philadelphia knowledgeable men judged that the cost of living had doubled during the war years.[88] Food prices began to moderate in 1763, but they resumed their upward flight by mid-1765. Country farmers welcomed the higher prices their produce commanded, but for urban artisans and laborers, who spent about half their wages on food, these were distressing times.[89]

The cost of firewood consumed only about 9 percent of the household budget but was essential to survival during the winter months. In all the seaport towns wood prices had begun to rise in the 1730s as the deforestation of the urban perimeters sent wood cutters to more distant places, increasing transportation costs.[90] But only during extraordinarily cold winters, such as in 1740-1741, did civic leaders find it necessary to launch public charity drives to provide firewood for the poor. Not until the late 1750s, when military demands for wagons in the frontier war crippled eastern transport facilities, did a critical situation develop in Philadelphia. In the winter of 1759-1760 the price of firewood shot up spectacularly, leaving laboring people in dire need. "Help! Help! Help!" cried a correspondent in the *Pennsylvania Gazette*. "Wood at £3-10 a cord, a Price never heard of . . . The widow hears a noise in her Yard, rises from her Bed at Midnight, from her Window sees a Thief, and asks him what he is doing; he answers, I must have Wood . . . The Rich engross . . . when perhaps two Hundred families have not a stick to burn."[91]

The average laboring-class family used five to ten cords of wood per winter.[92] A jump in price of even 10 shillings per cord was thus equivalent to three to six weeks' wages. In the winter of 1760-1761, as unemployment spread in the northern port towns, wood prices rose far more than this, reaching 40 to 50 shillings per cord in New York.[93] Many of the poor, reported the *Pennsylvania Gazette*, "are reduced to great Extremity and Distress" because of the high price of wood. Only a hastily formed Committe to Alleviate the Miseries of the Poor, going door to door to raise contributions and then providing free wood, saved hundreds of families in the town from freezing.[94] When bone-chilling weather returned in the winter of 1764-1765, the poor suffered miserably again. Notices in the newspapers recalled the winter of 1761-1762 and pleaded for the revival of the Committee to Alleviate the Miseries of the Poor.[95]

Along with food and firewood prices, taxes rose sharply during this period. The Seven Years War required massive military spending in spite of parliamentary grants to the colonies of about £1.4 million sterling. For decades Bostonians had been under a far heavier yoke of taxes than the propertied citizens in other cities. Now they saw taxes rise to ludicrous heights. In the peacetime years from 1750 to 1754 Bostonians paid town and provincial taxes that averaged £7,410 annually or about 55 shillings per taxable poll, the highest in history. Town taxes rose only modestly during the war years but provincial taxes to feed the military machine tripled, leaving taxpayers with annual taxes that averaged 88 shillings.[96] Governor Pownall reported in March 1758 that "the tax upon estates real and personal arises . . . in the town of Boston to 13s2d in the pound—a 66 percent tax on assessed value." Such a tax rate was unheard of, even in England where property owners were bemoaning the levies imposed to fight the Seven Years War. The same rate was imposed in 1759 and 1760.[97] For the next five years, with a huge war debt to pay off, the average Bostonian faced an annual tax bill of 89 shillings. But by this time a major part of the total levies were going uncollected.[98] Bostonians elected their tax collectors partially on the basis of their willingness to collect what they could, given a family's circumstances, and leave the remainder in arrears. In 1763, for example, more than £17,000 of the £31,120 imposed for 1761-1762 was still uncollected. For taxes levied from 1762 to 1766, totaling almost £60,000, nearly £18,000 went unpaid.[99] Bostonians were no sullen pack of tax dodgers but residents of a badly buffeted town where one-third of the 390 deceased inhabitants whose estates were inventoried between 1756 and 1765 left less than £25 personal wealth and less than £39 personal and real wealth.

New Yorkers and Philadelphians never felt the tax bite as did Bostonians, but both Pennsylvania and New York were obliged to impose unprecedented provincial taxes to meet the costs of military supplies and salaries. In Pennsylvania the war tax passed in 1756—and continued for the next twenty years—took 1.5 shillings per pound of assessed property from the pocket of every Philadelphian. This was more than triple the combined provincial, county, and city taxes paid in the prewar years and when added to spiraling local taxes meant that householders coughed up about 30 pence per pound of assessed property compared with the 4.5 pence they had paid from 1718 to 1750 and 7.5 pence from 1751 to 1755. Young unmarried men, who paid a head tax, faced aggregate taxes that rose from 13.5 shillings per year before 1750 to about 40 shillings after the onset of the Seven Years War.[100] In an economy where the journeyman's labor commanded 4 shillings per day, this meant about two weeks' income.

Gradually the fiscal burden on the laboring classes, especially after the recession beginning in 1760, became intolerable. Unable to extract even the smallest tax from families for whom firewood had to be provided by private or public relief, the assessors began lowering assessments. During the first half of the century the minimum assessment for married freemen in Philadelphia varied between £12 and £15. By 1756 the tax floor had been dropped to £8. In levying the heavy 18-penny provincial tax, the assessors initially set the minimum assessment at £4 but by 1767 they had halved it.[101] Even with these downward adjustments, hundreds of impoverished city dwellers could contribute nothing at all to the tax collectors. Such tax refugees represented less than 3 percent of the taxables in the period before 1740; in the 1740s and 1750s they rose to about 6.5 percent; and then, with the postwar depression, they totaled nearly 10 percent of the taxable population.[102] Philadelphia, which had been the fastest growing and most prosperous port town on the Atlantic seaboard, had by no means fallen to the state of Boston, as the personal estates left by its artisans show;[103] but its inhabitants could now appreciate what their Bay city cousins had endured for the last generation.

NOWHERE can the severity of the post-1760 depression be more clearly seen than in the rapid growth of a class of truly impoverished persons in the port towns. Boston was where the shadow of poverty had first fallen across the lives of substantial numbers of people and it was here that pauperism remained most deeply and unshakeably rooted. In 1757 the town estimated that about a thousand people were receiving poor relief, either as inmates of the almshouse or as out-pensioners.[104] The almshouse was crammed to capacity, especially during the difficult winter months, and officials prevented the problem from becoming even worse only by rigorously applying the warning out procedure. Never before 1753 had as many as a hundred people been warned out of Boston. With the onset of the war, which sent refugees from the frontier tramping the roads to Boston and sent many a poor war widow and her children from coastal towns toward what they hoped might be a bit of security in the capital city, the numbers began to rise sharply. In every year between 1753 and 1764 the number of those warned out exceeded 100; in two years it rose above 200; and in 1758, when the Massachusetts troops suffered heavy casualties at the battles of Ticonderoga and Fort Frontenac, the number reached 326. For the war period as a whole, warnings out totaled about 1,700, almost three times the number for the years from 1745 to 1752.[105]

It is not possible to ascertain the condition of all of these migrants. A number of them were disabled veterans; others were part of the mushrooming population of jobless, propertyless, drifting persons thrown up by the churning sea of economic dislocation in the early 1760s; and many were single women and widows, the latter invariably with several dependent children.[106] For most of these people jobs were unavailable. Yet they came, hoping against hope that in the province's largest town things would somehow be better.

Sterling expenditures for the poor, which had never exceeded £730 before 1751, rose rapidly on the eve of the war and reached £1,327 in

1756. By 1760 they had topped £1,600 and in 1764, driven upward even farther by a smallpox epidemic, they hit £1,999 sterling.[107] By 1764, when Boston began a mass inoculation program to combat the outbreak of smallpox, one-fifth of the 4,977 inoculated persons were described as poor.[108]

No statistics on expenditures in New York survive from this period. But there is little doubt that distress was acute among a growing number of citizens. New York's households were not widowed to the same extent as Boston's but hundreds of men had been idled and fell to the care of the town's poor relief officials. By January 1765 the churchwardens informed the common council that the monies raised for relief of the indigent "have been Long Since Expended" and the "distresses of the Poor" were so great that unless more money was made available immediately, the impoverished "must unavoidably perish" for want of food and firewood.[109] Taking a leaf from Boston's book, wealthy men in the city organized a Society for the Encouragement of Arts, Agriculture, and Economy, which sponsored a linen manufactory. But its attempt to put the jobless poor to work, though about 300 people were employed, was only a palliative which could not be sustained.[110]

Philadelphia confronted not only the unemployed and hard-pressed members of the lower artisanry but German and Scots-Irish immigrants as well.[111] The Quaker capital was the best equipped of any of the port towns to deal with the poor because in the early 1750s, as poverty began to spread, civic leaders had established the Pennsylvania Hospital for the Sick Poor. No project was closer to the heart of Benjamin Franklin. He waged a shrewd newspaper campaign based on a matching grants scheme that succeeded in extracting £2,000 from the assembly in 1751, after an equal amount had been raised by private subscriptions. Franklin contended that the care of the sick poor in Philadelphia would not cost one-tenth as much in a hospital as under the old system of out-relief and almshouse care. Moreover, to save the life of an injured or failing mariner or stocking weaver was to insure that his wife and children would not end up in the almshouse or on the out-pensioner rolls. Still another advantage, in a society where men of means were growing apprehensive at the prospect of a large and alienated lower class, was the tendency of such hospitals, as an English proponent suggested, "to give the poor in general grateful and honorable sentiment and inspire them with proper love and reverence towards their superiors and by consequence promote that harmony and subordination in which the peace and happiness of society consists." Following this line of thought, the managers of the hospital required discharged indigents to sign statements testifying to "the benefit they have received in this hospital to be either published or otherwise disposed of as the managers may think fit."[112]

Beginning in 1752, the hospital played an important role in holding down expenditures for the poor. The number of patients rose steadily and most of those treated were restored to the labor force. That so many of the patients were mariners testifies to the fact that disease and injury were common occurrences of the seagoing part of the lower class. For the hospital's merchant managers, who determined who should be admitted, the institution functioned admirably in keeping open the channels of trade by maintaining the health of those who kept ships at sea.[113] By all accounts, the hospital was an uncommon success, benefiting the lower-class laborer and the middle-class taxpayer alike.

The winter of 1761-1762 brought to an abrupt halt an era in which Philadelphia could rely on the hospital, a small almshouse, and a modest annual poor tax to meet the needs of the unfortunate. The depression, compounded by sharp price increases, emptied the larders of hundreds and put fuel beyond the reach of many. Into the breach jumped the Committee to Alleviate the Miseries of the Poor, whose records show that wood, blankets, and stockings were distributed to 329 "objects of Charity" in the southern half of the city. In all, more than 650 families were probably aided, about one of every five. Combined with 100 or more persons in the almshouse and about the same number who received aid in the Hospital for the Sick Poor, the rate of those proffered assistance rose to about five times the prewar rate. Most of these persons were recent immigrants or war veterans, but about one-quarter of the males on the committee's recipient list had been in the city at least since 1756.[114]

For four years after the numbing winter of 1761-1762 the overseers of the poor and men of wealth struggled to shore up the old system of relief while urging the provincial government to come to Philadelphia's rescue. The assembly listened to petitions in 1763 that "into rooms but ten or eleven Feet square . . . [we] have been obliged to crowd five or six Beds," while other needy persons were billeted in a nearby church.[115] But the legislature, unable to agree on a new measure, or preferring to let its capital city solve its own problems, took no action. By late 1764, when eleven immigrant ships arrived from Rotterdam and northern Ireland, the distress of the needy again became urgent. Attempts were made to employ the poor in a hastily erected linen manufactory, but this experiment had no greater success than in New York and Boston, although it employed about 200 poor women for several winters.[116]

In the bitter winter of 1764-1765, emergency measures were instituted again, private donations solicited, and the poor tax rate raised from 3 to 5 pence per pound of assessable wealth. The almshouse bulged with about 160 persons and another 150 received out-relief.[117] Conditions were still not nearly so bad as in Boston, but Philadelphia too now experienced economic derangement and social stress.

While the post-1760 depression severely wracked the poorest members of urban society, it also struck hard at many in the middle sector. The declining fortune of these artisans and petty entrepreneurs is harder to trace because circumstances did not deteriorate so badly for them that their names were inscribed in the almshouse admissions book, the warning out records, or the lists of those unable to pay taxes. Two hundred years later it is the poorest members of society who are most "articulate" in the extant records because it is they who received the care—or the opprobrium—of town officials.

The slippage of many established craftsmen and small shopkeepers is especially important because they were more politically conscious than those below them, who in many cases were recent immigrants, widows, or transient persons. These middling town dwellers were those who figured importantly in Boston's town meeting, who had often sat on New York's common council, and who formed the heart of Philadelphia's voluntary militia. A New York artisan, writing in August 1762, spoke movingly of their crumbling security. "A.B.," as he styled himself, was thankfully not one of the many unemployed in his town. But despite unceasing labor and frugal living he had fallen into poverty. He had trimmed every luxury from his household budget, but still "the Expence of living in the most frugal Way has increased so exorbitantly, that I find it beyond my ability to support my Family with my utmost Industry—I am growing every Day more and more behind hand, tho' my Family can scarcely appear with Decency, or have necessaries to subsist." What should he do? he asked his readers. Caught in a wage-price squeeze, he must "starve or be dishonest." His case, A.B. reminded his readers, "is really the Case with many of the Inhabitants of this City."[118]

If ALL urban dwellers had suffered equally in the aftermath of the Seven Years War, then the depression of the 1760s might have unified colonial urban societies. It might have served as a warning that while growing more powerful in numbers and productive capacity, they, as Americans, were becoming less powerful in their ability to control the violent fluctuations in the Atlantic economy. To a considerable extent this perception of the problem as externally caused did dominate thinking at the upper level of society, among merchants, large landowners, government officials, and lawyers. The drastic overhaul of imperial policy which Parliament instituted at the close of the war gave much credence to this point of view. It was apparent that an invigorated customs bureaucracy, cracking down hard on colonial smugglers, dried up profits on the illegal importation of French tea and sugar; that the establishment of vice-admiralty courts placed violators of the Navigation Acts beyond the forgiving attitudes of local juries made up of their peers; that the Currency Act of 1764, restricting the issuing of paper currency in New York and Pennsylvania, put a further damp on trade already shockingly depressed; and that the Stamp Act, passed in 1765, laid additional levies on heavily taxed urban dwellers, while also convincing many that even further fiscal burdens were in the offing. Many merchants and shopkeepers suffered heavy losses in the years after 1760, and for many of them the new parliamentary legislation and the contractionary actions of their British creditors were signals that a maturing American people must now expect their necks to be pinned to the ground by the paw of an insensitive British lion.

The common people were not shy about expressing this point of view, often in concert with their social superiors. But interwoven with this perception was another strand of thought. War, it was understood, had required financial sacrifice from everyone in the form of higher taxes. Furthermore, war had spilt much blood, primarily the blood of the lower class. That too was the usual way of things. But to many it was deeply disturbing that eight years of conflict had left the maritime centers with social pyramids that had greatly broadened bases, swarming with the poor, and lofty pinnacles where a few men stood high above their neighbors.

This social transformation is statistically measurable, though we can never obtain mathematical precison in these matters, given the selective survival of documents. In the inventories of estate and tax lists lies the silent record of the redefinition of class categories. Most notable is the parallel emergence of the fabulously wealthy and the desperately poor. The growth and commercialization of the port towns had all along been making possible the amassing of wealth by the few, and war accelerated the process by increasing the opportunities. In each city a handful of men in the waning years of the colonial period could boast of estates totaling £50,000 to £100,000 sterling. Samuel Waldo, Charles Apthorp, Thomas Hancock, and James Bowdoin in Boston; James DeLancey, John Watts, William Bayard, and John Cruger in New York; and Thomas Willing, James Hamilton, William Shippen, Israel Pemberton, Samuel Powel, William Allen, Joseph Turner, John Cadwalader, and John Mease in Philadelphia were some of those who reached this range.[119] Wealthy Philadelphians fared better than their Boston counterparts, as might be expected given Boston's long period of economic adversity, but in both towns the top 5 percent of taxpayers and decedents with inventoried estates controlled about as much wealth as the other 95 percent combined.[120]

These changes did not go unnoticed by eighteenth-century town dwellers. A kind of evidence far more palpable than profit and loss sheets was everywhere to be seen: the urban mansions built during the 1760s, the sharp rise in the number of four-wheeled coaches and carriages imported from London, and the burst of newspaper advertising by those who served the urban rich—wigmakers, silk dyers, retailers of expensive furniture, instructors of music and dancing. Wealthy Philadelphians such as Edward Shippen had for many years come home from trips abroad embarrassed at "how much we are excelled by those in Europe."[121] After 1750 these aspiring aristocrats were able to surround themselves with urbane elegance such that none could make slighting remarks about provincial rusticity. Benjamin Chew, the attorney general of Pennsylvania, spent more than £3,000 building his country seat outside of Philadelphia during the height of the postwar depression.[122] Brothers Charles and Alexander Stedman, Scottish immigrants twenty years before, were equally lavish in building Georgian showplaces in the city in 1765.[123] A few years later John Cadwalader, a wealthy merchant, spent £3,500 acquiring an elegant Philadelphia house, paid another £3,600 to enlarge and remodel it, and threw in another £1,500 for furnishings. Such grandeur made his old coach and harness look "but mean," as he put it, so he ordered his London agent to send him a dazzling new vehicle. Soon, Cadwalader was rolling through Philadelphia's cobbled streets behind six horses, with coachman Benjamin Ardle in command and two of his twelve slaves riding postilion.[124] In Boston, where fully half of the people died with less than £40 personal wealth and one-quarter with £20 or less, John Adams gasped at what he saw when invited to the house of a wealthy merchant. "Went over the House to view the Furniture, which alone cost a thousand Pounds sterling. A seat it is for a noble Man, a Prince. The Turkey Carpets, the painted Hangings, the Marble Tables, the rich Beds with crimson Damask Curtains and Counterpins, the beautiful Chimny Clock, the Spacious Garden, are the most magnificent of any Thing I have ever seen."[125] Ordinary people were not given tours of the stunning houses and spacious gardens of the new urban bashaws; but since it was their handicraft skills that created such mansions, the aristocratic life style could never be hidden, nor did the urban aristocrats wish it to be.

This wartime redistribution of wealth, which gave the lower classes not only a smaller share of the community's assets but in the years after 1760 also began to deteriorate seriously their absolute standard of living, was accompanied by a change in labor relationships as well as a shifting of economic power. One part of this was the attempt of some urban artisans, in the boom years of the late 1750s, to free themselves partially from the economic clientage that had traditionally prevailed in the cities. The decision to work on a per diem basis at a higher wage rather than accepting monthly or yearly employment at lower rates of pay was an important part of this striving to free oneself from paternalist structures of control. In a free labor market, the artisan moved from job to job, taking his chances of finding employment but commanding higher wages. Usually tied to this practice was the decision to provide one's own food rather than eating at the employer's table, thus receiving 1 shilling per day more for providing one's own "diet."[126] As has been pointed out in the English context, "to eat at one's employer's board, to lodge in his barn or above his workshop, was to submit to his supervision." An important part of the transition from an eighteenth-century paternalist labor system to the free labor system of the nineteenth-century factory was to convert these "non-monetary usages or perquisites . . . into money payments."[127]

We can see this entrepreneurial urge appearing in the boom era of the Seven Years War. The carpenters who worked for Isaac Norris, one of Philadelphia's wealthiest merchants and urban developers, had customarily taken their wages on a monthly basis with subsistence provided. Benjamin Morgan agreed in January 1753 to work for £3-2-5 per month on Norris's diet. He continued to work on these terms through mid-1755. With about twenty-six working days in the month, this figured to about 2.5 shillings per day. If he lost days because of injury or sickness, his pay was not docked. But in 1755, when the building of the Pennsylvania Hospital for the Sick Poor and large additions to the Statehouse created an unusual demand for artisans in the building trades, Morgan decided to ask for a daily rate at "his own diet," thus sacrificing security of employment but getting 3.5 shillings per day from Norris and 4 shillings for work at the Statehouse.[128] William Falk took the same chance in June 1756. Carpenters from Philadelphia had been in demand at Lake Ontario and Lake George to build the bateaux for carrying supplies in the northern campaigns against the French, so employment opportunities had never seemed brighter. "I now agree," wrote Norris in his account book, "to give him [Falk] after this 3/0 Per Day but not to be obliged to find him work on Rainy days and If I should have occasion to employ him in Winter . . . to give him 2/6 to the 25th day of March—and not at all engaged to find him in constant Employ." But the venturesome Falk soon suffered some kind of adversity and was obliged to come to Norris, cap in hand, and ask for a return to the lesser paid but more secure arrangement. "William after writing this Agreement," noted Norris, "changed his Mind and now requests that I advance him Mony to pay his House Rent and agrees to work at 2/6 Per Diem."[129]

The strivings of Benjamin Morgan and William Falk offer a small but crucial fragment of evidence which speaks to how laboring-class culture was changing in the second half of the eighteenth century. Commercial expansion and wartime opportunities gave many, especially in the upper ranks of the artisans, a chance to partake of the entrepreneurial spirit, to cut loose from the moorings of an older system. But many learned to their pain that greater freedom involved greater risks—and risks that employers gradually handed willingly over to them. In the postwar slump, many who labored with their hands tried to scurry back to the security of long-term contracts. Meanwhile, those who commanded the labor of others learned a lesson they would not forget. When times were bad, there was no advantage in making yearly contracts, including the provision of diet, either with artisans on a relatively short-term basis or with indentured servants and slaves on a long-term basis. Contractual labor meant mouths to feed and persons to pay through thick and thin. Converted to wage laborers, these persons could be paid at a higher rate in good times and simply released when business grew slack. Where they would go or how they would subsist became somebody else's problem.

Something of the new mentality of the free labor market can be seen in the operations of Philadelphia's Street Commissioners, appointed in 1762 to manage the paving and cleaning of the city's streets. The commissioners began by paying laborers 5 shillings per day, a high rate that reflected not only the unprecedented price of food but also the generally full employment in the city. By April 1763, as prices leveled off and the number of persons entering the city began to create an unemployment problem, the commissioners dropped the wage rate to 4.5 shillings per day; nine months later they lowered it to 4 shillings. Over the next four years, as unemployment became more and more widespread, the commissioners sank the wage rate by steps until it reached 3 shillings per day in 1768.[130] The traditional practice of paying a standard wage, regardless of business conditions, had given way to the modern concept that wage rates, like commodity prices, must respond to the impersonal laws of supply and demand.

If we can perceive important harbingers of the future in the breakdown of paternalist labor relations in Philadelphia, we can also see the persistence of the traditional world of laboring people in Boston. Long trapped in an economic backwater, Boston's leather apron men participated far less fully in the dawning entrepreneurial age. By the same token, they were the most remarkable of the port town inhabitants in perpetuating the highly symbolic and ritualistic culture of the laboring classes. The best window into their universe is through the Pope's Day celebration in Boston. Held every November 5 to commemorate the thwarting of the Catholic conspiracy in England, when Guy Fawkes attempted to blow up the House of Parliament in 1605, Pope's Day had become the high point of antipopery in New England. Also called Gunpowder Plot Day, this annual festival had special appeal on both sides of the Atlantic among urban artisans, especially of the lower ranks.[131]

In Boston, it was the artisans who began to commemorate the day with elaborate dramaturgical performances, including the erection of a large stage, drawn by men and horses, that paraded through the streets of the town. On the stage was a pageant of the infamous Gunpowder Plot. There sat the pope in an armchair, decked out in rich array, and behind him a gigantic effigy of the devil, covered with tar and feathers. Small boys danced around the pope, played cards, kissed the devil, and entertained street audiences through mocking popery and the Catholic Stuart Pretender, hated by Protestant Englishmen for his attempt to usurp the

English throne. For several years after Pope's Day was first celebrated in Boston, in the 1730s or earlier, artisans from the North End dominated the elaborate mummery. But South Enders were soon competing with them, parading through the streets with their own stage. What started out as friendly competition soon turned into gang warfare, as "formidable mobs collected, and furious battles were fought, with fists, clubs, stones and other missles."[132] The victorious party won the right to carry the opposition's pageantry to the top of a hill and burn it at night along with their own stage. As the years passed, artisans from the two ends of town formed paramilitary organizations with elaborate preparation preceding the annual event. Though not so intended, Pope's Day became a school for training lower-class leaders, for organizing men who worked with their hands, and for imparting to the lower element a sense of its collective power.

Boston's Pope's Day also involved the ritual of status reversal so well known all over Europe. November 5 became the day when youth and the lower class ruled, not only in controlling the streets of the town but also in going from house to house to collect money from the affluent for financing the prodigious feasting and drinking that went on from morning to night. These "forced levies" were handed up during the morning by well-to-do householders as a matter of course, for, as Isaiah Thomas, a young printer's apprentice, recalled some years later, "but few thought it quite safe to refuse."[133] Authorities in Boston made attempts to control the violence and indiscipline of Pope's Day, especially after melées when fatal injuries were inflicted, but in general they were powerless to change its character.

In its way, Pope's Day in Boston portrayed the reciprocal relationship of upper and lower classes. As in English cities, "rulers and crowd needed each other, watched each other, performed theatre and counter-theatre to each other's auditorium, moderated each other's political behavior."[134] The General Court, in trying to regulate the excesses of Pope's Day in 1753, spoke anxiously about how the yearly celebration tended "to encourage and cultivate a mobbish temper and spirit in many of the inhabitants, and an opposition to all government and order."[135] But it was allowed, for though social discipline was briefly shattered, one day's disorder was well worth the price if it prevented far more serious assaults on privilege. Who, in fact, knew what might be the result of an attempt to banish an artisan ritual that had become a tradition?

For the Boston gentry, there was much to be feared in the explosive power of the laboring classes. This kinetic force annually displayed itself on Pope's Day, taking symbolic form. But it could as easily surface on other occasions in expressly political ways, as it had in the antimarket action in 1737 and in the Knowles impressment riots a decade later. Or this energy could flow into religious enthusiasm, as during the turbulent times in 1740 and 1741 when the hot gospeling of the radical evangelists had drawn Bostonians by the thousands to the Common and sent them away full of disrespect for their betters. It is no wonder that upper-class guardians of the moral order and their allies, who had managed to enrich themselves during a long era of general economic hardship, might quiver at the bone-crushing street theater enacted by the artisanry each year and wonder how long the laboring class would continue to direct the ritualized mayhem inward upon themselves.

In an increasingly structured social system, where the distance between rich and poor was widening, the patrician elite could also attempt to demonstrate its power ritually through elaborate weddings, horseracing, fox hunting, dance societies, and other socially exclusive events and organizations. All of these manifestations of elite urban culture blossomed rapidly at mid-century.[136] Just as Pope's Day in Boston demonstrated the power and the distinctive cultural traditions of the laboring classes, these upper-class social events exhibited how far the wealthy had progressed in their emulation of the patrician conventions of Georgian England.

Yet, while they emphasized the growing void separating the elite from the lower echelons, the crystallizing upper-class cultural forms largely failed to exact deference from those of mean or middling condition. The power of those at the top could not be ignored, of course, for a large number of artisans, mariners, and laborers rented their houses, received employment, and borrowed money from the best situated men in their towns. But behind a mask of obeisance, required by the realities of an economic system where clientage was still widespread, lay an increasingly stormy visage. In the past an irreverent stance toward authority and high status, always dormant in colonial society, had surfaced episodically during times of stress. Egalitarian feeling had also grown extensively during the Great Awakening. Now, hostility toward men of great wealth intensified and the cultural hegemony of the elite, never firmly established, tottered precariously.

In effect, social structure and social attitudes were moving along divergent paths with the rise of egalitarian sentiment, concentrated in the laboring classes, accompanying the restructuring of urban society along more rigid class lines. For laboring people it was not so much that the opening of a chasm between rich and poor accentuated class differences, which by themselves bothered only the most utopian members of society. Rather, it was that the new wealth of the urban elite, in some not yet fully comprehensible way, was based on class exploitation. When each man could wrest a decent existence from the environment, virtually nobody challenged the concept of social hierarchy or even the accumulation of substantial wealth. But when hard work and frugal living no longer assured leather apron men the basic necessities of life, they began to fathom a connection between their plight and the simultaneous rise of some of their neighbors to towering wealth. By mid-century poverty in Boston had bred contempt for the rich in a number of political writers and fed the notion that great wealth and grinding poverty were organically connected. "From your Labour and Industry," proclaimed Phileleutheros for the mechanics, "arises all that can be called Riches, and by your Hands it must be defended: Gentry, Clergy, Lawyers, and military Officers, do all support their Grandeur by your Sweat, and at your Hazard." Yet heavy taxes, stagnation of trade, decay of the crafts, and wartime service "fall signally upon the middle and inferiour Ranks of Mankind."[137] Now such notions entered the consciousness of the laboring classes in the other port towns. "Some individuals," charged a New Yorker in 1765, ". . . by the Smiles of Providence, or some other Means, are enabled to roll in their four wheel'd Carriages, and can support the expense of good Houses, rich Furniture, and Luxurious Living. But is it equitable that 99, rather 999, should suffer for the Extravagance or Grandeur of one? Especially when it is considered that Men frequently owe their Wealth to the impoverishment of their Neighbors?"[138] This was the language of class consciousness, bred out of ancient feelings of the worth of leather apron men, nurtured by periodic adversity, and extended and clarified by the depressing aftermath of the Seven Years War. Direct political action by unlettered but not inarticulate people would follow hard upon such words.

10

The Intensification of Factional Politics

WARS HAVE always been engines of social change and the pattern of war-time boom and postwar bust, usually involving painful political adjustments, is not uncommon. So it was to be expected that the depression that enveloped the seaport towns beginning in 1760 should be accompanied by political turmoil. The activation of groups at all levels of society, the elaboration of the apparatus of party politics, the use of shrill rhetoric, and the crystallization of class consciousness had always proceeded most rapidly during periods of economic stress in the port towns and then receded with the return of better days. Each advance of a popularized form of politics had swept higher on the beach of traditional ways. But political control had never more than momentarily fallen from the grasp of those at or near the top.

It was not political power itself that the laboring classes yearned for, but an equitable system in which they could pursue their modest goals. Family, church, work, and community were still the linchpins of their existence; the exercise of political authority did not yet fit comfortably with their conception of their proper role. In moments when their economic security or their ideological commitment was threatened, they responded by attempting to influence, not dominate, politics, to redress grievances rather than dismantling the system inherited from their fathers.

Yet their periodic excursions into "radical" politics, in order either to conserve the corporate community or to prise open the doors of opportunity in the new entrepreneurial age, had a cumulative effect. A sense of their own power grew as their trust in those above them diminished and as their experience expanded in making decisions, exercising leadership roles, and refuting those who were supposed to be wiser because they were wealthier. Hence factional politics intensified. As never before, members of the lower ranks began to act for and of themselves, propelling forward their own leaders, making their muscle felt, and wreaking bitter violence against those they construed as their enemies.

Among the upper ranks also, especially merchants, the end of the war presented grave problems. England's decision to overhaul its system of imperial management—to tighten restrictions on trade, currency, the conduct of Indian affairs, and the judicial system—at precisely the time when economic depression was casting a pall over the port towns struck heavily at American traders. Merchants saw themselves caught between two pincers: first, the internal derangement of local economies that were now tied to the unstable international marketplace; and second, the grating effects of new policies imposed by imperial masters determined to extract greater contributions from colonial dependents. Gravely threatened, many merchants who by temperament were thoroughly conservative found themselves obliged to assume roles as protesters, propagandists, and, in the end, even revolutionaries. British imperial policy deeply divided the merchant communities and those who did protest sought support from below. The anomalies of the situation were manifold.

DURING the war years from 1755 to 1760 Boston and New York exhibited a political quietude that belied the situation that was rapidly developing. In Boston, despite serious economic difficulties, the political turmoil of the 1740s faded into the background. Governor Shirley learned that he could rule the colony by stitching together a rural majority in the General Court. Boston thus lost much of its importance as a political fulcrum. Elections for selectmen and representatives never drew as many people to the polls as had the marketplace controversy of the 1730s. Candidates for selectmen frequently went unopposed.[1] Conservative merchant allies of Shirley's successor in 1757, Thomas Pownall, won election to the House of Representatives.

Behind this unnatural calm lay two factors: the absence of a sizeable part of the laboring class, which had been mobilized for frontier warfare, and the inability of popular party leaders to formulate any kind of program for lifting Boston from the economic doldrums. Boston's popular politicians had always been more reactive than creative, fighting doggedly against threats upon the town meeting, measures to alter traditional methods of marketing, deflationary monetary policy, and impressment, but rarely fashioning programmatic solutions to structural weaknesses in the economy. They were the traditional conservators of the moral economy, the defenders of the common people, and sometimes the critics of the new wealth and commercialism. But other than their advocacy of a plentiful paper currency, they had no answers for setting the straitened economy to rights. Impotent to rectify the lack of a staple crop or Boston's waning position in the international commerce of the

Atlantic basin, they could only inveigh against the drive for power by the prerogative group or appeal to the past, to a simpler world where communality had stood above individuality.

In New York wartime politics were also unusually quiescent but for different reasons. Flush times, in contrast to Boston, almost eliminated divisive issues. When profits beckoned and everyone believed they could be a winner in the wartime sweepstakes, the ground for political contention all but disappeared. The assembly elected in October 1752 sat for more than six years, until December 1758, which meant that only once during the war years did New Yorkers so much as go to the polls for a provincial election. Moreover, they were content to let some of the city's wealthiest merchants do their lawmaking for them—John Cruger, William Walton, John Watts, and Paul Richards.[2] In local politics it was the same. In marked contrast to the tumultuous days of the 1730s, when artisans had flocked to purchase freemanship and captured control of the municipal corporation, the acquisition of voting rights between 1754 and 1760 fell to its lowest level in the colonial period. Likewise, the aldermanic councils of the 1750s were completely dominated by the mercantile elite.[3]

New York's only political turmoil during the war years emanated from opposition to British policies. A spat developed in the assembly in 1756 over the quartering of British troops in the city; a minor impressment riot in 1758 signified the discontent of waterfront New Yorkers, who had no wish to give up high wages on merchant ships or privateers for death duty in the British navy; and a merchant-inspired riot in 1759 sought to break a trade embargo clamped on the port by the British commander in chief, who was attempting to redirect foodstuffs bound for the French enemy in the Caribbean to his own troops.[4] All of these were minor fracases, however, mainly reflecting attempts to avoid the inconveniences of war while reaping profits from it. Lower-class Manhattanites kept alive the principle that the crowd had legitimate work to do in the streets when external authorities unrightfully imposed their will, but internal tensions were at a minimum during the years of fighting.

Only in Philadelphia did the war years roil the political waters. This was because only here was disagreement widespread on the advisability of pursuing the war and only here did this issue give a faction that had previously quested for power a golden opportunity to mount a political offensive. The years from 1755 to 1760 in Philadelphia politics bear investigation not only because they were stormy but also because they set in motion forces that would be greatly extended in the depression days that lay ahead.

The onset of war in 1755 immediately threw Pennsylvania's politics into confusion, for unlike the previous Anglo-French conflicts this one erupted in the colony's backyard. The French move to gain control of the

Ohio Valley and to capture the allegiance of the powerful Indian tribes there eliminated the possibility that the Quaker colony would be able to sit on the sidelines in this conflict. When Braddock's army was thrashed at the Monongahela in July 1755, all of western Pennsylvania, which had been rapidly filling with German and Ulster immigrants for a generation, was thrown into panic. Quaker pacifism seemed ludicrously inappropriate in such a situation. In a stroke the proprietary party, singularly unsuccessful in its quest for power and resigned after the early 1740s to making its weight felt through its control of appointive offices, saw the situation shifting in its favor. The German vote, so crucial in Pennsylvania, might now desert to the proprietary side, for Quaker foot-dragging in the legislature on war appropriations and a militia act for mobilizing provincial troops was all it would take, or so the proprietary leaders thought, to end the Quaker-German alliance. The Quaker "Wretches are, in the End, like to get their Reward," wrote Philadelphia merchant William Allen, a leader of the proprietary party and chief justice of Pennsylvania, "for they are heartily despised and hated by the People and particularly by the Germans, who were formerly much attached to them."[5]

The proprietary leaders overestimated their own political appeal, however. Germans had not forgotten the deprecatory remarks made earlier about them in proprietary quarters. What they wanted was not proprietary control of provincial politics but Quaker action on the war emergency. They got it by organizing marches on Philadelphia in November 1755. Seven hundred strong, they demanded what most legislators had already decided—that a militia must be formed and money appropriated to protect the western frontier.[6] Quakers soon began resigning from the assembly. They decided not to run in 1756, a pragmatic concession to the realities of the situation but by no means an abdication of political power since they continued to exert a strong antiproprietary influence on non-Quakers who ran in their places.[7] After 1755 the issue was no longer whether Pennsylvania would fight—it could not do otherwise unless it wished to abandon the colony—but on what conditions the war would be prosecuted. Among the several aspects of this problem, the most important were whether the vast proprietary estates should be taxed on the same basis as the land of ordinary Pennsylvanians in raising the enormous sums needed to prosecute the war and whether the militia should be organized on a volunteer basis with officers elected by the men in the ranks or should be a mandatory service with officers appointed by the proprietary governor.[8]

It would be tedious to follow the turnings and windings of these disputes, which kept Philadelphia's political atmosphere inflamed for most of the war years. In the end the proprietary party made only small inroads on the hegemony of the popular party and won only a few skirmishes, while losing the larger battles at the polls. Of greater importance is comprehending the transformation of the political consciousness of the city's people during the course of the war, for therein lay the beginning of a wholesale change that reached its climax in the postwar period.

At the heart of this transformation was the involvement of the broad mass of people in fiery political issues and the adoption of political stratagems that struck hard at the management of politics from above. This had occurred a generation before when William Keith had led the popular elements in a campaign to pull the town out of the painful depression of the 1720s. The reinitiation of popular politics in the late 1750s, by contrast, occurred during a period of almost unrivaled economic expansion. In both cases, the common threads were a quest for power by two contending factions and the identification by common people of issues that touched their lives. But whereas the conservative element in the 1720s had regarded it as unthinkable that men of education and substance should indulge in the popularization of politics, the proprietary leaders of the 1750s swallowed all such elitist pride and hotly pursued the "rabble" whom they despised. The artisans of Philadelphia found themselves courted simultaneously by both the assembly party, where Benjamin Franklin was assuming a major leadership role as the Quaker politicians retired, and the proprietary party.

At first, this broadening of the politically relevant sector of society was accomplished through resort to the press. *A Brief State of the Province of Pennsylvania*, a proprietary tract anonymously penned by William Smith, a young Anglican minister with political pretensions, appeared in Philadelphia in April 1755. It began a heated verbal war that not only politicized the mass of people but eventually brought all authority into disrepute as well. Smith openhandedly attacked the Quaker policies, accused the Friends of treason, warned of the imminent danger if the assembly party was not dismantled, and suggested barring Quakers from office and perhaps from voting as well. "Humphrey Scrouge" answered *A Brief State* with *Tit for Tat*, a pamphlet too vitriolic for any Philadelphia publisher to accept.

Then the paper war spread to the pages of the *Pennsylvania Journal*. From March to July 1756, with attention focused on the volunteer Militia Act passed by the legislature, the verbal combat intensified and the language became more abusive.[9] A Franklin supporter accused Smith of "inveterate calumny, foul-mouth'd Aspersion, shameless Falsehood, and insatiate Malice" and called this prominent Philadelphian, who was now also the president of the Philadelphia Academy, a "Frantick Incendiary, A Minister of the Infernal Prince of Darkness, the Father of LIES." Indicating that all rules of journalistic propriety had been cast aside, Smith's attacker charged that "the Vomitings of this infamous Hireling . . . betoken that Redundancy of Rancour, and Rottiness of Heart, which renders him the most despicable of his Species."[10]

Quakers who had dominated the assembly party for many years disavowed such calumny, despite the fact that they had been accused of treason and dictatorial behavior. But once the floodgates of literary assassination had opened, it proved impossible to close them again. Inevitably, the professional pamphleteer emerged on the scene as a new figure in politics. David James Dove, an ill-paid Philadelphia schoolteacher, seems to have been the first of this breed, a man ready to supplement his meager income by devising new ways of touching the fears and aspirations of the electorate through deception, innuendo, and scurrility. Dove was the hired pen behind many of the popular party's poisoned attacks, including a vicious assault in 1758 on the Philadelphia Academy, which engaged, he informed his readers, in "Violation of Truth, groveling Servility, Disaffection to our Country, Ingratitude to Benefactors, Infidelity to Friends, ill Breeding and Brutality," and retained as its chief tutor and president, "Dr. Cant," a man of "slovenly Dress, an awkward slouching Gait, and a blunt morose, crabbed, paedagogical Behaviour." Dove was so good at his work that he was soon in the hire of the side he was initially employed to attack.[11]

The point behind the bombardment of the public with inflammatory tracts and newspaper screeds was to move people to action—both in the formal political arena, where they were urged to cast their ballots for one candidate or the other, and in the streets, where public displays of collective power could be made. Franklin masterminded the conjoining of the two in his organization of the Philadelphia militia in December 1755. He began by showering the city with copies of his clever *XYZ Dialogue*, a fictionalized argument among three Philadelphians about the volunteer Militia Act where "X," an artisan in favor of the law, had all the best arguments. Having "prepared the public mind," Franklin went on to orchestrate a general election for militia officers in each of the city's ten wards and then staged an elaborate parade through the city of the thousand men who rallied to the colors of his private army.[12] As he had in 1747, Franklin created the sense that the mechanics of Philadelphia were its strength, that the choosing of militia officers was everyone's concern, and that the proprietary party was out of touch with the people.

The militia struggle politicized nearly every element of Philadelphia society. The nonsectarian Philadelphia Academy, where Franklin served as president of the board, became dominated by the Anglican supporters of the proprietary, who promptly drove Poor Richard out.[13] The proprietary leaders organized an independent militia, recruited five companies of supporters, and counterdemonstrated in the streets. Even Franklin's old organization of leather apron men, the Junto, became so obsessed with politics that its Anglican majority harassed supporters of the popular party into resignation.[14] Religious groups split along political lines and clergymen became parapolitical leaders. "What I am most concerned for & apprehensive of evil consequences from," wrote the rector of Christ Church to the Archbishop of Canterbury, "is the practice of some Clergymen here to intermix what is their true and real business with Politics in civil affairs and being so zealous therein as to blame and even revile those of their Brethren who cannot approve of their conduct in this particular."[15]

In this case, the clergyman in question was the Anglican William Smith. His political forays, which took the form of hard-hitting attacks on the Quaker party in 1756 and 1757, inspired the assembly to bring a libel suit against him early in 1758. No more dramatic representation of a politicized clergy can be imagined than the incarceration of Smith by the assembly in January of that year. During the course of a long trial and subsequent appeals to England, Smith carried out his clerical duties and political ambitions from the common jail in Philadelphia.[16] Franklin's great popularity carried many Anglicans away from the proprietary party and the fact that he was inveterately opposed by the leading Anglican in the city led eventually to a schism in the church. By 1759 about seventy Philadelphia Anglicans—the "lower sort of people," according to William Smith—split off to follow the revivalist preacher, William McClanaghan, a "follower of Whitfield's plan" and a man whose "stentorian voice," "strange extempore rhapsody," and "continual ringing . . . upon the words, Regeneration, instantaneous Conversion, imputed Righteousness, the new Birth, &c." deeply offended the conservative followers of the Church of England.[17]

Once they had determined to foray outside their customary strongholds—the courts, the proprietary offices, and the largely powerless city corporation—and to enter the arena of electoral politics, proprietary leaders were obliged to court the people. Quaker party writers heaped ridicule upon them for this, crying with glee that "Gentlemen of the best Fortune of that Party, thought it not Mean or dishonourable to enter the Houses of the lowest Mechanics to solicit their Opposition" to the militia law in 1756. Petitions were circulated door to door by the proprietary politicians in a move that made a mockery of their charges that the Quakers had always attempted to "sway the Mob at Elections."[18]

Essentially elitist in their view of society, the proprietary stalwarts were obliged by their determination to win at the ballot box to act contrary to their own beliefs. They regarded Franklin as "the chief author and Grand abettor of all the seditious practices in this Government," charged him with "infusing into the people's ears his Republican, Anarchical Notions," and tarred him as a man "of a Republican disposition and levelling Principles."[19] But they could not win the people's vote when they did not have the people's confidence. And how would the people's confidence be gained when proprietary leaders could not resist attacking Franklin and his followers, as did "Pensylvanus" in 1756, for paying "humble Court to the Multitude by putting them in Mind that the meanest of them has a Right to Civilities (that have never been denied to them) from the greatest."[20] Proprietary politicians hated this exaltation of ordinary Philadelphians, this attempt to "enflame the Minds of the People." They tried to convince the voters that the popular party was really run by "great Dictators," men who only wanted their votes in order to pursue their private ambitions and were intent upon "riveting their Chains on the People."[21] But ordinary Philadelphians were not listening to this argument. The disconsonance between proprietary attempts to appeal to the electorate and haughty condescension toward them was obvious. The people's reaction was duly registered in an unrelieved string of electoral defeats for the proprietary party in Philadelphia between 1754 and 1760.

WITH THE beginning of depression in mid-1760 a momentous new phase of politics began in the port towns. The economic slump brought no immediate response from those who sought office, for in truth neither popular nor prerogative leaders possessed a formula for economic recovery. In Philadelphia elections were unusually quiet from 1760 to 1763, which can be explained in part by the absence of any kind of proprietary party challenge to the assembly party and in part by the fact that the depression first affected those who were least incorporated into the political body—recent immigrants, transient mariners, and semiskilled former indentured servants returning from military service. In New York, the opposition Livingston party made a run at the incumbent DeLanceyites in 1761. With both sides recruiting hard, an unprecedented 1,447 voters turned out. But they split almost evenly between the Anglican DeLancey and Presbyterian Livingston party candidates, all of whom appealed to the artisan class but none of whom could offer anything more concrete than lawyer John Morin Scott's less than ringing promise that he was "the poor man's friend, and . . . freely espouses the widow's cause."[22]

As the postwar recession deepened, British imperial reform further impaired the urban economies. Customs officers swooped down on illegal traders and dampened trade. The tightening of credit in England created havoc among merchants who were overextended. The Sugar and Revenue Acts of 1764 imperiled the West Indian trade and constricted commerce generally by limiting the money supply. Buffeted and bewildered, urban politicians searched for answers but could devise nothing to combat unemployment and poverty other than linen manufactories, which proved unprofitable and unpopular with the poor.

While economic conditions worsened in all the northern port towns, the embers of political discontent burst into flames. Politics heated up

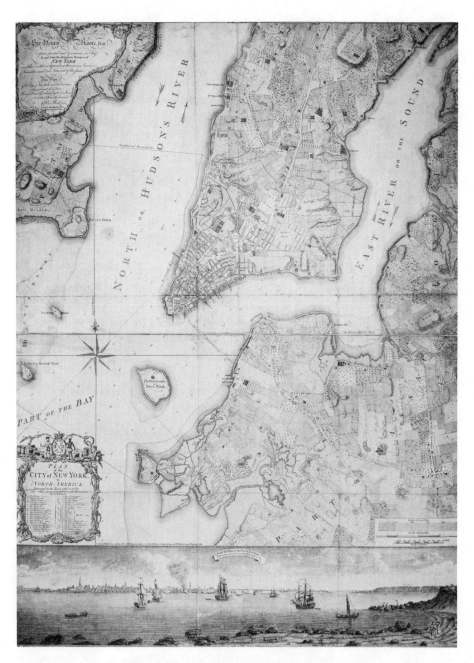

9. *Plan of New York in 1767 by Bernard Ratzer.*

not because popular leaders proposed economic programs attentive to the needs of laboring people but because of issues concerning the local exercise of political power. In Boston controversy began in 1760 when Thomas Hutchinson and his conservative merchant and lawyer followers decided that the time was ripe to renew attempts to dismantle the town meeting system of government. Known in the popular press as the "Junto," Hutchinson's group was composed of wealthy prerogative men who flocked to Governor Francis Bernard when he arrived as Governor Pownall's successor in August 1760. Most of them belonged to the Anglican church and many were related by blood or marriage. Among them were Eliakim Hutchinson, Andrew and Peter Oliver, Charles Apthorp, Robert Auchmuty, Samuel Waterhouse, Charles Paxton, Thomas Flucker, John Erving, Jr., Edmund Trowbridge, and Chambers Russell.

Such men of the court party had long rankled at the indignity of attending town meetings where laboring people outnumbered them. As the gulf between top and bottom grew, they became ever more convinced that the herd of common people was congenitally turbulent, incapable of understanding economic issues, moved too much by passion and too little by reason, and unfit to exercise political power. Governor Shirley had most cogently expressed this elite view in 1747. The main cause "of the Mobbish turn in this Town, is it's Constitution; by which the Management of it is devolv'd upon the populace assembled in their Town Meetings . . . [where] the meanest Inhabitants . . . by their Constant attendance there generally are the majority and outvote the Gentlemen, Merchants, Substantial Traders and all the better part of the Inhabitants; to whom it is Irksome to attend." Too many "working Artificers, Seafaring Men, and low sort of people," complained Shirley, added up to a "Mobbish Spirit."[23] Shirley was a man of aristocratic tastes, of course, but he had been a Boston resident since 1730 and hence was able to mirror the views of the provincial elite.

Poverty had erased a large part of the Boston lower class from the roll of voters in the years after Shirley penned this description and the town meeting had become a thoroughly unplebeian instrument by the 1750s, sending wealthy merchants to the General Court, electing many conservative selectmen, and generally supporting the policies of the well-liked Governor Pownall. But for the Hutchinson Junto this was not enough, especially when the arrival of Bernard, who drew them into his inner council, gave them fresh hopes of consolidating their power. Determined to succeed where earlier attempts to abolish the town meeting had failed, they mounted a campaign to elect four men to the General Court who would convince the legislature to pass a bill for changing Boston into a close corporation. A "Combination of Twelve Strangers," who called themselves "The New and Grand Corcas," warned the *Boston Gazette*, was designing to "overthrow the ancient Constitution of our Town-

Meeting, as being popular and mobbish; and to form a Committee to transact the whole Affairs of the Town for the future." In order to control the elections, the Junto would attempt to keep "tradesmen, and those whom in Contempt they usually term the Low lived People" from voting. If they could not successfully challenge their eligibility at the polls, they would attempt to buy their votes by threatening them with loss of jobs and arrest. On the eve of the election, a committee of artisans, working with the "old and true" Caucus of the popular party, urged Boston's laboring people to stand up to these threats. Artisans should "put on their Sabbath Cloathes, . . . wash their Hands and faces that they may appear neat and cleanly," and go to the polls. Calling the vote-jobbers of the aristocratic Junto "strangers," a term which the fiercely Puritan popular party leaders still used to depreciate adherents of the Church of England, the artisan committee exhorted the faithful to elect men of their own religious persuasion, who would represent their interests.[24]

With both parties courting the electorate, nearly a thousand voters turned out on May 13, 1760—more than had ever before voted in a provincial election. The result was indecisive. Royall Tyler, a rising light in the popular party, was elected but Benjamin Prat and John Tyng, two of the popular Caucus's candidates, lost their seats to moderates Samuel Welles and John Phillips, whom the Hutchinsonians supported.[25] Not since the marketplace issue of 1736-1737 had the populace been so aroused for an election, and as in those years it was the defense of the traditional modus operandi that energized the popular party.

In the period immediately after the 1760 election, James Otis made his meteoric rise in Boston's politics. The son of a country politician who had risen to prominence in the administrations of Shirley and Pownall, Otis had practiced law in Boston since 1750, made a propitious marriage to the daughter of a wealthy merchant, and obtained patronage appointments within the established system. But when Pownall's successor, Francis Bernard, decided to cast his lot principally with the Hutchinsonians of the court persuasion, both Otis and his father, still a power in the House, were eclipsed. Hutchinson had been appointed lieutenant governor in January 1758, and within a few months of Bernard's arrival in 1760 the death of Chief Justice Stephen Sewall left open the finest patronage plum that the governor could dispense. Otis's father believed he had the strongest claim to the next vacancy on the court, indeed, that it had been promised to him. When Hutchinson received the appointment in September 1760, the Otises and their supporters were enraged. It was at that point that a furious offensive began against the Hutchinsonians. The issue was power concentrated in the hands of those who in the popular party view had proved themselves incapable of serving the public good. The special target, the personification of grasping, self-serving power, was Thomas Hutchinson, who by the end of 1760 simultaneously held the positions of lieutenant governor, chief justice of the Superior Court of Judicature, member of the council, probate judge, and captain of Castle William in Boston harbor.[26]

Connected to the issue of narrowly concentrated power, which in Whig thought was a signal danger, was the writs of assistance case. It was here that reaction to new English regulations began to merge with purely local issues. Customs officials in Boston, under strict orders to crack down on years of evasionary tactics practiced by Boston's merchants, asked the Superior Court to renew the general search warrants under which the warehouses of suspected smugglers could be entered. Otis himself had been the deputy advocate general (chief prosecutor) of the vice-admiralty court in which indicted smugglers were tried; but he resigned his post, slipping free of a now onerous appointment that involved him in the strict new regulation of trade, and joined Oxenbridge Thacher as chief counsel for sixty-three Boston merchants opposing the writs.

The courtroom scene that took place in February 1761 was one of the most memorable in the colony's history. On the bench sat Chief Justice Hutchinson, Otis's bitter enemy. At the bar stood Thacher and Otis representing the merchant opponents of the writs. Arguing the case for the customs officials was Jeremiah Gridley, the craggy learned barrister who had been young Otis's mentor and friend. The legal issue at stake was whether such writs were still authorized by English law and, if so, whether or not the Massachusetts Superior Court could act as a court of exchequer in issuing such writs. If the answer was yes, then customs officials could reobtain such warrants, which lasted for as long as the reigning monarch lived, and use them during daylight to enter any premises in Boston, regardless of whether there was "probable cause" for suspecting illegal goods.[27]

Nothing was decided in court that day in February 1761, for Chief Justice Hutchinson, moving cautiously, adjourned the proceedings for nine months in order to obtain advice from London. In November, after hearing new arguments, he decreed that the writs were legal and authorized the court to issue them. But by this time the case itself had become secondary, for Otis's February oration before a packed courtroom had made him a popular hero. In arguing that Parliament was invading the fundamental rights of her colonists by passing trade laws that violated the "natural equity" of British subjects, Otis brushed aside the technicalities of the law and strode onto higher ground, "into the realm of political and social theory and the principles of British constitutionalism." The writs were not the real issue, he exhorted. What was really under question were the laws of Parliament that shackled the American economy, laws which made the writs necessary.[28] Writing years later, a young country lawyer who had only recently come to Boston recounted that the courtroom, as Otis spoke, "the child independence was then and there born [for] every man of an immense crowded audience appeared to me to go away as I did, ready to take up arms against writs of assistance."[29] John Adams may have romanticized Otis's peroration but he did not miscalculate Otis's effect on his Boston auditors. Three months later they elected him to the legislature.

The Otis-Hutchinson confrontation on imperial policy, carried out in the courtroom under a veil of legal niceties, was continued less politely in the context of local politics. For three years after the 1760 election Otis and other popular party writers filled the *Gazette* with vitriolic assaults on the Hutchinson clique. Hutchinson and his allies answered in kind in the conservative *Evening Post*. The Hutchinson-Oliver family network, charged Otis, had developed an incestuous political dynasty. Besides Hutchinson's multiple offices, his brother-in-law, Andrew Oliver, was the province secretary and Oliver's brother was on the Superior Court. Hutchinson's brother, as well as another relative, were judges on the Suffolk County Inferior Court and his nephew was register of the Probate Court and Secretary Oliver's deputy. The network extended on and on, into every corner of government. "Is not this amazing ascendancy of one Family," wrote John Adams, "Foundation sufficient on which to erect a Tyranny? Is it not enough to excite Jealousies among the People." It was this "very ambitious and avaricious Disposition" upon which Otis played in the public prints.[30] To it he added another charge: that Hutchinson had designed another devaluation scheme in 1761, which was an extension of the other fiscal measures he had concocted in the past, each of them undertaken in the name of fiscal stability, yet each somehow redounding to the benefit of men of money.[31]

Otis's campaign against Hutchinson and his circle has usually been interpreted as the product of family rivalry and the mounting tension over trade regulations. Catapulted to prominence in the writs of assistance case, Otis is depicted as the sulphurous orator and writer—either mad or brilliant, according to one's views—who in the early 1760s molded the opinion of the lower orders, called the "mob" into action, and orchestrated its actions.[32] It needs to be understood, however, that Otis was also reflecting opinion within Boston's laboring community. He mirrored as well as molded the views of ordinary citizens whose minds were well attuned to the dangers that aristocratic "reformers" represented. We trivialize the laboring-class mind by viewing it as so much dough to be kneaded by master rhetoricians and political manipulators. Otis did not need to create a feeling of alienation among the struggling ranks of Boston's artisans. That feeling was already there. Otis played to it with consummate skill. In his crusade against Hutchinson, Otis was, in fact, serving two masters—a large group of Boston merchants who had systematically evaded the trade laws and were battling the writs of assistance, and the laboring classes which had suffered in Boston for more than a generation. For the merchants Otis could offer concrete results: relief from the writs of assistance or, if that failed, legal defense combined with enough resistance within the House of Representatives to hobble the Bernard administration. For the laboring classes Otis had less to offer, for the popular party had no blueprint for economic reform. For now, the middle and lower ranks would have to be satisfied with searing verbal attacks on those who disdained the humble folk and totted up their profits while the poor suffered. Accordingly, Otis threw himself into vilifying the prerogative party and expounding Whig political theory passionately from 1762 to 1764.[33] If he was mad, as his opponents began to charge, it mattered little, for as one worried observer put it, "Massaniello was mad, nobody doubts it; yet for all of that, he overturned the government of Naples."[34]

In 1763 the Hutchinson circle made another attempt to strike at the town meeting system of politics over which they had all but lost control since the war years of the 1750s. Election messages in the *Evening Post* urged the electorate to "keep the Public Good only in View" while burying in "everlasting Oblivion" old prejudices and animosities. But this much said, the paper ran a scathing "exposé" of the popular party Caucus, which purportedly was written by a former member and thus took on the flavor of an inside report. Caucus leaders, it was explained, conducted all political affairs behind closed doors and in smoke-filled rooms. Convening several weeks before the town meeting, they "appoint town officers, and settle all affairs that are to be transacted at town meeting." Then, "for form sake," the Caucus leaders "prepared a number of warm disputes . . . to entertain the lower sort; who are in an ecstasy to find the old Roman Patriots still surviving." All townspeople were invited to speak at these open meetings, the writer alleged, but to oppose the decisions already made was to earn the "eternal animosity" of the back room managers, ending forever any chance of obtaining town office. Democracy, as practiced by the Caucus, was nothing but sham, mocked the *Evening Post* author.[35]

In fact, the Caucus did operate much as its critic charged. Invited into the inner sanctum, John Adams described how he had met in the sail loft of Tom Dawes where Caucus members "smoke tobacco till you cannot see from one End of the Garret to the other . . . drink Phlip I suppose, and . . . choose a Moderator, who puts Questions to the Vote regularly, and select Men, Assessors, Collectors, Wardens, Fire Wards, and Representatives are regularly chosen before they are chosen in the Town."[36] But this was no betrayal of participatory town politics in the eyes of the electorate because men from the middle ranks were included in the Caucus and it was what the town officers delivered rather than the Caucus's mode of operation that counted with them. Nor could they be swayed by broadsides that sarcastically accused popular politicians of mixing with the mechanics in order to get their votes. Attempting to discredit Royall Tyler, whom they nicknamed Pug Sly, the prerogative party plastered the town with a broadside containing an alleged conversation between Tyler and another aspirant for public office. "I can . . . tell you," said the supposedly duplicitous Tyler, "some of the steps I take two or three weeks before an election comes on. I send to the cooper and get all my casks put in order . . . I send to the mason and have some job done to my hearths or chimney; I have the carpenter to make some repairs on the roof or the wood house; I often go down to the ship yards about eleven o'clock, when they break off to take their drink, and enter into conversation with them. They all vote for me. When there is to be a [fire] engine [company] supper, I lay a plan to be invited; and they fix me at the head of the table and pay me as much homage as a demi-god: You would sometimes laugh your soul out, if you was to see how I work them poor toads."[37]

It was true of course that economic clientage existed. No less certain is it that popular party figures such as John Hancock cultivated the support of laboring men. But attempts to expose the Caucus as a dictatorial clique, made up of men who had no real interest in laboring families, failed miserably. Such electoral screeds faithfully reflected the elitist view that people were hopelessly dense, easily gulled by leaders such as Samuel Adams, James Otis, and Royall Tyler, and incapable of determining who best represented their interests. Following the 1763 attacks on the Caucus, 1,089 people went to the polls for town elections, a number never exceeded even in the tumultuous years of the following decade.[38] They drubbed the candidates favored by the court party. James Otis, the leading anti-Hutchinsonian, garnered the largest number of votes and was installed as moderator of the town meeting, equivalent to the leadership role in the antiprerogative party.

The bitter popular-prerogative party fight of the early 1760s, carried on before the Sugar and Stamp Acts embroiled Massachusetts in a violent contest with the mother country, revolved around a number of specific issues, including the replacement of William Bollan (a leading member of the governor's circle) as provincial agent in London; the establishment of an Anglican mission in the shadow of Harvard College, which for Congregationalists represented the growing strength and arrogance of those "strangers," who in olden days had persecuted their ancestors; and the multiple offices held by Hutchinson and his network of relatives. But more fundamentally, the struggle involved two competing conceptions of government and society. Developed during the controversies of preceding decades, these philosophies were spelled out in pungent language in the early 1760s.

James Otis, Samuel Adams, Royall Tyler, Oxenbridge Thacher, and many other respectable if not wealthy Bostonians espoused a vision of politics that gave credence to laboring-class views and regarded as entirely legitimate the participation of artisans in the political process. This was no new conception of the rightful political order but a very old one. The popular party leaders in the early 1760s merely followed in the footsteps of Oliver Noyes, the two Elisha Cookes, James Allen, and Thomas Cushing. The town meeting, open to almost all property owners and responsive to the propertyless as well, at least in theory, was the foundation of this system. Through the Caucus the town meeting was linked to shopkeepers, artisans, and laborers in a network of neighborhood taverns, fire companies, and clubs. By no means narrowly based or given over to a class view, the popular party embraced a wide variety of merchants, ship captains, petty entrepreneurs, lawyers, doctors, and clergymen, as well as a far larger number of artisans, merchant seamen, and laborers. Men of social standing filled the leadership roles and garnered most of the important elective posts—overseers of the poor, tax assessors, selectmen, and delegates to the House of Representatives. Lesser people filled minor offices and voiced their opinions at the town meetings where they were numerically dominant.[39] The poorest men, excluded from voting and officeholding, tried to make themselves heard informally by the patrician leadership. This, it needs to be emphasized, was popular, not radical, politics.

For the conservative merchants, lawyers, clergymen, and government appointees, led and epitomized by Thomas Hutchinson, the popular system spelled chaos. "Reform" for these men meant what it had since the early years of the century—paring back the power of the town meeting, substituting appointive for elective officeholders, restricting the freedom of the press, and breaking down the virulent anti-Anglican prejudice that still suffused the popular party. Like their opponents, some members of the prerogative party had suffered as Boston's economy stagnated after 1740. But many others had prospered. Whatever their economic record, they saw the best hope for commercial revival in handing over exclusive management of town government to the wealthy and well-born. To see James Otis addressing the assembled "mob" and "the Rage of Patriotism . . . spread so violently . . . thro' town and country, that there is scarce a cobler or porter but has turn'd mountebank in politicks and erected his stage near the printing-press from whence his oracular decisions have been stamp'd off and delivered to the world as infallible nostrums" was their vision of hell.[40]

Between 1761 and 1764 proponents of the popular and prerogative conception of politics engaged in a furious battle of billingsgate that filled the columns of the *Gazette* and *Evening Post*. It is easy to be diverted by the extreme forms which the scurrility took. Charges of "Racoon," "stinking Skunk," "Pimp," "wild beast," "drunkard," and dozens of other choice titles were traded back and forth in verbal civil war. But more important than the invective itself was the deep-seated, class-tinged animosity which the polemical pieces exposed: suspicion of laboring people and hatred of their leaders on the part of the Hutchinsonians; contempt and anger toward the wealthy, Anglican prerogative elite by the common people.

A few examples serve to indicate the depth of feeling. Thomas Pownall; the popular governor from 1757 to 1760, was satirized for ignoring the protocol of class divisions by executing public business without wearing the customary ruffled shirt and powdered wig, by going aboard ships in Boston harbor to talk with "common people about ship-affairs," and by mingling in the streets with the "dirtiest, most lubberly, mutinous, and despised part of the people."[41] The popular leaders, on the other hand, urged Bostonians to oppose "The Leviathan in power [Hutchinson], or those other overgrown Animals, whose influence and importance is only in exact mathematical proportion to the weight of their purses."[42] The popular Caucus, decried a Hutchinsonian, talked incessantly about the right "for every dabbler in politicks to say and print whatever his shallow understanding, or vicious passions may suggest, against the wisest and best men—a liberty for fools and madmen to spit and throw firebrands at those of the most respectable and most amiable character."[43] In a retort, James Otis, casting himself in the role of mechanic, gave voice to lower-class resentment at such defamation: "I am forced to get my living by the labour of my hand; and the sweat of my brow, as most of you are and obliged to go thro' good report and evil report, for bitter bread, earned under the frowns of some who have no natural or divine right to be above me, and entirely owe their grandeur and honor to grinding the faces of the poor, and other acts of ill gotten gain and power."[44] Anarchy, cried the conservatives in reply: "The day is hastening, when some who are now, or, have lately been the darling idols of a dirty very dirty witless rabble, commonly called the little vulgar, are to sink and go down with deserved infamy, to all posterity."[45] Such vilification of the lower class was a smoke screen, retorted a writer in the *Gazette*: the problem was that the rich were obsessed with money and "couldn't have the idea of riches without that of poverty. They must see others poor in order to form a notion of their own happiness." In what was once a flourishing town, "a few persons in power" attempted to monopolize politics and promoted projects "for keeping the people poor in order to make them humble."[46]

Drawn into verbal warfare, where newspapers and pamphlets were the weapons for arousing public opinion and gaining the support of the electorate, the prerogative elitists learned to give as good as they got. They claimed to hate the hurly-burly of political contention and decried the "personal invective" which the "modern Politician" was apparently obliged to wallow in, usually by engaging "hireling Scribblers" to turn out "downright scurrility and gross impudence" by the yard.[47] But, as in Philadelphia, the conservative mind proved at least as adept at scatalogical ribaldry as their allegedly irresponsible opponents. Three weeks after deploring the yellow journalism of Otis and his cronies in the *Gazette*, the prerogative party printed a mock report of a London criminal, "Hector Wildfire," in the *Evening Post.* "Wildfire," it was obvious to Boston readers, was James Otis. The report that he had been hanged at Tyburn and then removed for autopsy provided the Hutchinsonians with the scenario for their wildest fantasies. "Upon ripping open [Wildfire's] Belly, which was much distended, it was found to be fill'd with wind which rush'd out violently . . . There seemed to be a profuse quantity of liquor in the Gall Bladder, and so extremely corrosive that it ate the instruments of operation like aqua fortes." The doctors found that the heart was "very small and very hard," as if gnawed away by wasps. The lungs were ulcerated and tainted and the surgeons wondered that this diseased man had not "poison'd all those he had breath'd upon in his life time." The head had a double row of teeth, a forked tongue, a skull of "uncommon thickness," and a brain cavity so small that its contents would not fill a teacup. After dissection, the doctors threw the pieces of the body to "a kennel of hounds," who had since "run mad."[48]

The reciprocal animosity and mistrust that suffused the newspapers and pamphlets of the early 1760s reveals how deeply rooted were the social tensions that took seed as Boston's economy, declining in the previous generation, lay enfeebled at the end of the Seven Years War. The town was no longer one community, a corporate entity with several pyramidally arranged but interdependent parts. Only in the geographical sense did it remain a community at all; in social terms Boston had become fragmented, unsure of itself, ridden with internecine animosities. The court party was "modern" in its economic thinking, ready to take its chances in the free play of the international market economy and to welcome the new capitalist age. But its members looked backward in political terms, attempting to convince a broad electorate that the very men who had accumulated fortunes in an era when most had suffered were alone qualified to govern in the interest of the whole community. Lower- and middle-class Bostonians had heard prerogative men voice these ideas for half a century. They understood that each group promoted its particular interests and that aristocratic politicians who claimed to work for the commonweal could not be trusted. Such men employed the catchwords of the traditional system of politics—"public good," "community," "harmony," and "public virtue"—to cloak their own ambitions for aggrandizing wealth and power. The popular party leaders also employed these terms, and some of them wanted to return to what Samuel Adams would later call revealingly "a Christian Sparta"—a simplified, egalitarian society in which people were bound together by mutual obligation rather than the cash nexus. But the popular party, while sometimes looking backward nostalgically in its ideal of economic relationships, accepted a participatory form of politics, which alone, it thought, would guarantee economic justice and keep Boston faithful to its traditions.[49]

IN PHILADELPHIA also internal issues overshadowed the new British regulations as a source of conflict in the early 1760s. As in Boston, the political energy unleashed by internal conflict would be rechanneled into the resistance movement against England.

For Philadelphians the most galling problem of this era was the refusal of proprietor Thomas Penn to pay taxes on his vast proprietary estates. The Seven Years War obliged the assembly to impose heavy property taxes and Penn adamantly proclaimed his proprietary right, as he understood it, to exempt himself from such levies. The issue, in fact, offered Penn a golden opportunity to reverse the gradual encroachment of the legislative branch, dating back to the days of his grandfather, upon the proprietor's power. The assembly was stymied. It could not refuse to make military appropriations when, for the first time in Pennsylvania's history, war was laying in flames large portions of the colony; but unless they bowed to the proprietor's will, he would exercise his undoubted veto power over any appropriations bill.[50]

The Pennsylvania assembly twisted and turned but could not elude the proprietor's grasp. By 1757 they decided to send to England the only man they knew who could persuade a sphinx, Benjamin Franklin. His task was either to change the mind of Thomas Penn or convince the English government to overrule him. But even Franklin's magic was insufficient. By 1758, recognizing that, he began exploring another strategy—the direct assumption of Pennsylvania's government by the king. This had occurred briefly in the 1690s, during the first of the Anglo-French wars, and had been considered at other times. Moreover, the idea of voiding the proprietary charter jibed with the prevalent feeling in England that the four colonies in British North America still under proprietary or charter government were anachronisms. For four years Franklin schemed and dreamed in London but never brought the dismantling of proprietary rule any closer to reality. The Privy Council took some of the steam out of the movement for royal government by ruling in 1760 that Thomas Penn could not exempt his Pennsylvania estates from taxation; but the king's council also decreed that every Pennsylvania landholder must pay Penn his quitrents in sterling or in Pennsylvania money at the prevailing sterling exchange rate between Philadelphia and London. This was an advantage that Penn had sought for years, for the Pennsylvania money in which his rents were collected was worth only half to two-third of its sterling equivalent.[51]

This compromise solution to the problem of proprietary taxes and rents lay dormant in the early 1760s because with the war at an end—Pennsylvania saw no more of the fighting after the summer of 1758—the provincial government needed no new levies. So the assembly had no occasion to pass a revenue bill that included taxes on the proprietary estates but would have had to concede the payment of quitrents in sterling value. But in the summer of 1763 Pontiac's uprising in the transallegheny west brought war to Pennsylvania's frontier again. One after another the British forts in the Ohio Valley fell to this pan-Indian offensive and by June 1763, the Pennsylvania frontier lay under heavy Indian attack.

Once again, the assembly had to face the issue of troops and taxes. Franklin was back in Philadelphia by now, full of enmity for a proprietor whom he regarded as mercenary and dictatorial. The assembly voted small supply bills in order to put 700 provincial soldiers in the field, drawing not upon a general land tax but on liquor taxes, slave import duties, and other miscellaneous sources. The frontiersmen were far from satisfied. The troops performed abominably and the farmers, "becoming embittered because the authorities are taking not adequate measures for defense," became convinced that they would have to descend on Philadelphia with clubs and pitchforks to get their point across. "The people from the country are about to come to the city in droves and destroy everything in revenge," wrote one German clergyman.[52] Come they did, calling themselves the "Paxton Boys," but not before they murdered two bands of peaceful, Christianized Indians who lived about a hundred miles west of Philadelphia. Franklin called the Paxton Boys "White Savages" for their mass killing of innocent persons, but most Philadelphians displayed more concern for their own skins than those of Indians when they heard that the Paxtoneers meant to "pour out [their] Vials of Wrath and D[evili]sh[ne]ss on the Inhabitants of this City." Backs to the wall, the assemblymen prepared a bill for issuing £50,000 in paper money and raising 1,000 troops. At this point they caved in to the principle that the paper money issued to pay the troops could not be used to pay proprietary quitrents. The Paxton Boys reached the outskirts of Philadelphia several days later, on February 5, 1764, but by this time Franklin had performed his usual feat of organizing overnight a voluntary association of citizen soldiers for the city's defense.[53]

The dénouement of the Paxton affair was not civil war in Pennsylvania but "an epidemic of hyper-denominationalism" and a renewal of the movement to obtain royal government.[54] The Paxton Boys got the legislative action they wanted and returned to the frontier, Pontiac's

Rebellion was squelched by British troops, Franklin's personal army disbanded in Philadelphia, and the need for additional paper money disappeared. But the air had been dreadfully poisoned, first by the refusal of the resident governor, Thomas Penn's nephew, to sign the military revenue bill unless it contained a clause that would assess the proprietor's most valuable lands, such as vacant lots in Philadelphia, at the same rate as the poorest lands in the province; and second, by the Quaker-Presbyterian enmity that broke out over the march of the Paxtoneers on Philadelphia.

Thomas Penn readily conceded the first issue, once he heard that his nephew, misled by the proprietary attorney general in the colony, had insisted on such an inequitable provision. Nevertheless, the squabble greatly increased sentiment for royal government.[55] The second issue brought Quakers and Presbyterians to each other's throats because the Paxton Boys were known to be mostly Scots-Irish Presbyterians. Quakers interpreted their frontier lawlessness as one more sign of a trend they had feared for decades: a Presbyterian takeover of the colony. What began as a minor civil disorder that followed an unjustifiable murder of Christianized Indians now billowed up into verbal civil war in which Quaker and Presbyterian pamphleteers unloosed a barrage of philippics against each other such as never had been known. Quaker pamphleteers portrayed the descent of the Paxton Boys on Philadelphia as part of a global conspiracy, "the latest installment in a perpetual Presbyterian holy war against the mild and beneficent government of the Kings of England" that stretched back to the bloody Presbyterian uprisings in Scotland in the mid-seventeenth century. Giving as good as they got, Presbyterian writers attacked the Quakers for being "soft" on Indians, for encouraging them to maraud along the frontier, and for holding on to civil power when pacifist principles made its exercise during wartime hopelessly ineffectual. Venomous pamphlets streamed from Philadelphia's presses and passions became so heated that Franklin wrote friends that he never witnessed more "violent Parties and cruel Animosities" in his colony and feared that "civil Bloodshed" would soon occur.[56]

Proprietary policies and the Paxton Boys debacle generated so much heat in Philadelphia in the winter of 1763-1764 that they completely overshadowed the issue of trade regulation. Equally important, the bitter Quaker-Presbyterian split began to divide the laboring classes in the city along religious lines in a way that crucially affected Philadelphia's response to the Stamp Act. By March 1764, the animus toward proprietor Thomas Penn was so great that Franklin was able to revive the flagging campaign to obtain royal government and thrust it into the center of public concern.[57] Those who had followed Pennsylvania politics closely for the last generation could hardly miss the irony that the Philadelphia-centered assembly party was embarking on a campaign to obtain royal government at precisely the moment when royal authority was feared, suspected, and even despised as at no other time since Edmund Andros had ruled the Dominion of New England.

The renewed campaign for royal government politicized Philadelphia to an extraordinary degree. At the same time, it fixed the attention of the populace on the issue of externally imposed proprietary control when worsening economic conditions might have otherwise made that the focus of debate. Franklin himself took the leading role in orchestrating the "blitz" against proprietary government, working tirelessly in the assembly to obtain approval for twenty-six resolves against Thomas Penn and then inscribing a set of *Explanatory Remarks* to rally public support for this bill of indictment. Franklin's printing house published 3,000 broadside copies of the resolves and distributed them with an equal number of the *Explanatory Remarks*. After this softening up of the public mind the Franklinites called a mass meeting in early April for gathering signatures on a petition to the crown to assume the colony's government. Thus began the petition war between proprietary and antiproprietary factions, a battle that was paralleled by the most intense pamphleteering, speechmaking, and assembling of the public for open-air meetings in the city's history.[58]

For the proprietary party, the attack on proprietary government was more a blessing than a curse. Thoroughly defeated in its attempt to become a force in electoral politics at the beginning of the Seven Years War and quiescent ever since, it now had an issue, even if it was a negative one, upon which to appeal to the public. Franklin and the assembly party, in fact, were making the political mistake of their lives, for they set out to convince the public that royal government should be called in to protect people's lives, liberties, and property at the moment when most people believed that royal government, up and down the coast, had laid siege to traditional rights. The papers were filled with reports of the stamp duties about to be imposed without the colonies' consent, about a currency act that would abolish Pennsylvania's paper money, embraced since the 1720s as a boon to the colony's prosperity, about the vice-admiralty courts that would try violators of the Navigation Acts before a distant judge rather than local juries, and about the British men-of-war that patrolled Delaware Bay, searching every ship standing out from Philadelphia for illegal goods. "The way from Proprietary Slavery to Royal Liberty is easy," thundered Joseph Galloway, Franklin's political protégé, at a mass meeting to secure signatures for the royal government petition on March 31, 1764.[59] But the people proved hard to convince that "Royal Liberty" was making their lives easier. How could it do so if handed the executive branch of the colony's government?

The assembly party gathered signatures on petitions for royal government for three months before William Smith, their old Anglican nemesis, returned from England to organize the proprietary counterattack. But even with this head start and even drawing upon a generation of good will earned as the party of the people, Franklin and his friends were able to convince only about one-third of the adult males in Philadelphia to sign their petitions.[60] The unpopular proprietary party had by far the more popular appeal: keep provincial government out of royal hands.

The long-range outcome of the fierce politicking over royal versus proprietary government was a resounding defeat for the popular party opponents of Thomas Penn, who would retain his proprietary power until the outbreak of revolution. The short-range result was the defeat of Franklin and Galloway in the assembly election of October 1764—the only defeat Franklin ever suffered at the polls and, given his immense popularity, a reversal of public opinion almost unthinkable heretofore.[61] More important than either long- or short-range effects was the process itself. The campaign involved an extraordinary advance of the people-at-large into a position of importance. The Franklin forces began the ball rolling with mass meetings and door-to-door solicitation of signatures in April and May 1764. "Taverns were engag'd [and] many of the poorer and more dependent kind of labouring people in town were invited thither by night," wrote one proprietary critic. Some were induced to sign by "the eloquence of a punch bowl," others by "the fear of being turn'd out of business." Quakers went house by house in pairs, cajoling signatures against proprietary government. Going indiscriminately "into all the houses in Town without distinction," grumbed the proprietor's nephew, they emerged with the names of "a few Ship Carpenters and some of the lowest sort of people."[62]

Once the proprietary party got organized it too searched the lower social strata for support. Its counterpetitions, in fact, far outstripped those distributed by Franklin's stalwarts. Every white adult male in Philadelphia, and perhaps some others, found himself being courted by the leaders of the two political factions. It mattered not what his religion, class, or ideological position so long as he would sign. Never in Pennsylvania's history had the few needed the many so much.

As the battle thickened, pamphleteers reached new pinnacles of abuse and scurrility. Franklin was reviled as an intellectual charlatan who begged and bought honorary degrees in England, a corrupt politician intimately acquainted "With every Zig Zag Machination" (including a desire to become the first royal governor of the colony), and a lecherous old man.[63] His friends responded by labeling an opposition pamphleteer "A Reptile" who "like a Toad, by the pestilential Fumes of his virulent Slabber" attempted "to blast the fame of a PATRIOT." William Smith, coordinator of the opposition, was advertised to be a "consumate Sycophant," an "indefatigable" liar, and an impudent knave with a heart "bloated with *infernal Malice*" and a head full of "*flatulent Preach-*

*ments."*⁶⁴ As for the Presbyterians, a Franklinite pamphleteer renamed them "Piss-Brute-tarians (a bigotted, cruel and revengeful sect)."⁶⁵ Another hired pen reached the summit of scatalogical polemics when he suggested that now was the time for Smith, president of the Philadelphia Academy and a director of the Pennsylvania Hospital, to consummate his alliance with the proprietary pamphleteer David Dove, who "will not only furnish you with that most agreeable of all Foods to your Taste, but after it has found a Passage through your Body . . . will greedily devour it, and, as soon as it is well digested, he will void it up for a Repast to the Proprietary Faction: they will as eagerly swallow it as the other had done before, and, when it has gone through their several Concoctions, they will discharge it in your Presence, that you may once more regale on it, thus refined."⁶⁶ One shocked outsider wrote a friend in Philadelphia: "In the name of goodness stop your Pamphleteer's Mouths & shut up your presses. Such a torrent of low scurrility sure never came from any country as lately from Pennsylvan[i]a."⁶⁷

The torrent did not stop. The more scabrous the literature became the more widely it was distributed, often gratis, to all who would accept it. "There has not been a Week since you left," wrote one Philadelphian to a friend in May 1764, "but there has been One or more Pamphlets published & sold about the Streets."⁶⁸ Before the campaign was over more than thirty-five broadsides and pamphlets, not to mention scores of newspaper fusillades, filled the streets. Chief Justice William Allen, a man who had risen from sugar boiler to wealthy merchant, found himself called "Old Drip-pan," an adulterer who had slept with his Negro slaves for twenty years, and "a tricking Judge, and Presbyterian Jew." David Dove, the pamphleteer, stood accused of sodomy, misogamy, miscegenation, concupiscence, and the almost unheard of flaw of teratology. William Smith was charged with spreading venereal disease to his female slaves and Franklin too was charged with sexual irregularities.⁶⁹

It is difficult to know what to make of the volume of defamatory bile that poured from the presses in 1764 and 1765, for intense political factionalism, while it was bound to limber up the fingers of political writers, by no means required a descent into scatalogical character assassination or a description of sexual mayhem in the center of American Quakerism. Beneath the mudslinging, one suspects, lay the tension created by a combination of events: the economic depression of the early 1760s, the bitter disputes with proprietor Thomas Penn, the renewal of Indian attacks along the colony's frontier, the anger and anxiety created by the Paxtoneers, and the threat imposed by the restrictive new British policies. Never in the city's history had so many adversities torn simultaneously at the fabric of society. Never had answers to such intricate problems been so hard to find. The result seems to have been a pervasive uneasiness and irritability that, in the absence of clear-cut solutions to these problems, became transferred into party feuding and personal invective. "Neighbors, who from their Infancy, lived in the greatest Harmony," wrote one troubled Philadelphian, "cannot now spend an agreeable Evening together; and the agreement of Brethern, and even of Fathers and Sons who do not jump together in political judgements is rare."⁷⁰ At a time when colonists should be uniting to ward off external threats against their liberties, complained "Rusticus," they were engaged in "intestine Feuds and Animosities" and were "more intent on vilifying and abusing each other, than concerned about averting the Blow they are likely to receive." Philadelphia faced momentous issues but its "Disputants [were] losing sight of the great Object, and sinking into personal Abuse, and unparalleled Scurrility."⁷¹

Religious leaders were inevitably drawn into the fray. Foremost among them were the Presbyterian ministers, Gilbert Tennent, Francis Alison, and John Ewing. Neither they nor their religious brethren were fond of proprietary government, for in Philadelphia most of their parishioners were laboring men who cherished the party of Franklin and in the country most had felt oppressed by the extortionate officers of the proprietor's Land Office.⁷² But given the bitter Quaker attacks on Presbyterians and their conviction that the move for royal government was designed in part to insure the perpetuation of Quaker supremacy in the colony, these antiproprietary sentiments evaporated. Presbyterians put aside the last of their internal divisions that had originated in the era of the Great Awakening and began to organize as a pressure group. The first committees of correspondence in the revolutionary era were organized not in Boston by radical opponents of English policy but by Pennsylvania Presbyterians, who by May 1764 had created a colony-wide network in order to fight Franklin's campaign for royal government.⁷³

German religious leaders were also sucked into the political maelstrom. There had always been considerable tension between the German church groups—Lutherans and German Reformed—and the German sectarians—Moravians, Schwenkfelders, and other pietist groups. For many decades Quakers had enjoyed the support of most Germans, regardless of their religious leanings. But since the 1740s the more hierarchical, conservative church groups had very slowly been drawn toward the strongly Anglican proprietary party. The Anglicans now worked hard to convert them to the anti-royal government position. By the fall of 1764 Carl Wrangel and Henry Muhlenberg, the Lutheran church leaders in Philadelphia, and Christopher Sauer, Jr., and Heinrich Miller, the German printers, were in the fold. All of them wrote, translated, or printed anti-Quaker pamphlets for distribution in German neighborhoods and helped to harvest German signatures on petitions opposing royal government.⁷⁴

The disastrous campaign for royal government not only splintered the Germans of Philadelphia but also split the non-German laboring men of the city. This must have become obvious to those gathering signatures for the royal government petitions in the spring of 1764 because their door-to-door canvassing produced discouraging results. The proprietary party proved at least as successful in recruiting plebeian support.[75] Its leaders had castigated the Franklinites for prevailing among "those very generally of a low rank, many of whom could neither read not write," but by June 3, only a few weeks after distributing their counterpetitions, they obtained about 1,300 signatures in the city and county of Philadelphia.[76] Most of these must have come from the laboring class, which made up the bulk of the population.[77]

When the petition war merged into the annual assembly elections of October 1, the damage sustained by the assembly party became apparent. Heartened by their successful appeal to the laboring classes, and particularly to Germans and Presbyterians, the proprietary leaders redoubled their efforts as the election approached. William Smith joined a number of German church leaders to petition Thomas Penn for the appointment of German justices of the peace in the county courts and astutely arranged to place one Scots-Irish and two German candidates on the eight-man Philadelphia proprietary ticket.[78] "The design," wrote a party organizer, "is by putting in two Germans to draw such a Party of them as will turn the scale in our Favor." Another tactic was to disburse money liberally for the naturalization fees of recently arrived Germans, who thereby acquired voting privileges. Presbyterian clergymen "held Synods about the election, turned their pulpits into Ecclesiastical drums for politics and told their people to vote according as they directed them at the peril of their damnation," claimed one Anglican.[79] But Philadelphia's Anglican churches were also the scene of pre-election rallies, leading a "Gentleman from Transylvania" to charge that the Church of England clergymen had "prostituted their Temples . . . as an Amphitheatre for the Rabble to combat in." Beleaguered Quakers and Franklinites, accustomed to the solid support of laboring people, could only privately deplore the "unwearied Endeavours [of the proprietary leaders] to prejudice the minds of the lower class of people."[80]

Inflammatory rhetoric, a flood of polemical literature, the unabashed participation of the churches in politics, mobilization of social layers previously quiescent and unwelcome in political affairs—all combined to produce an election in which almost everybody's integrity was questioned and every public figure's use of power was attacked. Both sides presented themselves as true representatives of "the people." The effects were dramatic: a record number of Philadelphians, nearly 1,500, turned out for the election. The polls opened at 9 A.M. and remained open through the night as party lieutenants on both sides shepherded in the voters, including the infirm and aged, who were carried to the courthouse in litters and chairs. Officials did not close the polls until 3 P.M. on the second day.[81] A bit of postelection doggerel caught the spirit of the contest:

> A Pleasant sight tis to Behold
> The beggars hal'd from Hedges
> The Deaf, the Blind, the Young the Old:
> T' Secure their priveledges
> They're bundled up Steps, each sort Goes
> A Very Pretty Farce Sir:
> Some without Stockings, some no Shoes
> Nor Breeches to their A__e Sir.[82]

When the returns were counted, both Franklin and Galloway had lost in the city to men on the proprietary slate, and four of their ticket, all incumbents, had lost seats from Philadelphia County. Franklin, no longer sounding like a popular leader, did not doubt that he had been defeated by defecting Germans and "the wretched Rabble brought to swear themselves intituled to Vote" by proprietary opponents.[83] "They carried (would you think it!) above 1000 Dutch from me," Franklin lamented. Such bloc voting was described by the Lutheran minister Henry Muhlenberg, who confided in his diary that the "members of our Lutheran congregation assembled to discuss the election and then proceeded to the *court*house in an orderly group."[84] Presbyterians were the other defectors. They probably did not vote "to a man" for the proprietary candidates, as Chief Justice Allen averred, but they turned their backs on Franklin in considerable numbers.[85] How deeply the laboring ranks had been split is evident from the city vote: Franklin and his running mate garnered 707 and 669 votes respectively; their proprietary opponents received 815 and 786. The master-politician, who had so often in the past swung the public behind his programs for reform, had badly miscalculated sentiment among his own leather apron men, many of whom could not be dissuaded from the view, as it was later put, that "the little finger of the King was heavier than the loins of the Proprietor."[86]

Issues of local political control, broached during years when postwar recession and onerous new British policies had shaken the seaport economies, brought popular politics to a new pitch in the early 1760s. The prerogative party in Boston was almost entirely Anglican and highly aristocratic and therefore could make virtually no inroads on the strongly Congregational artisans and shopkeepers of that city. In Philadelphia, by contrast, the laboring ranks were composed of roughly equal numbers of Scots-Irish Presbyterians, Lutheran and Reformed Germans, and English Quakers so that when political issues had no specific economic content, such as the Paxton Boys' march and the dismantling of proprietary government, political unity among laboring men and petty entrepreneurs dissolved. Taking advantage of Franklin's quest for royal government and the Quaker-Presbyterian hostility that developed around the Paxton affair, the Anglicans were able to draw to their side, at least temporarily, a major part of the laboring classes. In New York the city's artisans and shopkeepers were also divided in the election of 1761, when Anglicans and Dutch Reformed voters were opposed by Presbyterians in a continuation of a long-standing religious split. But neither party was attempting to alter the ground rules of politics as in the other two cities, so New York was relatively unscathed by divisive local issues as the imperial crisis loomed.

In spite of the unique features of political life in each port town, there were aspects and effects of turmoil in the early 1760s that the cities shared. In each the elite was divided, their attempts to activate and obtain the support of the lower classes were unusually strenuous, the presses turned out polemical literature as never before, the clergy became deeply involved in politics, and electoral participation reached new heights. The full significance of these developments would not become apparent until local conflicts began to intersect with imperial issues. This convergence occurred with dramatic swiftness in the shocking events that took place in the summer and fall of 1765.

11

The Stamp Act in the Port Towns

ONLY THE ECONOMIC buffeting suffered by the seaport towns after 1760 and the build-up of antagonisms on local issues can fully explain the extraordinary response to the Stamp Act. Likewise, no sense can be made of the striking contrast between Philadelphia's reaction to the Stamp Act, as opposed to Boston's and New York's, without an understanding of the social circumstances and prior political experience of each city. History is full of exploitation and unpopular decisions by those who wield power, and the reaction of the populace is anything but uniform. So it was with the Stamp Act in America in 1765. Everywhere it was abominated, but opposition to it ranged from mass defiance to disgruntled submission.

The Stamp Act crisis in the cities is also a key to comprehending the course of revolutionary politics in the years that followed. The extraordinary disturbances in the northern cities show dramatically the merging of discontent over England's tightening of the screws on her American colonies with resentment born out of the play of local events. In 1765 the first signals of the dual revolution appeared. The defiance of authority and destruction of property by city people from the lower social ranks redefined the dynamics of urban politics and set the stage for a ten-year internal struggle for political control among the various social elements protesting English rule. The mass disorders surrounding the Stamp Act revealed to many in the urban patriciate the ghastly logic of four generations of political development in the American commercial centers and convinced them that the enemy within was as dangerous as the enemy without.

THE BOSTON PRESS had been filled for months with reports of the impending stamp duties. Parliament's intention in passing the Stamp Act was to make the Americans share in the cost of keeping 10,000 British regulars in North America as guardians of the frontiers and to remind the ill-disciplined colonial subjects that they were still beholden to the mother

country. No amount of colonial lobbying had altered Parliament's decision to put the Stamp Act in force on November 1, 1765. In an impoverished town that already bore a tax burden far greater than any place in
the British empire, the additional stamps, required on every newspaper,
pamphlet, almanac, legal document, liquor license, college diploma, and
pack of playing cards, were highly unpopular.

At dawn on August 14, Bostonians awoke to find an effigy of stamp
distributor Andrew Oliver, dressed in rags, hanging from a huge elm tree
at the crossing of Essex and Orange streets in the South End. Dangling
beside Oliver's image was a "Jack-Boot with a Head and horns peeping
out of the top" and painted green on the bottom—"a Green-ville sole,"
said a sign.[1] The green-soled boot was a clever symbolic conflation of the
unpopular Earl of Bute, the king's trusted adviser, and George Grenville,
First Lord of the Treasury and Chancellor of the Exchequer until June
1765. These two men were thought to have played the largest role in
fashioning the detested new imperial policies.

When Sheriff Stephen Greenleaf attempted to cut down the effigies at
the order of Chief Justice Hutchinson, he was surrounded by an animated
crowd. All day the town buzzed with rumors. Every farmer bringing
produce into town, across Boston Neck and along Orange Street, which
led to the center of town, was detained by the crowd until he had gotten
his goods "stamped." At the end of working hours, a mass of working
men began to form for a mock funeral. Their leader was Ebenezer Mac-
Intosh, a twenty-eight-year-old cordwainer and veteran of the Ticonderoga campaign in 1758. MacIntosh had been appointed fireman in
Engine Company No. 9 in 1760 and had emerged in the next few years as
the leader of the South End's Pope's Day company. He knew poverty at
first hand, for his mother had died when he was fourteen and his father,
for years a part of the tramping poor of eastern Massachusetts, had been
warned out of Boston two years later, in 1753, though he had served as a
soldier at Castle William in the 1730s and 1740s.[2]

With MacIntosh acting as "the principal leader of the mob," according
to the governor, the crowd cut down Oliver's effigy as dark came on and
carried it through the streets toward the Town House. Then the procession, which included "40 to 50 tradesmen, decently dressed at its head,"
turned down King Street toward the South End wharves where Oliver
had built a brick office in July, rumored to be the place from which
stamps would be distributed. It took less than thirty minutes to level the
building. The timbers were carefully saved, "stamped" in derision of the
Stamp Act, and carried to Oliver's luxurious house at the foot of Fort
Hill. At nightfall they were used to start a bonfire atop the hill. Oliver
had made it his business not to be home, but his brother-in-law Thomas
Hutchinson appeared and tried to reason with the people, by now in high
spirits and completely unopposed. Hutchinson's appearance only mad-

dened the crowd, which began to destroy Oliver's stable house and his coach and chaise—symbols of upper-class affluence. Later in the evening, when Hutchinson and the sheriff again tried to stop the destruction of property, they were driven off in a hailstorm of stones. For another four hours or so, the mob tore into Oliver's house, breaking windows and looking glasses, demolishing the elegant furniture, emptying the contents of the splendidly stocked wine cellar, and tearing up the gardens. Oliver promptly asked to be relieved of his commission as stamp distributor.[3]

Twelve days later it was Thomas Hutchinson's turn.[4] The crowd warmed up by attacking the luxurious houses of William Story, deputy register of the Vice-Admiralty Court, and Benjamin Hallowell, comptroller of customs. Then they moved across town to Hutchinson's mansion. Catching the chief justice and his family at the dinner table, the crowd smashed in the doors with axes, sent the family packing, and then systematically reduced the furniture to splinters, stripped the walls bare, chopped through inner partitions until the house was a hollow shell, destroyed the formal gardens in the rear of the mansion, drank the wine cellar dry, stole £900 sterling in coin, and carried off every moveable object of value except some of Hutchinson's books and papers, which were left to scatter in the wind. Led by MacIntosh, the crowd worked with almost military precision to raze the building, spending three hours alone "at the cupola before they could get it down," according to Governor Bernard.[5]

One of the first historians of the Revolution, Bostonian William Gordon, wrote that "Gentlemen of the army, who have seen towns sacked by the enemy, declare they never before saw an instance of such fury." Not a person in the city, neither private citizen nor officer of the law, attempted to stop the crowd. "The Mob was so general," wrote the governor, "and so supported that all civil Power ceased in an Instant, and I had not the least authority to oppose or quiet the Mob." The next day, tears in his eyes and barren of his judicial robes, Hutchinson appeared in his courtroom, an anguished man who had been savagely discredited in the town he believed he had dutifully served for thirty years.[6]

There is little argument that in pillaging the Boston mansions of Oliver and Hutchinson, and in storming the houses of William Story and Benjamin Hallowell, the crowd was demonstrating against the Stamp Act and the tightening of trade restrictions. But in conducting the most ferocious attack on private property in the history of the English colonies, the crowd was expressing its anger at far more than parliamentary policy. Stamp distributors were intimidated and handled roughly in many other towns, but nowhere else did the crowd destroy property on such a grand scale and with such exacting thoroughness. It is possible to explain this by adopting the traditional view that the crowd was led by middle- and

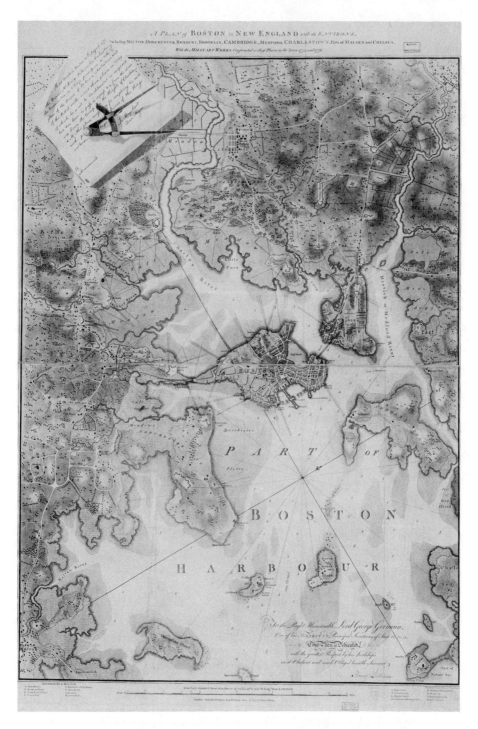

10. Plan of Boston in 1777 by Henry Pelham.

upper-class manipulators such as Otis and Samuel Adams, who were interested only in furthering their own political advantage. In this mechanical formulation, the crowd could never be self-activating, for thought and planned action could have their source only in the minds of educated persons. The mob went ransacking because they were told to do so.[7]

An understanding of what happened in Boston is better perceived by recognizing that laboring people, while looking to well-off leaders to articulate their grievances and to represent them as selectmen and representatives, were by no means powerless operatives, frenzied with liquor and dancing like puppets on the leading strings of men above them. Governor Bernard was sure that though MacIntosh directed the pillaging of Oliver's and Hutchinson's houses, he was "visibly under the Directions of Persons much his Superior." Bernard also spoke of forty or fifty "Gentleman actors" who retired from the scene at Oliver's house just before the destruction began.[8] This kind of coordination is believable because the Boston Caucus had made an effort following the bloody Pope's Day riot in November 1764 to fuse the two laboring-class companies from opposite ends of town into one force for political purposes. It is this struggle for control, in all probability, that lies behind the execution against MacIntosh and his cordwainer partner, Benjamin Bass, that was taken out by Samuel Adams just two days before the August 14 crowd action. The writ warranted the sheriff to collect a £10 12s debt from MacIntosh or attach his possessions for that amount. If he did not possess this much, the sheriff was to imprison him for his debt to Adams. We do not know what MacIntosh agreed to but some kind of bargain appears to have been struck because the deputy sheriff returned the warrant to the court endorsed "By order of the Creditor I Returne this Execution no part Satisfied."[9]

What can be seen in the Boston disturbances is the fragile and shifting relationship between different elements in the popular party. James Otis commanded the columns of the *Boston Gazette* and Samuel Adams directed the Caucus. But who controlled the streets? The effigies of Oliver, Bute, and the devil were prepared under the direction of some members of the Caucus who had formed themselves into the "Loyal Nine"—Benjamin Edes, printer of the radical *Gazette*; John Avery and Thomas Chase, distillers; John Smith and Stephen Cleverly, braziers: Thomas Crafts, a painter; and several more.[10] These were established tradesmen of the kind who had long suffered from Boston's sunken economy. However, the marches themselves and most of the carefully planned dirty work on the houses of the wealthy had been left to the lower artisans, laborers, and mariners, while the more "respectable" members of the alliance melted into the night. The crowd, led by a poor cordwainer, demonstrated its deep hostility to elitist oppressors such as Hutchinson, who had given his opinion in the last war that a £5 bounty offered the poor for enlisting was "extravagant."[11] Besides intimidating British official-dom and its colonial collaborators, which is probably all their leaders in-tended them to do, the crowd gave vent to years of resentment at the accumulation of wealth and power by the prerogative faction. Behind every swing of the ax and every hurled stone, behind every shattered crystal goblet and splintered mahogany chair lay the fury of a Bostonian who had read or heard the repeated references to an impoverished people as "rabble" and to the Caucus as a "herd of fools, tools, and sycophants," and who had suffered economic hardship while others fattened their purses. They had listened to their leaders condemn those "who grind the faces of the poor without remorse, eat the bread of oppression without fear, and wax fat upon the spoils of the people!"[12] They had heard it said over and over that "Luxury and extravagance are . . . destructive of those virtues which are necessary for the preservation of liberty and the happi-ness of the people."[13] They had burned inwardly at hearing some of the wealthy proclaim from their mansions that poverty was the best induce-ment for industry and frugality and that "the common people of this town and country live too well." And they had cheered James Otis when he replied that "I am of a quite different opinion, I do not think they live half well enough."[14] Now, in August 1764, they had some scores to settle. Slashing the canvas of the expensive paintings hanging in Hallowell's newly completed mansion, drinking imported wines from silver goblets at Oliver's house, and systematically destroying Hutchinson's elegant, pilastered brick mansion provided recompense to the "Rage-intoxicated rabble," as one young upper-class lawyer called them.[15] The "rabble" had lost faith that opportunity or equitable relations any longer prevailed in their town. If they could not change this, they could at least administer their own kind of rough justice upon those who judged them so harshly.

The political consciousness of the crowd and its use of the Stamp Act protests as an opportunity for an attack on wealth itself were remarked upon again and again in the aftermath of the August forays. The mob that had worked "with a rage scarce to be exemplified by the most savage people," wrote the governor, targeted fifteen additional houses in what was becoming "a War of Plunder, of general levelling and taking away the Distinction of rich and poor." Bernard warned that if "persons of property and consideration did not unite in support of government," by which he meant that a way must be found to employ the militia or a *posse comitatus* to control crowd actions, "anarchy and confusion" would continue in "an insurrection of the poor against the rich, those that want the necessities of life against those that have them."[16] On Sep-tember 10, two weeks after the destruction of Hutchinson's house, a Bos-ton merchant wrote that "the rich men in the town" were seized with apprehension and "were moveing their cash & valuable furniture, &c" to the homes of poorer friends who were above the resentment of the lower class. Another merchant confirmed that the "infernal Mob" was threatening "many of the most respectable Inhabitants with destruction to their Houses, Furnitur &c."[17]

Many of the Caucus leaders deplored the sacking of property on the night of August 26, while upholding the actions of August 14 as a legitimate defense of the people's rights. Violence in limited doses was all they were ready to prescribe. Intimidation of obnoxious officials, not class warfare, was what they wanted. The town meeting hurriedly expressed its "utter detestation of the extraordinary & violent proceedings of a number of Persons unknown against some of the Inhabitants" and agreed to form a "Military Watch, till the present unruly Spirit shall subside."[18] This was as far as the middle-class Caucus members and Whig merchants were prepared to go in expressing their dismay that the crowd had developed a mind of its own. Every effort by Hutchinson and the governor to indict the mob leaders, who could easily have been identified, were frustrated. No one stepped forward to claim the £300 reward offered for information leading to the conviction of the riot leaders.[19] A few warrants were issued for the arrest of some of the rioters and the justices of the peace began to hear testimony. MacIntosh was arrested by Sheriff Greenleaf, who knew him well since he was the master of Engine Company No. 9 and ironically had appointed MacIntosh to his company in 1760. But even before he could confine MacIntosh, who was soon to be titled "Captain General of the Liberty Tree," Greenleaf was informed by several high-ranking gentlemen that unless the shoemaker street general was immediately discharged, the citizens' watch would be canceled.[20] This set the tone for all further efforts to bring the ringleaders to book. A few other suspected rioters were indicted and jailed but all but three were sprung from confinement by an angry crowd within a few days. Hutchinson sighed that "there was no authority, which thought it advisable to make any inquiry after them," once they had escaped. Nor could the chief justice convince the grand jury that it was their duty to indict the three rioters who still remained in jail, so that by October 26 the Superior Court was obliged to release them.[21] As in the market riots of the late 1730s, the crowd proved that it was more than a match for the authorities when its members were apprehended or threatened with arrest.

Seen in the context of three generations of social and economic change in Boston, the Stamp Act riots provide the most illuminating example of how the molten metal of group consciousness and feeling was smithied out in the course of defying authority and restoring the "moral economy." Members of the Boston "mob" needed no upper-class leaders to tell them about the economic stagnation that had been affecting their lives and strangling their opportunities. Nor did they need to gut the homes of Oliver and Hutchinson in order to obtain the promise of these officials to hold the Stamp Act in abeyance. They did so because they were indeed in "a rage," as so many of the accounts expressed it. Their rage was directly connected to the conditions of their lives and the connection they perceived between their plight and the exercise of power by the prerogative elite.[22] The "rituals of detestation" carried out on the nights of August 14 and 26 marked the culmination of an era of mounting protest against oligarchic wealth and power.[23] At the same time they were attacks on the symbols of wealth and ostentatious displays of wealth rather than frontal assaults on "the basis of economic and social power."[24] In addition, the crowd actions demonstrated the fragility of the union between protesting city dwellers who occupied places in the lower strata of the laboring community and their more bourgeois partners, who in the uninhibited attacks on property saw their control melting away. It was Ebenezer MacIntosh who controlled the crowd, not Samuel Adams, James Otis, or any of the Loyal Nine.

This rapid emergence of MacIntosh was obvious to everyone in Boston by the time Pope's Day arrived, less than ten weeks after the destruction of Hutchinson's house. By this time the press was calling the cordwainer radical "Commander of the South [End]" and was giving him coverage for effecting a "treaty" with his North End counterpart whereby a peaceful and united Pope's Day parade would replace the traditional bone-breaking brawl. The governor described how "Captain" MacIntosh, or "General" MacIntosh as he was also referred to, splendidly decked out in a militia uniform of gold and blue, a gilt gorget on his chest, and a hat laced with gold on his head, led 2,000 paraders through the town on November 5.[25] Even MacIntosh's upper-class enemies were impressed. Peter Oliver, brother of the stamp distributor, called the orderly ranks of marchers a mob, but he described how MacIntosh marched them past the statehouse where "the General Assembly were sitting, to display his Power. If a Whisper was heard among his Followers, the holding up of his Finger hushed it in a Moment: & when he had fully displayed his Authority, he marched his Men to the first Rendevouz, & order'd them to retire peacably to their several Homes; & was punctually obeyed."[26]

It was no wonder, given the startling emergence of a heretofore unnoticed and obscure shoemaker, that the elite began to refer to MacIntosh as "a Massaniello."[27] Like the Neapolitan rebel of 1647, he had come from nowhere to take command of a force so powerful that it appeared nobody could stop it. With such forces at his command, how far might this man go?

By mid-December MacIntosh's power had become even more apparent. Several weeks before, Andrew Oliver's commission as stamp distributor had arrived from England, and although Oliver had previously promised that he would give up his commission, Bostonians wanted an immediate and unequivocal renunciation. The Sons of Liberty published an anonymous letter in the *Gazette* on December 16 asking for a public statement of resignation at high noon on the following day at the Liberty Tree. Oliver tried to satisfy his harassers by publishing in the same issue a statement that "He had taken no Measures to qualify himself for the Office, nor had he any Thoughts of doing it."[28]

This was not enough. The stamp resisters wanted not only resignation but public humiliation. Therefore they sent a letter to Oliver in the evening, again summoning him to the Liberty Tree at noon on the next day where he was publicly to reaffirm his resignation. Boston was in the middle of a northeaster which had deluged the town in winter rain and this only added to the ignominy being prepared. Oliver twisted and turned, offering on the morning of December 17 to resign at the courthouse—the home ground, as it were, of governmental authority. But the radicals would not hear of it. It was the Liberty Tree or else and none other than Ebenezer MacIntosh was sent to Oliver's house to march him across town to the Liberty Tree in the pelting rain.[29] Thomas Hutchinson tells us that "a great number" of people followed the mortifying march, probably hurling insults, as MacIntosh, at Oliver's right elbow, approached a waiting crowd of several thousand at the appointed place. With the shoemaker standing at his side and on the home turf of the radicals, Oliver ate humble pie. He concluded his resignation remarks with the bitterly ironic words that he would "always think myself very happy when it shall be in my power to serve this people."[30] The drenched crowd cheered and returned to their places of work. Thomas Hutchinson was left to reflect balefully that "This indignity to the third crown officer in rank in the province passed without notice from any authority. No grand jury would consider this as an unlawful assembly."[31] Having forced Oliver's resignation, the alliance of protesting merchants and shopkeepers, artisans, laborers, and mariners convinced the customs officers to open their doors for business, allowing the port-bound fleet to embark, in defiance of an act of Parliament, with unstamped clearance papers.[32]

IN NEW YORK and Philadelphia the growing resentment toward wealth and luxurious living, the rejection of an elitist conception of politics, the articulation of laboring-class interests, and the struggle for power within the emerging patriot movement also gained momentum in 1765. As in Boston, it was the extraordinary new vigor of urban laboring people in defining and pursuing their goals that raised the frightening specter of a radicalized form of politics and a radically changed society in the minds of many middle- and upper-class city dwellers who would later abandon the resistance movement against England that they had initially supported and led.

In New York, where the postwar depression wreaked havoc among hundreds of shipbuilders and mariners who had been essential to the town's impressive maritime advance during the war, resistance to the

Stamp Act began later than in Boston but followed a similar pattern. By late August sentiment among the lower people, especially maritime workers, had coalesced sufficiently to convince stamp distributor James McEvers, a wealthy merchant, to resign his post, fearing that "my House would have been Pillag'd, my Person Abused and His Majestys Revenue Impair'd."[33] McEvers had heard the news from Boston and realized that his considerable estate was in dire jeopardy unless he played willow rather than oak. By mid-September the stamp distributor for Maryland, who had fled to New York City after rough treatment by an angry mob, was sure that he was about to be attacked. A month later, when the English ship carrying the stamps for New York arrived, several thousand New Yorkers swarmed to the shoreline near the Battery where the ship was anchored, ready to do what was necessary to prevent them from being landed. On October 24, after a military regiment brought the stamps ashore in the dead of night and took them to Fort George, handwritten placards appeared throughout the town warning that "the first Man that either distributes or makes use of Stampt Paper let him take Care of his House, Person, and Effects. We dare. VOX POPULI."[34]

November 1 was the date when the Stamp Act went into force. Thereafter no ship could leave a colonial harbor without customs clearance documents to which the hated stamps had been properly affixed. As the fateful day approached, tension mounted. On October 31 the town's merchants met at Burns's City Tavern and agreed not to import any English goods while the Stamp Act was in effect. Simultaneously, artisans, mariners, and laborers met on the common and displayed their collective strength by marching down Broadway to Fort George and back in the most impressive show of lower-class·power since the days of Jacob Leisler. Badly split in the election of 1761, they were now showing strong signs of solidarity. The response of seventy-seven-year-old˙Governor Cadwallader Colden to all of this was an order to strengthen the fortifications at Fort George in preparation for a showdown with the mob. In past days, Colden had often been the upper-class tribune for laboring people who suffered at the hands of wealthy exploiters. Now, vested with executive authority, he came down squarely on the side of law and order.[35]

If action was what Colden craved, he did not have long to wait. On the night of October 31 the crowd assembled and soon was roaring through the streets, threatening the homes of suspected sympathizers of British policy. "Some thousands of windows Broke," wrote one British officer who watched the scene. This was only a warm-up for the next night. On November 1 a huge crowd assembled and agreed to deliver a strident message to the governor, calling him "The Chief Murderer of their Rights and Privileges" and warning that "you'll die a Martyr to your own Villainy, and be Hang'd like Porteis, upon a Signpost, as a Momento to a' wicked Governors, and that every Man, that assists you, Shall be, surely, put to Death."[36]

At nightfall the street theater began. As in Boston, it was meant to politicize participants and observers alike. Some 2,000 New Yorkers marched by flickering candlelight to Fort George where they strung up effigies of the devil and Governor Colden, the latter dangling with stamped paper in his hand and a drum on his back—an allusion to the legend that in his youth Colden had served as a drummer boy in the army of the Scottish Catholic Pretender to the English throne. After figuratively hanging the governor, the crowd cut down the effigy, carried it to his mansion, liberated his prize chariot, and with "the grossest ribaldry" paraded the effigy around the town in the coach. "The numbers of the Actors and Spectators," wrote one observer, "was inconceivably great and they went on with the greatest order, and now & then firing a pistol at the Effigy."[37] The celebration climaxed with a bonfire into which the shouting crowd hurled the governor's coach and two sleighs. Colden's effigy was hoisted atop the flaming heap.

Warming to their task, the people then surged through the streets to the house of Major Thomas James, commander of the 60th Regiment of Royal Artillery at Fort George. Hated for his outspoken defense of the Stamp Act and his promise that "the stamps would be crammed down New Yorkers' throats," James now felt the power of the crowd. Earlier they had threatened to bury him alive for his arrogance. Now, working as if they wished not to be compared unfavorably with their Boston brethren, the demonstrators gutted Major James's house. The windows and doors were eliminated in a trice; then the systematic destruction began. Furniture was reduced to kindling, china shattered on the ground, feather beds ripped open and flung to the wind, the wine cellar emptied, and the garden torn up. Not until 4 A.M. did the throng retire. "A great part of the Mob," wrote the governor, "consists of Men who have been Privateers and disbanded Soldiers whose view is to plunder the Town." By the next day a British officer was expressing his consternation that money was being "extracted from private people, or die"—a reversion to the traditional "forced levies" of England.

Four days later, still not mollified, the crowd regathered, this time to demand the surrender of the stamps that were housed at Fort George. Placards nailed up all over the town announced that "the sons of Neptune," in other words, seagoing men, would head the demonstration. So they did, leading several thousand people to the walls of the fort, taunting the guards to fire, and hurling insults liberally interspersed with bricks, stones, and garbage. The troops held their fire, and Colden, withdrawing from the brink, agreed to surrender the stamps to the city officials. A few days later, with 5,000 people lining the streets, the stamps were hauled in carts to the city hall and handed over to the mayor and aldermen.[38]

In New York no Masaniello arose from the anonymous masses to lead the crowd as in Boston. Leadership was more fragmented, resting mostly in the hands of a group of popular tradesmen and privateering captains who had risen from obscure backgrounds to small trader status during the Seven Years War. They included several ship carpenters, instrument-maker John Lamb, upholsterer Marinus Willett, ship captains Isaac Sears and Alexander McDougall, and schoolteacher Hugh Hughes. Styling themselves the "Sons of Liberty," they maneuvered for control of men in the lower ranks. Also contending for the allegiance of the laboring people were Whig merchants and lawyers William Smith, Jr., John Morin Scott, and William Livingston, the anti-DeLancey triumverate that had worked hard in the elections of 1761 to gain the artisans' support.[39] Following the "General Terror of November 1-4," the lawyers, closely tied to the city's Whig merchants, secured the backing of McDougall and then "went around to every part of the town," attempting to enlist the support of other sea captains and their lower-class followers.[40] Like their Boston counterparts, many Whiggish New Yorkers were deadly earnest about defeating the new trade policies of England and knew they could not do so without the support of those below them. But they were also coming to fear the awful power of the assembled artisans and their maritime compatriots. The interests of merchants, artisans, and laborers were not always identical. While they converged in specific instances such as forcing an annulment of the Stamp Act and defying new trade restrictions, the fissures between them relating to the internal governance of the city and management of its economy were not far beneath the surface.

The tension between upper-class Whigs and laboring-class radicals became more pronounced as events wore on in 1765. Even though the stamp distributor resigned his post, the law went into effect on November 1. This meant that thereafter any ship leaving port without stamped documents defied the king and Parliament. The alternatives for the American seaport dwellers were to maintain an embargo until British policy changed or to ship in defiance of the law. New Yorkers addressed this choice squarely on November 26 when the "freeholders, freemen, and inhabitants" met to decide on instructions to the city's representatives to the assembly, which was debating the issue. Such an open-air referendum was itself a radical innovation in New York, for it invited all the people to debate publicly and reach a decision on a momentous issue in a "town meeting" format that had been known previously only in Boston. The outcome of the meeting, however, was less than radical, for the Livingston Whigs, preferring passive resistance through embargo to active defiance of English law, gained control of the popular meeting and pushed through their embargo resolution.[41]

Thwarted at the "town meeting," the radicals found other ways to gain their objective. Pressure was exerted on the customs officials, who were doubtless reminded of the awful power displayed by the huge crowds earlier in the month. We have no details of this irregular politicking, but the actions of the customs officers speak volumes. One week after the public decision to maintain an embargo rather than ship in defiance of the Stamp Act, the port officers decided to open the port and clear ships without stamped papers. "This step," they wrote, "we thought more adviseable as we understood the Mob (which are daily increasing and gathering strength, from the arrival of Seamen, and none going out, and who are the people that are most dangerous on these occasions, as their whole dependance for a subsistence is upon Trade) were soon to have a meeting."[42] As in Boston, the lower ranks were feeling their power and beginning to take independent action. Breaking free of traditional ties to their betters, which had restrained them in the past, they groped for an autonomous voice and independent organizations.

In New York the radical and Whig camps were divided not only by differing viewpoints on how strenuously to oppose English policy and what tactics to employ but also by beliefs concerning the internal functioning of their society. New York had prospered during the Seven Years War whereas Boston had languished, and leaders such as Lamb, Sears, and McDougall, who were sons of artisans, had risen into the middle class whereas men such as Ebenezer MacIntosh had not. So it is not surprising that the voices raised against the wealthy were more muted in New York than in the capital of Massachusetts. Still, attacks on wealth, which reflected the strong strain of egalitarianism among radicals that was not shared by Whigs, began to emerge. Postwar depression had not cut so close to the bone as in Boston, but it had cut deeply enough to convince many that changes were necessary.

In one other way the storm clouds that gathered over New York were seeded differently than those over Boston. In the latter port, the radicals were wont to invoke the old Puritan ideals of community and to deplore the pursuit of private interest, still hoping, as one historian puts it, "to draw Massachusetts society together in a classless assertion of the public welfare."[43] New Yorkers, legatees of a far more utilitarian, less religiously oriented culture and part of an urban society where entrepreneurship had been legitimized by the successes of the Seven Years War, looked self-interest in the eye and made no apologies for it. "*Self Interest* is the grand Principle of all Human Actions," declared John Holt's radical *New-York Gazette;* "it is unreasonable and vain to expect Service from a Man who must act contrary to his own Interests to perform it . . . The publick Happiness is then in the most perfect State, when each Individual acts the most agreeably to his own Interest."[44] Here was an argument that could be aptly employed in the resistance to oppressive English policies. As "Freeman" observed, both the colonies and the mother country had interests that were legitimate to pursue and if "the benefit of one must necessarily be in the same degree hurtful to the others, then these two

Interests can never unite in the same government; their connection should be broken off, the jarring interest should be removed, or new modelled into Harmony & confidence with the Rest."[45] Quoting *Cato's Letters* a few months later, "Freeman" advised that "No Creatures Suck the Teats of their Dams longer than they can draw Milk from thence . . . nor will any Country continue their subjection to another only because their Great-Grandmothers were acquainted." Thus, "the radicals reduced reason to a mere calculation of personal interest," a formulation that would have drawn immediate howls from the likes of Samuel Adams or James Otis in Boston.[46]

THE REACTION of Philadelphians to the Stamp Act stands in stark contrast to the Boston and New York responses. Stamps were no less hated in Pennsylvania's capital and economic conditions had reached a depressing state by 1765 that might have been expected to fuel antistamp protests. But the city remained singularly free of the ritual processions, effigy burnings, and property destruction that characterized the other port towns. Philadelphia's stamp distributor was John Hughes, a baker turned merchant, one of Franklin's oldest friends, a brother of New York radical Hugh Hughes, and, until 1765, a stalwart of the popular assembly party.[47] Shortly after Franklin returned to England as the assembly's agent in November 1764 to prosecute the case against proprietor Thomas Penn, he learned of the impending stamp legislation. Franklin argued with Grenville, failed to convince him that the Stamp Act was unwise, and in the end capitulated to the minister's sop of asking Franklin to recommend a distributor for the Philadelphia region. Franklin chose Hughes.

By September 1765, Hughes was one of the least popular men in Philadelphia. He did not repair his reputation by voting on September 10 against sending a Pennsylvania delegation to the Stamp Act Congress in New York. In the election pamphlets that streamed from the press before the October 1 assembly election, the proprietary party charged that Hughes's patron, Franklin, had actually helped to write the Stamp Act in London.[48]

On the evening of September 16, when news arrived that George Grenville had resigned as chief minister, a celebrating crowd assembled at the London Coffee House, owned by Presbyterian William Bradford, printer of the *Pennsylvania Journal* and a member of the newly formed Philadelphia Sons of Liberty. Toasts to Grenville's ill health turned to cries that the houses of Franklin, Galloway, Hughes, and others involved in supporting the Stamp Act "should be level'd with the Street."[49] It appeared the angry crowd might emulate their Boston brethren until Joseph Galloway marshaled about 800 men, whom he had organized into an Association for the Preservation of the Peace. The association was really a private army of Franklin's artisan supporters and on cue they took their places in front of the threatened houses.

Now artisan faced artisan. The anti-Stamp Act crowd, according to Hughes, was made up of "the lower class," whipped up by "Presbyterians and proprietary Emissaries" led by Chief Justice William Allen's son; the Franklin-Galloway stalwarts were made up of two groups of ship carpenters, the White Oaks and Hearts of Oak, as well as many other "hones[t] good tradesmen," as Franklin's wife described them.[50] These mechanics had no love for the Stamp Act, but they had stood with Franklin for years—in civic associations that he had founded, in the volunteer militias organized in 1747 and 1755, in the impromptu military association hastily gathered to repel the marching Paxtoneers, and in the heated election of 1764. They hoped the rumors about their friend's complicity in the Stamp Act were simply part of the proprietary mudslinging campaign; in the meantime they intended to defend the property and family of Franklin and his friends.[51]

In Boston master artisans and petty entrepreneurs had organized powerfully in the Sons of Liberty, lower artisans and laborers of the South and North Ends had submerged their rivalry in the face of the threat of stamps, and a poor cordwainer had emerged to lead a united laboring citizenry. In Philadelphia, the royal government issue had deeply divided the working people, stunting the coalescence of artisans, and permitted upper-class leaders to retain control of both parts of a divided laboring population. Face to face with Franklin's artisan friends, the anti-Stamp Act crowd could only burn "a Figure that they call'd a Stamp-man" and then melt away into the night. Likewise, as printer William Bradford explained, "our Body of Sons of Liberty in this city is not declared numerous, as unfortunate dissentions in Provincial politics keep us a rather divided people."[52]

Two weeks after the anti-Hughes mob appeared Philadelphians went to the polls for an election even more tumultuous than the one in 1764. For months, Galloway and other assembly leaders had been working with a passion to reverse the defeats of the previous year. They left no stone unturned in an effort to recapture the allegiance of the defected Germans, paying naturalization fees, settling tavern bills, courting German leaders, and adding Michael Hillegas, a German merchant, to the assembly party slate. Equally important, the unpopular Hughes was purged from the ticket and one proprietary winner from 1764 was induced to switch over to the side of the assembly party. The proprietary party struggled to maintain their edge. They convinced Governor John Penn to appoint dozens of Presbyterian justices of the peace and to issue charters of incorporation to German churches, a reversal of a long-maintained proprietary policy. Proprietary leaders also worked hard on the "presbyterian and Dutch Tinkers and Cobblers," as one Quaker put it.

The city's presses again worked overtime to turn out campaign literature and the dirt peddlers did their best to improve on their performance in 1764.

The polls remained open for three days as nearly 2,000 voters, or about 80 percent of the tax-inscribed males, cast ballots.[53] When the votes were counted, the assembly party rejoiced to find that they had recouped most of their losses from the previous year. The deep division of laboring men was stunningly recorded in the vote for the city's two burgesses. Thomas Willing, a middle-of-the-road merchant, ran on both tickets, but the other place was hotly contested between James Pemberton, a venerable Quaker brought out of retirement by the Franklin-Galloway party, and George Bryan, the Presbyterian merchant who had defeated Franklin in 1764. Pemberton and Bryan each polled 902 votes, forcing a run-off election which Pemberton won later in October. Such an electoral turnout would never be duplicated during the revolutionary era in any port town, and never again would laboring-class voters be so divided.[54]

Two days after the election, the anti-Stamp Act crowd took to the streets again, this time to deal with the arrival of a ship bearing Hughes's commission and the province's stamps. Hughes was told that "if I did not immediately resign my office, my house should be pulled down and my substance destroyed." The artisan supporters of the Franklin party again formed a cordon around Hughes's house but this time they extracted from him, as the price of protection, a promise not to execute the Stamp Act "until the King's further pleasure was known, or until the act should be put into execution in the neighbouring provinces." In November a crowd tried once more to pry from Hughes an unconditional surrender of his commission but again the vertical division of laboring Philadelphians provided him with a protective shield that no other stamp distributor on the continent enjoyed.[55]

The issue of royal government in Pennsylvania was so aberrational and emotional that it diverted attention from the more fundamental issues of economic stagnation and British imperial policies, distorted the ideological positions of the proprietary and assembly parties, and divided those who in terms of economic interest had a natural affinity for each other. The assembly party, known for many decades for its defense of popular rights and its determined resistance against prerogative privilege, was the counterpart of the Adams-Otis "country" party in Massachusetts. In Philadelphia, motivated by its fierce hatred of Thomas Penn, it proceeded down the false road of seeking royal government. In order to "ingratiate themselves with the British ministry," which alone could shear Thomas Penn of his proprietorship, its leaders became "the apologists for and, as far as possible, the defenders of the royal prerogative as it ravaged colonial rights in the Stamp Act."[56] Thus, the popular party acted out of character in pursuing royal government and attempting to mute opposition to the Stamp Act. No less did the proprietary party reverse its traditional role. Given a golden opportunity to defeat its enemies, who had dominated electoral politics for decades, the Anglican-led conservative party of Philadelphia wooed the Scots-Irish Presbyterians and German Lutherans and Reformed, latching onto Stamp Act opposition as a means of expanding its political base. It was so uncharacteristic a role that even the more liberal proprietary party members squirmed. But, after all, how often did their old enemy Franklin blunder so monumentally?

Unnatural alliances can last only so long and politicians cannot act out of character forever. So it is not surprising that once the quest for royal government became recognized as a phantom goal, a false issue that obscured far more important problems, Philadelphia's occupational and religious groups began to realign in a way that brought together their material interests and ideological predispositions. Even as the Stamp Act protests were in progress, a reknitting of the laboring classes began. By early November, only a few days after the mass disturbances in New York, lower-class pressure forced Philadelphia's merchants to stop importing English goods until the Stamp Act was repealed. "So exasperated are the People," wrote Charles Thomson, who was becoming a leader of the radical Whigs in the city, "that to appease them and indeed for their own Safety the merchants are obliged to pawn their word and honour and give from under their hands that they will not import any more goods" until the English government backed down.[57] One of Philadelphia's wealthiest merchants believed his house would be gutted if he conformed to the Stamp Act and another anticipated "a deluge of blood" if merchants evaded the boycott of imported goods.[58]

Outgoing trade, along coastal routes and to the Caribbean, was a different matter. To shut it off would idle a large part of the maritime laboring force and the tradesmen connected to it. Therefore, as in the other ports, popular pressure was strong to clear outgoing ships without stamps affixed to their papers. "Our tradesmen begin to grow clamorous for want of employment [and] our city is full of sailors who cannot procure berths," wrote Benjamin Rush, an emerging radical leader with close ties to the laboring people. "Who knows," he continued, just one week after the port had been closed, "what the united resentments of these two numerous people may accomplish."[59] As in New York, it was the "clamor" of these men, along with pressure from some merchants, which within a few weeks after the Stamp Act took effect obliged port officials to issue clearances to ships without stamped papers.

By the summer of 1766 in Philadelphia the alliance of proprietary Anglicans and their Presbyterian supporters had cracked wide open. Presbyterians became convinced that the Anglicans were set upon establishing an American bishopric that would make life difficult for all dissenting groups; Anglicans became increasingly uncomfortable opposing policies devised in England; the disappearance of the royal government issue detached the Germans and Scots-Irish from their confederation with the proprietary party; and Quakers began to split between those who favored a conciliatory approach to the Anglo-American tension and those who counseled active opposition. Out of the kaleidoscopic shifting of groups a wholly new force was about to make its appearance in city politics—a Presbyterian led, artisan-based radical Whig party that would more nearly match the popular parties in Boston and New York.[60]

IN DECEMBER 1765, all of the northern seaports reopened for trade. Their doughty citizens could rejoice at having successfully resisted English authority, even if formal repeal of the Stamp Act would not come until the following year. But the sweet taste of victory among the upper-class merchants and lawyers who had attempted to lead the resistance movement was soured by the knowledge that in a number of instances the protest movement had slipped beyond their control. In working to counteract what they saw as a punitive British imperial policy, the Whig leadership of the port towns had welcomed the *vox populi* and the assembled force of the crowds. In fact, they could not do without them. But once the genie was out of the bottle, how could it be imprisoned again?

The "mob," of course, has been feared throughout history by both upper-class holders of power and intellectuals because it has been commonly assumed that the masses are irrational, are stirred into violent paroxysms by irresponsible rabble-rousers, and are indiscriminate in selecting their targets. Once unloosed, the mob is capable of almost anything. Hence, the assembled commonality was referred to over and over again by eighteenth-century writers, including many Whigs, as "the unthinking multitude," the "hellish crew," the "impassioned dregs of society," and other terms that reveal the elite view that people of the lowest ranks, who were most numerous in the crowds, were incompetent to calculate their own interests and act rationally to secure them. William Douglass was convinced that the Land Bank leaders in Boston in 1740 had succeeded in "debauching" the minds of unthinking people, "Instilling into them some pernicious Principles, destructive of all Society, and good Government," particularly, "that *common Consent*, or the Humour of the Multitude, ought to be the *Ratio Ultima* in every Thing."[61] William Smith, a wealthy lawyer in New York, explained that the assembly elections in 1743 were "conducted without tumult" because the leaders of the generality remained inactive "and thus the multitude were left to that torpor which generally prevails when they are uninfluenced by the arts and intrigues of the restless and designing sons of ambition." Peter Oliver, brother of the Boston stamp distributor, believed that the crowd in his city, like all mobs, was a "perfect Machine, wound up by any Hand who might first take the Winch."[62]

Such statements reflect two images of the revolutionary mobs in early America that have greatly influenced historical thinking: first, the manipulated mob, acting robotlike under orders from above, and second, the spontaneous, unprogrammatic, frenzied mob. Both of these models of mass action have been discredited in recent years by students analyzing crowd behavior on both sides of the Atlantic.[63] Here, it is only necessary to recognize that not everything written about mobs in the past is devoid of meaning. It is true that upper-class leaders tried hard to get crowds to do their bidding, sometimes with considerable success. No less certain is that urban dwellers of the lower classes often looked upward for leadership because deference was not yet dead and educated men in the upper ranks had money, organizational skills, and literary talents which were indispensable for successful protest movements. Nor is there reason to deny that the crowd, once it swung into action, could move beyond its initial purposes and defy those who thought they controlled it or even go out of control altogether. Enough is known about crowd psychology and the mind-altering effects of alcohol to accept the notion that the euphoria created by mass action and the contents of upper-class wine cellars were enough to sweep away caution and magnify deeply held feelings against those identified as high livers and oppressors.

The seaport crowds of 1765 can best be understood as large groups of disaffected citizens, drawn heavily but not entirely from the laboring ranks, who worked in purposeful and coordinated ways to protest British policies and express opposition to local oligarchies. Leadership among the crowds varied from port to port. In Boston, where poverty was most endemic and where the Pope's Day tradition and recurrent street demonstrations since the late 1730s had taught the laboring classes the basic lessons of organization and protest, the crowd leaders emerged from the lower social ranks and were tenuously tied to those above them. In New York, where poverty had arrived only in the wake of the Seven Years War and there was no recent history of crowd protests, the Stamp Act demonstrators were led by men somewhat higher up the social ladder —ship captains, master craftsmen, and even lawyers. In Philadelphia, where prosperity had also inhibited the development of class consciousness before 1760 and where local political issues divided artisans and shopkeepers, upper-class representatives such as Joseph Galloway and James Allen led the people.

In spite of these differences it is important to note that in all of the towns the struggle for political control was in a highly fluid state. Thomas Hutchinson, who was most comfortable in the presence of order and wealth, believed that a tight chain of command existed in Boston between the upper, middle, and lower ranks. It began, he said, with members of the Merchants Committee (established in 1763 to oppose the new trade restrictions); descended to the master craftsmen, who were organized through the Loyal Nine, several branches of the Caucus, and the fire companies; and finally tapped the laborers, mariners, servants, and even slaves.[64] Hutchinson was half right, correctly identifying the social layering in Boston and describing how Whig merchant leaders wished their political system to operate. But he overestimated the ability of the merchants and lawyers to control the crowd because he underestimated the self-energizing capabilities of common people. The attack on Andrew Oliver's house, carefully managed from above at least in its initial stage, conformed to his mechanistic vision of the chain of command. But the destruction of his own house proved that the crowd in the streets could follow its own dictates and its own leaders, moving far beyond what the "better sort" wanted. "The Boston Mob," wrote one observer, "raised first by the Instigation of Many of the Principal Inhabitants, Allured by Plunder, rose shortly after of their own Accord."[65]

In New York it was much the same. General Thomas Gage believed that "people of Property" had raised "the lower Class to prevent the Execution of the [Stamp] Law, and as far as Riots and Tumults went against Stamp-Masters . . . they encouraged and many perhaps joined them." The inferior people would not have stirred, opined Gage, except that "very great Pains were taken to rouse them," especially the sailors, who "are entirely at the Command of the Merchants who employ them."[66] Gage exaggerated the power of the merchants but soon altered his vision of the lower class as so much water to be pumped from a well by the propertied elite. After five days of tumult in New York, the "people of property," he wrote, "having no more influence over them [the crowd], began to be filled with terrors for their own Safety." Robert Livingston described how the vehemence of the demonstrations and the extensiveness of property destruction on October 31 and November 1 convinced the Whig lawyers, who thought they had a firm grip on the anti-Stamp Act movement, that their grasp of affairs was slipping.[67]

Both prerogative men and Whig leaders were capable of underestimating the self-activating capacity of the crowd. But by the end of 1765, a year of extraordinary significance in the social history of the port towns, the scales had been lifted from upper-class eyes. The momentous question at the end of that year, as the resistance movement against England began to lay bare signs of great internal stress, was this: if the "mob" controlled the streets, who would control the "mob"? The Whig leaders "began to be terrified at the Spirit they had raised," warned Gage, "to perceive that popular Fury was not to be guided, and each Individual feared he might be the next Victim to their Rapacity."[68] That, it was clear to men accustomed to political power and the obeisance of those beneath them, must not happen.

12

The Disordered Urban Economies

THE YEAR 1765 had been the most explosive in the history of the seaport towns. Urban dwellers deeply resented new British policies and opposed them violently. Local political factionalism produced bitter campaigns at the polls. Obscure men assumed leadership roles among the mass of ordinary people, upper-class Whiggish leaders maneuvered to maintain control of popular politics, and prerogative men shuddered at the welling up of leveling tendencies. The reopening of the northern ports at the end of the year revived commerce, and news that the Stamp Act had been repealed in May 1766 gave hope that the dispute with the mother country might be laid to rest. But optimism was short-lived, for the English crown swiftly signaled that it had no intention of permitting the Americans to go their own way, reaping benefits from membership in the empire but refusing to pay their share of the costs. Parliament passed new legislation in 1767 designed to bring the colonies to heel. The Townshend Acts levied duties on paper, lead, painters' colors, and tea. They also sent a board of determined customs commissioners to the colonies to enforce trade restrictions and suspended New York's assembly until that body adhered to the Quartering Act of 1765 by providing properly for British troops who had been garrisoned in the colony since the end of the Seven Years War.[1] From this moment forward the colonies and the parent country approached the brink of revolution.

The colonists did not become revolutionaries lightly, especially because they were part of the disunited set of territories that suffered a huge disadvantage with England in population, economic resources, diplomatic alliances, and military experience. It is no wonder, then, that the Americans engaged in a full decade of debate and internal struggle before making the decision to break the chains of English dependency and fight for independence. Those ten years of debate and confrontation engaged the energy of thousands of reasonable and well-meaning persons on both sides of the Atlantic·who strove to enunciate rational political principles, to find stable constitutional ground upon which to tread, and to formulate ideological positions that resonated convincingly within their political communities. At the same time, the crucial decade after 1765 produced the most violent economic fluctuations and the most difficult circumstances for people of all ranks that ever had been known in the port towns. Ideas are "a function of him who holds them, and of his position in his social milieu." Thus, because "political thought is integrally bound up with social life," we need to examine the way in which urban dwellers in different cities and in different social ranks were affected in the decade after 1765.[2] This involves grasping not only the effect of English policies on local economies but also the cumulative effect of long-range changes that were largely unrelated to decisions hammered out in London. By looking first at these silent streams of unplanned change we can better comprehend why the policies of the English government after 1765 were felt and interpreted as they were.

AMONG THE ALTERATIONS in the northern seaport towns in the last decade of the colonial era, none was more noticeable than sheer physical expansion. Philadelphia, which had grown steadily during the Seven Years War, spurted ahead spectacularly—from about 18,000 in 1765 to nearly 25,000 a decade later. New York, which had about 17,000 inhabitants at the end of the war against France, grew less impressively but reached 22,000 by 1771 and perhaps a few thousand more by the time of the Revolution. Only Boston failed to share in the rapid urban development, but even the Bay city ended thirty years of demographic stagnation by adding perhaps a thousand persons to its population, thus returning to the size it had been in the early 1740s.[3]

Impressive population increase does not necessarily mean economic vigor and demographic stagnation does not always connote economic decay, so we must look carefully into the meaning of these population figures. Rapid growth in Philadelphia and New York primarily reflected high immigration rates after the Seven Years War, but the newcomers came to port towns where for the first time there was no guarantee of work. Boston also attracted migrants, though they were not nearly so numerous as in the other northern ports and most were fleeing hard times in other New England towns rather than coming from overseas.[4] The other factor holding down Boston's population was the abnormally low birthrate throughout Massachusetts—the result, as Governor Bernard remarked in 1763, of the grievous loss of thousands of young prospective husband-fathers in the wars against the French.[5]

One immediate advantage of population growth for local economies was the spurring of the building trades. Work for construction artisans was sporadic at best in Boston, for in the decade after 1765 the number of houses increased by only about twenty per year. Nor were new churches and public buildings needed for a relatively static population.[6] In New York and Philadelphia, by contrast, construction boomed. The Manhattan port added about a thousand houses between 1765 and 1776 and Philadelphia's artisans erected more than twice this number. The roof beams were raised for more houses in 1774 in Pennsylvania's capital than in Boston during the entire prerevolutionary decade.[7] Expansion of this magnitude also created the need for churches and public buildings. While Boston's craftsmen erected only one major public building in the final decade of the colonial period, their counterparts in Philadelphia were building the "New College" for the emerging University of Pennsylvania, Carpenters Hall, new churches for the Anglicans, Lutherans, and Presbyterians, and the two largest structures erected in colonial America, the Bettering House and the Walnut Street Prison.[8]

The success of these Philadelphia construction tradesmen relative to their Boston cousins is indisputable, for it was systematically recorded in their inventories of estate. Among seventeen construction artisans whose estates were inventoried in Boston from 1766 to 1775 the median personal wealth left at death was £60 sterling; in Philadelphia, among nineteen artisans, it was £198. Only one Boston artisan left more than £80 worth of personal possessions while in the Quaker city eleven of the nineteen did. Seven of Boston's seventeen decedents left less than £24, the lowest figure recorded for any Philadelphia building construction craftsman.[9]

While Boston's construction artisans scrambled for work in the 1760s and 1770s, the fortunes of shipbuilding craftsmen brightened slightly from the dismal days of the 1750s. The Bay town had lost its dominance over New England shipbuilding many years before and would never again construct 10,000 tons in one year, as it had several times in the past. But from 1769 to 1771 an average of 7,664 tons of shipping was constructed in the colony. If Boston's share remained at the pre-1755 level, then about 2,700 tons of shipping slid down the ways each year.[10] Philadelphia's shipyards from 1769 to 1771 turned out an average of 2,073 tons per annum and in the next four years production jumped by more than half. Though exact figures are not extant, it appears that Philadelphia surpassed its New England rival in ship construction by the eve of the Revolution. Meanwhile, ship construction in New York fell badly, with the output in 1769 and 1770 dropping below 1,000 tons and averaging only 1,204 tons from 1769 to 1771.[11]

Boston's problems were also compounded by the loss of the fishing industry to outlying ports. At mid-century Boston had a considerable fishing fleet and exported as much fish as Marblehead and Salem combined. By 1763 only ten of Massachusetts's 301 fishing vessels were still operating out of Boston. During the decade before the Revolution its coastal rivals gained control of almost three-quarters of the colony's fish exports and the number of quintals shipped from Boston fell far below the previous level.[12]

Boston's economic decline relative to New York and Philadelphia can also be measured in the maritime traffic clearing the harbor. From 1714 to 1717 tonnage clearing New York was one-third that in Boston; on the eve of the Seven Years War it was half as much; from 1760 to 1762 it was 55 percent of the Boston total; and in the years immediately preceding the Revolution it reached 70 percent. Philadelphia had almost achieved parity with Boston by the early 1750s and a decade later the tonnage of ships entering and clearing the port exceeded that in Boston by nearly 40 percent. It was a supremacy that Philadelphia maintained up to the Revolution.[13]

In spite of its eclipse as North America's premier entrepôt, Boston staged a commercial recovery in the late 1760s and early 1770s. Tonnage clearing the harbor rose almost 40 percent in the last decade of the colonial period from the previous fifteen years and this must have meant regular employment for most of the town's large maritime labor force. Some confirmation of this can be found in the inventories of Boston's mariners, who left more worldly goods behind in the prerevolutionary decade than had their fellow tars in either of the two previous ten-year periods.[14]

Yet Boston could not halt its decline relative to Philadelphia and New York, for the latter two ports, especially Philadelphia, were the shipping points for prospering agricultural hinterlands that expanded rapidly after the Peace of Paris. Boston remained the commercial center for a relatively unproductive interior whose excess population, unable to extract a living from the thin New England soils, drifted off to the forests and rocky coastline of New Hampshire and Maine.[15] The people of Massachusetts by the end of the colonial period could not even feed themselves. The unusually detailed reports of the American inspector general from 1768 to 1772 show that the Bay colony was a large net importer of bread and flour, wheat, corn, beef, and pork. About 14 percent of its basic foodstuff requirements had to be purchased from other colonies. Massachusetts had become a net importer of food resources early in the eighteenth century, but whereas from 1714 to 1717 a population of 80,000 required only 2,100 bushels of imported grain, from 1761 to 1765 about 250,000 bushels were imported for only three times as many people.[16] In the early 1770s the reliance upon externally produced foodstuffs grew still heavier.

New York and Pennsylvania, on the other hand, were becoming the breadbaskets not only for colonies to the northward but also for England and southern Europe, where crippling droughts created an unprecedented demand for grains from the middle Atlantic region from 1764 onward. New York was able to export almost 30 percent of its own food requirements from 1768 to 1772 and Pennsylvania more than half.[17] Of course the merchant and mariner had employment whether their colony imported or exported foodstuffs. It was nonetheless true that all Bostonians operated in a regional economy that had reached the point of marginality while to the south the rich agricultural lands and high immigration rate created general economic expansiveness.

A MORE COMPLEX probing of commercial factors is needed before an explanation can be offered of how colonists in particular social categories responded to the epic question of the period—how should Americans resolve their disputes with England and how, if at all, should their society be internally reorganized in the process? After all, it was not only how many voyages he could send out each year that concerned the merchant, but where his goods might be marketed and what profit margin he could achieve. These matters hinged on trade policy set in England, the enforcement of customs laws, the availability of currency, the role of English traders in the American market, and the strength of overseas demand for American products. Similarly, the merchant seaman, sailmaker, or cooper was deeply concerned with English commercial regulation because steady employment depended largely on the state of the economy, which could be drastically affected by shifts in mercantile regulation. Living closer to the subsistence line, men in the laboring ranks also were deeply concerned with wages and prices because an unfavorable change in the relationship between them could undermine their economic security.

For merchants and large shopkeepers, the most troubling problem of the prerevolutionary decade was the growing domination of the American commercial process by English decision makers and English capital. To be sure, the colonial economy had always been the servant of the metropolitan master; that was what it meant to be a colony, to be "underdeveloped," to be a producer and exporter of foodstuffs and raw products and an importer and consumer of finished goods. Nobody expected economic sovereignty or even desired it. But as the colonial economies matured, restrictions on local development began to grate. In the wake of the Seven Years War, when these restrictions multiplied rapidly, the situation seemed less and less tolerable.[18]

Among the developments that northern merchants found worrisome was the growing tendency of British merchants to sell directly to shopkeepers or organize auctions for selling off English goods directly to the public. These "vendue sales," which had customarily been reserved for the disposal of damaged goods, became increasingly a part of commercial life in the northern ports. By cutting out the colonial middleman, this method of dumping goods on the American market struck directly at the interests of the seaboard merchant and shopkeeper. Vendue sales, complained one Philadelphian in 1772, "have gone near to deprive many an honest Family of a Living."[19] When Parliament passed the Tea Act in the following year it aroused bitter opposition precisely because it represented further intervention in the American marketing process. The Tea Act offered the urban consumer a lower price by allowing the East India Company to sell its product directly to the American public through its agents in the colonies. In considering the angry reaction of most northern merchants we must make allowances for the fact that many of them had trafficked profitably in smuggled Dutch tea, which was now to be undersold. But the Tea Act was also opposed because it was seen as an invidious plan to wrest control of the internal workings of the American economy from the hands of its own people. If the English got away with interventionism on tea, might they not do the same with other items imported from or through England or with all of them for that matter?[20]

A second cloud hanging over commercial activity was the increasingly heavy hand of British policymakers on the colonial currency system. The Currency Act of 1764, which strictly limited the authority of Pennsylvania and New York to emit paper currency, has been viewed "as a move to safeguard British investments in America, a move dictated by metropolitan, not colonial, needs."[21] In the northern port towns, especially New York and Philadelphia, the hard money drain was a fact of life, for no other way of making up for an excess of imports over exports existed than to ship gold and silver to the mother country. Locally issued paper money thus provided the circulating medium of local trade. When it was disallowed, internal trade shriveled up, hurting merchant and artisan alike and obliging traders to concoct ingenious schemes for issuing fiat money that might gain legislative approval and escape royal notice.[22] The years from 1767 to 1769 were especially difficult in this regard, with a number of Boston merchants, including John Hancock's younger brother, closing their doors and Philadelphians stunned by the collapse of Baynton, Wharton and Morgan, one of the city's largest houses, with liabilities of £94,000.[23]

Another aspect of the monetary problem was the erratic flow of British credit after the Seven Years War. Eyeing the dynamic growth of the colonial population, English and Scottish merchants at first vastly increased credit sales to American importers in order to spur the consumption of British goods. American merchants willingly increased their orders and passed their indebtedness on to retailers and consumers as book credit, where it became, in effect, a part of the colonial supply of money. Accepting credit in order to expand was not in itself a disadvantageous policy for the Americans, but it made borrowers far more vulnerable to cyclical swings in the British credit structure. Hence, during the English financial crises of 1762 and 1772, when sharp business contractions obliged British lenders to "repatriate their colonial assets," many seaboard merchants who were unable to meet the demands of their overseas creditors went bankrupt.

The credit crisis of 1772 was especially severe. Touched off by the collapse of a major London banking house in June of that year, it spread like a brushfire.[24] The bankruptcy rate doubled and panic reverberated throughout the Atlantic world, causing a "marked deterioration" of "debtor-creditor relations between the thirteen colonies and the mother country."[25] The scramble for liquidity was greatest among the southern planters, whose level of indebtedness was the highest in the colonies. But the northern commercial centers were also hard hit. Many merchants, through no fault of their own as they saw it, in fact because of forces entirely beyond their control, found themselves pinched. Haled into court for settlement of accounts and committed to debtors prison when they could not pay up, they began to lose faith in the violently cyclical behavior of the Anglo-American commercial system.[26]

The ultimate concern of merchants was profit itself. All other matters —vendue sales, currency supply, and credit—impinged upon the profit margin. Almost all of the new machinery for enforcing new commercial policies, including the reinvigorated customs service and strict new procedures for trying trade law violators in the admiralty courts, seemed to cut into profits. A number of merchants, as their inventories of estate testify, continued to flourish and a few, especially in Philadelphia, even amassed unprecedented fortunes. But for many more the road to commercial success seemed strewn with obstacles. Parliamentary legislation threatened the economic world that they had known and called into question the existing understanding of the proper relation of the colonies to the metropolis.[27]

To point out the tremendous concern of the merchants for the changes being imposed on their commercial life is not to maintain that their quarrel with England was not also over constitutional and natural rights. In fact, there was no compartmentalization in their minds between England's onerous new economic regulation and its encroachment upon the political rights of American subjects. Merchants saw a coordinated attack on their "lives, liberties, and property," as they so frequently phrased it, and in this juxtaposition of constitutional and material concerns can be seen the essential unity of their motives.[28] Thus John Dickinson, whose *The Late Regulations Respecting the British Colonies* (1765) was a straightforward indictment of English policy "on grounds of material self-interest narrowly defined," was also the author, two years later, of *Letters from a Farmer in Pennsylvania*, one of the most cogent constitutional arguments advanced in the prerevolutionary decade.[29] Dickinson had not changed but had penned two pamphlets that, while distinctly different in their thrust, were both part of an outlook where economic interest and ideological principles were so closely interwoven as to become virtually inseparable.

For the laboring classes economic life after 1765 was not always determined in the same ways as for merchants and shopkeepers, although there was often coincidence of interests. The sudden contraction of a merchant's credit meant demands upon artisans to settle accounts. If work had been slow, a laboring man in debt could find himself in court or even in debtors prison, where his problems quickly compounded because his earning power was then brought to a dead halt. But vendue sales, hated by many merchants, meant the availability of cheaper imported goods. Trade doldrums hurt merchants, artisans, and mariners, but they also tended to drive land values and house rents down, which eased budgetary pressures on laboring people who rented rooms or houses. The two ultimate arbiters of the artisan's existence were the availability of work and the purchasing power of his wages. Yet they are precisely the subjects about which we know the least. It will take much more research by historians to unearth enough detail to form a comprehensive understanding of these matters, but enough is already at hand to discern the outline of the problem and to chart the direction of change.

Even in the best of times seaport artisans understood that there was no such thing as full employment. In the preindustrial age the craftsman had no defense against inclement weather, shortage of working materials, lingering illness, and cyclical money shortage among employers and customers. The record of one ship carpenter who worked near Boston may have been typical: out of 710 consecutive days he worked only 296. Benjamin Rush noted in 1769 that few Philadelphia artisans were employed "the whole year around" because of the intermittency of consumer demand.[30]

The economic volatility of the late colonial period accentuated the uncertainty of the craftsman's work rhythms. When the postwar commercial depression bottomed out early in 1765, hopes revived for better times. But within a year substantial unemployment was reported in all the port towns. The Philadelphia Grand Jury lamented early in 1766 that many of "the labouring People, and others in low circumstances . . . who are willing to work, cannot obtain sufficient Employment to support themselves and their Families."[31] Reports of unemployment continued in 1767 and 1768, and by the end of the latter year forced sales of property reached an all-time high.[32] In New York "A Tradesman" complained bitterly in 1767 about unemployment and the suffering that must surely attend it. "What a dismal Prospect is before us: a long Winter, and no Work; many unprovided with Fire-wood, or Money to buy it; House-Rent, and Taxes high; our Neighbours daily breaking, their Furniture at Vendue on every Corner."[33] The situation reached its nadir in 1769 when New York property values declined by one-half or more and the prison bulged with insolvent debtors. Unemployment was still widespread in early 1770 when moonlighting British troops, working for cut-rate wages, brought a storm of protest from the artisan class.[34] In the same year a friend of Governor Hutchinson found many of the Boston laboring people "almost starving for want of Employment" and believed that in their desperation they would soon be "going to plunder the Rich and then cutting their throats."[35]

Commercial revival came later in 1770. But two years later the contraction of British credit was felt from the top to the bottom of the social scale. "Daily accounts of heavy failures among the Shopkeepers" were reported in Philadelphia in October 1773.[36] Unemployment spread again and the jails filled to overflowing with formerly respectable citizens who could not pay their debts. It is one of the ironies of the era that among the architectural wonders of Philadelphia and New York, admired by visiting Europeans on the eve of the war, were the spacious Walnut Street Prison in Philadelphia and Bridewell in New York, both of them built in the closing years of the colonial era because the existing jails could no longer hold the flocks of hungry inhabitants who stole for a living and the hundreds of tradesmen (and a few merchants as well) who were hustled behind bars for their inability to meet their creditors' demands.[37]

Another sign of economic difficulties was the rapid abandonment of bound labor in the last two decades of the colonial era. Bound labor may have become less prevalent because in hard times the amount of capital held by merchants and artisans fell, leaving them unable to purchase new servants as the indentures of former bondsmen expired. Among those who could still contract for the labor of others there was a growing preference for free labor. In uncertain times, those who still possessed the resources to command the labor of others learned that they were better off hiring labor when they needed it while remaining free of the obligation to maintain unremunerative workers during dull periods. A pool of free, floating contractable laborers better served the needs of small manufacturers and master artisans, although bound laborers who served as house servants were irreplaceable among the elite as symbols of affluence.

The importation of slaves dropped off sharply at the end of the Seven Years War in all three northern towns. By 1768 importations had virtually ceased in Philadelphia and Boston and the town meeting in the latter city was instructing its representatives to advocate the total abolition of the slave trade. In Philadelphia the number of slaves fell by almost half between 1767 and 1775 and the proportion of laboring males who were unfree dropped from about 60 to 35 percent.[38] In New York, where slaves had constituted about 20 percent of the population and 23.5 percent of the adult males in the 1730s and 1740s, they made up only 14 percent of the city's inhabitants and 15 percent of the adult males by 1771. In Boston the number of slaves dropped from 1,544 in 1752 to 811 in 1765 and probably fell below 500 by the outbreak of the war. Immigrating indentured servants entered the city at a trickle. On the eve of the Revolution bound laborers made up no more than 15 percent of those who labored with their hands.[39]

While employers phased out bound labor, artisans also helped to usher in a new labor system. As times grew hard, their resentment of slave labor competition increased. It is no coincidence that the strongest attacks on slavery in the prerevolutionary decade, excluding those by Quakers, who had made abolition a central part of their reformist zeal since the 1750s, were those by artisan spokesmen in the port towns such as James Otis and Nathaniel Appleton in Boston and Benjamin Rush and Thomas Paine in Philadelphia. Opposition to slavery was a part of the equalitarian message they were spreading; and for some, such as Rush, it fit perfectly with the evangelical insistence that American society must be reformed. While these early abolitionists were doubtlessly inspired by humanitarian concern for black slaves, we should not dissociate the appeal of their message in laboring-class quarters from the growing concern for economic security.[40] Nor should we overlook the demise of paternalist labor relations that was signified by those slave owners who answered the abolitionists' pleas by setting free their aged or infirm slaves who could no longer work, thus saving the shilling per day that it cost to feed a worthless laborer. This forced freedom became extensive enough in New York in 1773 for the legislature to pass a law imposing a £20 fine on the last owner of a freedman beggar—a measure taken more to keep the relief rolls down than to guarantee humane treatment for worn-out slaves.[41] Paternalistic relations between employer and worker, either black or white, were giving way to a system where cooler calculations of supply and demand governed the labor market and wage rates were determined not by custom but by market conditions.

The availability of work in the port towns was affected in one other entirely unprecedented way in the final decade before independence. Three times—in 1765-1766, 1767-1770, and 1774-1775—the three northern ports attempted to concert themselves in pledging not to consume or import British goods until their grievances were redressed. Tricity cooperation was never fully achieved but all the ports, for greater or lesser periods, curbed importations from England.[42] These boycotts hampered a number of artisans who relied on imported materials such as glass, glue, and certain metals but gave prospects for fuller employment to a far larger number of craftsmen whose domestic handicrafts were stimulated when English goods were banned. The "buy American" campaigns, which were initially designed to force repeal of odious English legislation, thus moved far beyond their original purpose. They became remedies for unemployment, raised embryonic visions of economic nationalism, and created the idea that artisans, through forging political pressure groups, could influence public policy in ways that enhanced their earning power. Hundreds of newspaper appeals to patriotism by artisans during a decade of dispute with England show that for laboring people, as for merchants, a concern for political rights was merged with efforts to solve economic problems.[43]

Whether he had employment or not, every artisan and laborer measured out his slender income in terms of the basic necessities of life that had to be purchased and the nearly fixed expenses, such as rent and taxes, that had to be paid. In an earlier chapter we examined how escalating food prices in the early 1760s placed those in the lower ranks of society in dire straits. Now, as the dispute with England became more acrimonious, the movement of prices made their final cyclical swing. In Philadelphia food costs began to drop in 1765 and reached a low point— still considerably above the level of the 1750s—in 1769. Then they began a climactic five-year climb that elevated the cost of a weighted nineteen-item diet 23 percent from 1769 to 1774. The managers of Philadelphia's Bettering House complained in the following year that they were paying twice as much for food items as they had in previous years.[44] New York prices followed a similar trend: a modest decline in the mid-1760s and then another punishing upswing at the beginning of the 1770s.[45]

The sharp rise in the price of provisions in New York and Philadelphia can be explained primarily by the conjunction of heavy foreign demand for grain during the early 1770s and a series of meager crops in the colonial wheat belt. With demand outstripping supply wheat reached 8 shillings per bushel in the summer of 1772 and flour rose to 20 shillings— double the prevailing prices of fifteen years before.[46] To make matters worse, the price peak nearly coincided with the second major commercial downturn of the period, which began in 1772 after the sudden contraction of British credit created a ripple effect all along the seaboard. Just as in the deep slump from 1760 to 1764, the recession came at a time when food costs for laboring families were rising sharply. There was no general *crise de subsistance*, but the situation was serious enough for the Philadelphia overseers of the poor to distribute thousands of loaves of bread.[47]

The cost of other items in the household budget—firewood, rent, and clothing—remained fairly stable during the waning years before war. But there was little respite from the taxes of the war period except in New York after 1767. In Massachusetts and Pennsylvania the huge war debt had to be retired by provincial land taxes scheduled into the 1770s and heavy local taxes were required to keep up with climbing poor relief expenses.[48]

As in the depression of the early 1760s, wage rates often failed to keep pace with price hikes and in fact fell among the least skilled laborers. Philadelphia's mariners, whose wages during the Seven Years War had risen to an all-time high of £4 and even £5 per month, saw their pay drop to traditional levels of £3 to £3.5 per month by 1763. Henceforth, the high level of immigration, which insured a plentiful supply of seagoing men, kept wages at this level.[49] Boston's mariners toiled for similar wages, which, even if berths had been available for twelve months a year, would not have provided the £35 sterling per annum that represented the minimum cost of board and lodging according to one newcomer to the town in 1771.[50] New York's mariners, who had commanded 5 shillings a day by 1758 and 6 shillings in the following year, also returned to the traditional £2 to £3 per month, a 50 percent decrease from the wartime heyday.[51] Laborers fared no better. The wartime boom had lifted their daily wage to 4 shillings and occasionally a bit higher. But amidst rising unemployment wages began falling in the mid-1760s. By 1769 laborers averaged barely 3 shillings per day in Philadelphia; in the early 1770s they were unable to earn even this much. With new immigrants arriving almost weekly and so many idle hands available, employers had no difficulty finding workers at these rates. The same laws of supply and demand that drove food prices up were driving wage rates down. A careful study of these trends shows that the earning power of Philadelphia's dock workers, chimney sweeps, watchmen, wood cutters, well diggers, street scavengers, porters, and the like fell a full 30 percent between the height of the Seven Years War and the outbreak of the Revolution.[52]

Wage levels in the building trades, at least in Philadelphia, remained stable in the last decade before the Revolution. Bricklayers, for example, who had averaged about 12 shillings per thousand bricks before 1755, customarily received 14 to 16 shillings per thousand during the Seven Years War and were able to hold on to these gains through the 1760s and 1770s. Stone masons' wages showed almost no movement, averaging about 4 shillings per perch from the 1720s on, although a few stonecutters who were engaged to do difficult jobs received somewhat more. Carpenters were the most successful of the building artisans in keeping wages abreast of price levels. Master carpenters, who commanded from 4 to 6 shillings a day in the first half of the century, increased their wages in the late 1750s to 6 to 7 shillings per day and may have done slightly better after the Peace of Paris.[53]

In the face of severe budgetary pressures it is not surprising that the seaport towns witnessed the most intense period of organizing in their history. Nor should it surprise us that those who were able to organize and present united fronts were best able to obtain higher wages. Two examples will suffice. Philadelphia's ship captains, who were closely tied to merchant shipowners, were able to protect the £7 (local currency) per month wage they had achieved during the Seven Years War throughout the remainder of the colonial period. The wages of ordinary seamen fell substantially, but those of ship captains did not. Without a master who could not only ply the seas but also operate skillfully in disposing of his cargo in the tricky West Indian markets no merchant's investment was worth much. Hence, sea captains were in a far better position to resist the erosion of their earning power. Operating from strength, they organized the Society for the Relief of Poor and Distressed Masters of Ships in 1765. Presumably a "friendly society" with charitable and fraternal purposes, the society, like its predecessor in Boston, the Marine Society of Boston in New England, seems to have played an important role in maintaining the £7 per month wage.[54]

Carpenters were also able to organize effectively and it is here that "the boundary line between the friendly society and the trade union came to be extremely shadowy."[55] Philadelphia's master carpenters had been organized since the 1720s and their most important function was fixing prices for "all new-fashioned Carpenter work." But in the difficult days of the 1760s, Philadelphia's journeymen carpenters, who most frequently hired out to master craftsmen, established their own company and attempted to set rates that would allow them a decent living. New York's carpenters organized in 1767 and Boston's some time before 1750. Philadelphia's ship carpenters were also organized effectively and we can presume that the political unity they displayed in 1765 in protecting the houses of Franklin and Hughes was matched by comparable solidarity on economic questions. As the Revolution approached organized artisans were able to obtain a measure of wage security.[56]

Within crafts that were less strategically located in the urban economy or whose members were less able to concert themselves, the struggle to keep wages abreast of rising prices usually met with less success. Many artisans contested the erosion of their economic security. Philadelphia's tailors organized in 1771. Three years earlier, journeymen tailors in New York struck because of a "late Reduction of . . . Wages" and announced that they could not support their families when their compensation was cut below 3.5 shillings per day with diet. Boston's butchers and tanners obtained "minimum-wage agreements" in 1766.[57] But Philadelphia's cordwainers, who relied on a small number of merchants for the hides they used in their trades, had little success in convincing the assembly in 1769 that their merchant suppliers, having engrossed the market and jacked up prices in order to inflate their own profits, ought to be regulated.[58] The cordwainers organized a craft guild in 1760, only faintly disguised by the title of Cordwainers Fire Company, and Philadelphia's tailors drew together in 1771 in order to fix prices at levels that would guarantee a decent subsistence. Neither of these groups, standing on the bottom rungs of the occupational ladder, had enough internal cohesion to achieve their goals. The reason was not only that "business in the clothing and leather trades was both highly competitive and easy to enter" but also that these were economic sectors where merchants controlled the supply of raw materials and could rarely be bested, either in the legislature when price-fixing regulation was sought or in the informal realm of daily face-to-face transactions.[59] In a period of general difficulties, men who worked in the least skilled occupations—mariners, laborers, cordwainers, tailors, and coopers—had far less success than those who occupied positions higher in the occupational hierarchy. This trend inexorably drove a wedge in the laboring classes, separating struggling lower artisans, who suffered greatly in the 1760s and 1770s, from upper artisans, who were able to maintain a degree of economic security and even forge ahead in some cases.

This internal stratification of the artisans, which had important political ramifications, can be seen in the occupational composition of Philadelphia's impoverished citizens in 1772. By that year 24 percent of the city's mariners, laborers, sawyers, and carters were receiving some form of poor relief. Among cordwainers the rate was 17 percent and among clothing workers, including breechesmakers, tailors, and weavers, it was 13 percent. In the better organized building construction trades only 9 percent of the artisans received relief and among those in maritime construction only 7 percent.[60] Patterns of house ownership display the same tendency. Only one of twelve mariners, one of nine laborers, and one of seven cordwainers, weavers, tailors, and breechesmakers owned a house. Among butchers, bakers, and the panoply of trades associated with house and ship construction the rate was one in three.[61] Escape from poverty was not guaranteed to anyone—even 9 of Philadelphia's 341 merchants were classified as poor—but the economic disorders of the late colonial period were clearly dividing the laboring ranks (where status differentiation had always been known) into those for whom poverty or marginal subsistence was endemic and those for whom economic security, however much it was threatened in this era, was usually possible.

In studying the momentous events that carried Americans into Revolution historians have understandably concentrated their attention on the dramatic events of the decade after the Stamp Act riots: New York's resistance to the Quartering Act of 1765, the Townshend Acts of 1767 and the nonimportation movement that followed them, the occupation of Boston by British troops in 1768, the Boston Massacre of 1770, the Tea Act of 1773 and the subsequent Tea Party, the Intolerable Acts of 1774, the convening of the Continental Congress late in that year, and, finally, the outbreak of armed hostility at Lexington and Concord in the spring of 1775. These were the events that occupied center stage in the unfolding drama. But beneath the surface social processes were at work that help us understand the origins of the American Revolution.

One important social change was the impoverishment of large segments of the urban populations. It is not necessary to promote the urban poor into the forefront of radical politics or to claim that the American Revolution was an uprising of the dispossessed in order to argue the importance of this pauperization to the general populace in the port towns. By and large those who reluctantly went to the almshouses or gratefully accepted out-relief from overseers of the poor were not actively involved in the radical movement. Many of them, including widows, children, the sick and elderly, were politically inert; among those who were not, political activism was usually limited to turning out for street demonstrations and other crowd actions. Such activities were, to be sure, indispensable to the patriot movement. But we must distinguish these people from the wage-earning laborers and mariners, and from the artisans, small shopkeepers, and struggling professionals who joined the Sons of Liberty, threw tea into Boston harbor, and enforced the nonimportation agreements. The impoverishment of the lower quarter or third of society was important to these middling men also because the spread of poverty at the bottom of society was accompanied by signs of crumbling economic security within the middling ranks. In their eyes, when indigency befell a large portion of the lowest laboring ranks, not simply the aged and infirm, it signified sickness in the body economic as surely as corruption foretold putridness in the body politic.

It would be inaccurate to depict the port towns as scenes of massive misery in the final decade of the colonial period. Overall, they remained dynamic commercial centers of a rapidly growing seaboard population. Ships entered and cleared the northern ports at record rates in these years and this high level of commercial activity spread rewards to the homes of many.[62] These signs of vigor cannot, however, disguise the fact that penury was the lot of a growing segment of the community and economic insecurity hovered at the doors of many more. This was evident in rising poor taxes, the overcrowding of the new almshouses, increases in forced sales of property and imprisonment for debt, and the rise of ethnic and occupational friendly societies which administered to hundreds of formerly "respectable" people whose pride would not allow them to be taken from their homes to workhouses and almshouses. Yet for all that was done to provide for the poor, the problem grew worse. Poor families sold their crude furniture on street corners in order to feed themselves, and when the furniture was gone simply broke into shops to steal the necessities of life.[63]

Urban poverty challenged the governing modes of thought in the northern towns, shook confidence in the internal economic system, and intensified class feeling. "He that gets all he can honestly, and saves all he gets (necessary Expenses excepted)," Poor Richard never tired of saying, "will certainly become RICH."[64] Laboring Bostonians had long before learned that this was an illusion and by 1772 it could provide no comfort for a growing pauper class in Franklin's city.

Local leaders had to face economic malaise just as surely as they had to confront English threats to American liberties. Hence, while Samuel Adams was dispensing impassioned rhetoric about British tyranny and the erosion of the rights of free-born English subjects in Boston, Overseers of the Poor Samuel Whitwell and Samuel Abbot were dispensing out-relief to 15 percent of the householders in their wards and sending others to the workhouse or almshouse.[65] New Yorkers learned about the Tea Act in 1773, at the same time their newspapers apprised them of a wave of thefts and breaking into shops and pointed out that 425 souls were jostling for space in the overcrowded almshouse while hundreds of others lived on out-relief.[66] The entire discussion of American constitutional rights, in other words, was carried out in urban locales where nagging poverty at the bottom of society and the crumbling of economic security in the middle gave rise to the most intense concern about the future and created a crisis in class relations.

URBAN WHIG LEADERS were embattled on two fronts: as they attempted to maintain control over the growing resistance against England, they also had to find solutions to local economic problems. In Philadelphia the attempt to come to grips with the burgeoning poverty problems began in 1763 when the assembly debated ways to reorganize the poor relief system. For three years the issue lay unresolved, probably because most of the rural legislators were not interested in expending provincial tax moneys to build a bigger almshouse and workhouse in Philadelphia. In 1764 a group of merchants raised subscriptions to erect a linen manufactory. By winter several hundred people were at work. But the project died within two years because it could not produce quality sail cloth, linen, and ticking as cheaply as English imports available in the shops.[67]

Two years later a group of Quaker merchants proposed a striking new plan for administering relief. The taxpayers, they argued, were now supporting a record 220 paupers in the overcrowded almshouse, the poor rates had become "extremely burdensome," and the linen manufactory was failing. Rather than hike poor taxes again, they proposed to incorporate a group of private citizens who, in return for raising a substantial sum for the construction of a large new almshouse and workhouse, would be given nearly complete control over the management of the poor. Calling themselves the Contributors to the Relief and Employment of the Poor and modeling their plan after the successful Pennsylvania Hospital for the Sick Poor, they proposed a new institution for the indigent. The "Bettering House," as it came to be called, would consist of an almshouse for the aged and disabled and a workhouse for the able-bodied poor. Into the workhouse would go all out-pensioners who had formerly received direct cash payments from the overseers of the poor. Gathered together, they could be clothed and fed inexpensively. More important, they could contribute to their own maintenance. The assembly, grateful that Philadelphians were proposing to solve their own problem, gladly consented.[68]

The Bettering House that rose on Spruce Street has been seen by historians as an expression of the charitable instincts of Philadelphians, especially of the Quakers who supplied the chief impetus for the new system.[69] The Society of Friends had early assumed a leading role in charitable work and now provided the fund raisers, most of the subscriptions, the architect, the builder, many of the construction artisans, and most of the managers of the new institution.[70] The historical focus has been on the building and its public-minded creators, not on the economic changes that were impoverishing the lower class or the shift in ideology that was now placing poor relief, heretofore conceived of as a public responsibility, in private hands. Although in some ways it was a monument to the philanthropic impulses of Philadelphia's Quakers, the Bettering House must also be understood as a response to the swelling ranks of immigrant and itinerant poor who were seeking work in the city, the increasing cost of relief, and the spreading notion that poor rates were rising because more and more people were content to live the life of the idler, the profligate, or the street beggar rather than pursue an honest trade. The Bettering House was, in fact, a cross between Boston's workhouse, whose book of rules the Quaker managers purchased, and the linen manufactory of the 1750s. Quaker leaders adopted a plan that was strikingly similar to the one which had proved a failure 300 miles to the north.[71]

The new approach to poverty in Philadelphia was not peculiar to Quakers, for the hand of Benjamin Franklin is highly visible in the organization of the Bettering House. As early as 1753, while in England, he had expressed the view that nothing was more responsible for creating poverty than poor relief itself—the view of Defoe and other English thinkers more than a half-century before.[72] Appointed to the assembly committee for reorganizing the poor law in 1763 and another for erecting a workhouse in 1764, Franklin was no doubt carefully heard, for he had an unmatched reputation as an architect of problem-solving urban institutions. The core of his thought can be grasped from letters he wrote shortly after his return to England in 1765. In response to warnings that the impending Stamp Act would increase the economic woes of an already straitened economy, Franklin replied that though the new tax would hurt a bit, "Frugality and Industry will go a great way towards indemnifying us." Shifting the onus to the laboring people of his city, Franklin added that "Idleness and Pride Tax with a heavier Hand then [sic] Kings and Parliaments."[73] Later in the year, angered when the London poor mobbed grain wagons in order to prevent wheat exports at a time when bread was scarce, Franklin publicly advised that "the more public provisions were made for the poor, the less they provided for themselves, and of course became poorer. And, on the contrary, the less was done for them, the more they did for themselves, and became richer." Because England led the world in caring for the poor, she also led the world in the creation of poverty. Repeal the poor laws by which the indigent were supported, he advised, and the poor would go back to work, abandoning the new national holidays they had proclaimed—St. Monday and St. Tuesday.[74]

Franklin's drastic proposal to eliminate poor relief was not adopted in Philadelphia, but the spirit behind his proposals was embodied in the decision to turn over to the Quaker merchants the management of the poor relief system with a new Bettering House as its centerpiece. Even the name of the institution indicated the growing tendency to regard the poor as flawed members of society who needed to be reformed rather than relieved. Confronting unprecedented economic dislocation, Philadelphia's leaders proposed to reduce the cost of caring for those who could not work, while rehabilitating the morals of those who would not work. "Employment and Wages to the diligent" would be provided and "the idle and slothful" "compelled to perform such Labour as might be best adapted to their Circumstances."[75] The old familial system of relieving want now gave way fo nonfamilial institutions—a change that reflected the emergence of the new social order.

Controlling the disbursement of all funds gathered under the poor tax laws, the Bettering House managers worked to end the payment of out-pensions by the overseers of the poor. "No person," warned the managers, "shall be paid any sum of Money by way of pensions out of the poor's fund (except in cases of extreme Sickness, Ages & of which the Managers shall have cognizance), but on examination if any person is entitled to the benefits of the Alms-house they shall be obliged to remove therein."[76] The managers were not able to stick to the letter of their announcement, but they drastically curtailed out-relief after the Bettering House opened in the fall of 1767. They faced considerable resistance to this policy, but in June 1769 decided to end "the Out-Pensions which they alledged would be a saving of the Publick moneys & be the Means of Obliging the Poor to come into the House of Employment & Alms-house."[77] Attempting to use fully their expensive and commodious new building, the Bettering House managers channeled all but about 15 percent of relief moneys into the institutional relief of people compelled to quit their abodes.[78]

The decision to end out-relief drew the managers into a heated dispute with the overseers of the poor. Drawn mostly from the ranks of established artisans and usually not members of the Society of Friends, the overseers were far closer to the needy in their neighborhoods. They understood the resentment of the non-Quaker poor who were being herded into a Quaker-dominated institution for their moral betterment. The fact that the Quakers had few poor of their own, since they were the best established economic group in the city and cared for their own indigent in a small Quaker almshouse, may have made the new policy all the more obnoxious.[79] By early 1768, less than six months after the Bettering House had opened its doors, the Quaker managers were complaining that the overseers were lax in levying and collecting the poor tax and were too influenced by the "Humours or Caprice of the People of their Respective Districts." What was really at issue was the attempt of the

Bettering House managers to force the poor into their institution. They had been stripped of their power to distribute out-relief, the overseers retorted, and were being pressured to send to the Bettering House persons who might make it through the winter with small sums of money and some firewood. Two years later the dispute still raged. The overseers objected to carting the infirm and aged to the Bettering House, decried the "Cruelty" of "breaking up many Familys" by sending members behind closed doors, and pointed out that because the Quaker managers were segregating men and women many husbands and wives were being miserably committed "to Live in a Separate State."[80]

Under attack, the Quaker managers issued a report to "silence the Clamours of the Mistaken and Captious who are endeavouring to lessen the Credit and thereby hurt the Usefulness of this Institution." They had placed hundreds of inmates under careful moral management, deprived them of "the use of Spiritous Liquors," taught them to work, and restored them to health.[81] Further to improve their public image, the managers started issuing annual reports containing statistics on inmate production. Those who read the fine print, however, would have noticed that, contrary to expectations, it was proving impossible to work the poor at a profit. The managers expended more each year to procure materials for manufacture and pay supervisory salaries than they received from selling the products of the inmates' labor.[82]

By 1775, after half a dozen years of controversy, all parties were thoroughly disillusioned: the Quaker managers, the overseers of the poor, the taxpayers, and the poor themselves. Robert Honyman, an English doctor, was surprised when a number of women "begged me to try to get them out" of what he had heard was a model institution.[83] The overseers of the poor, never reconciled to the abandonment of the familial relief system, engaged in a kind of sabotage by refusing to press their straitened neighbors for poor tax payments. Even though the managers of the Bettering House were able to obtain legislation in 1771 for imposing heavy penalties on delinquent overseers, tax collections fell further and further behind.[84] The rising price of provisions, in a period when the income derived from the poor taxes grew only slightly, reduced what the managers had to work with. As for the reform of dissolute persons, the Quaker philanthropists simply gave up. The poor entered the Bettering House, then ran away, and were returned "mostly as sick, naked, and burthensome as at first, and proceed this way with Impunity, as often as they please." Work could be extracted from few of them and so, the managers confessed, they "are entirely dead Weight."[85]

The attempts to deal with the poor revealed the limitations of Whig ideology as it applied not only to resisting new parliamentary policies but to internal social problems as well. Whig political theory had come to place a tremendous importance on natural rights, including the right to "unlimited individual appropriation."[86] In the American environment, especially in Philadelphia, where opportunity had been widespread for almost two generations before the end of the Seven Years War, this ideology of "possessive individualism" found widespread acceptance. Hard work and frugality had led to material success, not only for merchants, professionals, and extraordinary lower-class sons such as Benjamin Franklin, but also for scores of artisans. Hence, when poverty began to spread, the best established part of the community, whose ideas had been formed in a different economic milieu, subscribed fully to Franklin's notion, which was thoroughly Lockean, that "the best way of doing good to the poor is not making them easy *in* poverty, but leading or driving them *out* of it."[87]

The response of the poor tells much about how the concentration of cultural authority in the upper class was being deeply shaken in this troubled era. The poor—and many artisans who had not yet ascended so far as to lose touch with the problems besetting those at the bottom— staunchly resisted the ideology reflected in the Bettering House solution to poverty, even though it had the support of a wide range of city leaders. No amount of exhorting could convince the poor of the relevancy of maxims written in an era of full employment and lower prices. Aphorisms such as "God Helps those who help themselves" and "At the working man's house hunger looks in but dares not enter" continued to appear in *Poor Richard's Almanack* on the eve of the Revolution, but they applied little to the life situations facing the laboring poor.[88] Such people looked elsewhere for solutions as the poor have always done. The less rooted drifted in and out of Philadelphia in search of work, though that became more difficult after 1771 when a strict new residency law took effect. Those who had known better days and regarded themselves as respectable "declared in a Solemn manner that they would rather perish through want" than go to the Bettering House.[89] They scraped by as best they could, aided by friends, churches, and charitable societies. Those who could not escape confinement did as little labor as possible within the walls.[90] Never had the Philadelphia gentry committed themselves so fully to solving an urban problem, only to find that the recipients of their aid felt precious little gratitude and in fact strenuously resisted their moral management.

The failure of the poor to play the role assigned to them tells much about the deep fissures that were appearing in northern urban society. In New York, rather than acting the part of grateful supplicants, the poor looked to the affluent as an exploiting class that owed them relief, not because charity required it but because justice demanded it. It was the poor, one of their spokesmen wrote in 1769, "who, by their Industry heretofore, have contributed so much to make our Circumstances easy: It is to the meaner Class of Mankind, the industrious Poor, that so many of us are indebted for those goodly Dwellings we inhabit, for that comfortable Substance we enjoy, while others are languishing under the disagreeable Sensations of Penury and Want." The poor too often were treated as "objects of charity." Instead, they should be looked upon as "subjects of, or Dependents on our Justice."[91] Other writers pointed to the class injustice represented by the astounding increase in expensive carriages in New York—from five to seventy in four years after the Peace of Paris—while at the same time laboring people were selling their household goods to pay rents to rich landlords.[92]

IN ALL the northern seaports poverty and unemployment also inspired new attempts to do what had proved impossible in Boston in the 1750s: erect large buildings, fill them with spinning wheels and looms, recruit cheap labor, and manufacture cloth at a profit. What gave new hope to the promoters of these schemes were the nonimportation movements, which they believed would raise the demand for domestically produced cloth out of patriotic sentiment, and the shortage of English-produced material.[93] The hope of providing employment for the poor converged neatly with the desire to lower poor taxes and the effort to use economic boycott to pressure England into repealing repugnant policies. The problematic nature of these efforts tells much about the patriotism of the American consumer, the attitudes of investors in these private corporations, and the responses of those who were depended upon to bend their backs to a new kind of routinized, factory labor.

During the first nonimportation movement, which accompanied the Stamp Act protests, merchants in New York and Philadelphia set up cloth manufactories and recruited several hundred poor women to work there. Philadelphia's merchant elite subscribed more than £5,000, making theirs the best capitalized manufactory ever launched in the colonies. Both factories collapsed when the resumption of English imports in 1766 flooded urban markets with better quality goods and consumers made their preferences known.[94]

All three port towns tried cloth manufacturing again during the second nonimportation movement. New Yorkers revived their Society for Promoting Arts, Agriculture and Economy and employed "above three hundred poor and necessitous persons" by early 1768. In Philadelphia, the managers of the new Bettering House pre-empted the field by purchasing "sundry Looms, Wheels, Sleigh Geers, Shuttles &c" from the defunct linen manufactory and setting the poor to work. From the investors' point of view they had achieved the ideal situation: a captive labor force that worked without any wages and actually lived in the factory, which is what they intended the Bettering House to be.[95]

Boston moved more slowly. A committee appointed in October 1767 to study "what manufacture could . . . give a constant employ to the poor" reported that it was bootless to repeat the mistakes of the previous decades when the poor demonstrated that they would not work away from their homes for crumbs. The committee returned in January 1768 with a plan for using the old Manufactory House for the production of sail cloth and obtained the town's permission to proceed. But they did not get the £3,000 interest-free loan they requested and met a stone wall of opposition from Boston's wealthy. A promotional broadside was distributed and "Personal application [was made] to almost every Inhabitant that the Committee apprehended was of Ability to afford any Assistance." A mere £150 in pledges was all that could be secured and the scheme died aborning.[96]

Fund raising in Boston was no doubt crippled in part by the disillusionment with the earlier attempt at employing the poor. Many of the wealthy also saw it as an instrument of radical politics. The linen manufactory of the 1750s had been capitalized and directed primarily by the prerogative group, whose disdain for the lower class probably had something to do with the unwillingness of the poor to contribute their bodies to the experiment. The new scheme was directed by John Barrett, Meletiah Bourne, Edward Payne, Henderson Inches, and Ezekiel Goldthwait, all of them substantial merchants who had been involved in protest against the Revenue and Townshend Acts. For conservatives what could be the appeal of a plan to employ the poor under the supervision of those who might use them—or their husbands, brothers, and sons—as stone-throwing, property-destroying, law-defying crowds when they were not spinning and weaving? Peter Oliver, brother of Boston's stamp distributor, wrote contemptuously that the new clothmaking enterprise was "another scheme" concocted by the radicals "to keep up the Ball of Contention."[97]

In March 1769 the town meeting again considered "methods for employing the Poor." This time a committee proposed to teach large numbers of women and children to spin.[98] The new plan differed from its predecessors in several regards. First, no suggestion was made that the women and children should actually work in the manufactory; the presumption is strong that they were to remain in their homes, spinning yarn as household routines allowed. Second, the man who stepped forward to manage the project was William Molineux, one of the most important radical leaders in Boston. The fifth son of a prominent Dublin physician, Molineux had come to Boston in the 1740s and developed a substantial business as a hardware merchant. He suffered badly in the post-1760 depression. Never before involved in politics, he now entered the public arena and rose rapidly in radical Whig circles. As a key member of the radical infrastructure—he belonged to the North End Caucus, the Monday Night Club, the Long Room Club, and the Sons of Liberty— Molineux played a role second only to Samuel Adams in devising and coordinating strategies for thwarting Bernard's and Hutchinson's at-

11. View of Boston in 1774 by Paul Revere.

tempts to uphold royal policy. Whenever the crowd swung into action or whenever confrontations were staged with the governor or Tory merchants who refused to comply with the nonimportation agreements, Molineux was at the head of the crowd. Whereas the shoemaker MacIntosh had named his son Pascale Paoli after the Corsican revolutionary, the new director of Boston's legion of poor spinners was himself known as "Paoli" Molineaux.[99]

In March 1769 the town meeting voted an outright grant of £200 and a loan of £300 for Molineux to "hire School Mistresses to teach as many Persons to spin as are desirous to learn." He spent most of the money (and, according to Molineux, another £1,100, of his own) to build about four hundred spinning wheels and to repair the decayed Manufactory House. In the first year, "at least 300 Children and Women" learned to spin "in the most Compleat manner" and turned out 40,000 skeins of "fine Yarn, to make any kind of Women's wear." Next, Molineux built warping and twisting machines, looms for weaving cloth, hot and cold presses for finishing the material, and a dye house. Shortly after the town appointed him to a committee to confront Lieutenant Governor Hutchinson on the government's role in the Boston Massacre, the General Court granted Molineux a long-term, rent-free lease on the Manufactory House and £500 for the money he had advanced. Although the enterprise then became entangled in arguments between the council and House of Representatives and Hutchinson refused to sign the final bill, the manufactory continued under the House's auspices for the next few years.[100]

Molineux's direction of the cloth manufactory was far from crowned with success. Neither he nor anyone else could solve Boston's poverty problem or substantially lower the costs of poor relief. But because he made no attempt to coerce Boston's poor women into factory work and enjoyed great popularity among the lower classes he did better than his predecessors. Molineux could never by force of personality accustom Bostonians to repetitive, confining, year-round labor, nor could he solve the problem of the erratic supply of raw materials and the lack of technologically skilled personnel to carry on the difficult job of turning out cloth of fine quality. But he adjusted to these realities, suspending operations "through the winter's cold season," obtaining the services of English-trained "manufacturers" for dying and finishing the cloth, and leaving women and children in their homes rather than attempting to impose an industrial discipline on them.[101] His relative success also owes much to the Whig campaign to turn spinning into a patriotic activity and a symbol of defiance against England. Peter Oliver explained how "Mr. Otis's black Regiment, the dissenting Clergy, were also set to Work, to preach up Manufactures instead of Gospel" until the women and children of the town were absorbed in this "new Species of Enthusiasm, . . . the Enthusiasm of the Spinning Wheel."[102] Under radical Whig leadership the manufacture of cloth took on a political character and became a part of the self-denying zeal and reaffirmation of community by which well-to-do radical Whigs hoped to bind the lower classes to their leadership.

It was in Philadelphia that the attempt to manufacture cloth finally reached fruition in the last year before independence. The movement for domestic manufacturing had received a healthy impetus from the last nonimportation movement as the radical protests against England careered to a climax in 1774 and 1775. Also, the pool of impoverished and unemployed persons in the city had never been greater. Both of these factors were important in the success of the United Company of Philadelphia for Promoting American Manufactures. By themselves, however, they probably would not have guaranteed success and certainly not the kind of success that enabled the company to provide employment for nearly five hundred persons and to declare a dividend two years after its first meeting.

Three other factors allowed the company to succeed as had none of its predecessors in the port towns through a quarter-century of experimentation. First, the company made no attempt to bring poor women and children into a factory or to impose a discipline and time schedule upon them that ill-suited traditional attitudes toward work and family. Women spun at home, as time and familial responsibilities allowed, and brought their yarn to the factory where they were paid.[103] Second, this reversion to the old putting-out system enabled the company to avoid heavy capital expenditures for a large building to accommodate hundreds of spinners. Instead, it rented a house for a mere £40 per year for the looms and dying equipment. This allowed the company to begin operations within a month of incorporating itself and to put its money into equipment rather than buildings.[104] Third, the company was organized and operated by a group of middling men, many of them artisans, who came from mixed religious and ethnic backgrounds, had close ties to the poor in their neighborhoods, and were deeply involved in radical politics. The president of the company was Daniel Roberdeau, an important radical leader and shortly to be elected commander of the Pennsylvania militia. James Cannon, the "most important radical penman in Pennsylvania after Thomas Paine" and principal author of the radical Constitution of 1776, was secretary. The twelve-man Board of Managers included five members of the radical Committee of 100, elected five months after the company organized to enforce nonimportation.[105]

Such men stood far above the ruck in Philadelphia, but they differed strikingly from the wealthy merchant organizers who had launched a linen manufactory a decade before. More sensitive to the work rhythms of the laboring poor and closely involved in the emerging artisan-based political movement, they devised a system of cloth production that succeeded because it aided the poor without attempting to change their work environment or to talk about moral reform. While production figures plummeted at the Bettering House, run by wealthy Quaker merchants, they soared at the United Company of Philadelphia, run by popular leaders with close ties to the laboring people and an ability to convince them that spinning and weaving contributed to the defense of liberty in the face of a selfish and despotic crown.[106]

How URBAN dwellers perceived and experienced economic change after 1765 varied markedly according to their position in society. Thomas Hutchinson, who had riches aplenty but little peace of mind as he tried to govern Massachusetts from 1770 to 1774, blithely concluded that north of Maryland "you scarce see a man destitute of a competency to make him easy."[107] There were many others, equally oblivious to growing penury in their midst and possessed of that perpetual optimism which comes easily to those in comfortable circumstances, who saw nothing amiss in America and wished only for the trouble-making radicals to sink into oblivion. At the other end of the spectrum were pitiable persons such as John McCleary, who scratched out pathetic requests for assistance to the overseer of the poor in his North End ward: "I hope you will be so kind as to Lett Me have a Little wood for I have not had one Stick to burn since I wrote you before and I am almost perished with the Cold," or "the Room that I lye in is all over Run with water."[108] In between these two extremes stood the majority of merchant seamen, laborers, artisans, shopkeepers, professionals, and merchants of the port towns. For the most favorably positioned of them, onerous new trade regulations, restrictions on the issuing of paper currency, violent expansion and contraction of credit, heavy taxes, and strict customs enforcement "created a general sense of crisis in the economic order."[109] Trade continued, sometimes at very high levels, and artisan production continued, though unevenly. But the burdens of the mercantilist connection with England and the prospects for an independent economic order that the boycotts of the era aroused among urban artificers, along with the disturbing sight of poverty and unemployment among the lowest ranks, nurtured a profound uneasiness among many concerning the course of economic change and the future of their world. It was hard to ignore the fact that in all the cities the largest buildings erected after 1765 —cloth manufactories, almshouses, and prisons—were constructed to contain the impoverished, a growing criminal element spawned by poverty, and a noncriminal middle-class group whose only offense against society was an inability to weather the economic storms of the period. This was not the world of their fathers.

Among those in the lowest ranks, including most journeymen, apprentices, servants, laborers, and merchant seamen, a growing economic insecurity, which often turned to indigency in periods of unemployment or during the difficult winter months, fostered an equally strong disillusionment with the world as it existed. In part they directed their bitterness outward—at English press gangs that continued to plague seagoing men, at British soldiers who moonlighted on the waterfront at the expense of townsmen's wages, or at customs officers who cracked down on the customary petty smuggling of sailors. The disenchantment also had an internal focus, for the concurrent growth of wealth and poverty was not hidden from sight, the increase in transiency was equally visible, attempts to work the poor in cloth manufactories and poorhouses in order to improve their moral condition and reduce the taxes of the propertied were deeply resented, and consciousness was growing among those who labored with their hands that the "productive classes" had no community of interest with "unproductive" merchants and lawyers. Those who grew "rich by . . . a pernicious Trade," charged a New Yorker, did so "at the Expence and Ruin" of the people at large. "As a Proof of it we have only to look around us," he fumed, "to see some rolling triumphantly in their Coaches on the Profits gotten by a foreign Trade, out of the Unthinking and Unwary, whose Paternal Estates they have seized by the law, and the Bodies of those who have none crowd our Prisons, which of late Years have been obliged to be enlarged, whilst the Din and Noise of Prosecutions even tire our Courts of Justice."[110]

What was less obvious than the disordered state of the urban economies was what to do about them. The most sanguine of men believed that if England could be persuaded to return to the permissive mercantile system that prevailed before the Seven Years War, then all might be well again. Others, more given to reflections on the state of the people's morals than on the structure of the economy, believed that if denizens of the port towns would pull in their belts and live the frugal, virtuous lives of their forebears, then satisfaction and tranquillity would return. Still others counseled that Americans must become far more self-sufficient, reducing their imports from England through domestic manufacturing and thus providing more employment and balancing their trade. Whatever their analysis of the dark cloud that hung over the northern urban centers, virtually every person who lived through the tumultuous decade that led from resistance to rebellion understood that they inhabited an evermore precarious economic world. That is why it is necessary to grasp the day-by-day circumstances that urban people faced in order to comprehend the rise of a radical political consciousness in the prerevolutionary decade, the crumbling of the elite's cultural hegemony, and the final assaults on the old political order.

13

Revolution

THE REVOLUTIONARY impulse in the northern ports is best understood if ideological principles and economic interests are seen as intimately conjoined. Everyone, with the possible exception of a handful of ascetic recluses, has economic interests; and everyone, including the least educated members of the community, has an ideology, if that term is defined as a configuration of principles and values derived by a social group from its traditions and environment and applied to particular circumstances it confronts. Ebenezer MacIntosh, the debt-ridden street commander of the Boston crowd in 1765, knew how to measure the price of bread and the cost of imported English cloth against the wages he could earn at the cobbler's bench, just as Thomas Hutchinson, the wealthy merchant and government official, understood how the sterling exchange rate affected his margin of profit. Though their scale of economic operations differed tremendously, both men were part of a local economy whose fluctuations affected their well-being. Both men also had personal values and ideological commitments. One was lettered, the other not. But both were articulate in their disagreement on how social order, economic justice, and political liberty were best defined and achieved.

Like so many of New England's laboring poor, MacIntosh was fervently antipapist and only slightly less anti-Anglican. He was also convinced that affluence and self-indulgence had corrupted Boston's elite. He baptized his first-born son Pascale Paoli MacIntosh, and in this commemoration of the humble Corsican patriot can be seen the cast of his values. Hutchinson named no children after revolutionaries but embraced his own ideology no less warmly. Traditional English rights, including religious freedom, balanced government, limits on executive authority, and an electorate of substantial propertyholders formed the foundation of his thought. With lesser men keeping to their places and deferring to the judgments of their betters, social order would be maintained.[1]

The keepers of the past have explored the step by step alienation from

England and the final call to arms with exquisite care. Therefore, the concern here is not a detailed narrative on the coming of the War of Independence but the internal struggle for a new social order that many thought must accompany the severing of ties with England, if that contest, bloody and wrenching as all knew it must be, was to be worth the risk and pain. The argument is that the War of Independence in the port towns was accompanied by a profound social upheaval—a many-faceted crisis which was "like a powerful earthquake which . . . erupted along the lines of the deep faults that had existed within colonial society for generations, even when they went unobserved and remained inactive."[2]

WHILE INSISTING on the general relationship between the circumstances of their everyday lives and the susceptibility of people to particular ideas, it is not possible to define a series of self-contained, distinctly different ideological outlooks that existed in the cities. Nor is it possible to demonstrate a perfect correspondence between occupation or wealth and ideological outlook. However, two broad ideologies, which sometimes overlapped, can be defined, and several clusters of ideas that had not yet reached the level of all encompassing world views can be sketched.

The reigning ideology of eighteenth-century America was Whig, but its subscribers were by no means unified on all issues. One group, which can be loosely designated conservative Whigs, included a large part of the urban gentry, especially import-export merchants, important officeholders, many lawyers and clergymen, and a sprinkling of lesser men who by temperament or family ties were connected to this generally affluent group. By and large these men of wealth adhered to the canons of Whig political theory, including balanced government, the vital role of a legislature elected by propertyholders, and equal justice before the law. In the port towns they were often Anglicans from families whose wealth stretched back several generations and they often had close connections in England, both to large mercantile houses there and to important men in government. They openly espoused the world of international trade and capitalist relations and in this limited sense were "modernizers." In their social philosophy, however, they were profoundly conservative. Hierarchy and order imposed from above were at the heart of their social credo. They believed deeply that the "multitude, who have not a sufficient stock of reason and knowledge to guide them," should defer to their betters.[3] They were rationalists upon whom much Enlightenment thought had fallen, and they prided themselves for their roles as leaders of their communities.

These men appeared as placeholders and wealthy merchants around Thomas Hutchinson in Boston, as members of the Anglican-based, merchant-led proprietary faction in Philadelphia, and as the merchants and lawyers of the DeLancey party in New York. Thoroughly elitist in their beliefs, they valued balanced government instituted for the protection of property, of which they owned a great deal, and thought of elected legislators as political stewards of the general welfare rather than implementers of public opinion. They detested popular protest, which they saw not as the product of legitimate grievances among other groups in society but as the unloosing of "passion" by people who were unequipped to think clearly or responsibly. They abhorred social fluidity, which seemed to confound the natural hierarchical order that they said was ordained from on high. Their central problem after 1765 was how to keep resistance to English policies within orderly bounds and how, in the face of the awful affronts to authority and social order perpetrated by the Stamp Act demonstrators, to preserve their power in the provincial capitals as leaders and officeholders of the "court" party.[4] Many of them would become loyalists because they found the emerging "popular style of politics . . . simply incompatible with the rule of reason."[5] Others maintained a precarious neutrality during the war. Still others swallowed their distrust of a radicalized polity, shifted with the winds, and emerged during and after the war as leaders of a movement to reverse what they regarded as the dangerous excesses of the revolutionary era.

A second group of Whigs, who may be labeled liberals, was composed of some wealthy import-export merchants, many more local traders, ship captains, unpedigreed lawyers, non-Anglican clergymen, small manufacturers, and craftsmen, especially those in the more remunerative trades. They were striving men who had also embraced the bourgeois spirit of commercial life. Economic growth had meant opportunity for most of them and so long as the doors of opportunity were open, which most frequently meant access to capital and labor, they opted to participate in a social system that was by now only faintly disguising the pursuit of self-interest with traditional rhetoric about serving the public good. Many of them owned property, commanded the labor of slaves and indentured servants, and competed avidly in a world of credit, investment, and speculation. "Their loyalties," it has been aptly said, "lay with future possibilities. A return to the good old days of prescribed place and uncorrupted virtue held little appeal for them."[6] These were the men who led the opposition to the new regulation of economic life by England, including limitations on their right to issue paper money, attempts to eliminate American middlemen from certain sectors of international marketing, and interference with smuggling, which they viewed as an opening of channels of free trade in the face of monopolistic regulation.

In their political philosophy the liberal Whigs were far more open to participatory public affairs than the conservative Whigs, though they put definite limits on popular politics. In Boston they celebrated the town meeting as an instrument for guarding the people's liberties, whereas the conservatives condemned it as an exercise in mobocracy. In New York they almost always controlled the common council and other elected municipal offices. In Philadelphia they levied and collected the taxes, supervised poor relief, and spearheaded civic improvement projects. They were strongly Lockean in their belief that liberty was essentially the condition of being secure in one's property, which they held in modest to substantial amounts, and they had little desire to share political power with the unpropertied by extending the franchise or, in New York and Philadelphia, instituting a town meeting system of local government. Because they were themselves products of intergenerational mobility, they did not shrink from the ideal of social fluidity as did the conservative Whigs; but they distrusted the growing mass of propertyless and impoverished city dwellers below them and sometimes suspected that such people lacked the cardinal qualities of industry and frugality that accounted for their own success. If social stability, acceptance of capitalistic economic relations, and political stewardship were the identifying characteristics of the conservative Whigs, then equality of opportunity, an enthusiastic attitude toward the market economy, and political liberty were the badges of the liberal Whigs. Their central problem after 1765 was to lead the movement to resist British policy, employing those below them as necessary to create mass protest without losing control of the popular assembly parties which they dominated.

The second widely subscribed ideology in the cities was Evangelical. Though overlapping with Whig ideology at many points, especially in its advocacy of balanced government, electoral institutions, and freedom of speech and the press, the Evangelicals employed a different language of public discourse and had a different vision of the direction in which society ought to change. As among Whigs, they had internal divisions.[7] One part of their ranks, which may be called radicals, was composed of the lower elements in the urban social hierarchy—laborers, merchant seamen, and artisans in the least remunerative trades such as shoemakers, tailors, coopers, ship caulkers, and stocking weavers. Slaves and indentured servants were also in this group ideologically but in legal status stood by themselves. For all these people capitalist enterprise was of small concern, for they owned little property, were socially immobile (though geographically transient), had limited aspirations, and clung to traditional ideas of a moral economy where the fair wage and just price rather than free competition and the laws of supply and demand ruled economic affairs. Their ideology of productive labor was expressed by the shoemakers and tanners of Philadelphia, who wrote that their work had always gained them "a bare living profit," that few of them had prospered, "however industrious and attentive to [their] business, however frugal in [their] manner of living," but that nonetheless they had "been contented to live decently without acquiring wealth" because "our professions rendered us useful and necessary members of the community."

Family, pride in workmanship, religion, and community counted for more than capital accumulation. "Proud of [our] rank, we aspired no higher," they asserted.[8]

For men of this sort, who in Europe were called the laboring poor, elementary political rights and social justice rather than protection of property and constitutional liberties were the promises of revolution. They did not dream of rising to the status of merchants or lawyers, but they expected to make a living wage. Those who were unfree coveted their freedom. Many had been deeply infected by evangelical religion, drinking deeply from its egalitarian and communalistic wells. We have seen these people in action, working in Boston (along with many of their betters) to sabotage the public markets, stopping the exportation of grain when food was in short supply, defending themselves against impressment and attempts to coerce their labor in workhouses, and attacking the mansions of the wealthy during the Stamp Act disturbances. Their leaders were sometimes drawn from their own ranks, such as shoemakers Ebenezer MacIntosh in Boston and Samuel Simpson in Philadelphia, and sometimes from the middle stratum, where resided men such as Thomas Young, Alexander McDougall, and James Cannon, who themselves had risen out of poverty, retained bone-deep egalitarian notions, and still identified with the lowest ranks. Much of their consciousness harked back to the levelers of mid-seventeenth century England. They found their folk heroes in men such as Cornet George Joyce, an obscure tailor in Cromwell's army who even leveled a king in 1647 when he captured Charles I, urged his death, and, according to folklore, stood at the executioner's side when the ax fell.

A great social and economic distance separated these dispossessed and struggling residents of the port towns from the conservative Whigs, who saw them as "rabble" whose "idleness and profligacy" consigned them forever to self-imposed poverty.[9] In turn, the poor and unfree saw the mercantile elite as oppressors and believed that the laboring poor were "a vital part of God's great plan for the redemption of the world." Most of them would have agreed with Adam Smith, the great codifier of the rising philosophy of self-interest, that "Civil Authority, so far as it is instituted for the security of property, is in reality instituted for the defense of the rich against the poor, or of those who have some property against those who have none at all."[10] Less remarkable was the distance separating the radicals and the liberal Whigs. Sometimes they joined forces, but on other occasions in the prerevolutionary decade the agitation of the radicals alienated liberal Whigs and even drove a few of them into the loyalist camp, where they joined the conservative Whigs.

The second part of the Evangelical ranks was made up of a group of social reformers. Largely composed of clergymen, they included a sprinkling of middle-class doctors, lawyers, tradesmen, and teachers. They were far from unified in terms of prior social experience; what they had most in common was a highly moralistic temperament. They shared with Whigs a commitment to political liberty and the protection of property but simultaneously decried the Whig commercial spirit which they believed was corrupting American society. They perceived "that their society had been undergoing a drastic and frightening transformation" and that the connection with a decadent, materialistic mother country was injecting deadly poisons into the American bloodstream, as Americans, willingly or not, molded themselves in the image of the parent country. They anguished over the luxury, vice, and corruption that was loose in their midst and deplored "the way in which the society was moving and maturing, the distinctions of prestige and status that were arising, the rate and the nature of mobility, and the distribution of power and wealth." Their intention was to reverse the course of historical development, particularly to halt the growth of capitalistic activity. For them the Revolution was the millennium and their goal was to return society to its ascetic beginnings, where civic virtue, spartan living, and a disdain for worldly things had prevailed.[11]

It is necessary to maintain perspective in measuring the impact of the reformers. To some extent all revolutionary movements are millennial, calling forth new energy, a rebirth of society, a selfless dedication to the greater cause. It claims too much, however, to say that the port towns were broadly infected with the spirit of self-criticism and moral regeneration, as some historians have argued. Nor were most urban Americans driven to revolution by a "pervasive fear that they were not predestined to be a virtuous and egalitarian people."[12] Too much of the self-purifying impulse can be inferred when the pamphlets written primarily by clergymen and idealists, who saw the Revolution as the opportune moment for spiritual reawakening and moral rearmament, are taken to reflect the attitudes of the people at large. Those who had succeeded in the cities showed few signs of guilt over what they regarded as rewards earned through hard work and careful management of their affairs. This applies not only to merchants and lawyers but also to artisans such as those in Philadelphia who went on buying and reading—with no pangs of conscience and few thoughts that America was becoming like the Roman state on the eve of its fall—Franklin's almanac prescriptions on how to build a fortune. Reformer John Adams might groan at the "universal Spirit of Debauchery, Dissipation, Luxury, Effeminancy and Gaming" that he witnessed in Boston, but to most successful residents corruption meant upper-class restriction of their opportunities, not the accumulation of material comforts or participation in leisure activities by the elite.[13] The reformers' appeal cut across class lines to some extent, but their message resonated most notably among the dispossessed of the cities who had also been most affected by the Great Awakening a generation before.

Although, such matters cannot be quantified, it seems clear that the impulse to reverse the course of commercial development, returning to the state of the ancient Saxons or primitive Christians, was much stronger in Boston than in New York and Philadelphia. This can be explained in part by the hold of the seventeenth-century past on New England, where the sense of being God's special agents of destiny was much stronger than in the port towns to the south. The older Puritan ethic, with its suspicion of wealth and grudging tolerance for mercantile activity, persisted in Boston. Looking backward to ancestral virtue and communal attachment, some of the descendants of the Puritan founders saw the Revolution as an opportunity to restore dedication to the "Corporate Christian values that stressed denial more than opportunity and social order more than mobility."[14]

A certain historical logic also explains Boston's tendency to see the Revolution as the impending millennium, as the golden opportunity to recapture a world that once was. The winds of economic change that swept over the Atlantic world in the eighteenth century had blown much colder on Boston than on the middle Atlantic ports, and the passing of years had brought very little success, in fact a crumbling of economic security, to a large part of the populace. There was far more reason to reflect nostalgically on the precapitalistic past and engage in utopian dreaming of the world two thousand years before. Likewise, the millennial spirit of the Great Awakening had infected Boston far more than New York and Philadelphia, so it is not implausible that the Revolution would be seen in Boston as the final climactic campaign of Christian soldiers to purify society. The seeds of the utopianism that led Samuel Adams to believe that the Revolution might be the means of making Massachusetts over into a "Christian Sparta," where all would live simply and pretty much on a level, where public virtue would animate every citizen but where a due sense of subordination would still remain, fell on much less fertile ground to the south where, in the generation preceding the Seven Years War, a modest success at least had crowned the efforts of large numbers of city dwellers.

Even with these caveats we must look carefully at the ideas of the reformers, because in revolutionary situations those who speak for moral regeneration, root and branch reform, self-sacrifice, service to the common cause, and the possibility of perfecting society have a built-in advantage. To engage in revolution is to wipe clean the slate. Upon the fresh surface anything may be written, and those who speak for Novus Ordo Seclorum—a new civil polity—are hard to resist. The social and political ideology of these spokesmen provided a major part of the rationale for resisting English invasion of the liberties of Englishmen in America and a substantial part of the impetus for the reformation of American society. While resisting the Evangelical bias against the growth of commercial capitalism, many Whigs were tinged by the moral strictures of the reformers.

The reformers believed in what intellectual historians have called "classical republicanism" or "civic humanism"—a blend of the political theory of classical Greek and Roman writers with that of Renaissance masters such as Machiavelli, seventeenth-century English libertarians such as Harrington, Milton, and Sidney, eighteenth-century radical Whigs such as Trenchard, Gordon, Molesworth, and Hollis, and the French theorists Rousseau and Montesquieu.[15] The principal elements of their republicanism, which drew its original inspiration from classical antiquity, were the sacrifice of individual interests to the pursuit of the common good (a characteristic so central that it became encapsulated in the word "virtue"); balanced government, which provided stability while guarding against corruption by any element of society; a state of watchfulness against corruption; and the maintenance of a general equality in society, which would prevent the concentration of political power and the oligarchy or despotism that inevitably followed. Republicanism was not, however, a detailed plan of government. Although it shared with Whiggism a hatred of standing armies, a strong endorsement of freedom of speech and the press, frequent elections, the rotation of offices, and reliance upon the popularly elected branch of the legislature, it was, more fundamentally, an attitude toward government, toward society, and toward the character of the people. Thus, the main explicator of this genre of revolutionary republicanism has written that it "added a moral dimension, a utopian depth, to the political separation from England—a depth that involved the very character of their society."[16]

The clash between the Whig and Evangelical cast of mind can be seen in several elements of republicanism that were strongly resisted by broad segments of the urban populace. One point of tension was the republican notion that virtue, "the passion for pursuing the public good," was incompatible with the pursuit of private interest.[17] Especially in the cities, though to some extent throughout the colonies, Americans had been adhering to the competing notion that the public good in a market society was best served by each individual pursuing his or her own self-interest. This eventually became known as the ideology of economic liberalism, an elaborate defense of which was published in 1776 by Adam Smith. In the northern ports self-interested behavior, an anathema to republicanism, stemmed both from the acceptance of a growing body of English thought that no longer deemed self-sacrifice and altruism as good for either the body or soul of society and from a disbelief among lesser people that the elite, when it ruled, governed for the good of the whole society. Hence, in spite of the central place which service to the commonweal played in republican thought, many urban dwellers of entrepreneurial temperament, delivered "from the strictures of classical republicanism" by the newer belief "in a natural harmony of benignly striving individuals," elevated behavior on behalf of individual or group interests to the level of ideology. Here was where the reformers' republicanism "was caught between traditional concerns anchored in classical antiquity and the new conditions of an expansive commercial society."[18]

A second element of republicanism that never gained acceptance among most urban people was the notion that commerce corrupts. By definition the cities were commercial centers and thus were incapable of fulfilling the classical ideal of a society of sturdy yeomen, whose rustic honesty and commitment to the commonweal could not be eroded by the materialism and venality which commercial life in the cities spawned. Some of the eighteenth-century "commonwealthmen," the radical English writers who wove together the various strands of republican thought in their attacks on the corruption of Walpolean government in the Georgian era, had wrestled with this problem. While they sometimes grudgingly conceded commerce a place in producing the kind of national wealth that would insure political liberty, they remained suspicious of merchants, credit institutions, and the entire apparatus of finance capitalism. American republicanism remained ambivalent on the subject. Many of its agrarian exponents vilified the cities, scourged trade, and heaped abuse on the urban Whig gentility for their ostentation and affluence. But even farmers were tied into an Atlantic commercial network, so in the end most of the reformers "in the midst of a lingering rhetorical attachment to a classical, anticommercial Spartan ideal, . . . embraced an ideology of free trade that tied their republican hopes to the prospects for a burgeoning, invigorating intercourse with the rest of the world."[19]

The third element of republicanism that could not easily be digested by many in the cities was the emphasis on social equality. All of the republican writers from whom the colonial pamphleteers borrowed saw an organic connection between economic and political power. They regarded a general economic equality as absolutely essential to political freedom.[20] Wealth concentrated in the hands of a few led ineluctably to oligarchy, the rule of the few, for economic and political power were indivisible. Republicanism could flourish only in a society of independent, roughly equal citizens. The chances of achieving this were greatest in simple, agricultural societies where land was widely held and agrarian laws prevented the concentration of property. Such societies nurtured civic virtue because exploitative tendencies were held in strict check by the insistence on rough equality. Thus, James Harrington and Algernon Sidney, two of the most influential English writers of the late seventeenth century and men widely read by educated Americans, emphasized that

"Where there is inequality of estates there must be inequality of power," for "there is no maxim more infallible and holding in any science, than this in politics; that empire is founded in property."[21] Economic self-sufficiency was the heart of political freedom; without it one man was beholden to another for his living and inevitably fell prey to that man's political will. Inequality spawned dependency and dependency destroyed political liberty. The accumulation of wealth increased the ability of the rich to corrupt the body politic through money and power; conversely the impoverishment of laboring citizens deprived them of their political will.

The English "commonwealthmen" of the eighteenth century developed further the connections between wealth and political power. These writers, however, penned their tracts amidst great commercial expansion and the growth of financial institutions. Whereas writers such as Machiavelli, Harrington, and Sidney had argued for a generally equal distribution of landed wealth and had ignored the problem of commercial wealth, the commonwealthmen had to respond to the new world of joint-stock companies, overseas trade, the Bank of England, the increasing pervasiveness of the market in human relations, and the advocacy of self-interest as a positive regulator of human affairs. "Catonism," after the Roman Cato, is the name that Barrington Moore has employed to describe the anti-commercial philosophy of what in England and America become known as the "country party." "Antirationalist, antiurban, antimaterialist, and more loosely, antibourgeois," the writers of this persuasion called for moral regeneration, attacked corruption and upper-class self-indulgence, and invoked nostalgically a vision of a simpler society where a general equality among citizens safeguarded republican institutions.[22]

Among these commonwealthmen, John Trenchard and Thomas Gordon were the most important disseminators of ideas to Americans in the prerevolutionary generations. Their *Cato's Letters* were widely read and reprinted in the American press. Cato was a peculiar blend of the earlier repugnance to concentrated power and the advocacy of self-interest and gain. Cato never celebrated austerity and self-denial and was thoroughly Lockean in insisting that liberty was being secure in one's property, but also insisted that "A Free People are kept so by no other means but an equal distribution of property." A general economic equality was thus a precondition (and the only guarantor) of political liberty. "As Liberty can never subsist without Equality, nor Equality be long preserved without an *Agrarian* Law, or something like it; so when Mens Riches are become immeasurably or surprizingly great, a People, who regard their own Security, ought to make a strict Enquiry how they came by them, and oblige them to take down their own Size, for fear of terrifying the Community, or mastering it."[23]

Jean Jacques Rousseau was another eighteenth-century writer who came late enough upon the scene to confront the reality of capitalistic enterprise as a motive force in society. Available in translation in America just before the Revolution, Rousseau's *Social Contract* also emphasized that equality of economic conditions was essential to republican government. Rousseau went to the heart of the dual meaning of equality. He thought it fatuous to speak of that "apparent and illusory" equality before the law, the equality of opportunity, which "serves only to keep the poor man in his poverty and the rich man in his usurpation." True equality was equality of condition. A perfect leveling of estates was always beyond grasp and probably unnecessary and unwise; but in a true republic "no citizen is rich enough to be able to buy another, and none so poor as to be forced to sell himself."[24] Like other commonwealthmen, Rousseau believed that inequality led to dependent relationships, which in turn robbed citizens of political free will. Where there is economic inequality the rich have the real power and government is a sham, for all laws and institutions are controlled to their advantage and the disadvantage of the laboring poor.

For many Whigs in the cities, merchants foremost among them, the idea that a general equality of condition was a prerequisite to republican society was unacceptable. Given the course of colonial development, it could only be accomplished by a massive redistribution of property, and protection of property was one of the main incentives for resisting England. So equality and freedom, the latter defined as being secure in one's property, stood opposed to each other. Many of the Evangelicals, who wrote and published their pamphlets in the cities, minimized the issue of equality and concentrated instead on moral corruption and the need to reinstill a concern for the general welfare. John Adams was one of those who had read his republican theory carefully enough to understand the connection between economic inequality and political corruption. In preparing his *Dissertation on the Feudal and Canon Law*, one of the most powerful republican statements of the 1760s, Adams wrote that "Property monopolized or in the Possession of a few is a Curse to Mankind. We should preserve not an Absolute Equality—this is unnecessary, but preserve all from extreme Poverty, and all others from extravagant Riches." But Adams, caught between Whig and Evangelical modes of thinking, thought better of the statement, engaged as he was with wealthy Whig merchants in the early stages of resistance, and deleted it from his text.[25] He never again called for smoothing over the gradations of wealth. For the most part the reformers chose not to speak about structural inequalities, but concentrated on defects in the colonial character as it had evolved over past generations. Morality became the badge of the reformers and the radicals were left to bear the standards of equality.

It was the presence of different ideologies—sometimes overlapping, often antagonistic, none appearing in pure form, and all of them chang-

ing during these tumultuous years—that makes the urban experience
after 1765 so difficult to comprehend. It is also what made the resistance
movement and the social upheaval in the cities so difficult to control.
Samuel Adams, who had no commercial aspirations, might inveigh that
"Luxury & Extravagance are in my opinion totally destructive of those
Virtues which are necessary for the Preservation of the Liberty and Happiness of the People."[26] Yet Adams, though devoid of capitalistic urges,
was trying to lead a radical movement from New England's largest commercial center and had to work with John Hancock, who lived high on
the hill and stocked his cellar with the best Madeira wines. Hancock's
purse and prestige were vital to the success of the Massachusetts patriot
movement and he was not risking his life and fortune for a return to arca-
dian simplicity. Similarly, Benjamin Rush in Philadelphia believed that
revolution would usher in, if men would help it, the millennial Second
Coming and achieve the purification of American society, but Rush had
to march in step with John Dickinson, "penman of the Revolution," an
urbane lawyer with a country estate, a retinue of slaves, and a fondness
for the aristocratic lifestyle.

Different groups, in sum, began walking the road to revolution in the
port towns with different perceptions, rooted in prior experience and
values, of what a new society should look like. Every American who
joined the revolutionary movement was "inevitably compelled to expect
or to hope for at least some amount of reformation in American society."[27] But, depending on their position in society, they drew upon
republican theory selectively or drew upon alternative ideological traditions. Almost everyone, regardless of social position, religious temperament, or life experience seems to have imbibed the belief that cancers
were gnawing voraciously at England's republican vitals after the accession of George III in 1760. To this extent it is correct to say that a cluster
of values and ideas that revealed the incipient despotism of English policies was widely, almost universally, shared, although city dwellers
ranged from radical to conservative on how to confront the massive external threat. When we turn to ideas related to the reformation of American society, which was central to the revolutionary purpose, the univer-
sality of any single ideology fades away. Many city people were avid
participants in the new world of market relations, while others were
deeply anticapitalistic. Some hewed closely to the Whiggish insistence on
balance of government and the legislative power of propertyholders,
while others wished to change radically the meaning of political liberty
by conferring voting and officeholding rights upon the propertyless as
well as the propertied. Some imbibed a prophetic sectarian moralism fed
by the Great Awakening, while others were rationalists who deplored
popular enthusiasm in either religion or politics. Some defended slavery
passionately and others believed it a lesion which would eventually de-

stroy the body politic. Even within groups that shared the same attitudes toward economic activity, such as the merchants and higher artisans, acrid divisions could arise as the day of revolution drew near.

WHAT REMAINS is to examine how different groups in urban society—especially merchants, manufacturers and master craftsmen, and the lower levels of the laboring classes—struggled after 1765 to maintain or acquire political power in order to implement their vision of the future. The decade after the Stamp Act demonstrations involved a sharp clash between these groups, a growing feeling of class consciousness in several cities, and, in the process of resisting England, an attempt among those without political power to gain it in order to secure their own ends. Of utmost importance is to ascertain why the urban gentry was so successful in maintaining its hold on the levers of power in Boston, somewhat less so in New York, but in Philadelphia utterly lost control.

In Boston, where the Stamp Act disturbances had been most intense and the merchant-lawyer gentry had blanched as an impoverished shoemaker veteran of the Seven Years War gained control of the streets, the Whig leadership reasserted itself after 1765. "Captain-General" MacIntosh, who had led a crowd of 2,000 with military precision through the streets in November of that year, disappeared from sight as a crowd leader before another year passed. He lost his office of leather sealer in 1769, and shortly after the Boston Massacre in 1770 was languishing in debtors jail, where he had plenty of time to ponder why none of Boston's patriotic leaders stepped forward to provide the modest bail funds required to release him.[28]

The eclipse of MacIntosh does not signify that peace returned to Boston's streets. The arrival of the new Board of Custom Commissioners, which made its headquarters in Boston in 1767, the imposition of the hated Townshend duties in the same year, and the arrival of British troops to occupy the recalcitrant town in 1768 all kept the Massachusetts capital in a state of turmoil. Nor was organized violence against crown officials or crowd activity ended. The battering of customs official Benjamin Hallowell after his seizure of John Hancock's ship *Liberty* in 1768, the confrontation with British troops on the icy night of March 5, 1770, and the Tea Party in 1773 are only the most spectacular of a series of incidents that made Boston by far the most turbulent northern seaport in the climactic years prior to independence.

As the Whig leaders, themselves in flux, regained their influence with laboring people, they carefully drew a line between controlled violence directed at obnoxious crown officials and their supporters and mass violence that sprang from internal social grievances. James Otis, moderator of the town meeting in 1767, signified the suppression of interclass hostility by exhorting that "let our burthens be ever so heavy, or our grievances ever so great, no possible circumstances, tho' ever so oppressive, could be supposed sufficient to justify private tumults and disorders."[29] The *Boston Gazette,* the most influential paper among the laboring people, called repeatedly for "No Mobs or Tumults," and early in 1768 Samuel Adams, now emerging as the principal radical leader, assumed the name of "Populus" and wrote that the people should remain quiet and follow the *Gazette's* advice—"NO MOBS—NO CONFUSIONS—NO TUMULTS."[30] When effigies of Customs Commissioner Charles Paxton and Inspector General John Williams were discovered hanging from the Liberty Tree in the South End in March 1768, three members of the Loyal Nine cut them down before a crowd could assemble. Shortly after that an angry crowd, smashing windows and burning the property of customs officials in retaliation for the seizure of John Hancock's sloop *Liberty,* were dispersed by radical leaders who rushed to the scene crying "To your Tents O Israel."[31]

In the years after 1766 Samuel Adams, who came closer than any man in America to becoming a professional politician, emerged as the leader of the Whig resistance. Experienced in caucus politicking, a skilled newspaper polemicist, a man with deep roots among the artisans despite his Harvard degree, and possessed of "the vigor and *élan* of all great revolutionaries," he became the Whigs' most effective organizer and coordinator. Operating through the North End Caucus, the Masonic Lodge, the fire companies, and the taverns, he was shortly known in England as one of the most dangerous men in the colonies.[32]

Though Adams spoke the language of the "old Puritans," stressing the need for moral reform, an end to luxury and extravagance, and a return to the rustic simplicity of bygone days, his utopian vision did not prevent him from working effectively with Boston's Whig merchants. They sought the end of the tough new policy of trade regulation rather than the restoration of a "corporate Christian commonwealth," but Adams was willing to work with them first for the end of British tyranny and they probably had few fears that his romantic maunderings would ever gain much ground in New England's largest commercial center.[33] Thus, between 1766 and 1770 Adams served on town meeting committees with the most politically active merchants—Edward Payne, Ezekiel Goldthwait, John Rowe, Thomas Cushing, John Hancock, and William Phillips. Adams was particularly pleased to have secured the support—and to have opened the purse—of John Hancock. It was his largesse that financed many of the patriotic celebrations and feasts that kept politics on everyone's mind and helped to build interclass bridges during these years.[34]

Passage of the Townshend duties in 1767 put the revived Whig leadership to the test. Nonconsumption of British goods was the first response and proved to have a salubrious effect in unifying Boston's social ranks.

The BOSTONIAN'S Paying the EXCISE-MAN, or TARRING & FEATHERING

Plate I.

London Printed for Robt. Sayer & J. Bennett, Map & Printsellers, No. 53, Fleet Street, as the Act directs 31 Oct. 1774.

12. *The Bostonian's Paying the Excise-Man,
or Tarring & Feathering, 1774,
attributed to Philip Dawe.*

Adams reveled in it, for it was a means of drawing every member of the community into a political fellowship, a latter-day Puritan community covenant where the common goal was repeal of the Townshend Acts. At the same time, eschewing imported British finery would begin to "mow down luxury and high living in New England." Adams had always been offended by mercantile affluence in Boston—the "Decorations of the Parlor, the shining Side Boards of Plate, the costly Piles of China"—and liked to compare the ostentatious shows of wealth by Boston's rich with the humble rusticity of the Bay colony's founders.[35] Boston's merchants could afford to endure these barbs, for in nonconsumption they saw their best chance of reversing British policy. Their entire political clout in England was tied up with their connections to metropolitan merchants, who stood to lose a huge volume of orders annually if nonconsumption worked. For Boston's mechanics the economic boycott also had advantages because it provided the biggest boon to home manufacturing in that town's history. The same kind of economic boycott had been initiated in response to the Stamp Act and had garnered support among artisans who profited from this encouragement of domestic manufacturing.

Although the nonconsumption policy of December 1767 and the nonimportation agreement signed by most merchants four months later initially had a binding effect on the community, it also contained a potential for splitting the town apart. The effectiveness of economic boycott depended on stopping all goods at the water's edge and many merchants in Boston who were engaged in international trade and closely attached to the governor's interests had no intention of being bound by a community compact which had no force in law. Exhortation and insult could do only so much to change the minds of these high-placed men, who included many of the colony's largest importers, so in the end persuasion of a more physical kind proved necessary to seal Boston off from British imports. Thus the "no Mobs or Tumults" policy of the Whig leadership broke down. The street theater of 1765 began again but this time under the guidance of no impoverished shoemaker. Street brigades were used to terrify uncooperative importers and to disrupt the work of the reinforced customs corps, which was increasingly effective in stopping the smuggling of Dutch tea, French molasses, and other contraband goods that had built the fortunes of many Whig merchants and provided employment for hundreds of artisans in the town. Whig leaders in 1768 began resorting to crowd action to "rescue" goods seized by customs officials and to intimidate them from doing their work when illegal goods were about to be landed. But Whig leaders continued to promote the distinction between violence directed at external enemies—or their local agents—and violence inspired by demands for internal reform.[36]

During the years of nonimportation from 1768 to 1770 Whig leaders found two men who proved particularly effective in directing street crowds. The first was William Molineux, a small trader who had not been active in politics before the Stamp Act demonstrations but now assumed the mantle that Ebenezer MacIntosh had worn so briefly. The contrast between the two men is notable. MacIntosh was Scottish, poor, perpetually in debt, a war veteran, an engineman in one of Boston's fire companies, and, as a shoemaker, a toiler in the lower ranks of the artisan community. Molineux was from Ireland, the grandson of the lord lieutenant of that British colony, had felt no need to march off to fight the French, represented one of Boston's wealthiest merchants, Charles Apthorp, belonged to the Merchants Society, and had accumulated an estate that at his death in 1774 ranked him in the top 10 percent of Boston's inhabitants. Passionate for the Whig cause, given to both rhetorical and physical violence, and down to earth enough to mingle easily with lesser artisans and waterfront roughnecks, Molineux was firmly connected to the merchant leadership that still controlled the town meeting and worked hand in hand with the best established artisans and petty entrepreneurs who composed the Sons of Liberty. It was he who led nearly every mass action between 1768 and 1771—against John Mein, the irascible Tory publisher of the *Boston Chronicle*, against the importer William Jackson, who refused to abide by the nonimportation agreement, against Ebenezer Richardson, a customs informer who had fired into a crowd of demonstrators and had to be rescued from a street lynching by Molineux, and at numerous other street tumults.[37]

The second important street leader and intermediary between the Whig leaders and the laboring classes of Boston during these years was Thomas Young. Like Molineux, he was an outsider, having come in 1766 from Albany, New York, the son of immigrant Irish settlers in Ulster County. Young's hostility toward men of wealth and power, expressed earlier in his attacks on grasping landlords and speculators in New York, and his iconoclastic religious views made him an unlikely lieutenant of the merchant Whigs of Boston—a judgment that most historians have confirmed in describing him as a "flaming zealot," one of the "incendiaries of the lower order," "an eternal Fisher in Troubled Waters," and a "bawling New England Man . . . of noisy fame."[38] Shortly after his arrival, after playing a leading role in the Stamp Act demonstrations in Albany, he was thrust into the position of crowd leader. He sat repeatedly on committees of the Sons of Liberty, the town meeting, and the North End Caucus, led crowds to enforce nonimportation, and participated in the Tea Party. Like Molineux, he played a crucial role in halting undesired violence, as when he stood in the streets on the night of the Massacre in 1770 urging the crowd to return to their homes, or when he persuaded angry townsmen to abandon their pursuit of Customs Commissioner Benjamin Hallowell in 1774. Young was far more radical than the Whig leadership in Boston. Shortly after his arrival in Boston he was

writing in the papers that an "increase of property," which made its owners "haughty and imperious" and "cruel and oppressive," was the great
danger in government. "People of the lower ranks" must share political
power in order to restrict the grip of the rich and powerful, he wrote, and
the town should have a building commodious enough to hold "all that
chose to attend" the debates of the legislature.[39]

Young went far beyond the Whig leadership in his radical social thinking. Although not fully trusted, he was invaluable to them because his
extensive involvement with laboring people helped to bridge the social
distance between ranks. Young was a doctor and most of his ministra-
tions, like those of radical Benjamin Rush in Philadelphia, were among
laborers and artisans. He referred to the common people as "those worthy
members of society," the people who would "form the revolution of the
other ranks of Citizens."[40] With MacIntosh no longer at the center of
mass politics, men like Young and Molineux were vitally important to
Whig leaders because they were popular among the artisans and laborers.
The relationship was doubtless tenuous at times—both between these
middle-class intermediaries and the lower ranks and between the merchant leadership and the intermediaries. Laboring Bostonians at a number of moments broke free of their leaders and spontaneously acted on
their own, as in the waterfront brawls in 1769 and 1770 between ropewalk workers and moonlighting British soldiers. But the Whig leaders
had found street captains halfway between themselves and their more
radical social inferiors and had regained, even if precariously, their direction of affairs in the town.

The decision to repeal all of the Townshend duties except the one on
tea drove a wedge deep into the interclass Whig coalition in Boston in
1770. News of the impending repeal had already reached the colony in
December 1769, bringing many merchants to the verge of breaking
ranks. Some of them had seen enough violence, which had been increasing in intensity and could be put to other uses. Others, after nearly two
years of nonimportation, were eager to get black ink back on the columns of their ledgers. January 1, 1770 had been specified as the deadline
of the original agreement and when that day passed a number of merchants began selling goods which had been stored in warehouses for
months. Whig leaders responded by organizing the populace to descend
on the merchants' meetings so that they became "everyway a town meeting except in the mode of calling it."[41] "The Body of the People" was the
term employed to denote the assembled townspeople, who were exhorted
by the resistance leaders to attend the merchants' meetings at Faneuil
Hall, regardless of whether they were male or female, franchised or not,
free or bound. Four times in January 1770 the leaders around Samuel
Adams called meetings of "The Body," a term heavily laden with covenant implications. Anti-British leaders, the conservative *Boston Chroni-*

cle reported, went "trotting from house to house, to engage the master workmen to suffer their journeymen and apprentices to attend." Crowds reported at 1,200 to 2,000 responded.[42]

It is not likely that Boston's artisans had read the outpourings of Whig pamphleteers regarding the undermining of constitutional liberties by corrupt British ministers more carefully or more receptively than the Harvard-trained merchants and that therefore, while merchants compromised, they insisted on maintaining nonimportation until *all* the Townshend duties were removed. We can better comprehend the rift that appeared between merchants and mechanics by appreciating that most of the former had much to gain by resuming importation and most of the latter had much to lose. Hence it is not surprising that by the summer of 1770, when New York and Philadelphia merchants also resumed importing, conflict in Boston came to a head. Hancock was on the verge of defecting from the Adams-led resistance movement and by fall the interclass coalition verged on collapse. "Moderate merchants," claims Stephen Patterson, "dissociated themselves completely from the [popular] party," convinced that mercantile interest had nothing further to gain from nonimportation.[43]

The deep division in Whig ranks continued to grow in 1771 despite a commercial revival. Hancock moved farther away from the radical resisters, James Otis (now disabled by fits of insanity) wavered, Benjamin Church became an undercover "writer on the side of government," John Adams found reason to retire to the rustic charms of Braintree, and many merchants edged toward the newly appointed governor, Thomas Hutchinson. Samuel Adams was defeated in an election for registrar of deeds by merchant Ezekiel Goldthwait, a former committeeman in the resistance cause who now defected to the side of the conservatives. Hutchinson's supporters crowed "like dung-hill cocks" over Adams's defeat and his supporters saw their grasp of town politics slipping away.[44]

The Tea Act in 1773 widened the fissure in Whig ranks. As before, the most effective response to an obnoxious act was economic sanctions. Seeking the broadest possible base, the radical leadership convened The Body, defined as the entire community of concerned individuals. As many as 5,000 turned out to determine an appropriate response to threats upon their liberties. The Committee of Correspondence, formed late in 1772 to promote unified intercolony action, adopted nonimportation as its formal reply to the latest British outrage but took clandestine action of a less peaceful sort, organizing the destruction of £9,000 worth of tea.[45]

The crowds that gathered to decide what Boston should do with the tea consignees were enormous, reaching about 5,000 on several occasions. Governor Hutchinson believed that while men of wealth were present, the assemblages "consisted principally of the lower Ranks of the People" and sputtered that "even Journeymen Tradesmen were brought to increase the Number and the Rabble were not excluded."[46] Shrinking from these displays of popular force, the merchants tried desperately to head off a crisis with England by subscribing money to pay for the destroyed tea. At the same time they opposed the growing movement for nonimportation. England's response to the Tea Party was to pass the Coercive Acts, which closed Boston harbor until payment was made for the tea, virtually ended representative government in the province and town, and put Boston under the military rule of General Thomas Gage. Samuel Adams and his cohorts, organizing resistance through the Boston Committee of Correspondence, countered with "The Solemn League and Covenant," a community compact for boycotting all English goods.

The Solemn League and Covenant was pitched at the ordinary people and it explicitly denigrated the merchants, who were all but excluded from the meaning of community. "This effectual plan," wrote the Committee of Correspondence, "has been originated and been thus carried through by the two venerable orders of men styled Mechanicks and Husbandmen, the strength of every community." No longer trusting "mercantile Avarice," the committee carried the compact around the town, asking both men and women to sign it.[47]

Though some merchants held fast to the cause of radical resistance, most now concluded that they must repulse those who were moving the populace along a suicidal course. The majority of merchants, "whether of moderate or Tory persuasion, . . . determined that they must intervene to bring a halt to the Solemn League."[48] Determined to put matters to a test, they came in force to a town meeting in June 1774 called to discuss Boston's response to the Coercive Acts. Their intention was to censure and abolish the Committee of Correspondence. So many townspeople poured into Faneuil Hall that the meeting was adjourned to Old South Church. Speeches were made by both sides: Samuel Adams, Joseph Warren, William Molineux, Thomas Young, and Josiah Quincy, Jr., rose as popular leaders to defend the Solemn League and Covenant; conservative merchants Thomas Gray, John Amory, Ezekiel Goldthwait, Samuel Barrett, Edward Payne, and others thundered against it. The debate carried over to the next day when the radical Committee of Correspondence finally gained an overwhelming vote of confidence. The merchants trooped out, disheartened and bitter. One hundred and thirty seven of them promptly signed petitions protesting that the Solemn League would cripple Boston's trade. They were now irreparably divided from most of Boston's laboring people.[49] "The people of property, of best sense and character," wrote one conservative, "feel the tyranny of the [radical] leaders, and foresee[ing] the consequences of their proceedings, would gladly extricate themselves from the difficulties and distress they are involved in by making their peace with Great Britain, and speedily submitting to the conditions and penalties required."[50] Some merchants such as

Hancock and John Rowe attempted to maintain a middle position, opposing nonimportation and eschewing the radical resistance leadership yet not going over publicly to the Hutchinson circle. But Boston was now under military rule and the die was cast.

What is most remarkable about the turbulent years after 1765 is that laboring people in Boston, though defiant against the British and active in the streets as in no other port town, were conspicuously inactive as a separate group and made virtually no demands for an enlargement of their role in the political process. This is apparent in a number of ways. First, far more than in New York and Philadelphia the electorate continued to fill the important town offices—selectman, tax assessor, overseer of the poor, town meeting moderator—with merchants, doctors, and lawyers.[51] This was also true of the special committees appointed by the town meeting to recommend how the town should respond to such emergencies as the Massacre, the Tea Act, and the Port Act. The Committee of Correspondence and all the other ad hoc committees were routinely filled with professional men such as James Otis, Joseph Warren, Benjamin Church, and Thomas Young and the most anti-British merchants such as William Molineux, Nathaniel Appleton, Oliver Wendell, Caleb Davis, and Robert Pierpont.

Second, the artisans never organized a Mechanics Committee as in the other cities to push their own demands for internal reforms and made no demands for democratizing politics. The single change in the political modus operandi came in 1766 when the House of Representatives agreed to erect a public gallery. Although opening legislative debates to the public came to signify an altered relationship between the governed and their governors, the gallery in Boston was erected not at the demand of Boston's artisans but at the instigation of the voters of Cambridge. Moreover, it was agreed to not because citizens of the lower ranks were pushing the gentry legislators but because Whig politicians, seeking to broaden their support, decided to turn the House of Representatives into a "School of Political Learning," as Thomas Young put it.[52]

Third, the lower artisans and laborers seem to have made no demands in Boston for a broadening of the suffrage, which was narrower at the beginning of the 1760s than in either New York or Philadelphia. Even the sharp social animus that had burst forth in the 1750s and 1760s seemed to fade away. Lastly, artisan voices were conspicuously absent from Boston newspapers and broadsides. In both New York and Philadelphia after 1767 dozens of partisan pleas were specifically addressed to or signed by "A Tradesmen," "A Mechanic," "A Carpenter," or others who spoke for the laboring segment of urban society. In Boston this rarely occurred. It makes no difference whether artisans in the other seaports wrote these political appeals themselves or had others write for them; in either case they were beamed at laboring men as a group with their own interests to protect. In Boston, radical Whig appeals emanated from "Publius," "Americanus," "Publicola," and other spokesmen of the corporate whole.[53]

There are several reasons why challenges to gentry control in Boston receded after 1765. Of great importance was the presence of the British army. Highly visible since the first arrival of the Fourteenth and Twenty-ninth Regiments in 1768, the red-coated enemy (as well as a battery of customs officials and other royal bureaucrats) served to focus the attention of all Bostonians on the external crisis with England. If jobs along the wharves were scarce, Boston's laborers could blame moonlighting British soldiers. If political liberties were abridged, who was more culpable than the metropolitan government, which suspended the legislature and abolished the town meeting? Interclass hostility was thus muted by the presence of an adversary whom people in all ranks feared and detested. By the same token, as the town became more and more radical in confronting the British, attention was diverted from internal issues, which seemed less important because some of Massachusetts's most basic liberties were under attack.

No less important in the submersion of social tension between ranks was the ability of the radical resistance leaders to employ the struggle against the English as a means of reaffirming the ancient Puritan concept of corporate communalism. By insisting that Boston must fight as a community against British oppression and traitorous townsmen who knuckled under to British perversions of constitutional rights, Samuel Adams and other leaders were able to convince laboring people that they were essential to the struggle for freedom, even if they could not vote in the town meeting or in provincial elections. By a de facto inclusion of everyone in the political community the radical leadership pre-empted demands for a broadened suffrage or for artisan officeholders or for separate mechanics' organizations. This process began in 1767 when the nonconsumption pact was drawn up not by merchants, as in the case of the economic boycott of 1765, but by the town meeting, which then circulated the agreement "among the people for general signing."[54] In 1769 when Boston merchants began to break ranks on nonimportation, the resistance leaders began calling into action The Body of the People, which included not only those entitled to participate in the formal political process but everyone, regardless of age, sex, or rank. Especially in policing the nonimportation agreement in 1768 and 1769, the people at large assumed the functions of civil government, participating in ferreting out violators, fastening on them the opprobrium of the community, and coercing them to mend their ways. The humblest laborer on Boston's wharves, in fact, even teen-age children and slaves, became part of the political community when they daubed the houses of importers with Hillsborough paint, a peculiar recipe of body wastes, or pummeled zealous royal panjandrums who searched for smuggled goods. In this spirit, when some conservatives challenged the presence of unfranchised mechanics at an important town meeting in 1770, they were shouted down by men who argued that "if they had no Property they had Liberty, and their posterity might have property."[55]

By the early 1770s the Boston town meeting itself was frequently convened as The Body of the People. When that occurred, a restrictive body with "formal corporate status bound by law" became an informal but all-inclusive meeting of the people "bound only by its sovereign judgments."[56] Especially after 1770, when most of Boston's import merchants split from the resistance leaders, the artisans and laborers were drawn into the political process as part of The Body and even heralded as the heart of the opposition movement. In reinvoking the traditional covenant ideology of Puritan Massachusetts, which stressed "both structured order and a continuity with the past," a leadership which was radical in its opposition to England but mostly traditional in its social philosophy had found a means for including the people who had marched behind MacIntosh in 1765 and thus for "containing and controlling the American revolutionary impulse."[57]

A high degree of religious uniformity in Whig ranks and the ability of leaders such as Samuel Adams to turn the resistance movement into a kind of religious crusade also muted class discord and diverted attention from internal restructuring. Many of Boston's Anglicans supported Bernard's and Hutchinson's administrations, and substantial numbers of them became loyalists when fighting broke out. By definition this put them outside the "community." The rest of the people were not nearly so heterogenous in religion as in the other ports. To what was still largely a Congregational town Samuel Adams pitched a highly effective appeal that the "Virtue of our Ancestors inspires us" in resisting English tyranny. They were "Puritans," and "old Romans," Adams declaimed repeatedly, and his atavistic rhetoric did much to bind together in common cause people of the lower ranks and their middle- and upper-class superiors.[58] By 1774 the notion of an interclass crusade, in which politics, religion, and morality were inseparable, was summed up in the movement for the final economic boycott—carefully entitled "The Solemn League and Covenant." Every Bostonian knew that this was the name of the alliance of Scottish and English Puritans who had labored twelve decades before to reform the Anglican Church and finally rebelled against Charles I.[59] Now, all latter-day Puritans—women as well as men were exhorted to sign the covenant—must reform a corrupt England by denying themselves imported goods, an act not only of economic coercion but of self-denial. To sign the covenant was to participate in a purification rite which would return the signators to the straight path their ancestors had trod. Later in 1774 the Quebec Act, which established the Catholic religion and French law in the conquered Canadian territories, heightened the sense of drama regarding the necessity of Boston's Protestant people coming together in a body to resist the English government. The Quebec Act "enabled patriots of all kinds to complete the identification of themselves with the anti-Stuart rebellion of their ancestors. George III was Charles I or James II, the patriots were the Puritans, and the loyalists were 'the Guy Fawk's of the present day' who should be made 'to bow . . . and lick the Dust.' "⁶⁰

It was not only their receptivity to corporate ideology, the religious cast of the resistance movement, and the role they were given in The Body of the People that led Boston's laboring people to acquiesce to leadership from above in the decade after 1765. They were also well served, or at least as well as was possible in difficult circumstances, by the economic policies of their leaders. Nonimportation was not uniformly beneficial to artisans and laborers, as has been shown, but it benefited a very substantial number. For those who were hurt the resistance leaders did what they could through makework projects, primarily in textile production and in out-relief. The Whig leadership also exerted itself on behalf of shipbuilders. They rejected a petition to exempt certain items needed in ship construction from the nonimportation agreement of 1768, but appointed special committees of the town meeting to persuade men like Hancock to commission ships when employment was slack.⁶¹ When the Boston Port Act closed the harbor completely in mid-1774 laboring people were reduced to desperate straits; but by that time everyone was suffering and the Whig leaders could at least serve the laboring part of society by directing the collection and distribution of poor relief funds that flowed in from other colonies.⁶²

Thus the forging of class consciousness and demands for a new social order, which burst forth in 1765 and might have been expected to crystallize in the most turbulent and disordered decade in Boston's history, were halted in their tracks. Many merchants, appalled at the violence associated with resistance to England and divided from most artisans by the economics of nonimportation, moved into the loyalist camp or tried to maintain a neutral position. A larger number, including most of the lesser merchants and inland traders, held their ground and learned that the mechanics and merchant seamen would accept their leadership if, in the name of the corporate community, their needs and their political participation, even if not legitimized in law, were considered.

In New York the last decade before revolution witnessed the rapid growth of the techniques of popular politics, but Whig merchants and lawyers, both liberal and conservative, clung doggedly to political control until the final year before independence. This is puzzling at first glance because among the three northern ports New York had by far the most liberal franchise and hence the largest number of laboring men participating in electoral politics. Moreover, artisans were elected to important municipal offices as in no other city. Yet they could not unify after 1765 in order to wrest control of political power from the highly conservative mercantile elite. This was not, as in Boston, because resistance leaders smoothed over interclass hostilities by creating a spirit of The Body of the People or because they isolated most conservative merchants after 1770. In New York, the artisans did develop group consciousness, they gave vent to strong class feelings, and they deeply distrusted the men who occupied the leadership positions. But for reasons that were peculiar to New York, they were unable to use this collective identity to dislodge from political pre-eminence the city's wealthiest merchants, who held on until the shot heard around the world sent many of them into loyalist retirement.

In participating within the formal political arena New York's laboring men were far in advance of their Boston and Philadelphia counterparts during these years. At least two of every three free adult males could vote compared to less than half in Boston and Philadelphia, for freemanship was not tied to property ownership but was available upon payment of a modest fee if one were of age and satisfied the residency requirement. In the assembly elections of 1768 and 1769, 1,924 and 1,515 men respectively went to the polls—turnouts that were never matched proportionately to population in the other seaports.[63] Craftsmen were also elected to important city offices in substantial numbers. From 1761 to 1771 61 percent of the constables, collectors, and assessors elected were artisans, as compared with about 20 percent of the second-level officials in Boston and 46 percent in Philadelphia. Even more striking, 30 percent of the common councilmen chosen in New York from 1761 to 1775 were mechanics, whereas in Boston less than 10 percent of the selectmen and moderators were chosen from artisan ranks.[64] Such electoral power meant that "no candidate for public office, regardless of wealth and social standing, could afford to ignore the tradesmen and mechanics any more than he could voters of a higher status." One appalled patrician in the 1768 election noted that "every gentleman's table is now free and open to his friends, and he thinks it an honour to receive a visit from the meanest freeholder, nay condescends to shake hands with the dirtiest mechanic in the country."[65] It is also clear from reading the political broadsides and pamphlets in the elections of 1768 and 1769 that appeals for the votes of artisans and laborers were essential for winning office. Messages to the voters from "Jack Bowline and Tom Hatchway," from "Mr. Axe and Mr. Hammer," were distributed in the streets at election time and some of the appeals on nonimportation came from "A Mechanic" or "A Tradesman."[66]

Political power exercised outside formal political institutions also grew enormously in New York during the prerevolutionary decade. Mass meetings, where everyone had a voice, and house to house canvassing of the inhabitants became common. Thousands attended open-air gatherings around the issues of nonimportation in 1768, the quartering of British troops in 1769, the desire of merchants to abandon nonimportation in 1770, its reinstitution in 1773, and the Intolerable Acts in 1774. The spirit of mass decision-making was typified in 1769 by the urging of the popular leader Alexander McDougall, who rallied the populace to "assemble in the fields," hammer out a consensus on the issue of quartering troops, and then "go in a body to your members" (of the assembly) to insist that they follow the people's instruction.[67] In 1770, opposing factions decided to resolve the question of whether or not to resume importation by going door to door to question the inhabitants in what was perhaps the first public opinion poll in American history.[68] In both cases the will of the people was being determined quite apart from whether individuals were franchised or not.

Artisan participation, however, did not necessarily mean artisan power, as laboring men learned in 1770, when most New York merchants privately agreed to abandon nonimportation after Parliament rescinded all the Townshend duties except the one on tea. Two years earlier tradesmen had put teeth into the economic boycott by pledging not to patronize any merchant who violated the nonimportation pact. Enforcement was also carried out mainly by mechanics, who, operating under the directions of the Sons of Liberty, assumed the function of law officers. When news of the partial repeal of the Townshend duties arrived in April 1770, merchants with depleted inventories maneuvered to renew importations. Something of the upper-class sentiment for curbing the new power of the artisan enforcers of the boycott can be discerned in a broadside beamed at the laboring man of the city. "Nothing can be more flagrantly wrong than the Assertion of some of our Mercantile Dons that the Mechanics have no Right to give their Sentiments about the Importation of British Commodities . . . What particular Class among us has an exclusive Right to decide a Question of General Concern?"[69] Relations worsened in June and July, culminating in a street melee between importers and nonimporters, when most of the merchants voted to resume importation of nondutiable goods, ignoring the pressure of the artisans to maintain the boycott.

The unilateral decision of the merchants to renege on nonimportation ended illusions in New York that common interests bound classes together or that the election of artisans to municipal offices meant very much when the economic interests of the merchants were at stake. Artisans regarded the merchants' actions as a betrayal of a community compact and concluded that only through forming associations of their own and developing an independent voice could they hope to achieve their patriotic goals and defend their own economic interests. Nonimportation became the crucial test of whether the merchants could be trusted, whether different social ranks could work together under the leadership of the elite, whether class differences and competing interests could be set aside in a time of crisis.

Since the merchants had shattered the united front, the mechanics determined to act autonomously. A broadside issued on May 2, 1770, shortly after the merchants announced that they were placing new orders for boycotted goods, dripped with sarcasm at the defecting merchants. They had initially agreed to nonimportation, it was charged, in order "to collect in their debts, to vend their moth-eaten fragments, and to clear at least fifteen percent." Now, with nothing left on their shelves and "the increase of their private fortunes" involved, why should a riotous pack of mechanics deter them from chasing gold? Mechanics, in their view, were only "two legged pack horses . . . created solely to contribute to the ease and affluence of a few importers." and "a kind of beast of burden, who . . . may be seen in a state but should not be heard." After resuming importation, the merchants, it was recommended, should bend their efforts toward erecting a new manufactory where mechanics and their families, who were "innured to the severest bodily labour," would be compelled to work. When they expired, merchants could skin them and take their hides to the company tanyards. Another manufactory could be erected at the taxpayers' expense "for dressing, currying, and tanning the said hides" of laboring people and the profits could then be handed over to the merchants.[70] Productive labor, in this Swiftian satire, was now pitted against capitalist investment.

Despite growing class consciousness and alienation from the merchant gentry, New York's laboring men could not unite in these years. The artisan vote was deeply split in both 1768 and 1769 between the conservative DeLancey and moderate Livingston parties. In 1770, a house by house canvass produced 1,180 signatures for resuming importation and only 350 for maintaining the boycott, although the Sons of Liberty claimed that bribes or misunderstanding produced most of the signatures for resuming trade.[71] Even a repair in the rift within the Sons of Liberty in 1769 did not close the laboring ranks. It is these seemingly contradictory forces in motion—on one hand the presence of great laboring-class electoral power coupled with the advent of new forms of mass politics, and on the other hand the inability of artisans, laborers, and mariners to unite—that has confounded historians of New York for so long. Most frequently this enigma has been resolved by invoking the concept of "family loyalties"—the long tradition of personal loyalty from below to the Livingstons or the DeLanceys and their respective gentry associates.[72] In a sense this is true, but what did this loyalty consist of and was it consistent with the interests of laboring people, as they perceived them?

As in the other ports, artisans generally favored nonimportation because it gave them a protected market. Those who benefited especially
were artificers in the metal crafts and textile production, furniture-,
coach-, and instrumentmakers, and cordwainers, saddlers, hatters, and
glovers, who produced for the gentry who had previously purchased
these items from England.[73] Those whom nonimportation could not help,
and often hurt, were building craftsmen, the ship construction trades,
petty retailers, and some woodworkers such as coopers and turners.
They were hurt in a general economic decline, which, at least according
to the importing merchants, was the inevitable result of economic boycott. Mariners, who were numerous and extremely active in resistance
activities, were not affected much by nonimportation because, in spite of
the ominous sound of that policy for men who plied the seas, the volume
of tonnage in and out of New York did not decline during periods of
nonimportation, but was merely rechanneled in other directions or continued to England in items such as furs and grain, which were not included in the nonintercourse sanctions.[74] To some extent, then, merchants were probably able to obtain limited artisan support on ending
nonimportation because it was also in the interest of artisans in particular
trades.

Personal loyalty had another, more important dimension, which may
be labeled economic clientage. Many master artisans owned their own
houses and shops, worked independently to fill customers' orders, and
thus were at least partially insulated from economic pressure from
above. Far more numerous were those who were beholden to merchants,
lawyers, and urban landholders who controlled their rents, job opportunities, credit, and even personal affairs. Seventy percent of the mechanics who voted in the 1768 and 1769 elections or who obtained voting
rights in 1770 could not qualify to vote as freeholders—owners of £40 of
real property.[75] Most of these were tenants whose rent and house tenure
were at risk as they stepped to the polling place. For many others, such as
mariners and ship construction workers, jobs were at stake because merchants controlled the investment capital necessary for maritime construction and their ship masters could give or withhold berths as they pleased.
Even though the system of dependent labor was weakening, an extensive
network of economic clientage remained.

Economic dependency also existed in the other port towns, but in New
York it translated into political loyalty to an unusual degree because only
there was voice balloting, called viva voce voting, used instead of the
secret ballot. Even with secret balloting many artisans cast their votes as
their patron desired, for it was not easy to hide one's political preferences. But voice voting, where each shipwright, shoemaker, baker, and
laborer had to step forward and publicly announce his preference before
the assembled gentry, placed a tremendous constraint on the electoral

"preferences" of laboring men. Viva voce voting canceled out all of the supposedly greater political power which the more lenient franchise requirements and the tradition of artisan officeholding seemed to confer.

It was precisely the massive political arm twisting which viva voce voting allowed that led in 1769 to an all-out effort by New York's popular leaders and their laboring-class supporters to substitute a system of secret balloting such as had been used for decades in Boston and Philadelphia. In the previous year Oliver DeLancey and his wealthy cohorts had "posted themselves at the approaches to the City's election green" and "coaxed and bullied each voter as he strode to the poll" to announce his choice.[76] The three DeLancey candidates won between 53 and 60 percent of the mechanics' votes.[77] To insure that it was clear who had supported and who had opposed them the DeLanceyites took the extraordinary step of publishing the poll lists with the name of each voter and his political preferences inscribed. It may have been this intimidation that caused 25 percent of the laboring voters to stay away from the polls in 1769. Only the bakers and shoemakers held firm to Robert Livingston, whose mechanic vote dropped from 686 to 333, and it may be suspected that it was the relative immunity from economic retaliation of these artisans, who produced primarily for the laboring classes, that allowed them to vote according to their own dictates.[78] Among those who did go to the polls, "many of the poorer People," it was charged, "deeply Felt the Aristocratic Power, or rather the intolerable Tyranny of the great and opulent, who . . . openly threatened them with the loss of Employment, and to arrest them for Debt, unless they gave their Voices as they were directed."[79]

The campaign for secret balloting, led by the liberal Whigs, reached its height in late 1769 and early 1770. Newspaper and broadside writers argued that if this "antidote to Corruption" was passed by the assembly "no Man of Opulence will be able to procure a Seat . . . by an undue influence upon the Fears of the Electors." Secret balloting, wrote one advocate, would provide safeguards for "all honest Burghers and Tradesmen, who may incline to Vote contrary to the Sentiments, of their Employers or Landlords."[80]

Defenders of voice voting, who understood clearly what they stood to lose if electoral procedures were changed, especially with popularly selected extralegal committees playing a larger and larger role in making policy and enforcing community agreements affecting trade, fought back vigorously. The mechanics, led by smaller merchants such as Isaac Sears and Walter Franklin, called a rally of supporters for the secret ballot bill at the Liberty Pole, a nearly sacred symbol of the radical lower class, on December 27, 1769, but the conservative DeLancey group tore down the postbills advertising the meeting as fast as they were put up. The rally was rescheduled for December 29, and when opponents of secret ballot-

ing contested the size of the turnout another meeting at the Liberty Pole
was called. There "a most incontestible Majority" of the freemen and
freeholders "again Voted" to recommend the ballot bill to the city's four
representatives in the assembly.[81] A countermeeting, called by twelve of
the city's wealthiest merchants, half of whom would become loyalists
within six years, met at the Merchant's Coffee House on January 5. In
what their artisan adversaries called a design to see "how far commercial
influence would induce the common Artificers to acquiesce in the present
Deprivation of this most Inestimable Privilege" of secret balloting, the
merchants harangued the crowd and then asked for those who opposed
them to "draw off" to the side so they could be counted. This attempt to
isolate and identify men who would defy them led to violence, but in the
end, according to the mechanics, the "great and the mighty, and the rich,
and the long Whiggs and the Squaretoes" were outnumbered at least
three to two.[82]

In a final effort to sway New York's four DeLanceyite representatives,
each side conducted a petition drive for signatures. Spokesmen for the
laboring classes instructed their supporters to sign the petitions at the
houses of James McCartney, mariner, Henry Becker, carpenter, David
Philipse, wigmaker, and Jasper Drake, boatman. The conservative merchant group countered with a petition drive of their own and demonstrated that economic power still translated into political subservience by
obtaining the signatures of 1,007 "Freeholders and Freeman" who said
they wished to retain the voice voting system. New York's representatives, all wealthy merchants of the DeLancey faction, paid little heed to
the broad demand for reform, voting unanimously against the balloting
bill when the vote was taken in the assembly in January 1770. Even so,
the vote ended in a 12-12 tie, but went down to defeat on the speaker's
negative vote.[83]

Understanding how viva voce voting intimidated voters from the
lower ranks, especially in times of economic hardship when artisans and
laborers needed credit and employment, explains much about the failure
of laboring New Yorkers to unite. Hence, we see in a new light the house
by house poll in 1770, when merchants knocked on the doors of their
tenant-tradesmen, asked them how they wished to vote on ending nonimportation, and came away with a two-thirds majority in favor of resuming full commercial ties with England. Leaders of the lower ranks
attempted to instill courage in ordinary people by calling a meeting on
the common for resisting the petition until a more "general determination
upon this matter" could be reached, but the knocks on the door could not
go unanswered.[84] Petition in hand, the merchant was engaging in the
same kind of political arm twisting as occurred at the polls under voice
voting, even if the appearance of a house to house canvass was democratic.

After the detente in British-American relations in 1771 and 1772 the radical resistance leaders of New York, who had experienced such difficulties in coalescing the laboring men of the city, made their final push. When news of the Tea Act reached the city, Alexander McDougall and others distributed 1,500 copies of an *Association of the Sons of Liberty*, which condemned those who dared to accept consignments of East India Company Tea as traitors to their country and declared a boycott of their businesses. Two thousand New Yorkers stood in the rain at a mass rally in December 1773 to approve a total ban on tea. But tea leaves proved not to be the issue that could unite laboring men for either opposition to British policies or the promotion of internal reforms. Even though New Yorkers staged their own tea party, destroying a small shipment that Captain James Chambers attempted to smuggle into the city in April 1774, the radicals could not maintain their momentum. In fact, the tea episode so frightened conservative New Yorkers that they began an all-out effort to reassert their authority. A sworn foe "to *Cobblers and Tailors* so long as they take upon their everlasting and immeasurable shoulders the power of directing the loyal and sensible inhabitants of the city" declared the determination of propertied men to halt popular action. More and more the question became who would control the extralegal committees that were called into being by mass meetings of the people. "After the destruction of Captain Chamber's tea and some other violent proceedings of the pretended patriots," wrote Governor Colden, "the principal inhabitants began to be apprehensive and resolved to attend the meetings of the inhabitants when called together by hand bills."[85]

Another test of where political power resided came when New Yorkers had to decide how to respond to the closing of the port of Boston in May 1774. Broad commercial sanctions represented the most powerful response and by now all New Yorkers were aware of how such a policy would affect them. Almost as important was how a decision should be reached. It was apparent that merchants and mechanics were divided on the issue when separate meetings were called by the importing merchants and by "a number of respectable merchants and the body of mechanics." For several days the two groups contested the appointing of a committee to correspond with the Boston Committee of Correspondence and to hammer out a policy for New Yorkers. Indicative of their growing class consciousness, the artisans now formed a Mechanics Committee, which soon superseded the Sons of Liberty. It was this group that nominated a slate of twenty-five persons to correspond with Boston's resistance leaders and to enforce any new economic boycott. The Merchants Committee responded with a slate of fifty-one, which included some of the Sons of Liberty as a concession but was predominantly conservative. As an impasse with England approached, the citizens were asked to determine which slate should be presented for popular endorsement. Their choice was tantamount to determining who would formulate economic policy and rule the city, for many of the powers of government by now had fallen into the hands of the extralegal committees.[86] The young aristocrat Gouverneur Morris described "a great concourse of the inhabitants" who met on May 19 to contend "about the future forms of our government, whether it should be founded upon Aristocratic or democratic principles." Looking down on the crowd from a balcony, Morris described the scene: "on my right hand were ranged all the people of property, with some few dependents, and on the other all the tradesmen."[87]

The outcome of the meeting was a victory for the conservative merchants, whose Committee of 51 was chosen. According to McDougall, the merchants worked all day before the evening meeting to assemble "every tool who was under their influence as well those in trade as out of it."[88] Governor Colden agreed. "The principal inhabitants," he wrote to England, "being now afraid that those hot-headed men might run the city into dangerous measures, appeared in a considerable body at the first meeting of the people after the Boston Port Act was published here." Many of the merchants who agreed to serve on the Committee of 51 had never before participated in public affairs and were not eager to sit on extralegal bodies that were making de facto assumptions of authority. They were "induced to appear in what they are sensible is an illegal character, from a consideration that if they did not, the business would be left in the same rash hands as before."[89] The best the outmaneuvered popular leaders could do was to obtain agreement that a poll would be taken of the city to see if the Committee of 51 was acceptable to the majority of householders. When Isaac Sears, a lower-class leader, met with the head of the Merchants Committee, he could not reach agreement on who would conduct the polling—a critical issue in view of the power of merchants to dictate the vote of men dependent on them. Sears abandoned the referendum and conceded committee control of the city to the conservative merchants. "You may rest assured," wrote one jubilant patrician, "no non-im[portation], nor non-exportation will be agreed upon . . . The power over our crowd is no longer in the hands of Sears, Lamb, or such unimportant persons . . . Their power . . . expired instantly upon the election of the . . . Fifty-one."[90]

Though New York's conservative merchants squelched the commercial boycott and stifled the movement for internal reform, they had not reckoned with the possibility that their hard-won ground would be cut from under them by the First Continental Congress, which met in Philadelphia in the fall of 1774. New York's four delegates represented the sentiments of the victorious conservatives, but even this could not prevent the signing of a Continental Association which pledged all the colonies to adhere to a step by step cessation of commercial relations with Great Britain. This gave a tremendous boost to the mechanics of New York and they used it to secure nearly half of the places on the Committee of Sixty that was selected at the end of the year to enforce the association. By the following April, when fighting broke out at Lexington and Concord, public order was crumbling in New York and the DeLanceyites, who had controlled the extralegal committees, were resigning their places and establishing their credit with the loyalist element around the governor. They had held on tenaciously to the very end.[91]

Interclass relations in New York were affected by some of the same factors that pertained in Boston but were significantly different in several regards. In common with Boston was the presence of the British army. Among the poor and unemployed much of the resentment that might otherwise have been channeled into efforts to restructure society internally was directed at the soldiery, with whom lower-class New Yorkers were engaged in "a vigorous labor market rivalry." It was the vote of James DeLancey for the Quartering Act in 1769 that drove radical resistance leaders Sears and Lamb back to a union with McDougall and the moderate Livingston-led party. Their followers doggedly defended the Liberty Pole against royal soldiers in the fall of 1766, fought intermittently with the British garrison thereafter, and engaged in two bloody fights on Golden Hill and in Nassau Street in 1770 in New York's version of the fracases between troops and populace that led to the Boston Massacre in the same year.[92] Unemployment and high food prices were the issues for those in the lowest levels of the economy, but impressment by the British navy and moonlighting by British soldiers provided the most immediate focuses for their discontent.

A second reason for the absence of a strong artisan bloc in politics, despite growing class hostility, was the restriction that the lack of a secret ballot put on collective action. Laboring men rallied to the radical resistance leadership as best they could on issues such as nonimportation and control of the city's governing committees. When an opportunity for internal reform was at hand, such as the struggle for the secret ballot, they turned out in large numbers and provided leaders from their own ranks. But daily bread could not be compromised as easily as one's vote, so when they were forced by canvasses or public polls to declare themselves, some gave their support to those with economic power over them. Homogeneity within the laboring ranks was never entirely possible, given the complexities of economic boycotts, trade depressions, and the long-range division of masters and journeymen. But the sway of those who contracted for ships, developed urban real estate, rented property, and extended credit is more important in explaining the division of the laboring populace and the ability of the conservative merchants to maintain their political grip so long. What has frequently been called the political deference of laboring men or the cultural hegemony of the elite, in which lower-class people internalized the values of their superiors, can more accurately be described as a pervasive use of economic leverage from above.

Another factor retarding the coalescence of artisans and laborers as a class in New York was religious hostility, particularly between the Presbyterians and Anglicans. Historians have often observed that the Livingstons were the party of the Presbyterians while the Anglicans cleaved to the DeLanceys. Controversies between the two church groups had embroiled the city since the Kings College dispute of the 1750s and flared up again in the mid-1760s around the issue of establishing an Anglican bishop in America.[93] Religious ties were strong among many people and this factor cannot be ignored; but too much can also be made of it. Though their religious affiliations varied, shoemakers and bakers voted decisively for the Livingston party in 1768 and 1769, and cartmen unified behind the DeLanceyites in 1774 when the Committee of 51 was endorsed. These are clues (but only that until correlations between religious affiliation and occupation can be established) that the political preferences of laboring men were determined less by religion than by considerations of economic survival.[94] At the least, however, it can be said that the large degree of religious homogeneity that promoted interclass unity among Whigs in Boston did not exist in New York.

Gentry power in New York also owed something to the sheer strength of conservative merchants and professionals to resist pressure from below. More merchants in Boston joined the forces of resistance than in New York and the most flexible of them retained their power by convincing laboring people that their cause was one. A greater proportion of New York's merchants were diehard conservatives and wished to concede nothing to reformers, "I understand by all hands that you have an over-proportion of tories with you to any place on the continent," wrote Thomas Young to one of New York's Sons of Liberty. Animated "by fear of a civil war" and by anxiety that "the levelling spirit of New England should propagate itself into New York," the elite spoke not the language of covenant but the language of an embattled class.[95] Faced by what one of them referred to as a reptilian "mobility," which had demonstrated since the Stamp Act that ordinary people would employ their new-found power to "correspond with the other colonies, call and dismiss popular assemblies, make resolves and bind consciences of the rest of mankind, bully poor printers, and exert with full force all their other tribunitial powers," the patrician merchants and professionals exerted themselves and hung on as long as they could.[96] When it grew too late, they contributed themselves to the loyalist cause as in no other port town, leaving a partial vacuum into which artisan radicals could step.

Once war became a certainty and conservatives began abandoning New York, the city teemed with cries for social reform. When the drafting of a constitution was proposed, the Committee of Mechanics de-

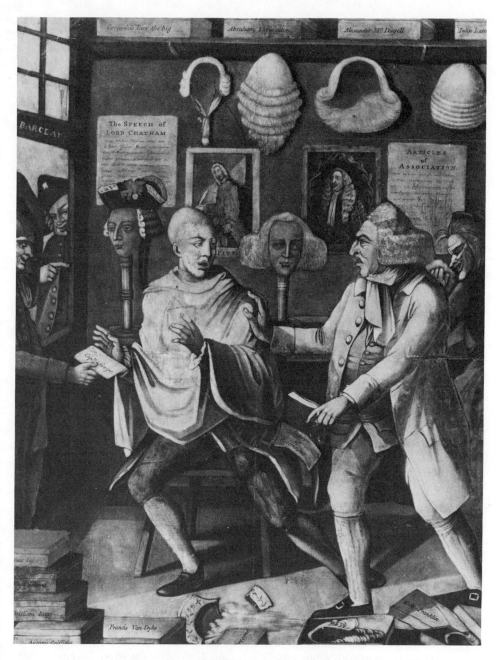

13. *The Patriotick Barber of New York, 1775,*
attributed to Philip Dawe.

manded popular ratification of any document produced and a provision for "an uncontrolled power to alter the constitution in the same manner that it shall have been received."[97] Artisans by the hundreds paraded in March 1776 to thank the Committee of Inspection for regulating prices of consumer items imported from the West Indies and insisted, in the face of opposition by the provincial assembly, that the people, not the assembly, should elect New York's representatives to the Continental Congress. Throughout the first half of 1776 the city's newspapers were filled with articles proposing annual assembly elections, rotation of offices, secret balloting, universal adult male suffrage, equal apportionment, popular election of local officials, and the abolition of slavery and imprisonment for debt. The city seethed in the last months before independence with artisan voices and artisan action, as the wealthy fled in anticipation of military occupation by the army of the Continental Congress and patriotic committees of inspection disarmed the Tories.[98]

In this belated release of radical political energy, lesser artisans, mariners, and laborers found themselves maneuvering for advantage with liberal Whigs, led by such men as John Jay, Philip Schuyler, James Duane, and Robert Livingston. Though these leaders had eagerly sought the support of the lower ranks in their opposition to English policies, they resisted pressure from below on internal issues, where they countenanced far less extensive reform than their social inferiors. In repulsing most of the demands of lower-class radicals, the liberal Whigs were greatly aided by the arrival of Washington's continental troops in the city in the spring of 1776. The flight of the most conservative element, which for so long had thwarted social reform, was accompanied by the arrival of a patriot army that turned New York into a center of military preparation.[99]

PHILADELPHIA was the northern port where artisans had participated least in political affairs before 1765 and where, during the Stamp Act crisis, they were so deeply split that one group of mechanics had opposed another group. Yet laboring men in Philadelphia coalesced so well after 1770 that this was the place where artisans most effectively infiltrated the extralegal committee structure and took the most radical steps to reform society internally.

Before 1770 artisans seldom held office in Philadelphia, except occasionally as overseer of the poor, street commissioner, or tax collector.[100] But artisan voices were rising in answer to economic insecurity, expressed in newspaper appeals from and to the mechanic segment of the community as a separate interest and in resentment of those who accumulated great wealth while laboring people suffered.[101] Writing in 1767, "Tom Trudge" told his auditors that he was only "one of those trudging dirty mortals whom irresistable destiny has almost ever obliged to walk on foot." Though humble and hungry, his sense of equity had not grown dull and it was mightily offended by paying an annual road tax that went primarily to pave the roads and remove the refuse in parts of the city where the well-to-do were concentrated. The poor, like himself, "sup on a cup of skim milk and have a parcel of half-naked children about our doors"; but rarely did they see the city dung carts come to their "penurious" alleyways. Why should they pay "for cleaning the yards of the opulent merchants and gentry"? The indignity was equal to the oppression, charged Trudge, and the matter called for redress.[102]

Philadelphia's artisans exerted themselves as a separate political entity for the first time in attempting to spur foot-dragging merchants of their city to adopt a nonimportation policy in the spring of 1768, as was being done in New York and Boston. Charges were rife that the Philadelphia importers were "contemptible to the last degree for their mercenary principles and abject pusillanimity" in refusing to join the economic boycott. Artisans did what they could to move the merchants, holding public meetings, publishing newspaper appeals, and organizing secondary boycotts of importing merchants.[103] It took until March 1769 for popular pressure to bring Philadelphia's merchants into the fold (a year after Boston and New York had adopted nonimportation), and by that time the disillusionment with them in the artisan community was widespread.

If any doubt remained among artisans regarding the absence of a natural community of interest between them and the merchants, it was shattered when the latter attempted to break free of the nonimportation agreement early in 1770. Philadelphia's leather apron men believed they had entered into these agreements in the spirit of community, where social boundaries separating person from person and rank from rank dissolved because all were working for a common goal. As in the other ports, Philadelphia's laboring men had participated widely in enforcing nonimportation, assuming the functions of civil government. Now, when the merchants wanted to abandon a policy that cut into their profits, they imperiously informed the mechanics that they had "no Right to give their sentiments respecting an importation" and called the artificers "A Rabble."[104] It took nothing more to convince the artisans that they must work independently for their objectives and even assume responsibility for setting and enforcing the community's goals. The change in the artisans' attitude in the spring of 1770 was "one of the most striking events in the history of Philadelphia in the eighteenth century." They had been "temperate and cooperative" before, but by May of that year, as merchants tried to scuttle the boycott, "it became apparent to them that they would have to strike out on their own if they were to obtain what they wanted."[105]

The artisans were not able to halt the merchants from resuming importations. But this is less important than the change of consciousness and the abrupt jettisoning of the customary reliance on merchant leadership that occurred. Artisans called a public meeting of their fellows in May 1770 and formed their own Mechanics Committee, four years before such an all-craft organization was established in New York. They were effective enough to delay the abandonment of nonimportation and showed how far deference toward the merchants had crumbled by promising in June that importing merchants "will be dealt with by the Mechanicks Committee."[106]

By the fall of 1770, although merchants were importing again, artisans were on the move. For the first time in many decades an artisan, proudly announcing himself as such, ran for sheriff. Artisans soon began to fill positions as tax assessors and collectors, wardens and street commissioners, and insisted on their right to participate equally with merchants and gentlemen in the nomination of assemblymen and other important officeholders. Addressing his "Brethern the Tradesmen, Mechanics, &c," an artisan who called himself "Brother Chip" gave notice that the day was over when laboring men would tamely endorse men nominated by the elite, who were always from the upper class. "If we have not the Liberty of nominating such Persons whom we approve, our Freedom of voting is at an End," wrote Chip. He occupied still more radical ground by asserting that it was "absolutely necessary" that one or two artisans be elected to the assembly from Philadelphia.[107]

The assembly election in 1770 was a turning point in Philadelphia politics. Brother Chip's strident call, published in the *Pennsylvania Gazette*, marked the beginning of a new political party, strongly Presbyterian and laboring class in composition, strongly radical in opposing British policies, and bent on restructuring society internally. The "White Oaks [ship carpenters] and Mechanicks or many of them," lamented Joseph Galloway, a leader of the collapsing assembly party that had dominated electoral politics for decades, "have left the old Ticket and 'tis feared will go over to the Presbyterians."[108] They did precisely this, leaving the assembly party in a shambles. Organizing a new ticket, which included tailor Joseph Parker, the first tradesman to run for the assembly since the 1680s, the emerging radical party won at the polls. "Many Threats, Reflections, Sarcasms, and Burlesques" were hurled against the artisans, according to one Philadelphia merchant, but this did little to deter them because secret balloting went far to keep them immune from the economic influence of those they offended.[109]

Possessing many votes and inspirited by success in electing their own kind to important offices, Philadelphia's artisans began pressing the legislature in 1772 for economic programs that would benefit them. Particularly, they opposed excise taxes on liquor. In a large public meeting, chaired by an artisan who crafted fishing tackle, they protested that the excise fell with greatest weight on "the middling and poorer Class of the inhabitants." Similarly, they declared that a Leather Act which drove up the price of skins "oppresses the Poor, by Shoes being considerably advanced in Price."[110] At a meeting in October 1772 artisans issued a call for publishing each week the full assembly debates and roll calls on important issues—a demand indicative of their distrust of patrician legislators and their determination to vote only for those who responded to their needs. They also challenged "the absurd and Tyrannical custom of shutting the Assembly doors during debate."[111] In Boston Whig leaders had opened legislative debates to the public in order to politicize them with resounding rhetoric. In Philadelphia the artisans, no longer believing in a community of interest between them and the merchant-lawyer elite, broke through the fiction that legislators acted most wisely and dispassionately when shielded from the hurly-burly of everyday opinion and pressure. Undivided as in New York, the artisans won legislative approval for the erection of public galleries in the assembly and for the weekly publication of assembly debates and roll calls. It was enough to leave some genteel Philadelphians muttering, "It is Time the Tradesmen were checked—they take too much upon them—they ought not to intermeddle in State Affairs—they will become too powerful."[112]

The power of a far more unified and aggressive artisan community than existed in New York or Boston showed itself dramatically in Philadelphia's response to the closing of Boston harbor in 1774. As in New York, conservative merchants and lawyers realized that they must assert themselves, both to head off another nonimportation movement and to prevent the extralegal committee system, to which more and more civil authority was falling, from slipping into the hands of radicals. Some of Philadelphia's popular leaders, such as Charles Thomson, joined hands with the more conservative merchants to construct a fusion ticket of nineteen candidates, composed primarily of well-to-do merchants, to act as a Committee of Correspondence for coordinating strategies of resistance with other cities. But the artisans called their own meeting, assembled 1,200 strong at the Statehouse on June 9, 1774, and forced their way into what they called the "Merchants Committee." Faced with this kind of artisan power, the Whig leadership made broad concessions. They dropped two merchant committeemen obnoxious to the artisans, added four Germans, including a baker and a tanner, and enlarged the committee with six other tradesmen put forward by the mechanics committee.[113] The resulting Committee of 43, which took over direction of the city's response to the Boston Port Act, marked the final demise of "the unquestioned control of local politics by the great import-export merchants." In contrast to the parallel New York Committee of 51, which was entirely composed of merchants and lawyers, the Philadelphia committee had artisans and small manufacturers sitting in about one-third of the places.[114]

This intercity contrast was equally evident in the committees elected in the northern ports after the Continental Congress scheduled a full-scale boycott of English trade in October 1774. Even the meeting in Carpenter's Hall rather than the Statehouse was a symbolic victory for artisan radicals and they accounted for thirteen of the twenty-four inspectors chosen to supervise the election of a sixty-six-person Committee of Inspection. Recognizing their growing strength, the mechanics put forward a ticket that "was thoroughly radical in character." It excluded every leading conservative from the Committee of 43 and gave places to artisans, shopkeepers, and minor merchants from the different religious groups and neighborhoods in the city. A conservative merchant slate, which included many of the older, wealthier, import-export merchants who had dominated politics in the past, went down to defeat.[115] Both of the tradesmen's main demands—one reflecting external concerns, one internal—had been fulfilled: that Pennsylvania commit itself unequivocally to an economic boycott and that the extralegal government by committee "include them in more than token numbers."[116]

The New York and Boston committees elected in November 1774 to enforce the Continental Association also represented a victory for the radical Whig resistance to the latest British policy, but the composition of the New York and Boston committees reveals the differences in the dynamics of internal social relations. In New York conservatives were forced to recognize the presence of the artisan radicals because the latter's demand for nonimportation, which they had successfully opposed locally, was put into effect by the Continental Congress. But the conservatives still had enough power to oblige the radicals to accept a fusion ticket rather than present the electors with a clear choice of slates, as in Philadelphia. The slate of sixty, moreover, included twelve merchants who would later become loyalists.[117] In Boston the Committee of 63 had none of the conservative merchants on it because the Whig leadership had no need to concede anything to a group that had been isolated from the majority of Boston's patriots for several years. Ten artisans, well-situated men like silversmith Paul Revere, sailmaker Norman Greenough, and blacksmith Richard Boylston, were also represented on the committee. But only in Philadelphia, where conservative merchants ran their own ticket, lost, and saw power shift wholly to the radical mechanics and their merchant allies, had artisans operating as a self-conscious group been able to grasp the levers of political action.[118]

The implications of this maturing of artisan consciousness became evident in the final year before independence. A new surge of radicalism, led by Thomas Young, James Cannon, Thomas Paine, and Timothy Matlack and centered in the thirty-one companies of the Philadelphia militia that had been organized in the spring of 1775, produced demands for the most radical reforms yet suggested in the colonies. The themes of curbing the individual accumulation of wealth, opening up opportunity, divorcing the franchise from property ownership, and driving the mercantile elite from power became explicit in a flood of polemical literature that swept over Philadelphia. "Our great merchants . . . [are] making immense fortunes at the expense of the people," charged a "Tradesman" in April 1775. Sounding the tocsin on economic inequality that English and European republican writers had stressed but genteel American Whigs saw fit to ignore, Tradesman argued that the merchants "will soon have the whole wealth of the province in their hands, and then the people will be nearly in the condition that the East-India Company reduced the poor natives of Bengal to." Men of this kind must be stopped in "their present prospect of making enormous estates at our expense." Once their "golden harvests" were put to an end, "all ranks and conditions would come in for their just share of the wealth." Tradesman doubtless exaggerated in claiming that some Philadelphia merchants made "from 15 to 20,000 pounds per month profit," but the hyperbole was itself a sign of the inequities felt in the laboring part of the community and the insistence that with independence must come greater economic equality.[119]

By the fall of 1775 the Philadelphia militia had become a school of political education, much in the manner of Cromwell's New Model Army. The militia "quickly developed a collective identity and consciousness, a sense of its own rights and grievances," and "became a center of intense political debate and discussion."[120] Organizing their own Committee of Correspondence, which included men of no previous political experience such as tailor Frederick Hagener and paperhanger Edward Ryves, the privates began exerting pressure on the provincial assembly to take a more assertive stand on independence. They also made three highly radical demands for internal change: first, that militiamen be given the right to elect all their officers, rather than only their junior officers, as the assembly had specified in the militia law; second, that the franchise be conferred on all militiamen, regardless of age and economic condition; and third, that the assembly impose a heavy financial penalty, proportionate to the size of his estate, on every man who refused militia service, using this money to support the families of poor militiamen.[121]

Though upper-class Whigs might call the militia privates "in general damn'd riff raff—dirty, mutinous, and disaffected," there was no denying the power of these men.[122] Generally from the lowest ranks of the laboring population, as opposed to the master craftsmen who had gradually, from 1770 to 1774, gained control of the extralegal committees, they played a major role in the creation of the radical Pennsylvania constitution of 1776. "An enormous proportion of property vested in a few individuals," they advised the Constitutional Convention, "is dangerous to the rights, and destructive to the common happiness of mankind, and therefore every free state hath a right by its laws to discourage the possession of such property." This clarion call for a ceiling on wealth was accompanied by the advice that in electing representatives the people should shun "great and overgrown rich men [who] will be improper to be trusted, [for] they will be too apt to be framing distinctions in society, because they will reap the benefits of all such distinctions."[123]

The greater ability of Philadelphia's laboring classes to organize and assert their collective strength was best exemplified in the move to broaden the franchise as well as break through the traditional concept that only property ownership—holding a "stake" in society, as it was commonly phrased—entitled one to political rights. In the other cities voices were raised occasionally for the political rights of the propertyless and the poor.[124] But only in Philadelphia, where a combination of artisans and lesser merchants captured control of the political process and then were themselves pressured from below by a highly politicized militia, was the franchise given to all taxpayers, regardless of whether they owned property. In a society where propertylessness was growing among the laboring classes, this was a break with the past of enormous significance. It swept away "the basic economic presupposition that the ownership of a specified amount of property was an essential guarantee of political competence."[125] Many avid patriots, such as Bostonian John Adams, were aghast at this, for, as the future drafter of the Massachusetts constitution said, "it tends to confound and destroy all distinctions, and prostrate all ranks to one common level."[126] That, of course, was what the radical architects of Pennsylvania's constitution had in mind.

In New York and Boston, where the franchise was broad but where economic derangements had impoverished many former propertyholders and hence disqualified them from voting, the Pennsylvania example of opening up political participation to all taxpayers was not followed. It is unlikely, in an era of intense politicization of all ranks, that former voters and those who had never voted but were involved in street demonstrations, open-air public meetings, and economic boycotts were not interested in the vote. Rather, it was the ability of the liberal Whig gentry, especially in Boston, to maintain control of the political process that prevented any move toward separating political rights from property ownership. When lawyers of middle-class background and moderate political views could not countenance the extension of the franchise to propertyless town dwellers, it was certain that no such expansion of the political community would be part of the internal reform of society until they lost control of the political process to those below them.

Why did group consciousness and class power proceed farthest in the city where laboring people had been most deeply divided and most politically inactive only eleven years before independence? One factor was the absence of the British army, which in Boston and New York had acted as a lightning rod for artisan discontent, especially in times of scarce employment, and had promoted interclass unity in the name of confronting a common enemy. Philadelphia never saw more than a token military force, while the other two cities faced British troops for most of the last decade before independence. To some extent this allowed for a preoccupation with internal matters that was not possible elsewhere.

A second factor was the ability of radical leaders, such as the small merchant Charles Thomson, schoolteacher James Cannon, itinerant physician and organizer Thomas Young, physician Benjamin Rush, apothecary Christopher Marshall, hardware retailer Timothy Matlack, and instrumentmaker David Rittenhouse, to overcome religious factionalism in what had always been a religiously heterogeneous town. In Boston religious homegeneity and the adroit promotion of political action by The Body of the People curbed the growth of class identity. In New York, Anglican-Presbyterian enmity, though probably not a major factor, could never be completely overcome by radical leaders such as Sears, McDougall, and Lamb. But in Philadelphia, the radicals came from every segment of the religious community and consciously worked to promote interdenominationalism by putting on the radical committee slates representatives of each ethnic and religious group.[127] Out of the shambles of the old assembly party of Galloway and Franklin, which had been partially discredited in 1765 for its weak stance on the Stamp Act and had been abandoned by artisans in 1770 over the nonimportation issue, rose a new popular party. It was often labeled "Presbyterian" by Quakers and Anglicans because they thought that was a way of discrediting it, but it enjoyed support from laboring men in all congregations except the Quakers. By 1776 it could be said that class identity rather than religious affiliation or an older association with either the proprietary or assembly party was the determining factor in how men made political choices.

A third factor promoting greater pressure for internal reform in Philadelphia than in either Boston or New York was the quality and ideology of radical leadership. By the eve of the Revolution Philadelphia not only was the home of radical native sons such as Matlack, Marshall, and Rittenhouse but also had attracted from distant places talented polemicists and organizers such as Cannon, who arrived from Edinburgh in 1765, Thomas Paine, who emigrated from England in 1774, and Young who arrived from Boston by way of Newport in the following year. Adding to the power of this group of egalitarian spokesmen was the talent and democratic commitment of William Goddard, who arrived from New York in 1767 to begin what soon became the most trenchant vehicle of artisan views in the colonies, the *Pennsylvania Chronicle*.[128] What is more, Philadelphia's radical leaders spoke a much different language than Samuel Adams in Boston. His goal was to return to the austere Christian commonwealth of the forefathers; theirs was to create a world in which the channels upward were clear, the concentration of political and economic power was shattered, and social justice did not give way to the contractual law of a society organized around market relations. Some of Philadelphia's leaders, including Rush and Paine, would later change their views, but in 1775-1776 they were at the core of an interdenominational, egalitarian circle with close ties to the lowest echelons of Philadelphia society.

Finally, the success of Philadelphia's laboring classes can be related to the partial vacuum of political leadership created by the withdrawal of Quakers from power. Violence in politics and the specter of war with England drove many Quakers, who had dominated the assembly party for years, into retirement, and the decision of the Society of Friends in December 1774 to enforce a policy of passive obedience and nonresistance (which soon took the form of disowning any Quakers serving on the quasi-governmental committees) sapped conservative Whiggism of much of its strength.[129] The weakness of the conservative press in Philadelphia, as contrasted with New York where *Rivington's Gazetteer* kept up a continuous offensive against radical attempts to transform politics well into the war years, is but one sign of conservatism on the run in Philadelphia. This galloping anemia was also related to the anxiety which the rising strength of the laboring classes evoked. In no other city did the propertied upper class see the radical point of view so vigorously articulated or feel the power of the artisans and those below them press so hard against traditional institutions. The soldiers of the militia, warned one frightened conservative, regarded "an Agrarian law" for redistributing property as "very agreeable." [130] The rapid disintegration of the non-Quaker proprietary elite of Philadelphia, which dominated the executive and judicial branches of government, was in no small part caused by the "madness of the multitude," the bringing of "all dregs to the top," as one of its members expressed it in 1775.[131] Conservative strength ebbed fastest where it was challenged directly by those who had developed their own consciousness and organizational base.

It is NOT within the compass of this book to analyze the revolutionary process that occurred after the outbreak of fighting in eastern Massachusetts in the spring of 1775. It is enough to note that the work of a new generation of historians has begun to demonstrate that much of the complexity and significance of the American Revolution is missed by portraying it primarily as a movement for independence and the creation of republican institutions. It was certainly that, but it was also a social upheaval involving "the rapid and often violent mobilization into public life of many different groups," the challenging of gentry control of public affairs, and the proposing of remedies for the social ills that many believed had beset American society.[132]

The burden of this book has been to show how the growth and commercial development of the northern seaport towns brought about multifaceted change involving the restructuring of social groups, the redistribution of wealth, the alteration of labor relations, the emergence of states of consciousness that cut horizontally through society, and the mobilization into political life of the lower ranks of laboring people. Haltingly it was recognized by many in the cities that the ligaments of the corporate society of the past had been torn in ways that struck at their opportunities, well-being, and sense that equity prevailed. In this century-long process there emerged no perfect crystallization of classes or class consciousness. But both master craftsmen and small retailers in the middle ranks and lesser artisans, merchant seamen, and laborers below them learned to define their interests and identify the self-interested behavior of those they had been taught to believe acted for the good of the whole. We have seen them beginning to struggle around the issues that were most palpable in terms of their daily existence and, in the process of struggling, developing a consciousness about their separate roles and their antagonistic interests with others in their communities.

Liberal theory, as imbided by historians, recognizes tension and conflict only in terms of the "explicit and unwarranted intrusion of authority upon individual [political] freedom."[133] But on a wide ensemble of issues —including political rights, but extending beyond them to wages and prices, charity, taxes, market and labor relations, and evangelical religion—the urban lower orders formulated distinctly different points of view from the ones held by those above them. It is necessary to reiterate that there was no unified ideology among those who worked with their hands or among those who did not. Urban society was much too fluid for that. Nor can it be said that there were no important areas where interclass agreement prevailed. Nevertheless, within their own cognitive structures, merchant seamen, artisans, and the poor, as well as merchants, shopkeepers, and professional men, saw their world changing. This led, as the Revolution approached, to the rise of a radical consciousness among many and to an interplay between calls for internal reform and insurgency against external forces that adversely affected the lives of city people. Challenges to the concentration of economic, political, and cultural authority ultimately shattered the equilibrium of the old system of social relations.

Although no social revolution occurred in America in the 1770s, the American Revolution could not have unfolded when or in the manner it did without the self-conscious action of urban laboring people—both those at the bottom and those in the middle—who became convinced that they must create power where none had existed before or else watch their position deteriorate, both in absolute terms and relative to that of others. Thus, the history of the Revolution is in part the history of popular collective action and the puncturing of the gentry's claim that their rule was legitimized by custom, law, and divine will. Ordinary people, sometimes violently, took over the power and the procedures of the constituted authorities. With wealth becoming far more concentrated at the top of urban society, plebeian urban dwellers forced their way into the political arena, not so much through the formal mechanisms of electoral politics as through street demonstrations, mass meetings, extralegal committees that assumed governmental powers, the intimidation of their enemies, and, in some cases, spirited defenses of traditional norms. This reordering of political power required a mental breakthrough, for it had to be accomplished in the face of a model of social relations, set by the elite, which claimed the superior wisdom and public mindedness of the educated and wealthy and prescribed deference as the customary and proper role of "inferior" people.

This shattering of the habit of obedience, advanced by the Great Awakening, proceeded far more rapidly in Boston in the second third of the century than in the other towns. Yet it relapsed after 1765, as traditional leaders, aided by the descent of a red-coated enemy on the community, reasserted themselves and as the people closed ranks in a reaffirmation of the spirit of covenant. In New York and Philadelphia the political leadership of the elite was challenged only sporadically until the end of the Seven Years War, when economic derangements and internal factionalism set the stage for the rise of laboring men to political power. But in all the cities those who labored with their hands, especially those who found it most difficult to weather the changes that had overcome their society, formed a picture of the social arrangements by which they lived. It was a picture that was political in its composition and increasingly vivid in its portrayal of the port towns as places where men struggled against each other rather than working harmoniously for the mutual good of the whole society.

APPENDIX
Tables
Figures

NOTES

INDEX

ABBREVIATIONS

BTR	*Reports of the Record Commissioners of the City of Boston*
CSM Pub.	*Publications of the Colonial Society of Massachusetts*
CSP Colonial	*Calendar of State Papers, Colonial Series, America and West Indies*
DAB	*Dictionary of American Biography*
HSP	Historical Society of Pennsylvania
MHS	Massachusetts Historical Society
MHS Coll.	*Collections of the Massachusetts Historical Society*
MHS Proc.	*Proceedings of the Massachusetts Historical Society*
NYCD	*Documents Relative to the Colonial History of the State of New York*
NYHS	New-York Historical Society
NYHS Coll.	*Collections of the New-York Historical Society*
PMHB	*Pennsylvania Magazine of History and Biography*
WMQ	*William and Mary Quarterly*, 3d ser.

Table 1. Occupational Structure of Philadelphia and Boston, 1685-1775

Occupation	Boston inventories 1685-1775 (no. and percent)	Phila. inventories 1685-1775 (no. and percent)	Phila. tax list 1772 (no. and percent)
Government	42 (1.52)	39 (2.79)	75 (2.14)
Colonial officers	11 (0.40)	7 (0.50)	14 (0.40)
Local officers	1 (0.40)	6 (0.43)	41 (1.17)
Unidentified "esquires" and "gentlemen"	30 (1.08)	26 (1.86)	20 (0.57)
Service	713 (25.77)	494 (35.31)	1,623 (46.34)
Professionals	77 (2.78)	43 (3.07)	122 (3.48)
apothecary, druggist	3	5	10
doctor, physician	30	20	34
lawyer, conveyancer	6	8	27
minister	10	8	17
musician, dancing master, artist	16	0	3
schoolmaster, professor	12	2	31
Retailers	48 (1.73)	23 (1.64)	67 (1.91)
bookseller, bookbinder	9	4	7
chandler, shipchandler	14	11	26
grocer, victualer	17	4	4
peddler, huckster, trader, fishmonger, milkman	8	4	30
Retail crafts	255 (9.22)	181 (12.94)	502 (14.33)
baker	29	28	104

(Continued)

Table 1 (Continued)

Occupation	Boston inventories 1685-1775 (no. and percent)	Phila. inventories 1685-1775 (no. and percent)	Phila. tax list 1772 (no. and percent)
butcher	15	10	54
confectioner, chocolate grinder	0	1	10
shopkeeper	137	95	159
tailor, breechesmaker, seamstress	67	44	157
tobacconist, snuffmaker	7	3	18
Building crafts	153 (5.53)	138 (9.86)	371 (10.59)
bricklayer	15	24	32
brickmaker	3	6	9
carpenter, housewright, wharfbuilder	81	65	202
glazier	9	6	4
joiner	23	29	67
mason, stonecutter, paver, plasterer	14	4	32
painter	8	4	25
Travel and transport	115 (4.16)	75 (5.36)	255 (7.28)
blacksmith, farrier, smith	61	24	88
carter, drayman	11	6	23
innkeeper, tavernkeeper	41	42	79
porter	2	3	65
Other services	65 (2.35)	34 (2.43)	306 (8.74)
barber	23	4	40

laborer, scavenger, watchman	29	16	253
perukemaker	11	8	0
sawyer, woodcorder	2	6	13
Industrial	405 (14.64)	214 (15.30)	781 (22.30)
Textile trades	24 (0.87)	28 (2.00)	125 (3.57)
dyer, silkdyer	3	3	9
feltmaker	7	5	0
hatter, bonnetmaker	6	7	70
weaver, stocking weaver	8	13	46
Leather trades	99 (3.58)	68 (4.86)	215 (6.14)
glover	1	2	5
saddler, harnessmaker, whipmaker	7	9	24
shoemaker, heelmaker, cordwainer	62	37	148
skinner	1	5	25
tanner, currier, leatherdresser	28	15	13
Food and drink processing	50 (1.81)	31 (2.22)	38 (1.09)
brewer, maltster	12	16	20
distiller, sugarboiler	32	11	17
miller, bolter	6	4	1
Shipbuilding crafts	116 (4.19)	36 (2.57)	131 (3.72)
blockmaker	10	3	7
caulker	2	2	7
mastmaker	6	1	4
ropemaker, rigger	16	6	12
sailmaker	12	3	14
shipwright, boatbuilder, ship joiner	70	21	87

(Continued)

Table 1 (Continued)

Occupation	Boston inventories 1685-1775 (no. and percent)	Phila. inventories 1685-1775 (no. and percent)	Phila. tax list 1772 (no. and percent)
Metal crafts	69 (2.49)	19 (1.36)	140 (4.00)
brassfounder, brazier	17	1	4
clockmaker, instrumentmaker, locksmith, watchmaker	6	5	73
goldsmith, jeweler, looking glass maker	19	1	16
gunsmith	12	1	5
pewterer, tinworker, tinker, coppersmith	11	3	20
silversmith	3	4	14
wheelwright	1	4	8
Furniture crafts and miscellaneous woodworkers	32 (1.16)	14 (1.00)	59 (1.68)
cabinetmaker, chairmaker, upholsterer, coachmaker	22	8	37
carver, lastmaker, saddle tree maker	6	5	19
turner	4	1	3
Miscellaneous trades	15 (0.54)	18 (1.29)	73 (2.08)
chinamaker, china mender	0	0	7
combmaker, brushmaker	0	1	7
printer, engraver, limner	2	2	19

potter	0	3	21
soapboiler, tallow chandler	11	8	4
staymaker	2	4	15
Maritime commerce			
Mariners	1,135 (41.02)	402 (28.73)	844 (24.10)
sea captain, pilot	647 (23.38)	136 (9.72)	375 (10.71)
seaman, sailor, flatman	153	38	174
shallopman	494	98	201
Merchants and ancillary trades	488 (17.74)	266 (19.02)	469 (13.42)
clerk, scrivener	12	8	32
cooper	61	28	99
merchant	415	230	338
Unclassified	472 (17.06)	250 (17.87)	179 (5.11)
Farmer, gardener, yeoman	45 (1.62)	43 (3.08)	27 (0.77)
Spinsters	93 (3.36)	29 (2.08)	27 (0.77)
Widows	334 (12.08)	178 (12.74)	125 (3.57)
Total	2,767	1,399	3,502

Source: Office of the Recorder of Wills, Suffolk County Courthouse, Boston (Boston inventories); Office of the Recorder of Wills, City Hall Annex, Philadelphia (Philadelphia inventories); Philadelphia City Archives, City Hall, Philadelphia (1772 tax list). The arrangement of occupations is taken, with modifications, from Jacob M. Price, "Economic Function and the Growth of American Port Towns in the Eighteenth Century," *Perspectives in American History,* 8 (1974), Appendix C. Both inventories and tax lists, especially for Philadelphia, greatly understate the number of ordinary seamen, who represented the most transient and impoverished part of seaport society. The number of seamen can be estimated at five times the number of sea captains.

Table 2. Mean Wages in Philadelphia and Boston, 1725-1775

Year	Phila. laborers shillings per day (Pa. currency)		Phila. seamen £ per month (Pa. currency)		Boston seamen £ sterling per month	
	Wage	Index[a]	Wage	Index[a]	Wage	Index[a]
1725	—	—	—	—	—	—
1726	—	—	—	—	—	—
1727	2.50	66	—	—	—	—
1728	2.50	66	—	—	—	—
1729	—	—	—	—	—	—
1730	—	—	2.63	69	—	—
1731	2.50	66	2.63	69	1.62	81
1732	—	—	3.00	79	1.20	60
1733	2.75	72	2.75	72	1.21	61
1734	2.50	66	—	—	1.10	55
1735	—	—	2.75	72	—	—
1736	—	—	2.50	66	1.20	60
1737	2.50	66	2.63	69	—	—
1738	—	—	—	—	—	—
1739	2.50	66	—	—	—	—
1740	—	—	—	—	1.20	60
1741	—	—	—	—	1.62	81
1742	—	—	—	—	1.70	85
1743	—	—	—	—	1.53	77
1744	2.50	66	2.50	66	1.65	83

Year						
1745	—	—	—	—	1.70	85
1746	2.50	66	—	—	—	—
1747	3.00	79	—	—	2.50	125
1748	—	—	—	—	—	—
1749	2.50	66	3.00	79	—	—
1750	3.00	79	2.96	78	—	—
1751	3.50	92	2.80	74	1.58	79
1752	3.41	90	2.69	71	1.58	79
1753	3.40	89	2.50	66	1.50	75
1754	3.25	86	2.75	72	1.39	70
1755	3.23	85	3.50	92	1.46	73
1756	3.50	92	—	—	1.46	73
1757	3.50	92	—	—	1.88	94
1758	3.42	90	4.50	118	1.75	88
1759	3.50	92	5.00	132	1.88	94
1760	4.47	118	—	—	1.97	99
1761	4.42	116	2.75	72	1.84	92
1762	3.80	100	2.75	72	2.00	100
1763	3.40	89	3.44	91	1.65	83
1764	3.25	86	3.25	86	1.78	89
1765	3.50	92	3.25	86	1.55	78
1766	4.00	105	3.38	89	1.69	85
1767	4.00	105	3.32	87	1.84	92
1768	3.82	101	—	—	1.80	90
1769	3.19	84	3.12	82	1.50	75
1770	3.38	89	—	—	1.35	68
1771	3.30	87	—	—	1.14	57
1772	3.12	82	—	—	1.20	60

(Continued)

Table 2 (Continued)

Year	Phila. laborers shillings per day (Pa. currency)		Phila. seamen £ per month (Pa. currency)		Boston seamen £ sterling per month	
	Wage	Index[a]	Wage	Index[a]	Wage	Index[a]
1773	2.60	68	—	—	1.54	77
1774	3.00	79	—	—	1.51	76
1775	2.80	74	—	—	1.91	96

Source: Philadelphia laborers: Minutes of the County Commissioners, 1718-1766, City Archives, City Hall, Philadelphia; Accounts for Building Addition to the Statehouse, 1750-1754. Norris of Fairhill Papers, HSP; Matron and Steward's Cash Books and Attending Managers Accounts, Records of the Pennsylvania Hospital for the Sick Poor, American Philosophical Society, Philadelphia; Minutes of the Commissioners for Paving Streets, 1762-1768, HSP; Minutes of the County Commissioners, 1771-1774, HSP; Billy G. Smith, "Struggles of the Independent Poor: The Living Standards of Philadelphia's 'Lower Sort' During the Last Half of the Eighteenth Century," unpub. ms., Table VIII.

Philadelphia seamen: Portledge bills (showing monthly rates of pay for ship's crews) in: Samuel Powel Papers, Ship *Tryall* Outfitting Bills, 1728-1745, HSP; Society Miscellaneous Collection, Boats and Cargoes, HSP; Gratz Collection. Miscellaneous Business Papers, HSP; Etting Papers, Ships and Shipping, HSP; Clifford Papers, Correspondence, II (1760-1762), HSP; Richard Waln Collection, Brig *Elizabeth* Accounts, HSP.

Boston seamen: Portledge bills in: Massachusetts Archives, LXIV, 177, 180, State House, Boston; Account Book of the Schooner *Jolly Robin*, Baker Library, Harvard Business School, Cambridge, Mass.; Joseph Prince Account Book, 1746-1754, Baker Library; John Erving Account Book, 1733-1745, Baker Library; Caleb Davis Papers, vols. 4, 6, 7, 7a, 7b, 7c, 7d, 8, 8a, 9, MHS; Sedgwick Papers, 1717-1761, Box 1, MHS; David Greenough Papers, Boxes 1 and 2, MHS; Thomas Hancock Papers, Boxes 3, 5, 23, New England Historic Genealogical Society, Boston; Bourn Papers, vol. 3, 5, 9, 10, Baker Library, Suffolk County Inferior Court of Common Pleas, Docket 1732-no. 319, 1733-no. 153, Social Law Library, Suffolk County Courthouse, Boston.

a. Base year is 1762. The number of observations for each year varies, so the mean wages presented here should be regarded as approximate. Seamen were customarily paid higher wages on African slave voyages, but there were not enough of these voyages to affect the mean in most years. Local currency in Massachusetts varied greatly in sterling value before 1750, so all wages for Boston seamen have been converted to sterling. Pennsylvania currency remained generally stable and can be converted to sterling by multiplying by .60.

Table 3. Distribution of Taxable Wealth in Boston, New York, and Philadelphia, 1687-1774 (percentage of taxable wealth in each decile group)

Decile group	Boston 1687	Phila. 1693	N.Y. 1695	N.Y. 1730	Phila. 1767	Boston 1771	Phila. 1774
Poorest 0-30	2.6	2.2	3.6	6.2	1.8	0.1	1.1
31-60	11.3	15.2	12.3	13.9	5.5	9.1	4.0
61-90	39.8	36.6	38.9	36.5	27.0	27.4	22.6
Richest 91-100	46.3	46.0	45.2	43.7	65.7	63.4	72.3
91-95	16.1	13.2	13.2	14.2	16.2	14.7	16.8
96-100	30.2	32.8	32.0	25.4	49.5	48.7	55.5
Schutz Coefficent	.49	.43	.46	.44	.61	.58	.66

Source: BTR, I, 91-133 (Boston, 1687); *PMHB*, 8 (1884), 85-105 (Philadelphia (1693); *NYHS Coll.*, 43 (New York, 1911), 1-35 (New York, 1695); New York City Archives Center, Queens College, Flushing, N.Y. (New York, 1730); Van Pelt Library, University of Pennsylvania, Philadelphia (Philadelphia, 1767); Massachusetts Archives, CXXXII, 92-147, State House, Boston (Boston, 1771); Pennsylvania State Archives, Harrisburg, Pa. (Philadelphia, 1774). Harlem has not been included in the New York data since the occupations of its inhabitants were not then urban in character. Southwark, adjacent to Philadelphia, has been included since its economy was urban and fully integrated with Philadelphia's, but the Northern Liberties has been excluded.

Table 4. Distribution of Personal Wealth among Boston and Philadelphia Decedents, 1685-1775 (percentage of wealth in each decile group)

Decile group	1684-99	1700-15	1716-25	1726-35	1736-45	1746-55	1756-65	1766-75
BOSTON								
Poorest 0-30	3.3	2.8	2.0	1.9	1.8	1.8	1.4	2.0
31-60	13.9	9.8	7.7	7.4	8.4	8.3	6.0	7.6
61-90	41.6	32.9	28.6	25.1	30.2	34.7	25.1	29.3
Richest 91-100	41.2	54.5	61.7	65.6	58.6	55.2	67.5	61.1
91-95	15.3	14.6	13.2	11.4	12.2	15.9	15.5	14.7
96-100	25.9	39.9	48.5	54.2	46.4	39.3	52.0	46.4
Number of inventories	304	352	314	358	318	532	390	390
PHILADELPHIA								
Poorest 0-30	4.5	4.9	3.9	3.7	2.6	1.5	1.1	1.0
31-60	16.5	16.9	11.1	11.9	9.3	5.5	6.0	4.7
61-90	42.6	37.0	38.1	30.6	36.8	22.9	32.4	24.4
Richest 91-100	36.4	41.3	46.8	53.6	51.3	70.1	60.3	69.9
91-95	14.7	16.3	15.7	13.0	20.7	13.8	16.5	14.1
96-100	21.7	25.0	31.1	40.2	30.6	56.3	43.8	55.8
Number of inventories	87	138	113	154	144	201	279	318

Source: Office of the Recorder of Wills, Suffolk County Courthouse, Boston (Boston inventories); Office of the Recorder of Wills, City Hall Annex, Philadelphia (Philadelphia inventories).

Table 5. Distribution of Personal Wealth in Boston and Philadelphia by Occupation, 1685-1775 (percentage of decedents in each wealth category)

Occupation	1685-1715		1716-1735		1736-1755		1756-1775	
	Boston	Phila.	Boston	Phila.	Boston	Phila.	Boston	Phila.
Merchants (N)[a]	121	41	90	57	123	66	120	103
£ 0-50[b]	10.7	4.9	17.8	1.8	11.4	1.5	10.0	3.9
51-200	20.7	12.2	38.9	15.8	37.4	16.7	30.8	9.7
201-400	20.7	34.1	22.2	29.8	20.3	19.7	23.3	10.7
401 and above	47.9	48.8	21.1	52.6	30.9	62.1	35.8	75.7
Professionals (N)	9	5	16	3	22	8	22	26
£ 0-50	33.3	0.0	12.5	0.0	31.7	12.5	31.8	11.5
51-200	33.3	60.0	68.7	33.3	40.0	25.0	36.4	26.9
201-400	22.2	20.0	6.3	0.0	9.1	12.5	27.3	7.7
401 and above	11.1	20.0	12.5	66.7	18.2	50.0	4.5	53.9
Shipbuilding artisans (N)	18	4	29	3	33	17	42	19
£ 0-50	22.2	25.0	48.3	33.3	54.5	29.4	57.1	36.8
51-200	61.1	25.0	37.9	66.7	36.4	41.2	38.1	36.8
201-400	16.7	0.0	6.9	0.0	3.0	5.9	2.4	10.5
401 and above	0.0	50.0	6.9	0.0	6.1	23.5	2.4	15.8
Building artisans (N)	27	29	40	20	36	37	42	44
£ 0-50	37.0	27.6	60.0	35.0	52.8	18.9	61.9	27.3
51-200	44.4	41.4	35.0	45.0	33.3	43.2	33.3	38.6
201-400	14.8	24.1	2.5	10.0	11.1	24.3	2.4	11.4
401 and above	3.7	6.9	2.5	10.0	2.8	13.5	2.4	22.7

(Continued)

Table 5 (Continued)

Occupation	1685-1715		1716-1735		1736-1755		1756-1775	
	Boston	Phila.	Boston	Phila.	Boston	Phila.	Boston	Phila.
Shoemakers and tailors (N)	*36*	*15*	*31*	*25*	*39*	*20*	*30*	*30*
£0-50	41.7	6.7	61.3	12.0	61.5	15.0	73.3	26.7
51-200	44.4	73.3	32.3	60.0	25.6	70.0	26.7	30.0
201-400	5.6	6.7	3.2	20.0	7.7	10.0	0.0	13.3
401 and above	8.3	13.3	3.2	8.0	5.1	5.0	0.0	30.0
Seamen and laborers (N)	*145*	*10*	*126*	*20*	*124*	*35*	*128*	*47*
£0-50	49.0	60.0	79.4	45.0	73.4	48.6	81.3	51.1
51-200	37.2	20.0	19.0	40.0	25.8	40.0	16.4	34.0
201-400	9.0	20.0	0.8	5.0	0.8	2.9	1.6	4.3
401 and above	4.8	0.0	0.8	10.0	0.0	8.6	0.8	10.6
Widows (N)	*56*	*24*	*75*	*34*	*95*	*34*	*109*	*85*
£0-50	53.6	20.8	45.3	17.7	62.1	14.7	53.2	21.2
51-200	35.7	41.7	45.3	58.8	28.4	32.4	33.9	36.5
201-400	5.4	25.0	6.7	14.7	3.2	23.5	10.1	11.8
400 and above	5.4	12.5	2.7	8.8	6.3	29.4	2.8	30.6

Source: Office of the Recorder of Wills, Suffolk County Courthouse, Boston (Boston inventories); Office of the Recorder of Wills, City Hall Annex, Philadelphia (Philadelphia inventories).
a. Number of decedents.
b. All values are in £ sterling.

Table 6. *Median Personal Wealth among Boston and Philadelphia Decedents, 1685-1775 (in £ sterling)*

Decile group	1685-99	1700-15	1716-25	1726-35	1736-45	1746-55	1756-65	1766-75
Poorest 0-30								
Boston	30	16	10	10	9	12	8	12
Boston[a]	34	23	15	12	12	17	13	19
Philadelphia	39	37	34	33	29	28	22	24
31-60								
Boston	129	55	40	36	38	52	38	50
Boston[a]	179	117	74	66	79	101	68	92
Philadelphia	140	137	107	104	114	96	117	113
61-90								
Boston	347	175	132	114	133	203	142	170
Boston[a]	538	368	307	240	328	396	292	497
Philadelphia	447	306	305	283	437	335	587	561
Richest 91-100								
Boston	992	685	529	489	501	843	986	826
Boston[a]	1,583	1,159	1,284	1,103	1,065	1,458	1,552	2,284
Philadelphia	959	957	1,064	1,051	1,931	1,815	2,795	2,961

Source: Office of the Recorder of Wills, Suffolk County Courthouse, Boston (Boston inventories); Office of the Recorder of Wills, City Hall Annex, Philadelphia (Philadelphia inventories).
a. Including real estate.

Table 7. Range of Personal Wealth among Boston and Philadelphia Decedents, 1685-1775 (in £ sterling)

Decile group	1685-99	1700-15	1716-25	1726-35	1736-45	1746-55	1756-65	1766-75
Poorest 0-30								
Boston	1-70	1-33	1-23	1-17	1-23	1-27	1-19	1-26
Boston[a]	1-86	1-55	1-33	1-26	1-34	1-50	1-31	1-43
Philadelphia	5-79	5-93	5-60	3-63	5-68	1-56	1-65	4-57
31-60								
Boston	72-206	34-102	24-78	17-65	20-78	28-102	20-67	27-77
Boston[a]	87-292	56-215	34-143	27-132	35-173	51-177	32-146	44-212
Philadelphia	79-246	94-189	64-222	65-180	69-189	56-183	65-252	57-229
61-90								
Boston	207-711	103-454	79-318	66-273	79-301	103-583	68-397	78-409
Boston[a]	307-1,151	217-736	146-653	138-690	174-720	179-984	149-758	215-1,249
Philadelphia	252-625	189-577	222-744	189-539	231-1,085	184-1,022	252-1,914	229-1,530
Richest 91-100								
Boston	728-2,634	460-4,078	356-6,422	275-9,046	305-5,496	592-3,389	405-6,538	422-3,095
Boston[a]	1,155-3,417	742-11,007	660-7,362	714-9,606	769-7,557	1,005-5,609	769-15,614[b]	1,293-5,138
Philadelphia	666-1,978	585-2,556	752-4,618	589-5,751	1,165-4,510	1,057-16,000	1,945-22,621	1,530-36,624

Source: Office of the Recorder of Wills, Suffolk County Courthouse, Boston (Boston inventories); Office of the Recorder of Wills, City Hall Annex, Philadelphia (Philadelphia inventories).
a. Including real estate.
b. Excluding the estate of Samuel Waldo, valued at £ 53,265.

Table 8. Ownership of Real Property by Boston Decedents, 1685-1775 (number and percentage of inventoried estates with real property in each decile group)

Years	Poorest 0-30	31-60	61-90	Richest 91-100	Number of inventories
1685-99	5 (5.5)	46 (50.5)	79 (86.6)	28 (90.3)	304
1700-15	4 (3.8)	46 (43.8)	76 (72.4)	32 (91.4)	350
1716-25	0 (0.0)	28 (29.8)	69 (73.4)	27 (87.1)	313
1726-35	2 (1.9)	23 (21.5)	78 (72.9)	33 (89.2)	358
1736-45	2 (2.1)	35 (36.8)	70 (73.7)	31 (96.9)	317
1746-55	7 (4.4)	61 (38.4)	106 (66.7)	49 (90.7)	531
1756-65	3 (2.6)	34 (29.0)	89 (76.1)	36 (94.6)	390
1766-75	7 (5.9)	40 (34.2)	95 (80.5)	38 (100)	390

Source: Office of the Recorder of Wills, Suffolk County Courthouse, Boston.

Table 9. Slave Ownership in Boston and Philadelphia, 1685-1775

Years	Number of slaves in inventories		Percentage of inventories with slaves	
	Boston	Phila.	Boston	Phila.
1685-99	41	27	11.5	9.2
1700-15	87	59	16.2	14.5
1716-25	72	50	16.9	21.2
1726-35	154	53	22.9	15.6
1736-45	171	82	28.9	18.1
1746-55	127	93	23.1	18.4
1756-65	114	123	17.9	15.8
1766-75	93	124	15.6	12.9

Source: Office of the Recorder of Wills, Suffolk County Courthouse, Boston (Boston inventories); Office of the Recorder of Wills, City Hall Annex, Philadelphia (Philadelphia inventories).

Table 10. Poor Relief in Boston, New York, and Philadelphia, 1700-1775

Years	Boston			New York			Philadelphia		
	Population	Average annual expenditure (£ sterling)	Expenditure per 1,000 (£ sterling)	Population	Average annual expenditure (£ sterling)	Expenditure per 1,000 (£ sterling)	Population	Average annual expenditure (£ sterling)	Expenditure per 1,000 (£ sterling)
1700-10	7,500	173	23	4,500	—	—	2,450	119	48
1711-20	9,830	181	18	5,900	249	32	3,800	—	—
1721-30	11,840	273	23	7,600	276	25	6,600	—	—
1731-40	15,850	498	31	10,100	351	21	8,800	471	49
1741-50	16,240	806	50	12,900	389	21	12,000	—	—
1751-60	15,660	1,204	77	13,200	667	39	15,700	1,083	67
1761-70	15,520	1,909	123	18,100	1,667	92	22,100	2,842	129
1771-75	15,550	2,478	158	22,600	2,778	123	27,900	3,785	136

Source: Boston: Overseers of the Poor Account Book, 1738-1769, MHS; annual reports of the town treasurer on disbursements to the overseers of the poor in BTR, passim; expenditures for 1727, 1729, 1734, 1735, and 1737 in BTR, XII, 108, 121-122, 178; for the period from 1700 to 1726 I have estimated poor relief costs at one-third of the town expenses (given yearly in BTR), the ratio that prevailed in the five years between 1727 and 1737 when poor relief expenses were recorded.

New York: Minutes and Accounts of the Church Warden and Vestrymen of the City of New York, 1696-1715, New-York Historical Society; Minutes of the Meetings of the Justices, Church Wardens, and Vestrymen of the City of New York, 1694-1747, New York Public Library; Petition of the vestrymen and church wardens of the City of New York, May 1776, in Peter Force, comp., American Archives, 4th ser., VI (Washington, D.C., 1846), 627.

Philadelphia: "Account of weekly . . . pay to the poor . . . 1709," HSP; Philadelphia Poor Day Book, 1739, HSP; Records of poor relief in 1758 in Christopher Marshall's Diary, 1774-1775, HSP; [Thomas Wharton], "A State of the Taxes paid by the . . . City of Philadelphia . . . for the support of their Poor . . . ," Wharton-Willing Papers, HSP; annual reports of poor relief expenditures (1768-1775) in Records of the Contributors to the Relief . . . of the Poor, Treasurer's Accounts, City Archives, City Hall, Philadelphia.

Table 11. Taxes in Boston, New York, and Philadelphia, 1695-1774 (£ sterling)

Years	Boston			New York			Philadelphia		
	Taxes/year (5-year average)	Annual tax per capita	Annual tax per taxable	Taxes/year (5-year average)	Annual tax per capita	Annual tax per taxable	Taxes/year (5-year average)	Annual tax per capita	Annual tax per taxable
1695-99	2,106	.324	1.504	167	.034	.190	180	.083	.450
1700-04	1,874	.280	1.339	214	.047	.223	159	.069	.379
1705-09	3,854	.494	2.471	674	.138	.648	278	.116	.632
1710-14	3,977	.444	2.209	467	.080	.423	459	.156	.820
1715-19	2,007	.209	1.004	242	.038	.192	369	.089	.486
1720-24	1,991	.189	.830	483	.069	.341	516	.097	.535
1725-29	2,550	.208	.850	596	.077	.420	372	.058	323
1730-34	2,024	.139	.595	319	.037	.217	582	.077	.434
1735-39	3,363	.204	1.050	325	.038	.210	729	.085	.473
1740-44	4,680	.282	1.671	532	.052	.333	870	.089	.468
1745-49	6,300	.391	2.520	2,081	.172	1.156	756	.064	.335
1750-54	7,410	.471	2.744	2,022	.153	1.064	1,632	.117	.653
1755-59	10,575	.675	4.406	4,892	.360	2.330	3,472	.225	1.253
1760-64	11,137	.714	4.455	4,460	.273	1.715	6,420	.367	2.058
1765-69	7,875	.507	3.150	4,215	.221	1.338	7,128	.383	2.147
1770-74	6,495	.393	2.498	2,581	.113	.698	8,484	.388	2.171

Source: Boston: The town's share of the provincial tax burden is given yearly in Abner C. Goodell and Ellis Ames, eds., *The Acts and Resolves, Public and Private, of the Province of the Massachusetts Bay*, 19 vols. (Boston, 1869-1922). Yearly town taxes are reported in BTR, VIII, XII, XIV, XVI, and XVIII.
New York: New York City's share of the provincial taxes levied by the assembly are given in *The Colonial Laws of New York*
(*Continued*)

Table 11 (Continued)

from the Year 1664 to the Revolution, 5 vols. (Albany, N.Y., 1894). Town rates are given annually in Minutes and Accounts of the Church Wardens and Vestrymen of the City of New York, 1696-1715, New-York Historical Society, and Minutes of the Meetings of the Justices, Church Wardens, and Vestrymen of the City of New York, 1694-1747, New York Public Library. From 1753 to 1775 the city taxes paid annually by James Beekman, which are recorded in his Account Book, Personal Affairs (1761-1796) and Receipt Book (1752-1802), New-York Historical Society, provide a means of charting approximate city taxes during these years. Town expenditures for the poor on the eve of the Revolution are reported in a petition of the vestrymen and church wardens to the Continental Congress, May 1776, in Peter Force, comp., *American Archives*, 4th ser., VI (Washington, D.C., 1846), 627.

Philadelphia: County tax rates have been gathered from Minutes of the Philadelphia County Commissioners, 1718-1766, City Archives, City Hall, Philadelphia, Minutes, 1771-1774, HSP, and Minutes 1774-1776, Tax and Exoneration Records, Pennsylvania State Archives, Harrisburg, Pa. Provincial taxes are summarized in Penn Papers: Accounts, and Provincial Tax for Philadelphia County, 1759-1768, HSP. City poor rates and other taxes for street paving, watch, and lamp have been reconstructed from tax receipts in Isaac Norris Journal, 1709-1716; Isaac Norris Ledger, 1709-1740; James Logan Cash Book, 1729-1736; Charles Norris Cash Books, 1735-1740, 1742-1755, and 1759-1764; Casper Wistar Receipt Book, 1754-1776; Isaac Norris Cash Book, 1735-1741; Samuel Coates Receipt Book, 1740-1758, all in HSP. The history of the watch, lamp, and pump tax is recounted in *To the Citizens of Philadelphia . . .* (Philadelphia, 1771).

Table 12. *Value of Massachusetts Paper Currency, 1685-1775*

Year	Price of silver per ounce in Mass. currency (shillings and pence)	Rate of exchange of Mass. currency on sterling	Multiplier (to convert Mass. currency to sterling)
1685-			
1704	6-8	129	.78
1705	7-8	148	.68
1706	8-0	155	.65
1707	8-0	155	.65
1708	8-0	155	.65
1709	8-0	155	.65
1710	8-0	155	.65
1711	8-4	162	.62
1712	8-6	165	.61
1713	8-6	165	.61
1714	9-0	174	.57
1715	9-0	174	.57
1716	10-0	193	.52
1717	10-0	193	.52
1718	11-0	212	.47
1719	12-0	232	.43
1720	12-4	239	.42
1721	13-0	252	.40
1722	14-3	277	.36
1723	15-0	290	.34
1724	16-3	318	.31
1725	15-6	300	.33
1726	16-0	310	.32
1727	16-0	310	.32
1728	17-3	332	.30
1729	20-0	386	.26
1730	20-0	386	.26
1731	18-9	360	.28
1732	20-0	386	.26
1733	22-0	426	.23
1734	25-6	494	.20
1735	27-6	530	.19
1736	26-9	515	.19
1737	27-0	520	.19
1738	27-6	530	.19
1739	28-0	540	.19
1740	28-0	540	.19
1741	29-0	560	.18
1742	29-6	570	.18

(*Continued*)

Table 12 (Continued)

Year	Price of silver per ounce in Mass. currency (shillings and pence)	Rate of exchange of Mass. currency on sterling	Multiplier (to convert Mass. currency to sterling)
1743	31-0	600	.17
1744	35-0	680	.15
1745	36-0	698	.14
1746	38-6	748	.13
1747	55-0	1060	.09
1748	57-0	1100	.09
1749	60-0	1160	.09
1750-75	6-10	133	.75

Source: Andrew McFarland Davis, *Currency and Banking in the Province of Massachusetts-Bay*, (2 vols. (New York, 1901), I, 368-370; Roger W. Weiss, "The Colonial Monetary Standard of Massachusetts," *Economic History Review*, 27 (1974), 586-587. I have supplemented and adjusted the values given by Davis and Weiss by utilizing silver prices given in the inventories of estate for Boston decedents.

Table 13. Taxable Inhabitants in Boston, New York, and Philadelphia, 1687–1775

Year	Boston		New York		Philadelphia	
	Population	Taxables	Population	Taxables	Population	Taxables
1687	6,000	1,330	—	—	—	—
1693	—	—	—	—	2,100	375
1695	—	—	4,750	761	—	—
1701	—	—	4,950	1,005	—	—
1708	—	—	5,110	1,064	—	—
1709	—	—	—	—	2,465	440
1720	—	—	—	—	4,885	872
1723	—	—	7,250	1,429	—	—
1728	12,650	3,000	—	—	—	—
1730	—	—	8,280	1,391	—	—
1733	15,075	3,500	—	—	—	—
1734	—	—	—	—	7,950	1,420
1735	15,925	3,637	8,650	1,556	—	—
1737	16,500	3,202	—	—	—	—
1738	16,700	3,395	—	—	—	—
1739	16,750	3,321	—	—	—	—
1740	16,800	3,043	—	—	—	—
1741	16,660	2,972	—	—	9,515	1,699
1745	16,290	2,660	—	—	—	—
1746	—	—	11,720	1,762	—	—
1750	15,890	2,400	—	—	13,720	2,450
1751	—	—	—	—		*(Continued)*

Table 13 (Continued)

Year	Boston		New York		Philadelphia	
	Population	Taxables	Population	Taxables	Population	Taxables
1752	15,730	2,786	—	—	—	—
1756	15,680	2,200	13,045	2,046	14,895	2,660
1760	—	—	—	—	17,060	3,047
1767	—	—	—	—	18,605	3,319
1769	—	—	—	—	19,445	3,414
1771	16,540	2,588	21,310	3,539	—	—
1772	—	—	—	—	21,880	3,907
1774	—	—	—	—	22,410	4,002
1775	—	—	—	—	24,180	4,434

Source: Boston: Lemuel Shattuck, *Report to the Commissioners of the City Council Appointed to Obtain the Census of Boston for the Year 1845* (Boston, 1846), p. 5; Evaluation of Suffolk County for 1752, Miscellaneous Bound Collection, XII (1749-1755), MHS; *BTR,* XII, 177-178, XIV, 12-14, 100, 280. The figures for 1728, 1733, and 1756 were contemporary approximations.

New York: For taxables through 1735, Bruce M. Wilkenfeld, "The Social and Economic Structure of the City of New York, 1695-1796" (Ph.D. diss., Columbia University, 1973), pp. 22, 28, 58-59, 80, 87, 122-123. The taxables for 1746, 1756, and 1771 have been estimated from the censuses for those years in Evarts B. Greene and Virginia D. Harrington, *American Population Before the Federal Census of 1790* (New York, 1932), pp. 99-102.

Philadelphia: For 1693 and 1709, *PMHB,* 8 (1884), 85-105, and 99 (1975), 3-19; for 1720 and 1751, *Votes and Proceedings of the House of Representatives, 1751-1752* (Philadelphia, 1752), pp. 51-54; for 1734, "Report of the Landholders in Philadelphia County . . . ," *"Publications of the Genealogical Society of Pennsylvania,* 1 (1895), 184; for 1741, John F. Watson, *Annals of Philadelphia . . .* (Philadelphia, 1881), III, 236; for 1756, Hannah Benner Roach, comp., "Taxables in the City of Philadelphia, 1756," *Pennsylvania Genealogical Magazine,* 22 (1961), 3-41; for 1760, Gertrude MacKinney, ed., *Votes and Proceedings of the House of Representatives . . . ,* in *Pennsylvania Archives,* 8th ser. (Harrisburg, Pa., 1931-35), VI, 5141; for 1767, tax assessors reports at the Van Pelt Library, University of Pennsylvania; for 1769 and 1774, tax lists in the Pennsylvania State Archives, Harrisburg, Pa.; for 1772 and 1775, tax lists in the City Archives, City Hall, Philadelphia.

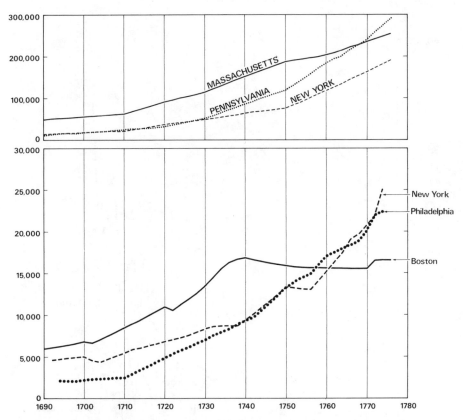

Figure 1. Population of Boston, New York, and Philadelphia, 1690-1776.

Source: Provincial population: *Historical Statistics of the United States, Colonial Times to 1970*, 2 vols. (Washington, D.C., 1975), II, 1168. Boston: John B. Blake, *Public Health in the Town of Boston, 1630-1822* (Cambridge, Mass., 1959), pp. 247-249 with corrections for 1765-1776 to account for the higher population for 1771 suggested in Allan Kulikoff, "The Progress of Inequality in Revolutionary Boston," *WMQ*, 28 (1971), 393. New York: censuses of 1703, 1723, 1731, 1746, 1749, 1756, and 1771 in Evarts B. Greene and Virginia D. Harrington, *American Population Before the Federal Census of 1790* (Gloucester, Mass., 1966; 1932), pp. 94-102. The 1737 data have been corrected because of large errors in the transcribing of the census, discussed in Gary B. Nash, "The New York Census of 1737: A Critical Note on the Integration of Statistical and Literary Sources," *WMQ*, 36 (1979). Philadelphia: Gary B. Nash and Billy G. Smith, "The Population of Eighteenth-Century Philadelphia," *PMHB*, 99 (1975), 366.

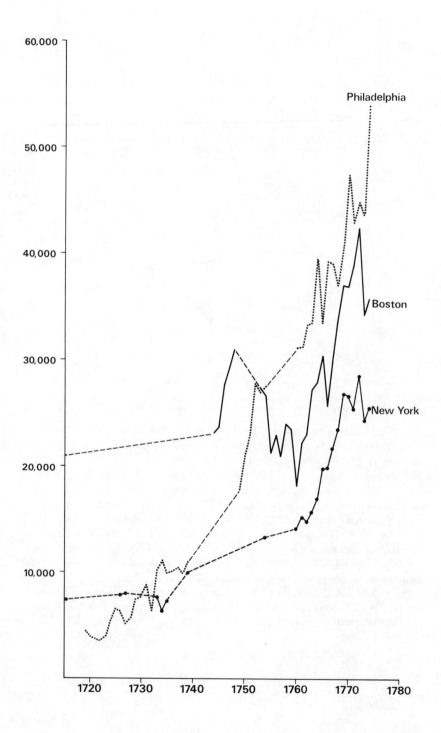

Figure 2. Tonnage of Ships Clearing Boston, New York, and Philadelphia, 1714-1775.

Source: For all years except as noted below tonnage data have been taken from *Historical Statistics of the United States, Colonial Times to 1970*, 2 vols. (Washington, D.C., 1975), II, 1180-1181.

All ports, 1760-1762: "An Account of the Number of Ships and Vessels entring Inwards and Outwards in the British Plantations . . . ," Manuscript Large Collection, MHS.

1767: Virginia D. Harrington, *The New York Merchant on the Eve of the Revolution* (Gloucester, Mass., 1964; 1935), p. 358.

Boston, 1744-1748: Shipping Register, 1744-1748, Boston Athenaeum, Boston, Mass. Data for only three quarters were registered in 1744 and 1748 so estimates for the fourth quarter were made on the basis of other years.

1753, 1756-1759: Murray G. Lawson, "The Routes of Boston's Trade, 1752-1765," CSM *Pub.*, XXXVIII (Boston, 1959), Table 1, following p. 85.

1773: "An Account of the Number of Vessels and Their Tonnage that have entered Inwards and Cleared Outwards," Jan. 5, 1773 to Jan. 5, 1774, Miscellaneous Bound Collection (1774-1774), MHS.

Philadelphia, 1773-1774: "An Aggregate and Valuation of the Exports from the Port of Philadelphia . . . 1771 to 1774, Taken from the Custom House Books," Society Miscellaneous Collection: Boats and Cargoes, HSP.

None of the data are completely accurate because some underreporting characterizes all Naval Office lists. Coastal trade and the activities of fishing vessels are not included.

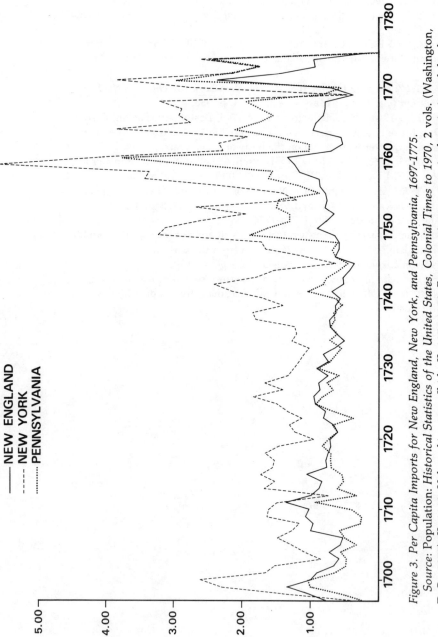

Figure 3. Per Capita Imports for New England, New York, and Pennsylvania, 1697-1775.

Source: Population: *Historical Statistics of the United States, Colonial Times to 1970.* 2 vols. (Washington, D.C., 1975), II, 1168. Value of imports: Ibid., II, 1176-1178. For correcting an error in the printing of the data for imports see Jacob M. Price's letter to the editor, *WMQ,* 34 (1977), 517. See also John J. McCusker, "The Current Value of English Exports, 1697 to 1800," *WMQ,* 28 (1971), 607-628. Value of per capita imports is given in sterling.

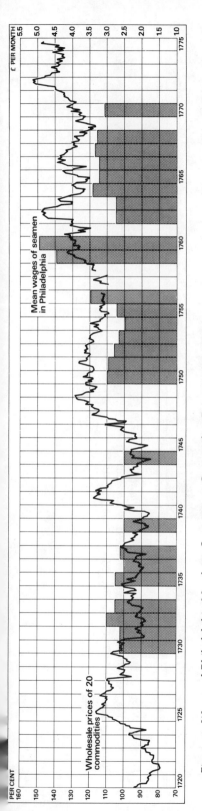

Figure 4. *Wages of Philadelphia Merchant Seamen vs. Commodity Prices, 1720-1775.*
Source: Wages: compiled from sources noted in Appendix, Table 2. Wages are given in Pennsylvania currency. Prices: Anne Bezanson, Robert D. Gray, and Miriam Hussey, *Prices in Colonial Pennsylvania* (Philadelphia, 1935), facing p. 294.

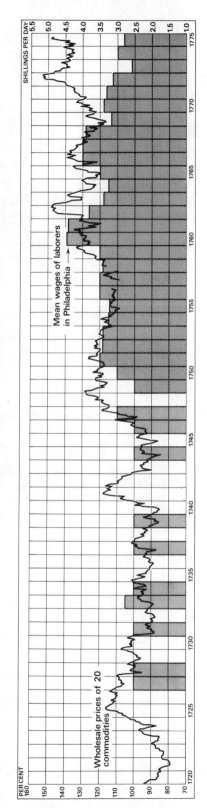

Figure 5. *Wages of Philadelphia Laborers vs. Commodity Prices, 1720-1775.*
Source: Wages: compiled from sources noted in Appendix, Table 2. Wages are given in Pennsylvania currency. Prices: Anne Bezanson, Robert D. Gray, and Miriam Hussey, *Prices in Colonial Pennsylvania* (Philadelphia, 1935), facing p. 294.

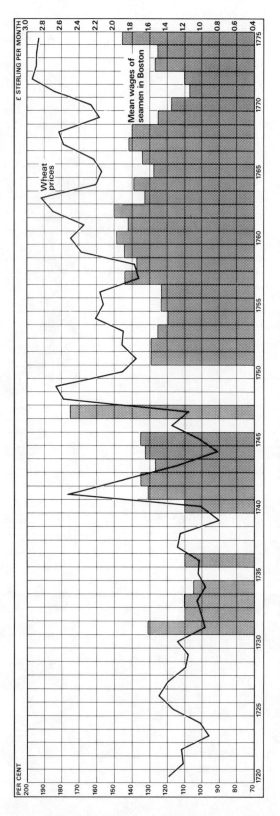

Figure 6. Wages of Boston Merchant Seamen vs. Wheat Prices, 1720–1775.

Source: Wages: compiled from sources noted in Appendix, Table 2. Prices: Arthur Harrison Cole, *Wholesale Commodity Prices in the United States, 1700–1861* (Cambridge, Mass., 1938), p. 117.

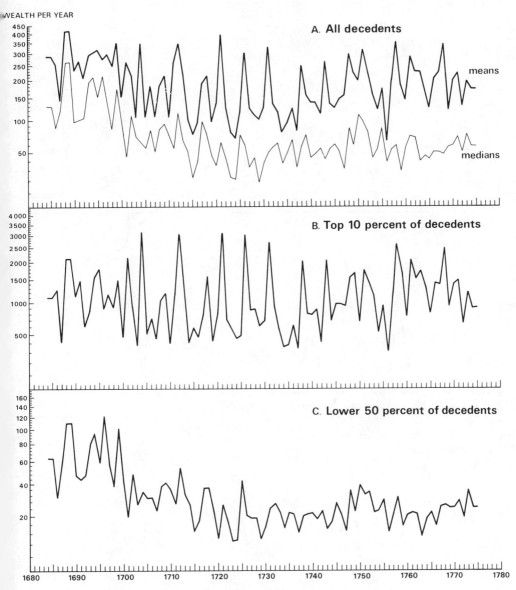

WEALTH PER YEAR

A. **All decedents**

means

medians

B. **Top 10 percent of decedents**

C. **Lower 50 percent of decedents**

1680 1690 1700 1710 1720 1730 1740 1750 1760 1770 1780

Figure 7. Mean Personal Wealth in Boston, 1690-1775.
Source: Inventories of estate in Office of the Recorder of Wills, Suffolk County Courthouse, Boston. Wealth per year is given in £ sterling.

WEALTH PER YEAR

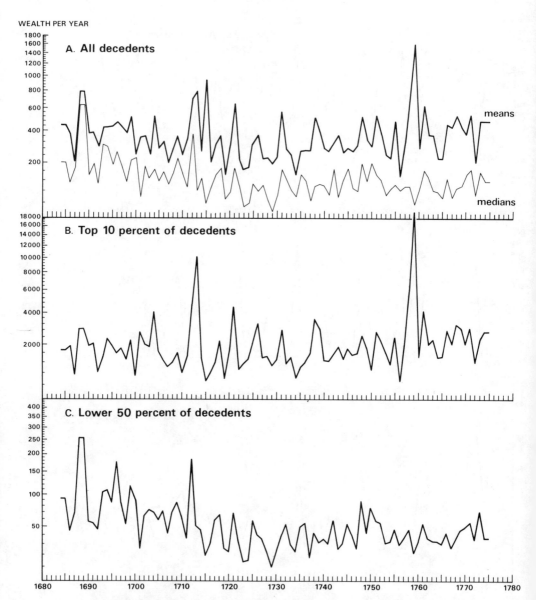

Figure 8. Mean Real and Personal Wealth in Boston, 1690-1775.
Source: Inventories of estate in Office of the Recorder of Wills, Suffolk County Courthouse, Boston. Wealth per year is given in £ sterling.

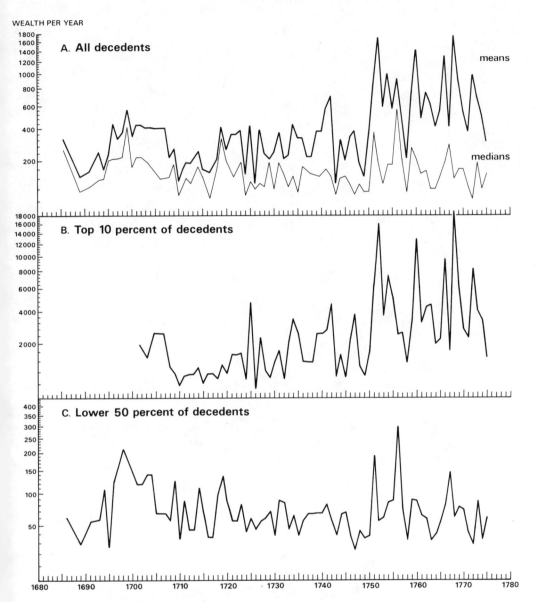

WEALTH PER YEAR

A. **All decedents**

means

medians

B. **Top 10 percent of decedents**

C. **Lower 50 percent of decedents**

Figure 9. Mean Personal Wealth in Philadelphia, 1690-1775.
    Source: Inventories of estate in Office of the Recorder of Wills, City Hall An-
nex, Philadelphia. The number of inventories for the years before 1701 is insufficient to provide data points for Figure 9B. In Figure 9C the data before 1701 have
been aggregated at two and three year intervals when necessary to provide a
minimum of five inventories for each data point. Wealth per year is given in £
sterling.

Notes

1. The Web of Seaport Life

1. A good general introduction to the functioning of the seaport towns is Carl Bridenbaugh, *Cities in the Wilderness: The First Century of Urban Life in America, 1625-1742* (New York, 1964; 1938) (hereafter Bridenbaugh, *Cities in the Wilderness*). Historical geographers and economic historians are altering our understanding of how colonial cities evolved and functioned. See, for example, Ronald Hoffman and Carville Earle, "Urban Systems in Colonial America: A Perspective," typescript; James T. Lemon, "Urbanization and the Development of Eighteenth-Century Southeastern Pennsylvania and Adjacent Delaware," *William and Mary Quarterly*, 3d ser., 24 (1967), 501-542 (hereafter *WMQ*); and Jacob M. Price, "Economic Function and the Growth of the American Port Towns in the Eighteenth Century," *Perspectives in American History*, 8 (1974), 123-186.

2. All of the existing estimates of population in the northern towns are flawed in some particulars; the most accurate are in W. S. Rossiter, ed., *A Century of Population Growth from the First Census of the United States to the Twelfth* (Washington, D.C., 1909), pp. 11, 78. For my own population estimates see Appendix, Figure 1.

3. For Lyon see Natalie Z. Davis, *Society and Culture in Early Modern France* (Stanford, Ca., 1975), p. 62; For Norwich, Wallace T. MacCaffrey, *Exeter, 1540-1660* (Cambridge, Mass., 1958), p. 12; for Latin American cities, Richard M. Morse, "Latin American Cities: Aspects of Function and Structure," *Comparative Studies in Society and History*, 4 (1962), 473-493.

4. Decadal population estimates for individual colonies can be found in *Historical Statistics of the United States, Colonial Times to 1970*, 2 vols. (Washington, D.C., 1975), II, 1168, and are represented in Appendix, Figure 1.

5. The topographical history of the port towns can be followed in Walter Muir Whitehill, *Boston: A Topographical History* (Cambridge, Mass., 1959); I. N. Phelps Stokes, *The Iconography of Manhattan Island, 1498-1909*, 6 vols. (New York, 1915-28); and Hannah B. Roach, "The Planting of Philadelphia: A Seventeenth-Century Real Estate Development," *Pennsylvania Magazine of History and Biography*, 92 (1968), 3-47, 143-194 (hereafter *PMHB*). On "bespoke

goods" see Carl Bridenbaugh, *The Colonial Craftsman* (Chicago, 1961), p. 147.

6. "Diary of James Allen, Esq., of Philadelphia," *PMHB*, 9 (1885), 185.

7. The history of the colonial family has burgeoned spectacularly in the last decade. Valuable works are too numerous to mention but among those with a demographic orientation the best is Philip J. Greven, Jr., *Four Generations: Population, Land, and Family in Colonial Andover, Massachusetts* (Ithaca, N.Y., 1970); among those with a nonquantitative cast the best is Edmund S. Morgan, *The Puritan Family: Religion and Domestic Relations in Seventeenth-Century New England* (Boston, 1944). A valuable history of an important Philadelphia family is Randolph Shipley Klein, *Portrait of an Early American Family: The Shippens of Pennsylvania Across Five Generations* (Philadelphia, 1975).

8. See the discussion by Rhys Isaac in "Dramatizing the Ideology of Revolution: Popular Mobilization in Virginia, 1774 to 1776," *WMQ*, 33 (1976), 358-362. Isaac draws heavily on Walter J. Ong, *The Presence of the Word: Some Prolegomena for Cultural and Religious History* (New Haven, Conn., 1967).

9. William Gouge, *Of Domesticall Duties* (London, 1622), cited in John Demos, *A Little Commonwealth: Family Life in Plymouth Colony* (New York, 1970), following p. xvi.

10. Quoted in Michael Kammen, *Colonial New York: A History* (New York, 1975), p. 129 (hereafter Kammen, *Colonial New York*).

11. Perry Miller, *The New England Mind From Colony to Province* (Cambridge, Mass., 1953), p. 179 (hereafter Miller, *New England Mind*). Two years before the Salem witchcraft trials an elderly Boston woman was arrested, tried, and executed as a witch after an accusation by a thirteen-year-old girl. Paul Boyer and Stephen Nissenbaum, *Salem Possessed: The Social Origins of Witchcraft* (Cambridge, Mass., 1975), p. 24n.

12. Robert V. Wells, *The Population of the British Colonies in America Before 1776* (Princeton, N.J., 1975), pp. 20-21. Nine years after the 1703 smallpox epidemic, Governor Robert Hunter reported resistance to a new census.

13. E. P. Thompson, *The Making of the English Working Class* (New York, 1963), p. 11. Thompson, "Eighteenth-Century English Society: Class Struggle without Class," *Social History*, 3 (1978), 150.

14. "A Modell of Christian Charity" (1630), *Collections of the Massachusetts Historical Society*, 3d ser., VII (Boston, 1838), 33 (hereafter *MHS Coll.*).

15. John Saffin, *A Brief and Candid Answer to a Late Printed Sheet . . .* (Boston, 1700), quoted in Stephen Foster, *The Solitary Way: The Puritan Social Ethic in the First Century of Settlement in New England* (New Haven, Conn., 1971), pp. 14-15 (hereafter Foster, *Solitary Way*).

16. Hugh Barbour, *The Quakers in Puritan England* (New Haven, Conn., 1964), p. 167, quoting John Whitehead, *A Manifestation of Truth in the Written Gospel-Labours* (London, 1704); Frederick B. Tolles, *Meeting House and Counting House: The Quaker Merchants of Colonial Philadelphia, 1682-1763* (Chapel Hill, N.C., 1948), pp. 110-111, quoting Robert Barclay, *An Apology for the True Christian Divinity* (Aberdeen, 1678).

17. Quoted in Marcus W. Jernegan, *The American Colonies, 1492-1750: A Study of Their Political, Economic, and Social Development* (New York, 1929), pp. 179-180.

18. J. G. A. Pocock, "The Classical Theory of Deference," *American His-*

torical Review, 81 (1976), 516-523. For an eloquent but overstated view of the deferential character of preindustrial English society see Harold Perkin, *The Origins of Modern English Society, 1780-1880* (London, 1969), pp. 17-56.

19. James A. Henretta, "The Study of Social Mobility: Ideological Assumptions and Conceptual Bias," *Labor History*, 18 (1977), 165-178.

20. Joseph J. Kelley, Jr., *Life and Times in Colonial Philadelphia* (Harrisburg, Pa., 1973), p. 48. Richard Pares analyzes the effects of weather on the North American-West Indies trade routes in *Yankees and Creoles: The Trade Between North America and the West Indies Before the American Revolution* (Cambridge, Mass., 1956), p. 18. Two accounts of the irregular pace of northern mercantile life are W. T. Baxter, *The House of Hancock: Business in Boston, 1724-1775* (Cambridge, Mass., 1945), pp. 184-220; and Virginia D. Harrington, *The New York Merchant on the Eve of the Revolution* (New York, 1935), pp. 76-125.

21. The irregularity of work for artisans and laborers lasted into the nineteenth century, as Bruce Laurie explains in " 'Nothing on Impulse': Life Styles of Philadelphia Artisans, 1820-1850," *Labor History*, 15 (1974), 343-344. Much can be learned on the subject from Keith Thomas, "Work and Leisure in Pre-Industrial Societies," *Past and Present*, no. 29 (1964), 50-66; and E. P. Thompson, "Time, Work-Discipline, and Industrial Capitalism," ibid., no. 38 (1967), 56-97.

22. Fernand Braudel, *Capitalism and Material Life, 1400-1800*, trans. George Weidenfeld (New York, 1973), p. x.

23. J. Hector St. John De Crevecoeur, *Letters from an American Farmer* (New York, 1957), p. 54.

24. Roger Williams to Major Mason, June 22, 1670, quoted in Francis Jennings, *The Invasion of America: Indians, Colonialism, and the Cant of Conquest* (Chapel Hill, N.C., 1975), p. 181.

25. Ibid.

26. On wage-price relatives see Victor S. Clark, *History of Manufactures in the United States, Vol. I, 1607-1860* (Washington, D.C., 1929), pp. 155-158.

27. Addison, *The Spectator* (1711), quoted in Maximillian E. Novak, *Economics and the Fiction of Daniel Defoe* (Berkeley and Los Angeles, 1962), p. 10.

28. On "St. Monday" see Thompson, "Time, Work-Discipline, and Industrial Capitalism," pp. 73-76. The weekly holiday was honored in England "almost universally wherever small-scale, domestic, and outwork industries existed," according to Thompson.

29. Quoted in Almon W. Lauber, *Indian Slavery in Colonial Times Within the Present Limits of the United States* (New York, 1913), p. 311.

30. Of 304 Boston estates inventoried between 1685 and 1699, 35 (11.5 percent) contained slaves. James A. Henretta reports a slave population of 150 in Boston in 1690. "Economic Development and Social Structure in Colonial Boston," *WMQ*, 22 (1965), 83n. Lorenzo J. Greene reports 400 in 1708. *The Negro in Colonial New England* (New York, 1942), p. 84. Both these figures are estimates.

31. Edgar J. McManus, *A History of Negro Slavery in New York* (Syracuse, N.Y., 1966), pp. 4-6, 11. The most thorough study is Thomas J. Davis, "Slavery in Colonial New York City" (Ph.D. diss., Columbia University, 1974).

32. The 1698 census is reprinted in Evarts B. Greene and Virginia D. Harrington, *American Population Before the Federal Census of 1790* (New York,

1932), p. 92 (hereafter Greene and Harrington, *American Population*); the 1703 census is in *The Documentary History of the State of New York*, ed. Edmund B. O'Callaghan, 4 vols. (Albany, 1849-51), I, 395-405.

33. *Some Considerations on the Keeping of Negroes, Part Second* (1762), in Phillips P. Moulton, ed., *The Journal and Major Essays of John Woolman* (New York, 1971), p. 237.

34. The classic study of these racial attitudes is Winthrop D. Jordan, *White Over Black: American Attitudes Toward the Negro, 1550-1812* (Chapel Hill, N.C., 1968). Edmund S. Morgan argues that it was the exploitative attitudes developed toward white indentured servants in Virginia that conditioned men to think of laborers as chattel. *American Freedom; American Slavery: The Ordeal of Colonial Virginia* (New York, 1975), chap. 2.

35. Gary B. Nash, "Slaves and Slaveowners in Colonial Philadelphia," *WMQ*, 30 (1973), 224-226.

36. Abbot Emerson Smith, *Colonists in Bondage: White Servitude and Convict Labor in America, 1607-1776* (Chapel Hill, N.C., 1947); Russell R. Menard, "From Servant to Freeholder: Status Mobility and Property Accumulation in Seventeenth-Century Maryland," *WMQ*, 30 (1973), 37-64.

37. Two studies of indentured servitude in Pennsylvania are Cheesman A. Herrick, *White Servitude in Pennsylvania: Indentured and Redemption Labor in Colony and Commonwealth* (Philadelphia, 1926); and Karl Frederick Geiser, *Redemptioners and Indentured Servants in . . . Pennsylvania* (New Haven, Conn., 1901).

38. Marion Balderston, "William Penn's Twenty-three Ships, with Notes on Some of Their Passengers," *The Pennsylvania Genealogical Magazine*, 23 (1963), 32n, 63n; "A Partial List of the Families Who Arrived at Philadelphia between 1682 and 1687," *PMHB*, 8 (1884), 328-340.

39. Richard B. Morris, *Government and Labor in Early America* (New York, 1965; 1946), pp. 363-389.

40. The only published estimates of the number of unskilled laborers are those of Jacob Price for the late eighteenth century (see n. 1). For my estimates, based on early eighteenth-century tax lists and inventories of estate, see Appendix, Table 1.

41. Carl Bridenbaugh's *Colonial Craftsman* is a general introduction to the subject.

42. Office of the Recorder of Wills, Inventories, Book A, 1682-1699, no. 199 (Stephen Coleman), Book B, 1699-1704, no. 17 (John Simons), City Hall Annex, Philadelphia; Suffolk County Probate Records, II, 449 (Thomas Smith), XIV, 122 (Richard Crisp), Suffolk County Courthouse, Boston.

43. In Philadelphia the mean personal wealth of goldsmiths and silversmiths whose estates were inventoried between 1690 and 1775 was £ 798 sterling; the mean for shoemakers was £ 216. In Boston 40.5 percent of tailors and weavers whose estates were inventoried owned a house or lot, whereas 73.1 percent of house carpenters did so. In a study of Philadelphians, Billy G. Smith has found only a weak correlation between wealth and "social age," as measured by the age of the oldest child in the household. "Up, Down, and Out in Late Eighteenth-Century Philadelphia," unpub. ms., pp. 11-12.

44. The Nathaniel Adams family history can be followed in the will and inventory of the first-generation Nathaniel, Suffolk County Probate Records, XI,

136, IX, 372, XVI, 340; his brother David, also a blockmaker, XVI, 34, 85; the will and inventory of Joseph (second generation), XXXIII, 52, XXXV, 330; and the appointment of a guardian for Nathaniel Adams (fourth generation), XXXV, 302, and John Adams, David Adams, and Elizabeth Adams, XXXV, 328-331.

45. William H. Whitmore and others, eds., *Reports of the Record Commissioners of the City of Boston*, 39 vols. (Boston, 1876-1908) (hereafter *BTR*); Robert Francis Seybolt, *The Public Schoolmasters of Colonial Boston* (Cambridge, Mass., 1939); Minutes of the Meetings of the Justices, Church Wardens, and Vestrymen of the City of New York, 1694-1747, New York Public Library.

46. Hamilton Andrews Hill, *History of the Old South Church (Third Church), Boston, 1669-1884*, 2 vols. (Boston, 1890), I, 417. In Massachusetts currency the salary allowed was £ 4.25 per week.

47. The merchants are the most thoroughly studied group in colonial urban history. Among the best works for the early period are Bernard Bailyn, *The New England Merchants in the Seventeenth Century* (Cambridge, Mass., 1955); Tolles, *Meeting House and Counting House*; Lawrence H. Leder and Vincent P. Carosso, "Robert Livingston: Businessman of Colonial New York," *Business History Review*, 30 (1956), 18-45; and Philip L. White, *The Beekmans of New York in Politics and Commerce, 1647-1877* (New York, 1956).

48. I have discussed the problems in using these sources, and ways of compensating for built-in distortions, in "Urban Wealth and Poverty in Pre-Revolutionary America," *Journal of Interdisciplinary History*, 6 (1976), 547-555, 566-574. For probate records and their use see also Gloria L. Main, "Probate Records as a Source for Early American History," *WMQ*, 32 (1975), 89-99; Main, "The Correction of Biases in Colonial American Probate Records," *Historical Methods Newsletter*, 8 (1974), 10-28; and Daniel Scott Smith, "Underregistration and Bias in Probate Records: An Analysis of Data from Eighteenth-Century Hingham, Massachusetts," *WMQ*, 32 (1975), 100-110.

49. See Appendix, Table 3.

50. Suffolk County Probate Records, XIII, 598; IX, 312.

51. Ibid., XIII, 311.

52. Including real estate, wealth in Boston ranged from £ 307 to £ 1,151.

53. Of the twenty-five real property owners, six held land and buildings worth less than £ 500 and nineteen, more than £ 500.

54. The best discussion of this for late seventeenth century is Foster, *Solitary Way*, pp. 127-152.

55. David J. Rothman, *The Discovery of the Asylum: Social Order and Disorder in the New Republic* (Boston, 1971), p. 4. The author provides a good discussion of early attitudes toward poverty, but, as subsequent chapters will show, I am at odds with him regarding the timing of changes in the eighteenth century.

56. See Appendix, Table 10 for the minimal expenses of poor relief at the beginning of the eighteenth century.

57. Bridenbaugh, *Cities in the Wilderness*, p. 84.

58. For an excellent discussion of Puritan attitudes toward wealth see Foster, *Solitary Way*, pp. 99-126; for Quakers consult Frederick B. Tolles, " 'Of the Best Sort but Plain': The Quaker Esthetic," *American Quarterly*, 11 (1959), 484-502.

59. See Appendix, Table 7. Edward Randolph, the most knowledgeable of

the English bureaucrats in the colonies in the late seventeenth century, believed that thirty Massachusetts merchants had fortunes of £ 10,000 to £ 20,000 in 1676. Samuel Eliot Morison, *The Maritime History of Massachusetts, 1783-1860* (Boston, 1921), p. 17. This was probably an exaggeration but it must be remembered that the extant inventories do not include the estates of all men and often exclude landholdings, sometimes vast, in other parts of the colony.

60. Some idea of the limited scale of mercantile operations can be gained from the shipping investments of Samuel Lillie, who Bailyn calls "easily the biggest shipowner in the western hemisphere" in 1707. In 1698 Lillie owned about 629 tons of shipping. At £ 7 per ton, which is a high estimate for the value of ships in New England in the late seventeenth century, this would be an investment of about £ 4,400. Bernard Bailyn and Lotte Bailyn, *Massachusetts Shipping, 1697-1714: A Statistical Study* (Cambridge, Mass., 1959), pp. 70, 128. For shipbuilding costs, I follow Jacob M. Price, "A Note on the Value of Colonial Exports of Shipping," *Journal of Economic History*, 36 (1976), 719-721. Lillie's investment may have been considerably lower if the cost of shipbuilding in Boston at this earlier period paralleled that in Philadelphia, where Isaac Norris paid £3.34 per ton for the 146-ton ship *Richmond* in 1722. Isaac Norris Letter Book, 1722-1724, p. 94, Historical Society of Pennsylvania, Philadelphia (hereafter HSP).

61. Bailyn, *New England Merchants*, p. 193.

62. Ibid., p. 195; Bridenbaugh, *Cities in the Wilderness*, p. 253.

63. Joyce Diane Goodfriend, " 'Too Great A Mixture of Nations': The Development of New York City Society in the Seventeenth Century" (Ph.D. diss., University of California, Los Angeles, 1975), p. 146. There were also seven Jewish traders.

64. This process is examined in Thomas J. Archdeacon, *New York City, 1664-1710: Conquest and Change* (Ithaca, N.Y., 1976), pp. 58-77. The 1695 tax list is in *Collections of the New-York Historical Society for the Year 1910* (New York, 1911), pp. 1-64 (hereafter *NYHS Coll.*).

65. Appendix, Table 7. The limited scope of mercantile activities in the early years of Philadelphia can be ascertained from the mercantile correspondence of one of the town's largest merchants, James Claypoole. Marion Balderston, ed., *James Claypoole's Letter Book, London and Philadelphia, 1681-1684* (San Marino, Ca., 1967); and the correspondence between William Frampton of Philadelphia and Charles Jones & Company, Bristol, in Early Letters from Bristol and Philadelphia, Am 2532, HSP.

66. Viola F. Barnes, "The Rise of William Phips," *New England Quarterly*, 1 (1928), 271-294; on Jones see Hannah Benner Roach, comp., "Philadelphia Business Directory, 1690," *Pennsylvania Genealogical Magazine*, 23 (1963), 97-97n.

2. The Urban Polity

1. Samuel Estabrook, *A Sermon Shewing that the Peace and Quietness Of a People Is a main part of the Work of Civil Rulers* . . . (New London, Conn., 1718), p. 18, quoted in Richard L. Bushman, *From Puritan to Yankee: Character and the Social Order in Connecticut, 1690-1765* (Cambridge, Mass., 1967), p. 5.

2. This problem is dealt with in sociological terms in Kai T. Erikson, *Wayward Puritans: A Study in the Sociology of Deviance* (New York, 1966).

3. This transition in thought is commandingly surveyed in J. G. A. Pocock, *The Machiavellian Moment: Florentine Political Thought and the Atlantic Republican Tradition* (Princeton, N.J., 1975).

4. William Douglass, *Summary, Historical and Political of the First Planting, Progressive Improvements, and Present State of the British Settlements in North-America* (Boston, 1749-51), quoted in Bernard Bailyn, *The Origins of American Politics* (New York, 1968), p. 59.

5. B. Katherine Brown, "The Controversy over the Franchise in Puritan Massachusetts, 1954 to 1974," *WMQ*, 33 (1976), 212-241 and a rebuttal by Robert E. Wall, "The Franchise in Seventeenth-Century Massachusetts: Dedham and Cambridge," ibid., 34 (1977), 453-458 are the latest additions to a very large literature on this subject. See also Stephen Foster, "The Massachusetts Franchise in the Seventeenth Century," Appendix A of *Solitary Way*, pp. 171-179.

6. Quoted in Darrett B. Rutman, *Winthrop's Boston: Portrait of a Puritan Town, 1630-1649* (Chapel Hill, N.C., 1965), p. 162.

7. Forty pounds sterling was equivalent to £53 4s "lawful money" in Massachusetts. If property was valued at 5 to 6 percent of its true worth, then anyone on the tax list assessed for more than about £3 would qualify. In a study of the 1687 tax list James Henretta calculates that 85.4 percent of all rated householders and 72 percent of all polls were above this line. "Economic Development and Social Structure in Colonial Boston," *WMQ*, 22 (1965), 76, 80. Brown, "The Controversy over the Franchise," p. 237 believes the assessors rated property at 6 percent of its true value. G. B. Warden, comparing the mean assessed value of real property with the mean value of property deed in 1687, concludes that real property was assessed at about 5 percent of its market value. "Inequality and Instability in Eighteenth-Century Boston: A Reappraisal," *Journal of Interdisciplinary History*, 6 (1976), 588.

8. For scattered voting statistics in this period see Brown, "The Controversy over the Franchise," p. 240. By 1690 there were about 1,100 adult white males in the town. On English suffrage, which recent scholarship has shown to be broader than previously believed, see Geoffrey Holmes, *The Electorate and the National Will in the First Age of Party* (London, 1976) and J. H. Plumb, "The Growth of the Electorate in England from 1600 to 1715," *Past and Present*, no. 45 (1969), 90-116.

9. Milton M. Klein, "Democracy and Politics in Colonial New York," *New York History*, 40 (1959), 237. In a disputed election in 1701 voters went to the polls in three wards that two years before had a total of 428 male taxpayers. The voters are listed in *Minutes of the Common Council of the City of New York, 1675-1776*, 8 vols. (New York, 1905), II, 163-178; the 1699 tax list is in *NYHS Coll., 1911* (New York, 1912), pp. 279-315.

10. Gary B. Nash, *Quakers and Politics: Pennsylvania, 1681-1726* (Princeton, N.J., 1968), pp. 42, 202-203 (hereafter Nash, *Quakers and Politics*).

11. The 1691 charter required £20 "ratable estate" in Massachusetts currency. As Robert Brown has shown, this was a higher qualification than the £40 sterling requirement for provincial elections until about 1713, when the depreciation of Massachusetts money began to reverse the restrictiveness of the two requirements. Robert E. Brown, *Middle-Class Democracy and the Revolution in Massachusetts, 1691-1780* (New York, 1969), pp. 80-87.

12. Rutman, *Winthrop's Boston*, chap. 3 and pp. 159-163 traces the evolu-

tion of the town meeting and its slow accrual of power in town affairs.

13. G. B. Warden, *Boston, 1689-1776* (Boston, 1970), pp. 31-32 (hereafter Warden, *Boston*). The percentage of males holding office gradually declined as the population grew, but even in 1748, when the adult white male population numbered about 3,500, at least 109 Bostonians held elective office, according to the list in William Douglass, *Summary, Historical and Political of the . . . Present State of the British Settlements in North-America* (London, 1750), I, 514.

14. The mixture of popular and hierarchical elements in local politics is explored in Edward M. Cook, Jr., *The Fathers of the Towns: Leadership and Community Structure in Eighteenth-Century New England* (Baltimore, 1976).

15. Arthur E. Peterson, *New York as an Eighteenth-Century Municipality Prior to 1731* (New York, 1917), pp. 14-33.

16. Nash, *Quakers and Politics*, pp. 129-130.

17. Warden, *Boston*, p. 28; Abner C. Goodell and Ellis Ames, eds., *The Acts and Resolves, Public and Private, of the Province of the Massachusetts Bay*, 19 vols. (Boston, 1869-1922), II, 30 (1715) (hereafter *Massachusetts Acts and Resolves*).

18. *BTR*, VIII, 12, 23.

19. Alan Everitt, "The Marketing of Agricultural Produce," in Joan Thirsk, ed., *The Agrarian History of England and Wales, 1500-1640* (Cambridge, Eng., 1967), pp. 569-570.

20. Jon C. Teaford, *The Municipal Revolution in America: Origins of Modern Urban Government, 1650-1825* (Chicago, 1975), p. 16.

21. Ibid., pp. 35-44.

22. Foster, *Solitary Way*, p. 157. Foster's discussion of Puritanism and democracy (pp. 155-172) assays the voluminous literature on the subject.

23. Quoted in Nash, *Quakers and Politics*, p. 39.

24. Foster, *Solitary Way*, p. 69.

25. Henretta, "Economic Development," p. 79; Nash, *Quakers and Politics*, chaps. 1-2.

26. For the occupations of Boston selectmen I am indebted to G. B. Warden. For the occupations of the New York aldermen see Joyce Diane Goodfriend, " 'Too Great A Mixture of Nations': The Development of New York City Society in the Seventeenth Century" (Ph.D. diss., University of California, Los Angeles, 1975), p. 172.

27. Understanding of the behavior of preindustrial crowds, formerly denoted "mobs," has been greatly altered by French and English scholars. The literature on the subject is now vast. For the applicability of this work to colonial America see Edward Countryman, "The Problem of the Early American Crowd," *Journal of American Studies*, 7 (1973), 77-90.

28. Roger Lane, *Policing the City: Boston, 1822-1865* (Cambridge, Mass., 1967), chap. 1; for New York see James F. Richardson, *The New York Police: Colonial Times to 1901* (New York, 1970), chap. 1.

29. Carl Bridenbaugh, *Cities in Revolt: Urban Life in America, 1743-1776* (New York, 1955), pp. 108-109 (hereafter Bridenbaugh, *Cities in Revolt*).

30. Pauline Maier, "Popular Uprisings and Civil Authority in Eighteen-Century America," *WMQ*, 27 (1970), 3-35, and Countryman, "Problem of the Early American Crowd."

31. Quoted in Foster, *Solitary Way*, p. 15.

32. Bailyn, *Origins of American Politics*, pp. 36-37. For the perpetuation of this body of thought in eighteenth-century Massachusetts see Stephen E. Patterson, *Political Parties in Revolutionary Massachusetts* (Madison, Wis., 1973), pp. 3-32. Patterson notes the wide gap between political rhetoric and political reality.

33. For a brief treatment of the Dominion of New England see Wesley Frank Craven, *The Colonies in Transition, 1660-1713* (New York, 1968), pp. 212-225. The standard work on the subject is still Viola F. Barnes, *The Dominion of New England* (New Haven, Conn., 1923).

34. For an account of Bostonians' reaction to Andros see T. H. Breen, *The Character of the Good Ruler: Puritan Political Ideas in New England, 1630-1730* (New Haven, Conn., 1970), pp. 141-150 (hereafter Breen, *Good Ruler*).

35. Two short accounts are David S. Lovejoy, *The Glorious Revolution in America* (New York, 1972), pp. 239-245; and Richard S. Dunn, *Puritans and Yankees: The Winthrop Dynasty of New England, 1630-1717* (Princeton, N.J., 1962), pp. 251-257.

36. Randolph to William Blathwayt, July 20, 1689, in Robert N. Toppan and Alfred T. S. Goodrich, eds., *Edward Randolph; Including His Letters and Official Papers 1676-1703*, 7 vols. (Boston, 1898-1909), VI, 289-290.

37. Quoted in Breen, *Good Ruler*, p. 151. Viola Barnes concludes that about a thousand men participated in the Town House action of April 18. This would be almost all the males over eighteen years of age in Boston at the time. Even allowing for consideration contingents from nearby communities such as Charlestown, and paring this estimate by a third, the crowd must have included a majority of Boston's men, and perhaps a good many women as well. Barnes, *Dominion of New England*, p. 242.

38. Quoted in Breen, *Good Ruler*, p. 159. Perry Miller argues that it was the Bostonians' need to prove themselves loyal to the crown, in the wake of their overthrow of Andros, that provided the chief incentive for mounting an expedition against French Canada in 1690. Miller, *New England Mind*, pp. 160-162.

39. Breen, *Good Ruler*, pp. 167-179.

40. Quoted in Miller, *New England Mind*, p. 156.

41. Randolph to Blathwayt, July 20, 1689, *Randolph Papers*, VI, 289-292. Dudley was also president of council under Andros. Thomas Hutchinson, a later chief justice of the colony, remembered Dudley in his history of Massachusetts as the most despised man in Boston at the time. *History of the Colony of Massachusets-Bay . . .* , I (London, 1760), 391-392 (hereafter Hutchinson, *History of Massachusets*). For Dudley's fate at the hands of the Boston crowd see also Everett Kimball, *The Public Life of Joseph Dudley: A Study of the Colonial Policy of the Stuarts in New England, 1660-1715* (New York, 1911), pp. 52-53.

42. Quoted in Breen, *Good Ruler*, pp. 171-172.

43. Ibid., p. 173.

44. Quoted ibid., p. 176. One observer described the crowd as "a rabble of two or three hundred." *Calendar of State Papers, Colonial Series, America and West Indies, 1689-1692*, ed. J. W. Fortescue (London, 1901), no. 310 (hereafter *CSP Colonial*).

45. Willard, *The Character of a Good Ruler* (Boston, 1694), quoted in

Breen, *Good Ruler*, p. 176. Breen and Stephen Foster have argued that the mid-1680s marked the turning point in Massachusetts society when a "widely accepted ideology," responsive political institutions, general prosperity, and social cohesion began to crumble. "The Puritans' Greatest Achievement: A Study of Social Cohesion in Seventeenth-Century Massachusetts," *Journal of American History*, 60 (1973), 5-22.

46. *The Happiness of a People in the Wisdome of their Rulers* (Boston, 1676), quoted in Foster, *Solitary Way*, p. 12.

47. Gershom Bulkeley, "Will and Doom" (1692), quoted in Breen, *Good Ruler*, p. 177. Bulkeley was at the far end of the political spectrum in New England at the time, representing what Perry Miller calls the "royalist" view. He was the son of Peter Bulkeley, one of the chief prosecutors of Anne Hutchinson in the 1636 Antinomian Controversy. See Miller, *New England Mind*, pp. 151-154.

48. Christopher Hill, *The World Turned Upside Down: Radical Ideas During the English Revolution* (New York, 1972), p. 11.

49. Ibid.

50. B. S. Capp analyzes the movement. *The Fifth Monarchy Men: A Study in Seventeenth-Century Millenarianism* (London, 1972).

51. For a study of apocalyptic radicalism in New England between 1630 and 1660 see J. F. Maclear, "New England and the Fifth Monarchy: The Quest for the Millennium in Early American Puritanism," *WMQ*, 32 (1975), 223-260. Maclear argues that the eschatological politics of the Fifth Monarchists, in its New England form, had nearly faded by 1660.

52. Quoted in Foster, *Solitary Way*, p. 14.

53. John Saffin, *A Brief and Candid Answer to . . . The Selling of Joseph* (Boston, 1700), quoted ibid., p. 15.

54. Miller, *New England Mind*, 48-51. Miller's treatment of economic and social change in late seventeenth-century New England is the best available on the subject.

55. Charles M. Andrews, ed., *Narratives of the Insurrections, 1675-1690* (New York, 1915), pp. 175-176.

56. Lovejoy, *Glorious Revolution*, pp. 251-257.

57. Ibid., pp. 336-340, 354-358. Moderates in Boston, although they had no reason to celebrate the artisan-oriented activities of Leisler, gratefully associated his anti-Catholic, anti-Dominion cause with their own. After Leisler was executed at the hands of the despised Dudley, Increase Mather, whose delegation to England had sought royal approbation from King William for the overthrow of Andros, wrote that Leisler and Milbourne "were not only murdered, they were barbarously murdered." *Documents Relative to the Colonial History of the State of New York*, ed. Edmund B. O'Callaghan and Berthold Fernow, 15 vols. (Albany, 1853-87), II, 250 (hereafter *NYCD*).

58. Thomas J. Archdeacon, *New York City, 1664-1710: Conquest and Change* (Ithaca, N.Y., 1976), pp. 97-122. Ethnic accommodation, especially at the upper levels of society, has been studied by Goodfriend in " 'Too Great a Mixture of Nations,' " chap. 5. Goodfriend gives less weight to ethnic tension than Archdeacon, but she too concludes that "the trend toward separation and heightened ethnic consciousness was unmistakable" in the late seventeenth century (p. 179).

59. Goodfriend has analyzed the surnames on the 1677 and 1695 tax lists and concluded that 67 percent of the taxpayers were Dutch in the former year and 58 percent in the latter year. Ibid., p. 139.

60. Jerome R. Reich, *Leisler's Rebellion: A Study of Democracy in New York, 1664-1720* (Chicago, 1953), pp. 76-86. Reich's treatment of Leisler has often been criticized for overemphasizing class conflict during the rebellion, but in fact it strikes a balance between class and ethnic factors and remains an invaluable study of this era. Reich's analysis corrects earlier interpretations of Leisler's movement as the revolt of the "near-greats" against the "greats." For a fresh and balanced account of the rebellion see Robert C. Ritchie, *The Duke's Province: A Study of New York Politics and Society, 1664-1691* (Chapel Hill, N.C., 1977), chap. 9.

61. "Abstract of Colonel Nicholas Bayard's Journal," *NYCD*, III, 601; Address of the Militia of New York to William and Mary, ibid., 584; Reich, *Leisler's Rebellion*, pp. 52-54.

62. Lovejoy, *Glorious Revolution*, pp. 282-284. It is difficult today, writes Lovejoy, to believe "that there was a monstrous Catholic plot to deliver England's colonies to the Pope"—a conspiracy hatched by James II in concert with Louis XIV and eagerly supported by the Catholic oligarchy in Maryland, the royal governors in Boston and New York, the French in Canada, and the disaffected Indian tribes. But such fears were real in New York, where Leisler, called by his adherents that "old Stander . . . of fervent Seale for the protestant Religion," lost no time in purging the colony of all Catholic influences, while he wrote to England of the many evidences of the Romish cancer that had infected the body politic.

63. Stephanus Van Courtlandt to Capt. Nicholson, Aug. 5, 1689, *NYCD*, III, 610; Reich, *Leisler's Rebellion*, p. 80.

64. "Representation of Ensign Joost Stol, Agent for the Committee of Safety of New-York," *NYCD*, III, 631.

65. Reich, *Leisler's Rebellion*, p. 71; Lovejoy, *Glorious Revolution*, p. 301; Andrews, ed., *Narratives of the Insurrections*, p. 336n.

66. For the occupations of the elected aldermen I am indebted to Joyce D. Goodfriend of the University of Denver.

67. Reich, *Leisler's Rebellion*, pp. 122, 128.

68. Nicholas Bayard to Francis Nicholson, July 23, 1689, *NYCD*, III, 599.

69. In 1698, in a tract written for the anti-Leislerians, it was claimed that the Leislerians "did force pillage, rob and steal" £13,959 of property in the city during Leisler's administration. *A Letter from a Gentleman of the City of New-York* (New York, 1698), reprinted in Andrews, ed., *Narratives of the Insurrections*, pp. 360-372. Andrews tentatively identifies the author as David Jamison, secretary of the anti-Leislerian council in that year, and claims that it was written at the request of the leading anti-Leislerians, Nicholas Bayard, William Nicolls, and Chidley Brooke (p. 358). The charge was partly denied and the amount of pillage disputed in *Loyalty Vindicated from the Reflections of a Virulent Pamphlet* . . . (New York, 1698), in Andrews, ed., *Narratives of the Insurrections*, pp. 375-401.

70. Stephanus Van Cortlandt to Francis Nicholson, Aug. 5, 1689, *NYCD*, III, 610.

71. Lovejoy, *Glorious Revolution*, pp. 298-300.

72. *A Letter from A Gentleman . . .* , in Andrews, ed., *Narratives of the Insurrections*, p. 364.

73. Lovejoy, *Glorious Revolution*, pp. 301-302; Archdeacon, *New York City*, pp. 109-115.

74. Chidley Brooke to Robert Southwell, April 5, 1691, Nicholas Bayard to John West, Jan. 14, 1689/90, *NYCD*, III, 757, 661; [Nicholas Bayard], *A Modest and Impartiall Narrative . . .* (London, 1690), in Andrews, ed., *Narratives of the Insurrections*, p. 323; Robert Livingston to Francis Nicholson, June 7, 1690, quoted in Lawrence H. Leder, *Robert Livingston, 1654-1728, and the Politics of Colonial New York* (Chapel Hill, N.C., 1961), p. 72.

75. Lovejoy, *Glorious Revolution*, pp. 298-300.

76. Julius Goebel, Jr., and T. Raymond Naughton, *Law Enforcement in Colonial New York: A Study in Criminal Procedure, 1664-1776* (New York, 1944), p. 83.

77. Gary B. Nash, "City Planning and Political Tension in the Seventeenth Century: The Case of Philadelphia," *Proceedings of the American Philosophical Society*, 112 (1968), 54-73.

78. Nash, *Quakers and Politics*, pp. 67-114.

79. Ibid., pp. 114-126, quotation p. 122.

80. Ibid., pp. 127-144.

81. Ibid., pp. 144-147; Jon Butler, " 'Gospel Order Improved': The Keithian Schism and the Exercise of Quaker Ministerial Authority in Pennsylvania," *WMQ*, 31 (1974), 431-452.

82. Nash, *Quakers and Politics*, pp. 147-153; Butler, "Keithian Schism," pp. 439-452; Ethyn Williams Kirby, *George Keith, 1638-1716* (New York, 1942), pp. 76, 85-87.

83. Robert Turner to Penn, June 15, 1692, quoted in Nash, *Quakers and Politics*, p. 154. Penn also expressed his view that Philadelphians were drawn to Keith more by personal than religious considerations. Ibid.

84. A fuller analysis is in Nash, *Quakers and Politics*, pp. 155-161. Butler, "Keithian Schism," pp. 431-439.

85. Penn to the Board of Trade, April 22, 1700 and Penn to Charlewood Lawton, Aug. 18, 1701, Penn Letter Book (1699-1703), HSP, quoted in Nash, *Quakers and Politics*, p. 162.

86. Quoted ibid., pp. 174-175.

3. The Seaport Economies in an Era of War

1. See Appendix, Figure 1 for more complete data and sources.

2. To chapters 3 and 4 of Curtis Putnam Nettels, *The Money Supply of the American Colonies before 1720* (Madison, Wis., 1934) should be added the recent work of historical geographer Douglas R. McManis, *Colonial New England: A Historical Geography* (New York, 1975).

3. For trade statistics see Appendix, Figures 2 and 3.

4. Appendix, Figure 1.

5. Bridenbaugh, *Cities in the Wilderness*, p. 178; Bernard Bailyn and Lotte Bailyn, *Massachusetts Shipping, 1697-1714: A Statistical Study* (Cambridge, Mass., 1959), pp. 102-105.

6. Calculated from data in Bailyn and Bailyn, *Mass. Shipping*, pp. 102-105.

7. Ralph Davis, *The Rise of the English Shipping Industry in the Seventeenth and Eighteenth Centuries* (London, 1962), pp. 66-68; Jacob M. Price, "A Note on the Value of Colonial Exports of Shipping," *Journal of Economic History*, 36 (1976), 705-706.

8. The Bailyns claim that the 544 owners represent one-third of the adult males in Boston at this time, but they do not calculate the coming of age of about 4 percent of the population a year, which increases the potential pool of Boston shipowners from their estimated 1,800 to about 2,800. *Mass. Shipping*, p. 56.

9. Ibid., pp. 63-64. This "decisive and significant change in the balance of ownership," the Bailyns assert, is confirmed by examining single-owner ships. In 1698 the two leading maritime investors held 29 percent of the tonnage in ships with undivided ownership; in the sixteen years after 1698 the same percentage of investors held about 55 percent of the tonnage of single-owner ships.

10. Bernard Bailyn, *The New England Merchants in the Seventeenth Century* (Cambridge, Mass., 1955), p. 195; Samuel G. Drake, *The History and Antiquities of Boston . . .* (Boston, 1856), p. 403n; Bailyn and Bailyn, *Mass. Shipping*, p. 69; Nettels, *Money Supply*, p. 93; Justin Winsor, ed., *The Memorial History of Boston, Including Suffolk County, Massachusetts, 1630-1880*, 4 vols. (Boston, 1886), II, 551. Belcher consolidated the fortune built upon wartime profiteering by taking as his second wife Hannah Walker, the daughter of Theophilus Frary, a wealthy Boston merchant, and widow of Isaac Walker, another merchant. She brought a minor fortune to the marriage.

11. Bailyn and Bailyn, *Mass. Shipping*, pp. 70, 34-35.

12. Ibid., pp. 70-71. The Bailyns note that Charles Hobby and Louis Boucher were among the other Boston merchants who declared bankruptcy during the war.

13. Boston-owned ships numbered 124 in 1698 according to the shipping register (Bailyn and Bailyn, *Mass. Shipping*, p. 79) and 194 in 1700 according to Governor Bellomont of New York (Nettels, *Money Supply*, p. 102). There is too large a discrepancy between these figures for both to be correct, but even taking the lower figure and reckoning six mariners per ship yields a total of 744 mariners in the town. Figures compiled from 1714 to 1717 on 1,247 ships clearing Boston show an average of 6.9 mariners per ship. *NYCD*, V, 618.

14. Herbert L. Osgood, *The American Colonies in the Eighteenth Century*, 4 vols. (New York, 1924), I, 434, 442. The lower figure was paid in the 1711 expedition. Francis Parkman, *A Half-Century of Conflict* (New York, 1962; 1892), p. 109 says recruits also received an enlistment bounty of £12 (Massachusetts currency).

15. The motives of recruits and the filling of quotas through impressment are discussed in George A. Rawlyk, *Nova Scotia's Massachusetts: A Study of Massachusetts-Nova Scotia Relations* (Montreal and London, 1973), chaps. 4-6.

16. Gerald S. Graham, *Empire of the North Atlantic: The Maritime Struggle for North America* (Toronto, 1950), p. 70. The fullest account is still Francis Parkman, *Count Frontenac and New France under Louis XIV* (Boston, 1880). Parkman says that 288 sailors and 400 to 500 militiamen were involved. John Gorham Palfrey, *History of New England*, 5 vols (Boston, 1865-90), IV, 49 states

that 700 to 800 men were involved.

17. Parkman, *Frontenac*, p. 246 says 2,200 men were recruited and notes that a land press was ordered by the governor when enlistments fell short. In one seaport town—Gloucester—two-thirds of the adult males were involved in the expedition. Parkman, *Frontenac*, chaps. 12-13 gives a detailed account of the Quebec assault.

18. Dummer, *A Defence of the New-England Charters* . . . (Boston, 1745; London, 1721), p.16. A modern authority, Howard H. Peckham, says that at least 230 men were lost in the 1690 expedition but this number is probably much too low. *The Colonial Wars, 1689-1762* (Chicago, 1964) pp. 36-38.

19. Quoted in Arthur H. Buffinton, "External Relations (1689-1740)," in Albert Bushnell Hart, ed., *Commonwealth History of Massachusetts: Colony, Province and State*, 4 vols. (New York, 1927-30), II, 76.

20. Jeremiah Dummer, *A Letter to a Noble Lord* . . . (Boston, 1712).

21. Dudley to Earl of Nottingham, Nov. 8, 1702, *CSP Colonial, 1702* (London, 1912), no. 1131; Dudley to Governor of Jamaica, Feb. 11, 1703, *CSP Colonial, 1702-03*, no. 319; Osgood, *American Colonies*, I, 401-402.

22. Nathaniel Cary to the Queen, March 15, 1705, *CSP Colonial, 1704-05*, no. 954; Gov. Joseph Dudley to Fitz-John Winthrop, July 26, 1704, *MHS Coll.*, 6th ser., III (Boston, 1889), 244; Palfrey, *History of New England*, IV, 269-270.

23. The reception of the troops in Boston, recounted by Wait-Still Winthrop, is quoted in Kenneth Silverman, ed., *Selected Letters of Cotton Mather* (Baton Rouge, La., 1971), p. 60.

24. Palfrey, *History of New England*, IV, 270-287; Parkman, *Half-Century of Conflict*, pp. 97-133; Buffinton, "External Relations," pp. 78-85; Osgood, *American Colonies*, I, 407-419.

25. William Douglass, *Summary, Historical and Political of the* . . . *Present State of the British Settlements in North-America* (London, 1750), II, 530. After examining the Massachusetts muster rolls in the Massachusetts Archives, Parkman concluded that "more than one in five of her able-bodied men were in active service in the summer of 1711." *Half-Century of Conflict*, p. 133n.

26. Cotton Mather, *The Bostonian Ebenezer* (Boston, 1698); Bridenbaugh, *Cities in the Wilderness*, p. 233.

27. Nettels, *Money Supply*, p. 255.

28. Dudley to the Board of Trade, April 8, 1712, *CSP Colonial, 1711-12*, pp. 258-260.

29. See Appendix, Table 11. Even before the heaviest military expenditures in 1710 and 1711 Cotton Mather was writing that "the back of the country [is] broken with insupportable expenses." Silverman, ed., *Letters of Mather*, p. 81.

30. Robert Quary to the Board of Trade, Jan. 10, 1708, quoted in Curtis P. Nettels, "The Menace of Colonial Manufacturing in the Old Colonial System," *New England Quarterly*, 4 (1931), 238n; Dudley to the Board of Trade, April 8, 1712, *CSP Colonial, 1711-12*, p. 260. Parkman wrote that "years passed before she [Massachusetts] recovered from the effects of her financial exhaustion." *Half-Century of Conflict*, p. 133n.

31. The best introduction to the initial experiments with paper money and deficit spending is Leslie V. Brock, *The Currency of the American Colonies, 1700-1764: A Study in Colonial Finance and Imperial Relations* (New York,

1975), pp. 1-64. A total of £82,000 in paper bills was issued between 1690 and 1702. The emissions are tabulated in Andrew MacFarland Davis, *Currency and Banking in the Province of Massachusetts-Bay*, 2 vols. (New York, 1901), I, 436 (hereafter Davis, *Currency and Banking*). The emissions from 1703 to 1716 are recorded on p. 443. For the amount of money in circulation each year see Brock, *Currency of the American Colonies*, pp. 591-592.

32. The entire question of monetary theory and practice in England was undergoing heated debate during this era. For a brilliant discussion of the topic see Joyce Oldham Appleby, "Locke, Liberalism and the Natural Law of Money," *Past and Present*, no. 71 (1976), 43-69.

33. Most conservatives at the time and most historians since have condemned the Massachusetts legislators for fiscal irresponsibility in issuing excessive amounts of paper money and deferring the retirement dates. None, so far as I know, have suggested what alternatives were available. For modern discussions of the problem see E. James Ferguson, "Currency Finance: An Interpretation of Colonial Monetary Practices," *WMQ*, 10 (1953), 153-180; Roger W. Weiss, "The Colonial Monetary Standard of Massachusetts," *Economic History Review*, 27 (1974), 577-592; and Herman J. Belz, "Paper Money in Colonial Massachusetts," *Essex Institute Historical Collections*, 101 (1965), 149-163.

34. Nettels, *Money Supply*, pp. 257n-258n; Davis, *Currency and Banking*, I, 88-89.

35. Tables of silver prices in Massachusetts currency are generally derived from the data in Davis, *Currency and Banking*, I, 368-370. See Weiss, "Monetary Standard of Massachusetts," pp. 586-587 for a slightly refined table and Appendix, Table 12 for my own refinements, based on values given in Boston inventories.

36. This explanation of the declining value of Massachusetts bills was later argued by Hugh Vance, a Boston merchant. See [Hugh Vance], *Some Observations on the Scheme* . . . (Boston, 1738) and *An Inquiry into the Nature and Uses of Money* . . . (Boston, 1740), in Andrew MacFarland Davis, ed., *Colonial Currency Reprints*, 4 vols. (Boston, 1910-11), III, 181-213 and 366-474 (hereafter Davis, ed. *Currency Reprints*). The ablest modern scholar of the problem concurs (Brock, *Currency of the American Colonies*, pp. 56-64). I am indebted to John Murrin of Princeton University for advice on this matter.

37. Quoted in Nettels, *Money Supply*, p. 258n.

38. For a wheat price series see Ruth Crandall, "Wholesale Commodity Prices in Boston During the Eighteenth Century," *The Review of Economic Statistics*, 16 (1934), 121.

39. Davis, *Currency and Banking*, I, 378.

40. *The Second Part of the South-Sea Stock, Being An Inquiry into the Original of Province Bills or Bills of Credit* . . . (Boston, 1721), in Davis, ed., *Currency Reprints*, II, 321. The author, in alluding to "the poor labourer," was doubtless speaking of artisans, who typically made 5 shillings a day at this time. Also see *The Present Melancholy Circumstances of the Province Consider'd* . . . [Boston, 1719], ibid., I, 359.

41. Crandall, "Prices in Boston," p. 121. It is likely that prices of imported commodities rose much faster because wheat prices were regulated by the town selectmen.

42. For the biases inherent in the inventories and the methodology employed for analyzing them see Gary B. Nash, "Urban Wealth and Poverty in Pre-Revolutionary America," *Journal of Interdisciplinary History*, 6 (1976), 548, 552-554, 583-584. The data in this paragraph are more fully tabulated in Appendix, Tables 5, 6, and 7 and Figures 7 and 8.

43. Appendix, Table 8. Because the inventories were more often left by well-to-do citizens than by those of slender means, these data undoubtedly overstate the extent of property ownership. It is likely that almost half the people in Boston were renters rather than owners of houses; of these a large majority were simply too poor to accumulate the £40 or so that even a modest structure cost at this time. For a fuller discussion of property ownership see G. B. Warden, "The Distribution of Property in Boston, 1692-1775," *Perspectives in American History*, 10 (1976), 81-130.

44. Among the poorest 30 percent of decedents, occupations have been identified for 77 of 91 from 1685 to 1699, 84 of 105 from 1700 to 1715, and 78 of 94 from 1716 to 1725.

45. William B. Weeden, *Economic and Social History of New England*, 2 vols. (New York, 1963; 1890), II, 576. The one modern historian to hark to Weeden's plea is Jesse Lemisch, "Jack Tar in the Streets: Merchant Seamen in the Politics of Revolutionary America," *WMQ*, 25 (1968), 371-407.

46. Occupational analyses of Boston in 1790 and Philadelphia in 1774 and 1780-1783 show mariners constituting about 7 to 9 percent of the urban labor force. Jacob M. Price, "Economic Function and the Growth of American Port Towns in the Eighteenth Century," *Perspectives in American History*, 8 (1974), 182. These figures, though accurately reflecting the number of mariners inscribed on the tax lists, understate the actual number living in the seaport towns. Many ordinary seamen, because of their poverty, transiency, and ability to escape the tax assessor's notice while not in port, do not appear on the tax lists. In the Boston inventories, mariners represent nearly half of the males whose occupations can be identified from 1685 to 1699, more than 40 percent from 1700 to 1715, and just under 40 percent in the following decade. Also see Appendix, Table 1.

47. Nettels, *Money Supply*, p. 71n; Weeden, *Economic and Social History*, II, 577, 887-889; "Wages in the Colonial Period," Bureau of Labor Statistics, *Bulletin*, no. 499 (Washington, D.C., 1929), pp. 95-96.

48. Suffolk County Probate Records, XX, 607 (Pell); XX, 53, X, 185 (Blin); and XIII, 5 (Fox), Suffolk County Courthouse, Boston.

49. Calculated from 617 inventories of mariners in the Suffolk County Probate Records.

50. For a fine study of Massachusetts widowhood see Alexander Keyssar, "Widowhood in Eighteenth-Century Massachusetts: A Problem in the History of the Family," *Perspectives in American History*, 8 (1974), 81-119. Keyssar, however, ignores war in his discussion of the high rate of widowhood. See especially pp. 98-99.

51. Mather, *Marah Spoken To* (Boston, 1718), p. 1, cited in Keyssar, "Widowhood," p. 98. Since female communicants usually outnumbered males by three to two, Mather's statement suggests that one-third of his female communicants were widows.

52. Published anonymously in 1719 and 1720, both pamphlets were prob-

ably written by John Colman, a Boston merchant. For the attributions, see Davis, ed., *Currency Reprints*, I, 365, 408.

53. For example, 1,247 ships with combined tonnage of 62,788 cleared Boston from 1714 to 1717 as compared with 646 ships with a tonnage of 22,392 from New York from 1715 to 1718. *NYCD*, V, 618.

54. Average annual clearances from New York were: 1705-1707, 120; 1708-1710, 138; 1711-1713, 151; 1714-1716, 194. Compiled from yearly data given in *CSP Colonial, 1716-17*, no. 470.

55. Arthur Buffinton, "The Colonial Wars and Their Results," in Alexander C. Flick, ed., *History of the State of New York*, 4 vols. (New York, 1933), II, 217; Richard A. Lester, *Monetary Experiments: Early American and Recent Scandinavian* (Princeton, 1939), p. 112. Lester lists paper money issues of about £67,000 between 1709 and 1717.

56. Charles McLean Andrews, *The Colonial Period of American History*, 4 vols. (New Haven, Conn., 1934-40), IV, 374 has stated the matter best: "After 1689 the colonists seemed less united than ever and less inclined to cooperate for mutual protection. They were living, as they had always lived, in groups far removed the one from the other, poor and insufficiently stocked with the materials for war, absorbed each in its own problems of government, maintenance, and defense. They were jealous, suspicious, and wanting in intercolonial confidence, disinclined to make sacrifices in a common cause, and ready 'by pretence or various pretences' to evade responsibility and ignore, if they could, the commands of the government at home."

57. Buffinton, "Colonial Wars," pp. 216-218.

58. Bernard Mason, "Aspects of the New York Revolt of 1689," *New York History*, 30 (1949), 174; Bellomont to Lords of Trade, Nov. 28, 1700, *CSP Colonial, 1700*, p. 676. Bellomont claimed that New York's trade doubled between 1688 and 1698—the era of King William's War. Bellomont to Lords of the Treasury, May 25, 1698, *NYCD*, IV, 317. Also see Herbert Alan Johnson, *The Law Merchant and Negotiable Instruments in Colonial New York, 1664 to 1730* (Chicago, 1963), pp. 9-10.

59. Buffinton, "Colonial Wars," pp. 218-219; Kammen, *Colonial New York*, pp. 151-152.

60. J. H. Owen, *War at Sea Under Queen Anne, 1702-1708* (Cambridge, Eng., 1938), pp. 55-70; Nettels, *Money Supply*, p. 93 calculates that £44,230 in bills of exchange were drawn at New York for provisioning military forces.

61. For an introduction to piracy see Osgood, *American Colonies*, I, chap. 16.

62. Nettels, *Money Supply*, p. 87n.

63. "A Letter to a Member of Parliament concerning the Suppression of Piracy," March 20, 1700, *MHS Coll.*, 6th ser., I (Boston, 1886), 221-222n.

64. Maximillian E. Novak, *Economics and the Fiction of Daniel Defoe* (Berkeley and Los Angeles, 1962), pp. 110-114, 144-149. Defoe also published a two-volume *General History of Robberies, and Murders of the Most Notorious Pyrates* (London, 1724-28), which was as much a defense as a criticism of piracy.

65. Nettels, *Money Supply*, p. 89n; Fletcher's complicity with the pirates is best recounted in James S. Leamon, "Governor Fletcher's Recall," *WMQ*, 20 (1963), 527-542; and John D. Runcie, "The Problem of Anglo-American Politics

in Bellomont's New York," *WMQ*, 26 (1969), 191-217.

66. Governor Lord Bellomont to Secretary Popple, July 7, 1698, cited in Jerome R. Reich, *Leisler's Rebellion: A Study of Democracy in New York, 1664-1720* (Chicago, 1953), p. 137.

67. Quoted in Nettels, *Money Supply*, p. 89n.

68. Reich, *Leisler's Rebellion*, pp. 136-144; Runcie, "Bellomont's New York," pp. 202-207.

69. Bellomont to Lords of the Treasury, Dec. 14, 1698, *NYCD*, IV, 438.

70. Thomas J. Archdeacon, *New York City, 1664-1710: Conquest and Change* (Ithaca, N.Y., 1976), pp. 52, 65. The customs records are published as *An Account of Her Majesty's Revenue in the Province of New York 1701-1709: The Customs Records of Early Colonial New York*, ed. Julius M. Bloch and others (Ridgewood, N.J., 1966).

71. Edward H. Hall, *The Philipse Manor Hall at Yonkers, New York* (New York, 1912), pp. 45-61; "Frederick Philipse," *Dictionary of American Biography*, ed. Allen Johnson, Dumas Malone, and others, 22 vols. (New York, 1928-58), XIV, 538 (hereafter *DAB*); Patricia U. Bonomi, *A Factious People: Politics and Society in Colonial New York* (New York, 1971), pp. 60-61 (hereafter Bonomi, *Factious People*). Philipse did not diminish his fortune by taking as his second wife in 1692 Catherine Van Cortlandt, widow of another of the seaport's wealthiest merchants, John Dervall.

72. Jacob Judd, "Frederick Philipse and the Madagascar Trade," *New-York Historical Society Quarterly*, 55 (1971), 354-355; Bellomont to Lords of Trade, July 22, 1699, *NYCD*, IV, 532.

73. Virginia Bever Platt, "The East India Company and the Madagascar Slave Trade," *WMQ*, 26 (1969), 548-553.

74. Judd, "Frederick Philipse," pp. 358-366.

75. Platt, "East India Company," pp. 551-554; Judd, "Frederick Philipse," pp. 366-374.

76. Kammen, *Colonial New York*, p. 174; *DAB*, XIV, 538.

77. Appendix, Table 3; Archdeacon, *New York City*, pp. 56, 148.

78. Ibid., p. 57 for wealth at death of Skelton and Marques. The tax list of 1699 is in *NYHS Coll., 1911* (New York, 1912), pp. 279-315. For the distribution of wealth see Appendix, Table 3 and Archdeacon, *New York City*, p. 56 for 1703.

79. Beverly McAnear, "Politics in Provincial New York, 1689-1761" (Ph.D. diss., Stanford University, 1935), pp. 271-280 (hereafter McAnear, "Politics in New York"). McAnear, the most thorough student of economic trends in this period, notes that a trade recession occurred in 1718-1720.

80. Kenneth Scott, "The Church Wardens and the Poor in New York City, 1693-1747," *The New York Geneaological and Biographical Record*, 99 (1968), 157-164. Raymond A. Mohl, "Poverty in Early America, A Reappraisal: The Case of Eighteenth-Century New York City," *New York History*, 50 (1969), 5-28.

81. Joyce Diane Goodfriend, " 'Too Great A Mixture of Nations': The Development of New York City Society in the Seventeenth Century (Ph.D. diss., University of California, Los Angeles, 1975), pp. 275n-276n.

82. *The Colonial Laws of New York from the Year 1664 to the Revolution*, 5 vols. (Albany, 1894), I, 507-508.

83. Petition of the Corporation of Philadelphia to the Assembly, 1710,

Penn Letters and Ancient Documents, III, American Philosophical Society, Philadelphia.

84. Appendix, Table 11.

85. The tax list of 1709 and the poor relief accounts are reprinted in Peter J. Parker, "Rich and Poor in Philadelphia, 1709," *PMHB*, 99 (1975), 3-19.

86. Nash, *Quakers and Politics*, pp. 137-138.

87. James Logan to Penn, Dec. 1, 1702, in Edward Armstrong, ed., *The Correspondence of William Penn and James Logan . . .* , 2 vols. (Philadelphia, 1879-80), I, 146.

88. Nash, *Quakers and Politics*, p. 253.

89. Appendix, Figure 3.

90. Nash, *Quakers and Politics*, pp. 320-321; Frederick B. Tolles, *Meeting House and Counting House: The Quaker Merchants of Colonial Philadelphia, 1682-1763* (Chapel Hill, N.C., 1948), pp. 127, 133.

91. Appendix, Table 6.

92. Appendix, Table 4.

4. *The Rise of Popular Politics*

1. Warden, *Boston*, p. 56. The Belcher incidents are recounted ibid., p. 66; Bridenbaugh, *Cities in the Wilderness*, p. 196; and Dirk Hoerder, *Crowd Action in Revolutionary Massachusetts, 1765-1780* (New York, 1977), pp. 54-55.

2. Charles Tilly, "Food Supply and Public Order in Modern Europe," in Tilly, ed., *The Formation of National States in Western Europe* (Princeton, N.J., 1975), p. 428. Tilly's discussion provides an excellent conceptual framework for considering urban food riots in colonial America.

3. *Diary of Samuel Sewall*, in *MHS Coll.*, 5th ser., VI (Boston, 1879), 280-281.

4. *Massachusetts Acts and Resolves*, I, 724-725.

5. *BTR*, IX, 194, 196.

6. *Diary of Cotton Mather, 1681-1708*, in *MHS Coll.*, 7th ser., VIII (Boston, 1911), 336.

7. Bridenbaugh, *Cities in the Wilderness*, p. 196; *BTR*, VIII, 99, 101, 104; XI, 194-197.

8. For a discussion of mercantilist economic thought and the "preservation of community in a market economy" see J. E. Crowley, *This Sheba, Self: The Conceptualization of Economic Life in Eighteenth-Century America* (Baltimore, 1974). In New York in 1666, 1667, and 1671 the governor and council had banned wheat exports to prevent bread shortages in the town. See Robert C. Ritchie, "London Merchants, the New York Market, and the Recall of Sir Edmund Andros," *New York History*, 57 (1976), 13-14.

9. John Gorham Palfrey, *History of New England*, 5 vols. (Boston, 1865-90), IV, 282. For economic regulation in New York City see Samuel McKee, Jr., "The Economic Pattern of Colonial New York," in Alexander C. Flick, ed., *History of the State of New York*, 4 vols. (New York, 1933), II, 253-256.

10. Alan Everitt, "The Marketing of Agricultural Produce," in Joan Thirsk, ed., *The Agrarian History of England and Wales, 1500-1640* (Cambridge, Eng., 1967), pp. 569-570; see also Tilly, "Food Supply," pp. 428-440, and C. R. Fay, "The Miller and the Baker: A Note on Commercial Transition, 1770-1837,"

Cambridge Historical Journal, 1 (1923), 85-91.

11. Joyce Appleby, "The Social Origins of American Revolutionary Ideology," *Journal of American History*, 64 (1978), 944.

12. For the pioneering study of this kind of crowd action see E. P. Thompson, "The Moral Economy of the English Crowd in the Eighteenth Century," *Past and Present*, no. 50 (1971), 76-136.

13. Dirk Hoerder, "People and Mobs: Crowd Action in Massachusetts During the American Revolution" (Diss., Free University of Berlin, 1971), p. 96.

14. Ibid., p. 97, quoting Council Records, VI, 38, Massachusetts Archives, State House, Boston.

15. Sewall Diary, *MHS Coll.*, 5th ser., VI, 281.

16. Quoted in Miller, *New England Mind*, p. 330.

17. Warden, *Boston*, p. 73; *BTR*, VIII, 55-56.

18. Dudley had spent thirteen years after being exiled from Boston in 1689 as chief justice in New York and then royal governor of the Isle of Wight. Appointed in 1702, he arrived amid rumors that he would be opposed by armed force. Warden, *Boston*, pp. 58-60.

19. For Dudley's "imperial" governorship see Breen, *Good Ruler*, pp. 226-238. Warden, *Boston*, pp. 60-67 also covers Dudley's venal and aristocratic administration. Among the activities of Dudley and his circle that aroused Bostonians were requests to the crown to establish royal courts in Massachusetts to decide cases without juries, attempts to have the Charter of 1691 replaced by one which curbed the legislative power and increased executive authority, and connivance with merchants in Boston who used flags of truce issued by the governor to sell supplies to the French troops in Canada whom New Englanders were fighting during Queen Anne's War. For the latter see George M. Waller, *Samuel Vetch: Colonial Enterpriser* (Chapel Hill, N.C., 1960), pp. 80-93.

20. Warden, *Boston*, pp. 68-73; Davis, *Currency and Banking*, II, 81-91.

21. *A Dialogue . . .* (Boston, 1714), in *Publications of the Colonial Society of Massachusetts*, 10 (*Transactions*, 1904-1906), 344-348 (hereafter *CSM Pub.*).

22. "My Son, fear thou the Lord . . . ," ibid., pp. 348-352.

23. Hutchinson, *History of Massachusets*, I (London, 1760), 175n-176n.

24. The opposition arguments can be followed in Paul Dudley, *Objections to the Bank of Credit Lately Projected at Boston . . .* (Boston, 1714), in Davis, ed., *Currency Reprints*, I, 239-262. Nearly thirty years earlier Paul Dudley's father and the elder Elisha Cooke had been partners in the first attempt to establish a private bank of credit in Boston. Herman Belz, "Paper Money in Colonial Massachusetts," *Essex Institute Historical Collections*, 101 (1965), 150.

25. *BTR*, VIII, 106, 115, 120.

26. Miller, *New England Mind*, p. 311.

27. Davis, *Currency and Banking*, II, 88-89.

28. Warden, *Boston*, pp. 80-95, and Davis, *Currency and Banking*, II, 89-101 give general accounts. Warden states that Elisha Cooke and Oliver Noyes, two of the strongest backers of the private bank, dropped their support following the defeat of the scheme by the town meeting (p. 82).

29. [John Colman], *The Distressed State of the Town of Boston Considered . . .* (Boston, 1720), in Davis, ed., *Currency Reprints*, I, 398.

30. The fiscal conservation of Andrew McFarland Davis, Charles Bullock,

and others who wrote at the turn of the century predisposed them to look unfavorably on paper money issues in Massachusetts and to equate local currency depreciation with the overissue of inadequately backed bills of credit. The Keynesian revisionism adopted by colonial historians on this issue is summed up in E. James Ferguson, "Currency Finance: An Interpretation of Colonial Monetary Practices," *WMQ*, 19 (1953), 153-180, although Ferguson and others of this school are notably weak in discussing the Massachusetts situation, where paper money devaluation was most serious. Joseph A. Ernst similarly avoids Massachusetts in his discussion of currency finance in *Money and Politics in America, 1755-1775: A Study in the Currency Act of 1764 and the Political Economy of Revolution* (Chapel Hill, N.C., 1973), pp. 3-17. The latest consideration of the problem is Roger W. Weiss, "The Colonial Monetary Standard of Massachusetts," *Economic History Review*, 27 (1974), 577-592. Weiss argues that Massachusetts had a "surprisingly stable" currency system, despite the vociferous criticisms of the inflation which paper money purportedly caused; but, like virtually every other writer on the subject, he concludes that "how the burden of inflation was distributed through the community we cannot say" (p. 590).

31. This is expressed in Appendix, Table 12 as the price of silver per ounce. Leslie V. Brock, *The Currency of the American Colonies, 1700-1764: A Study in Colonial Finance and Imperial Relations* (New York, 1975), p. 591 gives a table of New England bills of credit outstanding at the end of May each year. The amount rose from about £41,000 in 1707 to £219,000 in 1713 to £308,000 in 1721. Even at the latest date this represented only about £1.8 for each inhabitant of New England, which must be considered as a unified whole in currency matters since the paper money of Massachusetts, Rhode Island, New Hampshire, and Connecticut flowed freely within New England.

32. For a contemporary analysis of the effects of recession mixed with inflation see [Colman], *The Distressed State . . .*, in Davis, ed., *Currency Reprints*, I, 398-408.

33. *An Addition to the Present Melancholy Circumstances of the Province . . .* (Boston, 1719), in Davis, ed., *Currency Reprints*, I, 389.

34. [Colman], *The Distressed State . . .* , ibid., p. 399.

35. Ibid., pp. 400-407. At the time Colman wrote, the volume of New England bills in circulation had dropped from a high of £310,868 in 1717 to £276,859 three years later. This represented a 24.7 percent per capita decrease.

36. Most of the pamphlets are published in Davis, ed., *Currency Reprints*, I, 209-452 and II, 3-334.

37. *An Addition to the Present Melancholy Circumstances . . .* , ibid., I, 358-359. Also see the comments of Thomas Paine, *A Discourse shewing that the real first cause . . .* (Boston, 1721), ibid., II, 283-284; [Paul Dudley], *Objections to the Bank of Credit . . .* (Boston, 1714), ibid., I, 225; and Cotton Mather, *Concio ad Populum* (Boston, 1719), quoted in Foster, *Solitary Way*, pp. 132-134.

38. Ibid., p. 133.

39. Robert Middlekauff, *The Mathers: Three Generations of Puritan Intellectuals, 1596-1728* (New York, 1971), p. 358. The specific stand by Mather that incited the bomb thrower was his defense of smallpox inoculation. This too was unpopular with the lower class, who had no love for Mather.

40. John Colman, *The Distressed State of the Town of Boston Once More*

Considered . . . (Boston, 1720), in Davis, ed., *Currency Reprints*, II, 66-90.

41. *A Letter to an Eminent Clergy-Man* . . . (Boston, 1720), ibid., 233-234.

42. Quoted in Miller, *New England Mind*, p. 322.

43. Quoted ibid., p. 315.

44. Quoted ibid., p. 316. For the routine right of government to exercise censorship prior to publication see Clyde A. Duniway, *The Development of Freedom of the Press in Massachusetts* (Cambridge, Mass., 1906), chaps. 4-5.

45. Carl Bridenbaugh, "The Press and Book in Eighteenth-Century Philadelphia," *PMHB*, 65 (1941), 5.

46. Miller, *New England Mind*, p. 322. For discussions of the importance of printing as a weapon in the arsenal of political mobilization see J. R. Goody, ed., *Literacy in Traditional Societies* (Cambridge, Eng., 1968); and Elizabeth L. Eisenstein, "Some Conjectures About the Impact of Printing on Western Society and Thought: A Preliminary Report," *Journal of Modern History*, 40 (1968), 1-56. Stephen Botein, " 'Meer Mechanics' and an Open Press: The Business and Political Strategies of Colonial American Printers," *Perspectives in American History*, 9 (1975), 127-128 argues that "before the Revolutionary period the public forum was usually not open enough to permit regular communication of divergent and forceful opinion; since most of what issued from printer's presses was emphatically bland, there is little reason to think that a large part of their audience—whatever is exact size—'reacted' politically to what is read" (p. 129n). Even a casual reading of the thirty-five pamphlets published in Boston from 1714 to 1721 should convince most readers that a "regular communication of divergent and forceful opinion" was present with a vengeance in this town, and, while the economic thinking contained in the pamphlets was often muddy, the discourse was seldom "bland" or, as Botein argues (p. 130), "well insulated from stressful and discordant experience." Duniway says that the period from 1716 to 1723 marked the "last efforts to maintain censorship." *Freedom of the Press*, chap. 6.

47. Warden, *Boston*, p. 93.

48. Ibid., pp. 56, 60-62. Cooke is one of the most understudied figures in colonial history. Warden's book includes scattered material on him and recognizes his importance. See also the acidic sketch by Clifford Shipton in *Biographical Sketches of Those who attended Harvard College* . . . *with Bibliographical and other Notes*, IV (Cambridge, Mass., 1933), 349-356 (hereafter *Sibley's Harvard Graduates*), and the more neutral account by Edgar A. J. Johnson, *DAB*, IV (New York, 1930), 381-382.

49. Warden, *Boston*, p. 67.

50. G. B. Warden, "The Caucus and Democracy in Colonial Boston," *New England Quarterly*, 43 (1970), 19-45; Alan and Katherine Day, "Another Look at the Boston 'Caucus,' " *Journal of American Studies*, 5 (1971), 19-42.

51. See, for example, *Some Considerations Upon the several sorts of Banks* . . . (Boston, 1716), in Davis, ed., *Currency Reprints*, I, 340; and *The Distressed State* . . . , ibid., p. 407.

52. John Bridger to William Popple, July 9, 1719, *Documentary History of the State of Maine*, ed. James P. Baxter, *Collections of the Maine Historical Society*, 2d ser., X (Portland, Me., 1907), 127.

53. Warden, *Boston*, p. 96, citing *Peter Oliver's Origin & Progress of the*

American Revolution: A Tory View, ed. Douglass Adair and John A. Schutz (Stanford, 1967; 1961), p. 26.

54. Warden, *Boston,* p. 97.

55. Vote counts for General Court elections are given in *BTR* from 1717 on. For the period from 1717 to 1728 see *BTR,* VIII, 126, 132, 138, 153, 156, 164, 172, 184, 190, 198, 208, 212, 221. For scattered earlier returns recorded by Samuel Sewall see Sewall Diary, *MHS Coll.,* 5th ser., VI, 74, 77, 79, 253, 275, 303, 308; VII, 424-425, 478-479, 496.

56. Robert E. Brown argues that because of inflation, the requirement for voting in town elections, which was based on possession of a £20 rateable estate in Massachusetts money, was actually becoming less restrictive in this period. *Middle-Class Democracy and the Revolution in Massachusetts, 1691-1780* (New York, 1969), pp. 79-85.

57. I have defined a contest election as one in which a candidate was opposed and lost at least 25 percent of the vote.

58. Kenneth Colegrove, "New England Town Mandates; Instructions to the Deputies in Colonial Legislatures," *CSM Pub.,* 21 (1920), 411-449.

59. McAnear, "Politics in New York," pp. 200-201.

60. Ibid., pp. 145-147; *NYCD,* IV, 127-130.

61. John C. Runcie, "The Problem of Anglo-American Politics in Bellomont's New York," *WMQ,* 26 (1969), 212-216.

62. Bellomont to the Lords of Trade, Oct. 21, 1698, *NYCD,* IV, 400-401.

63. McAnear, "Politics in New York," pp. 167-173.

64. J. R. Pole, who did not study New York politics, regards the use of tickets in Boston in 1749 as "a daring step, perhaps not yet admitted as proper election tactics." *Political Representation in England and the Origins of the American Republic* (London, 1966), p. 70.

65. "The Burghers of New Amsterdam and the Freemen of New York, 1675-1866," in *NYHS Coll., 1885* (New York, 1886), pp. 60-71.

66. The voting statistics are in *NYCD,* IV, 508. Several dozen Orange County votes may have been included but even so the turnout was entirely unprecedented.

67. The names of the voters in the disputed election are given in *Minutes of the Common Council of the City of New York, 1675-1776,* 8 vols. (New York, 1905), II, 163-179. The tax list of 1699, arranged by wards, is in *NYHS Coll., 1911* (New York, 1912), pp. 279-315.

68. Thomas J. Archdeacon, *New York City, 1664-1710: Conquest and Change* (Ithaca, N.Y., 1976), p. 137.

69. Bellomont died in the spring of 1701 and was replaced briefly by his lieutenant governor, John Nanfan, before the arrival of Lord Cornbury in 1702.

70. Jerome R. Reich, *Leisler's Rebellion: A Study of Democracy in New York, 1664-1720* (Chicago, 1953), p. 156.

71. The best accounts of the Bayard-Hutchins trial are ibid., pp. 156-159; Herbert L. Osgood, *The American Colonies in the Eighteenth Century,* 4 vols. (New York, 1924), II, 57-60; and McAnear, "Politics in New York," pp. 190-194.

72. The clause stated that anyone who might "disturbe the peace good and quiet of this their Majestyes Government as it is now established shall be Deemed

and Esteemed as Rebells and Traitors." Reich, *Leisler's Rebellion*, p. 127.

73. Ibid., p. 158.

74. *A Proclamation* (New York, 1702).

75. McAnear, "Politics in New York," pp. 195-206; Osgood, *American Colonies*, II, 61-65.

76. *The Case of William Attwood . . . With a True Account of the Government and People of that Province; particularly of Bayard's Faction . . .* (London, 1703) in *NYHS Coll., 1880* (New York, 1881), pp. 290-291, 315-317.

77. For a brief account of Hunter's administration see Bonomi, *Factious People*, pp. 78-87. A fuller account is in Osgood, *American Colonies*, II, 97-118.

78. For example, Bonomi, *Factious People*, p. 79; Bernard Bailyn, *The Origins of American Politics* (New York, 1968), pp. 108-110.

79. The fullest analysis is in McAnear, "Politics in New York," pp. 265-286.

80. I have treated this period extensively in *Quakers and Politics*, pp. 181-208.

81. The question of equity jurisdiction and the role it played at the intersection of economic and political power is analyzed in Stanley N. Katz, "The Politics of Law in Colonial America: Controversies over Chancery Courts and Equity Law in the Eighteenth Century," *Perspectives in American History*, 5 (1971), 257-284.

82. Nash, *Quakers and Politics*, pp. 224-240.

83. Roy N. Lokken, *David Lloyd: Colonial Lawmaker* (Seattle, 1959) is a fine study of the popular leader.

84. The best study of Logan is Joseph E. Johnson, "A Statesman of Colonial Pennsylvania: A Study of the Private Life and Public Career of James Logan to the Year 1726" (Ph.D. diss., Harvard University, 1942).

85. James Logan to William Penn, ca. April and Aug. 10, 1706, in Edward Armstrong, ed., *The Correspondence of William Penn and James Logan . . .* , 2 vols. (Philadelphia, 1879-80), I, 137-139, 169. This section is drawn from Nash, *Quakers and Politics*, pp. 248-278.

86. Norris to Penn, Dec. 2, 1709, Norris Letter Book, 1709-1716, p. 112, HSP.

87. David Lloyd, "The Speaker's Vindication against James Logan's Invectives . . . ," in Armstrong, ed., *Correspondence of William Penn and James Logan*, II, 402-415 is the fullest statement of Lloyd's ideology. The quote is on p. 408.

88. Logan's political thought is enunciated in "The Secretary's Justification to the Assembly's Remonstrance," ibid., pp. 360-390.

89. Lloyd made the expulsion of Logan a prime political goal and in 1707 succeeded in convincing the assembly to proceed with articles of impeachment. The depth of the hostility can be measured in "Articles of Impeachment against James Logan," Feb. 25, 1706/07, Logan Papers, IV, 21, HSP; and Logan's "Answers to the Assembly's Articles of Impeachment," March 4, 1706/07, Logan Papers, IV, 35.

90. Logan to Penn, Nov. 22, 1704, *Pennsylvania Archives*, 2d ser., VII (Harrisburg, Pa., 1890), 16.

91. Isaac Norris to Penn, Oct. 11, 1704, Norris Letter Book, 1704-1706, p. 2.

92. Nash, *Quakers and Politics*, pp. 286-295.

93. *Votes and Proceedings of the House of Representatives of the Province of Pennsylvania*, ed. Gertrude MacKinney, *Pennsylvania Archives*, 8th ser., 8 vols. (Harrisburg, Pa., 1931-35), I, 426, 442, 637, 704; II, 947.

94. James T. Mitchell and Henry Flanders, eds., *The Statutes at Large of Pennsylvania from 1682 to 1801*, 18 vols. (Harrisburg, Pa., 1896-1915), II, 212-221.

95. Pole, *Political Representation*, p. 94.

96. Logan to Penn, Feb. 3, 1708/09, *Penn-Logan Correspondence*, II, 313.

97. Norris to James Logan, Aug. 29, 1710, ibid., II, 422.

98. Logan to Penn, Nov. 22, 1704, *Pennsylvania Archives*, 2d ser., VII, 16; Governor John Evans to Board of Trade, Sept. 29, 1707, *CSP Colonial, 1706-1708*, no. 1126.

99. Nash, *Quakers and Politics*, pp. 306-318.

100. Ibid., pp. 327-330.

5. The Urban Economies in an Era of Peace

1. See Appendix, Figure 1.

2. F. J. F. Schantz, Frank R. Diffenderffer, and others, *Pennsylvania—The German Influence in Its Settlement and Development*, pt. 7, *Proceedings of the Pennsylvania-German Society*, 10 (1900), 32-37.

3. Frederick B. Tolles, *James Logan and the Culture of Provincial America* (Boston, 1957), pp. 159-160.

4. Wayland F. Dunaway, *The Scotch-Irish of Colonial Pennsylvania* (Chapel Hill, N.C., 1944), pp. 28-42; R. J. Dickson, *Ulster Emigration to Colonial America, 1718-1775* (London, 1966). Some recent estimates of the volume of immigrant traffic through Philadelphia are given in James G. Lydon, "Philadelphia's Commercial Expansion, 1720-1739," *PMHB*, 91 (1967), 407-408. For economic conditions in Ireland in this period see L. M. Cullen, *An Economic History of Ireland since 1660* (London, 1972), chap. 2.

5. See Appendix, Figure 1.

6. John Duffy, *Epidemics in Colonial America* (Baton Rouge, La., 1953), pp. 50-51. One doctor, William Douglass, claimed that smallpox took 899 lives.

7. Ibid., pp. 52-54, 33, 36; John B. Blake, *Public Health in the Town of Boston, 1630-1822* (Cambridge, Mass., 1959), pp. 47-51.

8. Blake, *Public Health*, pp. 247-250. No American town, of course, suffered the mortality rate known in London, where at this time infant mortality reached 50 percent. Ralph Davis, *The Rise of the Atlantic Economies* (Ithaca, N.Y., 1973), p. 94.

9. Duffy, *Epidemics*, pp. 78-80.

10. For example, in Boston burials averaged 597 per year from 1729 to 1732 and 581 from 1738 to 1742. In Philadelphia during these same years deaths averaged 490 and 469. Beginning in 1730, when data is available for both cities, the crude death rate averaged as follows:

	Boston	Philadelphia
1730-32	43	42
1738-39	34	43
1740-44	35	40
1745-49	44	48
1750-54	40	47
1755-59	33	47

Blake, *Public Health*, Appendix II, pp. 248-249; Billy G. Smith, "Death and Life in a Colonial Immigrant City: A Demographic Analysis of Philadelphia," *Journal of Economic History*, 37 (1977), 871, 888.

11. Richard B. Morris, *Government and Labor in Early America* (New York, 1946), pp. 354-362.

12. Lawrence W. Towner, "The Indentures of Boston's Poor Apprentices: 1734-1805," *CSM Pub.*, 43 (1956-1963), 424; pauper apprenticing in Philadelphia can be followed in the Mayor's Court Records, City Archives, City Hall, Philadelphia.

13. Redemptioners, who borrowed money for the Atlantic crossing and repaid it through their labor in the colonies, came more often in families than did indentured servants.

14. Samuel D. McKee, Jr., *Labor in Colonial New York, 1664-1776* (New York, 1935), pp. 93-108. The advertisement was in the *New-York Weekly Journal*, June 27, 1737, quoted ibid., p. 105.

15. Logan to William Penn, Sept. 8, 1713, *Pennsylvania Archives*, 2d ser., VII (Harrisburg, Pa., 1890), 39.

16. Leonard Labaree, William B. Willcox, and others, eds., *The Papers of Benjamin Franklin* (New Haven, Conn., 1959———), I, 260 (hereafter *Papers of Franklin*).

17. For ship arrivals and number of passengers see Gary B. Nash, "Slaves and Slaveowners in Colonial Philadelphia," *WMQ*, 30 (1973), 227n-228n. For arrivals in 1749, *Poor Richard's Almanack for 1750 . . .* (Philadelphia, 1749). Franklin claimed that the twenty-four or twenty-five ships carried "about 12,000 souls," but this would mean 480 per ship, which is unlikely.

18. Bills of mortality, which distinguished race and religious affiliation, were published annually between 1747 and 1775 by the Anglican church in Philadelphia and are available, except for 1749 and 1750, on microcard as listed in Charles Evans, *American Bibliography: A Chronological Dictionary of all Books, Pamphlets and Periodical Publications Printed in the United States . . . 1639 . . . 1820* (Chicago, and Worcester, Mass., 1903-1959) (hereafter Evans, *American Bibliography*).

19. Nash, "Slaves and Slaveowners," pp. 227n-228n.

20. Two useful studies of indentured servitude in Pennsylvania are Cheesman A. Herrick, *White Servitude in Pennsylvania: Indentured and Redemption Labor in Colony and Commonwealth* (Philadelphia, 1926); and Karl Frederick Geiser, *Redemptioners and Indentured Servants in . . . Pennsylvania* (New Haven, Conn., 1901).

21. For an analysis of the extent of indentured servitude in Philadelphia I am indebted to an unpublished paper by Sharon V. Salinger, "Colonial Labor in

Transition: Indentured Servants in Eighteenth-Century Philadelphia." The 1745-1746 indentures are recorded in "Servants and Apprentices Bound and Assigned Before James Hamilton, Mayor of Philadelphia, 1745-1746," HSP. The number of taxable inhabitants in 1746 was about 2,075 (see Appendix, Table 13). Reducing the number of taxables by 5 percent to account for female taxpayers and increasing the result by 20 percent to account for males between sixteen and twenty-one years of age gives an approximate free male work force of 2,370 and a total white male work force of 3,250. The average length of indenture was about 4½ years, but because of runaways, premature deaths, and sales of servants outside the city, the average length of service has been estimated at 3½ years.

22. Quoted in Almon W. Lauber, *Indian Slavery in Colonial Times Within the Present Limits of the United States* (New York, 1913), p. 292.

23. Lorenzo J. Greene, *The Negro in Colonial New England, 1620-1776* (New York, 1942), p. 84. The 1742 ward census of Boston, reprinted p. 338, is in *MHS Coll.*, 3d ser., I (Boston, 1825), p. 152 (1846 edition). In 1708 Governor Dudley stated that there were about 400 slaves in Boston. John Daniels, *In Freedom's Birthplace: A Study of the Boston Negroes* (Boston, 1914), p. 5.

24. Greene, *Negro in New England*, pp. 50-51, 110-115. For one early attack on slavery as immoral see *Some Considerations Upon the several sorts of Banks . . .* (Boston, 1716), in Davis, ed., *Currency Reprints*, I, 346.

25. It seems likely that Negroes were undercounted in the 1742 census. In the two five-year periods preceding the census blacks and Indians represented 17.2 and 20.5 percent of all those buried in Boston. It is unlikely that the black mortality rate was more than twice as high as the rate for whites.

26. I have discussed this in "Urban Wealth and Poverty in Prerevolutionary America," *Journal of Interdisciplinary History*, 6 (1976), 583-584.

27. See Appendix, Table 9.

28. Slightly varying statistics on slave imports from 1701 to 1764 are presented in *Historical Statistics of the United States, Colonial Times to 1970*, 2 vols. (Washington, D.C., 1975), II, 1173 and James G. Lydon, "New York and the Slave Trade, 1700-1774," *WMQ*, 35 (1978), 382. The black and white population in New York City in eight censuses between 1698 and 1756 is given in Greene and Harrington, *American Population*, pp. 92, 95-101. But for errors of great magnitude in the 1737 census see Gary B. Nash, "The New York Census of 1737: A Critical Note on the Integration of Statistical and Literary Sources," *WMQ*, 36 (1979).

29. Edgar J. McManus, *A History of Negro Slavery in New York* (Syracuse, 1966), p. 27.

30. The household census for 1703 is in E. B. O'Callaghan, ed., *The Documentary History of the State of New York*, 4 vols. (Albany, 1849-51), I, 395-405.

31. For a discussion of these censuses see Robert V. Wells, *The Population of the British Colonies in America Before 1776: A Survey of Census Data* (Princeton, N.J., 1975), pp. 110-132. After about 1710 in New York City adult male slaves considerably outnumbered female slaves. The sex ratio (number of males per hundred females) varied between 121 and 142. Wells, *Population*, p. 122.

32. The figure of 30 percent is derived from the occupational analysis of the three port towns at the end of the colonial period in Jacob M. Price, "Eco-

nomic Function and the Growth of American Port Towns," *Perspectives in American History*, 8 (1974), 177-184.

33. Kenneth Scott, "The Slave Insurrection in New York in 1712," *New-York Historical Society Quarterly*, 45 (1961), 43-74.

34. Ferenc M. Szasz, "The New York Slave Revolt of 1741: A Re-Examination," *New York History*, 48 (1967), 215-230.

35. For the objections of Governors Hunter (1712), Cosby (1734), and Clarke (1737) see McManus, *Slavery in New York*, pp. 150-151 and Morris, *Government and Labor*, p. 183.

36. Three times between 1737 and 1743 artisans lobbied for statutory protection from the competition of slave labor. Beverly McAnear, "The Place of the Freeman in Old New York," *New York History*, 21 (1940), 421.

37. *The Mystery of Iniquity; In a Brief Examination of the Times . . . with Additions* (Philadelphia, 1730), p. 5. I have discussed more fully the Philadelphia involvement in slavery before mid-century in "Slaves and Slaveowners," pp. 223-228.

38. This is based on estimates that about 80 percent of the 885 indentured servants were males and 50 percent of the 900 slaves were males of working age. This gives a total of 1,150 bound male laborers. In a free white population of about 9,000 there would be about 2,250 males over sixteen. About 70 percent of them (1,575) occupied laboring roles (see Appendix, Table 1). Thus, bound laborers represented about 1,150 of 2,725 positions in the male laboring ranks.

39. Lorenzo J. Greene, *The Negro in Colonial New England* (New York, 1942), passim.

40. For a theoretical consideration of the colonial labor market and a discussion of the supply and demand sides of the labor curve in the Chesapeake region see Russell Menard, "From Servants to Slaves: The Transformation of the Chesapeake Labor System," *Southern Studies*, 16 (1977), 355-390.

41. *Some Considerations Upon the several sorts of Banks . . .* , (Boston, 1716), in Davis, ed., *Currency Reprints*, I, 343.

42. Abbot Emerson Smith, *Colonists in Bondage: White Servitude and Convict Labor in America, 1607-1776* (Chapel Hill, N.C., 1947), chaps. 2-3. David W. Galenson argues that servants exercised some choice in their destination but his evidence is based on a small sample of English servants who seem at best to have sometimes been able to avoid the West Indies. "British Servants and the Colonial Indenture System in the Eighteenth Century," *Journal of Southern History*, 44 (1978), 41-66.

43. In 1712 and 1773 a duty of £20 per slave was imposed. In 1725 and 1761 a £10 tax was levied. W. E. B. DuBois, *The Suppression of the African Slave Trade to the United States of America, 1638-1870* (New York, 1969; 1896), pp. 22-23.

44. Thomas [Moore?] to Lord Carteret, May 16, 1723, *CSP Colonial, 1722-1723* (London, 1934), p. 258. Seven years before an anonymous writer in Boston had stated that the inhabitants "have rather chosen to get Slaves" because servants "generally prove Run-aways, Thieves, or some way Disorderly." Davis, ed., *Currency Reprints*, I, 343.

45. Boston had 1,717 houses according to the 1742 census. If the ratio of about ten persons per house had not changed since 1720, the number of houses in

that year would be about 1,100. Among the public buildings erected in this period were Christ Church (1723), the Town Granary (1729), Hollis Street Meeting House (1731), Trinity Church (1735), Lynde Street Meeting House (1737), the Workhouse (1738), and Faneuil Hall and Market House (1742). Walter Muir Whitehill, *Boston: A Topographical History* (Cambridge, Mass., 1959), pp. 38-41.

46. For imports and exports, see Appendix, Figure 3. Property values are discussed in G. B. Warden, "The Distribution of Property in Boston, 1692-1775," *Perspectives in American History*, 10 (1976), 85-86, 123 (Table IV) where the mean value of 937 transfers of residential property between 1700 and 1719 was £107 and 1,372 transfers between 1720 and 1739 was £113.

47. Leslie V. Brock, *The Currency of the American Colonies, 1700-1764: A Study in Colonial Finance and Imperial Relations* (New York, 1975), pp. 591-592.

48. Richard A. Lester, *Monetary Experiments: Early American and Recent Scandinavian* (Princeton, 1939), pp. 7-10. Brock, *Currency of the American Colonies*, pp. 591-592, which records Rhode Island bills in circulation at £64,000 in 1726 and £466,000 in 1741.

49. Davis, *Currency and Banking*, I, 443; Joseph B. Felt, *An Historical Account of Massachusetts Currency* (Boston, 1839), pp. 110-111.

50. See Appendix, Table 12.

51. [Moore?] to Carteret, May 16, 1723, *CSP Colonial, 1722-1723*, p. 255.

52. New England's problems may have been compounded by the long depression in the British West Indies between about 1720 and 1745 caused by a slump in sugar prices. Marc Egnal argues that this caused a slowdown in demand for the produce of the northern colonies. "The Economic Development of the Thirteen Continental Colonies, 1720 to 1775," *WMQ*, 32 (1975), 205-208. By lumping the New England and mid-Atlantic colonies Egnal masks the fact that Pennsylvania and New York generally prospered in this period while Massachusetts began to languish. More work needs to be done to measure the effect of falling sugar prices on the economy of New England, but it appears that Massachusetts's problem was not in finding markets for its products but in the low per capita output of marketable commodities, or, to put it differently, the inability to cultivate a staple crop. For the "staple thesis," the relation of economic growth to the development of an intensive commodity export, see David Galenson and Russell Menard, "Economics and Early American History," Paper 77-4E, *Newberry Papers in Family and Community History* (Chicago, 1977), pp. 2-8.

53. Arthur Harrison Cole, *Wholesale Commodity Prices in the United States, 1700-1861* (Cambridge, Mass. 1938), p. 118. For butter see [William Douglass], *A Discourse Concerning the Currencies of the British Plantations . . .* (Boston, 1740), in Davis, ed., *Currency Reprints*, III, 329. We do not have adequate price series for Boston before 1752, but see Ruth Crandall, "Wholesale Commodity Prices in Boston During the Eighteenth Century," *Review of Economics Statistics*, 16 (1934), 117-128, 178-183. Crandall's statistics indicate that commodity prices in devalued (sterling) currency rose slowly from the end of Queen Anne's War to about 1719, fell modestly from 1719 to 1725, and then rose sharply through the 1730s. Price inflation was the result of two intersecting trends—currency depreciation and the cyclical patterns of prices relating to crop size and external demands for Massachusetts products such as grain and meat.

Thus, "Philo-Patriae" argued in 1724 that a drought had raised farm prices sharply but that in general they had "risen very little above what they were a Dozen or Fifteen Years ago." *New-England Courant*, Dec. 7, 1724. "Philo-Patriae" was apparently a spokesman for the rural interest. In comparing commodity price increases, which he set at 20 to 25 percent, with what he estimated as a 200 percent increase in the price of imported goods since the end of Queen Anne's War, he blamed Boston's merchants for the difficult times faced by people of modest means. "Such a supernumerary Shoal of Merchants," he expostulated, "are as Wens on the Body Natural, they suck the Sap and Nourishment from the Parts that are for Use and Ornament." John Wise, *A Word of Comfort . . .* [Boston, 1721] gives some prices for 1720 that also indicate an insubstantial increase in prices that year (Davis, ed., *Currency Reprints*, II, 178). Prices in 1727 are given in Felt, *Historical Account of Massachusetts Currency*, pp. 82-83. Data in Cole, *Wholesale Commodity Prices*, pp. 5-7, and Chart 2, indicate that most of the sharp increase in prices in the 1730s was due to accelerating depreciation of Massachusetts currency. The long-range trend of wheat prices from 1710 to 1740 was downward in all of the seaport towns (ibid., p. 14, Chart 5; pp. 30-31, Charts 10-11).

54. Carl Bridenbaugh, "The High Cost of Living in Boston, 1728," *New England Quarterly*, 5 (1932), 800-811. Bridenbaugh reprints the articles from the *New-England Weekly Journal*, Nov. 25 and Dec. 2, 1728, and *Boston Weekly News-Letter*, Dec. 12, 1728. Correspondence on the budgets was also printed in *Weekly Journal*, Dec. 9 and 16, 1728, and *News-Letter*, Dec. 12, 1728.

55. The deforestation of southern New England during the previous century had driven the price of firewood up steadily. Most of it came by boat from the coast north of Boston. Bridenbaugh, *Cities in the Wilderness*, pp. 151, 311-312. In 1726, 24,000 "loads" of firewood were brought into Boston at 51 shillings per cord (Massachusetts currency). Boston had by far the highest firewood prices of the three seaport towns. In 1740 one visitor noted that "their fuel is altogether wood, and it is one of the most expensive articles of housekeeping in Boston." "Bennett's History of New England," *MHS Proc., 1860-1862* (Boston, 1862), p. 114. I have allowed three cords of wood per family annually at 51 shillings per cord, the price in 1726. Spread over the year the firewood cost 3 shillings per week. House rent was usually calculated at one-sixth the value of the property (Warden, "Distribution of Property," p. 86n), which means that the average annual rent of all property transferred from 1720 to 1739 was about £19 sterling. I have taken half of that as the average rent of laboring-class families. Bridenbaugh says that artisans and shopkeepers paid average rents of £20 per year in the dock and waterfront area about 1720 and by 1740 double houses were renting at £40 to 50 per year. (*Cities in the Wilderness*, p. 308.) Some indication that £10 sterling per person per year is a conservative estimate of living costs can be derived from the fact that from Aug. 1739 to March 1741 the workhouse required £7.4 sterling annually per inmate in operating costs. *BTR*, XII, 237. I have used forty persons as the average workhouse population since the overseers reported that during most of this period the house held "Upward of Forty People." In London families of middling rank required about £50 per person annually and poor families about £10 per person. Dorothy Davis, *Fairs, Shops, and Supermarkets: A History of English Shopping* (Toronto, 1966), pp. 209-211, 213.

56. *New-England Courant*, Feb. 22, 1724/25. It was typical of commentaries on economic conditions in this period that the writer attributed the impoverishment of middling Boston families to their "going much above themselves at first" in purchasing imported European commodities. But at another point in this article the writer admitted that many heads of household could not find employment. By the late 1730s most economic writers had dropped the argument that overconsumption of European goods was at the root of Boston's problems and took a more structural approach to economic conditions.

57. *A Discourse Concerning the Currencies* . . . (Boston, 1740), in Davis, ed., *Currency Reprints*, III, 328. See pp. 356-357 for Davis's discussion of the writing of the pamphlet in 1739.

58. Ibid., p. 328. Douglass believed that butter was the best indicator of wage-price ratios "because it rises the most uniformly of all Provisions."

59. Hugh Vance, a Boston merchant, affirmed that "the chief of the labour of the Province has been paid for *in Shop-Goods*." [Vance], *An Inquiry Into the Nature and Uses of Money* . . . (Boston, 1740), in Davis, ed., *Currency Reprints*, III, 407. Vance believed that laboring-class wage earners were "great sufferers" because of the practice but attributed their losses not only to the discounted value of the shop notes, which bought less in goods than would an equivalent amount of money, but also to the fact that the notes were only good for shop purchases, which, he argued, "had introduc'd great Extravagances." This assumes that artisans could have saved part of their earnings, whereas my evidence suggests that most of them were having difficulty living on their wages. Another writer in 1740 called shop notes "a pernicious Practice and cheating Method." Davis, *Currency and Banking*, I, 94. See also the complaints in *A Letter from a Country Gentleman at Boston* . . . (Boston, 1740), in Davis, ed., *Currency Reprints*, IV, 30.

60. *Boston Weekly News-Letter*, Feb. 19, 1741; *Boston Weekly Post-Boy*, Feb. 23, 1741; Morris, *Government and Labor*, p. 196.

61. Appendix, Figure 6.

62. Warden, *Boston*, p. 121.

63. Hutchinson, *History of Massachusets*, II (Boston, 1767), 380-381, 394-395.

64. See Appendix, Table 13.

65. BTR, XII, 122, 178 (1737); XIV, 14 (1742).

66. Quoted in Bridenbaugh, *Cities in Revolt*, p. 79.

67. Compiled from inventories of 382 artisans in Suffolk County Probate Records. Also see Appendix, Table 5.

68. Suffolk County Probate Records, XXXVII, 111 (Faneuil); XXIX, 396 (Waldo); XXV, 242 (Clarke); XXXI, 444 (Stoddard); XXI, 455 (Mico); XXXIV, 31 (Townsend); and XXXIV, 241 (Cooke).

69. Carl Bridenbaugh, *The Colonial Craftsman* (Chicago, 1961), p. 145.

70. Annual intentions to marry are tabulated in Lemuel Shattuck, *Report to the Commissioners of the City Council Appointed to Obtain the Census of Boston for the Year 1845* (Boston, 1846), pp. 71-72. They were 19.8 per thousand inhabitants between 1710 and 1719, 19.3 per thousand from 1720 to 1729, and 15.3 per thousand in the following decade. The far from exact nature of eighteenth-century record keeping makes it advisable to regard any computations of this kind as evidence of broad trends rather than as an exact picture of collective

behavior. Annual figures on deaths and marriages were published in Boston newspapers in most years after 1704 and in summary form in 1753. These data were accepted by both Bostonians such as Thomas Prince, a local historian with an interest in demography, and English writers such as Richard Price. See James H. Cassedy, *Demography in Early America: Beginnings of the Statistical Mind, 1600-1800* (Cambridge, Mass., 1969), pp. 130, 184-186.

71. Infant baptisms were recorded in the newspapers beginning in 1732. They are tabulated in summary form in Shattuck, *Report*, pp. 71-72. For record keeping in Boston see Robert Gutman, *Birth and Death Registration in Massachusetts, 1639-1900* (New York, 1959).

72. Pennsylvania issues of paper money are given in Lester, *Monetary Experiments*, p. 88, Table 6; New York issues are listed in Virginia D. Harrington, *The New York Merchant on the Eve of the Revolution* (New York 1935), p. 352. See price level graphs in Cole, *Wholesale Commodity Prices*, pp. 14, 31.

73. Lydon, "Philadelphia's Commercial Expansion," pp. 401-418. For shipbuilding, Simeon J. Crowther, "The Shipbuilding Output of the Delaware Valley, 1722-1776," *Proceedings of the American Philosophical Society*, 117 (1973), 93-94.

74. See the value of annual imports in *Historical Statistics of the U.S.*, II, 1176.

75. Francis Rawle, *Ways and Means for the Inhabitants of Delaware to become Rich . . .* (Philadelphia, 1725), p. 11. For wheat prices see Anne Bezanson, Robert D. Gray, and Miriam Hussey, *Prices in Colonial Pennsylvania* (Philadelphia, 1935), pp. 9-11.

76. Francis Rawle, *Some Remedies Proposed for the Restoring the Sunk Credit of the Province of Pennsylvania* ([Philadelphia], 1721), pp. 6-7.

77. Logan to John Andrews, Aug. 14, 1722, quoted in Lester, *Monetary Experiments*, p. 66; Governor William Keith to the Lords of Trade, Dec. 18, 1722, *CSP Colonial, 1722-23*, p. 190. Also see [Francis Rawle], *A Just Rebuke to a Dialogue Betwixt Simon and Timothy* (Philadelphia, 1726), p. 15.

78. Lester, *Monetary Experiments*, pp. 68-71.

79. William Keith, *A Collection of Papers . . .* [London, 1740], quoted ibid., p. 70.

80. Ibid., pp. 93-101. Grain prices can be followed in Bezanson and others, *Prices in Colonial Pennsylvania*, pp. 10-17.

81. For shipbuilding see Crowther, "Shipbuilding Output of the Delaware Valley," p. 93, which shows average annual output in the 1720s (no data available for 1720-1721) of 667 tons and in the 1730s of 1,282 tons. For shipping and layover time see Lydon, "Philadelphia's Commercial Expansion," pp. 402-403. Lydon's statistics are derived from weekly shipping records published in the *American Weekly Mercury* from 1720 to 1728 and in the *Pennsylvania Gazette* from 1729 to 1739.

82. Lydon, "Philadelphia's Commercial Expansion," p. 402; Bezanson and others, *Prices in Colonial Pennsylvania*, pp. 20-29. Demand for Pennsylvania grain was especially heavy in Portugal and the Portuguese Atlantic Islands from 1734 to 1740.

83. *New-England Weekly Journal*, Aug. 12, 1735.

84. Harrold E. Gillingham, "Cesar Ghiselin, Philadelphia's First Gold and

Silversmith, 1693-1735," *PMHB*, 47 (1933), 244-259; the inventory of Ghiselin's estate is in the Office of the Recorder of Wills, City Hall Annex, Philadelphia.

85. John W. Jordan, "William Parsons: Surveyor-General and Founder of Easton, Pennsylvania," *PMHB*, 33 (1909), 340-346.

86. Based on an analysis of inventories in Office of the Recorder of Wills, City Hall Annex, Philadelphia. See also Appendix, Table 5.

87. Appendix, Table 5.

88. Alexander Mackraby to Sir Philip Francis, Jan. 20, 1768, *PMHB*, 11 (1887), 227.

89. I have analyzed the initial allocation of Philadelphia property in "City Planning and Political Tension in the Seventeenth Century: The Case of Philadelphia," *Proceedings of the American Philosophical Society*, 112 (1968), 55-70. For the subdivision of Front Street lots see Richard S. Dunn and Mary M. Dunn, "The Founding of Philadelphia," in Russell F. Weigley, *The History of Philadelphia, 1682-1982*, forthcoming.

90. Deed Book E1-5, pp. 185-188, John Test to Philip Richards, Feb. 3, 1685, City Archives, City Hall, Philadelphia.

91. The genealogy of the property, with references to the deed books, is traced in the file on 45-47 East Front Street, Philadelphia Historical Commission Archives, City Hall Annex, Philadelphia. The property values should be reduced by about one-third to convert them to sterling.

92. See, for example, the deeds for 104, 106, 112-114, and 118 Kenilworth Street, Philadelphia Historical Commission Archives.

93. Warden, "Distribution of Property," Table III, p. 121, tabulates a long-range decline in the involvement of craftsmen in Boston real estate in the 1730s and a decline of mariners in the market beginning in 1710. It is not surprising that this declining participation in property ownership should strike first at mariners, who would be the first to feel the effects of adverse wage-price trends.

94. Imports from England, which averaged £54,000 per year from 1715 to 1719, fell to £52,000 per year from 1720 to 1724. This was a 20.6 percent drop in per capita imports. See Appendix, Figure 3.

95. Quoted in Lester, *Monetary Experiments*, p. 117.

96. McAnear, "Politics in New York," pp. 361-365.

97. Governor George Clarke to the Lords of Trade, June 2, 1738, *NYCD*, VI, 116.

98. *The Account Stated* [New York, 1734], cited in McAnear, "Politics in New York," p. 363; *New-York Weekly Journal*, April 8, 1734; also see the response of "John Trusty," ibid., April 22, 1734, where it is claimed that "John Scheme" understated the degree to which shipping had decayed. One aspiring poet presented the situation in the *New-York Gazette*, Aug. 20, 1733, as follows:

> Pray tell me the cause of trade so dead,
> Why shops are shut up, goods and owners fled,
> And industrious families cannot get bread?

99. Governor Clarke to Lords of Trade, June 2, 1738 and Feb. 17, 1738, *NYCD*, VI, 116, 112. The years between 1734 and 1737 marked the low point in the slave trade for the preceding quarter century.

100. *New-England Weekly Journal*, July 21, 1735.

101. Speech of the governor to the assembly, April 5, 1737, quoted in Lester, *Monetary Experiments*, pp. 117-118. One out of eight persons admitted to freemanship in New York City in the early eighteenth century was a mariner or artisan engaged in ship construction, so the effect of the decline in shipping and shipbuilding was doubtless considerable. Samuel Mckee, Jr., "The Economic Pattern of Colonial New York," in Alexander C. Flick, ed., *History of the State of New York*, 4 vols. (New York, 1933), II, 268-269.

102. *New-York Weekly Journal*, March 28, 1737.

103. Appendix, Figures 1 and 3.

104. *Historical Statistics of the U.S.*, II, 1180; McAnear, who examined ship clearances in the first half of the eighteenth century, estimates that the depression of the 1730s cut trade with New England by about 50 percent and with the West Indies by about 20 percent. "Politics in New York," pp. 359-360.

105. Bridenbaugh, *Cities in the Wilderness*, p. 332.

106. Quoted from the preamble of the law authorizing the paper money issue by Lester, *Monetary Experiments*, p. 118. For the revival of trade, see Appendix, Figure 2 for ship tonnage and *Historical Statistics of the U.S.*, II, 1180 for the rising value of annual imports.

107. According to a report in the *New-York Weekly Journal*, March 28, 1737, a house that formerly rented for £30 now went for £20. Wheat in 1731 sold at an all-time low—about one-half of the price in 1719. Beef and pork prices also fell. McAnear, "Politics in New York," pp. 356-357.

108. *BTR*, XII, 122, 178.

109. *BTR*, VII, 135; *Massachusetts Acts and Resolves*, II, 756-758.

110. Bridenbaugh, *Cities in the Wilderness*, p. 393; Foster, *Solitary Way*, p. 147. For an analysis of the workhouse experiment, which concludes that the overseers were disguising its patent failure, see Stephen Edward Wiberly, Jr., "Four Cities: Public Poor Relief in Urban America, 1700-1775" (Ph.D. diss., Yale University, 1975), pp. 88-98.

111. *BTR*, XII, 121-122, 178; XIV, 13.

112. Figures for New York have been reconstructed from the Minutes and Accounts of the Church Warden and Vestrymen of the City of New York, 1696-1715, New-York Historical Society, New York; and Minutes of the Meetings of the Justices, Church Wardens, and Vestrymen of the City of New York, 1694-1747, New York Public Library. I have subtracted the salary of the clergymen for the Society for the Propagation of the Gospel, which was included in these expenditures, from the yearly totals. Also see Raymond A. Mohl, "Poverty in Early America, A Reappraisal: The Case of Eighteenth-Century New York City," *New York History*, 50 (1969), 8-13.

113. Christopher Sauer to _____, Dec. 1724, *PMHB*, 45 (1921), 259-261.

114. *Votes and Proceedings of the House of Representatives of the Province of Pennsylvania*, ed. Gertrude MacKinney, *Pennsylvania Archives*, 8th ser., 8 vols. (Harrisburg, Pa., 1931-35), III, 1931, 1950. The overseers' report was somewhat misleading since the poor from "foreign Parts" had long been entering Philadelphia. This was the first time, however, that they had disembarked in the middle of a depression when work was unavailable.

115. I have discussed this more fully, and indicated the sources, in "Poverty and Poor Relief in Pre-Revolutionary Philadelphia," *WMQ*, 33 (1976), 4-6.

116. David J. Rothman, *The Discovery of the Asylum: Social Order and Disorder in the New Republic* (Boston, 1971), pp. 3-5.

6. Political Unrest in the Interwar Period

1. Alan Everitt, "The Marketing of Agricultural Produce," in Joan Thirsk, ed., *Agrarian History of England and Wales, 1500-1640* (Cambridge, Eng., 1967), pp. 466-592, esp. 568-569.

2. Karen J. Friedmann, "Victualling Colonial Boston," *Agricultural History*, 47 (1973), 193-195. Boston's assize of bread was instituted in 1646, tightened in 1696, and bulwarked with stricter enforcement mechanisms in 1720.

3. Warden, *Boston*, pp. 53-54; *Massachusetts Acts and Resolves*, I, 237-239.

4. Warden, *Boston*, p. 56; *A Dialogue between a Boston Man and a Country Man* (Boston, 1714), in *CSM Pub.*, X (1904-1906), 345-348.

5. Colman, *Some Reasons and Arguments . . . for the Setting Up of Markets in Boston* (Boston, 1719). Colman argued that public markets would eliminate fraud and price fixing, which obliged the poor to "parcel out a cruel pittance" to dishonest vendors who "buy almost at any rate and then raise the price again as they please." *Some Reasons*, p. 6. Most of the lower class, however, apparently did not subscribe to this argument. Jon Teaford concludes that Bostonians "had profited from their peculiar form of commercial anarchy" for decades "and now they confronted a future of order and regulation with fear and misgiving." Jon C. Teaford, *The Municipal Revolution in America: Origins of Modern Urban Government, 1650-1825* (Chicago, 1975), p. 40.

6. The market proposals may also have been repugnant because they were accompanied by a new proposal to restructure town government, eliminating many of the elective offices. *Some Considerations Against the setting up of a Market in this Town* (Boston, 1733); *Trade and Commerce Inculcated . . .* ([Boston], 1731), in Davis, ed., *Currency Reprints*, II, 359-430, esp. 374, 404-405; *Boston Gazette*, Feb. 12, Feb. 19, 1733; Dec. 25, 1733; Jan. 8, 1733/34. For the 1729 grain riot see "The Diary of John Comer," *Collections of the Rhode Island Historical Society*, VIII (n.p., 1893), 78. A petition to the town meeting from ninety-three householders on Feb. 19, 1734 argued that the markets would be "a means of raising the prise of provisions." A group of petitions for and against the markets are in City Archives, Boston Public Library. I am indebted to Sharon Rodgers of Princeton University, who is studying the market controversy, for copies of these petitions.

7. Warden, *Boston*, pp. 102-118; Teaford, *Municipal Revolution*, pp. 42-43. John Colman had split with Elisha Cooke in 1720 and joined the prerogative party (Warden, *Boston*, p. 117). Craddock was Deputy Collector of Royal Customs.

8. Cooke was dismissed by Belcher in 1733. *Sibley's Harvard Graduates*, IV, 381. The best account of the conservative resurgence of the early 1730s is John Kern, "The Politics of Violence: Colonial American Rebellions, Protests, and Riots, 1647-1747" (Ph.D. diss., University of Wisconsin, 1976), pp. 189-199. Cooke nearly lost his assembly seat in 1732, barely beating out his conservative opponent on a second ballot after failing to achieve a majority of votes on the first. In the same year the town meeting failed to elect him to his usual role of

moderator, symbol of leadership for the popular party. *BTR*, XII, 31.

9. *BTR*, XII, 31, 46 for the 1732 and 1733 elections, which brought out 655 and 600 voters respectively.

10. *BTR*, XII, 46-49; Kern, "Politics of Violence," pp. 199-200; Warden, *Boston*, pp. 117-118 for the market committee.

11. *BTR*, XII, 46, 49, 64-65, 69, 80-81; Warden, *Boston*, pp. 118-121.

12. Warden, *Boston*, p. 120 argues that the revised plan included the odious and illegal allowance of work and trade on the Sabbath as a "sardonic way of taking the [conservative] reformers' project and turning it to their [the Cooke faction's] advantage."

13. *Boston Weekly News-Letter*, April 1, 1737.

14. *BTR*, XII, 119-124, 134. The high cost of provisions had led many Bostonians to leave town on Sundays to buy directly from farmers outside the city. Magistrates posted watches on the Neck, the narrow strip of land joining Boston to the countryside, but they were ignored and abused by the city dwellers. When Chief Justice Benjamin Lynde charged the grand jury to investigate the problem in 1738, he received no satisfaction. The jury foreman was Middlecott Cooke, son of Elisha Cooke, and the jury sidestepped the issue by reporting that they could not "discover the Actors of such crimes" but that the violators of the Sabbath were probably "young People Servants and Negros" (the groups usually indicted to divert attention from laboring-class disorders). The grand jury tried to reverse the tables by following this cover-up with charges against the wealthy, whose "Coaches & Chaises passing and repassing near [the churches] in the time of Service" was an affront to the town. Dirk Hoerder, *Crowd Action, in Revolutionary Massachusetts, 1765-1780* (New York, 1977), pp. 67-68, citing *BTR*, XIII, 223; XV, 2; and Records of the Superior Court of Judicature, 1737-38, f. 169, Suffolk County Courthouse, Boston.

15. Benjamin Colman to Samuel Holden, May 8, 1737, Colman Papers, II, Massachusetts Historical Society, Boston (hereafter MHS); Warden, *Boston*, p. 122. For the clerical disguise see Dirk Hoerder, "People and Mobs: Crowd Action in Massachusetts During the American Revolution" (Diss., Free University of Berlin, 1971), p. 99.

16. Colman to Samuel Holden, Jan. 25, 1737 and May 8, 1737, Colman Papers, II; Hoerder, *Crowd Action*, pp. 66-67.

17. The letters were published as part of Governor Belcher's proclamation condemning the rioters in the *Boston Weekly News-Letter*, April 21, 1737. John Kern, who treats the market riot in detail, argues that such militancy in Boston may have been galvanized by frequent newspaper reports of political violence in England in 1736, especially the opposition to the Gin Act and the famous Porteous Riot in Edinburgh. The Porteous Riot involved the execution of a folk hero, smuggler Andrew Wilson. When a huge crowd attacked the executioner, Captain John Porteous of the City Guard fired into the crowd and before the melee was over six lay dead and many more wounded. Porteous was convicted of murder and sentenced to die; when he received a royal stay of six weeks, many were convinced that a royal pardon would follow. On the day scheduled for his execution the Edinburgh crowd stormed the jail, captured Porteous, and hanged him themselves. Kern suggests that Bostonians may have drawn "upon an awareness of these British protest actions when they looked for ways to redress their own political grievances." "Politics of Violence," pp. 207-213, quote p. 207.

18. *Boston Weekly News-Letter*, April 21, 1737; see also Warden, *Boston*, pp. 121-122; and Hoerder, *Crowd Action*, p. 67.

19. Colman to Holden, May 8, 1737, Colman Papers, II.

20. Belcher to Richard Waldron, July 12, 1733, Dec. 3, 1733, *MHS Coll.*, 6th ser., VI (Boston, 1893), 324, 438. Forty years later Peter Oliver, the brother of one of the leading proponents of the public markets, still remembered Cooke as the "Cataline of that Aera." Douglass Adair and John A. Schutz, eds., *Peter Oliver's Origin & Progress of the American Revolution: A Tory View* (Stanford, 1967), p. 25.

21. Cotton Mather, *Lex Mercatoria; Or, the Just Rules of Commerce Declared . . .* (Boston, 1705). Mather, by the 1720s, had softened his criticisms of the elite and was far more intent on counseling the poor and declining families of Boston patiently to endure their lot since it was God's will. See [Mather], *Some Seasonable Advice unto the Poor . . .* [Boston, 1726]. On Colman see Charles W. Akers, "Religion and the American Revolution: Samuel Cooper and the Brattle Street Church," *WMQ*, 35 (1978), 479-480.

22. Bridenbaugh, *Cities in the Wilderness*, p. 70; John Palmer, *An Impartial Account of the State of New England . . .* (London, 1690), in *Publications of the Prince Society*, I (Boston, 1868), 53.

23. The *New-England Courant*, beamed at artisans and shopkeepers, was the principal opponent of inoculation. Miller, *New England Mind*, p. 335.

24. *Sibley's Harvard Graduates*, IV, 254, quoting David Dunbar to the Lords of Trade, Oct. 9, 1729, in *Documentary History of the State of Maine*, ed. James P. Baxter, *Collections of the Maine Historical Society*, 2d ser., X (Portland, Me., 1907), 441-442. A duel fought on Boston Common in 1728, which fatally wounded one participant, precipitated the move for a law against dueling. Miller, *New England Mind*, p. 306.

25. Bridenbaugh, *Cities in the Wilderness*, pp. 383, 389; *Boston Evening Post*, March 14, 1737.

26. Robert E. Brown presents data from which he infers that in Boston by 1776 not less than 56 percent of the adult white males could vote. He conspicuously avoids the voting totals which are continuously available after 1717 for selectmen and representative elections and for questions decided at town meetings. *Middle-Class Democracy and the Revolution in Massachusetts, 1691-1780* (New York, 1969), pp. 50-51, 57, 96. In 1734, after the most intensive campaigning in a generation on an issue that affected the daily purchase of food, only 916 Bostonians voted. In 1735 there were 3,637 polls (free white males above sixteen years of age). Since the legal voting age was twenty-one, the polls must be reduced by about 25 percent, leaving 2,729 men, about three times the number of voters.

27. E. P. Thompson, "Patrician Society, Plebeian Culture," *Journal of Social History*, 7 (1974), 403.

28. *The Christian Philosopher* (Boston, 1721), quoted in Joseph Dorfman, *The Economic Mind in American Civilization, 1606-1865*, 2 vols. (New York, 1946), I, 141.

29. Quoted ibid., I, 145. John Wise, the egalitarian clergyman from Ipswich, graphically described the psychological aspect of the problem in 1721: "Gentlemen! You must do by your [paper] Bills, as all Wise Men do by their Wives; Make the best of them . . . The great Skill is to cultivate the necessity and

make it a Happiness; for that end, Wise Men Love their Wives; and what ill-conveniences they find in them they bury; and what Vertues they are inrich't with they Admire and Magnifie. And thus you must do by your [paper] Bills for there is no doing without them . . . you must set them high in your Estimation; and by no ways [be] Prodigal of their Reputation, so as to vilify or run them down." *A Word of Comfort to a Melancholy Country* . . . (Boston, 1721), in Davis, ed., *Currency Reprints*, II, 192-195.

30. "Address in Opposition to Issuing More Paper Money," in "Letter-Book of Samuel Sewall," *MHS Coll.*, 6th ser., II (Boston, 1888), 235-289.

31. Robert Zemsky, *Merchants, Farmers, and River Gods: An Essay on Eighteenth-Century American Politics* (Boston, 1971), p. 3.

32. Alice Hanson Jones, "Wealth Estimates for the Southern Colonies about 1770," paper given at the Annual Meeting of the Organization of American Historians, April 12, 1973, pp. 2-3. Jones estimates mean wealth in the southern colonies at nearly four times that in New England and wealth in the middle colonies at about one-third more than in New England.

33. The best study of this process is Philip J. Greven, *Four Generations: Population, Land and Family in Colonial Andover, Massachusetts* (Ithaca, N.Y., 1970). For attempts to synthesize the recent work on rural New England see Kenneth Lockridge, "Land, Population, and the Evolution of New England Society, 1630-1790," *Past and Present*, no. 39 (1968), 62-80; and James A. Henretta, *The Evolution of American Society, 1700-1815: An Interdisciplinary Analysis* (Lexington, Mass., 1973), pp. 9-39, 95-107.

34. M. Eugene Sirmans, *Colonial South Carolina: A Political History, 1663-1763* (Princeton, N.J., 1966), pp. 108-122, 145-154, 185-186; Richard M. Jellison, "Paper Currency in Colonial South Carolina: A Reappraisal," *South Carolina Historical Magazine*, 62 (1961), 134-147. As in Massachusetts, paper money was first issued to support the expenses of war, in this case the 1702 expedition against Spanish St. Augustine. South Carolina paper bills depreciated even faster than those in Massachusetts. By 1712 they were worth only one-third their face value in sterling and by 1720 only one-fifth.

35. *A Word of Comfort to a Melancholy Country* . . . , in Davis, ed., *Currency Reprints*, II, 201-202. John Wise from neighboring Ipswich, known for his outspokenness, his hatred of arbitrary power, and his sympathy for laboring people, wrote in 1721 that the talk so easily bantered about regarding the common people's tendency to overspend on English luxuries was badly misdirected as an analysis of the economic problem to be faced. Did the critics want the people to "Live upon Ground-Nuts and Clams, and Cloath our Backs with the Exuviae, or Pelts of Wild Beasts"? If so, it would be possible to "lower our Expenses a great Pace; and renounce this branch of our Merchandize." On Wise see Breen, *Good Ruler*, pp. 251-261.

36. Davis, *Currency and Banking*, II, 122-125.

37. *The Melancholy State of this Province* . . . (Boston, 1736), in Davis, ed., *Currency Reprints*, III, 142.

38. Quoted in Dorfman, *Economic Mind*, I, 149.

39. For a short discussion see ibid., pp. 149-159.

40. *BTR*, VIII, 154-155; Warden, *Boston*, p. 96.

41. Boston became the first of the seaport towns to obtain a competitive

newspaper when James Franklin's *New-England Courant* appeared in 1721. The *Courant*, however, did not become an instrument of Cooke's faction; its principal target was the religious establishment, especially the Mathers. For opposing views on the role of newspapers in colonial politics see Lawrence H. Leder, "The Role of Newspapers in Early America: 'In Defense of Their Own Liberty,' " *Huntington Library Quarterly*, 30 (1966), 1-16 and Stephen Botein, " 'Meer Mechanicks' and an Open Press: The Business and Political Strategies of Colonial American Printers," *Perspectives in American History*, 9 (1975), 127-228.

42. Kenneth A. Lockridge, *Literacy in Colonial New England: An Enquiry into the Social Context of Literacy in the Early Modern West* (New York, 1974), pp. 13-43. For a discussion of the "country party" literature in the 1720s see Breen, *Good Ruler*, pp. 240-269. For press censorship see Clyde A. Duniway, *The Development of Freedom of the Press in Massachusetts* (Cambridge, Mass., 1906), chap. 6.

43. Among creditors, who might be expected to lose by currency depreciation, British merchants were the principal sufferers according to William Shirley's analysis in 1742. Davis, *Currency and Banking*, I, 172-173. The differential effects of price inflation need further study.

44. Bonomi, *Factious People*, pp. 75-97.

45. Immigrant craftsmen and merchants paid substantially more and their fees were increased after 1731. Freemanship technically gave a share of the monopoly in handicraft work and retailing to its holders and also conferred upon them the franchise and right to hold office. After 1686 the economic function of freemanship was never enforced, so New Yorkers "bought their freedom" only to enter the political arena. Beverly McAnear, "The Place of the Freeman in Old New York," *New York History*, 21 (1940), 418-425. The statistics on freemanship applications have been compiled from "The Burghers of New Amsterdam and the Freeman of New York, 1675-1866," *NYHS Coll., 1885* (New York, 1886), pp. 56-85, 99-113.

46. Bonomi, *Factious People*, pp. 87-97.

47. The most extensive treatment of Cosby's governorship is Stanley Nider Katz, *Newcastle's New York: Anglo-American Politics, 1732-1753* (Cambridge, Mass., 1968), pp. 61-163. Katz emphasizes the political crisis of the 1730s as a struggle at the top. Bonomi, *Factious People*, pp. 103-139 treats the politicization of society.

48. Katz, *Newcastle's New York*, pp. 23, 32-33.

49. Bonomi, *Factious People*, p. 112.

50. Quoted ibid., p. 113.

51. Stanley N. Katz, ed., *A Brief Narrative of the Case and Trial of John Peter Zenger, Printer of The New-York Weekly Journal, by James Alexander* (Cambridge, Mass., 1963), p. 20.

52. Ibid., p. 34. Zenger stands higher in historical memory than he did in his own time. His personal reputation in the affair can be measured by the fact that after the trial, while Hamilton was being carried by a noisy crowd through the streets to a banquet at the Black Horse Tavern, Zenger was taken unnoticed back to jail for a final night. Ibid., p. 77.

53. Andrew Fletcher [pseud.], *Vincit amor Patriae . . .* [New York, 1732]; other electoral appeals were Robert Dissolution [pseud.], *A Letter from a Gentle-*

man in the Country to his Friend in Town [New York, 1732]; [Alexander Campbell], *Maxima Libertatis Custodia Est* (New York, 1732); Alexander Campbell, *A True and Just Vindication of Mr. A.C. . . .* (New York, 1732); Portius [pseud.], *O Liberty, thou Doggess heavenly bright! . . .* [New York, 1732]; and Jacob Sydney [pseud.], *According to my Promise . . .* (New York, 1734).

54. *New-York Weekly Journal*, April 29, 1734; Sydney, *According to my Promise*. The importance of elective sheriffs was brought home in 1733 when Cosby's appointee in Westchester County tried to prevent the election of Lewis Morris by denying thirty-eight Quakers the right to vote unless they swore oaths of allegiance to the king, which their religious beliefs prohibited. Bonomi, *Factious People*, pp. 114-115.

55. Quoted ibid., p. 10n. Demands were made also for broadening the powers of the assembly, including the right to appoint an agent in London, fix fees of court and government officials, review the conduct of judges, and define the jurisdiction of courts. McAnear, "Politics in New York," p. 416.

56. It is clear from two lengthy lists of Lewis Morris's supporters in the town that the ethnic bloc voting of the Leislerian era had broken down and that artisans of French, English, and Dutch descent were aligning with the popular anti-Cosby party. Of the 297 surnames on the 1735 petition of "those agreeing to sustain Col. Morris" (Rutherfurd Collection, II, 75, New-York Historical Society), 44 percent are Dutch, 46 percent English, and 10 percent French. Two years later, on a petition "Demanding the removal of the sheriff," 49 percent of the surnames are Dutch, 44 percent English, and 7 percent French. E. B. O'Callaghan, ed., *The Documentary History of the State of New York*, 4 vols. (Albany, 1849-51), III, 292-294. I am indebted to Joyce Goodfriend, University of Denver, for an analysis of surnames.

57. William Smith, *The History of the Late Province of New-York, From its Discovery to the Appointment of Governor Colden, in 1762*, in *NYHS Coll., 1829* (New York, 1830), pp. 17-18. Erection of the poorhouse, while appealing to middle-class taxpayers and artisans who could gain employment from the project, probably alienated the poorest element, which understood that it meant the beginning of the end of out-relief.

58. McAnear, "Politics in New York," p. 426; *New-York Weekly Journal*, Oct. 28, 1734.

59. Timothy Wheelwright [pseud.], *Two Letters on Election of Aldermen* [New York, 1734].

60. Ibid.; *New-York Weekly Journal*, March 18, May 20, July 8, 1734.

61. Cosby to Newcastle, Oct. 26, 1732, quoted in Katz, *Newcastle's New York*, p. 84.

62. George W. Edwards, "New York City Politics Before the American Revolution," *Political Science Quarterly*, 36 (1921), 590; McAnear, "Place of the Freeman," p. 424.

63. *New-York Weekly Journal*, Oct. 7, 1734; *Valentine's Manuel . . . 1869* (New York, 1869), p. 851. These totals do not include the "Out" ward, later to become Harlem. Applications for freemanship rose sharply in 1731 and averaged sixty-seven per year for the next decade—almost twice as many as during the 1720s.

64. For population see Appendix, Figure 1.

65. Smith, *History of New-York*, pp. 34-35; *Letters and Papers of Cadwallader Colden*, in *NYHS Coll., 1917* (New York, 1918), p. 179. Colden's comments on the election were virtually duplicated in William Smith's account. William Smith Papers, III, 187-189, New York Public Library, quoted in I. N. Phelps Stokes, *The Iconography of Manhattan Island, 1498-1909*, 6 vols. (New York, 1915-1928), IV, 552. The 1739 election drew 631 voters and lasted until midnight. *New-York Gazette*, March 20, 1739.

66. The fullest account is in Katz, *Newcastle's New York*, pp. 91-132.

67. *A Word in Season* . . . [New York, 1736].

68. *New-York Gazette*, Sept. 19, Oct. 10, Oct. 17, 1737; Nicholas Varga, "New York Government and Politics During the Mid-Eighteenth Century" (Ph.D. diss., Fordham University, 1960), p. 253. Varga notes that this practice continued for nine years and then tailed off (p. 264).

69. *Many of the electors of the two, to the electors of the four* (New York, 1739), also printed in *New-York Weekly Journal*, March 19, 1739.

70. McAnear, "Politics in New York," p. 559; *New-York Weekly Journal*, March 18, 1733/34; May 20, July 8, July 15, 1734; March 3, 1735; May 30, 1737.

71. Smith, *History of New-York*, p. 41. A bill for triennial elections was first passed in 1734 but was vetoed in council. The council passed a similar bill in 1737 but it was disallowed in England by the Privy Council. Varga, "Government and Politics," p. 256.

72. [Lewis Morris], *Some Observations on the Charge Given by the Hon. James DeLancey . . . to the Grand Jury . . .* (New York, 1733); Alexander Campbell, *A True and Just Vindication . . .* (New York, 1732); *Heads of Articles of Complaint by Rip Van Dam . . . Against . . . William Cosby* (Boston, 1734).

73. Cosby to Newcastle, Dec. 17, 1733, quoted in Katz, *Newcastle's New York*, p. 75. In England Cosby was criticized for "appealing to the Country" in printed pamphlets—an undignified "wrong Step" on the part of a head of government, who should not compromise the dignity of descending to public debate. Bonomi, *Factious People*, p. 129.

74. Varga, "Government and Politics," p. 397. *New-York Weekly Journal*, Oct. 7, Oct. 21, Oct. 28, 1734.

75. *An Unanswerable Answer to the Cavils and Objections* . . . [New York, 1739]; *New-York Gazette*, Feb. 20, 1739; Carl L. Becker, "Nominations in Colonial New York," *American Historical Review*, 6 (1901), 272.

76. "History of Governor William Cosby's Administration," *Colden Papers*, IX, 298, in *NYHS Coll., 1935* (New York, 1936).

77. *New-York Gazette*, March 11, 1733/34, quoted in Patricia U. Bonomi, "The Middle Colonies: Embryo of the New Political Order," in Alden Vaughan and George Billias, eds., *Perspectives on Early American History: Essays in Honor of Richard B. Morris* (New York, 1973), p. 87.

78. [Wise], *A Word of Comfort to a Melancholy County* (Boston, 1721).

79. Richard Ashcraft, "Leviathan Triumphant: Thomas Hobbes and the Politics of Wild Men," in Edward Dudley and Maximillian E. Novak, eds., *The Wild Man Within: An Image in Western Thought from the Renaissance to Romanticism* (Pittsburgh, 1972), p. 143.

80. The following account of the Keithian era draws heavily upon Nash, *Quakers and Politics*, pp. 331-335 and Thomas Wendel, "The Keith-Lloyd Al-

liance: Factional and Coalition Politics in Colonial Pennsylvania," *PMHB*, 92 (1968), 289-305.

81. Logan to Henry Gouldney, Feb. 9, 1722/23, *Pennsylvania Archives*, 2d ser., VII (Harrisburg, Pa., 1890), 70-71. Five of Philadelphia's wealthiest merchants were swept from office in 1722: Richard Hill, Isaac Norris, Jonathan Dickinson, Clement Plumstead, and William Fishbourne. Two others, Samuel Carpenter and Robert Jones, lost their seats in the following year, completing the ousting of the old Quaker mercantile elite.

82. Norris to Joseph Pike, May 7, 1723, Norris Letter Book, 1716-1730, p. 329, HSP; Keith to the Lords of Trade, Dec. 18, 1722, *CSP Colonial, 1722-1723* (London, 1934), p. 190.

83. Richard A. Lester, *Monetary Experiments: Early American and Recent Scandinavian* (Princeton, 1939), p. 88.

84. Norris Letter Book, 1716-1730, pp. 369, 381, 395, 399.

85. *Votes and Proceedings of the House of Representatives of the Province of Pennsylvania*, ed. Gertrude MacKinney, *Pennsylvania Archives*, 8th ser., 8 vols. (Harrisburg, Pa., 1931-35), II, 1459-1460.

86. Logan, *The Charge Delivered from the Bench to the Grand Jury* (Philadelphia, 1723). The same analysis of poverty-producing and wealth-producing behavior was offered in a petition to the assembly opposing paper money in 1722. *Votes of the House of Representatives of Pennsylvania*, II, 1486-1496.

87. Lloyd, *A Vindication of the Legislative Power . . .* (Philadelphia, 1725).

88. *A Dialogue Between Mr. Robert Rich and Roger Plowman* [Philadelphia, 1725].

89. Norris to James Logan, Dec. 16, 1723, Norris Papers, II, 79-80, HSP; The Leather Apron Club was also called "The Tiff Club, which name they professedly Own from ye great use of that sottish liquor there." Norris to Joseph Pike, Oct. 28, 1728, Norris Letter Book, 1716-1730, pp. 515-516.

90. Logan to Andrew Hamilton, Feb. 24, 1724/25, Logan Letter Book, II, 270, HSP; Norris to Joseph Pike, June 22, 1724, Norris Papers, II, 84; Norris to Samuel Clement Norris, April 30, 1725, Norris Letter Book, 1716-1730, pp. 421-423. Before 1739, naturalization, which was necessary in order to vote, could be granted only by specific act of assembly naming the immigrants. By parliamentary legislation in 1739 aliens could be naturalized after swearing an oath or taking an affirmation of loyalty.

91. Jeremiah Langhorne to Andrew Hamilton and Clement Plumstead, Feb. 10, 1724/25, in Samuel Hazard, ed., *The Register of Pennsylvania*, VI (Philadelphia, 1830), 225-226; Norris to Stephen DeLancey, Feb. 12, 1722/23, Norris Letter Book, 1716-1730, pp. 326-327.

92. [Logan], *A Dialogue Shewing What's therein to be found* (Philadelphia, 1725).

93. Norris to John Askew, Feb. 15, 1724/25, Norris Papers, II, 89; Norris to Logan, Dec. 16, 1723, ibid., p. 80.

94. Logan to James Alexander, Oct. 23, 1749, Logan Letter Book, 1748-1750, p. 22. Logan was recalling an incident that occurred almost twenty-five years before, which indicates how searing the experience must have been to a man who regarded himself as one of Pennsylvania's chief assets.

95. The fullest statement of the ordinary Pennsylvanian's complaints

against an insensitive proprietary elite is William Keith's forty-five-page pamphlet, *The Observator's Trip To America, in a Dialogue between The Observator and his Country-man Roger* ([Philadelphia], 1726).

96. *A Modest Reply to the Speech of Isaac Norris . . .* [Philadelphia, 1727].

97. For the founding of the Carpenter's Company see Roger William Moss, Jr., "Master Builders: A History of the Colonial Philadelphia Building Trades" (Ph.D. diss., University of Delaware, 1972), pp. 76-91. Moss suggests that the company was founded in 1727 rather than 1724 and argues convincingly that its main function was price setting. Corporate privileges had been granted the tailors and cordwainers in Philadelphia in 1718.

98. [Logan], *A Dialogue . . .* (Philadelphia, 1725). By 1725 the German vote was regarded by the popular party as sufficiently important to reserve three of ten places on the slate of candidates for the city and county of Philadelphia for Germans.

99. Patrick Gordon to John Penn, Oct. 18 and Oct. 22, 1726; Logan to John Penn, Oct. 17, 1726, Penn Papers, Official Correspondence, I, 239, 247, 237, HSP; Norris to Jonathan Scarth, Oct. 21, 1726, Norris Letter Book, 1716-1730, pp. 474-475. Keith's followers were reluctantly dissuaded from burning Governor Patrick Gordon's proclamation against election day riots after Gordon replaced Keith in 1726.

100. David Barclay to Thomas Penn, [1728], Penn Papers, Official Correspondence, II, 43. The fullest account of the 1728-1729 paper money controversy and the defiant behavior of the Keithian faction is in Kern, "Politics of Violence," pp. 122-131.

101. Logan to Thomas Penn, April 24, 1729; Patrick Gordon to Springett and John Penn, May 2, 1729, Penn Papers, Official Correspondence, II, 54, 57; *Minutes of the Provincial Council of Pennsylvania*, 16 vols. (Philadelphia and Harrisburg, Pa., 1852-53), III, 352-355, 360-361.

102. Gordon to Springett and John Penn, May 2, 1729, Penn Papers, Official Correspondence, II, 57.

103. [Francis Rawle], *A Just Rebuke to a Dialogue betwixt Simon and Timothy . . .* (Philadelphia, 1726); [Rawle], *Ways and Means . . .* (Philadelphia, 1725); Logan, *A Dialogue* (Philadelphia, 1725); Norris, *A Speech Delivered from the Bench in the Court of Common Pleas . . .* [Philadelphia, 1727].

104. *A Modest Apology for the Eight Members* [Philadelphia, 1728]; *Remarks on the late Proceedings of some Members of Assembly at Philadelphia* [Philadelphia, 1728].

105. *Morris Morris's Reasons for his Conduct, in the Present Assembly, in the Year 1728* [Philadelphia, 1728].

106. *The Triumvirate of Pennsylvania; In a Letter to a Friend in the Country* [Philadelphia, 1729?]. This heated pamphlet is tentatively dated as 1725 in Evans, *American Bibliography*, I, 351, but internal evidence indicates that it was published in 1728 or 1729. Tolles believes it was published in 1729. *James Logan and the Culture of Provincial America* (Boston, 1957), p. 148. A detailed account of politics in the 1730s is given in Alan Tully, *William Penn's Legacy: Politics and Social Structure in Provincial Pennsylvania, 1726-1755* (Baltimore, 1977), pp. 3-22.

107. *American Weekly Mercury*, Dec. 21, 1733. In the following year Isaac

Norris was still complaining about the residual effects of artisan-oriented politics of the 1720s. The "usual care," he wrote to his son, "was taken to bring in Crowds of Journeymen & such like in opposition" at the assembly elections. Oct. 2, 1734, Copy Book of Letters, 1730-1735, Norris Papers.

108. *Pennsylvania Gazette,* March 24, April 1, 1736; *American Weekly Mercury,* April 8, 1736; *Pennsylvania Gazette,* April 15 and 22, 1736; *American Weekly Mercury,* April 22, 1736; *Pennsylvania Gazette,* April 29, 1736. "Z" was John Webbe, a conveyancer and lawyer in Philadelphia and editor of the short-lived *American Magazine.* This publishing project embroiled him in controversy with Franklin, who was launching a competitive journal, *The General Magazine,* at this time. *Papers of Franklin,* II, 263-269. For another statement of the emerging interest group ideology see "Constant Truman," *Advice to the Freeholders and Electors of Pennsylvania . . .* [Philadelphia, 1735].

109. Miller, *New England Mind,* p. 297.

110. Zemsky, *Merchants, Farmers, and River Gods,* pp. 69-72.

111. *A Just Rebuke to a Dialogue betwixt Simon and Timothy . . .* (Philadelphia, 1726).

7. The Renewal of War and the Decline of Boston

1. Joyce Appleby, *Economic Thought and Ideology in Seventeenth-Century England* (Princeton, N.J., 1978), p. xxx.

2. Appleby, "The Social Origins of American Revolutionary Ideology," *Journal of American History,* 64 (1978), 939. The political implications of the new economic thinking are presented in C. B. MacPherson, *The Political Theory of Possessive Individualism* (London, 1962).

3. Isaac Kramnick, *Bolingbroke and His Circle: The Politics of Nostalgia in the Age of Walpole* (Cambridge, Mass., 1968), pp. 201-202.

4. Nathan Rosenberg, "Mandeville and Laissez-Faire," *Journal of the History of Ideas,* 24 (1963), 183-196; William Letwin, *The Origins of Scientific Economics: English Economic Thought, 1660-1776* (London, 1963) and Albert O. Hirschman, *The Passions and the Interests: Political Arguments for Capitalism Before Its Triumph* (Princeton, N.J., 1977) also treat Mandeville's thought. The quote is from Appleby, "Social Origins of American Revolutionary Ideology," p. 944.

5. Quoted in Kramnick, *Bolingbroke,* p. 202.

6. M. Dorothy George, *London Life in the Eighteenth Century* (New York, 1965) is an excellent introduction to the topic.

7. John Carswell, *The South Sea Bubble* (London, 1960), passim. A convenient synopsis is in Kramnick, *Bolingbroke,* pp. 65-70.

8. Ibid., p. 67. The fullest treatment of the new role of credit is P. G. M. Dickson, *The Financial Revolution in England: A Study in the Development of Public Credit, 1688-1756* (London, 1967).

9. J. E. Crowley, *This Sheba, Self: The Conceptualization of Economic Life in Eighteenth-Century America* (Baltimore, 1974), p. 6.

10. Mather, *Theopolis Americana* (Boston, 1710), quoted in David Levin, ed., *Bonifacius: An Essay upon the Good* (Cambridge, Mass., 1966), p. xvii.

11. This does not mean that a dissenting voice was not heard. "New light" clergymen of the Great Awakening were much appalled by the accommodation of the "liberal" clergy to the new economic values.

12. The *asiento* granted England a thirty-year monopoly for supplying the Spanish colonies with slaves and allowed one English ship each year to trade with the Spanish in the New World.

13. For the European background to the Anglo-Spanish War, or the War of Jenkins' Ear as it is sometimes called, see Walter A. Dorn, *Competition for Empire, 1740-1763* (New York, 1940), pp. 122-126. A short account is Francis L. Berkeley, Jr., "The War of Jenkins' Ear," in Darrett B. Rutman, ed., *The Old Dominion: Essays for Thomas Perkins Abernethy* (Charlottesville, Va., 1964), pp. 41-61.

14. Howard M. Chapin, *Privateering in King George's War, 1739-1748* (Providence, R.I., 1928), passim. As early as June 1739, four months before war was formally declared, colonial governors had been authorized to issue letters of marque and reprisal. Douglas Edward Leach, *Arms for Empire: A Military History of the British Colonies in North America, 1607-1763* (New York, 1973), p. 210.

15. William B. Weeden, *Economic and Social History of New England*, 2 vols. (New York, 1963; 1890), II, 574n; William Douglass, *Summary, Historical and Political of the . . . Present State of the British Settlements in North-America* (London, 1750), I, 539-540.

16. John F. Jameson, ed., *Privateering and Piracy in the Colonial Period: Illustrative Documents* (New York, 1923), p. ix. Privateering was outlawed by international agreement in 1856.

17. Leach, *Arms for Empire*, p. 209.

18. James G. Lydon, *Pirates, Privateers, and Profits* (Upper Saddle River, N.J., 1970), p. 210.

19. Ibid., p. 212.

20. In a report to the Board of Trade in 1751, Jonathan Belcher, the former governor of Massachusetts, stated that 4,433 mariners manned the 657 ships that had cleared Massachusetts ports on foreign voyages and 5,090 mariners sailed aboard the 1,230 coastal vessels. This would be an average of 6.75 and 4.14 mariners per ship respectively. Belcher's report is in J. H. Benton, Jr., *Early Census Making in Massachusetts, 1643-1765 . . .* (Boston, 1905), pp. 18-26.

21. *BTR*, XIV, 98-99; Appendix, Figure 4.

22. Hancock to Miss Thomas and Adrian Hope, May 24, 1745, quoted in Joel A. Shufro, "The Impressment of Seamen and the Economic Decline of Boston, 1740 to 1760" (M.A. thesis, University of Chicago, 1968), p. 31. Hancock reported that "90 [shillings] per mo. for Sailors was offered to go to the Land [Newfoundland] and not to be had." This must have been sterling because in Massachusetts currency in 1745 90 shillings would have been the equivalent of 12s 6d, whereas normal wages were about 35 shillings per month.

23. Howard I, Chapelle, *The History of the American Sailing Navy* (New York, 1949), pp. 40-42; Hallowell died in 1773 with an estate of £1,706 sterling. Suffolk County Probate Records, LXXII, 354, 579-580.

24. *Sibley's Harvard Graduates*, VIII, 131.

25. Ibid.

26. Edward Edelman, "Thomas Hancock, Colonial Merchant," *Journal of Economic and Business History*, 1 (1928), 77-104; W. T. Baxter, *The House of Hancock: Business in Boston, 1724-1775* (Cambridge, Mass., 1945), pp. 45-61.

27. Ibid., pp. 67-68, 75-77.

28. Ibid., pp. 82-86. One major loss was the Iberian fish market, but the slack seems to have been taken up in increased sales to the West Indies, where a rapidly growing slave population created a growing demand for New England fish.

29. Ibid., p. 97. War contracting required good relations with the provincial governor. Thus Hancock, who had been a sharp critic of Governor Shirley, "outdid himself in soliciting the Governor's favor" once war began and turned from critic to supporter. John A. Schutz, *William Shirley: King's Governor of Massachusetts* (Chapel Hill, N.C., 1961), p. 84.

30. Ibid., pp. 97-98.

31. Ibid., pp. 98-110.

32. Ibid., p. 106. In 1748, Hancock's "cruel" tax bill amounted to £ 153 sterling and in 1751 about £124. At 1d per pound, the 1751 tax would indicate an estate of about £ 15,900. Ibid., p. 107n.

33. Ibid., p. 78n.

34. Shufro, "Impressment," pp. 23-42.

35. Gerald S. Graham, *Empire of the North Atlantic: The Maritime Struggle for North America* (Toronto, 1950), pp. 122-124; George A. Rawlyk, *Yankees at Louisbourg* (Orono, Me., 1967), pp. 46-47. The bounty and wages were in "new tenor" currency that had been recently issued. In sterling it was worth about one-half to two-thirds as much. Douglass claimed that 2,000 men of the 3,000 voted by the General Court were recruited for the 1746 campaign against Quebec, lured by a £ 30 (new tenor) bounty. *Summary*, I, 315, 344. The General Court would not allow the governor the power to impress men, as it had permitted in 1745.

36. The best account is Rawlyk, *Yankees at Louisbourg*, pp. 27-40. Governor Shirley himself had first opposed the plan when it was proposed by several zealous militarists who had been captured at Louisbourg but returned to Boston in 1744 as part of a prisoner exchange.

37. *The Importance and Advantage of Cape Breton truly Stated . . .* (London, 1746), p. 84, quoted in Graham, *Empire of the North Atlantic*, p. 127n. It was not by accident, as one historian has noted, that a stuffed cod was mounted above the speaker's chair in the Massachusetts House of Representatives. Jacob M. Price, "Economic Function and the Growth of American Port Towns in the Eighteenth Century," *Perspectives in American History*, 8 (1974), 141.

38. Rawlyk, *Yankees at Louisbourg*, p. 39.

39. Ibid., pp. 46, 174n. Rawlyk concludes that the recruitment was primarily from the lower class, although middle-class sons sought officer commissions on the assumption that they would be confirmed in England as regular army officerships, thereby entitling them to half-pay for life after demobilization.

40. Estimates vary on the number finally recruited, but this is the figure set by Governor Shirley in his official report to Newcastle, Secretary of State for the Colonies. Charles H. Lincoln, ed., *Correspondence of William Shirley, Governor of Massachusetts and Military Commander in America, 1731-1760*, 2 vols. (New York, 1912), I, 273. Thomas Hutchinson believed that 3,250 troops plus officers were sent initially and 400 more added later. *History of Massachusets*, II, 413, 418. This comports with William Douglass's estimate of 3,600. *Summary*, I, 350.

41. Shufro, "Impressment," p. 29, citing J. Osborne to William Pepperall and Peter Warren, Feb. 5, 1745, Belknap Papers, MHS.

42. L. Tyerman, *The Life of Reverend George Whitefield*, 2 vols. (London, 1877), II, 151.

43. Howard H. Peckham, *The Colonial Wars, 1689-1762* (Chicago, 1964), p. 91; Leach, *Arms for Empire*, pp. 217-218. Douglass, *Summary* (as printed in *Boston Evening Post*, Dec. 14, 1747) stated that not more than 50 of the 500 Massachusetts men on the Cartagena expedition returned.

44. Douglass, *Summary*, I, 350-351. Admiral Peter Warren, in command of the expedition, agreed with a casualty list of 2,000 and may have been Douglass's source. J. S. McLennan, *Louisbourg from Its Foundation to Its Fall* (London, 1918), p. 170n.

45. Otis Little, *The State of Trade in the Northern Colonies Considered . . .* (Boston, 1749, reprinted from London ed., 1748), p. 8; Douglass, *Summary*, I, 356, 510n; *Boston Independent Advertiser*, Feb. 8, 1748. I am estimating that one out of every ten men died in camp or while on garrison duty and that during four years of war at sea one-sixth of the 3,000 additional Massachusetts men recruited to man ships for the Louisbourg expedition or impressed into the royal navy, most of them from Boston and outlying ports, lost their lives. The figure of 3,000 sailors was cited by the Boston selectmen (*BTR*, XIV, 85) and was accepted by Little, *State of Trade*, p. 9. Looking back on the war in 1756, William Bollan, one of Massachusetts's most knowledgeable men, believed that one-third of the colony's adult males, or nearly 14,000 men, had served during the war. *Boston Evening Post*, July 14, 1756.

46. In the 1740s about 10 percent of the colony's inhabitants lived in Boston. Hence 300 to 400 fatalities would be proportionate to the total loss of life for the province as a whole. For casualty rates in the Revolution and the Civil War see Howard H. Peckham, ed., *The Toll of Independence: Engagements and Battle Casualties of the American Revolution* (Chicago, 1974), pp. 132-133.

47. *BTR*, XV, 369.

48. Although the even number 1,200 is suspicious, it may be a rounding of of an actual figure just below this number. A "lustration or census, called a valuation" was made "throughout the province" in 1742. Douglass, *Summary*, I, 524, 530.

49. *Boston Gazette*, Aug. 27, 1751. In a white population of 14,190 this suggests a total of 2,683 adult males and 3,836 adult females, a sex ratio of 70. Although this is an extraordinary imbalance, the 1765 census in Massachusetts revealed how profoundly a generation of war had skewed the sex ratio in all the maritime towns. Boston's sex ratio in that year was 81. By comparison the New York City sex ratio of adult whites was 78 in 1746 and 90 in 1749. This substantial difference in three years time suggests that the 1746 census did not count several hundred males who were at sea during the height of the privateering mania but were counted in 1749 after the return of peace. Greene and Harrington, *American Population*, pp. 99-100. The rise of widowhood also reflected in the inventories of estate. From 1736 to 1745 11.7 percent of the decedents were widows, but this climbed in the next two decades to 14.9 percent and 17.5 percent respectively. Since lower-class women are underrepresented in the inventories and since some lag can be expected before widows of King George's War would appear in the records, it seems likely that at least 25 percent of Boston's adult women were widowed.

50. Appendix, Table 13.

51. Hutchinson, *History of Massachusets*, II (Boston, 1767), 408-410, quoted in Rawlyk, *Yankee at Louisbourg*, p. 37.

52. By terms of the capitulation, the French civilians at Louisbourg were allowed to repatriate with their possessions. Thus, the plunder of the town was denied to the Massachusetts troops, who had been anticipating great rewards. French naval vessels entering the port (while the Anglo-American forces kept the French flag flying as a ruse) were condemned and auctioned off, but the proceeds went to the officers and crews of the English naval vessels. Leach, *Arms for Empire*, p. 242.

53. Appendix, Table 11. Douglass claimed in 1749 that "our taxes [are] from thirty to forty times more, than they were a few years ago." *Summary*, I, 537n.

54. Warden, *Boston*, pp. 128-129; Douglass, *Summary*, I, 314n; *BTR*, XIV, 99-101.

55. For prices, Arthur Harrison Cole, *Wholesale Commodity Prices in the United States, 1700-1861* (Cambridge, Mass., 1938), p. 5; for currency issues, Davis, *Currency and Banking*, I, 168. "New tenor" bills were set at four times the value of "old tenor" bills of the same denomination.

56. *Boston Evening Post*, Dec. 14, 1747. Even royal governors could be hurt. Governor Belcher complained bitterly in 1739 that the £1,300 salary voted him by the legislature was worth only £600 sterling, hardly sufficient to "live suitable to the Dignity of his Station." *Journals of House of Representatives of Massachusetts, 1739-1740* (Boston, 1940), p. 38. Shufro, "Impressment," pp. 36-37 notes that the constant threat of impressment during the war years raised food and fuel prices because the small craft that had traditionally brought food and firewood into Boston shunned the harbor. This hit with special force against the laboring poor who were least able to bear higher prices for food and fuel.

57. *Boston Evening Post*, Dec. 28, 1747, quoted in Herman J. Belz, "Currency Reform in Massachusetts, 1749-50," *Essex Institute Historical Collections*, 103 (1967), 68.

58. Davis, *Currency and Banking*, I, 172-202 treats debt legislation extensively.

59. Petition of a "Number of Inhabitants" to the town, Aug. 14, 1744, *BTR*, XIV, 57 and Selectmen's petition to the House of Representatives, May 28, 1746, *BTR*, XIV, 99-101. Economists have given scant attention to the differential impact of inflation, but for some suggestive formulations drawn from early nineteenth-century data in the cities see Jeffrey G. Williamson, "American Prices and Urban Inequality Since 1820," *Journal of Economic History*, 36 (1976), 303-333.

60. John Kern, "The Politics of Violence: Colonial American Rebellions, Protests, and Riots, 1647-1747" (Ph.D. diss., University of Wisconsin, 1976), p. 297. The wheat prices are derived from *BTR*, XV, XVIII, passim.

61. Nathaniel Appleton, *The Cry of Oppression* (Boston, 1748), p. 34.

62. Ibid., pp. 36-37.

63. *Boston Evening Post*, Feb. 1, 1748.

64. Flags of truce were "commissions from the Governors or judges in the British colonies authorizing them to visit the enemy colonies on the pretext of exchanging prisoners of war." Richard Pares, *Yankees and Creoles: The Trade Between North America and the West Indies Before the American Revolution* (London, 1956), p. 63.

65. *Boston Evening Post*, Feb. 1, 1748. Boston was not itself pure in respect to illegal trade. Massachusetts passed a law in 1744 prohibiting trade with the enemy in the West Indies but it lapsed after eleven months and was not renewed. Without intercolonial cooperation or a parliamentary statute, it was almost impossible to stop trade with the Spanish and French in the West Indies. For a discussion of this see Richard Pares, *War and Trade in the West Indies, 1739-1763* (London, 1963), chaps. 8-9; and Dorothy S. Towle, "Smuggling Canary Wine in 1740," *New England Quarterly*, 6 (1933), 144-154.

66. Whereas Massachusetts mustered about 9,000 men from 1739 to 1746, Pennsylvania sent about 900 men on the Cartagena expedition and one-third of them were indentured servants, who thus traded the rigors of servitude for death by yellow fever or starvation in the Caribbean. For the Canadian expeditions only about 400 volunteers mustered. Robert L. D. Davidson, *War Comes to Quaker Pennsylvania, 1682-1756* (New York, 1957), pp. 27-31, 44. New York raised five companies of volunteers (about 500 men) for the Cartagena assault and 1,600 men for the 1746 Quebec expedition. Douglass, *Summary*, I, 315, Gov. George Clarke to the Board of Trade, April 22, 1741, *NYCD*, VI, 185.

67. Pennsylvania appropriated small amounts of money: £ 3,000 in 1740 and £ 9,000 in 1746 or about 2s 4d per capita. Davidson, *War Comes*, pp. 33, 42, 44. New York was not quite so stingy, raising £45,000 or about 12s 10d per capita. *The Colonial Laws of New York from the Year 1664 to the Revolution*, 5 vols. (Albany, 1894), III, 577.

68. For the New York lotteries see Kammen, *Colonial New York*, p. 288. The Philadelphia lotteries, organized by Benjamin Franklin, are described in *Papers of Franklin*, III, 220-224, 229-231, 288-296.

69. Clarke to Board of Trade, Dec. 15, 1741, *NYCD*, VI, 207-209. The town, in fact, had just completed a three-month exercise in terrorism over an alleged slave conspiracy and had come through the harshest winter in memory—a time when food and fuel ran low and special funds were raised for alleviating distress among the poor. Kammen, *Colonial New York*, pp. 283-286.

70. *NYCD*, VI, 127, 511. For trade statistics see Appendix, Figure 3.

71. Lydon, *Pirates, Privateers, and Profits*, pp. 150-152; Howard M. Chapin, *Privateer Ships and Sailors: The First Century of American Colonial Privateering, 1625-1725* (Toulon, 1926), p. 12; Bridenbaugh, *Cities in Revolt*, pp. 61-62.

72. Lydon, *Pirates, Privateers, and Profits*, p. 154; Bridenbaugh, *Cities in Revolt*, p. 69.

73. *New-York Weekly Post-Boy*, June 20, 1748, cited ibid., p. 65.

74. Rawlyk, *Yankees at Louisbourg*, p. 50; Arthur Buffinton, "The Colonial Wars and Their Results," in Alexander C. Flick, ed., *History of the State of New York*, 4 vols. (New York, 1933), II, 226-229; Clinton to Newcastle, Nov. 18, 1745, *NYCD*, VI, 284-285. Most Massachusetts leaders believed that New York's Indian Commissioners had torpedoed the Oct. 1745 conference with the Iroquois by convincing the Indians to maintain their neutrality rather than join New Englanders in an assault upon the French.

75. The illegal fur trade is analyzed in Jean Lunn, "The Illegal Fur Trade Out of New France, 1713-60," Canadian Historical Association, *Report of the Annual Meeting . . . 1939* (Toronto, 1939), pp. 61-76. For the decline of the trade and the charges of the Clinton party see Thomas E. Norton, *The Fur Trade in*

Colonial New York, 1686-1776 (Madison, Wis., 1974), pp. 149-150, 181-191.

76. Bridenbaugh, *Cities in Revolt,* p. 63.

77. Powel to David Barclay, July 29, 1745, quoted in Anne Bezanson and others, *Prices in Colonial Pennsylvania* (Philadelphia, 1935), p. 33.

78. Ibid., 36, 50, 98-99, 104-106; Pares, *War and Trade,* pp. 492-494. For mariners' wages see Samuel Powel, Jr., to Thomas Hyam, June 12, 1740, quoted in Bezanson and others, *Prices in Colonial Pennsylvania,* p. 27, and Appendix, Figure 4.

79. Appendix, Figure 1.

80. Samuel Powel, Jr., to Henry Slingsby, Sept. 3, 1746, quoted in Bezanson and others, *Prices in Colonial Pennsylvania,* p. 125; also Richard Hockley to Thomas Penn, July 24, 1742, *PMHB,* 28 (1904), 31; and Bridenbaugh, *Cities in Revolt,* pp. 13-14, 21.

81. Appendix, Table 13. The number of taxables in 1746 is an estimate based on the number present in 1741 and 1751.

82. The names of taxables from whom collectors were unable to wring the minimum tax because of poverty are given in the manuscript minutes of the County Commissioners of Philadelphia. Three volumes of the Minutes, from 1718 to 1766, are in the City Archives, City Hall, Philadelphia. For decadal averages of those too poor to pay taxes in Philadelphia see Gary B. Nash, "Poverty and Poor Relief in Pre-Revolutionary Philadelphia," *WMQ,* 33 (1976), p. 25, Table III.

83. Ibid., pp. 5-6, 9. The winter of 1740-1741 is an exception to this statement. Bitter cold lasting for weeks in all the seaboard towns created distress that was partially alleviated through special committees and church collections.

84. Marc M. Egnal, "The Pennsylvania Economy, 1748-1762: An Analysis of Short-Run Fluctuations in the Context of Long-Run Changes in the Atlantic Trading Community" (Ph.D. diss., University of Wisconsin, 1974), pp. 97-114; McAnear, "Politics in New York," pp. 520-526; Virginia D. Harrington, *The New York Merchant on the Eve of the Revolution* (New York, 1935), pp. 290-291.

85. Simeon J. Crowther, "The Shipbuilding Output of the Delaware Valley, 1722-1776," *Proceedings of the American Philosophical Society,* 117 (1973), p. 93, Table 1.

86. In 1749 157 ships were registered in New York; in 1762 registrations climbed to 477. McAnear, "Politics in New York," p. 529. For the revival of shipbuilding also see Gov. George Clarke to Board of Trade, Dec. 15, 1741, *NYCD,* VI, 207.

87. In eleven years, from 1749 to 1760, the number of houses increased from 2,076 to 2,969. John K. Alexander, "The Philadelphia Numbers Game: An Analysis of Philadelphia's Eighteenth-Century Population," *PMHB,* 98 (1974), 324 assembles the extant data on houses in the town. In 1749, according to a report in the *London Magazine,* 120 houses, warehouses, and stores were built. Bridenbaugh, *Cities in Revolt,* p. 430. There was a sharp drop in the real estate market from about 1752 to 1754. "Land and losts will not sell for half as much as they would 4 or 5 years ago," reported Israel Pemberton, Jr., in May 1753. Egnal, "Pennsylvania Economy," p. 105.

88. Randolph Shipley Klein, *Portrait of an Early American Family:The*

Shippens of Pennsylvania Across Five Generations (Philadelphia, 1975), p. 66; Bridenbaugh, *Cities in Revolt*, p. 15.

89. For artisan wealth, see Appendix Table 5. Of 253 servants purchased by city dwellers in 1745-1746 80 percent were purchased by artisans, mariners, and laborers. I am indebted to Sharon V. Salinger for analyzing the occupations of those who purchased servants.

90. For statistics on early eighteenth-century shipbuilding see Bernard Bailyn and Lotte Bailyn, *Massachusetts Shipping, 1697-1714: A Statistical Study* (Cambridge, Mass., 1959), pp. 104-105, Table XVII. No systematic data exists after 1714 but for scattered years see Douglass, *Summary*, I, 510n, 538-540, and Weeden, *Economic and Social History*, II, 574. In 1742 the town meeting declared that building ships for sale in England was of "greatest Advantage" to the town and that ship construction "employed most of our Tradesmen." Quoted in Bridenbaugh, *Cities in Revolt*, p. 73.

91. Douglass, *Summary*, I, 540; BTR, XIV, 221. In 1756, the selectmen claimed in a petition to the General Court that during one (unspecified) year in the past 14,000 tons had been built. Petition of Town of Boston, Feb. 11, 1756, Massachusetts Archives, CXVII, 67-68.

92. BTR, XIV, 221, 238; Massachusetts Archives, CXVII, 67-68. For the Newport claim see Bridenbaugh, *Cities in Revolt*, p. 72. The selectmen's estimate in 1752 that two-thirds of all shipping was being built outside Boston is confirmed by the port records in the following year which show that of the 285 Massachusetts-built vessels clearing the harbor, 32 percent, with 37 percent of the total tonnage, were built in Boston. Murray G. Lawson, "The Boston Merchant Fleet of 1753," *American Neptune*, 9 (1949), 207-215. Of ships built since 1747, 35 percent of the tonnage came from Boston yards.

93. BTR, XIV, 220-222; Petition of the Town of Boston, Feb. 11, 1756, Massachusetts Archives, CXVII, 55-68. The decline in victualers and food processors must have represented a move to peripheral areas, for Boston's population could not have been fed unless the departing butchers and bakers continued to supply the city. The migration may have been triggered by forestalling.

94. Petition of the Town of Boston, April 1758, ibid., CXVII, 395-396.

95. W. T. Baxter, *The House of Hancock: Business in Boston, 1724-1775* (Cambridge, Mass., 1945), pp. 113, 127.

96. John Duffy, *Epidemics in Colonial America* (Baton Rouge, La., 1953), pp. 56-61. The quote is from the Rev. Thomas Smith of Falmouth (p. 58).

97. BTR, XIV, 239-240. By the end of the epidemic only 174 of 15,684 inhabitants had not been infected, either through inoculation or involuntarily. More than 10 percent of the uninoculated sick had died and it seems probable that these were concentrated in the lower class, where resistance to inoculation was strongest. Duffy, *Epidemics*, pp. 59-60.

98. John Lax and William Pencak, "The Knowles Riot and the Crisis of the 1740's in Massachusetts," *Perspectives in American History*, 10 (1976), 170-174; Dora Mae Clark, "The Impressment of Seamen in the American Colonies," *Essays in Colonial History Presented to Charles McLean Andrews by His Students* (New Haven, Conn., 1931), pp. 202-207. Boston merchants and mariners argued strenuously that a parliamentary act passed in 1707 permitted no impressment of mariners or others already in service aboard a privateer or mer-

chantman, or any person on land who was a resident of the colony. English officials maintained that this act expired in 1713 at the end of Queen Anne's War.

99. "I hate everything Eastward of Martha's Vineyard," wrote one Newport, Rhode Island shipbuilder, "as my men may be imprest." Quoted in Bridenbaugh, *Cities in Revolt,* p. 72. Shufro, "Impressment," pp. 20-42, and Lax and Pencak, "Knowles Riot," pp. 163-216 are the fullest accounts of impressments in Massachusetts during this era. However, I do not accept Shufro's argument that impressment was the most important factor in Boston's economic decline.

100. *BTR,* XIV, 85.

101. *Industry and Frugality Proposed as the Surest Means to Make Us a Rich and Flourishing People . . . With Some Cursory Reflections on Charity so far as it Regards our Distributions to the Poor* (Boston, 1753), pp. 8-10.

102. Lawrence W. Towner, "The Indentures of Boston's Poor Apprentices: 1734-1805," *CSM Pub.,* 43 (1956-1963), 417-468, quote p. 433.

103. Calculated from a chronological listing of all indentures ibid., pp. 435-467.

104. Josiah Benton, *Warning Out in New England, 1656-1817* (Boston, 1911), pp. 5-52.

105. Bridenbaugh, *Cities in the Wilderness,* p. 392.

106. "Persons Warned Out of Boston, 1745-1792," Records of the Boston Overseers of the Poor, MHS.

107. Douglas Lamar Jones, "The Strolling Poor: Transiency in Eighteenth-Century Massachusetts," *Journal of Social History,* 8 (1975), 28.

108. Based on my analysis of the Warning Out Book for these years. G. B. Warden has argued that the influx of transients into Boston after 1745 indicates that opportunity in the town was improving, thus attracting persons from other parts of the colony. All of the evidence on shipbuilding, poor tax increases, tax abatements, and net population decline suggests the opposite. As Appendix, Figure 1 indicates, Boston's population was declilning for several decades after 1740; given the increase in in-migrants, this meant a very heavy outflow caused by war, smallpox, and the loss of shipbuilding to satellite ports. It is not unusual for the jobless and poor to move toward the city in times of depression, even though the city may itself be deeply mired in economic difficulties. For Warden's argument: "Inequality and Instability in Eighteenth-Century Boston: A Reappraisal," *Journal of Interdisciplinary History,* 6 (1976), 592-593.

109. Jones, "Strolling Poor," p. 33, Table 3 reports that the itineracy rate in Essex County from 1750 to 1754 was 56 percent higher than in 1739-1743. The heavy out-migration among lower-class Bostonians is apparent from the muster rolls at the beginning of the Seven Years War. Of the 165 recruits for the Crown Point expedition in 1756 who gave Boston as their place of birth, 97 (58.8 percent) were at that time residing in other Massachusetts towns. Massachusetts Archives, XCIV, 161-555.

110. Foster, *Solitary Way,* p. 138; Kenneth A. Lockridge, *Literacy in Colonial New England: An Enquiry into the Social Context of Literacy in the Early Modern West* (New York, 1974), p. 33.

111. *BTR,* XIV, 222. In the severe winter of 1740-1741 special contributions to help the poor were raised in all the seaport towns. Boston, with a population

of about 17,000, gathered £237 sterling, while Philadelphia, with about 9,000 inhabitants, collected £136—a roughly comparable figure. For the Boston collections, Douglass, *Summary*, I, 542; for Philadelphia, Nash, "Poverty in Philadelphia," p. 6.

112. Charles W. Akers, "Religion and the American Revolution: Samuel Cooper and the Brattle Street Church," *WMQ*, 35 (1978), 480-485; Samuel Cooper, *A Sermon Preached in Boston, New-England before the Society for Encouraging Industry and Employing the Poor* . . . (Boston, 1753).

113. *BTR*, XIV, 222, 240. The selectmen were doubtless wrong. By the early 1750s Boston was spending annually about £1,000 sterling to support several hundred people in the almshouse and workhouse and hundreds of others on out-relief. Exeter, England, with a population of about 15,000 at mid-century, spent some £2,900 sterling per year on poor relief—about 2.5 times as much as Boston on a per capita basis. W. G. Hoskins, *Industry, Trade and People in Exeter, 1688-1800* . . . (Manchester, 1935), pp. 144-145. But scattered estimates of poverty in French towns such as Amiens, Lyon, and Aix-en-Provence, which were much larger than Boston, suggest that the New England capital had indeed reached a point comparable to western European market towns. See Cissie C. Fairchilds, *Poverty and Charity in Aix-en-Provence, 1640-1789* (Baltimore, 1976), pp. 75-76. In Rouen in 1777, the *hôpital général* cared for about 2,000 in a population of 87,000. Olwen H. Hufton, *The Poor of Eighteenth-Century France, 1750-1789* (London, 1974), p. 150.

114. Robert Zemsky, *Merchants, Farmers, and River Gods: An Essay on Eighteenth-Century American Politics* (Boston, 1971), pp. 311-313 calculates the average assessment by region in 1756 and 1764 but his "tax inequity score" for each region does not take account of the per capita wealth of the taxpayers.

115. *Durable Riches* (Boston, 1695) and *Concio and Populum* (Boston, 1721), quoted in Foster, *Solitary Way*, pp. 135, 137.

116. In 1656 a group of subscribers privately raised money to buy materials with which to set unemployed youths to work. Ibid., p. 147. In 1700, the selectmen spent £500 (£390 sterling) for a "Stock to set the poor on work." *BTR*, VIII, 3. The work program in 1700 was the outcome of a law passed in the previous year for "setting the Poor to work in workhouses." Albert Bushnell Hart, *Commonwealth History of Massachusetts: Colony, Province and State*, 4 vols. (New York, 1927-30), II, 266-267.

117. William Petty, *Economic Writings*, ed. Charles Hull (Cambridge, Eng., 1899), I, 274-275. The main treatment of this English movement is Dorothy Marshall, *The English Poor in the Eighteenth Century: A Study in Social and Administrative History* (London, 1926). Also see her "The Old Poor Law, 1662-1795," *Economic History Review*, 8 (1937), 38-47.

118. Marshall, *The English Poor*, pp. 22-51; A. W. Coats, "Economic Thought and Poor Law Policy in the Eighteenth Century," *Economic History Review*, 2d ser., 13 (1960-61), 46-50; Sidney and Beatrice Webb, *English Local Government From the Revolution to the Municipal Corporations Act, I: The Parish and the County* (London, 1906). For Bellers see John Bellers, *Proposals for raising a College of Industry* (London, 1695) and *Essays about the Poor, Manufactures, Trade, Plantations, and Immorality* . . . (London, 1699).

119. *BTR*, XII, 104-105, 111, 114, 116, 156, 159-162, 165-168, 172; Briden-

baugh, *Cities in the Wilderness*, p. 393; Foster, *Solitary Way*, pp. 147-148. The fullest account of the workhouse is in Stephen Edward Wiberly, Jr., "Four Cities: Public Poor Relief in Urban America, 1700-1775," (Ph.D. diss., Yale University, 1975), pp. 88-98.

120. *BTR*, XII, 273 for financial report. The 1742 count is in *MHS Coll.*, 3d ser., I (Boston, 1846), 152. Even in 1768, when poverty expenditures were greater, there were only forty persons in the workhouse. Bridenbaugh, *Cities in Revolt*, p. 320.

121. *BTR*, XII, 159-160. According to a census taken in 1756 the almshouse, completed in 1686 and not nearly as large as the new workhouse, held 148 inmates in thirty-three rooms. City of Boston, Indentures, 1734-1757, City Clerk's Office, City Hall, Boston. A list of 126 subscribers to the workhouse fund is in *BTR*, XII, 180-183. Kern, "Politics of Violence," pp. 233-234 identifies many of the subscribers as prerogative men.

122. "Bennett's History of New England," *MHS Proc., 1860-1862* (Boston, 1862), pp. 116-117.

123. Wiberly, who has analyzed the admissions records of the almshouse and workhouse, shows that women and children outnumbered men about three or four to one. "Four Cities," pp. 94-95.

124. *BTR*, XII, 234-241 for the rules of the workhouse.

125. Wiberly emphasizes that the workhouse was a financial failure, costing the town more per indigent than out-relief. "Four Cities," pp. 95-97.

126. In its promotional pamphlet, *The Society for Encouraging Industry . . . Articles of Incorporation . . . with a List of Subscribers* (Boston, 1748, reprinted 1754) it was pointed out that "the most immediate Advantage" to be gained by the scheme "is that which will arise" when "Many Thousands of the poor are taught to support themselves." A corollary benefit was that the price of labor—"so much and justly complained of"—would fall. A. P. Usher believed that the society's name and their expression of concern for the plight of the poor "were mostly an indirect way of expressing an ambition to make good use of cheap labor." Hart, *Commonwealth History of Massachusetts*, II, 408. The only more extensive published account—antiquarian but filled with useful documentary material—is William R. Bagnall, *The Textile Industries of the United States . . .* (Cambridge, Mass., 1893), pp. 28-37.

127. In 1754 it was claimed that sheep were not widely raised in Massachusetts because of the long winters (*The Society for Encouraging Industry . . .* [Boston, 1754], p. 1) but Usher disputes this (Hart, *Commonwealth History of Massachusetts*, II, 407), and he is supported by the 1735 tax valuation, which counted 130,001 sheep of at least one year. *Papers of Franklin*, III, 440.

128. Edward L. Parker, *The History of Londonderry . . .* (Boston, 1851), pp. 36-39, 48-50. The author does not indicate when the linen industry began but implies that the Londonderry settlers brought their wheels and looms with them. The linen production was apparently carried out as a home industry. In 1748, when the Boston plan became known, the Londonderry town meeting quickly passed an ordinance regulating carefully the quality of linen and putting a Londonderry label on all linen products of the town. It seems likely, in view of this protective measure, that they refused help to the Bostonians, either in teaching them how to build looms or showing them how to weave, bleach, and stretch

linen. Such uncooperativeness was a form of economic protectionism but it may also have been a belated settling of scores, for when the Ulster immigrants arrived in Boston in five ships in the fall of 1718 the town refused to succor some 300 impoverished souls who had insufficient money and provisions to carry them through the winter. Parker, *Londonderry*, pp. 37-38; *BTR*, XIII, 41-42, 46; *Massachusetts House Journals, 1718-1720* (Boston, 1921), pp. 83, 106 for 150 bushels of Indian meal contributed to the immigrants by the General Court.

129. *Society for Encouraging Industry*, p. 3. For the growth of the Irish linen industry see George O'Brien, *The Economic History of Ireland in the Eighteenth Century* (Dublin, 1918), pp. 189-207; W. H. Crawford, "The Rise of the Linen Industry," in L. M. Cullen, ed., *The Formation of the Irish Economy* (Cork, [1969]); and Conrad Gill, *The Rise of the Irish Linen Industry* (Oxford, 1925).

130. Bagnall, *Textile Industries*, pp. 29-31.

131. Edith Abbott, an authority on the subject, says that in the "latter half of the eighteenth century many women were regularly employed spinning at home for purchasers who were really commission merchants"; that "the most important occupations for women . . . before the establishment of the factory system were spinning and weaving"; and that while "it is impossible to make any estimate of the number of women who did such work . . . it is quite safe to say that spinning for the household was a universal occupation for women." *Women in Industry: A Study in American Economic History* (New York, 1909), pp. 19-20. These statements are based primarily on the assumption that what was widely practiced in England must have been carried to America. I do not challenge the extensiveness of household spinning and weaving in rural areas. But it is clear from the absence of wheels and looms in the thousands of Boston household inventories that have survived from this period and from the discussion about the need to establish spinning schools in 1718 that urban women and children were not accustomed to spinning and weaving. In 1720 a town-appointed committee recommended the founding of seven spinning schools for children, offered an interest-free loan of £300 (old tenor) to anyone who would start such schools, and found no takers. In 1721 Daniel Oliver, a wealthy merchant, erected a spinning school at his own expense, but little came of it. Bagnall, *Textile Industries*, pp. 17-18. A generation later, in 1750, it was advertised that "several Spinning Schools in this Town" would open shortly and children would be taught free. *Boston Evening Post*, Dec. 17, 1750. This is additional proof that the daily work of urban women did not include spinning and weaving.

132. Edward Winslow, "The Early Charitable Organizations of Boston," *New England Historical and Genealogical Register*, 44 (1890), 100-103 reprints the initial list of subscribers, but incorrectly gives 1735 as the year when the United Society for Manufactures and Importation was established. This error is noted in Bagnall, *Textile Industries*, p. 29. For importing Irish weavers and the opening of the manufactory see *Boston Evening Post*, July 9, Dec. 10, 1750. The United Society may have leased a part of the workhouse, for the building was located, according to the Dec. 10 notice, on the common "below the seat of Thomas Hancock," which fits the location of the workhouse.

133. The pamphlet was published in Dublin and reprinted in London in 1749.

134. *A Letter from Sir Richard Cox.* The quoted passages are from pp. 7 and 16. Cox neglected to state that the impoverishment of many Irish towns was attributable to the Woollen Act of 1699, which placed prohibitive tariffs on woolens imported from Ireland to England. This accomplished the desired effect of crushing the Irish woolen industry, which was eventually replaced by linen manufacturing. For Cox, see *Dictionary of National Biography*, ed. Leslie Stephens and Sidney Lee, IV (London, 1917), 1339-1340.

135. Gill, *Rise of the Irish Linen Industry*, pp. 91, 122-137.

136. *Papers of Franklin*, V, 233n-234n. According to Collinson, Franklin "proposed the same Plan to some Ingenious publick spirited Friends." I assume Collinson referred to friends in Boston, for Philadelphia had no sizeable poverty problem at this time. The Bostonians, of course, already had a linen production scheme underway.

137. *Boston Gazette*, Aug. 27, 1751.

138. *Report of the Committee for the Society for Encouraging Industry . . .* (Boston, 1752).

139. *Boston Weekly Post-Boy*, Feb. 12, 1752; Chauncy, *The Idle-Poor Secluded from the Bread of Charity*, p. 19.

140. *Report of the Committee of the Society . . .* (Boston, 1752); Cooper also hinted at financial problems in 1753 when he urged subscribers not to weary of doing well and predicted a "fair Prospect of *reaping*" in the future. *A Sermon Preached*, p. 34.

141. *BTR*, XIV, 234-235; *Massachusetts Acts and Resolves*, III, 680-682. Most of the £2,246 expended in purchasing land and erecting the Manufactory House was advanced by Thomas Gunter, a Roxbury merchant. Gunter was to be repaid from luxury tax receipts.

142. "An account of the cost of the Linen Manufactory House . . . ," Massachusetts Archives, LIX, 391-394 shows that most artisans and suppliers were paid in Sept. 1753.

143. *Boston Gazette*, Aug. 14, 1753, quoted in Richard B. Morris, *Government and Labor in Early America* (New York, 1946), p. 517. The public spinning exhibition and the attempt to induce lower-class women to spin by using upper-class daughters as examples of this kind of civic duty were taken straight from Richard Cox's description of his Irish linen experiment.

144. Barnard, *A Sermon Preached before the Society . . .* (Boston, 1758). In an appendix to the sermon, the "Committee of the Society" repeated the old pitch that linen production was unusually well suited for Boston's problem, for "the greatest Part of the Labour is done by Women and Children, who have no other Employment and can therefore work cheaper at this." They closed with a final plea for contributions so that the poor could "maintain themselves by their Industry, instead of their being maintain'd by others in Idleness, the Pest of Society, and the Mother of every Vice." The number of looms is noted in Ezekiel Price Papers, nos. 314-315, MHS.

145. By early 1756 the society had received only £312 sterling from the carriage tax. Wiberly, "Four Cities," p. 100. Gunter's involvement and subsequent attempts to recover his money can be followed in a series of petitions and actions by the General Court in Massachusetts Archives, LIX, 281-294, 427-428, 431, 441-442, 452-457, 494-499, 509-510, and *Massachusetts House Journals, 1758-*

1759 (Boston, 1963), pp. 56-57, 249, 262, 314; *1759-1760* (Boston, 1964), p. 48. Gunter began petitioning for recovery of his loan in June 1758 but the House stalled for a year before deciding to put the manufactory on the auction block. Elisha Brown had been hired by the society to supervise operations in the early 1750s. Ezekiel Price Papers, no. 317. The Price Papers contain what remains of the society's records.

146. Ezekiel Price Papers, nos. 314, 318.

147. *BTR*, XVI, 226-227; Thomas Barnard, in *A Sermon Preached . . .* (Boston, 1758), p. 23 admitted that linen was cheaper to import than weave domestically but asked his auditors to reject "the stale Objection, of the Cheaper Importation of Linnen" in view of the social advantages to be gained. In their initial petition to the General Court for a provincial subsidy, the society wrote at length on the subsidies in Ireland that had launched the linen industry there. Alice Clark concludes that wages paid women for spinning flax in England were never sufficient for their maintenance. Spinning, as a make-work project, was abandoned as unprofitable in Bristol as early as 1654. "The flaw in all these arrangements was the fact that spinning remained in most cases a grant in aid, and could not, owing to the low wages paid, maintain a family, scarcely even an individual, on the level of independence." Clark adds, "Women could not maintain themselves by the wages of flax spinning; still less could they, when widows, provide for their children by this means." *The Working Life of Women in the Seventeenth Century* (London, 1919), pp. 134-137. The linen industry in northeastern Ireland became successful after heavy subsidies, which reached £20,000 a year by 1711, were provided by the Irish Parliament. Alfred S. Moore, *Linen* (New York, 1922), pp. 34-43.

148. E. P. Thompson, "Time, Work-Discipline, and Industrial Capitalism," *Past and Present*, no. 38 (1967), 56-97 analyzes this problem brilliantly, although without distinguishing the special problems pertaining to women's work.

149. Patricia Branca, "A New Perspective on Women's Work: A Comparative Typology," *Journal of Social History*, 9 (1976), 133. I have also been guided by Olwen Hufton, "Women and the Family Economy in Eighteenth-Century France," *French Historical Studies*, 9 (1975), 1-22; Mary Lynn McDougall, "Working-Class Women During the Industrial Revolution, 1780-1914," in Renate Bridenthal and Claudia Koonz, eds., *Becoming Visible: Women in European History* (Boston, 1977), pp. 255-279; Theresa M. McBride, "The Long Road Home: Women's Work and Industrialization," ibid., pp. 280-295; and Elizabeth H. Pleck, "Two Worlds in One: Work and Family," *Journal of Social History*, 10 (1976), 178-195.

150. New York: Greene and Harrington, *American Population*, p. 101; Philadelphia: Gary B. Nash, "Slaves and Slaveowners in Colonial Philadelphia," *WMQ*, 30 (1973), 246 for the total number of slaves and servants, one-third of whom were female; Boston: Benton, *Early Census Making in Massachusetts*, following p. 71.

151. The census of 1765, in Benton, *Early Census Making in Massachusetts*, indicates 1,676 houses in the city. In 1742 there were 1,719 houses. *BTR*, XIV, 369-370. The ratios are taken from Lemuel Shattuck, *Report of the Committee of the City Council Appointed to Obtain the Census of Boston for the Year 1845* (Boston, 1846), p. 54. The ratio in New York has been calculated by extrapolat-

ing the population for 1753 from the censuses of 1749 and 1756 and dividing by the number of houses in 1753 as specified by Thomas Pownall, the governor of Massachusetts, in Lois Mulkearn, ed., *T. Pownall, A Topographical Description of the Dominions of the United States of America* . . . (Pittsburgh, 1949), p. 44. For Philadelphia I have used the house count as given in John K. Alexander, "The Philadelphia Numbers Game: An Analysis of Philadelphia's Eighteenth-Century Population," *PMHB*, 98 (1974), 324 and the population figures calculated in Billy G. Smith, "Death and Life in a Colonial Immigrant City: A Demographic Analysis of Philadelphia," *Journal of Economic History*, 37 (1977), 865.

152. The society reported that 489 yards had been woven for them and 340 yards for private persons. "Report of the Committee . . . ," *Boston Evening Post*, Feb. 19, 1753. In the quarterly report a year earlier, the society noted that 1,772 yards had been produced, more than twice as much. *Report of the Committee . . . Feb. 1752* [Boston, 1752].

153. *Boston Evening Post*, Feb. 19, 1753; Cooper, *A Sermon Preached*, p. 33; Memorial of Andrew Oliver et al. to the Governor and Council, May 1753, Massachusetts Archives, LIX, 381-383.

154. Ezekiel Price Papers, no. 318. John Hancock and John Barrett were buying cloth procured from independent weavers and were thus competing directly with the manufactory. Ibid., no. 329. In 1752, 72 percent of the cloth woven had been produced for the society. *Report of the Committee . . . Feb. 1752*.

155. This was the conclusion of a committee appointed by the town meeting in 1768 to analyze the failure of the manufactory. *BTR*, XVI, 226-227. The society's records show that spinners could process 100 pounds of flax per year and were paid 3 shillings, 9 pence per pound (Massachusetts money). Ezekiel Price Papers, no. 322. This works out to 7.2 shillings a week, not enough to buy food for even one person.

156. Chauncy, *A Sermon Preached* . . . (Boston, 1752), pp. 9-17; *Industry and Frugality Proposed* . . . (Boston, 1753), p. 10.

157. Cooper, *A Sermon Preached*, p. 23. Some of the older ideology, which charged the rich with responsibility for alleviating the distress of the unfortunate, still persisted. The *Boston Gazette* reprinted an essay on poor relief from the *New-York Gazette* in 1751 that urged people of means to buy from artisans and shopkeepers who had fallen upon hard times, even if it meant paying a bit more, and to sell the necessities of life to the poor below the prevailing rates. *Boston Gazette*, Aug. 27, 1751.

158. *BTR*, XIX, 38.

8. Religious Revival and Politics at Mid-Century

1. *New-York Gazette*, Feb. 20-27, March 13-20, 1739, cited in Carl L. Becker, "The History of Political Parties in the Province of New York, 1760-1776," *Bulletin of the University of Wisconsin*, II (1909-1910), 18.

2. Richard Peters to Thomas Penn, Aug. 25, Nov. 17, 1742, Peters Letter Book, 1737-1750, HSP.

3. *Pennsylvania Gazette*, Sept. 12, 19, 26, 1754. The issue that gave the proprietary faction an opportunity for electoral success was war appropriations,

for Pennsylvania's frontier was in flames and the Quaker-dominated assembly refused to vote for military supplies.

4. [William Smith], *A Brief State of the Province of Pennsylvania . . .* (London, 1755), p. 26. J. R. Pole calls this a "closed primary." *Political Representation in England and the Origins of the American Revolution* (London, 1966), p. 102.

5. *New-York Weekly Post-Boy,* Oct. 17, 1743, June 24, 1745, Nov. 30, Dec. 7, 14, 21, 1747; *New-York Gazette,* Jan. 18, Feb. 15, 1748; *New-York Evening Post,* Jan. 11, 18, 1748.

6. *Pennsylvania Gazette,* Sept. 6, 27, 1744; *American Weekly Mercury,* Aug. 16, 23, Sept. 6, 13, 20, 1744.

7. Paul S. Boyer, "Borrowed Rhetoric: The Massachusetts Excise Controversy of 1754," *WMQ,* 21 (1964), 328-351.

8. Beverly McAnear, "American Reprints Concerning King's College," *Papers of the Bibliographic Society of America,* 44 (1950), 301-339.

9. William Alexander to John Stevens, Aug. 23, 1750, Alexander Manuscripts, Box IX (Stevens), NYHS; Kammen, *Colonial New York,* p. 245.

10. A few examples will establish the point. In 1735 Lewis Morris paid one penny per sheet for 250 copies of a screed printed in London. Stanley N. Katz, "A New York Mission to England: The London Letters of Lewis Morris to James Alexander, 1735 to 1736," *WMQ,* 28 (1971), 462. In 1764 and 1765 Franklin and Hall in Philadelphia printed 3,000 copies of the two-page *Explanation and Remarks on the Assembly Resolves* for £8; 1,000 copies of Governor William Franklin's one-page *The Answer to the Invidious Charges of the Proprietary Party . . .* for £2-5; and 2,000 copies of *An Address to the Inhabitants of Pennsylvania* for £3-5. George S. Eddy, "A Work Book of the Printing House of Benjamin Franklin and David Hall, 1759-1766," *New York Public Library Bulletin,* 34 (1930), 580, 587-588. Converted to sterling, these prices indicate that political literature could be obtained at about one-sixth of a penny per sheet. Prices of a few lengthier tracts confirm the view that political literature was relatively inexpensive to print. The twenty-three-page *Interest of City and County to Lay No Duties . . .* (1726) sold in New York for 4 pence, and Cadwallader Colden's reply, which ran to thirty-five pages, went for 6 pence. *Money the Sinews of Trade* (sixteen pages) could be purchased in Boston in 1731 for 4 pence, and in Philadelphia a few decades later William Smith's lengthy anti-Quaker tracts, printed in London, retailed at 1 shilling and 1 shilling, 6 pence respectively. Although it is difficult to ascertain how broadly these pamphlets were disseminated, it is clear that many political leaders thought the distribution far too wide for the good of the country. As early as the 1720s the hard money faction in Boston was decrying the "abundance of Letters" distributed, with a fiery pamphlet entitled *News from Robinson Crusoe's Island* by the popular faction (*Reflections upon Reflection . . .* [Boston, 1720], in Davis, ed., *Currency Reprints,* II, 116). In the same year the author of *A Letter to an Eminent Clergyman* complained that "the Country has been overrun with pamphlets" (ibid., 229). More significant, it was revealed in Philadelphia in the 1730s that election pamphlets and broadsides were commonly read aloud to the assembled crowd at the polls, a practice also noted in 1754 by the *Pennsylvania Journal,* which wrote that *To the Freemen of Pennsylvania* "came out on the Election morning in half sheets which was dispers'd among the

Electors of this and the other Country's" (Oct. 10, 1754). From all this evidence, admittedly scattered and incomplete, it seems safe to assume that political leaders were reaching large audiences in the cities by mid-century. Indeed, it is hard to imagine that anyone living in an urban center was left untouched by the widely available tracts, broadsides, and newspapers.

11. William Currie, *A Treatise on the Lawfulness of Defensive War . . .* (Philadelphia, 1748), p. iii; Carl Bridenbaugh and Jessica Bridenbaugh, *Rebels and Gentlemen: Philadelphia in the Age of Franklin* (New York, 1965), p. 54. *Papers of Franklin,* III, 240n, 243n.

12. Franklin to Joseph Galloway, Feb. 17, 1758, *Papers of Franklin,* VII, 374; *A View of the Calumnies lately spread in some Scurrilous Prints against the Government of Pennsylvania* (Philadelphia, 1729). Franklin came close to changing his mind concerning the beneficial effects of the political press when he became the target of a savage offensive in 1764, but he could not have forgotten that his brother, publisher of the *New-England Courant,* was the object of the first attempt to muzzle a Boston newspaper in 1721.

13. James DeLancey, *The Charge . . . To the Gentlemen of the Grand-Jury for the City and County of New-York . . .* (New York, 1733); and *The Charge . . . to the Gentlemen of the Grand-Jury . . .* (New York, 1734).

14. *Letters and Papers of Caldwallader Colden,* IV, 122, 161, in *NYHS Coll., 1920* (New York, 1921). Governor Clinton decried the opposition "Grubsheet" that appeared before the 1752 election but promised to "come out with a hummer next Week" himself. Clinton to Robert Hunter Morris, Jan. 21, 1752, Robert Hunter Morris Papers, New Jersey Historical Society, Newark.

15. Peters to John Penn, Oct. 20, 1741, Peters Letter Book, IV, 18, quoted in Paul A. W. Wallace, *Conrad Weiser, 1696-1760, Friend of Colonist and Mohawk* (Philadelphia, 1945), p. 115.

16. Smith to Thomas Penn, May 1, 1755, Penn Papers, Official Correspondence, VII, 31, HSP.

17. James DeLancey, *The Charge . . . to the . . . Grand-Jury . . .* (New York, 1734), p. 7.

18. Colden to Gov. George Clinton, Dec. 27, 1748, *Letters and Papers of Cadwallader Colden,* IV, 185.

19. For a suggestive essay see Natalie Zemon Davis, "Printing and the People," in *Society and Culture in Early Modern France* (Stanford, Ca., 1975), pp. 189-226.

20. Boyer, "Borrowed Rhetoric," pp. 341-344.

21. Thomas Gordon, *The Craftsman: A Sermon . . .* (New York, 1753), pp. iii-xiii, xxv, xxvi. The anti-Anglican rhetoric was a part of a lengthy introduction to the New York printing of Gordon's 1720 English radical pamphlet. Also see the introduction by Milton M. Klein, ed., *The Independent Reflector; Or, Weekly Essays on Sundry Important Subjects* (Cambridge, Mass., 1963), pp. 3-15; and Klein, "Church, State, and Education: Testing the Issue in Colonial New York," *New York History,* 45 (1964), 291-303.

22. *Pennsylvania Journal,* April 22, 1756.

23. *New News from Robinson Crusoe's Island . . .* ([Boston], 1720), in Davis, ed., *Currency Reprints,* II, 134.

24. Isaac Norris to Robert Charles, Nov. 10, 1740, Norris Letter Book,

1719-1756, HSP; Richard Peters to Thomas Penn, Aug. 25, 1742, Peters Letter Book 1737-1750.

25. Letter of the Quarterly Meeting [of Friends] of Philadelphia to the Meeting for Sufferings, London, May 15, 1755, in Dietmar Rothermund, *The Layman's Progress: Religious and Political Experience in Colonial Pennsylvania, 1740-1770* (Philadelphia, 1961), p. 175; Governor Robert Morris to the Secretary of State, Aug. 25, 1755, *Minutes of the Provincial Council of Pennsylvania*, VI (Harrisburg, Pa., 1851), 600.

26. The debate can be followed in a series of nine pamphlets published in 1748. See, for example, William Currie, *A Treatise on the Lawfulness of Defensive War* (Philadelphia, 1748); Gilbert Tennent, *The Late Association for Defence, Encourag'd* . . . (Philadelphia, 1748); and John Smith, *The Doctrine of Christianity, As Held by the People Called Quakers* . . . (Philadelphia, 1748).

27. Rothermund, *Layman's Progress*, 129-130; the splitting of congregations over political questions was described contemporaneously in letters from Richard Peters to Thomas Penn, April 29, 1756, Penn Papers, Official Correspondence, VIII, 79; and Peters to Thomas Penn, April 25 and June 1, 1756, in Rothermund, *Layman's Progress*, pp. 179-180.

28. "Philo-Reflector" in preface to Thomas Gordon, *The Craftsman* (New York, 1753), pp. ii, v. The charge that the launching of King's College was a conspiracy to gain civil and religious hegemony in New York was made at length by *Independent Reflector*, nos. 18 and 19, in Klein, ed., *The Independent Reflector*, pp. 178-190. For the founding of the *New-York Mercury* see Alfred L. Lorenz, *Hugh Gaine: A Colonial Printer-Editor's Odyssey to Loyalism* (Carbondale, Ill., 1972), pp. 7-20.

29. Quoted in Alan Heimert, *Religion and the American Mind from the Great Awakening to the Revolution* (Cambridge, Mass., 1966), p. 15.

30. William G. McLoughlin, *New England Dissent, 1630-1833: The Baptists and the Separation of Church and State* (Cambridge, Mass., 1971), p. 329.

31. Ibid., p. 335.

32. Not the least of the ironies of the Awakening was that the Friends were generally unfriendly to the Awakeners, who shared so much with the seventeenth-century Quaker enthusiasts. See Frederick B. Tolles, "Quietism Versus Enthusiasm: The Philadelphia Quakers and the Great Awakening," *PMHB*, 69 (1945), 26-49.

33. Of the many biographies of Whitefield, the best are L. Tyerman, *The Life of Rev. George Whitefield*, 2 vols (London, 1877); Arnold A. Dallimore, *George Whitefield: The Life and Times of the Great Evangelist of the Eighteenth Century Revival* (London, 1970); and Stuart C. Henry, *George Whitefield (1714-1770): Wayfaring Witness* (New York, 1957).

34. Quoted in Bridenbaugh, *Cities in the Wilderness*, p. 424.

35. *Pennsylvania Gazette*, Nov. 8, 15, 29, 1739; April 17, 1740; *A Continuation of the Reverend Mr. Whitefield's Journal* . . . (London, 1741), pp. 343-345, 407-409; Dallimore, *George Whitefield*, pp. 432-434, 438-440, 479-482, 486-487. Although Whitefield's crowd estimates might be suspect, Benjamin Franklin, after listening to him speak from the courthouse steps to a large crowd in Philadelphia, calculated that the evangelist could be heard at a distance of two city blocks. In his own account, Franklin "computed that he might well be heard by

more than thirty thousand. This reconciled me to the newspaper accounts of his having preached to twenty-five thousand people in the fields." Max Farrand, ed., *The Autobiography of Benjamin Franklin* (Berkeley and Los Angeles, 1949), p. 132.

36. William Howland Kenney, 3d, "George Whitefield, Dissenter Priest of the Great Awakening, 1739-1741," *WMQ*, 27 (1969), 80-83.

37. John William Raimo, "Spiritual Harvest: The Anglo-American Revival in Boston, Massachusetts, and Bristol, England, 1739-1742" (Ph.D. diss., University of Wisconsin, 1974), pp. 64-76. Colman is quoted on p. 73.

38. Heimert, *Religion and the American Mind*, p. 50. The Boston crowd estimates vary. What Whitefield calculated as a crowd of 4,000 in the Brattle Street Church (a figure that seems unlikely), the *Boston Weekly News-Letter* (Sept. 25, 1740) called "a vast Congregation." The *News-Letter* reported that on the next day Whitefield preached to 5,000 on the common and on the following day "to at least 8,000 Persons" in the fields. See Dallimore, *George Whitefield*, pp. 529-535 for other estimates as well as Whitefield's journal of the 1739-1741 trip, which were published by Benjamin Franklin in Philadelphia. Edwin Scott Gaustad, the main authority on the Awakening in New England, claims that during his Boston sojourn Whitefield preached to "about six thousand persons" at the New North Church. *The Great Awakening in New England* (New York, 1957), p. 27. Many historians, including Gaustad, claim that 30,000 heard Whitefield's farewell sermon, but the *Boston Weekly News-Letter*, Oct. 16, 1740, said 20,000. Even if we accept the lowest estimates, it is certain that Whitefield drew crowds unlike any seen before or after in prerevolutionary America.

39. Quoted in Justin Winsor, ed., *The Memorial History of Boston, Including Suffolk County, Massachusetts, 1630-1880*, 4 vols. (Boston, 1886), II, 233.

40. Ibid., II, 235; Perry Miller, *Jonathan Edwards* (New York, 1949), pp. 166-167.

41. Kenney, "George Whitefield," p. 86.

42. Raimo, "Spiritual Harvest," pp. 88-111 analyzes the position of each Congregational clergyman.

43. Kenney, "George Whitefield," pp. 86-90. Attacks on Whitefield had been printed in the colonial press from the outset of his American pilgrimage. Most of these came from fellow Anglicans, such as Alexander Garden of Charleston, South Carolina, and Archibald Cummings and Richard Peters of Philadelphia. See Kenny, "George Whitefield," pp. 79-86. The coverage of these disputes in the Boston press is detailed in Raimo, "Spiritual Harvest," 123-140; and M. A. Yodelis, "Boston's First Major Newspaper War: A 'Great Awakening' of Freedom," *Journalism Quarterly*, 51 (1974), 207-212.

44. Quoted from George Whitefield's journal by Tyerman, *George Whitefield*, I, 434-435.

45. Miller, *Jonathan Edwards*, p. 166.

46. Eugene E. White, "The Decline of the Great Awakening in New England: 1741 to 1746," *New England Quarterly*, 24 (1951), 36. For an extensive account of Gilbert Tennent and the Presbyterian origins of the Great Awakening in the middle colonies see Leonard J. Trinterud, *The Forming of an American Tradition: A Re-examination of Colonial Presbyterianism* (Philadelphia, 1949).

47. Quoted in Miller, *Jonathan Edwards*, p. 166.

48. Timothy Cutler to Zachary Gray, Sept. 24, 1743, quoted in White, "Decline of the Great Awakening," pp. 37-38. Scurrilous attacks on Whitefield were by now filling the Boston press. See Gaustad, *Great Awakening in New England*, pp. 29-34 and Raimo, "Spiritual Harvest," pp. 123-140.

49. McLoughlin, *New England Dissent*, pp. 330, 332.

50. The career of the neglected Davenport is sketched in Franklin B. Dexter, *Biographical Sketches of the Graduates of Yale College*, I (New York, 1885), pp. 447-450 and C. C. Goen, *Revivalism and Separatism in New England, 1740-1800* (New Haven, Conn., 1962), pp. 19-27.

51. Bostonians were warned of the hideous effects of Davenport's preaching in Connecticut in the *Boston Weekly Post-Boy*, Sept. 28, 1741. A defense of him appeared in the following issue, Oct. 5, 1741.

52. *Boston Evening Post*, July 5, 1742. Davenport's assault on Boston can also be followed in Joseph Tracy, *The Great Awakening: A History of the Revival of Religion in the Time of Edwards and Whitefield* (Boston, 1842). Tracy's account is filled with documentary evidence and remains one of the most important sources of studying the Great Awakening.

53. White, "Decline of the Great Awakening," p. 40.

54. *Boston Evening Post*, Aug. 2, 1742; Miller, *Jonathan Edwards*, p. 172.

55. Miller, *Jonathan Edwards*, p. 176; *Boston Evening Post*, Aug. 2, 1742.

56. *Boston Evening Post*, Feb. 8, 1742, quoted in Raimo, "Spiritual Harvest," p. 126; Miller, *Jonathan Edwards*, p. 173, quoting Chauncy, *Enthusiasm described and caution'd against* . . . (Boston, 1742), p. 15.

57. On Nov. 10, 1740 Thomas Fleet, conservative printer of the *Boston Evening Post*, published a letter from England accusing the evangelist Benjamin Ingham of promoting the communal ownership of property. Raimo, "Spiritual Harvest," p. 126. By 1740, Alexander Garden of Charleston was warning that the evangelists would spread in America the "Ruin and Desolation" of the "Oliverian Days" in England, when social levelers had made a play for power. Edward Wigglesworth, Hollis Professor at Harvard College, also saw a possible re-enactment in New England of the Fifth Monarchy uprising. Garden, *Regeneration, and the Testimony of the Spirit* . . . (Charleston, 1740), p. 23 and Wigglesworth, *A Letter to the Reverend Mr. George Whitefield* . . . (Boston, 1745), pp. 3-4, quoted in Heimert, *Religion and the American Mind*, p. 92.

58. The exception is Goen, *Revivalism and Separatism*. Even those historians who are friendly to the Great Awakening, such as Trinterud and Gaustad, speak of Davenport's "mad evangelizing" and call him an "archfanatic." Trinterud, *Forming of an American Tradition*, p. 113; Gaustad, *Great Awakening in New England*, p. 36. The most important question does not concern Davenport's emotional balance but his extraordinary appeal in certain social sectors of society.

59. *Boston Evening Post*, Aug. 2, 1742.

60. It is difficult to estimate what proportion of Boston's population attended or belonged to one of the town's sixteen churches. Church records for eight of the nine Congregational churches show aggregate annual admissions before the Great Awakening of about 50 per year, which is roughly one-fifth of the Bostonians who came of age each year. Admissions rose to 240 annually in

1741 and 1742. Raimo, "Spiritual Harvest," p. 113, Table IV. In 1761 two Boston ministers estimated that about one-fourth of the families were still unchurched. Bridenbaugh, *Cities in Revolt*, p. 352. It is impossible to be precise but clearly a substantial part of the town was unchurched on the eve of the Awakening. It seems likely that among the poorest Bostonians this may have been especially true. Cotton Mather had complained in the 1720s that sailors and young people were leaving his church and almost all accounts of the Great Awakening talk about the special appeal it held for the young and dispossessed. A great many of the latter seem to have been drawn toward the messianic and radical preachers such as Davenport, as they have been at other points in history.

61. For a study of the social context of evangelical fervor in another setting see Rhys Isaac, "Preachers and Patriots: Popular Culture and the Revolution in Virginia," in Alfred F. Young, ed., *The American Revolution: Explorations in the History of American Radicalism* (DeKalb, Ill., 1976), p. 139.

62. Goen, *Revivalism and Separatism*, pp. 10-12.

63. *Boston Evening Post*, March 8, 1742. Two years later Crosswell became the pastor of some 500 persons who withdrew from Boston's Congregational churches as Separates following the general denunciation of the Great Awakening that accompanied Whitefield's return to New England. *Sibley's Harvard Graduates*, VIII, 390-404; Goen, *Revivalism and Separatism*, pp. 57, 97.

64. Whereas evangelical Methodism in England was seen by upper-class leaders as having the potential for imposing a new work discipline on the laboring classes by draining off psychic, emotional energy on Sundays so that the factory work routine could be strictly observed on workdays, the opposite was true in the early stages of the American Great Awakening. E. P. Thompson, *The Making of the English Working Class* (New York, 1963), pp. 350-400. One of the most frequent criticisms of the Awakeners was that they ignored their daily tasks. One of Whitefield's critics in Philadelphia complained in 1740 that "field preaching prevails with the vulgar here so much, that industry, honest labor, and care for their families, with many seems to be held as sinful, and as a mark of neglect for the salvation of their souls." *Boston Weekly Post-Boy*, June 23, 1740. Leonard Labaree has analyzed this criticism of the Awakening, concluding that the elite deeply feared that the craze for revival meetings would "interfere with the long hours of good hard work that were the proper weekday occupation of the 'multitude' " and that the "ministerial rebukes" against shunning daily labor "were, in part at least, an expression of conservative class-consciousness." Leonard W. Labaree, "The Conservative Attitude Toward the Great Awakening," *WMQ*, 1 (1944), 342-343. Also see Heimert, *Religion and the American Mind*, p. 53.

65. Harry S. Stout, "Religion, Communications, and the Ideological Origins of the American Revolution," *WMQ*, 34 (1977), 527.

66. Quoted in Goen, *Revivalism and Separatism*, p. 29. Charles Chauncy made explicit the link between the Awakeners and the Antinomians in the introduction to his influential attack on the Awakeners, *Seasonable Thoughts on the State of Religion in New England . . .* (Boston, 1742), pp. iii-xxx and criticized the social composition of the exhorters: "There are among these exhorters, babes in age as well as understanding. They are chiefly, indeed, young persons, sometimes lads, or rather boys; nay, women and girls; yea Negroes have taken upon

them to do the business of preachers." *Seasonable Thoughts*, p. 236; also see Chauncy, *A Letter from A Gentleman in Boston, To Mr. George Wishart, One of the Ministers of Edinburgh, Concerning the State of Religion in New-England* (Edinburgh, 1742), pp. 9-10. Ebenezer Turell was another who published against lay exhorting and especially against preaching by women. See *Mr. Turell's Directions to his People with Relation to the present Times . . .* (Boston, 1742). Crosswell defended preaching by women in *A Letter . . . to the Rev. Mr. Turell, In Answer to his Directions to his People . . .* (Boston, 1742).

67. Mr. Brockwell to the Secretary [of the Society for the Propagation of the Gospel], Feb. 18, 1741/42, in William Stevens Perry, ed., *Papers Relating to the History of the Church in Massachusetts, 1676-1785* (n.p., 1873), p. 353.

68. McLoughlin, *New England Dissent*, p. 352 and Stout, "Religion and the Revolution," pp. 519-541.

69. The standard account is George A. Billias, "The Massachusetts Land Bankers of 1740," *University of Maine Studies*, 2d ser., 74 (1959). Much can still be learned from a contemporary tract, *An Account of the Rise, Progress and Consequences of the Land Bank . . .* ([Boston], 1744), and from Davis's analysis in *Currency and Banking*, I, 129-133; II, 130-167, 182-218.

70. The Silver Bank proposal was published on Dec. 28, 1739 and the Land Bank proposal on Mar. 10, 1740. Silver Bank bills were issued Aug. 1, 1740 and Land Bank bills on Sept. 19, 1740. Davis, *Currency and Banking*, II, 130-132, 143-144.

71. Robert Zemsky, *Merchants, Farmers, and River Gods: An Essay on Eighteenth-Century American Politics* (Boston, 1971), p. 119.

72. John A. Schutz's biography, *William Shirley: King's Governor of Massachusetts* (Chapel Hill, N.C., 1961) draws a sensitive picture of Shirley's accession and his attempt to mediate the crisis.

73. *Post[s]cript To a Discourse concerning the Currencies of the British Plantations in America* ([Boston, 1740]), in Davis, ed., *Currency Reprints*, IV, 59-60.

74. Billias, who is at pains to dismantle an earlier interpretation of the Land Bank as a class-based interest group, points out that its principal proposers were well-established men such as merchants John Colman, Peter Chardon, William Stoddard, and Robert Auchmuty. He further emphasizes that 90 percent of the identifiable Land Bank subscribers came from outside Boston. It must be remembered, however, that approximately 90 percent of the colony's population resided outside the provincial capital and that while the leaders of the Land Bank might have been lesser merchants, the bank itself was an instrument for solving a long-standing monetary problem which most common people believed robbed their purses while wealthy merchants, associated with the Silver Bank, prospered. Only by comparing the Land and Silver Bank subscribers can we begin to get a firm sense of which interests were served by each. John Kern, who has attempted such an analysis, reports that the Silver Bankers were predominantly prerogative men, many of whom had also subscribed to the Merchants Notes of 1733 and held the most prestigious town offices—selectman, auditor, and overseer of the poor. The Land Bank subscribers were predominantly popular party men, who had not subscribed to the Merchants Notes and held lesser local offices such as assessor and collector. "The Silver Bank," Kern concludes, "may be

added to the cluster of programs for municipal incorporation, regulated markets, and the Work House, programs by which prerogative party adherents sought to regulate economic and political behavior in Boston and Massachusetts. John Kern, "The Politics of Violence: Colonial American Rebellions, Protests, and Riots, 1647-1747" (Ph.D. diss., University of Wisconsin, 1976), pp. 239-243. All four Boston representatives to the General Court voted against the Land Bank's right to issue bills on June 24, 1740 and were re-elected in 1741. *Journals of the House of Representatives of Massachusetts, 1740-1741* (Boston, 1942), p. 47. I am indebted to Catherine Menand for pointing this out and for other insights from her unpublished paper, "The Land Bank Controversy of 1740."

75. Many of the reports on incipient civil war are in Massachusetts Archives, CII, 155, 159-168. Belcher wrote in the spring of 1741 that "there is at present a great scarcity of all kinds of grain, beyond what I can remember for forty years past." This was an interesting lapse of memory, for the warehouses of Belcher's father were ransacked in 1710 when his engrossing of country grain supplies had created an urban shortage. Belcher to Thomas Hutchinson, May 11, 1741, *MHS Coll.*, 6th ser., VII (Boston, 1894), 387. One of Boston's largest grain merchants, James Bowdoin, was apprehensive enough about a grain riot to advertise that he was neither exporting grain nor buying up large quantities to raise the price nor attempting to withhold it from Land Bank subscribers. *Boston Evening Post*, May 18, 1741.

76. Quoted in John C. Miller, "Religion, Finance, and Democracy in Massachusetts," *New England Quarterly*, 6 (1933), 33.

77. White, "Decline of the Great Awakening," p. 49.

78. Quoted in Miller, "Religion, Finance, and Democracy," p. 48.

79. [William Rand], *The Late Religious Commotions in New-England considered* . . . (Boston, 1743), p. 13; Douglass, *A Post[s]cript* . . ., in Davis, ed., *Currency Reprints*, IV, 78. Rand was dismissed from his pastorate by his parishioners in Hampshire County in 1745 for his shrill attacks on the Awakeners. *Sibley's Harvard Graduates*, VI, 550-551.

80. William G. McLoughlin, *Isaac Backus on Church, State, and Calvinism: Pamphlets, 1754-1789* (Cambridge, Mass. 1968), p. 1.

81. [William Rand], *The Late Religious Commotions*, p. 18.

82. Alan Heimert and Perry Miller, eds., *The Great Awakening: Documents Illustrating the Crisis and Its Consequences* (Indianapolis and New York, 1967), p. lxi.

83. Jonathan Mayhew, *Seven Sermons* . . . *Preached at a Lecture* . . . *in August, 1748* (Boston, 1749), quoted in Heimert, *Religion and the American Mind*, p. 252; Jonathan Edwards, *A Dissertation Concerning the Nature of True Virtue* . . . , in *The Works of Jonathan Edwards*, 10th ed. (London, 1865), quoted in Heimert, *Religion and the American Mind*, p. 252.

84. Gilbert Tennent, *Brotherly Love Recommended, by the Argument of the Love of Christ* (Philadelphia, 1748), quoted in Heimert, *Religion and the American Mind*, pp. 298-299.

85. Gilbert Tennent, *A Solemn Warning to the Secure World from the God of Terrible Majesty* [Boston, 1735], pp. 56-57, 102, quoted in Heimert, *Religion and the American Mind*, pp. 306, 32.

86. Ibid., p. 306; also see pp. 31-34.

87. Ibid., p. 253.

88. Charles Chauncy, *The Idle-Poor Secluded from the Bread of Christian Charity by the Christian Law* . . . (Boston, 1752), p. 6.

89. Edwards, "Christian Charity: or, the Duty of Charity to the Poor, Explained and Enforced," in Edwards, *Works*, II, 164-165, quoted in Heimert, *Religion and the American Mind*, p. 250; Holyoke, *The Duty of Ministers* . . . . (Boston, 1741), quoted in Heimert, *Religion and the American Mind*, p. 33.

90. Ibid., p. 32. Edwards was second to nobody in the intellectual history of the Great Awakening, but his direct impact on the laboring people of the cities was probably minimal, for he never preached there. His importance to the social history of the Awakening lies in his pointed indictments of commercialism, affluence, disregard for the poor, and elitist pride. These attacks, which were influential in the radical social thought of evangelists who preached in the port towns, are dealt with in Heimert, *Religion and the American Mind*, pp. 30-34, 246-253.

91. Ibid., p. 93.

92. Ten of the 1744 attacks are listed in Tyerman, *George Whitefield*, II, 131-140. For the Harvard College excoriation see Goen, *Revivalism and Separatism*, pp. 56-57. It was published in Boston in 1744 as *The Testimony of the President, Professors, Tutors, and Hebrew Instructors of Harvard College, against George Whitefield*.

93. Heimert, *Religion and the American Mind*, p. 32.

94. Only the slaves, representing about one-fifth of New York's population and one-tenth of Philadelphia's, were comparable to the struggling lower elements in Boston. And to the slaves, gathered together, the revivalists could never preach, especially in New York, where after the suspected black conspiracy in 1741 all assemblies of Negroes were strictly forbidden.

95. Kenney, "George Whitefield," p. 81; Charles Hartshorn Maxson, *The Great Awakening to the Middle Colonies* (Chicago, 1920), pp. 13-14. Some in New York later opined that the 1741 black conspiracy was traceable to "the great encouragement the negroes had received from Mr. Whitefield" during his visit to the city. Daniel Horsmanden, *The New-York Conspiracy, or A History of the Negro Plot* . . . (New York, 1810; reprinted and edited by Thomas J. Davis, Boston, 1971), p. 360. I am grateful to David Lovejoy for pointing out this reference.

96. Maxson, *Great Awakening*, pp. 47-50; Tracy, *Great Awakening*, p. 52. The most recent student of the Awakening in New York concludes that "Whitefield's success at New York . . . was but a pale imitation of his triumph in Philadelphia," with crowds 5,000 to 7,000 in the spring of 1740 and much smaller gatherings that fall. Martin Ellsworth Lodge, "The Great Awakening in the Middle Colonies" (Ph.D. diss., University of California, Berkeley, 1964), pp. 185-186.

97. Lodge interprets the Great Awakening in Pennsylvania primarily as an institution-building phenomenon, with evangelists stepping into a vacuum where the established churches had not proved "capable of fulfilling the religious needs of a rapidly expanding population." Unlike New England, where Harvard and Yale had been training a clergy adequate to the needs of the region's population, the middle colonies suffered a severe shortage of ministers and consequently an inadequate network of established religious institutions. It was to this need that the Awakening primarily addressed itself. Martin E. Lodge, "The Crisis of the

Churches in the Middle Colonies, 1720-1750," *PMHB*, 95 (1971), 195-220. This thesis is confirmed in a study of the German communities of the region. John B. Frantz, "The Awakening of Religion among the German Settlers in the Middle Colonies," *WMQ*, 33 (1976), 266-288. Neither Lodge nor Frantz study Philadelphia in particular, leaving the history of the revival in that town a subject about which much remains to be learned.

98. Maxson, *Great Awakening*, p. 62; *Pennsylvania Gazette*, Nov. 13, 1740.

99. Heimert, *Religion and the American Mind*, p. 49 concludes that "In the decades after the Awakening the appeal of evangelical religion remained most enduring in those parts of the colonies that suffered economic difficulty." The same might be said for the years from 1741 to 1745 after the apogee of enthusiasm connected with Whitefield's 1740 tour had been reached. In Philadelphia a brief flurry of newspaper articles revealed mild class antagonism in the spring of 1740 but the comments did not go much beyond an argument over whether the Awakening was assailed by the "Better Sort" and whether the enthusiasts were "a stupid Herd, in whom the light of Reason is extinguished" or were "industrious Tradesmen" and "laborious Ploughmen." Lodge, "Great Awakening," pp. 228-230.

100. Anglican attacks on Whitefield were plentiful of course, but these mainly involved doctrinal disagreement. The highly explosive Presbyterian schism of 1741, which forms another chapter of the Great Awakening story in Pennsylvania, is covered fully in Trinterud, *Forming of an American Tradition*.

101. *Papers of Franklin*, II, 241n.

102. *Pennsylvania Gazette*, June 12, 1740, reprinted ibid., II, 287-288.

103. Lodge, "Great Awakening," p. 230 concludes that the Awakening "was almost purely a religious phenomenon. Its motives, aims, and even its social effects remained always within a religious context." This may overstate the matter somewhat, but the contrast with Boston is evident.

104. The two most thorough accounts of the Knowles riot are Kern, "Politics of Violence," pp. 256-284; and John Lax and William Pencak, "The Knowles Riot and the Crisis of the 1740s in Massachusetts," *Perspectives in American History*, 10 (1976), 163-216. I have drawn extensively on both accounts, although they differ in their perspectives.

105. Dora Mae Clark, "The Impressment of Seamen in the American Colonies," *Essays in Colonial History Presented to Charles McLean Andrews by His Students* (New Haven, Conn., 1931), pp. 202-207.

106. Details on the violent history of impressments in Boston before 1747 are given in Joel A. Shufro, "Boston in Massachusetts Politics, 1730-1760," (Ph.D. diss., University of Wisconsin, 1976), pp. 187-209; Kern, "Politics of Violence," pp. 258-272; and Lax and Pencak, "Knowles Riot," pp. 174-182. The impressment of men from small coastal vessels that carried firewood and produce to Boston became a factor in the rapid rise of prices in the early 1740s because the coasters were reluctant to come to the town if it meant risking impressment. H.M.S. *Shirley*'s log lists more than ninety men impressed off Boston in 1745-1746. Jesse Lemisch, "Jack Tar in the Streets: Merchant Seamen in the Politics of Revolutionary America," *WMQ*, 25 (1968), 383-384.

107. Lax and Pencak, "Knowles Riot," pp. 184-196. Hutchinson's estimate of the crowd is in *History of Massachusets*, II, 431; the governor's instructions to

the militia are in Orders to Col. Jacob Wendell, Nov. 17, 1747, Wendell Family Papers, 1691-1846, MHS, quoted in Kern, "Politics of Violence," p. 305.

108. *BTR*, XIV, 217; Shirley to Josiah Willard, Nov. 19, 1747, *Correspondence of William Shirley, Governor of Massachusetts and Military Commander in America, 1731-1760*, ed. Charles H. Lincoln, 2 vols. (New York, 1912), I, 406; Hutchinson, *History of Massachusets*, II, 431.

109. Lax and Pencak, "Knowles Riot," pp. 196-200. Knowles's statement, as recalled by a ship's carpenter, Joseph Ballard, is in *CSM Trans.*, III (Boston, 1920), 232. Eleven men, nine of them mariners and laborers, were indicted for disturbing the peace. Three were convicted, one of whom was pardoned. Lax and Pencak, "Knowles Riot," pp. 199-200.

110. *An Address to the Inhabitants of the Province of Massachusetts-Bay* . . . (Boston, 1747), pp. 4-5. The pamphlet was ready for publication by Nov. 23 but an attempt to suppress it delayed publication until a week later.

111. Lax and Pencak make a case for Adams's authorship, but this remains in doubt. "Knowles Riot," pp. 204-205. Kern, "Politics of Violence," p. 339n points out that John Wise, the most radical libertarian of the 1720s, had used the pseudonym "Amicus Patraie" in 1721 in his fiery attack on the conservative court party and that the author may have chosen this name to draw upon the popular party tradition of the previous generation.

112. *Boston Independent Advertiser*, Jan. 25, 1748. For the founding of the paper by a club of men sworn to secrecy see William V. Wells, *The Life and Public Services of Samuel Adams* . . . , 2 vols (Boston, 1865), I, 15-16. The club may have been the revived Boston Caucus. Adams's father had been a close political ally of Elisha Cooke, Jr., one of the earliest members of the Caucus (Wells, *Adams*, I, 3), and had apprenticed his son to Thomas Cushing, Cooke's successor as head of the popular party. *Sibley's Harvard Graduates*, X, 422. Cushing was elected moderator of the town meeting and served in that role, which usually signified leadership of the antiprerogative party, until his death in 1746.

113. *Boston Independent Advertiser*, Feb. 8, 1748. Also see the essay on "Loyalty and Sedition" in Wells, *Adams*, I, 17 and specifically attributed to Adams.

114. There are good accounts of the Shirley administration and the handling of the currency question in Schutz, *William Shirley*, chap. 7 and Zemsky, *Merchants, Farmers, and River Gods*, chap. 6. The most incisive account is Malcolm Freiberg, "Thomas Hutchinson and the Province Currency," *New England Quarterly*, 30 (1957), 190-208. It should be supplemented by Herman J. Belz, "Currency Reform in Massachusetts, 1749-50," *Essex Institute Historical Collections*, 103 (1967), 66-84. A table of paper money emissions during the 1740s is in Davis, *Currency and Banking*, I, 168.

115. Kilby to Gov. William Shirley, Jan. 1748, Massachusetts Archives, XX, 408, quoted in Belz, "Currency Reform," p. 79. By the summer of 1748 a correspondent in the *Boston Weekly News-Letter* was fuming: "So the Money that the brave Sons of *New-England* bitterly earned with Sweat and Blood, and Unspeakable fatigue, shall be immediately snatch'd out of their Hands; not they nor their Children hardly any Thing the better for it." *News-Letter*, July 7, 1748.

116. *Boston Weekly News-Letter*, Nov. 25, 1748, quoted in Joseph Dorfman, *The Economic Mind in American Civilization, 1606-1865*, 2 vols. (New

York, 1946), I, 161; Hutchinson, *History of Massachusets*, III, 8. It is difficult to say how many artisans and laborers would have been affected. Their position depended on whether or not they were debtors and, if so, at what point in the inflationary process they had contracted the debt. The exchange rate established for the redemption of paper money was 44 shillings old tenor Massachusetts currency for one ounce of silver.

117. *Boston Evening Post*, Dec. 18, 1749. The rhetoric smacks of the two Samuel Adamses, senior and junior. Five years before, the senior Adams had been a member, and probably the drafter, of a tax policy committee of the town that brought in a report bitterly opposed to fiscally contractionary proposals drafted by Thomas Hutchinson. "We cannot suppose," the report read, that the people of Boston would agree to "have our Bread & Water measured out to Us by those Who Riot in Luxury & Wantonness on our Sweat & Toil and be told by them that we are too happy, because we are not reduced to Eat Grass with the Cattle." *BTR*, XIV, 58-60. The report was not accepted by the town meeting. Hutchinson had first put forward plans for returning to a specie standard in 1736. Already a wealthy man (with a dowry of "at least £5,000 sterling" acquired at marriage), he was roundly hated by the popular faction. Freiberg, "Hutchinson and the Currency," p. 192.

118. The popular party charged that the Massachusetts trade recession following the Peace of Aix-la-Chapelle in 1748 was the result of the conservatives' redemption plan. The slump can also be attributed to the contraction of the economy, as supply contracts dried up and British spending in New England ended, and to the decreased productivity of a colony drained of one-fourth of its male labor force. Freiberg, "Hutchinson and the Currency," pp. 203-204; and, for a more extensive analysis of the redemption issue, Shufro, "Boston in Massachusetts Politics," pp. 239-263. The *Boston Evening Post* reported widespread unemployment on April 2, 1750 and seven weeks later one bitter critic charged that the redemptionists' "great Goddess Silver" was soon "a poor broken despised Idol" and urged voters to vote from office those "who have almost eat out the very Vitals of the Body Politick." *Boston Evening Post*, May 21, 1750.

119. For the 1749 election, where Hutchinson got only about 200 of the 684 votes cast, see *BTR*, XIV, 161. A pre-election fusillade decrying the "shifting the People's Property, the Foundation and Cause of Power, into the Pockets of those, who have thereby been enabled to raise Prerogative to an enormous Height," reminded the voters that the Roman agrarian law was the best safeguard of liberty, and warned that the people's rights would be lost concurrent with the "growing Poverty of the People, by the Shifting of Property." *A Letter to the Freeholders* . . . (Boston, 1749).

120. Hutchinson recalled his hasty retirement to Milton sixteen years later in a letter to his friend William Bollan, Dec. 27, 1765, Massachusetts Archives, XXVI, 187. See also *Boston Independent Advertiser*, Sept. 18, 25, 1749.

121. The fire at Hutchinson's was noted in *Boston Gazette*, May 2, 1749, and in *The Diary and Letters of His Excellency Thomas Hutchinson*, ed., Peter O. Hutchinson, 2 vols. (London, 1883-86), I, 54. His brother-in-law, Peter Oliver, also a wealthy merchant of the administration party, was certain that "interested Men set the Canaille to insult him; which they did in the most open Manner in the publick streets, threatening him not only with Words but with

Sticks." *Peter Oliver's Origin & Progress of the American Revolution: A Tory View*, ed. Douglass Adair and John A. Schutz (San Marino, Ca., 1961), p. 32. Hutchinson was also hated because two years before, during the Knowles Riot, he had lined up behind the governor in attempting to disperse the crowd in the name of law and order, and had been a member of the committee that drafted a report condemning the riot. His election as tax collector, an office from which he was exempt by law as a member of the governor's council, was reported in the *Boston Weekly Post-Boy*, Dec. 25, 1749. Also elected as tax collectors were James Bowdoin, Andrew Oliver, Samuel Welles, and Edmund Quincy, well-known leaders of the conservative faction. *BTR*, XIV, 166-167. The regularly elected tax collectors refused to serve, some indication of the kind of paralysis of government that the Adams-led popular party was now prepared to engage in.

122. Vincent Centinel [pseud.], *Massachusetts in Agony: Or, Important Hints To the Inhabitants of the Province* . . . (Boston, 1750), pp. 3-5, 8, 12-13.

123. *Sibley's Harvard Graduates*, VIII, 467. Quincy, a supplier of the garrison at Louisbourg, had just returned from France and England where he had procured contracts to supply the French garrison at Louisbourg after it was surrendered by the British at the Treaty of Aix-la-Chapelle in 1748 and reoccupied by the French. Quincy also received the contract to supply the British garrison at Cape Sable at the southern tip of Nova Scotia. For a few Boston merchants war and peace could be equally profitable and Louisbourg, in either English or French hands, could be a source of profits.

124. Bonomi, *Factious People*, pp. 140-144; Stanley Nider Katz, *Newcastle's New York: Anglo-American Politics, 1732-1753* (Cambridge, Mass., 1968), chaps. 7, 8.

125. See, for example, *New-York Gazette*, Jan. 25, 1748, and *New-York Weekly Post Boy*, Jan. 27, 1752. For a few of the pamphlets and broadsides see those listed in Evans, *American Bibliography*, nos. 5461, 5791, 5984, 6524, 6526, 6597, 6618, 6699, 6809, 6865, and 40561.

126. *New-York Weekly Post Boy*, Dec. 28, 1747, quoted in McAnear, "Politics in New York," p. 659; "Address to The Freeholders . . . ," in *Letters and Papers of Cadwallader Colden*, III, 326-327, in *NYHS Coll., 1919* (New York, 1920).

127. "Address to The Freeholders . . . ," ibid., III, 313-314.

128. Colden Letter Book, I, 451, quoted in Milton M. Klein, "The American Whig: William Livingston of New York" (Ph.D. diss., Columbia University, 1954), p. 232. A good account of Clinton's attempt to build a party that could recruit broad support is in Bonomi, *Factious People*, pp. 158-166.

129. Ibid., p. 161; the charge against DeLancey is from Clinton to Newcastle, Oct. 11, 1748, quoted in Katz, *Newcastle's New York*, p. 171.

130. *NYHS Coll., 1885* (New York, 1886), pp. 140-183 for admissions to freemanship between 1740 and 1755. *New-York Evening Post*, June 24, 1745 for the electoral count.

131. McAnear, "Politics in New York," pp. 721-733. McAnear points out that the DeLancey candidates in New York City ran unopposed in 1748 and in a by-election of Oct. 1751. Ibid., pp. 661, 709.

132. Ibid., pp. 535-536; *New-York Weekly Mercury*, Dec. 24, 1753, Jan. 7, 14, 21, 1754; *New-York Weekly Post Boy*, April 22, 1754; *New-York Gazette*,

Jan. 14, April 22, 1754.

133. Theodore Thayer, *Pennsylvania Politics and the Growth of Democracy, 1740-1776* (Harrisburg, Pa., 1953), pp. 9-24.

134. Arthur D. Graeff, *The Relations Between the Pennsylvania Germans and the British Authorities (1750-1776)* (Philadelphia, 1939), pp. 61-63. Also see Glenn Weaver, "Benjamin Franklin and the Pennsylvania Germans," *WMQ*, 14 (1957), 536-559.

135. James Hamilton to Thomas Penn, Nov. 8, 1750, Penn Papers, Official Correspondence, V, 88; [William Smith], *A Brief State*, p. 40. The attempts of the proprietary party to recruit the German vote in the early 1740s can be followed in the letters of the party leaders, James Allen and Richard Peters, to John Penn and Thomas Penn, in Penn Papers, Official Correspondence, III.

136. Smith, *A Brief State*, pp. 27-28, 33. In 1741 Weiser published *A Serious and Seasonable Advice to our Countrymen ye Germans in Pensilvania* (Philadelphia, 1741) but Sauer countered with a last minute paper in German, distributed at the polls. "Every Dutchman [was] furnish'd with it & they came down to ye Election with so much zeal for ye old Assembly that all ye arguments in ye World wou'd have had no Effect upon them." Richard Peters to Thomas Penn, Oct. 8, 1741, Peters Letter Book, 1737-1750.

137. The 1739 vote is recorded in *American Weekly Mercury*, Sept. 27, 1739. The 1740 vote is ibid., Oct. 2, 1740. The pseudonymous author of *An Answer to an invidious Pamphlet intituled, A Brief State of the Province of Pennsylvania . . .* (London, 1755) wrote that 1740 was the first year in which the Quaker party attempted to mobilize large numbers of Germans at the polls (pp. 65-66). For the authorship of the pamphlet see Benjamin H. Newcomb, *Franklin and Galloway: A Political Partnership* (New Haven, Conn., 1972), pp. 29n-30n.

138. William Allen to John Penn, March 27, 1741, Penn Papers, Official Correspondence, III, 143; Smith, *A Brief State*, pp. 27-28.

139. For two interpretations of the riot see Norman S. Cohen, "The Philadelphia Election Riot of 1742," *PMHB*, 92 (1968), 306-319 and William T. Parsons, "The Bloody Election of 1742," *Pennsylvania History*, 36 (1969), 290-306. The most intense pamphleteering since the late 1720s had preceded the election. See Evans, *American Bibliography*, nos. 4987, 5034, 5075, 40284, 40307, 40319, and 40271.

140. Richard Hockley to Thomas Penn, Nov. 1, 1742 and Nov. 18, 1742, Penn Papers, Official Correspondence, III, 241-243; Richard Peters to Thomas Penn, Nov. 17, 1742, Peters Letter Book, 1737-1750.

141. Pennsylvania Assembly Committee report, Sept. 11, 1753, in *Papers of Franklin*, V, 47. In 1743, for example, William Allen, a proprietary leader, ran in the Philadelphia election and received 3 of the 1,028 votes cast. Isaac Norris to Robert Charles, Oct. 2, 1743, Norris Letter Book, 1719-1756, HSP. In 1750, a record number of voters turned out—more than 2,000; but this was "occasion'd by a Contest for the Sheriff's Place." John Smith to Elizabeth Hudson, Oct. 10, 1750, John Smith Correspondence, 1740-1770, p. 27, HSP.

142. This episode is ably told in Robert L. D. Davidson, *War Comes to Quaker Pennsylvania, 1682-1756* (New York, 1957), chap. 4.

143. *Papers of Franklin*, III, 200-201.

144. Ibid., 184, 205.

145. Ibid., 202.

146. *A Word in Season* . . . (Boston, 1748), in Davis, ed., *Currency Reprints*, IV, 357, 362.

9. Prosperity and Poverty: The Seven Years War and Its Aftermath

1. Max Savelle, "Diplomatic Preliminaries of the Seven Years' War in America," *Canadian Historical Review*, 20 (1939), 22-25; Lawrence Henry Gipson, *The British Empire Before the American Revolution*, vol. V, *Zones of International Friction; North America, South of the Great Lakes Region, 1748-1754* (New York, 1939), chaps. 1-6; Randolph C. Downes, *Council Fires on the Upper Ohio: A Narrative of Indian Affairs in the Upper Ohio Valley until 1795* (Pittsburgh, 1940), chaps. 3-4.

2. Douglas Edward Leach, *Arms For Empire: A Military History of the British Colonies in North America, 1607-1763* (New York, 1973), p. 310.

3. Gipson, *Zones of International Friction*, pp. 113-166.

4. For a good short account see Leach, *Arms for Empire*, pp. 357-360, 362-369.

5. The military history of the American phase of the Seven Years War is most comprehensively covered in Gipson, *The British Empire Before the American Revolution*, vol. VI, *Years of Defeat, 1754-1757*, and vol. VII, *The Victorious Years, 1758-1760* (New York, 1965).

6. Gerald S. Graham, *Empire of the North Atlantic: The Maritime Struggle for North America* (Toronto, 1950), pp. 165, 171-172; Herbert L. Osgood, *The American Colonies in the Eighteenth Century*, 4 vols. (New York, 1924), IV, 395, 435, 452.

7. Virginia D. Harrington, *The New York Merchant on the Eve of the Revolution* (New York, 1935), pp. 290-302.

8. W. T. Baxter, *The House of Hancock: Business in Boston, 1724-1775* (Cambridge, Mass., 1945), pp. 129-146; Stanley McCrory Pargellis, *Lord Loudoun in North America* (New Haven, Conn., 1933), p. 84n. For some shady dealings and windfall profits attributed to New York and Boston merchants see ibid., pp. 135-141.

9. Benjamin H. Newcomb, *Franklin and Galloway: A Political Partnership* (New Haven, Conn., 1972), p. 46.

10. Pargellis, *Lord Loudoun*, p. 290n.

11. Philip L. White, *The Beekmans of New York in Politics and Commerce, 1647-1877* (New York, 1956), pp. 361-407, 641.

12. *Historical Statistics of the United States: Colonial Times to 1970*, 2 vols. (Washington, D.C., 1975), II, 1176, Harry Berg, "Economic Consequences of the French and Indian War for the Philadelphia Merchants," *Pennsylvania History*, 13 (1946), 185-193.

13. Harrington, *New York Merchant*, p. 303.

14. William Smith Papers, II, 412, New York Public Library, quoted in McAnear, "Politics in New York," p. 526.

15. James DeLancey to William Pitt, March 17, 1758, *NYCD*, VII, 343; Stuyvesant Fish, *The New York Privateers, 1756-1763: King George's Private Ships which cruized against the King's Enemies* (New York, 1945), pp. 54-82.

16. James G. Lydon, *Pirates, Privateers, and Profits* (Upper Saddle River,

N.J., 1970), pp. 157-159; Harrington, *New York Merchant*, pp. 303-305.

17. Bridenbaugh, *Cities in Revolt*, pp. 63-64, 335, 338.

18. Harrington, *New York Merchant*, p. 308. Lydon, *Pirates, Privateers, and Profits*, pp. 157-159. Lydon's analysis shows that an average of eighty-one prizes per year were taken from 1756 to 1759. This dropped to nineteen per year in the last four years of the war.

19. Harrington, *New York Merchant*, pp. 308-309; Victor L. Johnson, "Fair Traders and Smugglers in Philadelphia, 1754-1763, *PMHB*, 83 (1959), 125-149; Thomas C. Barrow, *Trade and Empire: The British Customs Service in Colonial America, 1660-1775* (Cambridge, Mass., 1967), pp. 160-173.

20. Milton M. Klein, "The Rise of the New York Bar: The Legal Career of William Livingston," *WMQ*, 15 (1958), 348-349; Gipson, *The Great War for Empire*, vol. VIII: *The Culmination, 1760-1763* (New York, 1965), p. 81. Spence's account of his mistreatment is in Philadelphia Custom House Papers, III, 345, HSP.

21. Richard Pares, *War and Trade in the West Indies, 1739-1763* (London, 1963), pp. 426, 437-446.

22. Barrow, *Trade and Empire*, pp. 160-163; Nicholas B. Wainwright, "Governor William Denny in Pennsylvania," *PMHB*, 74 (1950), 457-472; Pares, *War and Trade*, pp. 446-468.

23. Hamilton to William Pitt, Nov. 1, 1760, in Gertrude S. Kimball, ed., *Correspondence of William Pitt when Secretary of State with Colonial Governors and Military and Naval Commanders in America*, 2 vols (New York, 1906), II, 352.

24. Virginia D. Harrington, "The Merchants Ledger," in Alexander C. Flick, ed., *History of the State of New York*, 4 vols. (New York, 1933), II, 334.

25. *New-York Mercury*, Aug. 7, 1758, cited in Richard B. Morris, *Government and Labor in Early America* (New York, 1946), p. 194.

26. William S. Sachs, "The Business Outlook in the Northern Colonies, 1750-1775" (Ph.D. diss., Columbia University, 1957), pp. 97-98.

27. Gerard Beekman to Powel and Wiley, Nov. 19, 1756, in Philip L. White, *The Beekman Mercantile Papers, 1746-1799*, 3 vols. (New York, 1956), I, 285.

28. Gipson, *The Victorious Years*, pp. 69-70; Earl of Loudoun to Duke of Cumberland, June 22, 1757, in Stanley McC. Pargellis, ed., *Military Affairs in North America, 1748-1765* (New York, 1936), p. 376.

29. Jesse Lemisch, "Jack Tar in the Streets: Merchant Seamen in the Politics of Revolutionary America," *WMQ*, 25 (1968), 383; Paul L. Ford, ed., *The Journal of Hugh Gaine, Printer*, 2 vols. (New York, 1902), II, 8-9.

30. For New York mariners' pay see Jesse Lemisch and John K. Alexander, "The White Oaks, Jack Tar, and the Concept of the 'Inarticulate,' " *WMQ*, 29 (1972), 122, 124. For mariners' wages in Philadelphia see Appendix, Table 2.

31. *NYHS Coll., 1891* (New York, 1892), pp. 503-504, 513, 516; Gipson, *The Victorious Years*, p. 70.

32. Lord Loudoun to the Duke of Cumberland, June 22, 1757, in Pargellis, *Military Affairs*, p. 376.

33. Lydon, *Pirates, Privateers, and Profits*, pp. 124, 197.

34. Ibid., p. 208; Lemisch, "Jack Tar," p. 397n for estimates of the number

of seamen. Many privateersmen were countrymen who did not live in the city but flocked there only to ship out on the sea raiders. Loudoun's estimate of 3,000 privateering sailors in 1757 was roughly 75 for each ship. If that average applied to all of New York's 224 privateers and each sailor served on two ships during the war, then about 8,400 men were involved.

35. Theodore G. Thayer, "The Army Contractors for the Niagara Campaign, 1755-1756," *WMQ*, 14 (1957), 34.

36. John Gorham Palfrey, *History of New England*, 5 vols. (Boston, 1865-90), V, 159; Osgood, *American Colonies*, IV, 395, 435, 452.

37. In 1753 there were 1,991 houses in New York. Thomas Pownal, *A Topographical Description of the Dominions of the United States of America . . .* , ed. Lois Mulkearn (Pittsburgh, 1949), p. 44. In 1760, according to Bridenbaugh, there were about 2,600 houses. *Cities in Revolt*, p. 226. The number of houses in Philadelphia grew from about 2,300 in 1753 to 2,969 in 1760. John K. Alexander, "The Philadelphia Numbers Game: An Analysis of Philadelphia's Eighteenth-Century Population," *PMHB*, 98 (1974), 324. Construction craftsmen's wages moved up from about 4 to 5 shillings per day during the war. This can best be traced in the ledgers and account books of master carpenter Isaac Zane and merchant Isaac Norris (1752-1761), HSP.

38. From 1714 to 1717 ship clearances from Boston had averaged 415 annually. From 1753 to 1755 they averaged 447 per year. For tonnage see Appendix, Figure 2.

39. Joel A. Shufro, "Boston in Massachusetts Politics, 1730-1760" (Ph.D. diss., University of Wisconsin, 1976), pp. 216-217.

40. *BTR*, XIV, 280; Shufro, "Boston in Massachusetts Politics," pp. 296-297, 330 for codfish exports.

41. Writing in the *Boston Gazette*, June 9, 1755, "J.T." described the growing cost of supporting the poor and the flight of well-to-do persons.

42. The reports of various craft leaders to the selectmen regarding the decline of their trades are in Massachusetts Archives, CXVII, 58-60, 67. The selectmen's petition to the legislature, based on these reports, is in *BTR*, XIV, 280-281.

43. *BTR*, XIV, 303; for another report of widespread unemployment, indebtedness, and economic decay see *Boston Gazette* April 18, 1757.

44. For seamen's wages see Appendix, Figure 6. Wages for seamen serving on the province ship were lower than for merchant seamen, ranging from 27 to 40 shillings per month. This was less than half the rate paid in New York. Boston ship carpenters on provincial service commanded about 30 shillings per month in 1755 but about double that after 1757, when the demand for bateaux builders on Lake Champlain and Ontario brought real gains to this craft. The Massachusetts wages still did not compare with the £12 per month (£9 converted to Massachusetts currency) paid in New York. For provincial wage rates see *Journals of the House of Representatives of Massachusetts, 1754-1755* (Boston, 1956), p. 285; *1757* (Boston, 1960), p. 334; *1758-1759* (Boston, 1963), p. 190; *1761* (Boston, 1966), p. 58.

45. William B. Weeden, *Economic and Social History of New England*, 2 vols. (New York, 1963; 1890), II, 678.

46. For commodity prices in Boston see Ruth Crandall, "Wholesale Commodity Prices at Boston, 1700-1795," in Arthur Harrison Cole, *Wholesale Com-*

modity Prices in the United States, 1700-1861 (Cambridge, Mass., 1938), p. 7 and Chart 4. Wheat prices are charted in Appendix, Figure 6.

47. For bankruptcy notices see Bridenbaugh, *Cities in Revolt*, p. 61. The town report is in *BTR*, XIV, 302.

48. Calculated from the annual report of town treasurer regarding disbursements to the overseers of the poor, in *BTR*, passim, and Overseers of the Poor Account Book, 1738-1769, MHS. For comparative figures on poor taxes in the three seaports see Gary B. Nash, "Urban Wealth and Poverty in Pre-Revolutionary America," *Journal of Interdisciplinary History*, 6 (1976), 555-558.

49. For tax flight, Baxter, *House of Hancock*, p. 135, and *Journals of the House of Representatives of Massachusetts, 1757* (Boston, 1961), p. 133. Mary Roys Baker, "Anglo-Massachusetts Trade Union Roots, 1130-1790," *Labor History*, 14 (1973), 394-395 notes the £3,000 loan.

50. Baxter, *House of Hancock*, p. 130.

51. Gipson, *The Victorious Years*, pp. 71, 145; Pargellis, *Lord Loudoun*, pp. 99-100, 235n; Osgood, *American Colonies*, IV, 377. Population figures are from *Historical Statistics of the United States, Colonial Times to 1970*, 2 vols. (Washington, D.C., 1975), II, 1191.

52. Memorial of William Bollan to the King, April 11, 1764, quoted in Palfrey, *History of New England*, V, 143n. For a full report on the 8,000 men raised for various kinds of provincial service in 1755 see Massachusetts General Court to William Bollan, Sept. 26, 1755, *Correspondence of William Shirley, Governor of Massachusetts and Military Commander in American, 1731-1760*, ed. Charles H. Lincoln, 2 vols. (New York, 1912), II, 285.

53. For the increase in antipapist sermon literature at mid-century see Nathan O. Hatch, *The Second Cause of Liberty: Republican Thought and the Millennium in Revolutionary New England* (New Haven, Conn., 1977), pp. 39-43.

54. Records detailing the compensation of Philadelphia masters whose servants enlisted in the British army are in "List of Servants Belonging to the Inhabitants of Pennsylvania & Taken into His Majesty's Service, 1757," HSP (copy of original at Henry Huntington Library, San Marino, Ca.).

55. "Muster Rolls of the New York Provincial Troops," *NYHS Coll., 1881* (New York, 1882), pp. 162-167, 170-175, 206-213, 292-309, 374-379. At one critical point in the war, after the surrender of Fort William Henry in Aug. 1757, 700 volunteers from the city enlisted to march to the relief of their captured compatriots. *New-York Mercury*, Aug. 22, 1757, printed ibid., pp. 512-513. Muster rolls for Philadelphia in 1757 and 1758 are printed in *Pennsylvania Archives*, 2d ser., II (Harrisburg, Pa., 1890), 484-485, 487-488, 491-494.

56. Based on an occupational analysis of the muster rolls cited in note 55. I am indebted to Ronald Schultz of the University of California, Los Angeles for analyzing the New York data. Mariners and laborers composed 48 and 60 percent respectively of New York's and Philadelphia's units. When the lower artisans (shoemakers, tailors, and weavers) are added, the percentages rise to 64 and 76 respectively.

57. Massachusetts Archives, XCIV, 161, 193, 333. Bounties offered in Massachusetts and New York are listed below. The Massachusetts bounties have been extracted from the *House Journals*; the New York bounties from "Muster

Rolls for the New York Provincial Troops," *NYHS Coll., 1881*. The New York values have been reduced by one-fourth because of the difference in par exchange for the two currencies. See "A State of the Exchange in the British North American Colonys . . . ," in Pargellis, *Military Affairs*, p. 42.

Year	Massachusetts	New York
1755	2s 8d to 8s	£ 1 4s 5d
1756	16s	£ 3 15s
1757	16s	£ 3 15s
1758	£ 1 6s 8d	£ 7 10s
1759	£ 10 6s 8d	£ 11 5s
1760	£ 9	£ 11 5s
1762	£ 9	£ 11 5s
1763	£ 7	£ 7 10s

58. Alan Heimert, *Religion and the American Mind from the Great Awakening to the Revolution* (Cambridge, Mass., 1966), p. 91.

59. Muster Rolls for Crown Point Expedition, Massachusetts Archives, XCIV, 140-568. I am indebted to Sally McMahon of Brandeis University for analyzing these lists.

60. Massachusetts Archives, XCIV, 14-127 (1755); XCV, 1-206 (1756); XCV, 246-552 and XCVI, 2-48, 52-88 (1757); XCVI, 181-534 and XCVII, 5-70 (1758); XCVII, 87-235 (1759); XCVIII, 154-417 (1760). The age of recruits is based on the lists for 1756, 1759, and 1761, where the ages of 775 Boston men are given.

61. J. H. Benton, Jr., *Early Census Making in Massachusetts, 1643-1765* . . . (Boston, 1905), pp. 74-75. Boston's adult sex ratio (males to females) was .814, an imbalance approximated in other maritime towns such as Marblehead (.836), Ipswich (.787), and Gloucester (.836).

62. Ibid.

63. Bridenbaugh, *Cities in Revolt*, pp. 101-102; *Boston Post-Boy*, April 28, 1760.

64. Warden, *Boston*, pp. 149-151. The records of losses, which categorize the victims as rich, middling, and poor, are in Am 1809, Boston Public Library. Another report, listing 439 "sufferers" and the aid distributed to each, is in *BTR*, XXIX, 89-100.

65. £ 13,317 was distributed to the fire victims and much of this must eventually have gone to artisans in the building trades in wages. Bridenbaugh, *Cities in Revolt*, p. 102.

66. Appendix, Figure 2.

67. Barrow, *Trade and Empire*, pp. 160-185; Arthur M. Schlesinger, *The Colonial Merchants and the American Revolution, 1763-1776* (New York, 1968; 1918), pp. 15-60.

68. Leslie J. Thomas, "Partisan Politics in Massachusetts during Governor Bernard's Administration, 1760-1770" (Ph.D. diss., University of Wisconsin, 1960), pp. 25-51. What made the molasses duty even more unacceptable was the fact that after the British captured Guadaloupe in 1759 and Martinique in 1761 the sugar trade from these French islands became duty-free, since they were regarded, until the Peace of Paris, as British possessions. By 1762 thirty-six Boston

vessels had entered from the French sugar islands. Dorothy Burne Goebel, "The 'New England Trade' and the French West Indies, 1763-1774: A Study in Trade Policies," *WMQ*, 20 (1963), 333. In addition, a lucrative provisioning trade from Boston and satellite ports to the French Windward Islands, allowed by the French in 1763, was strangled by orders from England about the time the Sugar Act of 1764 was taking effect. Goebel, " 'New England Trade,' " pp. 343-348.

69. Schlesinger, *Colonial Merchants*, p. 57. Adding to Boston's difficulties in 1764 was another smallpox epidemic, which left business at a standstill from Jan. to April. *Journals of the House of Representatives of Massachusetts, 1764-1765* (Boston, 1971), pp. 56-57; Samuel G. Drake, *The History and Antiquities of Boston* (Boston, 1856), pp. 677-678. Drake, writing at mid-nineteenth century, considered 1764 a year "of great depression to the town."

70. A. E. Brown, *John Hancock, His Book* (Boston, 1898), pp. 61-62, quoted in Sachs, "Business Outlook," p. 132n.

71. *Boston Post-Boy*, June 3, 1765, cited in Schlesinger, *Colonial Merchants*, p. 57; Bridenbaugh, *Cities in Revolt*, p. 281.

72. James and Drinker to John Clitherall, May 9, 1760, James and Drinker Letter Book, 1759-1762, HSP. The fullest analysis of the depression is in Marc M. Egnal, "The Pennsylvania Economy, 1748-1762: An Analysis of Short-Run Fluctuations in the Context of Long-Run Changes in the Atlantic Trading Community" (Ph.D. diss., University of Wisconsin, 1964).

73. *The Late Regulations respecting the British Colonies . . .* (Philadelphia, 1765), quoted in Marc Egnal and Joseph A. Ernst, "An Economic Interpretation of the American Revolution," *WMQ*, 29 (1972), 17, where the postwar depression is also analyzed.

74. The number of immigrant ships is taken from Ralph Beaver Strassburger, *Pennsylvania German Pioneers: A Publication of the Original Lists of Arrivals in the Port of Philadelphia from 1727 to 1808*, ed. William John Hinke, I (Pennsylvania German Society, *Publications*, 42 [Norristown, Pa., 1934]), pp. xxix-xxxi; and R. J. Dickson, *Ulster Emigration to Colonial American, 1718-1775* (London, 1966), Appendix E.

75. The Cherokee, Delaware, and Shawnee resistance movements of 1758-1761 and Pontiac's pan-Indian movement of 1763-1765 have not been sufficiently explored as possible causes of the bottling up of the new immigrants flooding into the colonies after 1760. For information on these Indian resistance movements see Downes, *Council Fires on the Upper Ohio*; David H. Corkran, *The Cherokee Frontier: Conflict and Survival, 1740-1762* (Norman, Okla., 1962); and C. A. Weslager, *The Delaware Indians: A History* (New Brunswick, N.J., 1972).

76. James and Drinker to Devonshire and Reeve, Dec. 14, 1763, quoted in Arthur L. Jensen, *The Maritime Commerce of Colonial Philadelphia* (Madison, Wis., 1963), p. 121; Egnal, "Pennsylvania Economy," pp. 217-224; Sachs, "Business Outlook," pp. 128-131.

77. The number of houses in Philadelphia, including Southwark and the Northern Liberties, grew from 2,969 to 4,474 between 1760 and 1769. Alexander, "Philadelphia Numbers Game," p. 324. In 1772 about 11 percent of Philadelphia's artisans were in the house construction trades. See Appendix, Table 1.

78. Harrington, *New York Merchant*, pp. 316-324; Gipson, *The Culmination*, p. 188.

79. Watts to Francis Clarke, Jan. 2, 1762, *Letterbook of John Watts: Merchant and Councillor of New York*, in *NYHS Coll., 1928* (New York, 1929), p. 6.

80. Watts to Scott, Pringle, Cheap and Co., Feb. 5, 1764, ibid., p. 228.

81. Sachs, "Business Outlook," p. 133.

82. Quoted in Harrington, *New York Merchant*, p. 323.

83. The continuing vigor of the shipbuilding industry can be inferred from the rise the ship registrations from 477 (19,514 tons) in 1762 to 709 (29,132 tons) in 1772. Harrington, "The Merchant's Ledger," in Flick, ed. *History of New York*, II, 334. Between 1753 and 1766 the number of houses in New York increased from 1,991 to 3,223. Almost all of this construction must have come during the war, for in 1764 the *New-York Gazette* reported that there were more unrented houses in the city than at any time in the previous seven years. After the war the city's population grew very slowly. The number of houses in 1753 was reported in Pownall, *A Topographical Description*, p. 44. For a count of houses by ward and the *Gazette* report see Esther Singleton, *Social New York under the Georges, 1714-1776* (New York, 1969; 1902), p. 4.

84. Edward Shippen to James Hamilton, Sept. 22, 1760, Balch Papers, HSP.

85. Marc Egnal, "The Business Cycle in Colonial America," paper presented at the Annual Meeting of the Organization of American Historians, April 18, 1975, pp. 5, 24.

86. Anne Bezanson and others, *Prices in Colonial Pennsylvania* (Philadelphia, 1935), pp. 14-15, 18-19, 38-39, 397, 403. William S. Sachs, "Agricultural Conditions in the Northern Colonies Before the Revolution," *Journal of Economic History*, 13 (1953), 275-276.

87. Billy G. Smith, "Struggles of the Independent Poor: The Living Standards of Philadelphia's 'Lower Sort' During the Last Half of the Eighteenth Century," unpub. ms., Table VI.

88. "Plebeanus" is quoted in Max G. Schumacher, *The Northern Farmer and His Markets during the Late Colonial Period* (New York, 1975), pp. 136-137. Rising food prices in New York are also treated in Harrington, *New York Merchant*, pp. 283-284. Wholesale commodity prices at New York closely paralleled those in Philadelphia. See Herman M. Stoker, "Wholesale Prices at New York City, 1720-1800," Cornell University Experimental Station *Memoir* no. 142, pt. II (Ithaca, N.Y., 1932). For the doubling of living costs in Philadelphia see Franklin to Richard Jackson, March 8, 1763, *Papers of Franklin*, X, 209. Franklin wrote that many items, including house rent, had tripled since 1757 when he had left Philadelphia for England.

89. Sachs, "Agricultural Conditions," pp. 284-285. A series of poor crops in England and southern Europe greatly increased the demand for American grains beginning in 1764.

90. By 1763 Philadelphia's most famous naturalist, John Bartram, claimed that Pennsylvania lands had been cleared "quite to the mountains (about one hundred miles inland). "What our people will do for fencing and firewood fifty years hence, I can't imagine." Quoted in Bridenbaugh, *Cities in Revolt*, p. 232.

91. *Pennsylvania Gazette*, Jan. 10, 1760.

92. Firewood consumption is difficult to measure and varied greatly with weather conditions. But larger homes probably used about twenty-five cords in a

normal winter, with lower-class families, living in much smaller quarters, consuming one-quarter to one-third as much. Smith, "Struggles of the Independent Poor," p. 16.

93. *New-York Gazette*, Jan. 22, 1761, cited in Bridenbaugh, *Cities in Revolt*, p. 233.

94. For a fuller description of the wood stamp program instituted in the winter of 1761-1762 see Gary B. Nash, "Poverty and Poor Relief in Pre-Revolutionary Philadelphia," *WMQ*, 33 (1976), 12-13. For a Philadelphia wood prices series see Nash, "Up From the Bottom in Franklin's Philadelphia," *Past and Present*, no. 77 (1977), p. 75n.

95. *Pennsylvania Gazette*, Jan. 24 and 31, 1765; Nash, "Poverty and Poor Relief," p. 14.

96. Appendix, Table 11.

97. Quoted in Palfrey, *History of New England*, V, 159. For 1759 and 1760, Bridenbaugh, *Cities in Revolt*, p. 220.

98. Jonathan Mayhew, *God's Hand and Providence to be Religiously Acknowledged . . .* (Boston, 1760). p. 18.

99. Ibid. Twice, in 1757 and 1764, the General Court agreed to rebate £ 4,000 in taxes, convinced by the town that the capital had been "brought to the brink of utter Ruin." Baker, "Anglo-Massachusetts Trade Union Roots," p. 395.

100. Appendix, Table 11 charts the rise of the total taxes paid by Philadelphians in this era. The land tax in New York, at 4 shillings per pound of assessed property, was almost three times as high as in Philadelphia. Sachs, "Agricultural Conditions," p. 280n.

101. Nash, "Up From the Bottom," p. 77.

102. The names of those excused from taxes were recorded annually in the Philadelphia County Commissioners Minutes, 1718-1766, City Archives, City Hall, Philadelphia; Minutes, 1771-1774, HSP; Minutes, 1774-1776, Tax and Exoneration Records, Pennsylvania State Archives, Harrisburg, Pa.

103. Appendix, Table 5.

104. *BTR*, XIV, 302.

105. Nash, "Urban Wealth and Poverty," 560-564. From 1745 to 1752 an average of 61 persons a year were warned out of Boston. From 1753 to 1764 the average was 173 per year.

106. In 1747, of the 101 in-migrants, 85 percent were married couples and their children. By the height of the war, in 1759, single men and women and widows had begun to take the places of these wandering families, composing 34 percent of the 190 persons warned out. For a fuller analysis see Nash, "Urban Wealth and Poverty," pp. 562-564.

107. Calculated from the Overseers of the Poor Account Book, 1738-1769, MHS and the annual reports of the town treasurer, beginning in 1754, in *BTR*, passim.

108. James Freeman Notebook, June 29, 1764, MHS.

109. *Minutes of the Common Council of the City of New York, 1675-1776*, 8 vols. (New York, 1905), VI, 403-404.

110. Harrington, *New York Merchant*, pp. 146, 331; William R. Bagnall, *The Textile Industries of the United States* (Cambridge, Mass., 1893), p. 52; Schlesinger, *Colonial Merchants*, p. 77.

111. For a table of arriving passenger ships carrying Scots-Irish and Germans see Gary B. Nash, "Slaves and Slaveowners in Colonial Philadelphia," *WMQ*, 30 (1973), 233.

112. For an excellent account of the founding of the hospital see William H. Williams, "The 'Industrious Poor' and the Founding of the Pennsylvania Hospital," *PMHB*, 97 (1973), 431-443. The quotes are from p. 436.

113. Nash, "Poverty and Poor Relief," pp. 7-8. From 1753 to 1757 the hospital treated an average of 53 sick poor annually. In the next two five-year periods the average number treated rose to 128 and 292 respectively.

114. Of the 125 males listed in the committee's disbursement ledger, 32 have been located on the 1756 tax list, which is reprinted in *Pennsylvania Genealogical Magazine*, 22 (1961), 10-41, or on lists of those excused in that year from the county tax in the Philadelphia County Commissioners Minutes, 1747-1766, City Archives, City Hall. Most of these earlier residents who received special aid in 1761-1762 were mariners, tailors, cordwainers, or laborers.

115. *Votes and Proceedings of the House of Representatives of the Province of Pennsylvania*, ed. Gertrude MacKinney, *Pennsylvania Archives*, 8th ser., 8 vols. (Harrisburg, Pa., 1931-35), VII, 5506, 5535-5536.

116. Two broadsides announced the plans for the linen manufactory and spelled out the unemployment problem: *Whereas the Number of Poor In and Around this City* . . . [Philadelphia, 1764] and *A Number of the Inhabitants of this City* . . . [Philadelphia, 1765]. See also *Pennsylvania Journal*, Nov. 28, 1765, Jan. 23, 1766, and *Papers of Franklin*, XI, 314-316, XIII, 252.

117. Nash, "Poverty and Poor Relief," p. 14.

118. *New-York Gazette*, Aug. 26, 1762. For a general treatment of the plight of the middle ranks see Bridenbaugh, *Cities in Revolt*, chap. 7.

119. For New York fortunes see Harrington, *New York Merchant*, pp. 126-135, and Harry B. Yoshpe, *The Disposition of Loyalist Estates in the Southern District of the State of New York* (New York, 1936), pp. 29, 123-131. For Hancock and Bowdoin see respectively Baxter, *House of Hancock*, pp. 223-224, and *Sibley's Harvard Graduates*, XI, 514. For Philadelphians see Carl Bridenbaugh and Jessica Bridenbaugh, *Rebels and Gentlemen: Philadelphia in the Age of Franklin* (New York, 1965), p. 199. Other fortunes are recorded in the inventories, although the absence of data on real estate in the Philadelphia inventories hides much of the wealth of Philadelphia's wealthiest men.

120. Appendix, Tables 3, 4, and 7; Figures 7, 8, and 9.

121. Bridenbaugh and Bridenbaugh, *Rebels and Gentlemen*, p. vii.

122. Margaret B. Tinkcom, "Cliveden: The Building of a Colonial Mansion." *PMHB*, 88 (1964), 3-36.

123. George B. Tatum, *Philadelphian Georgian: The City House of Samuel Powel and Some of Its Eighteenth-Century Neighbors* (Middletown, Conn., 1976), pp. 5-6, 145. In 1769, buffeted by economic misfortune, Charles Stedman sold his mansion for £3,150 to Samuel Powel.

124. Nicholas B. Wainwright, *Colonial Grandeur in Philadelphia: The House and Furniture of General John Cadwalader* (Philadelphia, 1964).

125. L. H. Butterfield, ed., *Diary and Autobiography of John Adams* (New York, 1964), I, 294.

126. For an excellent discussion of this in the house construction trades see

Roger W. Moss, "Master Builders: A History of the Colonial Philadelphia Building Trades" (Ph.D. diss., University of Delaware, 1972), pp. 143-146.

127. E. P. Thompson, "Patrician Society, Plebeian Culture," *Journal of Social History*, 7 (1974), 384.

128. Norris Account Book, 1752-1761, pp. 12, 22-25, HSP. Isaac Zane hired journeymen carpenters for £27 and £35 per year, diet included, at this time. Moss, "Master Builders," p. 143. The unemployment compensation that went with yearly contracts is discussed on pp. 144-145.

129. Norris Account Book, 1752-1761, p. 35.

130. Minutes of the Commissioners for Paving Streets, 1762-1768, HSP. This was a 33 percent drop in wages during a six-year period when the household budget of laborers dropped about 13 percent. Smith, "Struggles of the Independent Poor," Table VI. Almost all the laborers employed by the Street Commissioners have Scots-Irish names.

131. Alfred F. Young, "Pope's Day, Tar and Feathers, and 'Cornet Joyce, jun.': From Ritual to Rebellion in Boston, 1745-1775," unpub. ms., pts. I and II. The next three paragraphs are drawn principally from Young's pathbreaking investigation of artisan culture in Boston during the late colonial years.

132. Ibid., pt. I, p. 4.

133. Ibid., pt. II, pp. 19-20. Thomas's remark, quoted at p. 19, is from "Memoir of Isaiah Thomas," in Thomas, *The History of Printing in America*, 2 vols. (Albany, 1874), I, xxix.

134. Thompson, "Patrician Society, Plebeian Culture," p. 396.

135. *Massachusetts Acts and Resolves*, III, chap. 18 (1752-1753).

136. The best guide to these elite social conventions and institutions is Bridenbaugh, *Cities in Revolt*, chaps. 6 and 9; Bridenbaugh and Bridenbaugh, *Rebels and Gentlemen*, passim; and Stephen Brobeck, "Revolutionary Change in Colonial Philadelphia: The Brief Life of the Proprietary Gentry," *WMQ*, 33 (1976), 410-434. For a study of the way in which the elite employed these social conventions in an attempt to maintain cultural hegemony see T. H. Breen, "Horses and Gentlemen: The Cultural Significance of Gambling among the Gentry of Virginia," *WMQ*, 34 (1977), 239-257.

137. *An Address to the Freeholders and Inhabitants of Massachusetts-Bay* (Boston, 1751), pp. 5-6. The pamphlet was taken almost verbatim from *Cato's Letters*, no. 69, first published in book form in London in 1724; but its virtue, Phileleutheros explained, "is not altogether lost by crossing the Atlantic."

138. *New-York Gazette*, July 11, 1765, quoted in Bernard Friedman, "The Shaping of the Radical Consciousness in Provincial New York," *Journal of American History*, 56 (1970), 794.

10. The Intensification of Factional Politics

1. For example, BTR, XIV, 267 (1755); XIV, 302 (1757); and XVI, 1 (1758). Politics under governor Shirley are surveyed by Robert Zemsky, *Merchants, Farmers, and River Gods: An Essay on Eighteenth-Century American Politics* (Boston, 1971), chap. 6.

2. Bonomi, *Factious People*, Appendix C. Watts replaced Cornelius Van Horne upon the latter's decease, just after the assembly of 1752 convened.

3. The rate of gaining freemanship has been calculated by comparing the number of freemen admitted, as listed in *NYHS Coll., 1885* (New York, 1886),

pp. 179-195, with the estimated adult white male population. A slightly lower rate may have occurred from 1703 to 1711, in the years following the mass admission to freemanship of 271 New Yorkers in 1702. Never again would even half this many be admitted in a single year.

4. Stanley McCrory Pargellis, *Lord Loudoun in North America* (New Haven, Conn., 1933), pp. 198-200.

5. Allen to William Beckford, Nov. 28, 1755, William Allen Letters, 1753-1770, Burd-Shippen-Hubley Papers, HSP. For a more detailed treatment see Ralph L. Ketcham, "Conscience, War, and Politics in Pennsylvania, 1755-1757, *WMQ*, 20 (1963), 416-439.

6. Arthur D. Graeff, *Relations Between the Pennsylvania Germans and British Authorities (1750-1776)* (Philadelphia, 1939), pp. 138-139. For a description of the march see Robert H. Morris to Thomas Penn, Nov. 28, 1755, *Papers of Franklin*, VI, 279-284.

7. Richard Bauman, *For the Reputation of Truth: Politics, Religion and Conflict among the Pennsylvania Quakers, 1750-1800* (Baltimore, 1971), pp. 19-34.

8. James H. Hutson, *Pennsylvania Politics, 1746-1770* (Princeton, N.J., 1972), pp. 6-40.

9. [Smith], *A Brief State of the Province of Pennsylvania . . .* (London, 1755). "Humphry Scourge" has been identified as a "Triumvirate of young Turks composed of Joseph Galloway, George Bryan, and William Franklin. Benjamin H. Newcomb, *Franklin and Galloway: A Political Partnership* (New Haven, Conn., 1972), p. 29. For another attack on the Quakers see *New-York Mercury*, no. 168. The Quakers disclaimed *Tit for Tat*, which was published in New York. *Papers of Franklin*, VI, 390n.

10. *Pennsylvania Journal*, April 22, 1756. Smith counterattacked in the issue of May 20 and in *A Remonstrance of Obadiah Honesty . . .* (Philadelphia 1757). For a general account see Ralph L. Ketcham, "Benjamin Franklin and William Smith: New Light on an Old Philadelphia Quarrel," *PMHB*, 88 (1964), 142-163.

11. [David James Dove], *The Lottery* [Germantown, 1758], pp. 5-6; on Dove see Joseph Jackson, "A Philadelphia Schoolmaster of the Eighteenth Century," *PMHB*, 35 (1911), 315-332.

12. The "Dialogue between X, Y, and Z" is reprinted in *Papers of Franklin*, VI, 295-306. The election for militia officers, held from Dec. 22 to 24, was reported in the *Pennsylvania Gazette*, Dec. 25, 1755. The militia act, reprinted in *Papers of Franklin*, VI, 269-273, was so ambiguously worded that although it stated that "it shall and may be lawful for the Freemen of this Province to form themselves into Companies . . . and for each company, by a Majority of Votes, in the Way of Ballot, to chuse its own Officers," Franklin admitted in the "Dialogue between X, Y, and Z" that "Persons who never intended to engage in the Militia, even Quakers, may meet and vote in the Choice of Officers." Apparently, the entire electorate went to the polls to choose officers. Contrary to James H. Hutson's view that they chose "obscure men" ("An Investigation of the Inarticulate: Philadelphia's White Oaks," *WMQ*, 28 [1971], 12), well-known merchants and master artisans were chosen, most of them occupying positions in the top quarter of the tax list of 1756.

13. Ketcham, "New Light on an Old Quarrel," pp. 151-154.

14. *Papers of Franklin*, VI, 415-418; Hugh Roberts to Franklin, June 1, 1758, ibid., VIII, 83.

15. Robert Janney to the Archbishop of Canterbury, Nov. 27, 1758, Horace Wemyss Smith, ed., *Life and Correspondence of the Rev. William Smith*, 2 vols. (Philadelphia, 1880), I, 185.

16. William Renwick Riddell, "Libel on the Assembly: A Prerevolutionary Episode," *PMHB*, 52 (1928), 176-192, 249-279, 342-360; William S. Hanna, *Benjamin Franklin and Pennsylvania Politics* (Stanford, Ca., 1964), pp. 134-137.

17. William Smith to Archbishop Secker, Nov. 27, 1759, in Smith, ed., *Life and Correspondence of William Smith*, I, 220-227. The Anglican split can be followed in the documents in William Stevens Perry, ed., *Papers Relating to the History of the Church in Pennsylvania, 1680-1778* (n.p., 1871), pp. 295-311, 320-323.

18. [Joseph Galloway], *A True and Impartial State of the Province of Pennsylvania* (Philadelphia, 1759), p. 61; [Smith], *A Brief State*, p. 14n.

19. William Allen to _____, quoted in Theodore Thayer, *Pennsylvania Politics and the Growth of Democracy, 1740-1776* (Harrisburg, Pa., 1953), p. 90; Richard Hockley to Thomas Penn, Aug. 22, 1755, quoted in James H. Hutson, "Benjamin Franklin and Pennsylvania Politics, 1751-1755: A Reappraisal," *PMHB*, 93 (1969), 309n.

20. *Pennsylvania Journal*, March 25, 1756. "Pensylvanus" wrote that because the people in their legislative capacity had too much power and the executive too little, "the lower Sort are not respectful enough of the better Sort; hence the Laws are lax and the Execution of them more so."

21. Ibid., April 15, 1756.

22. *New-York Weekly Mercury*, Feb. 16, 1761. The vote was reported ibid., Feb. 23. Nine years later the *New-York Gazette* reported that there are "above 1500" qualified voters in the city, so virtually every eligible person must have voted in 1761. An account of the election is in William Kelly to Robert H. Morris, Feb. 22, 1761, Robert H. Morris Papers, Box 3, Alexander Library, Rutgers University, New Brunswick, N.J.

23. Shirley to the Lords of Trade, Dec. 1, 1747, *Correspondence of William Shirley, Governor of Massachusetts and Military Commander in America, 1731-1760*, ed. Charles H. Lincoln, 2 vols. (New York, 1912), I, 418.

24. *Boston Gazette*, May 5, May 12, 1760.

25. *BTR*, XVI, 40. Prat and Tyng had taken an unpopular stand in the preceding year, voting to send Thomas Pownall home in the province ship which was build to protect the fishing fleet and coastal trade. *Sibley's Harvard Graduates*, X, 231-232; VII, 598.

26. The best account is Ellen E. Brennan, *Plural Office-Holding in Massachusetts, 1760-1780: Its Relation to the "Separation" of Departments of Government* (Chapel Hill, N.C., 1945), pp. 25-73.

27. John J. Waters, Jr., *The Otis Family in Provincial and Revolutionary Massachusetts* (Chapel Hill, N.C., 1968), pp. 120-125; Hiller B. Zobel, *The Boston Massacre* (New York, 1970), pp. 13-14.

28. Bernard Bailyn, ed., *Pamphlets of the American Revolution*, I (Cambridge, Mass., 1965), 411.

29. William V. Wells, *The Life and Public Services of Samuel Adams . . . ,* 2 vols. (Boston, 1865), I, 44.

30. L. H. Butterfield, ed., *Diary and Autobiography of John Adams* (New York, 1964), I, 260.

31. Hugh F. Bell, "A Personal Challenge': The Otis-Hutchinson Currency Controversy, 1761-1762," *Essex Institute Historical Collections*, 106 (1970), 297-323.

32. The best discussions of Otis's political career from 1761 to 1765 is Waters, *Otis Family*, pp. 132-152.

33. *A Vindication of the Conduct of the House of Representatives . . .* (Boston, 1762) and *The Rights of the British Colonies Asserted and Proved* (Boston, 1764).

34. Bailyn, ed., *Pamphlets of the American Revolution*, I, 414, citing William Tudor, *The Life of James Otis of Massachusetts* (Boston, 1823), p. 172n.

35. "An Impartial Account of the Conduct of the Corkass By a Late Member of that Society," *Boston Evening Post*, March 21, 1763. The Caucus was also attacked in the issues of March 14 and March 28.

36. Butterfield, ed., *Diary of John Adams*, I, 238.

37. *The Conversation of Two Persons under a Window* [Boston, 1765]; a slightly different version is in Tudor, *Life of Otis*, 91-92.

38. *BTR*, XVI, 88.

39. G. B. Warden, "The Caucus and Democracy in Colonial Boston," *New England Quarterly*, 43 (1970), 19-33; Alan and Katherine Day, "Another Look at the Boston 'Caucus,' " *Journal of American Studies*, 5 (1971), 19-42.

40. *Boston Evening Post*, March 7, 1763.

41. Tom Thumb [Samuel Waterhouse], *Proposals for Printing, . . . by Subscription the History of Vice-Admiral Thomas Brazen . . .* ([Boston], 1760).

42. *Boston Gazette*, Dec. 28, 1761; [Oxenbridge Thacher], *Considerations on the Election of Counsellors, Humbly Offered to the Electors* ([Boston], 1761).

43. *Boston Evening Post*, March 14, 1763.

44. *Boston Gazette*, Jan. 11, 1762, Supplement.

45. *Boston Evening Post*, March 14, 1763.

46. *Boston Gazette*, Feb. 28, 1763.

47. *Boston Evening Post*, Feb. 14, 1763.

48. Ibid., March 7, 1763.

49. Stephen E. Patterson discusses the "antipartisan theory and partisan reality" of this period in *Political Parties in Revolutionary Massachusetts* (Madison, Wis., 1973), chap. 1.

50. Hutson, *Pennsylvania Politics*, pp. 6-40.

51. Ibid., pp. 41-70; Newcomb, *Franklin and Galloway*, p. 66 calls the trade-off of proprietary taxes for sterling quit-rent payments "the Franklin-Mansfield agreement."

52. Hutson, *Pennsylvania Politics*, pp. 71-80. The quotes from Muhlenberg are on pp. 79-80.

53. Ibid., pp. 80-92; Brooke Hindle, "The March of the Paxton Boys," *WMQ*, 3 (1946), 461-486. The quotation is taken from [Anon.], *The [P]axton Boys, A Farce* (Philadelphia, 1764), in John R. Dunbar, ed., *The Paxton Papers* (The Hague, 1957), p. 161.

54. Hutson, *Pennsylvania Politics*, p. 103.

55. Ibid., p. 119.

56. Ibid., pp. 96-104, quotation p. 97. Many of the pamphlets in the fiery

Quaker-Presbyterian paper war are collected in Dunbar, ed., *Paxton Papers*.

57. The campaign for royal government is analyzed in detail in Hutson, *Pennsylvania Politics*, pp. 122-177.

58. Franklin followed *Explanatory Remarks* with *Cool Thoughts on the Present State of Public Affairs*. Both Pamphlets are in *Papers of Franklin*, XI, 134-144 and 153-173, along with other materials relating to his public opinion offensive.

59. Quoted in Hutson, *Pennsylvania Politics*, p. 126.

60. Hutson works out the mathematics of the signature gathering, ibid., pp. 127-128.

61. Even his prolonged absence in England from 1756 to 1762 did not keep Franklin from being elected to the assembly as a representative for Philadelphia.

62. *The Plain Dealer . . . No. III* (Philadelphia, 1764), in Dunbar, ed., *Paxton Papers*, p. 369; William Bingham to John Gibson, May 4, 1764, Shippen Family Papers, VI, 97a, HSP; John Penn to Thomas Penn, May 5, 1764, Penn Papers, Official Correspondence, IX, 220, HSP. Penn claimed the petitions were carried around the town by merchant Thomas Wharton, silversmith Philip Syng, and barber Philip Knowles—a neat cross-section of the upper, middle, and lower classes.

63. [Hugh Williamson], *What is Sauce for a Goose is also Sauce for a Gander* [Philadelphia, 1764], in *Papers of Franklin*, XI, 380-384. A sampling of the electoral polemics is ibid., pp. 369-390. Much of the pamphlet literature is described in J. Philip Gleason, "A Scurrilous Colonial Election and Franklin's Reputation," *WMQ*, 18 (1961), 68-84.

64. *The Scribbler . . .* ([Philadelphia], 1764), in *Papers of Franklin*, XI, 387-390.

65. [Isaac Hunt], *A Letter From a Gentleman in Transilvania To his Friend in America . . .* (New York, 1764), p. 4.

66. [Isaac Hunt], *A Humble Attempt at Scurrility* (Philadelphia, 1765), pp. 36-37.

67. Samuel Powel to George Roberts, Nov. 24, 1764, quoted in Gleason, "A Scurrilous Election," p. 82n.

68. William Bingham to John Gibson, May 4, 1764, Shippen Family Papers, VI, 97a.

69. [Hunt], *A Humble Attempt at Scurrility*, pp. 39-41; [Anon.], *A Conference Between the D . . . L and Doctor D . . E* [Philadelphia, 1764]; [Anon.], *Exercises at Scurrility Hall . . .* (Philadelphia, 1764); *An Answer to the Plot* [Philadelphia, 1764]; [Williamson], *What is Sauce for the Goose*.

70. *Observations on a Late Epitaph . . .* (Philadelphia, [1764]).

71. *Pennsylvania Gazette*, Feb. 6, 1765.

72. Hutson, *Pennsylvania Politics*, pp. 153-154, 130-131.

73. Ibid., pp. 155-156; Samuel Purviance, Jr., to James Burd, Sept. 10, 1764, Shippen Family Papers, I.

74. Hutson, *Pennsylvania Politics*, pp. 162-167; Theodore Tappert and John W. Doberstein, trans. and eds., *The Journals of Henry Melchior Muhlenberg*, 3 vols (Philadelphia, 1942-45), II, 91, 99-102, 106-107, 123. For some of the pamphlets Sauer printed in German see Evans, *American Bibliography*, nos. 9575, 9578, 9828.

75. The campaign for royal government also lost laboring-class support because three of the popular party leaders—Isaac Norris, Joseph Richardson, and John Dickinson—fled the ranks on this touchy issue. David L. Jacobson, "John Dickinson's Fight against Royal Government, 1764," *WMQ*, 19 (1962), 64-85.

76. John Dickinson, *A Speech Delivered in the House of Assembly . . .* (Philadelphia, 1764), p. iv. The statement is contained in a preface to Dickinson's pamphlet written by William Smith. The proprietary party had also inveighed against the Franklin-Galloway petition gatherers who appealed to the lower class in John Dickinson, *A Reply to a Piece called the Speech of Joseph Galloway . . .* (Philadelphia, 1764), pp. 32-33; and [Williamson], *The Plain Dealer; Number II, or, A Few Remarks upon Quaker Politicks . . .* (Philadelphia, 1764), p. 7.

77. How many more signatures were obtained in Philadelphia during the summer of 1764 is unclear but it was probably enough to exceed the 1,650 votes that the pro-royal government leaders were able to harvest. Hutson, *Pennsylvania Politics*, pp. 127-128.

78. Newcomb, *Franklin and Galloway*, pp. 94-98; Hutson, *Pennsylvania Politics*, pp. 173-175.

79. Samuel Purviance, Jr., to James Burd, Sept. 10, 1764, Shippen Family Papers, I; Hugh Neill to the Secretary of the Society for the Propagation of the Gospel, Oct. 18, 1764, Perry ed., *History of the Church in Pennsylvania*, p. 365.

80. [Hunt], *A Letter From a Gentleman in Transilvania*, p. 10; James Pemberton to John Fothergill, Oct. 11, 1764, Pemberton Papers, HSP.

81. Tappert and Doberstein, eds., *Journals of Muhlenberg*, II, 122-123; William B. Reed, *Life and Correspondence of Joseph Reed*, 2 vols. (Philadelphia, 1847), I, 36-37; William Logan to John Smith, Oct. 4, 1764, John Smith Papers, HSP; *Papers of Franklin*, XI, 390-391. For another account of the election see Newcomb, *Franklin and Galloway*, pp. 97-100.

82. *The Election Medley* (Philadelphia, 1764). The "Steps" refers to the two-way staircase that led to the balcony of the courthouse where voters cast their ballots. The "trial for the stairs" had become a familiar part of election-day jousting in Philadelphia. Sister Joan de Lourdes Leonard, "Elections in Colonial Pennsylvania," *WMQ*, 11 (1954), 393-394.

83. For the election results see *Papers of Franklin*, XI, 394. Franklin was defeated twice—in the Philadelphia county election, where he ran thirteenth among fourteen candidates and in the city election, where he ran third among four candidates. Philadelphia voters cast ballots in both the county election, where eight assemblymen were elected, and in the city election, where two burgesses were elected to the assembly. Franklin's comment on the election was included in his *Remarks on a Late Protest . . .* (Philadelphia, 1764), in *Papers of Franklin*, XI, 434. William Smith retorted in *An Answer to Mr. Franklin's Remarks on a Late Protest* (Philadelphia, 1764) that the "wretched Rabble" that Franklin claimed had defeated him were the "industrious Germans." Thus Franklin and Smith reversed positions from the 1750s on ethnic stereotyping.

84. Franklin to Richard Jackson, Oct. 16, 1764, *Papers of Franklin*, XI, 397; Tappert and Doberstein, eds., *Journals of Muhlenberg*, II, 122-123.

85. Quoted in Hutson, *Pennsylvania Politics*, p. 171. Another report sighed that "the riotous Presbyterians" had deprived Franklin of his assembly seat by "Illicit Arts and Contrivances." Peter Collinson to Lord Hyde, Oct. 11,

1764, Collinson-Bartram Papers, American Philosophical Society, Philadelphia.

86. The city election results are recorded in Isaac Norris Journal, 1764, Rosenbach Foundation, Philadelphia. The quotation is from William Allen, as paraphrased in Edmund S. Morgan and Helen M. Morgan, *The Stamp Act Crisis: Prologue to Revolution* (New York, 1963; 1953), p. 308.

11. The Stamp Act in the Port Towns

1. Alfred F. Young, "Pope's Day, Tar and Feathers, and 'Cornet Joyce, jun.': From Ritual to Rebellion in Boston, 1745-1775," unpub. ms., pt. III, 2.

2. The best account of the Aug. 14 demonstration is Dirk Hoerder, *Crowd Action in Revolutionary Massachusetts, 1765-1780* (New York, 1977), pp. 97-101. On MacIntosh see George P. Anderson, "Ebenezer Mackintosh, Stamp Act Rioter and Patriot," *CSM Pub.*, 26 (1924-1926), 15-64.

3. Young, "From Ritual to Rebellion," pt. III, 3-4. One account says that the crowd had perpetrated "some small insults such as breaking the windows of the kitchen" but would have stopped "had not some indiscretions been committed by his [Oliver's] friends within which so enraged the people that they were not to be restrained from entering the house." James Freeman Notebook, 1745-1765, MHS. The presence of tradesmen was noted by Hutchinson, *History of Massachusets*, III (London, 1828), 120.

4. On Aug. 17 a crowd had appeared at Hutchinson's house but had been persuaded to leave. For an analysis of the events leading up to Aug. 26 see Hoerder, *Crowd Action*, pp. 101-104.

5. Ibid., pp. 104-110; Young, "From Ritual to Rebellion," pt. III, 5-7.

6. William Gordon, *The History of the Rise, Progress, and Establishment of the Independence of the United States of America . . .*, 4 vols. (London, 1788), I, 178. The legislature later passed an act reimbursing Hutchinson for £3,195 damages but the law was disallowed. Anderson, "Mackintosh," p. 34n. This was the beginning of a period so psychologically traumatic for Hutchinson that twenty months later he suffered a serious nervous breakdown. Bernard Bailyn, *The Ordeal of Thomas Hutchinson* (Cambridge, Mass., 1974), p. 28.

7. For analyses of how historians of revolutionary America have treated the crowd see Edward Countryman, "The Problem of the Early American Crowd," *Journal of American Studies*, 7 (1973), 77-90; and Jesse Lemisch, "Radical Plot in Boston (1770): A Study in the Use of Evidence," *Harvard Law Review*, 84 (1970), 485-504.

8. Quoted in Leslie J. Thomas, "Partisan Politics in Massachusetts During Governor Bernard's Administration, 1760-1770," (Ph.D. diss., University of Wisconsin, 1960), pp. 181-182.

9. Hoerder, *Crowd Action*, p. 96.

10. Gordon, *History of Independence of the United States*, I, 175.

11. On the morning of Aug. 26 many prominent Bostonians, including Hutchinson, heard that the mob would attack his house and those of Bernard, Story, and Hallowell. Ebenezer Parkman Diary, Aug. 26, 1765, MHS; Hiller B. Zobel, *The Boston Massacre* (New York, 1970), p. 33.

12. [Samuel Waterhouse], *Proposals for Printing by Subscription the History of Adjutant T. Trowel and J. Bluster* [Boston, 1764]. Evans, *American Bibliography*, IV, 82 gives 1766 as the date of publication but the internal references to Otis being elevated to moderator of the town meeting, which occurred in 1763,

indicate that the pamphlet was published in 1764. For the comments of the popular party leaders, *Boston Gazette,* Jan. 11, 1762, Supplement, and April 4, 1763.

13. Henry A. Cushing, ed., *The Writings of Samuel Adams,* 4 vols. (New
York, 1904-08), IV, 67; John C. Miller, *Sam Adams: Pioneer in Propaganda*
(Stanford, Ca., 1960; 1936), pp. 19, 84-86.

14. Hutchinson said the poor lived too well in his article on devaluation in
the *Boston Evening Post,* Dec. 14, 1761. He was quoted and refuted by Otis in
Boston Gazette, Dec. 28, 1761, also printed in William Tudor, *The Life of James
Otis of Massachusetts* (Boston, 1823), p. 99-100.

15. Edmund S. Morgan and Helen M. Morgan, *The Stamp Act Crisis: Prologue to Revolution* (New York, 1963; 1953), pp. 164-167. Thomas, "Partisan
Politics," p. 178n. Hallowell's mansion cost £ 2,000 sterling according to Bernard. Bernard to Thomas Pownall, Aug. 23, 1765, Sparks Manuscripts, IV, 15-
17, Houghton Library, Harvard University. For the "rage-intoxicated rabble" see
Josiah Quincy, Jr., *Reports of Cases Argued in the Superior Court . . . Between
1761 and 1772 . . . ,* ed. Samuel M. Quincy (Boston, 1865), p. 169.

16. Bernard to the Board of Trade, Aug. 31, 1765, in William Cobbett, ed.,
The Parliamentary History of England, XVI (London, 1813), 129-131; Bernard to
Halifax, Aug. 31, 1765, Francis Bernard Papers, IV, 158-160, Houghton Library,
Harvard University, quoted in Bailyn, *Hutchinson,* p. 37n.

17. James Gordon to William Martin, Sept. 10, 1765, *MHS Proc.,* 2d ser.,
XIII (1899-1900), 393; Henry Lloyd to William Butler, Aug. 29. 1765, quoted in
Hoerder, *Crowd Action,* p. 109.

18. *BTR,* XVI, 152.

19. Anderson, "Mackintosh," p. 38. Nor had anyone claimed the £ 100
reward offered for information leading to the conviction of those who attacked
Oliver's house. Zobel, *Boston Massacre,* p. 32.

20. Anderson, "Mackintosh," pp. 25, 29. Nathaniel Coffin, a prerogative
man and wealthy merchant, led a delegation to confer with the sheriff. That one
of Hutchinson's own circle would argue for MacIntosh's release indicates the
apprehension of the wealthy. *Sibley's Harvard Graduates,* XI, 368.

21. Hoerder, *Crowd Action,* pp. 111-113; Thomas Hutchinson, "A Summary of the Disorders . . . ," Massachusetts Archives, XXVI, 182-184.

22. The long-held grudges against Hutchinson were evident even to him. A
month after the destruction of his house he admitted that some of those who in
1749 and 1750 had "threatened me with destruction" had "retained their rancor
ever since and are supposed to have been aiders and abettors if not actors in the
late riot." Hutchinson to Henry Seymour Conway, Oct. 1, 1765, Massachusetts
Archives, XXVI, 155.

23. The phrase is borrowed from Rhys Issac, "Dramatizing the Ideology of
Revolution: Popular Mobilization in Virginia, 1774 to 1776," *WMQ,* 33 (1976),
372.

24. Dirk Hoerder, " 'Mobs, a Sort of Them at Least, Are Constitutional':
The American Revolution, Popular Participation, and Social Change," *Amerika-
studien,* 21 (1976), 303.

25. Pauline Maier, *From Resistance to Revolution: Colonial Radicals and
the Development of American Opposition to Britain, 1765-1776* (New York,
1972), p. 70.

26. Douglass Adair and John A. Schutz, eds., *Peter Oliver's Origin & Pro-*

gress of the American Revolution: A Tory View (Stanford, Ca., 1967), p. 54.

27. Ibid.; Hutchinson to Thomas Pownall, March 8, 1766, Massachusetts Archives, XXVI, 207-214.

28. Quoted in Morgan and Morgan, *Stamp Act Crisis*, p. 180.

29. Anderson, "Mackintosh," p. 43.

30. Quoted in Morgan and Morgan, *Stamp Act Crisis*, p. 181.

31. *History of Massachusets*, III (London, 1828), 140.

32. Morgan and Morgan, *Stamp Act Crisis*, pp. 181-182.

33. Quoted in F. L. Engelman, "Cadwallader Colden and the New York Stamp Act Riots," *WMQ*, 10 (1953), 560-565. For McEvers see Harrington, *New York Merchant*, pp. 24, 30, 132.

34. Engelman, "New York Stamp Act Riots," pp. 566-569; Robert R. Livingston to Gen. Robert Monckton, Nov. 8, 1765, *MHS Coll.*, 4th ser., X, (Boston, 1871), 559-561; Montressor Journal, *NYHS Coll.*, *1881* (New York, 1882), p. 336.

35. Engelman, "New York Stamp Act Riots," pp. 569-570.

36. Montressor Journal, p. 336; Engelman, "New York Stamp Act Riots," pp. 560-561, 571-572.

37. Ibid., pp. 571-573; Livingston to Monckton, Nov. 8, 1765, *MHS Coll.*, 4th ser., X, 559-562. The remainder of this paragraph is reconstructed from Livingston's account and those of Montressor, as cited in note 34 above, and General Thomas Gage, in a letter to Secretary of State Henry Seymour Conway, Nov. 4, 1765, in Clarence E. Carter, ed., *The Correspondence of General Thomas Gage*, 2 vols (New Haven, 1931-1933), I, 71. Engelman provides the best secondary account of the Stamp Act demonstrations in New York.

38. Engelman, "New York Stamp Act Riots," pp. 575-577.

39. Maier, *From Resistance to Revolution*, p. 69; Roger J. Champagne, "The Military Association of the Sons of Liberty," *New-York Historical Society Quarterly*, 41 (1957), 338-350; Champagne, "Liberty Boys and Mechanics of New York City, 1764-1774," *Labor History*, 8 (1967), 115-135.

40. Roger J. Champagne, *Alexander McDougall and the American Revolution in New York* (Schenectady, N.Y., 1975), p. 14.

41. Jesse Lemisch, "New York's Petitions and Resolves of December 1765: Liberals vs. Radicals," *New-York Historical Society Quarterly*, 49 (1965), 313-326.

42. Quoted in Morgan and Morgan, *Stamp Act Crisis*, p. 209. For the split in the Sons of Liberty over the question of exporting without stamps see Champagne, "Liberty Boys," p. 121.

43. Stephen E. Patterson, *Political Parties in Revolutionary Massachusetts* (Madison, Wis., 1973), p. 56.

44. *New-York Gazette*, April 4, 1765, quoted in Bernard Friedman, "The Shaping of the Radical Consciousness in Provincial New York," *Journal of American History*, 56 (1970), 789-790.

45. *New-York Gazette*, June 6, 1765, quoted ibid., p. 790.

46. *New-York Gazette*, Sept. 26, 1765; Friedman, "Radical Consciousness," p. 792.

47. Benjamin H. Newcomb, *Franklin and Galloway: A Political Partnership* (New Haven, Conn., 1972), p. 115. Hughes was one of two pro-royal gov-

ernment candidates who escaped defeat in the election of 1764.

48. For Franklin's role see Verner W. Crane, "Benjamin Franklin and the Stamp Act," *CSM Pub.*, 32 (1933-1937), 56-77. David Hall, Franklin's old printing partner, wrote him that he was implicated in the Stamp Act in the minds of many. Hall to Franklin, Sept. 6, 1765, *Papers of Franklin*, XII, 259.

49. [Samuel Wharton] to Franklin, Oct. 13, 1765, *Papers of Franklin*, XII, 315-316; Benjamin H. Newcomb, "The Stamp Act and Pennsylvania Politics," *WMQ*, 23 (1966), 265.

50. Hughes to Franklin, Oct. 12, 1765, *Papers of Franklin*, XII, 301; Deborah Franklin to Franklin, Nov. 3, 1765, ibid., p. 353. Hughes had written Franklin on Sept. 8, 1765 that he doubted he could "escape the Storm of Presbyterian Rage." Ibid., p. 264.

51. The best account is James H. Hutson, "An Investigation of the Inarticulate: Philadelphia's White Oaks," *WMQ*, 28 (1971), 11-19. I find much to agree with in Jesse Lemisch and John K. Alexander's objections to Hutson's characterization of the ship's carpenters as politically conservative and representative of the laboring classes in general. "The White Oaks, Jack Tar, and the Concept of the 'Inarticulate,' " *WMQ*, 29 (1972), 109-136.

52. Joseph Galloway to Franklin, Sept. 20, 1765, *Papers of Franklin*, XII, 270; William Bradford to New York Sons of Liberty, Feb. 15, 1766, quoted in Francis Von A. Cabeen, "The Society of the Sons of Saint Tammany of Philadelphia," *PMHB*, 25 (1901), 439.

53. The election is fully reported in Newcomb, *Franklin and Galloway*, pp. 119-125. For "Tinkers and Cobblers" see Hutson, *Pennsylvania Politics*, pp. 198-199.

54. More than 4,300 voters from the city and county of Philadelphia went to the polls, about 500 more than in 1764. In the city 1,973 ballots were cast. The vote for county assemblymen is given in *Papers of Franklin*, XII, 291n; the vote count for city burgesses is in Franklin Papers, LXIX, 98, American Philosophical Society. The German leader Muhlenberg described how 600 German voters assembled at the German schoolhouse and then "marched in procession to the *courthouse* to cast their votes"—an impressive example of ethnic bloc voting. Theodore Tappert and John W. Doberstein, eds., *The Journals of Henry Melchior Muhlenberg*, 3 vols. (Philadelphia, 1942-45), II, 73. Franklin was informed that "every Mechanick" who has been associated with turning back the Stamp Act demonstrators had voted for the assembly ticket. But the 902 votes for the opposition demonstrate the impressive laboring vote for the proprietary party. Samuel Wharton to Franklin, Oct. 13, 1765, *Papers of Franklin*, XII, 316.

55. Hughes to the Stamp Commissioners, Oct. 12, 1765, in *Pennsylvania Journal*, Sept. 4, 1766, Supplement. These events are covered fully in Morgan and Morgan, *Stamp Act Crisis*, pp. 313-324. Benjamin Rush reveals that an effigy of Hughes was hung from a gallows in the city. Rush to Ebenezer Hazard, Nov. 8, 1765, in L. H. Butterfield, ed., *Letters of Benjamin Rush*, 2 vols. (Princeton, N.J., 1951), I, 18.

56. Hutson, *Pennsylvania Politics*, p. 200.

57. Thomson to Welsh, Wilkinson & Co., Nov. 7, 1765, *NYHS Coll., 1878* (New York, 1879), pp. 5-6.

58. Arthur L. Jensen, *The Maritime Commerce of Colonial Philadelphia*

(Madison, Wis., 1963), p. 161.

59. Rush to Ebenezer Hazard, Nov. 8, 1765, in Butterfield, ed., *Letters of Benjamin Rush*, I, 18.

60. Hutson, *Pennsylvania Politics*, pp. 214-243 traces the emergence of a Presbyterian-led, artisan-supported radical party.

61. Douglass, *A Letter to [a] Merchant in London . . .* (Boston, 1741), in Davis, ed., *Currency Reprints*, IV, 76.

62. Michael G. Kammen, ed., *The History of the Province of New-York by William Smith, Jr.*, 2 vols. (Cambridge, Mass., 1972), II, 61; Adair and Schutz, eds., *Peter Oliver's Origin & Progress*, p. 65.

63. For considerations of "concepts of crowd behavior" see Hoerder, *Crowd Action*, pp. 1-20; Gordon S. Wood, "A Note on Mobs in the American Revolution," *WMQ*, 23 (1966), 635-642: and the works cited in note 7 above.

64. Hutchinson to Thomas Pownall, March 8, 1766, in Edmund S. Morgan, ed., *Prologue to Revolution: Sources and Documents on the Stamp Act Crisis, 1764-1766* (New York, 1973), p. 125. By 1767 the popular Caucus had two and possibly three components. See Alan and Katherine Day, "Another Look at the Boston 'Caucus,' " *Journal of American Studies*, 5 (1971), 19-42. The Days mistake the "New and Grand Corcas" of 1760, the Hutchinsonian clique striving to abolish the town meeting, as part of the popular Caucus.

65. Gage to Conway, Sept. 23, 1765, in Carter, ed., *Correspondence of Gage*, I, 67.

66. Gage to Conway, Dec. 21, 1765, ibid., I, 78-79.

67. Gage to Conway, Nov. 8, 1765, ibid., I, 72-73; Livingston to General Monckton, Nov. 8, 1765, *MHS Coll.*, 4th ser., X (Boston, 1871), 563.

68. Gage to Conway, Sept. 23, 1765, in Carter, ed., *Correspondence of Gage*, I, 67. The best overall account of the Stamp Act crisis in New York and the struggle for control within both radical and conservative factions is Carl L. Becker, *The History of Political Parties in the Province of New York, 1760-1776* (Madison, Wis., 1960; 1909), pp. 23-52.

12. The Disordered Urban Economies

1. For the Quartering Act and the colonial response see John Shy, *Towards Lexington: The Role of the British Army in the Coming of the American Revolution* (Princeton, N.J., 1965), pp. 250-258. The fullest treatment of the establishment of the new American Board of Customs Commissioners is Thomas C. Barrow, *Trade and Empire: The British Customs Service in Colonial America, 1660-1775* (Cambridge, Mass., 1967), chaps. 10-11.

2. Karl Mannheim, *Ideology and Utopia: An Introduction to the Sociology of Knowledge* (New York, 1955; 1936), pp. 56, 125.

3. See Appendix, Figure 1.

4. By the end of the colonial period the mortality rate in Philadelphia was substantially higher than in Boston. Billy G. Smith, "Death and Life in a Colonial Immigrant City: A Demographic Analysis of Philadelphia," *Journal of Economic History*, 37 (1977), 884-888. But the very high immigration rate in Philadelphia overwhelmed the higher mortality rate in driving upward the city's population. The number of immigrant ships entering Philadelphia each year is given in Gary B. Nash, "Slaves and Slaveowners in Colonial Philadelphia," *WMQ*, 30 (1973),

233. The total for 1772 should be twenty-three instead of thirteen as given. From 1764 to 1768 ninety-one immigrant ships, carrying some 20,000 passengers, entered Philadelphia. Boston received 2,380 immigrants during the same period. James A. Henretta, "Economic Development and Social Structure in Colonial Boston," *WMQ*, 22 (1965), 83. See also Mildred Campbell, "English Emigration on the Eve of the American Revolution," *American Historical Review*, 51 (1955-56), 8 for the virtual cessation of overseas migration to Boston in the 1770s.

5. Bernard to the Board of Trade, Sept. 5, 1763, in J. H. Benton, Jr., *Early Census Making in Massachusetts . . .* (Boston, 1905), p. 55.

6. The number of houses increased between 1765 and 1771 from 1,676 to 1,803. Allan Kulikoff, "The Progress of Inequality in Revolutionary Boston," *WMQ*, 28 (1971), 393, Table V. By 1770 seventy houses stood empty, which must have discouraged further construction. Bridenbaugh, *Cities in Revolt*, p. 228. The only new public buildings constructed during these years were a prison erected in 1767 and a courthouse built in 1769. Samuel Adams Drake, *Old Landmarks and Historic Personages of Boston* (Boston, 1900), p. 78; Bridenbaugh, *Cities in Revolt*, p. 230.

7. Bridenbaugh, *Cities in Revolt*, pp. 224, 226. The increase in New York can be estimated by using ratios of people per house for 1753, when there were 1,991 houses, and for 1766, when there were 3,223, and dividing this figure into the estimated population in 1776. For the number of houses in 1766 see Esther Singleton, *Social New York Under the Georges* (New York, 1969; 1902), p. 4. The number of houses in Philadelphia is given in John K. Alexander, "The Philadelphia Numbers Game: An Analysis of Philadelphia's Eighteenth-Century Population," *PMHB*, 98 (1974), 325. For the number built in 1774, ibid., 48 (1924), 235.

8. Bridenbaugh, *Cities in Revolt*, p. 229.

9. Based on an analysis of inventories in Office of the Recorder of Wills, Suffolk County Courthouse, Boston, and Office of the Recorder of Wills, City Hall Annex, Philadelphia.

10. David MacPherson, *Annals of Commerce . . .* , 4 vols. (London, 1805), III, 570. Of the ships built in Massachusetts from 1747 to 1753 and clearing Boston harbor in the latter year, 35 percent were constructed in the capital city. Murray G. Lawson, "Boston Merchant Fleet of 1753," *American Neptune*, 9 (1949), 207-215. Thomas Hutchinson related that after 1764 John Hancock "built, and employed in trade, a great number of ships," thereby giving the town an economic shot in the arm and not, incidentally, hurting his reputation with "a great number of tradesmen" who obligingly chose him as selectman, town meeting moderator, and representative. W. T. Baxter, *The House of Hancock: Business in Boston, 1724-1775* (Cambridge, Mass., 1945), p. 259. The volume of shipping built from 1769 to 1771, however, was only about 500 tons per year more than in 1755, when the selectman complained of a great decrease in shipbuilding from previous years.

11. MacPherson, *Annals of Commerce*, III, 570. The figures for Philadelphia given by Simeon J. Crowther, "The Shipbuilding Output of the Delaware Valley, 1722-1776" *Proceedings of the American Philosophical Society*, 117 (1973), 93 are somewhat higher than MacPherson's. I have used them because they are based on manuscript ship registrations at HSP.

12. William S. Sachs, "The Business Outlook in the Northern Colonies, 1750-1775" (Ph.D. diss., Columbia University, 1957), 184-187; James F. Shepherd and Gary M. Walton, *Shipping, Maritime Trade, and the Economic Development of Colonial North America* (Cambridge, Eng. 1972), pp. 168-170. From 1768 to 1772 Boston shipped about 342,000 quintals of fish compared with 856,000 quintals from Salem and Marblehead. A report of the number of fishing vessels operating from each Massachusetts port is in Ezekiel Price Papers, I, 59, MHS.

13. See Appendix, Figure 2.

14. See Appendix, Figure 2 for tonnage and Table 5 for mariners' wealth.

15. An overview of this process is presented in Kenneth Lockridge, "Land, Population, and the Evolution of New England Society 1630-1790," *Past and Present*, no. 39 (1968), 62-80; see also Jacob M. Price, "Economic Function and the Growth of American Port Towns in the Eighteenth Century," *Perspectives in American History*, 8 (1974), 145-149.

16. David Klingaman, "Food Surpluses and Deficits in the American Colonies, 1768-1772," *Journal of Economic History*, 21 (1971), 553-569. Klingaman's work builds upon Max George Schumacher, *The Northern Farmer and His Markets During the Late Colonial Period* (New York, 1975).

17. Klingaman, "Food Surpluses," p. 562; Sachs, "Business Outlook," p. 176; Anne Bezanson, *Prices and Inflation During the American Revolution, Pennsylvania, 1770-1790* (Philadelphia, 1951), pp. 73-77. Parliament amended the corn laws in 1766 to allow American grains to enter duty free.

18. Still a classic on the subject is Arthur M. Schlesinger, *The Colonial Merchants and the American Revolution, 1763-1776* (New York, 1968; 1918). It has been refined and reformulated in some respects by Marc Egnal and Joseph A. Ernst, "An Economic Interpretation of the American Revolution," *WMQ*, 29 (1972), 3-36, and Ernst, *Money and Politics in America, 1755-1775: A Study in the Currency Act of 1764 and the Political Economy of Revolution* (Chapel Hill, N.C., 1973).

19. *Pennsylvania Gazette*, Jan. 9, 1772. Colonial tenderness about vendue sales is discussed in Marc Egnal and Joseph A. Ernst, "An Economic Interpretation of the American Revolution," *WMQ*, 29 (1972), 15-18, and Arthur L. Jensen, *The Maritime Commerce of Colonial Philadelphia* (Madison, Wis., 1963), pp. 123-124.

20. The Tea Act and American opposition are carefully examined in Benjamin W. Labaree, *The Boston Tea Party* (New York, 1964).

21. Ernst, *Money and Politics*, p. 359.

22. Virginia D. Harrington, *The New York Merchant on the Eve of the Revolution* (New York, 1935), pp. 333-341; Charles M. Andrews, "The Boston Merchants and the Non-Importation Movement," *CSM Pub.*, 19 (1916-17), 179-191; Sachs, "Business Outlook," pp. 200-207; Ernst, *Money and Politics*, pp. 207-210.

23. For bankruptcies in New York see Philip White, *The Beekmans of New York in Politics and Commerce, 1647-1877* (New York, 1956), pp. 414-415; for Hancock's brother, W. T. Baxter, "A Colonial Bankrupt: Ebenezer Hancock, 1741-1809," *Bulletin of the Business History Society*, 25 (1951), 115-124.

24. Ernst, *Money and Politics*, p. 356; Richard B. Sheridan, "The British

Credit Crisis of 1772 and the American Colonies," *Journal of Economic History*, 20 (1960), 161-186.

25. Ibid., 172-174, 161.

26. Sachs, "Business Outlook," p. 229. For a good view of one mercantile house attempting to stay afloat in the buffeting storms of this era see White, *Beekmans of New York*, chap. 14. White characterizes the period as one of "far more violent flunctuations" and a "generally much lower level of business" (p. 408).

27. Every student of the colonial merchants, including Charles Andrews, Arthur M. Schlesinger, Virginia D. Harrington, William Sachs, Stephen G. Patternson, and Arthur L. Jensen, see merchants reacting primarily against direct threats to their economic welfare. Only those who study the pamphlet literature of this period without specific reference to merchants argue that the protests against English policy orginated in a fear of British despotism and a British desire to snuff out American political liberties.

28. For a discussion of this interplay of economic interest and ideology see Stephen E. Lucas, *Portents of Rebellion: Rhetoric and Revolution in Philadelphia, 1765-1776* (Philadelphia, 1976), chaps. 2-5.

29. Bernard Bailyn, ed., *Pamphlets of the American Revolution*, I (Cambridge, Mass., 1965), 666.

30. Joseph A. Goldenberg, *Shipbuilding in Colonial America* (Charlottesville, Va., 1976), p. 71; Rush to _____, Jan. 26, 1769, quoted in Charles S. Olton, *Artisans for Independence: Philadelphia Mechanics and the American Revolution* (Syracuse, N.Y., 1975), p. 31.

31. *Votes and Proceedings of the House of Representatives of the Province of Pennsylvania*, ed. Gertrude MacKinney, *Pennsylvania Archives*, 8th ser., 8 vols. (Harrisburg, Pa., 1931-35), VII, 5830.

32. Bettering House Managers to the Assembly, Feb. 9, 1768, ibid., 6149-6150; sheriff's sales of property, which had averaged about 40 per year from 1756 to 1762 rose to an average of 187 per year from 1766 to 1769. Marc Egnal, "The Business Cycle in Colonial America," paper presented at the Annual Meeting of the Organization of American Historians, April 18, 1975, p. 24.

33. *New-York Journal*, Dec. 17, 1767. Another writer described the widespread forced sale of property to satisfy debts and pointed to "our Prisons crowded with Debtors." *The Commercial Conduct of the Province of New-York Considered* . . . (New York, 1767), p. 5. Gov. Henry Moore to Lord Hillsborough, May 14, 1768, *NYCD*, VIII, 72.

34. Moore to Hillsborough, July 11, 1769, *NYCD*, VIII, 176; Harrington, *New York Merchant*, p. 341; Ernst, *Money and Politics*, pp. 251-260; and *To the Public. Whoever seriously considers the impoverished State of this City* . . . [New York, 1770].

35. Nina Tiffany Moore, ed., *Letters of James Murray, Loyalist* (Boston, 1901), p. 132.

36. Quoted in Bridenbaugh, *Cities in Revolt*, p. 276.

37. Carl Bridenbaugh and Jessica Bridenbaugh, *Rebels and Gentlemen: Philadelphia in the Age of Franklin* (New York, 1965), pp. 249-253; George William Edwards, *New York as an Eighteenth-Century Municipality, 1731-1776* (New York, 1917), pp. 59, 103. In 1759 New York had built a new jail, thought to

be commodious, but within a decade it was filled to overflowing.

38. For Philadelphia: Nash, "Slaves and Slaveowners," pp. 231-239; for Boston: Arthur Zilversmit, *The First Emancipation: The Abolition of Slavery in the North* (Chicago, 1967), p. 100. The number of slaves imported yearly from 1768 to 1772 in Massachusetts and Pennsylvania is given in John J. McCusker, "The Rum Trade and the Balance of Payments in the Thirteen Continental Colonies" (Ph.D. diss., University of Pittsburgh, 1970), pp. 558, 570. For New York, where slave importations fell to less than half their former volume, see the yearly figures in *Historical Statistics of the United States, Colonial Times to 1970*, 2 vols. (Washington, D.C., 1975), II, 1173. The best analysis of the changing composition of the labor force in any of the port towns is Sharon V. Salinger, "Colonial Labor in Transition: Indentured Servants in Eighteenth-Century Philadelphia," paper presented at the Annual Meeting of the Organization of American Historians, April 1978.

39. New York: Greene and Harrington, *American Population*, pp. 98-102; Boston: *Papers of Franklin*, IV, 337 for black population in 1752; Benton, *Census Making in Massachusetts*, unpaginated, for population in 1765. Henretta, "Economic Development and Social Structure," p. 83 for indentured servants entering Boston. There is no way of knowing how many remained in the city.

40. Quaker abolitionism in this era can be followed in Thomas E. Drake, *Quakers and Slavery in America* (New Haven, Conn., 1950); and Sydney V. James, *A People among Peoples: Quaker Benevolence in Eighteenth-Century America* (Cambridge, Mass., 1963). Otis's attack on slavery was a little-noticed part of his famous excoriation of British colonial policy, *The Rights of the British Colonists Asserted and Proved . . .* (Boston, 1764).

41. *The Colonial Laws of New York from the Year 1664 to the Revolution*, 5 vols. (Albany, 1894), V, 533-534.

42. For an example of articles banned see Schlesinger, *Colonial Merchants*, pp. 107-108. The full power of these boycotts was never achieved because merchants built up their inventories prior to signing nonimportation pacts and then worked their inventories down during the boycott period.

43. Olton, *Artisans for Independence*, pp. 25-32; Lucas, *Portents of Rebellion*, pp. 40-42; and Schlesinger, *Colonial Merchants*, pp. 64-65, 107-111, 121-124, 130-131, 146-152, 482-502, 517-518, 553-554.

44. Smith, "Struggles of the Independent Poor: The Living Standards of Philadelphia's 'Lower Sort' in the Last Half of the Eighteenth Century," Table 1, p. 6; Almshouse Managers Minutes, Nov. 3, 1775, Records of the Contributors of the Relief . . . of the Poor, City Archives, City Hall, Philadelphia.

45. Arthur Harrison Cole, *Wholesale Commodity Prices, in the United States, 1700-1861* (Cambridge, Mass., 1938), pp. 13-16. William S. Sachs, "Agricultural Conditions in the Northern Colonies before the Revolution," *Journal of Economic History*, 13 (1953), 287-289 reports that even after grain prices fell in New York in 1765 there was "persistent agitation" to prohibit the exportation of grain and other foodstuffs until prices dropped to a level that the laboring poor could afford. No adequate price series exists for Boston but a three-commodity series for rum, fish, and molasses shows a more modest upturn from 1768 to 1771 and then an equivalent decline in the next five years. Cole, *Wholesale Commodity Prices*, p. 7.

46. Anne Bezanson and others, *Prices in Colonial Pennsylvania* (Philadelphia, 1935), pp. 46-47.

47. Minutes of the Overseers of the Poor, 1768-1774, City Archives, City Hall, Philadelphia. See especially entries for Jan. 27, 1772, March 9, Nov. 1, Dec. 13, 1773; Feb. 28, Oct. 17, 1774; Feb. 1, March 1, April 5, 1775.

48. Appendix, Table 11. City taxes in Philadelphia continued to climb in the 1770s, leaving property owners with the stiffest tax bills in the city's history on the eve of the Revolution. For a personal record of tax payments in Boston from 1754 to 1773 see Papers of Samuel Abbot, Box 13, Andover-Newton Theological Seminary (on loan to Baker Library, Harvard Business School).

49. Smith, "Struggles of the Independent Poor," pp. 30-42 and Table VIII; Appendix, Table 2.

50. Appendix, Table 2. For the cost of room and board, Ann Hulton, *Letters of a Loyalist Lady* (Cambridge, Mass., 1927), p. 42.

51. Jesse Lemisch, "Jack Tar vs. John Bull: The Role of New York's Seamen in Precipitating the Revolution" (Ph. D. diss., Yale University, 1962), pp. 29, 195n. The demand for seamen in New York fell rapidly after the decline of privateering in 1760. In the previous year 5,670 mariners (not all of whom lived in the city) had sailed out of New York. In 1762, the number had dropped to 3,552—a 37 percent decrease. By 1772, while the city was growing, the merchant seamen population declined another 5 percent to 3,374. The data on the number of mariners is provided in Lemisch, "Jack Tar vs. John Bull," p. 54.

52. Smith, "Struggles of the Independent Poor," Tables I, VIII, pp. 23-27; Appendix, Table 2.

53. Wages for the building trades have been drawn from widely scattered sources for Philadelphia, including Treasurer's Accounts, Records of the Contributors to the Relief . . . of the Poor, City Archives, City Hall: Matron's and Steward's Cash Books and Treasurer's Accounts, Pennsylvania Hospital Records, American Philosophical Society, Accounts for the addition to the Statehouse, Norris of Fairhill Papers: General Loan Office, Miscellaneous Account Books, HSP; Isaac Zane Ledgers, 1748-1759, Isaac Norris Cashbook, 1752-1761, and building records for the houses of Benjamin Chew and John Cadwallader, all at HSP; the records of the Friendship Carpenters Company, American Philosophical Society; the bridge building accounts in the Minutes of the Philadelphia County Commissioners, 1718-1766, City Archives, and Minutes, 1771-1774, HSP.

54. The records of the Ship Masters Society are at the HSP. According to an account in *Pennsylvania Journal*, April 4, 1771, the organization began as the Sea Captains Club and was not incorporated as the Society for the Relief of Poor and Distressed Masters until 1770. By 1774 it had a capital fund of £2,200 and was disbursing about £100 per year. *Pennsylvania Journal*, May 25, 1774. Annual reports were published in the *Pennsylvania Gazette*, usually in April.

55. Richard B. Morris, *Government and Labor in Early America* (New York, 1946), p. 198.

56. Ibid, pp. 143-144; Mary Roys Baker, "Anglo-Massachusetts Trade Union Roots, 1130-1790," *Labor History*, 14 (1973), 387. On Philadelphia's ship carpenters, see James H. Hutson, "An Investigation of the Inarticulate: Philadelphia's White Oaks," *WMQ*, 28 (1971), 3-25; Jesse Lemisch and John K. Alexan-

der, "The White Oaks, Jack Tar, and the Concept of the 'Inarticulate,' " *WMQ,*
29 (1972), 109-134, and the reply by Hutson on pp. 136-142.

57. Morris, *Government and Labor,* p. 196; Baker, "Anglo-Massachusetts
Trade Union Roots," p. 387; Olton, *Artisans for Independence,* pp. 13-15 shows
examples of wheelwrights organizing in 1763 and silversmiths in 1767.

58. Olton, *Artisans for Independence,* pp. 14-18.

59. Ibid., p. 16. Olton argues that most craft organizations in Philadelphia
failed because controlled competiton was "inappropriate to the conditions of the
marketplace." I see the goal of these groups as a living wage rather than controlled competition per se, and believe that the "conditions of the marketplace"
that rendered them unsuccessful were not governed by any ideological predis-
position against craft organizations but the superior power of merchants and
others in defeating artisan proposals for price regulation by the legislature.

60. These figures have been calculated by reconstructing the occupational
composition of the adult, free males in the city from the 1772 tax list, as supplemented by the several hundred individuals who do not appear there but whose
names can be recovered from the records of public and private officials who dispensed aid to the poor—the overseers of the poor, the managers of the Bettering
House, the directors of the Pennsylvania Hospital for the Sick Poor, the county
commissioners, and the governing boards of the churches and charitable societies. All estimates of the extent of poverty must be regarded as conservative because many indigents who did not receive public aid were assisted by churches
and fraternal societies whose charitable efforts cannot be traced in extant records. It is important to note that colonial tax lists invariably omit the lowest
layer of the population—the 5 to 10 percent of the city's residents who were at sea
and maintained no permanent home in the port, the wandering poor who had not
yet established residence, the institutionalized poor, and those declared as non-
taxables because of extreme poverty. In Boston, figures on taxable inhabitants
probably underestimate by at least 20 percent the number of free adult males.

61. Renters are distinguished from house owners on the 1772 tax list. The
long-range trend in all the port towns was toward a concentration of property
ownership.

62. See Appendix, Figure 2.

63. Bridenbaugh, *Cities in Revolt,* pp. 302-303 reports waves of theft and
breaking into shops in New York in 1762 and 1773. Bridenbaugh astutely notes
that "It seemed to many law-abiding persons that the age of violence had arrived
when they assessed the grave effects of the postwar period and realized what a
large number of unemployed seafarers and women of the lower class had turned
criminals, and it was small comfort to them that the situation resembled on a
provincial scale that of the great cities of contemporary Britain." Ibid., p. 300.
For other reports of poverty driving large numbers of New Yorkers to crime see
New-York Mercury, Feb. 18, 1774, and Patrick M'Robert's observation that
there were "above 500" prostitutes in one part of the city. This would be about
one of every 2.5 white women above age sixteen at the time. *A Tour through
Part of the North Provinces of America,* ed. Carl Bridenbaugh (New York, 1935),
p. 5.

64. *Papers of Franklin,* III, 308.

65. Account of Payments to the Poor, April 1769-March 1771, Wards 2

and 12, Records of the Boston Overseers of the Poor, MHS: Account Book of Samuel Abbot [Overseer of the Poor for Ward 2], 1770-1775, Papers of Samuel Abbot, Baker Library, Harvard Business School.

66. *New-York Gazette*, March 30, 1772, March 15, 1773.

67. *Votes of the House of Representatives of Pennsylvania*, VII, 5506, 5535-5536, 5694; for the linen manufactory: *Pennsylvania Journal*, Nov. 28, 1765; *Papers of Franklin*, XI, 314-316; XIII, 252; *Whereas the Number of Poor In and Around This City . . .* [Philadelphia, 1764], and *A Number of the Inhabitants of This City . . .* [Philadelphia, 1765]. On the failure of the factory see William R. Bagnall, *The Textile Industries of the United States . . .* (Cambridge, Mass., 1893), p. 60.

68. Gary B. Nash, "Poverty and Poor Relief in Pre-Revolutionary Philadelphia," *WMQ*, 33 (1976), 14-15.

69. Bridenbaugh and Bridenbaugh, *Rebels and Gentlemen*, pp. 232-235; Frederick B. Tolles, *Meeting House and Counting House: The Quaker Merchants of Colonial Philadelphia, 1682-1763* (Chapel Hill, N.C., 1948), p. 71; James, *A People among Peoples*, pp. 210-211.

70. Of the original treasurer and twelve managers of the organization, eleven were Quakers. Of twenty-eight new members after 1766, at least twenty-five were Quakers and twenty-one of them were merchants. Quakers also predominated among the large contributors to the corporation. See Catalog of the Contributors to the Relief and Employment of the Poor, AM 366, HSP. The special committees that had been formed to relieve the poor in the harsh winters of 1761-1762 and 1764-1765 were more diverse in religious and occupational composition.

71. Stephen Edward Wiberley, Jr., "Four Cities: Public Poor Relief in Urban American, 1700-1775" (Ph.D. diss., Yale University, 1975), pp. 110-111. The purchase of the "Rules and Orders" of the Boston workhouse is recorded in Treasurer's Accounts, Records of the Contributors to the Relief . . . of the Poor, I, 13, City Archives, City Hall, Philadelphia.

72. Franklin to Richard Jackson, May 5, 1753, and to Peter Collinson, May 9, 1753, *Papers of Franklin*, IV, 479-486; also "To the Printer of the London Chronicle," Dec. 30, 1758, ibid., VIII, 214-215. In his autobiography, written after the Revolution, Franklin noted that he was much influenced in his early thought by reading Defoe. For English approaches to poverty in this period see Dorothy Marshall, *The English Poor in the Eighteenth Century* (London, 1926), pp. 22-51; Joyce Oldham Appleby, *Economic Thought and Ideology in Seventeenth-Century England* (Princeton, N.J., 1978), chap. 6; A. W. Coates, "Economic Thought and Poor Law Policy in the Eighteenth Century," *Economic History Review*, 2d ser., 13 (1960-61), 46-50; and Daniel A. Baugh, "Poverty, Protestantism, and Political Economy: English Attitudes toward the Poor, 1660-1800," unpub. ms.

73. Franklin to Charles Thomson, July 11, 1765, *Papers of Franklin*, XII, 208.

74. "On the Price of Corn, and Management of the Poor," *London Chronicle*, Nov. 29, 1766, in *Papers of Franklin*, XIII, 512-516. Franklin's views were elaborated two years later in an essay "On the Laboring Poor," *Gentleman's Magazine*, 38 (1768), 156-157, in *Papers of Franklin*, XV, 103-107. Franklin's

advice to the Philadelphia poor is all the more remarkable because he had returned to the city from Nov. 1762 to Nov. 1764 and thus knew at first hand the effects of the postwar depression. In "On the Laboring Poor," "Poor Richard" carried his animus against the indigent to the extreme, arguing sophistically that the rich spent nearly all their income on goods and services that gave employment to the poor; therefore, "our labouring poor do in every year receive *the whole revenue of the nation.*" What more could the wealthy do for the poor, especially if the laboring classes wasted their money "expensively at the alehouse" rather than employing their time "cheaply at church"?

75. *Votes of the House of Representatives of Pennsylvania,* VII, 6148. The Bettering House solution may also owe something to Thomas Wharton, a wealthy Quaker merchant whose unpublished "A Proposal for Building a Work House in the City of Philadelphia" was written about 1764. It is in Wharton-Willing Papers, HSP.

76. Almshouse Managers' Minutes, June 16, 1769, City Archives, City Hall, Philadelphia.

77. Minutes of the Overseers of the Poor, June 15, 1769, City Archives; Wiberly, "Four Cities," pp. 73-75 analyzes the curtailment of out-relief.

78. Ibid., pp. 75-76. In Boston, where the almshouse could not accommodate all the needy, about one-third of all relief moneys went to out-pensioners.

79. A comparison of the occupations and wealth of the overseers and Bettering House managers in one year makes the difference between them clear. In 1769 the managers included seven merchants, one shopkeeper, and one attorney. Seven were Quakers, one a Baptist, and one is undetermined. From 1770 to 1775 all the managers were Quakers. In 1769 the overseers of the poor were composed of two merchants, three carpenters, one baker, hatter, lastmaker, watchmaker, stonecutter, distiller, and cooper. The average assessment of the 1769 managers on the 1772 tax list was £154; that of the overseers was £45.

80. *Votes of the House of Representatives of Pennsylvania,* VII, 6148-6149, 6097-6099. Wiberly, "Four Cities," pp. 188-197 gives details on the dispute. The overseers complaints are recorded in their Minutes, Jan. 22, 1770, City Archives.

81. Almshouse Managers' Minutes, Jan. 22, 1770, City Archives.

82. Wiberly, "Four Cities," pp. 115, 120-123 where the output of the Bettering House is analyzed. Also see Nash, "Poverty and Poor Relief," pp. 26-27.

83. Philip Padelford, ed., *Colonial Panorama 1775: Dr. Robert Honyman's Journal for March and April* (San Marino, Ca., 1939), p. 18.

84. A new poor law passed in 1771 imposed heavy penalties on delinquent overseers, but the annual reports of the Bettering House managers show that tax collections were falling farther and farther behind. In 1775 poor taxes for 1773 were still being submitted. See Nash, "Poverty and Poor Relief," p. 24, n. 63 for data on the failure of the poor tax revenues to keep up with the growing number of poor and the rising price of provisions.

85. Almshouse Managers' Minutes, Nov. 3, 1775, City Archives. For the efforts of the managers to solve the poverty problem in 1776 see their petition to the assembly for a new poor law in *Votes of the House of Representatives of Pennsylvania,* VIII, 7393. The first historian of the Bettering House wrote that it became "somewhat an epithet of contempt." Charles Lawrence, *History of the Philadelphia Alms House and Hospital* (Philadelphia, 1905), p. 23. Wiberly,

"Four Cities," p. 202 concludes that the Bettering House managers were "unique among urban relief officials" in "their lack of direct contact with the poor as well as their apparent dearth of sympathy for the needy." The fact that so many of the poor were fairly recent immigrants, as opposed to the poor in Boston who were mainly indigenous, helps to explain this callousness. By 1775 the Bettering House managers were £2,000 in debt and were seeking another hike in the poor taxes. Almshouse Managers' Minutes, Nov. 3, 1775, City Archives.

86. C. B. MacPherson, *The Political Theory of Possessive Individualism* (Oxford, 1962), p. 221.

87. "On the . . . Management of the Poor," *Papers of Franklin*, XIII, 515.

88. *Papers of Franklin*, II, 140, 168.

89. Minutes of the Overseers of the Poor, June 15, 1769, City Archives. The poor law of 1771 conferred the right of settlement upon migrants who had paid taxes for two years instead of one year, or had rented a house worth at least £10 per year rather than £5, and required newcomers to present a certificate of residency from the overseers of the poor in the last place of habitation. *Statutes at Large of Pennsylvania*, VIII, chap. 635.

90. Annual production figures were given in the yearly reports of the Contributors to the Relief of the Poor, published in the *Pennsylvania Gazette*, usually in May. Dividing the yards of cloths produced by the monthly average of women in the Bettering House gives a rough estimate of productivity. The yards woven annually per woman were 98 in 1769-1770, 100 in 1770-1771, 94 in 1771-1772, 81 in 1772-1773, 63 in 1773-1774, 60 in 1774-1775, and 15 in 1775-1776, when most of the looms may have been sold to the United Company of Philadelphia, which was establishing a new cloth factory in the city.

91. *New-York Gazette*, Nov. 13, 1769; see also Dec. 17, 1767.

92. *New-York Gazette*, Aug. 13, 1767. In the next issue (Aug. 20) it was claimed that not more than thirty carriages and coaches existed in the city and most of these belonged to government officials, British army officers, and recent wealthy immigrants from England and Ireland. But in 1770 Pierre Eugene Du Simitière, the Swiss observer of the American scene, listed sixty-two carriages of which fifty-three belonged to long-familiar families such as the Livingstons, Watts, Crugers, and DeLanceys, "List of New York Coachowners, 1770," Du Simitière Papers, HSP. For an analysis of a similar phenomenon in Philadelphia see Robert F. Oaks, "Big Wheels in Philadelphia: Du Simitière's List of Carriage Owners," *PMHB*, 95 (1971), 351-362.

93. The Sugar Act of 1764 abolished drawbacks on exported foreign linens, which raised prices in the colonies and gave further hopes that domestically produced linen could be made profitably. Merrill Jensen, *The Founding of a Nation: A History of the American Revolution, 1763-1776* (New York, 1968), p. 48.

94. New York: Bagnall, *Textile Industries*, pp. 52-53; *New-York Gazette*, Dec. 20, 1764. Philadelphia: *Papers of Franklin*, XI, 314-316; XIII, 252.

95. New York: Bagnall, *Textile Industries*, pp. 53-54; *New-York Journal*, Feb. 2, 1768. Philadelphia: Treasurer's Accounts, Records of the Contributors to the Relief . . . of the Poor, I, 12, City Archives.

96. *BTR*, XVI, 226-227, 231-236, 249; Bagnall, *Textile Industries*, pp. 37-41; Wiberly "Four Cities," pp. 105-106; *Proposals for Carrying on a Manufacture in the Town of Boston for Employing the Poor . . .* (Boston, 1768). Records relat-

ing to the revival of the manufactory are in Ezekiel Price Papers, MHS.

97. All were former overseers of the poor except Goldthwait. For some of the radical Whig committees on which these men served see Samuel G. Drake, *The History and Antiquities of Boston* . . . (Boston, 1856), pp. 729, 732, 738, and 764. Goldthwait was connected to the earlier enterprise as one of the executors of Thomas Gunter's estate: Massachusetts Archives, LIX, 490-492. Oliver's remark is in Douglass Adair and John A. Schutz, eds., *Peter Oliver's Origin & Progress of the American Revolution: A Tory View* (Stanford, 1967), p. 63.

98. BTR, XVI, 275-277; Bagnall, *Textile Industries*, pp. 42-50.

99. Historians have neglected Molineux, one of Boston's most important radicals during the prerevolutionary decade. For hints about his character and career see Hiller B. Zobel, *The Boston Massacre* (New York, 1970), pp. 157-159, 165-167, 176, 202-204; John C. Miller, *Sam Adams: Pioneer in Propaganda* (Stanford, Ca., 1960; 1936), p. 87; and Esther Forbes, *Paul Revere and the World He Lived In* (Boston, 1942), pp. 120-121. Peter Oliver wrote of Molineux that "by minding the Rioting Business more than his own, he had reduced his Circumstances to a Low Ebb," but this seems to invert the relationship between economic woes and political radicalization. Adair and Schutz, eds., *Peter Oliver's Origin & Progress*, p. 117. For Molineux's ancestry see Nellie Z. D. Molyneux, *History Genealogical and Biographical of the Molyneux Families* (Syracuse, N.Y., 1904), pp. 134-135, 145, 152-153, 169. Molineux's uncle was the distinguished philosopher and scientist of the same name who had argued passionately for Ireland's legislative independence from England in *The Case of Ireland's Being Bound by Acts of Parliament in England, Stated* . . . (Dublin, 1698).

100. BTR, XVI, 275-277; Bagnall, *Textile Industries*, pp. 42-49.

101. Ibid., p. 43.

102. Adair and Schutz, eds., *Peter Oliver's Origin & Progress*, pp. 63-64.

103. Bagnall, *Textile Industries*, pp. 63-72. On "near five hundred employed" in spinning *for* rather than *in* the factory see *Pennsylvania Packet*, Oct. 16, 1775. Shares in the United Company rose in value from £10 to £17 between 1775 and 1777.

104. Bagnall, *Textile Industries*, p. 67.

105. For an analysis of the social backgrounds of the managers see Richard Alan Ryerson, *The Revolution Now Begins: The Radical Committees of Philadelphia, 1765-1776* (Philadelphia, 1978), pp. 112-114.

106. It is possible that many women who otherwise would have had to accept confinement in the Bettering House stayed in their homes in the last year before revolution because of the wages they obtained from the United Company. The plummeting of cloth production at the Bettering House also suggest this. But the number of women admitted to the Bettering House from May 1775 to May 1776 (183) was actually higher than in the previous twelve-month period (152). It seems more likely that the United Company purchased the looms and other weaving equipment from the Bettering House sometime in late 1775 or early 1776, although I find no reference to this in the Treasurer's Accounts, City Archives.

107. Hutchinson to Richard Jackson, Oct. 20, 1767, quoted in Bernard Bailyn, *The Ordeal of Thomas Hutchinson* (Cambridge, Mass. 1974), p. 97.

108. John McCleary to Samuel Abbot, Feb. 12, March 6 and 13, 1771, Papers of Samuel Abbot, Box 14, folder 18, Baker Library.

109. Joseph A. Ernst, "Economic Change and the Political Economy of the American Revolution," in Larry R. Gerlach, ed., *Legacies of the American Revolution* (Provo, Utah, 1978), p. 107.

110. *The Commercial Conduct of the Province of New-York Considered* . . . (New York, 1767), pp. 11-12.

13. Revolution

1. The best account of MacIntosh's ideology, much of which must be inferred from his actions, is George P. Anderson, "Ebenezer Mackintosh: Stamp Act Rioter and Patriot," and "A Note on Ebenezer Mackintosh," *CSM Pub.*, 26 (1924-26), 15-64, 348-361. Hutchinson's ideology is portrayed in Bernard Bailyn, *The Ordeal of Thomas Hutchinson* (Cambridge, Mass., 1974), although Bailyn ignores Hutchinson's insensitivity to economic dislocation and lower-class suffering in Boston.

2. Philip Greven, *The Protestent Temperament: Patterns of Childrearing, Religious Experience, and the Self in Early America* (New York, 1977), p. 335.

3. An entrance into the mind of this group can be gained by consulting Greven's analysis of "The Genteel," in *Protestant Temperament*, Part Four, and Alan Heimert's analysis of the "Liberals" or "Rationalists" in *Religion and the American Mind from the Great Awakening to the Revolution* (Cambridge, Mass., 1966). These two studies, although not entirely complementary, are invaluable. That this group also subscribed to many elements of Whig thinking is made clear by Mary Beth Norton in "The Loyalist Critique of the Revolution," in *The Development of a Revolutionary Mentality* (Washington, D.C., 1972), pp. 127-148.

4. Bernard Friedman, "The Shaping of the Radical Consciousness in Provincial New York," *Journal of American History*, 56 (1970), 786.

5. For revealing biographical portraits see Bailyn, *Ordeal of Thomas Hutchinson* and Carol Berkin, *Jonathan Sewall: Odyssey of an American Loyalist* (New York, 1974). A collective portrait is presented in William H. Nelson, *The American Tory* (New York, 1961).

6. Joyce Appleby, "The Social Origins of American Revolutionary Ideology," *Journal of American History*, 64 (1978), 943.

7. In positing a distinct ideological division between Whigs and Evangelicals I follow Heimert's *Religion and the American Mind*, although, as will be clear below, I make greater distinctions within the ranks of Evangelicals than he allows.

8. *To the Inhabitants of Pennsylvania in General, and Particularly Those of the City and Neighbourhood of Philadelphia* (Philadelphia, 1779).

9. This view was distilled in a Thanksgiving sermon published in Boston in 1766 that could have caused little thanksgiving among the poor of that town. It was "plain to observe," declaimed Henry Cumings, "that the poverty and want of most people among us, originate either from indolence, or intemperance, or some particular expensive vices to which they are addicted." Quoted in Heimert, *Religion and the American Mind*, p. 434.

10. William G. McLoughlin, "The American Revolution as a Religious Revival: 'The Millennium in One Country,' " *New England Quarterly*, 40 (1967), 102. Adam Smith, *The Wealth of Nations*, ed. E. Cannan (New York, 1937), p. 674.

11. Gordon S. Wood, *The Creation of the American Republic, 1776-1787* (Chapel Hill, N.C., 1969), pp. 108, 113. Edmund S. Morgan, "The Puritan Ethic and the American Revolution," *WMQ*, 24 (1967), 3-43 is a seminal essay on this subject; but also see Heimert, *Religion and the American Mind*, chap. 9; Cushing Strout, *The New Heavens and New Earth: Political Religion in America* (New York, 1974), chap. 4; Catherine L. Albanese, *Sons of the Fathers: The Civil Religion of the American Revolution* (Philadelphia, 1976); and Wood, *Creation of the American Republic*, pp. 91-124.

12. Wood, *Creation of the American Republic*, p. 108.

13. Quoted in Greven, *Protestant Temperament*, p. 336.

14. H. James Henderson, "The Structure of Politics in the Continental Congress," in Stephen G. Kurtz and James H. Hutson, *Essays on the American Revolution* (Chapel Hill, N.C., 1973), p. 183.

15. Scholarship on this subject in the last twenty years is voluminous. I have found especially useful Caroline Robbins, *The Eighteenth-Century Commonwealthman* (Cambridge, Mass., 1959); Bernard Bailyn, *The Ideological Origins of the American Revolution* (Cambridge, Mass., 1967); and J. G. A. Pocock, *The Machiavellian Moment: Florentine Political Thought and the Atlantic Republic Tradition* (Princeton, N.J., 1975). For a review of the literature see Robert E. Shalhope, "Toward a Republican Synthesis: The Emergence of an Understanding of Republicanism in American Historiography," *WMQ*, 29 (1972), 49-80.

16. Wood, *Creation of the American Republic*, p. 47.

17. Pocock, *Machiavellian Moment*, p. 472. Those who have written on expressions of republican thought in the prerevolutionary decade have not considered how receptivity to it varied with the historical experience of different sectors of colonial society. See W. Paul Adams, "Republicanism in Political Rhetoric Before 1776," *Political Science Quarterly*, 85 (1970), 397-421, and Pauline Maier, "The Beginnings of American Republicanism, 1765-1776," in *Development of a Revolutionary Mentality*, pp. 99-117.

18. Appleby, "Social Origins of Revolutionary Ideology," p. 956; Drew R. McCoy, "Benjamin Franklin's Vision of a Republican Political Economy for America," *WMQ*, 35 (1978), 606.

19. Ibid., p. 621. McCoy's discussion of how the "republican ideology was riddled with tensions and ambiguities" adds greatly to the work of Wood and Pocock. The impasse for capitalist city dwellers may have been obvious for those who read essays such as Lord Chesterfield's "Account of the Government of the Republic of the Seven United Provinces," which was reprinted in the *Pennsylvania Ledger*, Feb. 10, 1776. Chesterfield argued that "The Necessary principle of a Republic, Virtue, subsists no longer there. The great riches of private people (though the public is poor) have long ago extinguished that principle." Quoted in Adams, "Republicanism in Political Rhetoric", p. 416.

20. The centrality of equality of condition to republican society is almost totally ignored in Robbins, *Commonwealthman* and Bailyn, *Ideological Origins*. The theme is recaptured in Pocock, *Machiavellian Moment*, Wood, *Creation of the American Republic*, and, most extensively, in J. R. Pole, *The Pursuit of Equality in American History* (Berkeley and Los Angeles, 1978).

21. Charles Blitzer, ed., *The Political Writings of James Harrington* (New York, 1955), p. 98.

22. Barrington Moore, Jr., *Social Origins of Dictatorship and Democracy: Lord and Peasant in the Making of the Modern World* (Boston, 1966), p. 496.

23. [John Trenchard and Thomas Gordon], *Cato's Letters: or, Essays on Liberty, Civil and Religious*, 6th ed. (London, 1755), II, 16; III, 207-208.

24. Paul Merrill Spurlin, *Rousseau in America, 1760-1809* (University, Ala., 1969), chap. 6; Frederick Watkins, trans. and ed., *Rousseau: Political Writings* (Edinburgh, 1953), pp. 24, 55,; also see pp. 324-325.

25. Robert J. Taylor, ed., *The Papers of John Adams*, I (Cambridge, Mass., 1977), pp. 106-107n.

26. Harry Alonzo Cushing, ed., *The Writings of Samuel Adams*, 4 vols (New York, 1907), IV, 67.

27. Wood, *Creation of the American Republic*, p. 91.

28. Dirk Hoerder, *Crowd Action in Revolutionary Massachusetts, 1765-1780* (New York, 1977), p. 141; Anderson, "Ebenezer MacIntosh," pp. 27, 51-53.

29. Hoerder, *Crowd Action*, p. 155.

30. Ibid., p. 156; also see Pauline Maier, "Revolutionary Violence and the Relevance of History," *Journal of Interdisciplinary History*, 2 (1971), 123.

31. Hiller B. Zobel, *The Boston Massacre* (New York, 1970), p. 75.

32. William A. Williams, "Samuel Adams: Calvinist, Mercantilist, Revolutionary," *Studies on the Left*, 1 (1959-1960), 57; also see Pauline Maier, "Coming to Terms with Samuel Adams," *American Historical Review*, 81 (1976), 12-37.

33. Williams, "Samuel Adams," pp. 50-52, 57.

34. On demonstrations, celebrations, and other social events see Philip Davidson, *Propaganda and the American Revolution* (Chapel Hill, N.C., 1941), chaps. 5, 10, and 11.

35. John C. Miller, *Sam Adams: Pioneer in Propaganda* (Stanford, Ca., 1960; 1936), pp. 195-196.

36. Hoerder, *Crowd Action*, pp. 204-243; for another treatment of violence associated with nonimportation, from the perspective of law and order breaking down, see Zobel, *Boston Massacre*, pp. 60-86.

37. Miller, *Sam Adams*, pp. 87, 188, 191, 202, 208-209, 218, 236; Zobel, *Boston Massacre*, pp. 49, 157-159, 164-169, 172, 176, 202-204. For two of Molineux's threats—one to kill himself and one to kill importers with his own hands—see Pauline Maier, *From Resistance to Rebellion: Colonial Radicals and the Development of American Opposition to Britain, 1765-1776* (New York, 1972), p. 129, and Hoerder, *Crowd Action*, p. 218.

38. Pauline Maier, "Reason and Revolution: The Radicalism of Dr. Thomas Young," *American Quarterly*, 28 (1976), 229-249. The following paragraph also draws upon David Hawke, "Dr. Thomas Young—'Eternal Fisher in Troubled Waters': Notes for a Biography," *New-York Historical Society Quarterly*, 54 (1970), 6-29, and Henry H. Edes, "Memoir of Dr. Thomas Young, 1731-1777," *CSM Trans., 1906-1907* (Boston, 1910), pp. 2-54.

39. Maier, "Radicalism of Dr. Thomas Young," pp. 229, 245.

40. Ibid., pp. 245-246.

41. Stephen E. Patterson, *Political Parties in Revolutionary Massachusetts* (Madison, Wis., 1973), pp. 67-68.

42. Miller, *Sam Adams*, pp. 206-207. On The Body of the People see also

Warden, *Boston*, pp. 218-220, 243-244, 286, and Richard D. Brown, *Revolutionary Politics in Massachusetts: The Boston Committee of Correspondence and the Towns, 1772-1774* (New York, 1976; 1970), pp. 161-162.

43. Patterson, *Political Parties*, p. 70; Hoerder, *Crowd Action*, pp. 216-217; Miller, *Sam Adams*, pp. 248-249, 256.

44. Miller, *Sam Adams*, pp. 248-249; L. H. Butterfield, ed., *Diary and Autobiography of John Adams*, II (New York, 1964), 10-11.

45. The fullest treatment of the Tea Act and the response in the port towns is Benjamin Woods Labaree, *The Boston Tea Party* (New York, 1964). On the Solemn League and Covenant see also Miller, *Sam Adams*, pp. 297-312.

46. Hutchinson to Lord Dartmouth, Dec. 2, 1773, quoted in Hoerder, *Crowd Action*, p. 258.

47. Miller, *Sam Adams*, p. 302; Brown, *Revolutionary Politics*, p. 193.

48. Patterson, *Political Parties*, p. 83.

49. Ibid., pp. 83-85; Arthur M. Schlesinger, *The Colonial Merchants and the American Revolution, 1763-1776* (New York, 1968; 1918), pp. 320-323, Brown, *Revolutionary Politics*, pp. 194-199.

50. Ann Hulton to _____, July 8, 1774, *Letters of a Loyalist Lady* (Cambridge, Mass., 1927), p. 73.

51. Table A indicates the occupation distribution of elected selectmen and moderators in Boston and aldermen and councilmen in the New York. Philadelphia's aldermen and councilmen were not elected. Table B shows the occupational distribution of elected second-level officials. Philadelphia's overseers of the poor were appointed by the Mayor's Court.

Table A: Elected Major Officials in Boston and New York

| | Boston selectmen and moderators | | | New York alderman and assistants | | |
Years	Merchant	Professional	Artisan	Merchant	Professional	Artisan
1761-65	78.0%	17.1%	4.9%	72.5%	8.7%	18.8%
1766-70	71.2	17.3	11.5	65.2	4.3	30.4
1771-75	85.0	5.0	10.0	55.2	4.5	40.3

Table B: Elected Second-Level Officials in Boston and Philadelphia

| | Boston overseers of the poor and assessors | | | Philadelphia overseers of the poor and assessors | | |
Years	Merchant	Professional	Artisan	Merchant	Professional	Artisan
1761-65	73.0%	9.4%	17.6%	57.9%	2.6%	39.5%
1766-70	69.0	8.6	22.4	43.1	3.1	53.8
1771-75	66.7	8.9	24.4	50.0	2.4	47.6

52. Miller, *Sam Adams*, p. 110; J. R. Pole, *Political Representation in England and the Origins of the American Republic* (London, 1966), pp. 69-70.

53. The one instance of what seems to be a printed address from the Boston artisans—*Trademen's Protest against the Proceedings of the Merchants Relative to the New Importation of Tea* [Boston, 1773]—was actually written by administration merchants trying to influence artisans at the important town meeting on

Nov. 5, 1773 to oppose the radicals' demand for stopping all tea importations. Hoerder, *Crowd Action*, pp. 255-256; Labaree, *Tea Party*, pp. 110-112.

54. Schlesinger, *Colonial Merchants*, p. 106.

55. Quoted in Miller, *Sam Adams*, p. 207.

56. Brown, *Revolutionary Politics*, p. 162.

57. Heimert, *Religion and the American Mind*, pp. 425-426.

58. Miller, *Sam Adams*, pp. 302, 305.

59. Brown, *Revolutionary Politics*, pp. 191-192.

60. Alfred F. Young, "Pope's Day, Tar and Feathers, and 'Cornet Joyce, jun.': From Ritual to Rebellion in Boston, 1745-1775," unpub. ms., pt. VII, 1. The reference to Guy Fawkes is from Maier, *From Resistance to Revolution*, p. 274. For a full analysis of how the Quebec Act fed antipopery in New England see Charles H. Metzger, *The Quebec Act: A Primary Cause of the American Revolution* (New York, 1936).

61. Hoerder, *Crowd Action*, p. 216; *BTR*, XVIII, 13, 20.

62. Charles Chauncy probably overstated the case when he pleaded that 15,000 in Boston were "poverty struck." *A Letter to a Friend, Giving a Concise but Just Representation of the Hardshps and Suffering of the Town of Boston* (Boston, 1774), p. 6.

63. Roger Champagne, "Liberty Boys and Mechanics of New York City, 1764-1774," *Labor History*, 8 (1967), 124-129.

64. Ibid., pp. 129-130 for New York. The incidence of artisan officeholders in Boston and Philadelphia are my own calculations. A carpenter ran for the assembly in New York in 1768 but garnered only 12 percent of the vote. Champagne, "Liberty Boys," p. 130.

65. Ibid.; *New-York Journal*, Feb. 18, 1768, as quoted in Champagne, "Liberty Boys," p. 130.

66. Bonomi, *Factious People*, pp. 242, 252-255; "New York Broadsides, 1762-1779," *New York Public Library Bulletin*, III (1899), 25-28.

67. Bonomi, *Factious People*, p. 268. The growth of mass meetings and other popular forms of politics is traced in Carl Lotus Becker, *The History of Political Parties in the Province of New York, 1760-1776* (Madison, Wis., 1960; 1909), chaps. 2-5.

68. Ibid., p. 90.

69. Quoted in Schlesinger, *Colonial Merchants*, p. 220. Nonimportation in New York is discussed ibid., pp. 217-227; Roger J. Champagne, *Alexander McDougall and the American Revolution in New York* (Syracuse, N.Y., 1975), pp. 34-37; and most extensively in Becker, *Political Parties*, pp. 53-94.

70. *Proposals, for Erecting and Encouraging a new Manufactory* [New York, 1770].

71. Becker, *Political Parties*, pp. 90-91; Champagne, *McDougall*, pp. 36-39. A second poll by the merchants produced only 794 signatures "including all ranks and both sexes" according to a protest by radical leaders Isaac Sears and John Lamb, Philip S. Foner, *Labor and the American Revolution* (Westport, Conn., 1976), p. 107. Also see *New-York Journal*, June 21, July 26, and Aug. 2, 1770 for denials that a majority in the city favored importing.

72. Roger Champagne, "Family Politics Versus Constitutional Principles: The New York Assembly Elections of 1768 and 1769," *WMQ*, 20 (1963), 57-79.

For a rebuttal which argues that artisans pursued their own interests as best they could see Bernard Friedman, "The New York Assembly Elections of 1768 and 1769: The Disruption of Family Politics," *New York History*, 46 (1965), 3-24.

73. Imported items which citizens were asked to boycott are given in *The Committee Appointed by the Inhabitants . . .* [New York, 1768].

74. See Appendix, Figure 2.

75. Champagne, "Liberty Boys," p. 126.

76. Nicholas Varga, "Election Procedures and Practices in Colonial New York," *New York History*, 41 (1960), 267, citing *New-York Journal*, April 12, 1770. For the extraordinary manipulation of voters in the 1768 and 1769 elections see Champagne, "Family Politics Versus Constitutional Principles," pp. 59-60, 67-68.

77. Champagne, "Liberty Boys," pp. 132-133.

78. *A Copy of the Poll List, of the Election for Representatives . . .* (New York, 1768); Champagne, "Liberty Boys," pp. 129, 132.

79. *All the Real Friends of Liberty . . .* [New York, 1770].

80. Quoted in Friedman, "The New York Assembly Elections of 1768 and 1769," pp. 17-18.

81. *To the Public* [New York, 1769]; *All the Real Friends of Liberty* [New York, 1770].

82. *To the Independent Freeholders and Freemen of this City . . .* [New York, 1770]; *All the Real Friends of Liberty* [New York, 1770]. The loyalists who were among the merchant signers of the broadside are identified in Becker, *Political Parties*, p. 128n.

83. *Advertisement* [New York, 1770]; *New-York Gazette*, Jan. 8, 1770; Bonomi, *Factious People*, p. 275.

84. Champagne, *McDougall*, p. 37.

85. Quoted in Becker, *Political Parties*, p. 111n. Becker's treatment of the Tea Act and the response in New York is the fullest on the subject. Ibid., pp. 95-111. See also, Schlesinger, *Colonial Merchants*, pp. 291-294.

86. Becker, *Political Parties*, pp. 105-111; Champagne, *McDougall*, pp. 52-66. Twenty-five members of the Committee of 51 had worked to halt non-importation in 1770. Schlesinger, *Colonial Merchants*, pp. 329-330; Becker, *Political Parties*, p. 116n.

87. Reprinted in Kammen, *Colonial New York*, p. 344.

88. Quoted in Champagne, "New York and the Intolerable Acts," *New-York Historical Society Quarterly*, 45 (1961), 201-206.

89. Colden to Lord Dartmouth, June 1, 1774, in Peter Force, comp., *American Archives*, Fourth Series, 6 vols. (Washington, D.C., 1837-1843), I, 372-373; and Colden to _____, Sept. 7, 1774, quoted in Schlesinger, *Colonial Merchants*, pp. 328-329.

90. Quoted in Becker, *Political Parties*, p. 116n. This incident is also analyzed in Bernard Mason, *The Road to Independence: The Revolutionary Movement in New York, 1773-1777* (Lexington, Ky., 1966), pp. 27-31.

91. Ibid., chaps. 2-4; Becker, *Political Parties*, chaps. 5-7.

92. Lee R. Boyer, "Lobster Backs, Liberty Boys, and Laborers in the Streets: New York's Golden Hill and Nassau Street Riots," *New-York Historical Society Quarterly*, 57 (1973), 281-308. The quote is on p. 282.

93. For example, Champagne, "Family Politics Versus Constitutional Principles," p. 58. The 1769 election produced many pamphlets aimed at wooing voters on the basis of religion (see ibid., p. 74), but Champagne concludes that "the idea that the campaign was really over religious issues is phony."

94. Champagne, "Liberty Boys," p. 133; Mason, *Road to Independence*, p. 28n.

95. Thomas Young to John Lamb, Nov. 19, 1774, quoted in Champagne, *McDougall*, p. 74; Becker, *Political Parties*, p. 117n quoting John Adams.

96. Gouverneur Morris to John Penn, May 20, 1774, quoted in Kammen, *Colonial New York*, p. 343.

97. "The Respectful Address of the Mechanicks in Union . . .", quoted in Edward Countryman, "Consolidating Power in Revolutionary America: The Case of New York, 1775-1783," *Journal of Interdisciplinary History*, 6 (1976), 659.

98. Staughton Lynd, *Class Conflict, Slavery, and the United States Constitution* (Indianapolis, 1967), pp. 92-95; Countryman, "Consolidating Power," pp. 659-660; Mason, *Road to Independence*, pp. 148-177.

99. Alfred F. Young, *The Democratic Republicans of New York: The Origins, 1763-1797* (Chapel Hill, N.C., 1967), pp. 14-17.

100. Charles S. Olton, *Artisans for Independence: Philadelphia Mechanics and the American Revolution* (Syracuse, N.Y., 1975), pp. 49-51.

101. There are scores of appeals from men signing themselves "tradesman," "mechanick," or "artifier" in the *Pennsylvania Gazette*, *Pennsylvania Chronicle*, *Pennsylvania Evening Post*, *Pennsylvania Packet*, and *Pennsylvania Ledger* in the last years before revolution. These are uncommon in New York before 1774 and virtually nonexistent in the Boston newspapers.

102. *Pennsylvania Chronicle*, March 27, 1767. For further complaints about the inequitable use of tax funds see Sept. 18 and Oct. 2, 1769.

103. *New-York Journal*, Oct. 6, 1768, reprinted in *Boston Gazette*, Oct. 24, 1768. The best account of the nonimportation movement in 1768 is Arthur L. Jensen, *The Maritime Commerce of Colonial Philadelphia* (Madison, Wis., 1963), pp. 171-181.

104. *To the Free and Patriotic Inhabitants of the City of Phila. and Province of Pennsylvania* (Philadelphia, 1770), quoted in Olton, *Artisans for Independence*, p. 43.

105. Ibid., p. 45. In a broadside a "Tradesman" wrote that artisans who suffered from nonimportation "are but few, when compared to the Number of those who have recieved great Benefit from it." Quoted in Hutson, *Pennsylvania Politics*, p. 234. The merchants on the other hand "dread a further continuance of the non-importation agreement, as [they] see with grief and astonishment that if they continue one year longer the vend for British manufactures will be ruined in future, as industry, manufacturing and economy gain ground every hour, which will finally render English goods unnecessary." *Pennsylvania Chronicle*, June 18, 1770, quoted in Olton, *Artisans for Independence*, p. 44.

106. *Pennsylvania Chronicle*, July 5, 1770, cited ibid., p. 45.

107. Olton, *Artisans for Independence*, pp. 50-52. "Brother Chip" lectured the elite in the *Pennsylvania Gazette*, Sept. 27, 1770.

108. Galloway to Benjamin Franklin, Sept. 27, 1770, *Papers of Franklin*,

XVII, 228. For the emergence of the new party see James H. Hutson, *Pennsylvania Politics, 1746-1770* (Princeton, 1972), pp. 236-243 and Richard Alan Ryerson, *The Revolution Is Now Begun: The Radical Committees of Philadelphia, 1765-1776* (Philadelphia, 1978), pp. 25-38, 177-206. Ryerson corrects Hutson's overemphasis of the Presbyterian control of the new party.

109. Olton, *Artisans for Independence*, p. 53. William Goddard, a printer, was nearly elected to the assembly in 1772.

110. Olton, *Artisans for Independence*, pp. 54-55; Hutson, *Pennsylvania Politics*, p. 242.

111. *A Trademan's Address to his Countrymen* (Philadelphia, 1772); the public gallery issue was first raised in 1764 but had been opposed by popular party leaders Galloway and Franklin. *Votes and Proceedings of the House of Representatives of the Province of Pennsylvania*, ed. Gertrude MacKinney, *Pennsylvania Archives*, 8th ser., 8 vols. (Harrisburg, Pa., 1931-35), VII, 5557-5560.

112. *Pennsylvania Gazette*, Sept. 22, 1773, quoted in Olton, *Artisans for Independence*, p. 56.

113. Ryerson, *Revolution Is Now Begun*, pp. 79-86; Olton, *Artisans for Independence*, pp. 59-62.

114. Ryerson, *Revolution is Now Begun*, p. 87; Olton, *Artisans for Independence*, pp. 62-63.

115. Ryerson, *Revolution Is Now Begun*, p. 95.

116. Olton, *Artisans for Independence*, p. 71.

117. Becker, *Political Parties*, pp. 166-168. Fewer than 100 citizens turned out in New York at the meeting called to endorse the fusion ticket. The Philadelphia Committee of Inspection included only three persons who would later become loyalist. Robert F. Oaks, "Philadelphia Merchants and the Origins of American Independence," *Proceedings of the American Philosophical Society*, 121 (1977), 430. For its occupational makeup see Ryerson, *Revolution Is Now Begun*, p. 181, Table 12.

118. The Boston Committee of 63 is listed in *MHS Proc.*, 2d ser., XII (Boston, 1899), 139-142. On the Philadelphia committee see Olton, *Artisans for Independence*, pp. 73-74, and Ryerson, *Revolution Is Now Begun*, pp. 128-131.

119. *Pennsylvania Packet*, April 30, 1776.

120. Eric Foner, *Tom Paine and Revolutionary America* (New York, 1976), p. 64.

121. Olton, *Artisans for Independence*, p. 74; Foner, *Tom Paine*, p. 65; Ryerson, *Revolution Is Now Begun*, pp. 133-134, 138-145, 160-162.

122. Quoted in Foner, *Tom Paine*, p. 63.

123. *An Essay on a Declaration of Rights . . .* (Philadelphia, 1776); *To the Several Battalions of Military Associators . . .* (Philadelphia, 1776). For a general discussion of the eruption of egalitarian sentiment see Foner, *Tom Paine*, pp. 123-126.

124. For example, in New York see *New-York Journal*, Aug. 18, 1774 and June 20, 1776, and Merrill Jensen, *The American Revolution Within America* (New York, 1974), pp. 72-74.

125. Pole, *Political Representation*, p. 273. The issue of broadening the franchise was first raised in April 1776. Olton, *Artisans for Independence*, pp. 76-77, and Foner, *Tom Paine*, pp. 125-126.

126. Quoted in Pole, *Political Representation*, p. 273n.

127. Ryerson, *The Revolution Is Now Begun*, pp. 94-95, 178-206.

128. Arthur M. Schlesinger, *Prelude to Independence: The Newspaper War on Britain, 1764-1776* (New York, 1965), pp. 118-122; Benjamin H. Newcomb, *Franklin and Galloway: A Political Partnership* (New Haven, Conn., 1972), pp. 148-159, 213-227.

129. Ryerson, *The Revolution Is Now Begun*, pp. 103-115; for a more extensive analysis see Richard Bauman, *For the Reputation of Truth: Politics, Religion, and Conflict among the Pennsylvania Quakers, 1750-1800* (Baltimore, 1971), chaps. 8-9.

130. Quoted in Foner, *Tom Paine*, p. 120.

131. Stephen Brobeck, "Revolutionary Change in Colonial Philadelphia: The Brief Life of the Proprietary Gentry," *WMQ*, 32 (1976), 410-434. The quotes, from the diary of James Allen, are on p. 431.

132. Edward Countryman, " 'Out of the Bounds of the Law': Northern Land Rioters in the Eighteenth Century," in Alfred F. Young, ed., *The American Revolution: Explorations in the History of American Radicalism* (DeKalb, Ill., 1976), p. 57.

133. Joyce Appleby, "Liberalism and the American Revolution," *New England Quarterly*, 49 (1976), 6.

Index

Adams, John, 258, 276, 277, 344, 357, 380; *Dissertation on . . . Law*, 349
Adams, Nathaniel, family (Boston), 17
Adams, Samuel, 488n117
Adams, Samuel, Jr., 299, 326, 488n117; and Boston Caucus, 278, 296; and "Christian Sparta," 281, 345, 381; vs. Hutchinson, 278, 333; populistic politics of, 224, 278-279, 305, 307, 350, 352-353, 356-357, 358, 360, 361, 489n121
Addison, Henry, 12
Africa: trade with, 14, 69, 70, 78
Albany, N.Y., 65, 178, 186
Albany Congress (1754), 234
Alexander, James, 141-143, 147, 177, 236
Alison, Francis, 288
Allen, James (Boston), 279
Allen, James (Philadelphia), 310, 490n135
Allen, William, 257, 267, 287, 290, 306, 490n141
American Weekly Mercury, 155
Amory, John, 358
Andros, Sir Edmund, 80, 285; Boston uprising against, 38, 40-45, 48, 76, 86
Anglican church (Church of England), 309, 314, 340; animosity toward, 38, 135, 202, 204, 207, 274, 278-280, 339; and immigrants, 230, 288, 308; and Kings College controversy, 199, 202-204, 372; merchant elite and, 80, 273, 290, 361; Presbyterians vs., 204, 271, 289, 291, 308, 372, 381; vs. Quakers, 268-270, 285. *See also* Boston; Protes-

tantism; Religion
Appleby, Joyce, 162
Appleton, Nathaniel, 175, 321, 359
Apprenticeship, 5, 15-16, 36, 58; poverty and, 105, 184-185; slavery replaces, 109. *See also* Education; Indentured servants; Labor; Slavery in northern colonies
Apthorp, Charles, 169, 236, 257, 273, 355
Artisans: appeal to and mobilization of vote of, 35, 80, 87, 91, 142-144, 150-155, 274, 276-279, 363, 374; economic controls on, 32, 47, 78, 83, 259, 324; Franklin's Junto of, 105, 121, 269, 290; group consciousness of, 363, 374-378, 380; intergenerational continuity of, 17; internal stratification of, 325, 363, 365-366, 371-372, 380; merchant elite vs., 47, 50-52, 141, 375-376, 378; as officeholders, 34, 35, 47, 100, 359, 360, 363, 364, 376; vs. private interests, 148; and secret ballot, 367-368, 371-372; and slave competition, 107, 109-110, 260, 321; social status of, 16-17, 58, 258-263, 342-343; and Stamp Act, 293, 296-298, 301, 303, 304, 305-308, 310-311; war prosperity of, 240, 241. *See also* Labor; Mechanics Committee(s); Political life and power; Social class; Wages; Wealth, distribution of
Association of the Sons of Liberty (broadside), 369
Auchmuty, Robert, 273, 483n74